£16.99

his book is to be returned on

EUROPE

1760–1871

Terry Morris
Richard Staton
Sally Waller
Series editor: Derrick Murphy

Collins Educational
An Imprint of HarperCollinsPublishers

Published by Collins Educational
An imprint of HarperCollins*Publishers* Ltd
77–85 Fulham Palace Road
Hammersmith
London W6 8JB

www.**Collins**Educational.com
On-line Support for Schools and Colleges

© HarperCollins*Publishers* Ltd 2000
First published 2000

ISBN 0 00 327 132 3

Terry Morris, Richard Staton and Sally Waller assert the moral right to be identified as the authors of this work.

British Library Cataloguing in Publication Data
A catalogue record for this book is available from the British Library.

Edited by Steve Attmore
Design by Derek Lee
Cover design by Derek Lee
Map artwork by Tony Richardson
Picture research by Celia Dearing
Production by Kathryn Botterill
Printed and bound by Bath Press

Contents

Study and examination skills

This chapter of the book is designed to aid Sixth Form students in their preparation for public examinations in History.

- Differences between GCSE and Sixth Form History
- Extended writing: the structured question and the essay
- How to handle sources in Sixth Form History
- Historical interpretation
- Progression in Sixth Form History
- Examination technique

Differences between GCSE and Sixth Form History

- **The amount of factual knowledge required for answers to Sixth Form History** questions is more detailed than at GCSE. Factual knowledge in the Sixth Form is used as supporting evidence to help answer historical questions. Knowing the facts is important but not as important as knowing the factual knowledge supports historical analysis.

- **Extended writing is more important in Sixth Form History.** Students will be expected to answer either structured questions or essays.

Structured questions require students to answer more than one question on a given topic. For example:

> 1. In what ways did Napoleon I change the way France was governed?
>
> 2. How successful was Napoleon in bringing political stability to France between 1799 and 1814?

Each part of the structured question demands a different approach.

Essay questions require students to produce one answer to a given question. For example:

> To what extent was the unification of Italy, between 1859 and 1870, due to the intervention of foreign powers?

Similarities with GCSE

- Source analysis and evaluation

The skills in handling historical sources, which were acquired at GCSE, are developed in Sixth Form History. In the Sixth Form sources have to be analysed in their historical context, so a good factual knowledge of the subject is important.

● **Historical interpretations**

Skills in historical interpretation at GCSE are also developed in Sixth Form History. The ability to put forward different historical interpretations is important. Students will also be expected to explain why different historical interpretations have occurred.

Extended writing: the structured question and the essay

When faced with extended writing in Sixth Form History, students can improve their performance by following a simple routine that attempts to ensure they achieve their best performance.

Answering the question

What are the command instructions?
Different questions require different types of response. For instance, 'In what ways' requires students to point out the various ways something took place in History; 'Why' questions expect students to deal with the causes or consequences of an historical question.

Are there key words or phrases that require definition or explanation?
It is important for students to show that they understand the meaning of the question. To do this, certain historical terms or words require explanation. For instance, if a question asked 'how far' a king or politician was an 'innovator', an explanation of the word 'innovator' would be required.

Does the question have specific dates or issues that require coverage?
If a question mentions specific dates, these must be adhered to. For instance, if you are asked to answer a question on the foreign policy of Russia it may state clear date limits such as 1800 to 1855. Also questions may mention a specific aspect such as 'domestic', 'religious', 'social' or 'economic'.

Planning your answer

Once you have decided on what the question requires, write a brief plan. For structured questions this may be brief. This is a useful procedure to make sure that you have ordered the information you require for your answer in the most effective way. For instance, in a balanced, analytical answer this may take the form of jotting down the main points for and against an historical issue raised in the question.

Writing the answer

Communication skills
The quality of written English is important in Sixth Form History. The way you present your ideas on paper can affect the quality of your answer. Since 1996 the Government (through QCA) have placed emphasis on the quality of written English in the Sixth Form. Therefore, punctuation, spelling and grammar, which were awarded marks at GCSE, require close attention. Use a dictionary if you are unsure of a word's meaning or spelling. Use the glossary of terms you will find in this book to help you.

The introduction
For structured questions you may wish to dispense with an introduction altogether and begin writing reasons to support an answer straight away. However, essay answers should begin with an introduction. These should be both concise and precise. Introductions help 'concentrate the mind' on

the question you are about to answer. Remember, do not try to write a conclusion as your opening sentence. Instead, outline briefly the areas you intend to discuss in your answer.

Balancing analysis with factual evidence
It is important to remember that factual knowledge should be used to support analysis. Merely 'telling the story' of an historical event is not enough. A structured question or essay should contain separate paragraphs, each addressing an analytical point that helps to answer the question. If, for example, the question asks for reasons why the Revolutions of 1848 in Austria began, each paragraph should provide a reason for the outbreak of war.

Seeing connections between reasons
In dealing with 'why'-type questions it is important to remember that the reasons for an historical event might be interconnected. Therefore, it is important to mention the connection between reasons. Also, it might be important to identify a hierarchy of reasons – that is, are some reasons more important than others in explaining an historical event?

Using quotations and statistical data
One aspect of supporting evidence that sustains analysis is the use of quotations. These can either be from an historian or a contemporary. However, unless these quotations are linked with analysis and supporting evidence, they tend to be of little value.

It can also be useful to support analysis with statistical data. In questions that deal with social and economic change, precise statistics which support your argument can be very persuasive.

Source analysis

Source analysis forms an integral part of the study of History. In Sixth Form History source analysis is identified as an important skill in Assessment Objective 3.

In dealing with sources you should be aware that historical sources must be used 'in historical context' in Sixth Form History. Therefore, in this book sources are used with the factual information in each chapter. Also, a specific source analysis question is included.

Assessment Objectives

1 knowledge and understanding of history

2 evaluation and analysis skills

3 a) source analysis in historical context

  b) historical interpretation

How to handle sources in Sixth Form History

In dealing with sources a number of basic hints will allow you to deal effectively with source-based questions and to build on your knowledge and skill in using sources at GCSE.

Written sources

Attribution and date

It is important to identify who has written the source and when it was written. This information can be very important. If, for instance, an historical source was written by Otto von Bismarck, explaining how and why he amended the Ems telegram of 1870, this information will be of considerable importance if you are asked about the usefulness or reliability of the source as evidence of Bismarck's behaviour during the unification of Germany.

It is important to note that just because a source is a primary source does not mean it is more useful or less reliable than a secondary source. Both primary and secondary sources need to be analysed to decide how useful and reliable they are. This can be determined by studying other issues.

Is the content factual or opinionated?

Once you have identified the author and date of the source it is important to study its content. The content may be factual, stating what has happened or what may happen. On the other hand, it may contain opinions that should be handled with caution. These may contain bias. Even if a source is mainly factual, there might be important and deliberate gaps in factual evidence that can make a source biased and unreliable. Usually, written sources contain elements of both opinion and factual evidence. It is important to judge the balance between these two parts.

Has the source been written for a particular audience?

To determine the reliability of a source it is important to identify to whom it is directed. For instance, a public speech may be made to achieve a particular purpose and may not contain the author's true beliefs or feelings. In contrast, a private diary entry may be much more reliable in this respect.

Corroborative evidence

To test whether or not a source is reliable, the use of other evidence to support or corroborate the information it contains is important. Cross-referencing with other sources is a way of achieving this; so is cross-referencing with historical information contained within a chapter.

Visual sources

Maps

Maps which appear in Sixth Form History are either contemporary or secondary sources. These are used to support factual coverage in the text by providing information in a different medium. Therefore, to assess whether or not information contained in maps is accurate or useful, reference should be made to other information. It is also important with line written sources to check the attribution and date. These could be significant.

Statistical data and graphs

It is important when dealing with this type of source to check carefully the nature of the information contained in date or in a graph. It might state the information in old forms of measurement such as pre-decimal currency: pounds, shillings and pence. One pound equalled 20 shillings, or 240 pence. It might also be stated in foreign currency, such as thalers in Austria or livres in France. Be careful to check if the information is in index numbers. These are a statistical device where a base year is chosen and given the figure 100. All other figures are based on a percentage difference from that base year. For instance, if 1800 is taken as base year for the production of iron it is given a figure of 100. If the index number for 1815 is 118 it means that iron production has risen 18% since 1800.

An important point to remember when dealing with data and graphs over a period of time is to identify trends and patterns in the information. Merely describing the information in written form is not enough.

Historical interpretation

An important feature of both GCSE and Sixth Form History is the issue of historical interpretation. In Sixth Form History it is important for students to be able to explain why historians differ, or have differed in their interpretations of the past.

Availability of evidence

An important reason is the availability of evidence on which to base historical judgements. As new evidence comes to light, an historian today may have more information on which to base their judgements than historians in the past. For instance, sources for late 18th and early 19th-century Europe include state papers, including government papers on meetings and policies on individual issues. Occasionally, new evidence comes to light that may influence judgements about modern European history.

The archaeological study of industrial sites, such as early 19th-century railway lines in Germany and France, provide historical evidence of the early Industrial Revolution in those countries.

'A philosophy of history?'

Many historians have a specific view of history that will affect the way they make their historical judgements. For instance, Marxist historians – who take the view from the writings of Karl Marx, the founder of modern socialism – believe that society has been made up of competing economic and social classes. They also place considerable importance on economic reasons in human decision making.

The role of the individual

Some historians have seen past history as being moulded by the acts of specific individuals who have changed history. Napoleon I, Giuseppe Garibaldi or Otto von Bismarck are individuals who changed the course of history. Other historians have tended to 'downplay' the role of individuals; instead, they highlight the importance of more general social, economic and political change. Rather than seeing Napoleon I, Garibaldi or Otto von Bismarck as individuals who changed the course of history, these historians tend to see them as representing the views of wider social, religious or economic groups.

Placing different emphasis on the same historical evidence

Even if historians do not possess different philosophies of history or place different emphasis on the role of the individual, it is still possible for them to disagree because they place different emphases on aspects of the same factual evidence. As a result, Sixth Form History should be seen as a subject that encourages debate about the past based on historical evidence.

Progression in Sixth Form History

The ability to achieve high standards in Sixth Form History involves the acquisition of a number of skills:

- Good written communication skills

- A sound factual knowledge

- Evaluating factual evidence and making historical conclusions based on that evidence

- Source analysis

- Understanding the nature of historical interpretation

- Understanding the causes and consequences of historical events

- Understanding the themes in history which will involve a study of a specific topic over a long period of time

- Understanding the ideas of change and continuity associated with themes.

Students should be aware that the acquisition of these skills will take place gradually over the time spent in the Sixth Form. At the beginning of the course the main emphasis may be on the acquisition of factual knowledge, particularly when the body of knowledge studied at GCSE was different.

When dealing with causation students will have to build on their skills from GCSE. They will not only be expected to identify reasons for an historical event, but also to provide a hierarchy of causes. They should identify the main causes and less important causes. They may also identify that causes may be interconnected and linked. Progression in Sixth Form History will come with answering the questions at the end of each sub-section in this book and practising the skills outlined through the use of the factual knowledge contained in the book.

Examination techniques

The ultimate challenge for any Sixth Form historian is the ability to produce quality work under examination conditions. Examinations will take the form of either modular examinations taken in January and June or in an 'end of course' set of examinations.

Here is some advice on how to improve your performance in an examination.

- *Read the whole examination paper thoroughly*
Make sure that the questions you choose are those for which you can produce a good answer. Don't rush – allow time to decide which questions to choose. It is probably too late to change your mind half way through answering a question.

- *Read the question very carefully*
Once you have made the decision to answer a specific question, read it very carefully. Make sure you understand the precise demands of the question. Think about what is required in your answer. It is much better to think about this before you start writing, rather than trying to steer your essay in a different direction half way through.

● *Make a brief plan*

Sketch out what you intend to include in your answer. Order the points you want to make. Examiners are not impressed with additional information included at the end of the essay, with indicators such as arrows or asterisks.

● *Pace yourself as you write*

Success in examinations has a lot to do with successful time management. If, for instance, you have to answer an essay question in approximately 45 minutes then you should be one-third of the way through after 15 minutes. With 30 minutes gone, you should start writing the last third of your answer.

Where a question is divided into sub-questions make sure you look at the mark tariff for each question. If in a 20-mark question a sub-question is worth a maximum of 5 marks then you should spend approximately one-quarter of the time allocated for the whole question on this sub-question.

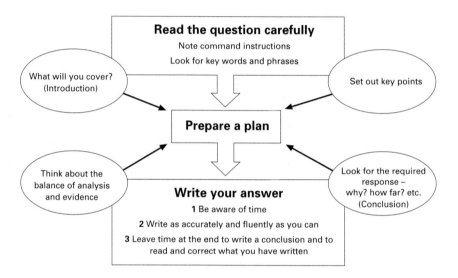

Europe, 1760–1871: a synoptic assessment

Key Issues

- *Why did the structure and role of government activity change, 1760–1871?*

- *How far did European international relations change, 1760–1871?*

- *In what ways, and why, did society and the economy change in Europe, 1760–1871?*

1.1 In what ways did ideas about government and society change between 1760 and 1871?

Absolute monarchy: The King or Queen has total control over the country. This power is believed to be ordained by God and the monarch rules with the support of the noble classes.

Tsar: Title of the emperor of Russia. Also spelled Czar and Tzar. Believed to be a shorted form of Caesar (Roman emperor).

Liberalism: This idea, spread by the French Revolution, encouraged personal and economic freedom. Personal freedom included the right to property, freedom of speech and worship, and the freedom to participate in politics. The term came to imply resistance to autocratic rule and liberals favoured government by an elected, representative assembly.

Nationalism: The growth and spread of loyalty towards a nation, rather than an individual ruler.

In 1760 the dominant form of government in most of Europe was **absolute monarchy**. This form of state organisation was based on the rule of a hereditary monarch who was the sole source of political power. Such an idea was reinforced by the belief that hereditary monarchs had been chosen and were responsible to God. Historians such as Nicholas Henshall have suggested that the amount of political power held by a monarch was not always complete and unchallenged. Nevertheless, the *ancien régime* rulers of the mid-18th century possessed a degree of political power unknown in the early 21st century.

By 1871 several states were still absolutist in structure. The most important of these states was the Russian Empire. The **Tsar** of Russia, in political terms, was still answerable only to God. Another major state with this form of government was the Ottoman Empire. However, between 1760 and 1871, a major change took place in most European states.

The period 1760–1871 was dominated by competing ideas about the organisation of government and society. Conservatism was a set of ideas that wished to preserve the type of society associated with absolutist monarchy. Absolute monarchy supported a society where large-scale landowners (the aristocracy) possessed considerable political power, usually in the regions of a state. Before the French Revolution, France under Louis XVI was regarded as the best example of this type of state. From 1815 to 1848, Prince Metternich (Chancellor of the Austrian Empire) was the main defender of European conservatism. Throughout the whole period, Russia was Europe's most conservative state. Nicholas I (Tsar 1825–55) was known as the 'policeman of Europe' because of his defence of conservative ideas.

This was challenged by **liberalism** and **nationalism**. Both ideas were products of a major change in European ideas about politics, society and culture known as the 'Enlightenment'. Enlightenment ideas grew in influence during the 18th century. These ideas formed the basis of the major political movements that helped to undermine and, ultimately, destroy the *ancien régime*. The French Revolution of 1789–99 can be seen as a product of the Enlightenment.

Liberalism was a set of ideas that wished to see political power within a state shared between a monarch and the wider population. Some liberals wanted political power to be limited to those in society who owned property. For instance, in Britain in 1832, and again in 1867, the right to vote in parliamentary elections was based on a property qualification. Most of the Liberals who participated in the 1848–49 European Revolutions shared this view of society. To them, **peasants** and factory workers did not possess either the property or the education to participate in politics. More radical liberals wished to see the creation of democracy (one man, one vote). Only in France, during the early 1790s and during the Second Republic (1848–52), was democracy put into practice.

Peasants: Farm labourers who rented land from a landowner. They were, mostly, illiterate (unable to read and write) and poor.

National/Liberal revolts and risings, 1820–49

Republic: A country whose system of government is based on the idea that every citizen has equal status, so that there is no king or queen and no aristocracy.

For most of the period 1760–1871 liberalism was associated with nationalism – a set of political ideas which suggested that states should consist of people with a common language, culture or race. In 1760, no state could be described as a 'nation state'. Instead, loyalty within a state was to a monarch rather than to 'the nation'. Those republics that did exist were not nation states. Switzerland comprised French, German, Italian and Romansh (Latin) speaking people. The republics of Genoa and Venice, in Italy, had an elected monarch known as the Doge.

The first state based on the principles of liberalism and, to a lesser extent, nationalism was not in Europe at all but was founded by Europeans – the United States of America (USA). The United States' Constitution of 1787 abolished monarchy, creating a **republic** from 13 states. Political power was divided between an elected President and a national parliament (Congress). In addition, political power was also divided between a national government and state governments.

Within Europe, France was the first state to combine these two ideas. The creation of the First French Republic in September 1792 combined support for a French national state with the creation of a National Assembly. So radical was the change brought about by the creation of the First French Republic that the French revolutionaries abolished the traditional calendar – 1792 became Year 1! Perhaps the most famous, or notorious, aspect of these changes was the French Revolutionary Terror of 1792–94, when thousands of aristocrats were put to death. The most significant victim of the Terror was King Louis XVI who was executed in January 1793.

Socialism: A set of political beliefs and principles whose general aim is to create a system in which everyone has an equal opportunity to benefit from the country's wealth.

Throughout the period 1789–1871 European monarchs feared the spread of liberalism and nationalism. Both ideas would undermine their authority and could, ultimately, lead to their overthrow. Following the overthrow of Napoleon I, in 1815, Europe was affected by outbreaks of liberal, national revolutions. In 1820–21, 1830–32 and 1848–49 revolutions took place across Europe.

1. How did Conservatism differ from Liberalism in Europe between 1760 and 1871?

2. In what ways did liberalism and nationalism challenge the ways European states were governed and organised between 1760 and 1871?

3. To what extent did the Enlightenment bring about fundamental change in Europe between 1760 and 1871?

Most revolutionary leaders wanted to create political regimes based on the parliaments elected by the property-owning classes. In virtually every case, the revolutions were defeated. Only in France, in 1830 and in 1848, was a political regime overthrown by revolution. One of the reasons for the continued failure of liberal revolution was the lack of military power and opposition from peasants and urban industrial workers. Even in France after 1830 and 1848 urban industrial workers tried, but failed, to seize political power. The most serious outbreak of revolutionary violence in Europe after 1799 occurred in France in 1871: the Paris Commune. The Commune was a rising of the population of Paris against the liberal republican government created as a result of France's defeat in the Franco–Prussian War. The Communards looked back to the example and ideas of the French Revolution of 1792–94. The political idea that attracted the urban workers of Paris in 1848 and in 1871 was **socialism**. This idea suggested that economic wealth within society should be distributed more equally among members of society. In 1848, the German socialists Karl Marx and Friedrich Engels produced 'The Communist Manifesto' calling for all industrial workers in Europe to unite against the wealthy classes. Although socialism was to become a popular and powerful political force in the late 19th and 20th centuries, by 1871 it was still in its infancy.

1.2 How far did the structure of government change in Europe between 1760 and 1871?

During the period 1760–1871 the structure and role of government changed considerably in western and central Europe. In eastern Europe,

Zemstva: Elected local government institutions in rural areas of Russia, established in 1864. The functions of the *zemstva* included the administration of primary education, public health, poor relief, local industry and the maintenance of the highways.

Serfdom: The social and economic system by which the land was owned by the wealthy classes but cultivated by serfs (peasants).

Suffrage: The right of people to vote in order to choose a government or a national leader.

1. **Explain how rule solely by a monarch was changed in Europe between 1760 and 1871?**

2. **How important were parliaments in the government of European states by 1871?**

most notably Russia and the Ottoman Empire, political power remained in the hands of ruler. Even here, in 1864, elected local government was introduced in Russia in the form of local *zemstva*.

The most notable change in the structure of government was the rise in importance of national, elected assemblies in decision making. In Britain, in 1760, parliament played an important role in the government of the country. By that date, it was accepted that the Prime Minister had to command support from the majority of the House of Commons. The King had the power to create parliamentary seats. He also had the power to offer MPs government jobs. As a result, for most of George III's reign (1760–1821) parliament followed the views of the reigning monarch. By 1871, the political role of the British monarch had declined considerably. Queen Victoria (1837–1901) became a constitutional monarch who, by the time of her death, reigned but did not rule. In 1871, the Prime Minister was the Liberal, William Gladstone, whom Victoria disliked intensely. Monarchic-controlled government had been replaced by parliamentary government. The extension of the right to vote, in 1832 and 1867, aided this process.

In France, parliamentary government had become established. Between 1830 and 1852, the French national parliament played an important part in government. However, under Napoleon I (1799–1815) and Napoleon III (1852–70) France was, in reality, a dictatorship.

In central Europe the absolute power of monarchs had been adversely affected by the impact of the French Revolutionary and Napoleonic Wars (1792–1815). As Napoleon's armies crossed Europe to reach as far as Moscow in 1812, the French Emperor abolished **serfdom** and the Holy Roman Empire. By 1815, central Europe had been transformed into the German Confederation of 38, later 39, states. Many of these states had their own national parliaments. The most notable exceptions were the two Germanic 'Great Powers', Prussia and Austria. Instead they possessed local Diets, assemblies dominated by the aristocracy. Although the 1848–49 revolutions in Central Europe failed to overthrow any state, they did lead to changes within them. In Prussia, a national parliament elected by a three-class **suffrage** appeared in 1848. In Austria, conflict between the ruling Habsburg family and the Hungarians led to the creation of the Compromise, or *Ausgleich*, of 1867. This created the new state of Austria-Hungary. Each half of the Empire possessed its own elected national assembly.

By 1871, every state in Europe, with the exception of Russia and the Ottoman Empire, had a national parliament. In Britain, control of the House of Commons resulted in control of government. In states like the newly-created German Empire, parliament had an advisory role only. Of the five Great Powers, in 1871, only Britain and France possessed parliamentary government; Germany, Austria-Hungary and Russia were states where the ruling royal family still possessed considerable political power.

1.3 To what extent did European international relations change between 1760 and 1871?

In 1760, the five Great Powers of Europe – Britain, France, Austria, Russia and Prussia – were all engaged in the Seven Years' War (1756–63). These states were regarded as 'great powers' because of their military strength. An important aspect of 18th-century international relations was the 'balance of power'. This idea aimed at preventing any one state dominating Europe. No one Great Power possessed the ability to dominate the other four.

Throughout the 18th century, two major conflicts between the Great

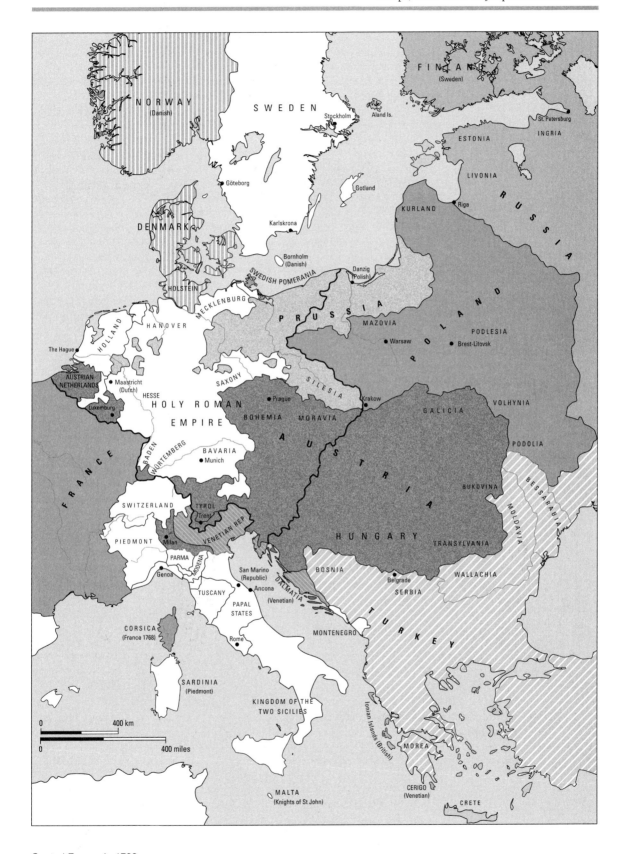

Central Europe in 1789

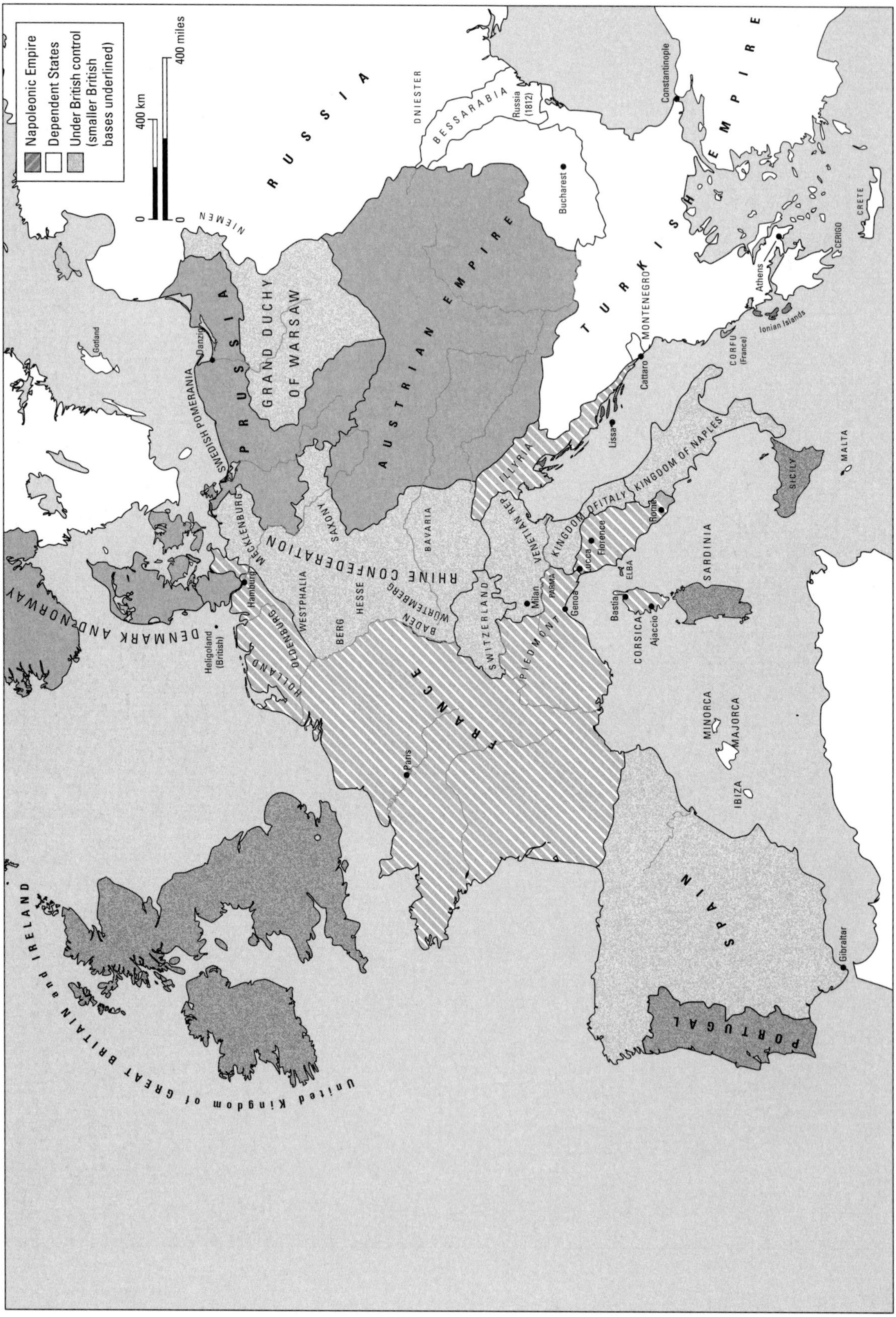

Napoleonic Empire
Dependent States
Under British control (smaller British bases underlined)

400 miles
400 km

RUSSIA

DNIESTER
BESSARABIA
Russia (1812)
NIEMEN
Bucharest

TURKISH EMPIRE
Constantinople

CRETE
CERIGO
Athens
Ionian Islands
CORFU (France)
MONTENEGRO
Cattaro

GRAND DUCHY OF WARSAW
Danzig
SWEDISH POMERANIA
P R U S S I A
Gotland

AUSTRIAN EMPIRE

ILLYRIA
Lissa
KINGDOM OF NAPLES
SICILY
MALTA

MECKLENBURG
Hamburg
SAXONY
RHINE CONFEDERATION
BAVARIA
VENETIAN REP
KINGDOM OF ITALY
Rome

WESTPHALIA
BERG
HESSE
WÜRTEMBERG
BADEN
SWITZERLAND
Milan
PARMA
Lucca
Florence
ELBA
SARDINIA

OLDENBURG
HOLLAND
Heligoland (British)
DENMARK AND NORWAY

PIEDMONT
Genoa
Bastia
CORSICA
Ajaccio

FRANCE
Paris

SPAIN
Gibraltar
MINORCA
MAJORCA
IBIZA

PORTUGAL

IRELAND
United Kingdom of GREAT BRITAIN and

Europe in 1811

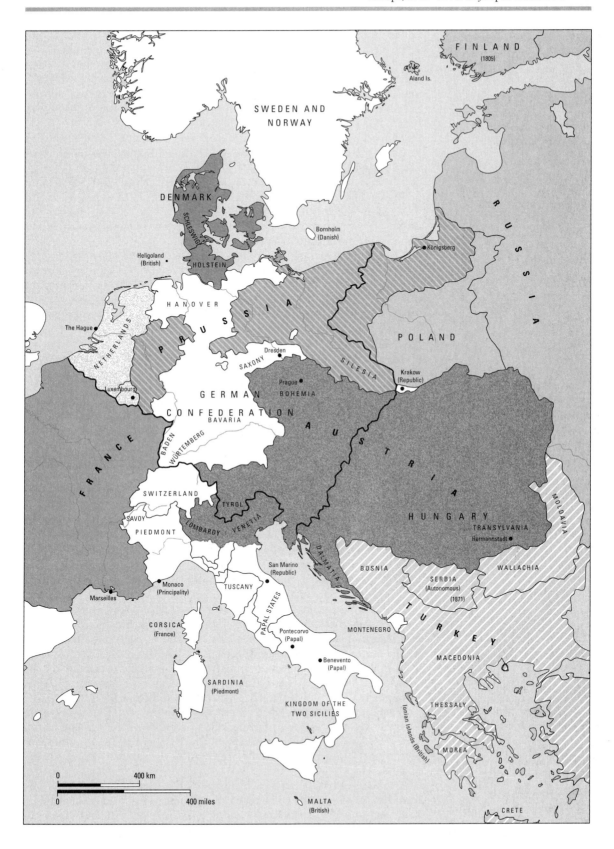

Central Europe in 1815

Study the three maps on pages 15–17.

1. In what ways did the political map of Europe change between 1789 and 1811?

2. To what extent was the political map of Europe in 1815 similar to the political map in 1789?

Powers took place. Britain and France were at war 1701–13, 1744–48, 1756–63, 1778–83 and 1793–1815. Britain and France's conflict was mainly over colonial possessions. The British and French fought each other in North America, the Caribbean and India. In addition, from 1714, the Kings of England were also Electors of the German state of Hanover. British armies in the 18th and 19th centuries not only fought to defend Britain but also the King's German possessions.

The other major Great Power conflict was between Austria and Prussia – the two Germanic powers. This conflict reached its height when King Frederick the Great of Prussia invaded the Austrian province of Silesia in 1740. Austria and Prussia fought each other 1740–48 and 1756–63. This does not mean that Austria and Prussia were not able to find agreement on some issues. From 1772 to 1796 Austria, Prussia and Russia co-operated in partitioning the large, but politically weak, eastern European state of Poland.

The European internal system was transformed by the French Revolution and the rise of Napoleon I. From 1792, old animosities between the Great Powers were put aside because of the greater threat of the French Revolution. From 1792 to 1815 Britain, Austria, Prussia and Russia allied together at various times. Initially, these Great Powers allied together to stop the spread of French Revolutionary ideas. From 1799, they allied together against Napoleon I. From 1799 to 1815 Napoleon I dominated European international relations. His military campaigns of 1805–06 defeated Austria, Russia and Prussia. By 1810, France dominated the European continent from Portugal to the Russia border.

Napoleon I's eventual defeat between 1814 and 1815 was the result of considerable co-operation between the European states. The Fourth Coalition of Powers against Napoleon (1812–15) was made up of Britain, Austria, Prussia, Russia and Sweden.

The highlight of European international co-operation took place in Vienna in 1814–15 – a new balance of power based on the five Great Powers of the 18th century. The political map of Europe (see page 17) was redrawn to help ensure that a recurrence of the Napoleonic Wars could not occur. To maintain European peace the Great Powers agreed to work in concert (together) to resolve any major European crisis. The Concert of Europe worked successfully to end the Greek War on Independence (1830–32), the Belgian Revolt (1830–39) and conflicts in the Ottoman Empire (1840 and 1841). From 1815 to 1854 war between European Great Powers was avoided.

However, between 1854–71, European international relations were transformed. From 1854 to 1856 Russia fought Britain, France and the Ottoman Empire in the Crimean War. This conflict occurred as a result of **the Eastern Question** and the European 'balance of power'.

The Eastern Question was an international problem created by the widespread belief that the Ottoman Empire was in a state of collapse. Britain feared Russia would gain territory and influence if this took place. This would result in an alteration in the European balance of power in Russia's favour. Already, during the Greek War of Independence (1821–32) and the Mehemet Ali crises (1831–33 and 1839–41), problems within the Ottoman Empire almost resulted in war between the Great Powers.

The Crimean War had a major impact on international relations. The most important was the end of the Holy Alliance. This international agreement had united Austria, Russia and Prussia since 1815. The main aim of the alliance was to prevent the success of liberal revolutions in Europe. In 1849, the Hungarian revolution within Austria was defeated with the aid of the Russian army. In 1855, at the height of the Crimean War, Austria

The Eastern Question: Term applied to the issues raised by the decline and disintegration of the Turkish Empire in the 19th century. The most important of these was the question of which states would fill the power vacuum left by the decline of Turkish power in the Balkans, and what the impact would be upon the balance of power in that part of the world.

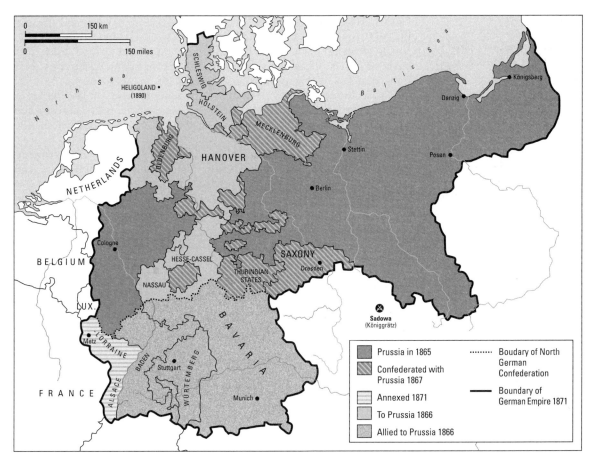

The unification of Germany

allied itself with Britain and France against Russia. From 1855 to the
creation of the Three Emperors' Agreement of 1873, Russia did not
become involved in European international relations.

The end of the Holy Alliance helped to bring about the two most
important developments in international relations between 1815–1914 –
the unification of Italy and the unification of Germany. The unification of
Italy began with the defeat of Austria by France in 1859. From 1859 to
1861 the Italian state of Piedmont-Sardinia and Italian nationalists led by
Guiseppe Garibaldi united most of the Italian peninsula.

Of great significance was the unification of Germany. The old rivalry
between Prussia and Austria reappeared in the 1860s. Prussia wanted to be
co-equal in importance with Austria within the **German Confederation**.
When this could not be achieved through diplomacy, war broke out
between Austria and Prussia in 1866. Prussia's crushing victory resulted in
the Prussian domination of Europe. In 1870–71, the Franco–Prussian War
led to the creation of the German Empire when the three South German
states of Baden, Bavaria and Würtemberg agreed to fight on Prussia's side
against the French.

In both the unification of Italy and of Germany, Russia took no active
part to preserve the Treaty agreed at Vienna in 1814–15. Britain actively
encouraged the unification of the Italian **peninsula**. The British saw Italy
as a possible ally against France in the Mediterranean.

By 1871, European international relations had been transformed. Since
the Middle Ages central Europe, in the form of Germany and Italy, had
been divided into a large number of small states. Both areas had been the

1. What was the 'balance of power', as applied to European international relations?

2. Why were the European Great Powers willing to co-operate with each other in the period 1760–1871?

3. Why were European international relations transformed between 1792 and 1815 and between 1854 and 1871?

battlegrounds of large powers such as France, Spain, Sweden and Austria. By 1871, both areas were united into large states. Germany, in particular, had now replaced France as Europe's most important Great Power. Ever since the reign of Louis XIV (1643–1715) France had been Europe's most important state. This position reached its height under Napoleon I. In 1870–71, France lost its position in dramatic fashion. At the battle of Sedan (September 1870), the French Emperor, Napoleon III, was captured by the Prussians. Between 1870 and early 1871, Paris was besieged by the Prussians and forced to surrender.

Although Germany was the dominant Great Power on the continent, Britain was Europe's only world power. Although Britain lost its American colonies between 1775–83, it still controlled a large world empire. The centrepiece was the British Indian Empire. In addition, Britain had colonies in every continent. It dominated world trade and had Europe's most industrial economy.

1.4 How did warfare develop between 1760 and 1871?

Blockade: To prevent goods and armies from reaching a particular country or place.

The changes in international relations were influenced by changes in warfare. The most effective aspect of warfare in the period 1760–1871 was British sea power. The Royal Navy laid the foundations for and maintained the British Empire and British dominance of trade. By 1760, the Royal Navy had established itself as Europe's most successful navy. In 1759, in the Seven Years' War, the Royal Navy defeated the French Atlantic fleet at the battle of Quiberon Bay and the French Mediterranean fleet at Lagos Bay.

These victories contained the basic ingredients of British success. Sailors in the Royal Navy were better fed and had a higher morale than their French or Spanish counterparts. This allowed the Royal Navy to **blockade** enemy naval bases, such as Brest in France, for long periods. The ability to blockade enabled the British army to conquer French Canada in 1759–60. In the Napoleonic Wars, the Navy successfully blockaded French-occupied Europe.

The other ingredient for success was the quality of naval officers. A naval career was one way a person of modest means could rise to a position of authority. The best example was Horatio Nelson (1758–1805), the son of a Norfolk parson. Nelson's command of naval strategy and tactics helped to defeat Napoleon's navy off Egypt in the battle of the Nile in 1798. His most spectacular victory was at Trafalgar on 21 October 1805. Nelson destroyed the combined fleets of France and Spain, the second and third largest navies in the world after the Royal Navy. Trafalgar confirmed Britain's control of the seas, which was to last beyond the First World War. Britain's naval dominance was enhanced by the Treaty of Vienna (1814–15), which gave Britain important naval bases across the world. Britain acquired the Cape of Good Hope, Mauritius, Ceylon (Sri Lanka), Malta and the Ionian Islands off western Greece.

Even the development of naval technology, with the appearance of steam-driven ships, did not diminish British naval power. In the 1830s, the Royal Navy blockaded the river Scheldt. This forced Holland to accept Belgian independence. In the 1850s, the Navy helped Britain to win the Crimean War. Only in 1859 did a naval scare occur. In that year the French launched the world's first ironclad ship, 'La Gloire'. By the early

1860s, Britain had launched the first true battleship, 'HMS Warrior', to reconfirm British naval power.

In land warfare the most important developments occurred in military tactics. The individual who transformed these was Napoleon I. His spectacular military career from 1797 to 1815 displayed his ability to use field artillery effectively. More importantly, it showed his ability to organise and move troops around the battlefield. Napoleon introduced the 'Corps' as a basic unit of army organisation.

However, what gave French Revolutionary and Napoleonic armies the edge over their rivals was conscription (compulsory military service). Beginning with *La Levée en masse*, in 1793, the French were able to raise large armies. By 1805 Napoleon was commanding a force of 150,000 men. Well led, well provisioned and well armed, these large forces gave the French spectacular military success from the battle of Valmy in 1792 until the battle of Leipzig in 1813,

Even after Napoleon I's death, in 1821, Napoleonic tactics dominated European military thinking up to 1871. However, military tactics were overtaken by the development of weaponry. By the 1860s the French and Prussians had developed breech-loading muskets which allowed infantry to fire more rapidly over greater distances. This development led to considerable loss of life.

The Franco–Austrian War of 1859 was noted for its bloody battles of Magenta and Solferino. By the time of the Franco–Prussian War of 1870–71, mass infantry attack – a feature of Napoleonic tactics – proved both ineffective and costly in terms of lives.

Even more important than changes in weaponry were changes in transportation. The development of railways and their efficient use by the army gave Prussia the military edge in the 1860s. The Prussians were able to concentrate their forces quickly and effectively. It was a decisive factor at the battle of Sadowa (Königgrätz) in the Austro–Prussian War of 1866. It also enabled the Prussians to defeat France in 1870–71.

1. Why was Britain the dominant naval power in Europe between 1760 and 1871?

2. To what extent was France the main military power in Europe between 1760 to 1871?

1.5 How great was the change in Europe's economy and society between 1760 and 1871?

Feudal obligations: Peasants had to perform a number of duties by law, such as working for the landowner, free of charge, during harvesting or giving the landowner a proportion of their produce.

In 1760, Europe was a continent heavily dependent upon agriculture. The vast majority of the population lived and worked on the land as peasants. For most of this population a form of serfdom existed. In France, this involved **feudal obligations** to landowners. In the Austrian Empire it took the form of the *robot* (labour service).

In Russia over 80% of the population were serfs – the property of their owners. The lack of freedom and the failure of harvests led to peasant revolt. These revolts were spontaneous, short lived and excessively violent. Peasants attacked millers (who were believed to have secretly stored food) and landowners. The most serious peasant uprising in the mid-18th century occurred in 1763 in Russia: the Pugachev Rebellion. It was defeated by Catherine the Great of Russia.

Industry was usually limited to towns where a guild system operated. Each industry, such as shoemaking, was controlled by a guild, which regulated working practices and wage rates.

By 1760, Europe was a major participant in world trade. Britain, France, Spain, Portugal and Holland had all gained considerable wealth from trading with the Americas, Africa and Asia. A significant feature of European trade was the Atlantic slave trade. A triangle of trade, where Europeans sold their home-produced goods in west Africa for slaves which were sold for tobacco, cotton and sugar in the New World. Britain dominated this trade by 1760. Ports like Bristol and Liverpool acquired considerable wealth as a result.

By 1871, European society had gone through considerable change. Serfdom and feudal obligations on peasants had been swept away. In France, change came with the French Revolution of 1789. For western and central Europe, feudal obligations were abolished by the advancing French Revolutionary and Napoleonic armies. The 1848 Revolutions brought an end to the *robot* in Austria and feudal obligations in eastern Prussia. However, it took till 1861 for serfdom to be abolished in Russia. Even then the former serfs had to pay 'redemption' payments to their former masters over 49 years.

The most significant social change occurred with industrialisation. Beginning in Britain a revolution occurred in manufacturing. Machines in textile production increased production by such a margin that cost of production dropped significantly. Also the new machines could be operated by semi-skilled workers. Highly skilled handloom weavers faced economic ruin as a result.

By 1815 Britain had become the manufacturing centre of Europe. New cities such as Manchester arose because of the boom in the textile industry, notably cotton. Other cities such as Birmingham grew wealthy through engineering and metal production. Unique to British industrialisation was the use of canals as the major transport system. Britain's industrial might helped make Britain one of Europe's Great Powers.

Industrial change brought social change. Large numbers of rural workers flocked to new industrial cities. Living in poor housing and working long hours factory workers became an important social class. Even more important were the new wealthy middle class which had grown rich as a result of the growth of trade and manufacturing. In Britain this rising middle class led the campaign for the extension of the right to vote in 1830–1832 and the demand for free trade in the 1840s.

Industrial change also affected much of Europe after 1815. In France, the growth of factories and mass production led to the economic ruin of the guilds and skilled workers. It was this social group which was important in the 1848 French Revolution. It was also important within Germany during the 1848–49 Revolutions.

The development of railways and the telegraph helped to reduce distance and to speed up the transmission of news. In the 1848 Revolutions the news of the fall from power of the Austrian Chancellor, Metternich, was so rapid that it precipitated revolution in other parts of the German Confederation with days.

In Germany, economic change was aided by the creation of the *Zollverein* (customs union) in 1834. Under the leadership of Prussia, and excluding Austria, the *Zollverein* brought economic unity to Germany. It helped to pave the way for eventual political union under Prussia in the 1860s.

By 1871, industrialisation had reached the Low Countries (Belgium and Holland), parts of France and much of Germany outside Austria. It meant that during the remainder of the 19th century economic power would have an important impact upon military power. This led to the dominance of Britain in naval power and Germany in land warfare.

1. In what ways did industrialisation affect Europe between 1760 and 1871?

2. How important was economic and social change in producing political change in Europe between 1760 and 1871?

1. Assess the importance of the change in political ideas, economy, society and warfare to the development of European international relations between 1760 to 1871.

2. What do you regard as the most important changes in European History between 1760 and 1871?

Give reasons to support your answer.

The Enlightenment and Enlightened Despotism

Key Issues

- *How important was the Enlightenment?*

- *Did the Enlightenment present a coherent programme of change?*

- *How far did Enlightened ideas affect existing ideas about absolute monarchy?*

Framework of Events

The Enlightenment

1734	Voltaire publishes *The Philosophical Letters*
1748	Montesquieu publishes the *Spirit of the Laws*
1762	Rousseau publishes *The Social Contract*
1763	Beccaria's work on justice is published – *Crime and Punishment*
1772	The *Encyclopédie* (collected works of the *philosophes*) is completed
1774–6	Turgot, a Physiocrat, becomes *Controlleur-Général* in France

Austria and Joseph II

1765	Joseph becomes co-Regent with his mother, Maria Theresa
1780	Joseph assumes sole power
1781	Toleration for Protestants; Joseph abolishes serfdom; penal code is introduced
1782	Papal visit. Toleration for Jews
1784	District Commissioners are appointed
1787	Administrative reforms in Belgium
1788	War with Turkey. Revolts in Hungary
1789	Tax and Agrarian Law. Belgium revolts
1790	Reforms cancelled. Joseph dies.

Catherine the Great

1762	Catherine becomes Tsarina
1764	Church lands taken over by the state
1767	Legislative Commission called
1773–5	Pugachev revolt
1775	Local Government reform
1785	Charter of Nobility/Charter of the Cities
1786	Statute of Popular Schools
1790	Catherine's anti-Revolutionary suppression
1796	Catherine dies.

Overview

THE term 'Enlightenment' refers to the outpouring of ideas which sent shock waves throughout Europe from the middle of the 18th century. As historian E. N. Williams states, in *The Ancient Regime in Europe* (1970), it burst 'in a shower of brilliant concepts' and led to feverish intellectual debate across the continent. Europe was a continent dominated by the actions of kings, queens, nobles and clergy. The 18th century witnessed a challenge to existing ideas about absolute monarchy. Some monarchs, such as in France, clung to old beliefs. Others, such as Joseph II of Austria or Catherine the Great of Russia, recognised that they had a duty to serve the state and to reform it. For once, historians cannot be blamed for attaching the label the 'Enlightenment' to that period. Contemporaries used the term *le siécle des lumiéres* ('the enlightened age') because they realised that this was an exciting time to be enquiring, philosophising and reasoning. As the printing presses got to work and as discussions took place in coffee-houses, clubs, literary associations or among **salon society**, there was an awareness that new ways of looking at the world were being formulated. Jean D'Alembert called it a 'lively intellectual ferment'; but where was it leading?

It is easier to identify what the intellectuals of the Enlightenment disliked rather than decide what they were actually proposing. Perhaps this is hardly surprising. It was never the intention of the French *philosophes* to suggest policy; it was certainly their intention to question, argue and reason. As historian Hugh Dunthorne, in the Historical Association pamphlet 'The Enlightenment' (1991), puts it: 'For all its party-spirit, the movement produced no generally accepted programme and its leading members were famous for disagreeing with one another.' Their ideas were complex, as were the geographical, social and political contexts in which they wrote. Few ideas united them. Things were certainly different in Britain, in France, in Italy or in Germany.

However, it is possible to identify broad features which were common to the thinkers of the Enlightenment and which highlight changes in mentality which were taking place throughout Europe. What were these features?

Salon society: Fashionable ladies and gentlemen drawn from the noblesse (nobility) who met socially in salons or public lounges either at Court or in the houses of the wealthy. The salons were places of gossip, gambling and talk of the Enlightenment.

Philosophes: These writers of the Enlightenment sought to question traditional assumptions about society, the Church and **absolutism**.

Absolutism: In theory, this political system meant that the ruler was 'absolved' from accountability to his fellow men – he or she was answerable only to God.

2.1 What was the Enlightenment?

A sense of enquiry and criticism

Jean le Rond d'Alembert (1717–1783)
A French mathematician who worked closely on the great work of the Enlightenment, *Encyclopédie*, with Denis Diderot. D'Alembert framed several mathematical theorems and principles (including d'Alembert's principle) and devised the theory of partial differential equations.

It was the central nature of the Enlightenment to criticise and to enquire – and the range of targets selected for scrutiny was very wide. The *philosophes* did manage to agree on one matter – they contributed to the collection of their works, the *Encyclopédie*, published in 28 volumes and completed by 1772.

Denis Diderot, its co-editor, set out the aims of the Enlightenment: 'Everything must be examined, everything must be shaken up, without exception.' Little escaped their attention. As T.C.W. Blanning notes, in *Joseph II and Enlightened Despotism* (1970), there was nothing new about the attack on existing assumptions, ideas and institutions. But there was a new intensity and passion about it.

This search for new truths would shake the confidence of the establishment, particularly the Catholic establishment. The thinkers refused to

The Inquisition: A Catholic tribunal set up by Rome to root out heresy.

Revocation of the Edict of Nantes 1685: Louis XIV revoked the edict (law) granting some limited toleration of Huguenots (Protestants) within the French State. Following this, Huguenots were persecuted and forcibly converted to Catholicism.

Artisans: People whose work requires skill with their hands, such as painters and sculptors, carpenters and engravers.

Judicial torture: A 'confession' was extracted on the orders of Catholic judges. In fact, Jean Calas' only crime was being a Protestant. His name was eventually cleared.

Tithes and church taxes: The clergy received special dues, including tithes, which amounted to about 8% of a peasant's annual crop. See Chapter 3.

Utilitarianism: The belief that the greatest happiness of the greatest number should be the guiding principle of conduct.

accept the unproved dogmas (stated opinions) of the Churches or the Scriptures. The Church's insistence that it was itself the exclusive repository of all truth and knowledge had already been undermined. Scientific enquiry threatened the Church. The **Inquisition** had been called to suppress Galileo's theory that the sun was at the centre of the universe, an idea which was contrary to Church teaching. Questions were being asked about Catholic beliefs. Printing presses poured out attacks on Church dogmas, abuse and injustices. The bishops were attacked for their worldly wealth, loose morals and privileges. The Church seemed to encourage superstition and intolerance.

The **Revocation of the Edict of Nantes** which suppressed the French Huguenots (Protestants) and led to the emigration of thousands of skilled **artisans** was further evidence of a backward-looking Catholic Church. The celebrated case of Jean Calas, a Huguenot wrongly executed for murder after **judicial torture**, was further evidence of injustice carried out by a corrupt legal system. **Tithes and church taxes** contributed to the burden on peasants. Monasteries attracted particular contempt. The portly monks – isolated, rich and surrounded by holy 'relics' – were the subject of scorn. Many contemporaries would have agreed when Voltaire (see page 30) dismissively noted that 'they (monks) sing, they drink, they digest'. The Catholic Church controlled education and did its best to prevent the spread of new ideas – the work of its censors saw to that. The enlightened thinkers had a different agenda.

A sense of human progress

Enlightened thinkers sought to liberate 'man' from the narrow teachings of the Church. They shared a faith in the possibility of human progress and improvement – people should no longer be satisfied with their lot just because 'God had ordained it thus'. Thought was given to the 'general good' – promoting people's happiness in this life rather than in the after-life. Education could help people to realise their talents and to become useful citizens. Everything was subjected to the test of **utilitarianism** – useful laws and useful institutions were needed to improve the welfare of society. And this would be achieved by an army of officials. They would spread the benefits of reform introduced by a ruler who would regard himself as the 'first servant of the state'.

A sense of reason

A revolution in philosophy was driven by René Descartes, Isaac Newton and John Locke. When Newton proposed his laws on motion in his book

René Descartes (1596–1650)
French philosopher and mathematician who believed that commonly accepted knowledge was doubtful because of the subjective nature of the senses. He attempted to rebuild human knowledge using as his foundation *cogito ergo sum* ('I think, therefore I am'). Descartes identified the 'thinking thing' (i.e. the human soul and consciousness).

Isaac Newton (1642–1727)
English physicist and mathematician who laid the foundations of physics. He studied at Cambridge University, where he became a professor at the age of 26. Newton sat in the parliaments of 1689 and 1701–2 as a Whig. As master of the Royal Mint he carried through a reform of coinage. In 1665 he began to investigate gravitation inspired, so legend has it, by seeing an apple fall from

a tree. A by-product of his experiments with light and prisms was the development of the reflecting telescope.

John Locke (1632–1704)
English philosopher who studied at Oxford. He practised medicine before becoming secretary to the Earl of Shaftesbury in 1667. Locke fled to Holland in 1683 where he lived until the 1688 revolution brought William of Orange to the

English throne. Locke's 'Second Treatise on Civil Government' (1690) helped to form contemporary ideas of liberal democracy. This theory supposed that governments derive their authority from popular consent, so a government may be rightly overthrown if it infringes such fundamental rights of the people as religious freedom.

Principia Mathematica, his ideas about gravity, and the movement of the planets soon became popular throughout Europe.

The idea of observation and arriving, through scientific reasoning, at an understanding of the laws which govern Nature, quickly caught on. Newton's success in using this approach lit the path which others would follow. He showed that there were alternatives to accepting blindly the assertions of the Church. But the *philosophes* still had a belief in God – He had not been discarded; nor was there any intention of this happening. God was acknowledged as part of Nature. As the creator, God still had a role in the universe along with the laws which made it work. However, God was no longer the all-powerful and sole force.

A sense of upheaval

Descartes declared he would 'accept as true nothing that I did not know to be evidently so'. Politics, society and economics were not going to escape criticism. If the Church was being challenged, so was **divine right monarchy**. The mystical powers of the King (for example, his claim to cure diseases by the laying-on of hands) were likely to fail the application of scientific reasoning. Once divine right was undermined, absolutism was also likely to be challenged. Absolutism 'absolved' the monarch from earthly accountability because he would ultimately answer to his God. If this was questioned, on what authority was the power of the ruler now based? And was absolutism so beneficial?

It was not a coincidence that some of the *philosophes* were **anglophiles**. Both Voltaire and Montesquieu (see page 29) appreciated that the English model reflected Enlightened thinking and that England's emergence as a world power and industrial nation owed nothing to absolutism. Why should it? The defenders of an absolutist system argued that it guaranteed strong government and military pre-eminence, as it enabled the complete mobilisation of the resources of the state. England, however, appeared to be achieving similar results with a monarch who shared power with parliament. Knowledge of other ancient civilisations was likely to make Europeans question the assumption that they were more advanced. Books told of cultures outside Europe, perhaps in China or Arabia, Rome or Greece. Europe's ruling families no longer felt assured that they were centre stage – the Catholic Church and absolutist rulers ought not to have sounded so self-satisfied, claiming that they alone had all the answers. Enlightened thinkers did not accept that the state should be run purely in the interests of one royal family. Critical voices were heard more regularly as the century wore on.

If the purpose of the ruler was being re-examined, so was the purpose of **privilege**. Did privilege fulfil a useful role, thinkers asked? Did the privileges of the Church, **nobility**, **guilds** and **municipal corporations** safeguard the rights of the individual citizen? Or did they detract from the general good by encouraging exploitation of one individual by another? How might the greatest happiness and a sense of progress be achieved when one group of citizens overburdened and forced the rest into following them? How might injustice be prevented when the privileged few could maintain their position at other people's expense?

Those who defended privilege were regarded as the enemies of progress. John Locke's 'Second Treatise on Civil Government' (1690) proposed the idea of a social contract between government and governed. 'Man' had a right to basic freedoms and security. The ruler was responsible for maintaining such natural laws. In a **civil society**, there was mutual consent and agreement about these fundamental rights – power was a trust from the community. When laws were applied according to reason,

Divine right monarchy: Traditionally, Kings claimed to be appointed by God and thereby act as his representatives on Earth.

Anglophiles: People who love all things Anglo-Saxon (English).

Privilege: Nobles and clergy had particular rights – for instance, they could claim to be tried in special courts and to have tax exemption.

Nobility: Traditionally, the noble class fought to defend the realm. It consisted of a privileged, landed and titled group of people.

Guilds: Groups of skilled craftworkers organised themselves into guilds (groups) to protect prices and wages.

Municipal corporations: Ruling bodies of towns and cities, often controlled by one powerful, wealthy family.

Civil society: Based on the theory that the governed consented to the rule of an administrator who would provide security and a 'natural order' in society – liberty, self-preservation and the right to own property. Power in a civil society was not derived from God but from the agreement and trust of the governed.

> *What does this source reveal about the attitudes of the Enlightenment towards the law and the reform of justice in the 18th century?*

In this engraving from one of Beccaria's books, the figure of Justice turns away from capital punishment towards the tools used by criminals sentenced to hard labour.

the individual should be protected against injustice and arbitrary rule. The rule of law should protect the citizen, but who should safeguard the law? Should it be the King, who also created the law? It became a fundamental principle of enlightened thinking that those who enact the law should not have the power to enforce and apply it. Hence a 'separation of powers' was proposed – that the ruler should be separate from the judiciary – to prevent despotism (see page 29), and to impose checks and balances on the power of the monarch.

Similarly, when Cesare Beccaria wrote about justice in 1764 he called for a fairer legal system. This included equality before the law, and an end to torture and capital punishment. Laws, he said, needed to be simpler and fairer.

But did the writers of the Enlightenment present a clear and organised programme? No. In matters of detail there were major differences between the *philosophes*. However, in general their writings were optimistic, benevolent, reflective and committed to making laws which guaranteed progress and the greater good. None of this might reasonably be regarded as revolutionary.

Humanitarianism: The concern that humanitarians have for the welfare of humankind. Humanitarians work for the welfare of humankind in the hope that life will be improved and there will be less suffering and pain.

Orphanages: Places where children who are orphans (have no parents or guardians) are looked after.

Emancipation of serfs: Freeing peasants from having to work for an overlord, so that they can live their own lives.

1. **In what ways did the Enlightened challenge traditional ideas in 18th-century Europe?**

2. **How far was the Enlightenment a 'revolutionary' movement?**

Enlightened beliefs

These include:

- the rule of law
- welfare and the general 'good'
- progress
- efficient administration
- better education and poorhouses
- toleration
- abolition of torture and persecution
- **humanitarianism**
- a free press, the founding of **orphanages**, the **emancipation of serfs**
- the abolition of privilege.

2.2 What were the main ideas of the writers of the Enlightenment?

The Physiocrats

This group of writers aimed to resolve the apparent contradiction between authority on the one hand and defending people's freedoms on the other. How was it possible to ensure the rule of law (which was necessary to protect people's security and rights) while at the same time preserving civil liberty? In which case, were 'enlightened' and 'despotic' two mutually exclusive and contradictory concepts? The Physiocrats defended the concept of 'legal despotism'. They argued that only a strong ruler with authoritarian powers could maintain the natural order of things. They defined the natural order as the people's right to self-preservation, liberty, private property, and to buy and sell in a free market without hindrance. According to historian Norman Davies, in *Europe – A History* (1970), 'The celebrated slogan *'pauvres paysans, pauvre royaume'* ('poor peasants, poor realm') encapsulated the revolutionary notion that national prosperity could only be assured through the personal prosperity and liberty of all.'

Physiocrats, who included François Quesnay (who wrote his 'Tableau Economique' in 1758) and Anne[1] Turgot (French *Controlleur-Général*, 1774–76) then set about arguing how this prosperity might be assured. In a concerted attack on **mercantilism**, they aimed to abolish restrictions and remove obstacles to economic freedom. These included abolishing monopolies, guilds, tariffs and, most of all, the privileges of the wealthy. It would need despotic power to cut through the self-interest of these privileged groups. With obstructions removed, the state would flourish. **Serfdom** would be abolished. A single land tax would be

Mercantilism: An economic theory based on strict state regulation to obtain wealth by stimulating exports and restricting imports. Subsidies and monopolies would help exports, while tariffs would stop foreign competition.

Serfdom: The social and economic system by which the land was owned by the wealthy classes but cultivated by serfs (peasants).

---

[1] Anne was a man's name at this time.

'**Legal despotism**': When a King adopted powers in order to introduce Enlightened reforms against the wishes of self-interested groups in society.

Laissez-faire: The belief in free trade and that government interference should be kept to a minimum.

Montesquieu (1689–1755)
Born Charles de Secondat: nobleman and magistrate. Montesquieu became President of the parlement of Bordeaux. His major works included *Lettres Persanes (Persian Letters)*, published in 1721 and *De l'Esprit des Lois (Spirit of the Laws* 1748). He was a defender of privilege and nobility, and proposed the 'separation of powers'.

Index: A list of books banned by the Catholic Church.

Despotism: The rule of states by individuals whose power is not limited by reference to a constitution.

Veto: To decide officially that a scheme or plan must not be put into action and to have the power to prevent it being put into action.

Tyranny: Cruel and unjust rule by a person or small group who has complete power over everyone else in the country.

paid by all, with the landlord paying his fair share. Efforts would be made to stimulate 'natural' products since the wealth of the nation depended on agriculture, fisheries and forestry rather than gold (as mercantilists believed). Expanding grain production would prevent famine and encourage the growth of the population, which would increase taxable wealth.

It needed '**legal despotism**' to overcome the forces of privilege, combined with economic freedom based on *laissez-faire* principles. The ruler would merely have to follow the natural order to win the consent of the people. The assumption was that the best government was the least government. Apparently, Quesnay's reply to Louis XV when asked what he would do if he was king was '*Rien*' (nothing). Other Enlightened thinkers did not agree, as they were convinced that the human condition could be transformed by enlightened law-making. Some historians, such as Fritz Hartung in *Enlightened Despotism* (1957), have dismissed the influence of the Physiocrats. Hartung claims that their practical effects were nil.

Turgot had the chance to put Physiocratic ideas into practice and failed. He was dismissed after only two years when his reforms aroused anger from privileged groups (see page 55).

However, there is another case to answer. While no European ruler directly implemented Physiocratic ideas, it would be wrong to assume that they made no impact on those rulers who read them, especially if they were receptive to change. *Laissez-faire* and free trade were widely accepted in the 19th century, and Joseph II eagerly embraced 'legal despotism'.

We will now look at three of the more important *philosophes*.

What were Montesquieu's ideas?

Montesquieu had the most influence on political ideas of all the philosophes. His books were very popular. *De l'Esprit des Lois*, despite running to 22 volumes, was a bestseller and the Catholic Church lost no time in banning it by placing it on the **Index**. Montesquieu's approach was conservative. What really concerned him was how to develop a political system which would prevent despotic rule. He disapproved of absolutism. Instead, political processes must be in place to restrain the ruler. His views were used by French parlements to voice their opposition to Louis XVI. Montesquieu influenced the constitution formulated by the Americans following their successful rebellion against George III. His language 'was conceived essentially as a safeguard against **despotism** rather than as an instrument of progress' (G.R.R. Treasure, *The Making of Modern Europe 1648–1780*, 1985). He was far from a revolutionary. Monarchy and the defence of privilege were guiding principles. A mixed monarchy provided the best basis for the defence of people's rights and liberties. Paradoxically, he had travelled widely and despite studying the English political constitution (which he admired) he mistakenly thought that it represented a 'separation of powers'.

According to Montesquieu, the monarch would administer the laws (and have the power to **veto** them). An assembly with two houses would make the laws, while an independent judiciary would ensure that the laws were obeyed. A privileged nobility was guaranteed power under this constitution through one of the assemblies. Montesquieu foresaw a kindly monarchy acting in accordance with reason to protect the people and avoid the misery of war. He warned against intolerance and **tyranny**.

Montesquieu claimed that such things as climate, religion, social practices and historical customs shaped 'a general spirit' of law. This differed from state to state. He was more interested in trying to understand the ways in which people were governed. He left it to others to advocate radical change. This did not stop him criticising absolutism, the clergy and financial abuse. His *Lettres Persanes* (1721) claimed to be the letters written by a visitor to Paris from Persia. It was a device that not only enabled Montesquieu to escape the censor, but also to score points against the establishment. Most of all, Montesquieu offered a practical political model – other writers were less constructive.

What were Voltaire's political ideas?

Voltaire's witty use of ridicule or sarcasm exposed obvious cases of injustice, such as that of the Huguenot Jean Calas. He had no time for the Catholic Church, which he regarded as the worst example of an intolerant institution. His prejudices in matters of faith resulted in the Church preventing him from having a Christian burial. 'If God did not exist it would be necessary to invent Him' was just one of his many attacks on established religion.

Voltaire contributed to the *Encyclopédie* (see page 39) and in his *Lettres philosophiques* (1734) he spread Newton's ideas. Historians have questioned Voltaire's reputation as a thinker and philosopher. Essentially, he was a merciless campaigner and a satirist. He spread ideas in a style which made them popular. His writing made fun of tyrants and the clergy. Voltaire has been criticised for not presenting clear Enlightened policies. This is hardly surprising as it was never his intention to present either practical alternatives or clear ideas about a perfect society. He was a critic. His greatest achievement was to emphasise the importance of reason and toleration.

Voltaire believed that if a ruler was wise and fair, then checks and balances were unnecessary. He hated the idea of 'government by the masses' – or by *la canaille* (rabble) as he referred to them. Instead, Voltaire proposed the continuation of absolute monarchy. He knew that power could be abused (as in a tyranny). But there would be a select group of nobles to assist the ruler. The approval of absolutism was in contrast to other *philosophes*, although he shared the view that privileged nobility should take part in government.

Judgements of Voltaire are varied. His popularity contributed to the way in which existing ideas were challenged. On the other hand, he sometimes went too far. He is not above criticism himself. He was a wealthy man – and part of his wealth came from the slave trade and from his estates at Ferney where he lived as feudal lord, claiming tax exemption and exacting dues from his peasants. He built a church for his peasants despite attacking the existence of God. He also courted the favour of Frederick the Great of Prussia and Catherine the Great of Russia. He accepted their **patronage**. He even accepted Frederick's hospitality in Potsdam for three years. However, Voltaire never missed the opportunity to attack despotism. In his book *Candide* he mocked the King of Bulgaria (in reality, Frederick the Great) for the futility of military discipline and warfare. Voltaire was part of the spirit of the Enlightenment but he did not have much in common with fellow *philosophes* – as the next section will show.

Did Rousseau encourage tryanny?

'Man is born free, but everywhere in chains.' Rousseau's *The Social Contract* delivered this powerful statement. His idea of human equality and the 'natural' goodness of each individual lay at the heart of this remarkable man's philosophy. Yet he has been accused of encouraging and justifying tyranny. Why?

Rousseau was appalled by the repressive nature of French absolutism and by the extent of poverty in Paris amid the wealth of the aristocracy. In

---

'Voltaire' (1694–1778)
Pen name of François Arouet, one of France's most intimidating and influential writers. He abandoned a training in law to make a living as an author. Early experiences gave him a sharp focus for his attacks on intolerance, privilege and the abuse of the law. He spent 11 months in the Bastille after insulting the duc de Rohan. Once that ***lettre de cachet*** was cancelled, Voltaire travelled to England. The more liberal society he found there was more to his liking. Although his fame spread across France, his writings were frequently banned or subjected to the censor's pen.

Lettre de cachet: Royal decree ordering arrest and imprisonment without trial.

Patronage: The willingness of wealthy or powerful sponsors to commission works from creative artists or to encourage writers to develop their ideas.

Jean-Jacques Rousseau (1712–1778)
French philosopher and writer. Born in Geneva to a watchmaker's family. Although he left when he was 15, Geneva provided a model which shaped his ideas. If his autobiography, *Confessions*, is to be believed, he never settled anywhere for long; instead he had a dissolute and isolated life, much of it spent around Paris or in exile in Holland, Switzerland or England, escaping the attentions of the French authorities for writing banned works.

his 'Discourse on Inequality' he wrote that 'Money, though it buys everything else, cannot buy morals and citizens'. He rejected the Church's dogma on original sin because he asserted that children were born as innocents into a corrupt and rotten world. For Rousseau, 'civilisation' was blamed for the evils of society. 'Man' in his natural state was peaceful, free, equal and part of a supportive community.

Rousseau never suggested that society should go 'back to nature' or that the clock should be turned back. Nevertheless, in *Emile* (published in 1762) he showed how a boy could still lead a good, moral life if he was given the right education. This would allow the individual to learn and develop naturally.

There was a sense of emotion here which was missing from some of the writings of the Enlightenment. Rousseau's bestseller *La Nouvelle Héloïse* (1761) argued that, while reason was important to the human condition, so were people's inner feelings. This book was, after all, the story of an ill-fated couple – the love between a nobleman's daughter and a poor man.

It was *The Social Contract* (1762) which received public condemnation, forcing him into exile (not for the first time). Rousseau drew on the example of Geneva, a small city-state in which many adult males participated in government. He grappled with the same political dilemma as others – how could individual freedom and rights be maintained by a government which had power and authority over the people? Rousseau proposed that the direct participation of all people would give the government the authority to run the state. He thought that all citizens should meet in assemblies to discuss laws and either choose or sack the government. Everybody had to be involved in this ideal of democracy – the people would give consent to the laws, and the interests of all would be guaranteed. Mass meetings would hardly be popular with the crowned heads of Europe – nor with Voltaire. The idea of electing a parliament to represent the views of the people was rejected. From these mass assemblies, those who ran the government would understand 'the General Will' – which laws were best for the whole community. This wise group of administrators would act unselfishly and in accordance with common sense. This 'General Will' represented obvious truths – so obvious that those who disagreed would have to be disregarded. Indeed, Rousseau argued that laws were in the interests of all, so the 'General Will' would be imposed.

Rousseau's views would certainly promote democracy but were unlikely to work in all but small communities. Unfortunately, French Revolutionaries re-interpreted Rousseau's views and used them to justify dictatorship. During the 'Terror', Maximilian Robespierre defended his actions and the use of the guillotine on the grounds that he understood the 'General Will'. Hence the 'Terror' would safeguard the Revolution and the best interests of all. Rousseau's reputation suffered as a result.

However, nothing could be further from his true intentions. Rousseau rejected despotism and resolutely defended the individual. He disagreed with other *philosophes* who argued for some form of monarchy. His ideas did not really take root, although some American Revolutionaries were influenced by him. In the development of political ideas, Rousseau played his part in putting the case for democracy and the direct participation of people in government. This is what made him so different.

1. In what ways did these writers of the Enlightenment disagree?

2. How fundamental were these disagreements?

2.3 What was the impact of the Enlightenment?

The historian Lord Acton delivered a series of lectures in 1890. He was in no doubt that the Enlightenment brought real progress.

> 'The years that followed the Seven Years' War were a time of peace for a greater part of the continent, in the course of which a memorable change took place. It was the age of what may be called the Repentance [regret] of monarchy. That which had been selfish, oppressive and cruel became impersonal, philanthropic [giving freely] and beneficent [helping other people]. The state was employed for the good of the people. It was still despotism but enlightened despotism. It was influenced by the great writers – Locke, Montesquieu, Turgot … There was a serious tendency to increase popular education, relieve poverty, build hospitals, promote wealth, free serfs, abolish torture and to encourage academies and the like. Attempts were made to reform prisons. Laws were codified. The movement was almost totally universal …'

Few contemporary historians would take this extreme position. The idea of a sudden turning point in the 1760s, when rulers abandoned what had gone before and accepted a new set of principles by which to rule their states, is not supported by the evidence. Certainly not in France, as you will read in Chapter 3.

The Enlightenment and the enlightened despots

What impact did the Enlightenment have on European rulers?
There is no agreed view about the extent to which rulers believed the way they acted was because of the Enlightenment. Hartung's definition of enlightened despotism as 'a form of government strongly influenced by the philosophy of the Enlightenment' has the virtue of being clear but rather too broad. It would encompass any ruler who had read the works of the *philosophes* and then took steps to attack the church, end torture, codify the law, tolerate other religions, improve the lot of peasants, encourage education and culture, and free industry and trade from stifling regulation. They undermined the *status quo*, and the belief in divine right monarchy. They attempted to modernise the administration so that they could be the 'first servant of the state' and thereby drive through reforms more quickly and effectively.

Status quo: Keeping things unchanged.

Ultimately, the historian takes a leap of faith – that rulers who were genuinely receptive to the ideas of the Enlightenment might well adopt these in some form to suit their particular states. Attitudes of mind changed as a result of direct contact with the philosophes. This would include Joseph II of Austria, (1780–1790), Catherine the Great (1762–1796) and Frederick the Great (1740–1786). Rulers of smaller states were similarly affected, such as Leopold of Tuscany and Margrave (Marquis) Charles Frederick of Baden.

Some historians have argued that it is difficult to discern any direct impact the Enlightenment might have had. M.S. Anderson, for instance, argued in *Europe in the Eighteenth Century* (1961) that it was impossible for any ruler to stick rigidly to one set of ideas because they were too busy trying to sort out the problems they had inherited. 'Most European rulers could not afford the luxury of close adherence to one ideology even one so loosely defined as the Enlightenment.' The political, economic, social and military characteristics of their states were so complex and powerful that each ruler had little time or energy to implement philosophical theories. Neither were they prepared, apart from Joseph II, to face the upheaval required to implement radical reforms. Rulers such as Frederick the Great merely used the ideas of the *philosophes* to justify policies undertaken for 'reasons of state'. *Raison d'état* (reason having to do with state security) involved increasing the power of the state so rulers could pursue an aggressive foreign policy. The attacks on the Church and the streamlining of the administration might be seen as attempts to improve the wealth and efficiency of the state. The attacks on privilege would assist in modernising government so it could be more successful in war.

It is important to recognise the compromises rulers had to make. The realities of trying to rule large empires meant that practicalities had to be placed before theories. Joseph II, Frederick the Great and Catherine the Great each built on what had gone before. The Enlightenment, by itself, did not lead the monarchs to reform. Often their predecessors had taken huge steps – Frederick William I in Prussia and Maria Theresa in Austria, for example, both introduced key administrative improvements without any influence from the *philosophes*. Nevertheless, it is impossible to read the correspondence between, for example, Voltaire and Frederick the Great or Catherine II, without recognising that they had genuine interest in each other's work. As S.J. Lee notes, in *Enlightened Despotism* (1978), 'this was largely a marriage of convenience'. It suited each side. Voltaire never denied that he flattered monarchs – they provided protection, patronage and a feeling of importance which derived from the association. The monarchs, on their part, could draw on the ideas of *philosophes* and implement those which were realistic according to the situation in which they found themselves. It would never be possible to act entirely on the *philosophes*' suggestions. Catherine the Great recognised this, although Joseph II failed to grasp the realities of power. The 'art of the possible' therefore baffled him.

These rulers are something of a contrast. Joseph aimed to impose enlightened principles through despotic means. For him, the Enlightenment was not open to question. Catherine, however, recognised the limitations on her **autocracy**. She realised what could and could not be achieved if she were to maintain her grip on power. The case could be made that Joseph was an 'enlightened despot', while Catherine aimed for an Enlightened monarchy. The final part of this chapter will explore this idea.

Autocracy: Government of a country or empire by one person who has complete power. Any dissent is usually dealt with harshly.

1. Why is Lord Acton's view of the Enlightenment now outdated?

2. Why is it difficult to assess the impact of the Enlightenment?

2.4 Did Joseph II of Austria succeed in imposing the Enlightenment throughout his Empire?

What influences shaped Joseph II's view on monarchy?

The young Joseph, despite his mother's hostility to the Enlightenment, was well read in the writings of the *philosophes*. It is impossible to discount the effects that they had on the young Prince, particularly his Professor of Law,

Joseph II of Austria (1780–1790)
When only three months old, Joseph was thrust onto the political stage. His mother, Maria Theresa, had become Empress of Austria in the previous year. She had inherited a weak state paralysed by debt, dithering old ministers, a poor army and an administration which was ineffective and inefficient. In 1741, a disastrous event took place which would overshadow Maria Theresa's reign and that of her son. Frederick the Great attacked Austria and seized its richest province – Silesia. Maria appeared in front of the Hungarian **Estate** with Joseph in her arms and appealed for taxes and military support. In order to regain Silesia, Maria Theresa was forced to reorganise her state for war.

Estate: A representative assembly of nobles, through which they exercised power.

Karl Martini. Joseph's teenage *Rêveries* (diaries), written when his political views were forming, show him eager to modernise the Empire and to adopt an enlightened but despotic approach in order 'to do good'. But he would have to wait. Maria Theresa ruled until 1765 when her husband, Francis of Lorraine, died. Joseph became co-regent with his mother until 1780 when she died. She was cautious, pragmatic, and never dazzled by the Enlightenment. Over-enthusiastic proposals for reform were quickly suppressed, and Joseph chafed under his mother's restrictions. There was no disguising the fact that Joseph wanted action. On the death of Maria, Baron Risbeck wrote: 'As soon as Joseph stands alone at the helm, a revolution will take place here …'. In 1780 he was 39 and a cold, single-minded individual, probably not likeable, and certainly arrogant to the point where he thought he was incapable of making mistakes.

Joseph was impatient. He was intolerant of criticism. His intention to impose a whirlwind of reform, attempting 100 years of change in 10 years, would cause major problems.

What kind of state did Joseph inherit?

Geography was the stumbling block. The Empire was far flung (see map). Each area had its own Estates and the nobles who sat on them were stubbornly independent. They blocked centralised rule and, despite Maria Theresa's attempts to streamline the administration of the Austrian homelands, only a limited amount had been achieved. The Roman Catholic Church also hindered progress. It had immense power and had no wish to see enlightened principles adopted, particularly towards Protestants. The Church was determined to maintain the *status quo*.

Austria was mainly agricultural with a sparse and illiterate population. The economy failed to prosper, and the different languages, laws and culture within the Empire made the prospect of reform difficult. Parts of

The Austrian Empire under Joseph II

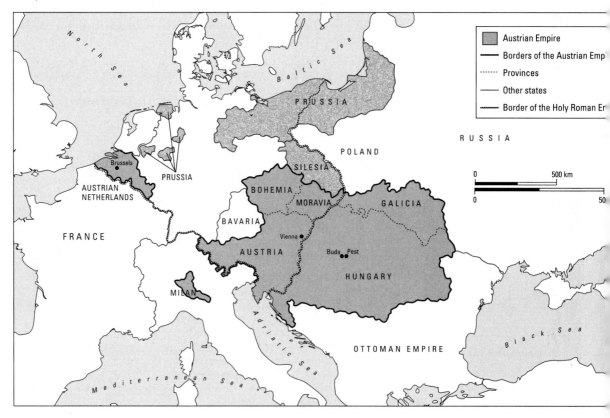

Semi-independent: Both areas had Estates or assemblies that exercised significant powers above those exercised from Vienna.

Robot: Peasants were forced to provide free labour for their landlord.

Unitary state: Centralised administration throughout the empire, with laws imposed by decree.

Bureaucracy: Administrative system operated by a large number of officials following rules and procedures.

Dominions: Areas controlled by a ruler.

Joseph's Habsburg lands did not welcome Imperial interference, particularly the Austrian Netherlands and Hungary which were **semi-independent**.

Maria Theresa had attempted modest reforms, and there is a case for arguing that Joseph introduced little that was original. His government and education reforms built on work started by his mother. Although Hungary, Italy and Belgium had been hardly touched, Austrian provincial administration was modernised and the Estates bypassed. Small steps were taken to extend state supervision of the Church – their courts were supervised. In 1774, a General Education Regulation set up a national system of schools and, the following year, there was a move to limit the amount of forced labour (the *robot*) which a serf had to complete. Joseph wanted the *robot* to be abolished but his mother insisted on it being limited to three days a week. This law, called the Urbarium, had to be withdrawn when internal revolts threatened the safety of the state. Again, Joseph and his mother had argued about the measure. To his disappointment, serfdom remained intact. Nevertheless, Joseph would take up many of these threads when he achieved power.

What were the main influences on Joseph II?

In some respects Joseph II admired Frederick the Great of Prussia who had modernised and centralised his own scattered lands and forged a **unitary state**. But there again, Frederick had seized Silesia from the Austrian Empire. Frederick, then, was both an enemy and a model. He considered himself 'the first servant of the state' and Joseph adopted a similar view. Joseph felt he had a duty to achieve the supreme good, to create a more humane state, to prevent the abuse of privilege and to promote public welfare. He considered his authority was a trust from the people. Despite the unappealing sides to his character, he had an idealistic view of human equality and disliked snobbery and privilege. It was not unknown for him to venture out into the streets and engage ordinary people in debate.

However, his methods provoked hostility – in his single-minded pursuit of change he would accept no criticism. There would be no compromise with the forces of privilege ranged against him – short-term despotism would cut through that. Nor would there be any separation of powers – the ruler would need to monopolise power for the benefit of all. Joseph could not wait for practical results. In 1780, he had been made to wait before applying his vision, and his health was now failing. He had no time to lose. It was not what he did, it was the way that he did it which caused a crisis at the end of his reign.

How did Joseph attempt to create a unitary state?

Joseph's vision of a more humane and efficiently run state would depend on a centralised, well-run **bureaucracy**. Only through this would new laws be passed and the forces of privilege swept away. Uniformity would be imposed and traditional self-interest destroyed. Such was the diverse nature of his **dominions** that control from Vienna had to be assured and an army of civil servants would carry out the urgent task of reform. Everywhere Joseph turned, there were local Estates or municipal councils with powers which posed obstacles to the smooth execution of laws from Vienna – local bodies would be swept away.

1. Even in Austria and Bohemia, at the heart of the Empire, authority was divided. Here, Joseph built on his mother's tightening of control. A single Chancellery was introduced to have an overview of all areas of government, chaired by the Emperor. Only foreign policy (where Maria's old minister, Prince Wenzel Anton von Kaunitz, retained a say

in policy), the army and justice were outside the Chancellery's authority. Local government was streamlined and six administrative units (governments or *gubernia*) were set up. The surviving local Estates lost nearly all of their influence.

2. Hungary was further away from Vienna and virtually independent. Maria Theresa had confirmed the local powers of Hungarian nobles in exchange for assistance against Frederick of Prussia. Nobles were in control everywhere. Although the national parliament was rarely called, noble families had a stranglehold on county assemblies which controlled the administration, the Church, schools and justice. Indeed Hungarian justice was something of a scandal – it was both unfair and barbaric. The execution of 115 gypsies in 1782 for alleged **cannibalism** is often quoted as one of the more shocking cases of the abuse of legal powers. Furthermore, Hungary did not pay a fraction of the taxation which was due given the size of the province. Joseph was determined to impose a more humane and unified system.

Cannibalism: Eating the flesh of living things of the same type (e.g. humans eating humans).

Reforms began in 1784 to a predictably hostile response. In Hungary the following reforms were introduced:

● Joseph refused a coronation in Budapest and the ancient Crown of St Stephen was transferred from Hungary to Vienna in 1784. Nationalist passions were inflamed because of this.

● German was decreed as the official language. It was more useful if all official documents were written in one language. But, again, national pride had been assaulted. However, the Hungarian Diet (government) conducted business in Latin.

● Hungarian assemblies declined in importance and their authority was transferred to ten provincial Austrian Commissars.

● Conscription (compulsory military service) was introduced.

● Courts were run by Austrian officials not Hungarian nobles.

● If all this was not enough to provoke a revolt, the final straw was a proposal to end nobles' tax exemption. Austria was at war with Turkey (1788–90) and Joseph needed resources urgently. Instead of coming to his aid, Hungarian nobles rebelled in 1789 and appealed to Prussia for assistance.

3. In the Austrian Netherlands (Belgium), Joseph had much to gain from the co-operation of the ruling elite. The province was passive, paid generous taxes and serfdom did not exist.

Joseph could not let things alone. He visited Belgium and found the process of government complex, inefficient and unclear. Local estates had wide powers and 'within each province, the privileged groups of a bygone era kept Belgian life in a state of self-satisfied stagnation: clergy, nobility, universities, town councils and guilds and so on' (E. N. Williams). Insensitive to the interests of nobles and office holders, Joseph began the process of reform in 1787. Once again, the German language decree was introduced and local Estates lost their powers. A General Council implemented orders from Vienna and provincial government was in the hands of nine German-speaking **intendants**.

Intendants: Royal officials who carried out orders directly from Vienna.

Once again, the onset of the Turkish war brought fears that privileges would be under attack. By 1789 the Austrian Netherlands, too, had exploded with civil disobedience and insurrection.

4. Joseph's Italian territories – Lombardy and Milan – were not immune from the drive to impose reform by edict. If the law and the economy were to be modernised then obstructive, privileged oligarchies (government by few) would have to be destroyed. Milan was the home of Cesare Beccaria. Where better to introduce enlightened justice?

In 1786 ruling bodies were abolished: the Senate (in Lombardy) and the Council of Sixty (in Milan). Once again, Vienna ruled through *intendants*. New administrative districts and new courts of law were introduced.

Even Enlightened thinkers were shocked by the radical and rapid nature of these reforms. Economist Pietro Verri wrote that Joseph knew the system was rotten but, in destroying all laws and practices, he made the 'remedy worse than the malady. He took no account of opinion … and made men feel all the unlimited power of a monarch who recognises no other standard than his own will.'

Joseph had committed the major error of losing the support of his nobles. Other monarchs, such as Louis XIV or Frederick the Great, understood the truth behind Montesquieu's dictum, 'No nobles, no King, no King, no nobles'. Nobles were the keystone to maintain the stability of the state and the monarchy. Joseph ignored this at his peril.

Could the civil servants cope with the pace of change?
The civil servants had to deal with over 17,000 of Joseph II's decrees, long hours and a demanding master. They failed to cope and Joseph hurled abuse at them for what he assumed was their lazy and unco-operative behaviour.

They were spied on, bullied and files were compiled on their work. In 1784, District Commissioners were appointed in the provinces to ensure that no one was ignoring his decrees. In the teeth of a storm of protest, Joseph was determined to see these administrative changes through. In Austria, at least, the unitary state stood a chance; elsewhere it was unlikely to succeed. Was a programme of forcing enlightened reform on people by edict doomed to fail? Was it Joseph's ideas which were at fault or his methods? Before reaching a conclusion, how were other reforms greeted? Which were the most lasting of Joseph's reforms?

How did Joseph use the law?
Joseph's legal reforms are usually considered a great success. They lasted into the 20th century. Characteristically, they are a mixture of humanity and the severe application of reason. The latter, however, did introduce a darker side to aspects of Imperial justice.

Initially, Joseph II continued Maria Theresa's work by drawing on the ideas of Beccaria and his own law professor, Martini. Most remarkably, the Penal Code (1781) and Code of Criminal Procedure (1788) introduced equality under the law (nobles receiving the same punishments as everyone else) and abolished the death penalty.

Appeal courts gave a chance for a re-trial. To prevent those accused of crime languishing in prison for too long, charges had to be brought within 24 hours and presented to a judge within three days. Some punishments were banned, such as mutilation, branding and the use of stocks. Some crimes that related to spiritual practices, such as witchcraft, were regarded as less severe and were no longer punishable by death. Nobles were deprived of duelling as a method by which gentlemen might resolve a dispute – it was banned. The quality of justice did not escape scrutiny. The Order of Civil Procedure (1781) gave Vienna the power to supervise church and local courts, while judges were required to pass law examinations. Children and the insane were no longer regarded as criminally responsible.

These were remarkable advances, and historians often make comparisons with justice elsewhere. Historian T.C.W. Blanning points out, in *Joseph II* (1984), that Joseph was 'a model of rationality' compared with government in France where a child could have his tongue cut out for blasphemy.

Nevertheless, there was another side. Capital punishment may have been abolished but prison and hard labour were savage. Forcing a convicted murderer to pull barges up the river Danube was not only more useful, but also made a lasting example of the guilty party. Reference will be made later to the expanding activities of the secret police, which operated outside the law.

Overall though, Joseph had introduced a more humane justice system.

How did Joseph change education and welfare?

Education policy continued along the lines introduced during the co-Regency. The reforms appear enlightened enough as Austria provided a level of education unequalled anywhere in Europe. The reality reflects a utilitarian and penny-pinching, miserly attitude. Joseph had no appreciation of education for its own sake. Intellectual pursuits were a means to an end – expanding the frontiers of human knowledge was not enough.

State education had specific purposes – to teach obedience, to break the grip of the Catholic Church on education, to further the use of German throughout the Empire, and to provide a steady stream of trained civil servants. There were only enough places at university for the number of vacancies in the civil service.

Amadeus Mozart, too, suffered in the name of utilitarianism when his pension was terminated. It was a sad reflection on Joseph's enlightened policies.

Education

- Compulsory education for primary school age children but still only 30% attended.

- Fines were levied for non-attendance.

- Schools would provide civil servants, farmers or soldiers, and housewives.

- There was a much smaller number of secondary schools with 60 'gymnasia' for able boys subject to fees being paid.

- Only four universities survived Joseph's cuts.

- German was spoken widely in schools and 'non-useful' subjects like Music were not taught.

---

1. **In what ways was Joseph II more interested in utilitarian reform than humanitarian reform?**

2. **To what extent did these changes reflect the Enlightenment?**

In contrast, Joseph introduced a wide range of welfare reforms which went far beyond those elsewhere in Europe or those proposed by Enlightened writers. From virtually no provision, Joseph set up orphanages, hospitals, institutions for handicapped people as well as foundling homes (for illegitimate children). **Lunatic asylums** were run along liberal and humanitarian lines. Where hospital provision existed, the very poor didn't pay. This forms an impressive record.

How did the Church fare?

The Enlightened writers reserved particular venom for the Catholic Church. It was rich, privileged, intolerant and an obstacle to reform. Its beliefs were based on dogma and superstition – not reason. Its censors

Lunatic asylums: Hospitals for those with mental illnesses.

Metaphysical: Relating to theories about what exists and how we know that it exists – often based on the abstract or superstitious.

Papacy: The position, power and authority of the Pope, including the length of time that a particular person holds this position.

Dissolution of contemplative orders: The closing of monasteries which were devoted to prayer study rather than 'good works'.

Relics: Things which are kept because they are associated with a saint, often a body or part of it. They are thought to be holy.

were out in force to suppress the *Encyclopédie* and its like. Joseph hated the way it anchored Austria in the past.

However, Joseph's motives were more complex. It is true that Joseph could see the practical advantages of encouraging skilled workers from abroad who might be Protestants. He recognised that the Church could do useful work in the community, although he felt its wealth might be better spent on welfare and 'good' works. Joseph understood how education ought to be liberated from the **metaphysical**. Yet he had no wish to destroy the Church. He was a devout man who observed religious practices with the same grim sense of duty he applied to many other aspects of his life. In many ways Joseph II strengthened the Church – he built over 1,000 churches in Hungary, for example, and paid particular attention to improving the training of priests.

However, Joseph wanted religious policy on his own terms. The Church had to play its part in the 'unitary state'. Politically, that led to an attack on the influence of the **Papacy**. Not only did the Church claim special status, virtually a 'state within a state', but the Pope exercised authority over Joseph's subjects from outside the state. Given Joseph's view that the clergy should serve the state and their interests should be national, there was bound to be trouble.

None of this was likely to happen unannounced. Apart from the writings of the *philosophes*, which Joseph allowed to circulate freely, his mother had agreed to attacks made by her trusted minister, Kaunitz, on church wealth, privileges, courts and Papal influence. Not for the first time, Joseph would push these early changes to the limit.

Reform was not half-hearted. The first moves were to undermine links with the Papacy. Joseph was uncompromising. The first visit by a Pope to Austria for 350 years took place in 1782. No good came of it, except to advertise the popularity of Pope Pius VI at Joseph's expense.

Attacks on monasteries had begun as early as 1781 with the **dissolution of contemplative orders**. These amounted to around one-third of the total number of monasteries. As far as Joseph's strict logic was concerned, they had made no contribution to poor relief or welfare. The monks and nuns were given pensions, and the buildings put to use as schools, prisons or lunatic asylums. The sale of land and property brought in large revenues – equivalent to a year's taxation.

Joseph took matters a step too far. His interference in daily religious life was badly received. The simple faith of peasants was soon shaken, although Joseph's faith in his own infallibility was unshakeable. The test of utility was applied rigorously to whatever Joseph considered superstitious. **Relics**, statues, paintings, processions and candles were cleared out. German, not Latin, would be spoken. In 1784, coffins were banned in favour of burial sacks.

Joseph never quite grasped the damage he had done to the peasants' personal faith – so much so that everything else the Emperor attempted was automatically damned. He built churches so that no one was more than one hour's walk away from one. Priests were paid a decent salary and tithes were abolished. Colleges taught priests to pay less attention to the superstitious side of Christianity and more to practical welfare. It was also the priest's duty to teach obedience to the state. The priest was expected to be the mouthpiece for the government's enlightened instructions from the pulpit: everything from farming to not drinking contaminated water. Joseph's efforts were not appreciated. 'The unitary state may have borne a distinct resemblance to a workhouse but at least it was a co-operative effort' (Blanning in *Joseph II*).

These changes were deeply unpopular with ordinary people. So were Joseph's attempts at toleration. Once again he had the best of intentions and religious toleration was not unknown elsewhere in Europe. Frederick the Great had introduced it. Joseph showed concern for the oppression suffered by minorities and a pragmatic eye for the benefits of attracting useful immigrants.

The Edict of Tolerations for Protestants (1781) attracted 150,000 Protestants to the Empire and was a success. But in 1782 the Edict of Toleration for Jews created outrage and was even disliked by Jews themselves. They hated conscription and, although Joseph was in favour of assimilating them into the state, the Jews wished to cling to their separate identity. They were relieved of the need to wear the yellow Jewish armband but they feared a dilution of their status as 'chosen' people. Christians were outspoken in their opposition. Despite all this, the Jews did benefit the Empire and there would be no turning the clock back after Joseph's death.

These religious changes were profoundly significant and, for many, profoundly disturbing. Joseph may have had everybody's best interests at heart, but they detested him for it.

Religion

● Papal influence in Austria was completely weakened. Bishops would have to swear to obey the state and links with the Papacy were severely constrained. Imperial permission was needed before any appeals to Rome could be made or before papal communications were published. No foreign bishop was allowed authority inside Austrian borders.

● The Edict of Toleration for Protestants only allowed private worship but did give them equality under the law, of education and entry into professional careers.

● The Edict Relating to Jews tried to remove their social stigma and encourage them to play a full part in the economics of the state and to become obedient servants. It included the same rights as those granted to Protestants but with some limitations. Synagogues (Jewish places of worship) were not allowed – nor was Hebrew in official documents. Jewish children could attend state schools but would be liable to conscription too.

Attacks on the guilds and the economy

The drive toward the unitary state brought a sustained attack on guilds (see page 26). To Joseph, guilds represented a privileged group who prevented progress and performed no useful service except in their own self-interest. Price-fixing, establishing monopolies and limiting membership were all characteristics of the guilds – and their days were numbered.

Many were abolished. Foreign workers were brought in and trade opened up. In general, Joseph's economic polices were a mixture of the the old and the new. He was keen to follow Physiocratic ideas of **free trade**, removing restrictions on industry and internal customs. The exception was Hungary, which was treated like a colony – customs separated it from the rest of the Empire. Otherwise, strands of mercantilism keep re-emerging. Efforts were based on a better transport system (roads and harbours), immigration of skilled workers and incentives for factory owners. Imports were controlled by tariffs – and predictably fell victim to retaliation when tariffs were placed by other government on goods from the empire.

Free trade: A system that encourages the free flow of imports and exports. It is exempt from import tariffs.

Results were modest. Silesia's loss was a constant handicap and everywhere agriculture dominated. Industry was of workshop scale, although tax income increased by over one-third. The most cherished project of the Enlightenment – a single land tax paid by all – was introduced but it had to be quickly withdrawn (see later).

Regrettably, Joseph's work was undone by a disastrous war against Turkey which left a mountain of debt (equivalent to four years' taxation) for the next Emperor, Leopold.

Nobles, privileges and serfs

Perhaps this is the area of policy where Joseph's judgement was at its worst. To Joseph, serfdom cast the darkest shadow over the Empire and it had always been at the heart of disagreements between him and his mother. Again, Joseph mixed humanitarianism with an awareness that serfdom was not useful – it damaged the state by depressing the economy. Agricultural developments were held back, rural poverty was never able to stimulate demand in other sectors of the economy. In common with the *ancien régime* elsewhere, the least able to pay taxes paid the most, while those able to pay did not.

Ancien régime: System of government or state of affairs in France before the Revolution.

Maria Theresa had, in the end, achieved nothing to alleviate the burden on serfs. She was too concerned about not upsetting the nobles to take effective action. Joseph had no such qualms. Indeed, he was more than pleased to treat their social status with disdain. In 1781, a group of decrees made steps towards freeing serfs from their bonds and turning them into freeholders. In theory, these decrees appeared to be a turning point. Reality was different. Until steps were taken to abolish the robot, Austria would remain gripped by serfdom.

Joseph set an example by ridding his Crown lands (including those of the Church) of serfdom. The nobles failed to follow suit. Undeterred, Joseph planned the boldest step of all. In 1789, the Tax and Agrarian Law was introduced. Presumably to the rapture of the *philosophes*, it proposed to replace all taxes, tithes and the *robot* with a single land tax, paid by all. The *impôt unique* would be imposed from above, by decree. Surveys of landholdings (to assess taxation) were carried out, at the point of a sword, causing resentment. Nobody wanted the new law, not even the group of people who were likely to benefit most – the peasants.

Serfdom: 1781 Decrees

● Serfdom was abolished.

● The hold of nobles over serfs was weakened.

● Serfs could leave their village without permission.

● The Penal Patent limited the powers of nobles to punish serfs through the manor courts e.g. higher approval was needed for jail sentences of more than 8 days.

● Serfs had the right of appeal against landlords via a free advocate (lawyer).

● Peasants were allowed to buy land.

Seigneurial dues: For landowners, particularly in rural France, the collection of dues from villagers was regarded as a major item of income.

Why was there opposition to Joseph II's reforms?

Without question, nobles hated the land tax. They would lose their tax privileges, the *robot* and **seigneurial dues** without receiving any compensation. Joseph was deaf to criticism. Indeed he revelled in threatening the nobles if they blocked reform. Louis XIV or Frederick the Great would not have made the same error of judgement. There was a mutual dependency between monarch and privileged orders – the nobles' support for the Crown added stability and underpinned its legitimacy. Attacking privilege would deprive the monarch of his or her mainstay – without privilege conflict was bound to occur.

The serfs' opposition is, perhaps, more difficult to grasp. However, only 20% of serfs were included in the reform – the rest felt excluded and their hopes of an end to the *robot* dashed. The peasants were also in the dark about Joseph's true intentions. They were already suspicious of conscription and were angry at the Emperor's religious reforms. They feared what might happen next. On the face of it, peasants would only pay 30% of their income – a great improvement on previous crippling rates of taxation. But still peasants and nobles rose in revolt.

The French Revolution had already de-stabilised Europe and the army was caught up in a bitter war against Turkey. Conditions for radical reform were not favourable. The Tax and Agrarian Law had to be suspended and the army sent in to crush the revolts. Joseph's single land tax experiment had failed. Here was another example of the way his reign was to end in disappointment and reaction.

Was Joseph II a failure?

Many of Joseph's reforms not only outlived him, but were remarkable advances. The law was most enlightened, Austria was the best schooled country in Europe, and there was no question of reversing the changes in religion. The Catholic Church was no longer the force it had been. The sheer extent of Joseph's legislation was spectacular by any measure. Welfare measures brought more humane treatment to many. However, there was the unmistakable feeling, at the end of the reign, that all his efforts were crumbling.

The Empire was in open revolt. Belgian riots increased from 1787 onwards and, by 1789, the Emperor's troops had been expelled. Hungary's protests were predictable. It was already seething from the administrative restructuring and economic changes which had injured Hungarian pride by reducing its status to little more than a colony. The imposition of the German language and rule from Vienna were regarded as intolerable. Tariffs depressed its economy. But the last straw was the tax decree, and not only in Hungary, for anger and frustration boiled over everywhere. How much of this was Joseph's fault? In Joseph's defence, the nature of the Empire made it difficult to establish a modernised, unitary state.

The geography of the dominions made communications and direct rule from Vienna very difficult. Attitudes of mind were deeply provincial. Each province had distinctive culture, language and traditions. They had no desire to change. Why should they alter the *status quo* on the orders of German officials? Their loyalties and horizons were parochial (based on their own local affairs). Joseph's mother had grasped that to steamroller the provinces into change would cause nothing but trouble. The noble-serf relationship was deeply engrained and produced a static society. It proved beyond Joseph's capabilities to impose a revolution from above, by decree.

Three weeks before he died, the tax decree and the abolition of the *robot* were abandoned. Many administrative changes were reversed and Joseph offered to restore the nobles and the Estates. Joseph had relied on an army of officials to carry out his edicts. They were unequal to the task. He criticised them for their laziness and conservatism, although the way he treated them did not encourage selfless devotion to duty. They were nagged, punished, spied on and overworked.

Here, then, is Joseph cast as the villain. Many of his difficulties were of his own making. He never understood why his efforts to improve the human condition of his subjects were rejected. He was arrogant enough to dismiss the opposition and to plough on regardless. Compromise did not occur to him. Time and again his tactics were at fault. Frederick the Great complained that Joseph made the mistake of taking the second step before the first. His actions certainly lost him the support of nobles and clergy – normally the bedrock of the state. Their outlook could not have been less radical. The attacks on the Church, the establishment of provincial Estates and the ultimate threat of the land tax caused the privileged orders to abandon the Crown. Joseph could not be trusted to defend their interests so they turned to insurrection instead.

Heresy: The rejection of the doctrines and authority of the Roman Catholic Church.

Peasants should have supported him, but his religious policies were so deeply resented that Joseph was associated with **heresy** and the anti-Christ. The system of conscripting peasants to the army added to the sense of outrage. By the time the Tax and Agrarian Law was proposed, Joseph was condemned both for doing too little and for going too far. Some serfs were left out of the reforms and others were fearful of them.

It was foreign policy that began the crisis at the end of the 1780s. Joseph was a disastrous diplomat and a hopeless soldier. T.C.W. Blanning describes his foreign policy as 'muscular but mindless'. Joseph failed to win more than 34 square miles of Bavarian land from Frederick the Great. His efforts to swap Belgium for Bavaria were an embarrassment. And in 1787, war against Turkey left him with a legacy of debt and retreat.

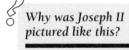

Why was Joseph II pictured like this?

Joseph II is shown behind a plough.

Radicalism: The belief that there should be great or extreme changes in society.

1. What were Joseph II's successes and failures?

2. How far was the nature of his dominions responsible for Joseph II's failures?

As the Empire began to collapse, taxation and conscription were intensified, as was the economic crisis. There were bread riots in 1788. It brought a reversal of Enlightened thinking. As a flood of pamphlets criticised Joseph, he turned to measures to bolster his despotism. Censorship was imposed. Spies were everywhere and the activities of the secret police, under Count Pergen, expanded alarmingly. At times, the rule of law was cast aside in favour of imprisonment without trial.

When **radicalism** was spreading its influence from France, Joseph's subjects were taking urgent steps to maintain as much of the *status quo* as possible. They had had enough. Joseph was thoroughly hated; he had lofty ideals for humanitarian reform and to impose his view of human equality. But his grimly utilitarian outlook was imposed regardless of the opposition of those who were his natural allies in society.

Joseph would have regarded himself as a failure. This was a harsh judgement, but typical of a ruler who would grant no concessions nor waver from his vision of the unitary state.

2.5 Why have historians differed in their interpretations of Catherine the Great?
A CASE STUDY IN HISTORICAL INTERPRETATION

Catherine was a complex figure. At times she could be enlightened, at others autocratic. The historian G.R.R. Treasure regards her as the prophet of the Enlightenment – industrious, genuine and devoted to the service of the state. At other times the *philosophes* disapproved of her.

Catherine seemed overwhelmed by the conservative forces at work in 18th-century Russia. In which case, her claims to be an Enlightened monarch are no more than a **propagandist** at work. These are extreme views to adopt. Catherine knew the realities of power. She probably achieved what she could in the circumstances. She knew she was treading a dangerous path and there were 'moments when it is not necessary to be too precise'.

Propagandist: A person who spreads propaganda (exaggerated or false information) for, for example, a political group or for personal ends.

Was there a progressive shift away from Enlightened thinking during the early part of her reign?

The religious changes started by her husand, Peter III, were confirmed and concluded. In 1764, all monasteries were abolished and all church property was run by the state. There was to be no religious persecution –

Catherine the Great (1762–1796)

Catherine, a German princess, came to power after her husband, Peter III, was butchered by the brother of one of her numerous lovers. 'I shall reign or perish,' she told the British Ambassador. It would take all her skill to survive; brought to power by a palace revolution, she might easily have become the victim of any one of the aristocratic factions which vied for power. Catherine was a remarkable figure – energetic, determined and intelligent. She was well versed in the works of the Enlightenment, writing regularly to Voltaire, Diderot and Montesquieu.

When aged 15, Catherine married the man who would become the future Tsar Peter III. The marriage did not work – Peter rejected her at Court. In 1762, Peter succeeded to the throne but he lasted only a few months. Palace guards overthrew him and Catherine was declared Tsarina.

She inherited a militaristic state, economically underdeveloped, without an efficient administrative structure and dominated by serfdom. The civil service was totally inadequate and the government barely functioned at all.

Catherine's Instructions included:

- Article 9: 'The Sovereign is absolute'

- Article 13: 'What is the true End of Monarchy? Not to deprive people of their natural liberty; but to attain the supreme good.' Voltaire, not surprisingly, loved it.

Zemstvo: An elected assembly consisting of all classes in Russia. It was the first time such a commission had been called to talk about Russia's laws. Catherine's set of instructions to the *Zemstvo* were called the *Nakaz*.

a sign of the Enlightenment. Catherine was certainly enlightened, but she recognised that the take-over of Church lands would be of immense practical benefit – she gained enormous wealth plus over one million serfs. The Church was also in no position to prevent this. Peter the Great had weakened the Church and made it almost a department of state in 1725. However, this policy was largely a success judged purely on the enlightened grounds that religious intolerance barely existed in Russia by the end of Catherine's reign.

In 1767, Catherine called together representatives of Russia in a legislative commission or *Zemstvo*. It was to discuss Russia's laws in an attempt to rationalise them. Two years' hard work went into the instructions for this assembly. Many threads are apparent – some fashionable, some autocratic. Catherine said there should be more freedom for peasants and torture should be abolished. Voltaire praised her to the skies. The commission's results, though, were a disappointment. Few laws were drafted and participants seemed hell bent on preserving their privileges. It did teach Catherine the limitations on her power and how she would need to be cautious in maintaining the support of the nobility by not proceeding too radically.

Subsequent events were to prove her right.

The Pugachev Revolt

Between 1773 and 1775, a serious Cossack revolt, led by Emelian Pugachev, took place. Pugachev pretended to be Peter III. Serfs flocked to join him; so did Cossacks who wished to remain independent. The fact that nobles were killed, towns were sacked and that thousands of serfs took part in it shook Catherine and the aristocracy. Its scale was threatening – it impressed upon Catherine the importance of having a solid basis of support amongst the nobility. Subsequent reforms granted nobles extensive powers over serfs. Catherine is accused of failing to deal with serfdom and repression was savage. Pugachev, though, did promote administrative change – and, in 1775, efforts were made to impose a framework of order, efficient institutions and administrations. In this sense, Catherine's vision was enlightened.

- In 1775, the government was overhauled. Peter the Great's provinces were too large and the administration too cumbersome. Catherine set about decentralising by splitting Russia into better-sized units. Fifty *gubernia* (governments) were set up, each with a governor who was directly responsible to Catherine. Each *gubernia* was split into districts and this enabled local decisions to be made. Nobles dominated the whole system. Enlightened writers applauded this streamlining process, particularly since each *gubernia* had a board responsible for finance, industry, schools, hospitals and poor relief. Catherine the Great's structure survived well into the 19th century, although she was always short of efficient, trained civil servants, and corruption continued to be widespread.

- Russian laws were extended to conquered areas.

- In 1785, Catherine tried to stimulate the urban economy and the spirit of enterprise by publishing the Charter of the Cities. A governor would supervise an elected committee to run each city and a group of professional civil servants would assist.

- As fears of a violent civil war receded after the Pugachev Revolt, it was clear that 'the whole affair sealed the knot that tied Catherine to her nobility' (G.R.R. Treasure). The Charter of Nobility of 1785 (see panel on page 47) confirmed the nobles' privileges. Did it greatly increase their power as has been claimed? Probably not. At least it placed their rights and obligations within a proper structure. Even the voluntary nature of state service was more in appearance than reality. Catherine could summon them to 'spare neither labour nor life' when necessary. Crucially, she controlled the nobles through her personally appointed Provisional Governors.

When Catherine wrote to the *philosophes* she made it clear that she detested serfdom. But she knew it was not within her power to abolish it. Indeed, Catherine contributed to further enserfment. Not only did nobles gain absolute rights over them, but 800,000 Crown serfs (who were not overburdened by obligations) were handed over to nobles and favourites.

The pull of tradition had proved too strong and the rigid social structure, based on the noble–serf relationship had asserted itself.

What happened to the economy and education?

In some aspects of economic life Catherine 'was a true daughter of the Enlightenment'. There was industrial and commercial growth based on order, stability and the liberalisation of the economy. All privileges, monopolies and regulations were swept aside. Trade more than quadrupled (1762–96) and Russia became the world's largest pig-iron producer. However, at the heart of Russia's difficulties was backward agriculture based on serfdom. Nothing was done to solve rural poverty by granting land to the serfs, thereby stimulating production and demand. Farming techniques were primitive and the Russian middle class never developed sufficiently to take trade out of the hands of foreign merchants. By the time of Catherine's death, industry was in decline and debt, because of war and an expensive court, was growing.

Education might have helped. The Statute of Popular Schools (1786) planned a network of elementary and high schools. By her death, 288 had been built. It may appear impressive but their impact was limited. Nor is there any evidence that Catherine was in favour of educating serfs.

The end of the reign

By the late 1780s, Catherine's position in Russia was secure. Her critics point to the lack of progress on serfdom and her increasingly reactionary views. Catherine despised the activities of the French Revolutionaries. She called the National Assembly 'fools masquerading as philosophers'. 'I am an autocrat by profession,' she said and she meant it. Russian students were withdrawn from France, just in case dangerous ideas spread eastwards.

In 1790, Alexander Radishchev, a young nobleman, violently attacked serfdom in a book, *Diary of a Journey from Moscow to St Petersburg.* Catherine's reaction was swift. He was charged with treason and was sent into exile in Siberia.

Police burnt books, papers were censored and spies were widely used. It would be easy to conclude that Catherine had abandoned the Enlightenment, but at least she had given Russia a more cultured and westernised aristocracy. Art and literature flourished. The country was better administered and had a framework of laws and institutions. Catherine's achievements were considerable. Reality prevented her from doing more. She no doubt realised that, in the wake of the Pugachev Revolt, abolishing serfdom was beyond her powers.

1. Why have historians differed in their views on Catherine the Great?

2. Is there a case for defending Catherine the Great's record as an Enlightened monarch? Explain the arguments both for and against this.

The Charter of the Nobility 1785

It agreed that nobles:

- would have their titles protected
- could only be tried by other nobles
- were exempt from paying taxes
- could travel abroad without permission
- had the right of Assembly every three years
- commitment to state service was now voluntary.

 ## Source-based questions: Enlightened Despotism

SOURCE A

Royal authority is sacred ... absolute ... subject to reason. God establishes Kings as his ministers and reigns over people through them. The person of the King is sacred. The prince need render account to no one for what he orders.

Bishop Bossuet, 'Political lessons to be drawn from the scriptures', 1670

SOURCE B

Absolute government is inconsistent with Civil Society. If the King has both legislative and executive power in himself alone, there is no judge to be found, no appeal is open to anyone.

John Locke, 1690, from 'An Essay concerning the true original extent and end of Civil Government'

SOURCE C

The new rationalism meant that the ruler was more willing to justify his authority. He no longer sheltered behind the term 'Divine Right'. Instead he placed more emphasis on the monarch as a servant of the state. Only by this total dedication could he hope to rule the state.

'Enlightened Despotism' by S J Lee, 1978 (from Aspects of European History)

SOURCE D

Montesquieu could not tolerate the absolute aristocracy of France, but praised the mixed monarchy of Great Britain ... which separated the legislative and executive. The French Constitution was absolutist and contrary to nature for it could not adapt itself to the changing needs of the community.

Phyllis Doyle, A History of Political Thought, 1963

1. Study the sources and explain what is meant by the following highlighted phrases. Use your knowledge of absolutism and the Enlightenment to help you explain your answer.

(a) 'Divine Right' (Source C)

(b) Civil Society (Source B)

(c) 'mixed monarchy' (Source D)

2. Study Source A. How useful is this source in understanding the arguments that were used to justify absolutist government?

3. In what ways did the Enlightenment undermine the concept of absolutism? Use all the sources and the information in this chapter to help you answer this question.

The origins of the French Revolution

3.1 What was the *ancien régime*?

3.2 What was France like before the French Revolution?

3.3 Was the French economy in crisis by 1789?

3.4 How far were members of the French monarchy responsible for the outbreak of revolution in 1789?

3.5 Were Enlightened ideas important in bringing revolution?

3.6 How did French governments deal with the financial crises of the 1770s and 1780s?

3.7 The calling of the Estates-General: What caused the revolution to slip out of the hands of the privileged classes?

3.8 Historical interpretation: Why have historians differed in their view of why the French Revolution began in 1789?

Key Issues

● How far was the authority of Louis XVI undermined by the social and economic problems facing France in the late 18th century?

● What was the impact of the Enlightenment on absolute monarchy in France?

● How successfully did Louis XVI respond to the problems faced?

Framework of Events

1740–48	The War of Austrian Succession
1756–63	The Seven Years' War
1771	Exile of *parlements*
1774	Louis XV dies; Louis XVI becomes King
1774 –76	Turgot is *Controlleur-Général*
1776	The Six Edicts
	The onset of economic depression
1777–81	Necker is Director-General
1778–83	The American War of Independence
1783–87	Calonne is *Controlleur-Général*
1786	Calonne warns the King of imminent bankruptcy
1787	The Assembly of Notables
1787–88	Brienne is *Controlleur-Général*
	May Edicts
	Revolt of the Nobles
	Estates-General called for 1789 Necker's return
1789	Bread crisis
	Estates-General meet
	Tennis Court Oath.

Overview

Estates-General: An assembly, called during an emergency, which consisted of the three Estates of France – clergy, nobility and bourgeoisie, and peasantry. Each class was represented. Decisions taken by the Estates-General had legitimacy (see page 156) and real authority.

Bourgeoisie: A French term, originally indicating those who lived in towns, but increasingly being understood to mean those members of the middle classes who lived by trade, investment and speculation.

Guillotined: Executed. A guillotine was a device used in France. A sharp blade was raised up on a frame and dropped on to a person's neck.

I N 1789, King Louis XVI called a meeting of the **Estates-General**. This consisted of representatives from the clergy, nobles, **bourgeoisie** and peasants. Louis had effectively given up. He no longer felt in a position to reform the government's finances or get France out of the cycle of debt and revolt which was crippling it.

Louis was faced by the possibility of bankruptcy and by the instability caused by the revolt of that class which had always been the King's greatest support – the nobles. Why was the monarchy being challenged and why did it prove incapable of solving France's problems?

Louis XVI (1754–1793) Grandson of Louis XV and son of Louis the Dauphin. He became King of France in 1774. He was dominated by his queen, Marie Antoinette. French finances fell into such confusion during his reign that, by 1789, the Estates-General had to be called and the French Revolution began. Louis XVI lost his personal popularity in June 1791 when he attempted to flee the country. In August 1792, Parisians stormed the Tuileries palace and took Louis prisoner. He was deposed in September, tried in December, sentenced for treason in January 1793 and **guillotined**.

3.1 What was the ancien régime?

As the historian William Doyle writes in *Origins of the French Revolution*, published in 1989:

> 'The *ancien régime* was what the revolutionaries thought they were destroying in and after 1789. *Ancien* means not so much "old" as "former" ... By early 1790, *ancien régime* had become the standard term for what had existed before the Revolution.'

Historiography: Different historical views by historians. Another term for historical interpretation.

There was no certainty that the *ancien régime* was destined to end in revolution. The revolution has acquired such epic status in **historiography** as a great 'turning-point' that it is easy to assume that everything that preceded it must inevitably form the 'causes of the Revolution'. French society and government were riddled with problems. It is just as valid to remind ourselves that contemporaries on the verge of revolution in 1789 not only failed to agree on what measures of reform should be adopted but also were deeply conservative. How did long-term problems faced by the *ancien régime* interact with events in the 1770s and 1780s?

In France, Divine Right was the foundation of monarchy. As the Bishop of Meaux claimed in the 17th century, 'Royal authority is sacred ... God establishes Kings as His ministers, and reigns through them over the nations ... . All power comes from God ... Princes therefore act as ministers of God, and His lieutenants on earth .... The royal throne is not the throne of a man, but the throne of God himself.'

This classical statement of Divine Right kingship formed the basis of Louis XVI's claims to absolute power. Kings were not accountable to any earthly power, although it was perfectly understood that, if the King failed to act according to reason, then he would face the judgement of God. As the source of all legal authority in the kingdom, Louis would also act as

'**Despots**': Rulers who act as tyrants and are accountable to no one, so act in a harsh and cruel way.

Chief executive: An efficient administrator who mobilises the resources of the state.

Protector: The guardian of the privileges of the First and Second Estates (see pages 51–55).

Intendants: In France, these royal officials acted as the 'King in the provinces'. They had to enact every new government edict on top of their traditional functions. These included the engaging and supervision of troops, the overseeing of the collection of taxes, and providing constant intelligence especially about municipal corporations and *parlements*.

Pays d'état: Six ancient areas of France that retained powerful assemblies.

Autonomy: Control or government of a country or area by itself rather than by others.

Customary law: In the north of France, law was based on tradition or custom.

Roman law: In the south of France, laws were based on those of ancient Rome.

Chief Judge. It was essential that he should maintain the law and those customs and rights previously accepted by the Crown. This included protecting the various rights and privileges of his different subjects. In fact, the King's position rested entirely upon his legitimacy, as the eldest legitimate son in line to the succession. Just as the privileged orders recognised Louis' fundamental rights to the succession, so he in turn would recognise their fundamental liberties and privileges. As the King was chief noble and landowner, these mutual ties were accepted. Hence the powers of the Crown were heavily circumscribed. These Kings of France were not allowed to behave as arbitrary and irresponsible monarchs – as '**despots**'.

However, there was a dilemma, which became increasingly apparent during the 18th century. Effective government could be seen to mean efficient administration. Privileges, such as tax exemption, hindered government. On the one hand, how could the King maintain the law and customs of France while, on the other hand, increasing his power to run the State government more efficiently? An effective **chief executive** rather than a **protector** of privilege would run the risk of being called a 'despot', or a tyrant. Louis XIV ('the Sun King'), until the final years of the reign, succeeded in avoiding this type of criticism. However, neither Louis XV nor Louis XVI had the Sun King's ability. They were neither determined nor resourceful enough to seize the initiative and introduce reforms to stem the revolutionary tide that would eventually engulf the monarchy.

The Enlightenment (see Chapter 2) had already undermined Divine Right monarchy, although both Kings failed to grasp this, so government remained archaic. There was a contradiction between the King, who claimed to be the source of earthly power, and the forces of privilege and customary right that prevented him from exercising that power. The historian Alfred Cobban argued in *History of Modern France* (1957) that such a 'system' based on personal government did not add up to an effective administrative system.

Neither could the King exercise complete control over all aspects of government. Such were the complexities of administration that there were areas where the King's oversight of ministers was in name only. At least Louis XIV had the good sense to use ministers of ability. During the reign of Louis XVI, a minister was more concerned with the preservation of his post and safeguarding his reputation. The 'system' relied to a large degree on the work of *intendants* – the instruments of the King's administration in each of the 34 *généralités* that made up provincial France. It is true they were men of quality, but dreadfully overworked. Anne Turgot, the *Controlleur-Général*, complained that their role consisted of the 'constant tidying of endless lumber'.

It was another feature of the confused administration that *intendants* shared authority with other individuals or groups. In the six areas of France known as *pays d'état*, the assemblies or estates had significant **autonomy** to vote a '*don gratuit*' (free gift) on their own decision. Provincial Governors, usually nobles of standing, combined military powers with authority to deal with the local *parlements*. The *intendants* could not always be guaranteed resolute support from Versailles – which was where Louis XVI seemed to be isolated.

Intendants were no substitute for a proper civil service. All they had to rely on was the *officier's* class, who had mostly bought their posts and who used their positions for personal gain. Their capacity for delay meant that the government's own officials could well hinder the smooth running of the government. Alfred Cobban called it 'absolutism qualified by indiscipline'.

Although the King was Chief Judge, applying the law was by no means straightforward. Law differed significantly, from the largely **customary law** in the north to the **Roman law** of the south. Courts were slow, inefficient and corrupt. As the King was unable to hear all appeal cases, they were delegated to 13 sovereign courts, or *parlements*. The Paris Parlement was the most important of these and became the focus of persistent opposition to the Crown. Their magistrates were all **noblesse de robe**. The Paris Parlement had long held the view that it was the guardian of the nation's interests against arbitrary monarchy, claiming the right to remonstrate against royal edicts and amend them, before giving a final seal of approval by registering them. They would emerge in the 18th century as a powerful force – although how powerful is still open to debate.

The King's financial system was chaotic. There was widespread abuse of the tax system and many groups in society were exempt from tax. Without a Central Treasury or efficient accounting system, the King was always financially embarrassed by debt. The administration lacked coherence and uniformity. Slow communications made it difficult to execute government business effectively. The King was hemmed in on all sides by limitations to his authority. No wonder Napoleon Bonaparte commented on 'this chequered France, more like 20 Kingdoms than a single State'.

Noblesse de robe: These people had bought their status as a noble. They made up the judicial elite.

1. What were the limitations of absolutism?

2. To what extent was absolutism just a myth?

3.2 What was France like before the French Revolution?

The First Estate: to what extent did the clergy support the Crown?

The First Estate of the realm was the clergy. Their pre-eminence was guaranteed. Not only was the throne occupied by 'The Most Christian King' and pillar of the Catholic Church, but also the clergy carried out important functions throughout society. Bishops and Archbishops rubbed shoulders with Cardinals and *noblesse* at Court. Some Churchmen, such as Loménie de Brienne, accepted high office. The King made appointments to senior church posts and this was an accepted career route for the sons of the nobility. Indeed great wealth was to be had, particularly since **pluralism** was still practised. From Bishops at the top of the ecclesiastical ladder down to village *curés*, the clergy had a distinct social and religious status. It, in turn, added stability to absolute monarchy – a monarchy that clung to Divine Right as the basis for its authority.

The church was also enormously rich, owning about 10% of all the land in France – second only to the King. Bishops, too, had a position to maintain. They amassed great wealth not only from their own sees but also by drawing from parish **tithes**. All clergy enjoyed privileges similar to the nobility.

However, a closer look reveals stresses within the clergy, and an **ambivalent** attitude to the Crown. Firstly, antagonisms existed between curés and upper clergy (socially superior and extremely wealthy – some Archbishops earned 500 times more than a *curé*). Jealousy about clerical income was only part of this hostility. The upper clergy who were unpopular because of pluralism made the most of their social exclusivity, while the *curés* worked hard and closely with the lower orders, most of whom were peasants. Village priests shared something of their precarious existence and understood the weight of taxation and **feudal dues** on their flocks. Historians have ascribed 'democratic' ideas to parish priests (an odd concept so far removed from the 20th-century political vocabulary), although there is evidence in the *cahiers* of 1789 that *curés* wished to participate more in the running of the Church. They were exasperated by the abuse of the tithes, and by the bishops who demanded unquestioning obedience. Animosities spilled over into matters of faith. Lower clergy continued to be **Gallican**, unlike their clerical masters. Many of these

Pluralism: The practice of holding more than one church office or benefice at the same time.

Curés: Poor parish priests who earned less than 1,000 livres a year.

Tithes: About 8% of the crop produced which was paid to the clergy.

Ambivalent: Unclear whether they approve of something or do not approve of it.

Feudal dues: Monies paid to the landlord or noble (see page 53).

Cahiers: Lists of complaints recorded in 1789 in France.

Gallican: In favour of the independence of the French Church from Papal interference.

tensions were not new, but they could well have been made worse by the radicalism that increased in 1789.

Secondly, how important was the Church to the King? It was certainly a keystone in the *ancien régime*. King and upper clergy shared the assumption that God had ordained the order of things and that was that. It was this kind of attitude, alongside the wealth of some clerics, which attracted the attention of the *philosophes* (see page 24). They reserved particular spite for the clergy, blaming them for perpetuating superstition, dogma and privilege.

The Church also faced repeated campaigns waged against it by the King. It resisted him successfully, as it was very much a 'state within a state'. Its income was a closely guarded secret and, instead of paying taxes, it paid an annual *don gratuit* (free gift) which it negotiated with the King and was normally quite modest. The Assembly of the Clergy undertook the negotiations. It met every five years and it proved a formidable body. Even under the 'grand monarch' Louis XIV, the Assembly of the Clergy met at regular intervals and its representations were always carefully considered. Subsequent attempts by the government to make an assault on the Church's wealth were always beaten off.

In 1780, there was a proposal to value Church property so it could be taxed. Nothing came of it; the clergy had plenty of experience of passive resistance, closing ranks in the face of unwelcome interference.

The Second Estate: a divided nobility?

Nobles dominated French society. They were a tiny group. Historians estimate that nobles made up probably around 1% of the total French population. But they had immense wealth, owning between one-third and one-quarter of all the land as well as having a stranglehold on important positions of power. They were bishops and archbishops of the Church, army officers, judges and magistrates of *parlements*, King's ministers and *intendants*.

A booming economy up to the mid-1770s had enabled the nobility to take over high positions in the state. A century earlier, Louis XIV had reduced the nobility to nonentities at the palace of Versailles, trapped by court etiquette to playing out rituals which emphasised the pre-eminence of the King at the expense of the nobility. How things had changed! The *noblesse* had taken over most positions of State and were perfectly placed to safeguard their privileges and status, and to defend their self-interest if they were ever threatened by the government.

Decadent: Having low standards, especially low moral standards.

Revolutionaries were keen to keep an image of the nobility as a single, exclusive class, living a **decadent** life of luxury while viewing the rest of society with snobbish disdain. In 1789, they led the 'aristocratic reaction' to defend their privileges from being undermined by the Crown's ministers and from the challenge of the bourgeoisie. A declining nobility fought back against a rising bourgeoisie (see page 49), so the argument ran. Much of this is mythology and does not bear close analysis.

Firstly, did the nobility constitute a single class? In theory, they defended the King's realm because their sons provided officers for the army while their families drew income from the land in gentlemanly fashion. They would take snobbish satisfaction from studying their family trees that would stretch back into the mists of time.

Reality was very different.

Fortunes differed widely. The historian William Doyle notes in *Origins of the French Revolution* (1989) that only 250 families probably had incomes of over 50,000 livres a year which would support a lavish lifestyle of crippling expense at Versailles. At the other end of the scale, probably

20% had less than 1,000 livres, meaning that they were almost indistinguishable from peasants. It is hardly surprising that the concept of the nobles as a single class has been challenged. Such differences nurtured resentments that were never far from the surface. What privileges did nobles enjoy and how could anyone join their ranks?

Nobility could be conferred by birth. This was an accepted principle by which estates and titles were either handed down to the eldest son (the legal idea of primogeniture), or granted by the King's will, perhaps to someone who had come to the assistance of the Crown financially or militarily. Birth was widely acknowledged as the true mark of blue-blooded nobility. Just as the King's right of succession to the throne was never questioned, so neither was the right of the *grandes noblesse* to confer title, privileges and property on their sons. They had the bloodlines to prove it.

Ennoblement: The right to purchase noble status.

Nevertheless, **ennoblement** could be conferred by purchasing a post in the government's administration or in the law. If kept in the family for two or three generations, the title became hereditary. It may have taken time, then, before 'full' status was acquired, but there was no shortage of demand – 2,477 joined the ranks between 1774 and 1789. If one's purse was particularly deep, then purchasing the position of King's Secretary brought instant hereditary nobility. In all, probably between 30,000 and

---

The Second Estate

1. *Noblesse d'épee* ('nobles of the sword')

- These were Princes of the blood.

- They were resident at Court.

- They numbered about 4,000.

- They held honorary and ancient titles, with family trees going back hundreds of years, to before 1400.

- Many had high rank in the Church and Army or held Provincial Governorships.

2. *Noblesse de robe* ('robe nobles')

- These were office holders in the government.

- They were King's ministers, magistrates and judges of the *parlements* or sovereign courts.

- They were vital to the work of government, the law and in the raising of taxation and finance.

- As a class, robe nobles were considered inferior to those of the sword.

3. Provincial nobility

- These were conservative and parochial.

- Some had old feudal titles and continued to live in their chateaux off rents and seigneurial dues.

- They led gentlemanly lives in rural France.

4. Others

- These included the *hobereaux* (proud nobles but poor). As they often had to work in their own fields, barely scratching a living, they were the objects of scorn in the fashionable salons in Paris.

50,000 had become recently ennobled in the 18th century. Given the large numbers of nobles, it is difficult to estimate what proportion this constitutes, but the current view is about one-quarter. It is not easy, therefore, to defend the myth of an exclusive caste when membership of the nobility was so open.

Aside from the recognisable honour of being 'noble', a title brought numerous privileges, particularly tax exemption. Nobles recognised that they should serve the Crown, either in the army or administration, and it was in their interests to maintain the *ancien régime* that was serving them so well.

Nevertheless, when challenged, would the members of the Second Estate prove capable of defending themselves? Apparently not. Everything from petty snobbishness and jealousy to downright antagonism prevented them from working with each other to defend their status and privileges. It is worth pointing out that co-operation between robe and sword was not unheard of. Members of ancient families, financially drained by lavish court expenses, could find marriage to less distinguished nobility worth their while. Inter-marriage and new forms of creating wealth blurred the distinctions between those who had gained their title by birth and those who gained them by **venality**. It was accepted that venality not only provided valuable income for the King, but was also an effective method of preventing dangerous social tensions from developing by providing a route for the bourgeoisie to rise up the social ladder and achieve their social aspirations. These are perfectly valid arguments. However, there is no disguising the hostilities between different groups of nobles who didn't need much of an excuse to start backbiting.

Extravagant, fashionable, proud and arrogant they may have been, but court nobles were able to petition the King personally. Provincial squires (*hobereaux*) were rejected by the Parisians, and scorned for dressing like peasants. Meanwhile, bourgeoisie with neither a family tree nor a distinguished record of military service were leapfrogging them by purchasing offices, which gave them a social status to which they had no right by birth. To the provincial gentry and the old order, money could never enable an upstart to acquire the habits and gentlemanly outlook required by those who lived 'nobly'. Nor would there be any love lost between 'robe' and 'sword' nobles. The *Ségur Ordinance* (1781) was a deliberate attempt by the old nobility to prevent the recently ennobled from becoming army officers, thus closing down the most prized career route for those who knew that social ambitions would stand or fall on whether or not they won approval in military service. Frustrations and hostilities were, then, often based on money, status and snobbery. It is easy to overpaint this picture for reality is seldom as clear cut. For contemporaries, however, these impressions were very real and remained a potent force.

The precise impact of the Enlightenment continues to be debated (see Chapter 2). Here, again, the nobility reflected all shades of opinion. It is likely that most nobles saw no reason to embrace reformist ideas (even if they were completely aware of them) and thereby challenge an *ancien régime* that enshrined their privileges. Church and government also provided career opportunities for their sons. There are numerous documented examples of magistrates in *parlement* exercising their powers of censorship over 'dangerous' plays and books. On the other hand, there was a minority (e.g. the Marquis de Lafayette) who were eager to engage in debate in fashionable salons, literary societies, academies and wherever the Enlightened ideas flourished. Once again the chasm which separated conservative, self-satisfied *noblesse* from liberal thinkers would make it difficult for the Second Estate to act with any sense of purpose or find acceptable leaders when the Estates-General met in 1789.

Venality: The system by which posts and titles could be purchased.

Ségur Ordinance: This law stated that no one could become an army officer unless they could prove that they had been nobles for a minimum of four generations.

Marie Joseph de Motier, Marquis de Lafayette (1757–1834)
French soldier and politician. He fought against Britain in the American Revolution (1777–79 and 1780–82). During the French Revolution he sat in the National Assembly as a constitutional royalist and, in 1789, he presented the Declaration of the Rights of Man. After the storming of the Bastille, Lafayette was given command of the National Guard. He fled the country in 1792 after attempting to restore the monarchy and was imprisoned by the Austrians until 1797. He supported Napoleon Bonaparte in 1815 and played a leading part in the 1830 revolution. He was a popular hero in the USA – cities of Lafayette in Louisiana and Indiana are named after him.

Why should the nobility have felt concerned about their apparent disunity? Nobles were the leaders of society and there seemed little, even on the eve of revolution, to dent their confidence. The lower orders might strike or riot, but usually it was just in protest about wages or bread prices. The *philosophes*, apart from Rousseau, recognised the central role of an educated elite of nobles in government and society. This was hardly surprising given that many of them had noble titles, wrote for a noble audience and relied on noble patronage and support (see page 30). Pierre Beaumarchais' play *The Marriage of Figaro*, once banned for its anti-noble sentiments, was performed in 1784, but only with noble backing and there was no shortage of aristocrats who wanted to see it. The nobles had little to fear so it seems. They felt assured and they dominated the government, which clearly could not carry on without them. The question is why were they consumed by the revolution so quickly?

Nobles' privileges

The most significant privilege was tax exemption. They did not pay *taille* (the most common direct tax) nor the salt tax (*gabelle*). They were exempt from forced labour on the roads (*corvée*), they could wear a sword in public places and could be tried in special courts. Also, despite the purist view of nobility that involved a duty to serve in the army, noble status did grant exemption from troops being billeted on them.

Third Estate: the bourgeoisie and peasants

Problems of defining the Third Estate bedevil studies of the period. It consisted of bourgeoisie and peasants.

Who were the bourgeoisie?

Marxist: Based on Marxism, the ideas of Karl Marx (1818–1883), author of *Das Kapital*, often called the manifesto of Communism. Karl Marx claimed that history is the product of class struggle.

Rentiers: People who live on income from property or investments.

This seems a crucial question given the **Marxist** view (see page 75), now treated with scepticism, that it was this class which gave the initial impetus to the revolution. At the risk of over-simplification, they were not regarded as labourers or peasants, nor were they nobles. They made their living largely in towns, where their wealth derived from trade investments or skills, or from inheritances. They managed small enterprises, bought and sold goods, or positions, financed others, invested or were professional people. Marxists thought the bourgeoisie included *rentiers*, lawyers, financiers, doctors, shopkeepers, ship-owners, commercial traders, low-ranking office holders, craftworkers, shopkeepers, and small-scale manufacturers. The range is so wide as to defy any further kind of generalisation. This did not stop Marxists from lumping them together as one class. It is tempting, in this pre-revolutionary period, to look for evidence of tensions within the bourgeoisie and between the bourgeoisie and the class they displaced, the *noblesse*. These tensions certainly existed but, according to historian J.H. Sherman in *France before the Revolution* (1983), 'There was no fundamental hostility between the bourgeoisie and the nobility before the Revolution.'

Lacking any sense of belonging to a particular class, the bourgeoisie sought to join another – the *noblesse*. To gain social status and esteem involved rapidly shedding their past, particularly when their ancestors had been involved in trade and commerce. Being 'trade' was socially unacceptable and, in an intensely snobbish culture, was not regarded as an activity fit for gentlemen to pursue. Strict rules prohibited nobles

Capitalism: Economic system based on the theory that possession of capital or money leads to the making of profits through the power of investment.

Grandees: The *grandes noblesse*, or high-born sword nobles.

from dabbling in commerce, although these had been eroded by the mid-18th century, as a significant but small group of nobility invested in **capitalism**. Demand for posts that brought ennoblement never slackened, despite the increasing expense of these kinds of offices: 6,500 families in France became *anoblies* (newly ennobled) during the 18th century. The dividing lines between the rich bourgeoisie and the nobility were becoming blurred. Venality seemed to suit everyone: the Treasury raised income; older noble families could be supported by 'new money' through inter-marriage with *familles anoblies*; the bourgeoisie could aspire to, and achieve, social mobility; and, all the time, noble values were being asserted.

The upper bourgeoisie did not stop there. They copied their social superiors by buying up land (probably about 25% of all land in the country) and thereby acquiring seigneurial rights. However, beneath the surface there were deep social tensions. Ennoblement of bourgeois families offended the pride of **grandees** with ancient titles who never accepted the idea that true nobility could be bought. The economic boom had made the division between businessmen and the non-commercial bourgeoisie (lawyers, office-holders and *rentiers*) rather more obvious.

As commerce prospered, particularly overseas trade, so there was an energy and assurance amongst those involved in it. They were impatient about the forces of privilege that hindered them, such as guilds, municipal immunities, customs dues, government regulation and tax exemptions. More importantly, the social ambitions of the rich were frustrated as the government was selling fewer and fewer offices after the 1730s. When the Depression squeezed their incomes, the government seemed to be conspiring against them by signing commercial treaties that opened markets to foreign competition. In 1784, the French West Indies trade was opened up and, in 1787, Charles-Alexandre de Calonne (*Controlleur-Général* of Finances 1783–7) opened the French market to British textiles.

Nevertheless, rich businessmen became richer, while the poorer non-commercial bourgeoisie became poorer. Office-holders and investors in *rentes* (government stocks) must have felt especially aggrieved and jealous. *Rentiers* felt undermined by the economic downturn of the late 1770s. Office-holders struggled to come to terms with their inability to compete for ennobling offices with the wealthiest businessmen. Just short of 40,000 venal *officiers* were suffering a decline in the value of their posts and falling profits. Not all these posts conferred ennoblement – some only conferred it after the family had been *officiers* for several generations. There were just too many of them. The historian E.N. Williams notes, in *The Ancient Regime in Europe* (1970), that the city of Angers had 53 judicial courts, with insufficient business to support its lawyers. They would have endured the arrogance of *les anoblis* or the superior magistrates of *parlement* who looked down on those who dealt with minor cases in lower courts. All of these frustrations amount to little more than froth up to 1788. The bourgeoisie supported the *noblesse* without argument during the events that led to the calling of the Estates-General. Their language also attacked 'tyranny'. However, when the forms of voting for the Estates-General (see page 49) were being debated and the nobility revealed their naked self-interest, the bourgeoisie assumed a role more dynamic than ever before.

The peasant

Gross fermiers: These farmers leased larger areas of land, over 200 acres (80 hectares). They employed workers or sub-let land to poorer tenants.

The term 'peasant' covers a wide range of groups, from **gross fermiers** to landless labourers. Peasants comprised 80% of the total population of France and most of the semi-agricultural, semi-industrial wage earners at the bottom of the heap bore the brunt of dues and taxes which probably led to the handing over of over 40% of their income.

As the King ran into increasing debt, peasants paid more, particularly after 1749. There was no escape – no peasant was exempt from taxation and, to make matters worse, tax-exempt nobles or bourgeoisie would buy land. The total paid by a village was normally sub-divided amongst the taxable population. Hence, when it came to paying the total amount owed, a larger proportion fell on the peasants to pay. As economic conditions worsened in the 1770s, dues had to be squeezed out with ruthless regularity. By far the largest burden in their cost of living was the increase in rents paid on each plot of land. For the landlord (who might normally be a noble, but increasingly was a member of the clergy or bourgeoisie), putting up rents, when the depression struck in the 1700s, was an effective and profitable answer to declining incomes.

It was also widely accepted that local *seigneurs* could demand feudal dues. Once again, they varied regionally. What is uncertain is how much criticism there was of **feudalism**, as a system. Apparently, there was little. Peasant revolts were spontaneous and involved the specific venting of anger against local dues, courts and *seigneurs*. Peasants' horizons were narrow, both physically and intellectually. But they would stretch to the local town, where the bourgeois moneylenders and profiteers preyed on the rural poor. It was towns that would pay only modest prices for peasants' goods – the *cahiers* of 1789 included plenty of complaints about the urban bourgeoisie.

Feudalism: A system in which people are given land and protection by lords and, in return, work and fight for them.

Feudal rights

These could consist of the following:

- The landlord could run his own seigneurial court and exact punishments for the infringement of his feudal rights, such as enforcing dues for using the lord's oven, mill, wine-press and stretch of river for fishing or area of wood for hunting.

- Harvest dues were payable and the *seigneur* could exact heavy fines when the ownership of land or houses changed.

It was difficult for peasants to escape from this cycle of economic misery. Urban capitalists exploited those peasants engaged in semi-industrial activities. For the great mass who eked out a living on the land, locked into primitive methods, there was little prospect of earning more money or feeding the rising population.

Agriculture was backward. The revolution in farming techniques taking place in Britain seemed to bypass the French countryside, where farmers were locked into old fashioned and ineffective practices. Admittedly there were exceptions, such as Flanders where that bane of farmers' existence, the **fallow**, had been discarded. Eighteenth-century writers were well aware of the doleful effect of leaving land uncultivated so the soil might recover.

A spiral of low productivity began, with the need to feed more hungry mouths and grow more arable crops. This led to a reduction in the number of animals kept, and less and less manure to fertilise soil which had already been over-ploughed.

It is remarkable that enough food was produced to feed the population, although it seems clear that this could only be achieved by pressing more land into use rather than by improving crop productivity.

Fallow: Under this system, large areas of land were left unused for sometimes two or three years. This merely led to pressure on the fields in use to produce more, and the downward spiral would begin again.

Enclosure: A process where some landowners put hedges around large fields and created bigger and more productive units of farming.

Laboureurs: They were better-off peasants who were more than self-sufficient. They grew a modest surplus which could be sold for profit. They might own 25 acres, probably about 40 animals and they probably owned a plough.

There were formidable obstacles in the way of change, even if anyone had thought it worthwhile to do so. Peasants were not keen to make improvements that would catch the eye of the tax collector, while landowners preferred to push up rents (easily done when there was such demand for land). The death of the head of the family usually meant that estates were divided up between the surviving sons, making it more difficult to farm the smaller plots.

The trend in Britain was towards **enclosure**, which had enabled farmers to introduce new, and specialised, crops. In France there was opposition, which slowed the urgent need for change. *Laboureurs*, particularly, needed common land grazing and they put paid to numerous plans for enclosure.

It is worth noting that the poor state of rural transport, before the advent of railways, made it almost impossible to move goods to the markets where they could get decent prices.

As the cost of living rose, many semi-landed peasants took refuge in waged employment. But this was just at the time when so many others were doing the same and, as prices rose, wages failed to keep pace. With no shortage of labour, it is likely that rising wages lagged far behind rising prices, possibly by up to one-third.

It is a feature of rural society that groups of migrant, landless peasants were an unwelcome sight. However, up to 1788, these groups of peasants played no significant part in the unrest that started the King's crisis and the calling of the Estates-General. But when the harvests failed in 1788, these lower orders became a force to be reckoned with.

Millions of peasants had barely enough land to guarantee their survival and they lived a nightmare existence of semi-starvation. In the year of a good harvest they might scrape through. They made ends meet, living from hand to mouth on tiny plots of land. They might try to earn wages from a rich farmer or weave cloth in their homes for the bourgeois industrialist from the town. Many had to migrate in search of work; they may have borrowed heavily and, when they defaulted on their payments, the urban bourgeois moneylenders would dispossess them.

It didn't take much of an economic downturn to expand the ranks of the landless labourers. They begged, and drifted into criminality for casual work.

Tax farmers: Collectors of *gabelle* (salt tax) who paid for the right to collect the tax. This gave the monopoly for collecting *gabelle* in a particular area.

Taxes and dues paid by peasants

Taille: the main direct tax

Gabelle: salt tax, collected by **tax farmers** who had bought the monopoly to collect the tax in particular areas.

Tithes: the proportion of each year's crop paid to the Church. Normally around 8% of all produce, but in Brittany it could be up to 25%.

Corvée (forced labour on the roads): extremely unpopular even when peasants could pay a money tax to avoid it.

Was life any better in the towns?

There was no shortage of friction between town and country. The urban bourgeoisie provided loans to peasants in debt. They then acquired that land when the debtors were in default, so the towns got the blame for expanding the class of landless workers. Markets were carefully supervised so that peasants, who had already paid substantial transport costs,

1. How serious were the tensions between the First, Second and Third Estates?

2. How far did social tensions threaten the stability of the state?

did not always receive the prices for their goods that they would have wished.

The guilds were an obvious target as they clung to ancient privileges that enabled them both to control prices and output, and to protect themselves from outsiders who might try to undercut their trade.

Rural labourers and urban workers alike were the victims of long hours, falling standards of living, unemployment, and bread prices which rose alarmingly after the disastrous 1788 harvest. Bread consumed over three-quarters of an urban worker's wages in 1789, which was the final ingredient in an already difficult situation.

3.3 Was the French economy in crisis by 1789?

Growth of population in France

1700 – 22,000,000
1789 – 28,000,000

Colonies: Countries controlled by a more powerful country, which uses the colony's resources in order to increase its power.

The problems faced by the economy and by successive *Controlleurs-Général* in trying to meet government expenditure, intensified the conflict within French society. There was a turn for the worse in August 1786 when Calonne, the *Controlleur-Général*, reported to Louis XVI that bankruptcy was staring the government in the face. Debts had been rising steadily since the King's accession, but by 1786 the estimated shortfall in the royal finances amounted to 25% of the Crown's yearly income. What had brought France to this situation? Had this happened recently, or did it represent a gradual deterioration in finances that had affected the *ancien régime* over decades?

Potentially, France was a prosperous country. The population was growing (see panel), dragging the economy slowly behind it. Trade flourished, particularly with the **colonies** (quadrupling since 1715), and industrial production doubled. Up to 1776, the French economy had been enjoying boom conditions. 'The sickly 17th century was finally over, and gone were the depressed prices and stunted trade, the slumps and the famines', wrote historian E.N. Williams in 1970. Even peasants must have noticed a difference; widespread famine no longer stalked the land.

However, by 1776 the boom was almost over, and the onset of an economic depression would dash people's expectations of better times. What they had enjoyed, they would clearly miss. Under the strains and stresses of depression, the weaknesses of government finance and the economy would re-emerge.

Investment in agriculture continued to stagnate. France was still dominated by local village markets, backward agricultural practices and poorly developed transport. Mechanisation and factory-scale production lagged behind European rivals. Britain had 200 cotton mills in 1789, while France had eight, and was hence in no position to compete. France's financial structure was hardly robust. During Louis XV's minority, under the Regency of Philip, duc d'Orléans, France's venture into state banking was a spectacular failure. This was in sharp contrast to England where, from 1694 onwards, the Bank of England underwrote the cost of the Spanish Succession War. John Law's bold scheme was to develop a state bank of France, which would issue notes and credit, and control the collection of taxation and the distribution of investments. All this depended on the success of colonial enterprise and, when investments in Louisiana failed, the bubble burst. Those who had speculated in John Law's schemes found their investments worthless, all of which left a legacy of suspicion against a banking system.

France was left without a system of financing credit to raise capital. As a result, the old abuses of the tax system returned. Absolutism had proved incapable of reforming its confusing, corrupt and inefficient finances. It was unequal to the task of protecting investments. Hence the old ways seem safer. Tax-farmers collected indirect taxes in return for generous commissions. *Officiers* who collected the *taille* had purchased their post, so their self-interest was paramount. There was always a shortfall between the amount collected and the amount the government received in taxation. Its own officials saw themselves as independent contractors with the discretion to use the King's money to conduct private business. The King continued to be short of revenue and had to fall back on short-term loans from numerous speculators, many of whom were its own *officiers*. Hence, servicing these loans (paying the interest) could easily absorb government spending for years into the future.

Of course, while the King was seen as the guarantor of privilege – as he had to be – the government was unable to tax those specific groups in society who possessed most of the country's wealth. Tax exemption on such a scale made it unlikely that the Crown's financial problems would ever by solved. None of this was helped by the ambition of the bourgeois entrepreneurs, which was to leave the wealth-creating sector and become ennobled, and exempt from tax.

1. What were the fundamental weaknesses of the French economy before 1789?

2. How did the depression of the late 1770s increase France's financial difficulties?

Scale of debt of the French government	One of the problems faced by *Controlleurs-Général* was the absence of accurate accounting methods and precise figures of revenue and expenditure. Without a state bank or central treasury, bookkeeping was completely unreliable.
1763 50 million livres 1774 40 million livres 1786 112 million livres	

3.4 How far were members of the French monarchy responsible for the outbreak of revolution in 1789?

It is difficult to measure the significance of the role of an individual against long-term historical trends. The role played by Louis XVI continues to be a source of argument.

On balance, the historian J.H. Shennan in *France before the Revolution* (1983) places emphasis on the historical context: 'Royal failures of will and character are not to be dismissed, though they are only of limited significance when weighed against the enormous pressures which inevitably destroyed the *ancien régime*.'

On the other hand, in *A History of Modern France Volume 1* (1957), Alfred Cobban sees the failure to reform 'in terms of the personality of the ruler. If Louis XV had been unequal to his responsibilities, Louis XVI was to be even more so. He gives the impression of being one of the most uninterested and uninteresting spectators of his own reign.'

William Doyle, in *Origins of the French Revolution* (1989) also takes the view that Louis XVI *was* the King, so ultimately the failure to support reform was his.

Louis XVI might have had a keen sense of duty to serve God and his people, but he is seen as too diffident, too lacking in will to either introduce reforms or to support reforming ministers. He clung to the belief in Divine Right and personal monarchy at a time when the tide had turned in favour of the Enlightenment which had sown the seeds of doubt about such outdated ideas.

This man, who was keen to court approval, was too easily blown off course by pressure groups and factions at Court. His lack of self-belief paralysed government and did not encourage firm decision making. John Hardman's view is kinder. He sees Louis XVI as intelligent and hard

Counsel: The King's ministers were traditionally accused of giving the monarch poor advice or 'counsel'; Louis XVI retained some popular loyalty because of this – at least for a while.

Intrigues: Secret plans that are intended to harm someone's reputation, career, friendship etc.

Marie Antoinette (1755–1793)
Queen of France from 1774; daughter of Empress Maria Theresa of Austria. Married Louis XVI of France in 1770. Her reputation for extravagance helped to provoke the French Revolution. She was tried for treason (October 1793) and guillotined.

War of Austrian Succession: Following Maria Theresa's succession to the throne of the Austrian Empire, Prussia and France fought Britain and Austria.

Twentieth: A 5% levy supposedly paid by all.

1. How far were Louis XVI's problems of his own making?

2. 'Louis XVI was a weak king. But it was the weakness of the French monarchy in general which really undermined the government.' How far do you agree with this statement? Explain your answer.

working – and not entirely to blame for the slow working of French government. Interestingly enough, Louis retained some credibility up to 1789 because, when the finger of blame was pointed, it was at the King's ministers and advisers who had given him poor '**counsel**'.

Louis XVI's lack of interest seemed to be confirmed by the often-repeated story about his reluctance ever to leave Paris and Versailles. The exception was one visit to Cherbourg and the naval dockyards.

Joseph II of Austria – who was never one to avoid blunt comment – wrote: 'The King [Louis XVI] can change his ministers, but he can never become master of his business. Petty **intrigues** are treated with the greatest care and attention, but important affairs, those which concern the state, are completely neglected.'

While Louis remained uninterested, his wife, Marie Antoinette, was completely the opposite.

It is difficult to imagine such an ill-matched couple. Marie Antoinette played a large part in undermining the prestige of the monarchy. She was conceited, flippant and unpopular. Unlike her husband, she was self-willed and impulsive to such an extent that her extravagance became legendary. Despite the need for strict economies in court expenditure, she managed gambling debts of half a million livres in one year and became known as 'Madame Déficit'. She treated her husband with contempt, shunned Court ritual and surrounded herself with favourites. Clearly, Rousseau's vision of rural simplicity appealed to her – withdrawing into her *jardin anglais* (English garden), she dressed as a shepherdess and thereby isolated herself from powerful factions of nobles at Court. She made few attempts to win over these influential representatives of privilege.

Enemies at court incited pamphlet writers to publish stories about a host of lovers chosen from the eligible men of Versailles. Neither was she disinclined to meddle in affairs of state, ensuring that the interests of her brother, Joseph II of Austria, were kept to the forefront – hence her title, '*l'Autrichienne!*' ('the Austrian woman').

None of this helped the standing of the royal family. It wasn't long before Louis XVI was taking decisions that would later prove unwise. As the costs of warfare rose, the failure to raise taxes and finance efficiently led to extraordinary measures. The **War of Austrian Succession** (1740–48) and the Seven Years' War (1756–63) forced *Controlleurs-Général* to adopt emergency measures to stave off debt. A new tax, the **Twentieth**, was levied in 1749 and again throughout the Seven Years' War in 1756, 1760 and 1763. The Assembly of the Clergy managed to claim exemption after staunch resistance. French help for the rebels during the American War of Independence merely added to the scale of debt. When another Twentieth was imposed between 1783 and 1786, it was looking less and less like a temporary measure. The year it was due to end coincided with Calonne's warning to Louis XVI. Privilege seemed to be under attack – and amidst their squeals, it wasn't long before the King was being attacked as a 'tyrant' and a 'robber'. The Crown seemed to be failing in one of its primary duties – the defence of privilege.

3.5 Were Enlightened ideas important in bringing revolution?

The Enlightenment made people less easy to govern. Although the Enlightenment did question and raise doubts about the old order, its spread and impact are uncertain. The ideas of the *philosophes* (see Chapter 2) were fashionable in the salons of Paris, but they never amounted to a programme of reform. They never caused a revolution. However, when the old order began to crumble and when authority began to lose control, the Enlightenment made it easier to express arguments for the attacks on the monarchy. In the meantime, the catastrophic financial crisis would plunge France into chaos.

The Enlightenment and the French Revolution

It would be tempting to see the Enlightenment as a cause of the French Revolution. New ideas burst upon the public, which then undermined the *ancien régime*. However, it would be a gross error of judgement to assume that just because these philosophical ideas preceded the Revolution they were a cause of it.

There is a case for saying that standards of literacy and the readership of books, journals, papers and so on were increasing during the second half of the 18th century. However, this was not mass readership. The *philosophes* addressed genteel, polite society. Their writings were meant for educated **aristocrats** and the wealthy bourgeoisie who were buying into the nobility. Only Rousseau believed in general participation in government; others in the Enlightenment movement, whose backgrounds were almost entirely noble, never intended that their ideas should reach the masses. Instead, readers populated fashionable salons, coffee-houses, provincial academies and literary societies. According to historian T.C.W. Blanning, in *The French Revolution, Class War or Culture Clash?* (1998), 'The French Enlightenment was a movement of the educated elite.' Prices of published works remained high and purchasing was confined to the well-to-do. Attendance at lectures and debating societies was the fashion and conferred the mark of social approval. As the printing presses poured out one enlightened tract after another, demand grew – as did the spirit of debate.

The government of Louis XVI recognised the threat to the established order. Freer criticism sapped confidence as people recognised the alternatives to the *status quo*. Censorship tightened and spies were everywhere. But, as the historian William Doyle argues, in *The Origins of the French Revolution* (1989), the government was losing control of informed public opinion. If there was an emerging political culture in late 18th-century France, it was becoming apparent that the monarchy was losing its legitimacy (i.e. the bond of mutual consent between governed and the government). The German sociologist, Max Weber, argued in the 19th century that legitimacy could be defined either as traditional, legal or charismatic. The Enlightenment was busy challenging traditional assumptions; and if Divine Right underpinned the religious basis of Louis XVI's power then it, too, was collapsing. If the *philosophes* agreed on anything it was that they despised the metaphysical.

The French King continued to be sanctified at his coronation by holy water. His claim that he could cure scrofula (a skin disease) by the laying-on of hands reinforced his 'spiritual' power. The Enlightenment discredited not only this but also his reputation as an inspirational national leader. Opposition to the King and the contempt for his wife were increasing. The Queen was accused of being a whore. This undermined the dignity of the monarchy.

Aristocrats: People whose families have a high social rank, especially those who hold a title. Their wealth is passed down the generations by inheritance.

More seriously, the government was losing its grip on national sovereignty. The monarch's credibility depended on military glory and the defence of the nation's interests. French defeats during the Seven Years' War served to show that France's status as a leading power was declining. The Crown stood accused of being incapable of defending national sovereignty and the privileges of the leading members of society. The 'tyrants' could not safeguard the nation – or so it appeared.

Notwithstanding the fact that France was becoming more difficult to rule, the impact of the Enlightenment was limited. The *philosophes* had no agreed, coherent programme. They were critics, not policy makers. They may have been a power in salons and coffee-houses, but beyond this, there is no evidence that they carried much weight. The *cahiers* of 1789, which listed grievances from every class, reveal a conservative society that lacked the commitment to radical change. The *philosophes* (apart from Rousseau) were not in favour of abolishing the monarchy, nor did they wish to destroy the aristocracy and what it stood for. Even Voltaire understood that '20 folio volumes (of the *Encyclopédie*) will never make a revolution'. Nevertheless, a growing number of historians argue that when the first steps in the revolution had begun, the Enlightenment provided the language, concepts and ideas in shaping what was to come. As Hugh Dunthorne states in *The Enlightenment* (1991):

'… When in France the Third Estate had broken with the Estates-General and set itself up as the core of a new National Assembly – only then did the Enlightenment become a dominant influence, providing justification for revolutionary action and guidance in the making of a new political order.'

1. How were the ideas of the Enlightenment spread through France?

2. How important were Enlightenment views in bringing revolution to France by 1789?

3.6 How did the government deal with the financial crises of the 1770s and 1780s?

Remonstrances: Protests about a royal edict, which *parlement* was trying to change or stop.

Edict: A royal proclamation or decree.

Lit de justice: When the King would attend *parlement* to ensure the registration of an edict, often of a financial nature.

Bold, firm actions might have saved France. But Louis XVI was unlikely to rise to the challenge. As historian William Doyle (1980) puts it, 'It was not the strength of opposition that prevented the Crown from reforming, but the inertia, the uncertainty and irresolution of the Crown itself'.

It is easy to be critical of one of Louis XVI's first decisions – the restoration of *parlements* in 1774. Parlement had ambitions to act as the mouthpiece of the privileged *noblesse*. It mounted determined and persistent opposition to the Crown. However, these claims have been rather overdone. At this stage they acted cautiously, aware that they had spent three years in the wilderness, abolished by Louis XV's minister, Count René-Nicolas Maupeou. Their powers were very limited. **Remonstrances** could only be presented after an **edict** had been registered, and within one month. Anyway, a *lit de justice* was usually sufficient to dismiss any obstructions that they placed in the path of financial edicts. It is true that *parlement* would become increasingly troublesome – but that seemed not to be critical in the 1770s.

Louis XVI lived out an isolated, narrow life at Versailles, lacking the knowledge or drive to see through reforms. He was surrounded by ministers who had risen successfully through the system – so why criticise it? There was an inbuilt inertia among those who counselled the King – an inbuilt defence mechanism against suggesting anything too radical which might change a system that they had exploited to get to the top. It would take a man of ideas and exceptional ability to see beyond all this and support reforming ministers. Louis XVI was not that man.

Versailles tended to be dominated by intrigue and faction. Ministers needed to maintain their support at Court or risk damaging their reputation and losing royal favour. It was a game of survival and intrigue to cast doubt on an opponent's views. Louis XVI's first minister, the Comte de Maurepas, was remarkably successful at defending his position by ensuring that rivals were discredited if they endangered his hold on power. He did so until 1781. One minister who fell victim to this courtly intrigue was Anne Turgot.

Why was Turgot's political career so short?

The Physiocratic belief in 'natural products' explains one of Anne Turgot's first actions. On the assumption that a free market would stimulate demand productions and taxable wealth, Turgot swept away those regulations that hindered the free circulation of grain. The only regulations that survived were those which guaranteed that Paris would not go short of grain – not to do so would have been catastrophic.

As it was, the experiment was not a success. The 1774 harvest was poor, prices rocketed and the rioting which followed in Northern France – sometimes known as the Flour War – made Turgot's position vulnerable.

Undeterred, more reforms were planned. A General Land Tax paid by all was the only answer. Turgot's Six Edicts in 1776 (see below) were met by howls of protest. The Paris Parlement emerged to defend privilege from attack. Remonstrances followed which poured scorn on this 'inadmissible system of equality'. It took a *lit de justice* to quieten the Parlement and force the registration of the Six Edicts. However, Maurepas and Louis XVI's nerves were about to fail. Shaken by the protest against the troublesome Physiocrat, Turgot was dismissed. His work was dismantled. Was Parlement to blame? Probably not. Turgot had been undone by lack of support in the face of his enemies at Court. In France, then, an attempt to introduce enlightened reforms collapsed because of the weakness of the King. The historian John Lough draws an interesting comparison with Austria and Joseph II, where the opposite was the case.

E.N. Williams takes the view that with Turgot's fall, 'the point of no return in the downfall of the *ancien régime* had now been passed. The ministers who followed either made the financial position worse by leaving alone the constitutional issue of privilege, or exacerbated the constitutional struggle by attempting financial reform.'

Six Edicts 1776

Amongst these were well-meaning attempts to move the burden of taxation from poorer sections of society to the more wealthy.

- Unnecessary offices were to be abolished.

- Free trade in grain was to include Paris.

- Monopolistic guilds were to be abolished (opening up restrictive industries to those who had previously been excluded).

- The *corvée* was to be replaced with a General Land Tax paid by all.

Did Necker fair any better?

If intrigue at court undermined Turgot, it brought Jacques Necker to Maurepas' attention. He was financially astute, a man of business, with connections amongst the *philosophes*, but without too many risky ideas which would shake the confidence of financiers.

This was the key to Necker's success. He faced the prospect of another monetary crisis. Between 1778 and 1783, France intervened in the American War of Independence, supporting the struggle of the colonists against Britain. The irony that the French, representing an absolute monarchy, were backing American revolutionaries who wished to gain their liberty from a traditional monarch, George III, was not lost on contemporaries. Young noblemen returned as heroes, talking about 'the growing awakening of liberty, seeking to shake off the yoke of arbitrary power'. French patriots had been successfully associated with rebels who sought to establish a republic with elected, representative institutions. Their ideas were not new – what was new was that they were being put into practice. The declaration in the American constitution – 'we the people' – put **egalitarian** principles, which were being more openly discussed in France. It was the language of resistance and it was fashionable. Divine Right monarchy was under fire. None of this would make a revolution in France – but it added to the sum of enlightened ideas that made people question and challenge the *status quo*.

Behind each crisis was finance. The American War of Independence was an expense the Crown could ill afford. It was left with a huge debt and Necker, as Director-General, had little room for manoeuvre. Economies would make virtually no impact on that scale of debt. Attacking tax exemption and privilege, perhaps via a General Land Tax, had proved fatal for Turgot. Increasing taxes appeared unacceptable as the perception in France, and particularly Paris, was that the burden was already enormous and increasing.

In the first place, Necker attempted a few reforms that followed a familiar trend: abolition of posts, attempted Court economies to cut down on extravagance, and reorganisation of the public accounts. There were plans for provincial assemblies that came to nothing because of opposition from the *intendants*. Some historians, such as John Lough in *Eighteenth-Century France* (1960), consider these changes timid. Others, such as J.F. Bosher in *French Finances 1770–1795* (1970), regard them as more important. Attempting to reduce venality, and appointing officials who were paid and accountable to the government, was long overdue. So were Necker's moves towards a Central Treasury to control all income and spending.

However, Necker's great talent was raising loans without increasing taxation. In this way, he avoided hostility from the Paris Parlement, which had already proved itself to be the self-interested guardian of privilege. He raised 520 million livres between 1777 and 1781, at interest rates between 6% and 10%. The interest on the debt was huge, but Necker had no trouble in finding investors.

It certainly paid for the American War. In order to convince investors that the government was creditworthy Necker produced his balance sheet, called the *compte rendu*, in 1781. This remarkable publication succeeded in enhancing Necker's reputation, and in deceiving investors into thinking their money was safe. It showed that the King's ordinary peacetime accounts were 10 million livres in credit. However, there was no mention of the wartime accounts that showed 200 million livres spent helping the American Colonists. The *compte rendu* was only a temporary success.

Necker's enemies at court were gathering. Maurepas was jealous although Necker didn't help. In attempting to gain a seat on the *conseil d'en haut* (high council) as well as taking control of the spending of the Ministers of War and Marine, Necker was thought to be over-reaching himself. Other ministers said they would resign and, not for the first time, a minister who had promised to make constructive reforms was abandoned. The King failed to support Necker, who was removed from office.

A less charitable interpretation accuses Necker of causing his own

Machiavellian: A term describing a form of political activity that is guided by cynical self-interest and advantage, rather than by any form of abstract principle. The term derived from the 15th-century Italian, Niccolo Machiavelli, who was an advocate of such political activity.

downfall. He knew time was against him and loans were drying up. Without these, Necker had run out of options. Perhaps this is too **Machiavellian**. Nevertheless, the public was disappointed. His reputation lived on to haunt subsequent *Controlleurs-Général*. He had apparently proved that finance could be raised without any need for increased taxes or economies.

The scene was set for further difficulties in the 1780s. The economy was beset by crisis after crisis. Successive *Controlleurs-Général* either increased taxes, levied another *vingtième* (Twentieth), or continued borrowing at very high rates of interest. Venality was rife and **tax farmers** revolted to protect their contracts. Financiers scrambled for the profits to be made from loaning money to the Crown – *officiers* and even ministers joined in.

The onset of depression in the late 1770s and 1780s witnessed a series of unhappy coincidences. As the population rose, pressure on grain stocks began to tell and prices inevitably rose too. Workers spent more and more of their income on bread, while wages failed to keep pace. When matters were at their worst, bread could account for 60% of income. Food riots were sporadic but intense. Customs posts put up around Paris led to disturbances in 1785 and 1786. Troops were used in Lyon against strikers – clear evidence that the textile industry was in crisis as demand slumped. The economic historian Trénard discovered that in 1789, 18,000 workers in Lyon made ends meet only through public charity.

How could the government raise sufficient revenue without invading the tax privileges of the nobility and clergy? It couldn't. Was it feasible to attack the edifice of tax exemption and release vital money? The dilemma was that, on the one hand, the Crown could not afford to carry on without doing so. But on the other hand, it may have been beyond the ability of the Government to undermine privilege seriously, such was the opposition from the First and Second Estates, as well as the grip of speculators on royal finances. Given the weakness of the Crown and the failure of will at Versailles, it was unlikely that anyone would be able to cut through the administrative chaos, sweep away financial abuse, and introduce some efficiency to the tax system.

Undeterred, Calonne, the confident *Controlleur-Général* appointed in 1783, attempted just that. Initially, he did as others had before – borrowed on a huge scale. A generous public works programme, such as building a new harbour Cherbourg, took place. Such spending made it appear that all was well. Interest rates were as high as 16% and repayments were made promptly – in this way confidence was restored. But only for a time.

Calonne managed to raise over 400 million livres. However, by 1786, it was getting tougher to raise the loans. The most recent *vingtième* was due to end, while even optimistic speculators knew that the government would have difficulty maintaining the repayments.

A drastic problem required a drastic solution. With the deficit of expenditure over income standing at 112 million livres, Calonne presented to the King his 'Summary of a Plan for the Improvement of the Finances'. Reform was to take place on a hitherto unheard of scale.

What did Calonne propose?

- A general land tax to be paid by all; even the nobles, church and *pays d'état* would not be exempt.
- Abolition of temporary taxes such as the capitation and *vingtième*.
- Assemblies to be elected by landowners to work out the level of taxation to be paid, as long as *intendants* agreed.

- Abolition of the *corvée*.

- Abolition of internal customs, allowing free trade in grain.

- Reduction of the *taille*.

Turgot had been dismissed for proposing much less. In the meantime, there were loans to be repaid. Even if Calonne did manage to persuade the King to support his reforms, there would be a shortfall of 32 million livres in the budget. To meet this, Calonne reckoned on borrowing even more.

Assembly of Notables: Such a group last met in 1626 and consisted of important bishops, archbishops and *noblesse*.

None of this was likely to gain the approval of Parlement, so in order to gain the appearance of support for his measures, Calonne called an **Assembly of Notables**. This Assembly of privileged groups would, the *Controlleur-Général* incorrectly assumed, give approval to his ideas. All 144 were specially chosen in an attempt to decide the outcome beforehand. When it met in early 1787, Calonne's plans quickly ran aground. The clergy schemed tirelessly to ensure they maintained their tax exemption. The land tax was greeted with suspicion. The underlying difficulties sank Calonne. The Notables were not convinced that things were so bad that radical reform was required and Calonne himself was the subject of persistent intrigue from his enemies. Necker did not waste time in defending his own reputation when Calonne suggested that previous borrowing had brought France to the current crisis.

Calonne's approach didn't help. He ignored criticisms of his reforms and swept aside the legitimate concerns about the land tax voiced by some of the Notables. Calonne went into print characterising the Notables as the representatives of selfishness who were fighting a rearguard action to maintain their privileges. Nobody was impressed. The Notables could have been persuaded to agree to many of the proposals, particularly the need for a fairer distribution of taxation. However, Calonne didn't listen. Historian J.H. Shennan, in *France before the Revolution* (1983) emphasises that Calonne 'had made his reputation as an *intendant* and was associated in the Notables' eyes with that "ministerial despotism" which they detested'. Calonne proved that he had no liking for *parlements*. The Notables were clearly suspicious and refused to co-operate with him. Calonne's support ebbed away and the King, not for the first time, sacked his minister in April 1787. How might a plan of reform gain national acceptance?

The King recognised the merits in the reform proposals. Should he act as an enlightened despot and carry through reform amid accusations of acting like a tyrant? Or should he act as constitutional monarch and try to gain the backing of a representative assembly, bearing in mind that such an assembly would represent privilege? Louis XVI would find no answer to this dilemma.

**Loménie de Brienne
(1727–1794)**
Archbishop of Toulouse and member of the Assembly of Notables. This intelligent cleric was to act as *Controlleur-Général* until the late summer of 1788 when he was replaced by Necker.

The new minister was a Notable, Loménie de Brienne. This able man knew reform was needed although he suffered fatal blows before he had time to implement them.

His first act was to adopt Calonne's plans. Some changes were made to meet criticisms of the land tax made by nobles. Despite these, Brienne found that the Assembly, which he had used so effectively to obstruct Calonne, was now obstructive towards him. The publication of government accounts brought home the seriousness of the crisis to many Notables. They concluded that the government had handled affairs with incompetence and pressed for the calling of an Estates-General.

Brienne needed new taxes. He was clearly not going to get them, and the demands for a meeting of the Estates-General reflected a breakdown in trust in the government.

In May, the Assembly of Notables was dissolved and Brienne turned to the Paris Parlement to register his reforms. Its reaction was predicable enough – its impact on what followed, in a volatile situation, would shake the *ancien régime*.

How serious was the clash between the government and the Parlement?

The answer was 'serious enough', and Brienne knew it. There had to be a solution to the debt crisis; without it there would have to be increased taxation and Brienne foresaw disorder and opposition. Calls for a meeting of the Estates-General had now developed a momentum that would be difficult to stop. In the meantime, attention turned to the Paris Parlement.

Brienne had to act. In July 1787 his reforms were sent to the Paris Parlement to be registered. Not surprisingly, in view of the reaction of the Notables (many of whom sat in *parlement*) some of the reforms were greeted with protests.

The Paris Parlement, with provincial *parlements* tracking in its wake and copying the lead taken in the capital, was now voicing some ambitious claims. It talked of its right as an 'assembly of citizens' to speak for the nation; that it stood between King and people as the guardian of fundamental rights and laws against tyranny. Its language reflected the views of Montesquieu (a mixed monarchy where an assembly would moderate the Crown's powers) and Locke (a social contract linking the duty of the King to the will of the nation).

There seemed little doubt that the Parlement's stand was very popular. The atmosphere in the capital was extremely tense.

When Brienne's plans for a land tax and higher stamp duty were turned down, he imposed them using a *lit de justice* to force their acceptance. Parlement declared the session null and void, repeating the demand that

To what extent does this cartoon accurately reflect the threat to the noble order in 1787?

A French cartoon of 1787. The caption read: 'My friendly nobles, I have called you here to ask with what sauce you want to be eaten?' Reply: 'We do not want to be eaten at all!'

only an Estates-General could now approve and consent to the kind of tax changes the government wanted.

Events gathered pace. In August 1787, the magistrates of Parlement were sent into exile at Troyes, by order of the King. The government lost any chance it might have had to raise new taxes when provincial parlements also refused point blank to register Brienne's edicts. Public clamour was ferocious. Agitation and protest in the streets of Paris were becoming a habit. Clearly, finances were in chaos and the King's hands were forced. In September, the Parlement of Paris returned from exile confident that it had restricted those ministers willing to use royal despotism to force through new taxes at will. The land tax was to be abandoned. The *vingtième* would be extended, new loans raised and the King finally agreed to the calling of an Estates-General – but only by 1792.

If there was a hint that King and parlement had been reconciled, it quickly evaporated. The King wanted the new loans passed without a vote. In November, *lettres de cachet* exiled the duc d'Orléans and imprisoned two magistrates for speaking out against Louis XVI during a royal session of *parlement*. It sparked a winter of further discontent, a cold war of Remonstrances and constant harassment, until May 1788, when matters came to a head. Parlement dared to act as the champion of the fundamental 'rights of the Nation'.

Further arrests of leaders of *parlement* took place and the May Edicts (see insert) were forced through. No further evidence of the tyrannical use, or abuse, of power was needed. Soldiers were sent to terminate an all-night session of protest. The after-shock of the May Edicts was felt throughout France. Historians refer to this as the 'Revolt of the Nobles'.

May Edicts

- The registration of laws was transferred to a plenary court of nobles, *officiers* and magistrates chosen by the King.

- This plenary court also took over from *parlement* the right to remonstrate.

- The legal work of *parlements* was transferred to lower courts.

- The number of judges at the Paris Parlement was to be reduced.

- The Edicts were forcibly registered.

Brienne's Government

Historians are still divided about Brienne. Some recognise that here was an intelligent, enlightened thinker but that he lacked the drive and determination to see through necessary reforms. Others recognise that Brienne, along with Guillaume de Lamoignon, head of the judiciary, planned an impressive programme of change. Some of this was linked to the Enlightenment: such as codification of the law, religious toleration and expanding education. Other changes were vital if finances were to be put into better order: a central treasury to control income and expenditure and the abolition of *officiers'* posts related to taxation and finance. This was the only way of wresting control of government taxation away from those who exploited it for private profit.

The Paris Parlement issued a statement on 3 May 1788. It claimed that:

● *Lettres de cachet* were illegal.

● The Estates-General must meet.

● Only the Estates-General could agree new taxes.

● Imprisonment without trial was illegal.

How important was the Revolt of the Nobles of 1788 in bringing revolution?

How would magistrates react – submit or resist? The answer was never in doubt and the most violent stage of the pre-Revolutionary period was reached. Royal authority outside Paris appeared to be collapsing. Remonstrances poured out from provincial assemblies opposing the judicial changes. The Assembly of the Clergy joined in the chorus of disapproval and voted only a quarter of the government's request for its *don gratuit*. Pamphlets attacking Brienne and Lamoignon poured from printing presses. Historians can find no shortage of evidence of disturbances, many of them fuelled by the privileged.

Nobles incited rioting in Bordeaux, Dijon and Pau. In Toulouse, royal officials were intimidated. The *intendant* was attacked in Brittany, where plans were made for defence against royal troops. At Rennes, the *intendant* was besieged in his house. In Grenoble, royal troops were pelted with stones and roof slates. Both in Franche-Comté and Provence, the Estates met for the first time since the 17th century.

What did all this amount to? So much was froth and excitement, but little else. Royal troops certainly remained loyal and, in July 1788, there were few serious signs of Paris backing the nobles. The risings were uncoordinated and sporadic, like many that had come and gone before.

However, collapse was just around the corner. With tax collection breaking down and *intendants* doing nothing about it while feeling abandoned by Versailles, confidence in the government had completely disappeared. In August, short-term loans dried up. By 16 July, Brienne stopped all payments from the Royal Treasury. Its business could not be conducted as it had no cash flow. Finance, once again, had dealt the blow. It was as close to bankruptcy as made no difference. Brienne could delay no longer. He called an Estates-General to meet on 1 May 1789. If he had hoped that this might help to raise confidence and finance, he was mistaken. He resigned, to be replaced on 25 August by the one man who was still regarded as a magician when it came to raising loans – Necker.

The nation expected salvation. Proposals for reforms, including the May Edicts, were abandoned. In September, *parlement* returned in triumph to Paris. Loans would be raised, but Necker had decided to take no further action until the Estates-General met. For the Crown, it was an admission of defeat. *Parlement* had admitted that it could not reform state finances and Louis XVI had surrendered his responsibilities.

The nobles and *parlement* have been blamed for this. In the end, however, Louis had been the central architect of his own demise.

What decisions now faced Necker and the government?

1. Why did it prove so difficult to solve the financial crisis?

2. What part did (a) the King, (b) the nobles, (c) the parlements, (d) Controlleurs-Général, and (e) the financial crisis play in the events which led to the calling of the Estates-General?

3.7 The calling of the Estates-General: what caused the revolution to slip out of the hands of the privileged classes?

Honoré, Comte de Mirabeau (1749–1791)
French politician, from a noble Provençal family. He had a stormy career before the French Revolution – was imprisoned three times and spent several years in exile. In 1789 Mirabeau was elected to the Estates-General. His eloquence won him the leadership of the National Assembly. He wanted to establish a parliamentary monarchy based on the English model. From May 1790 he secretly acted as political adviser to Louis XVI.

The Comte de Mirabeau may well have complained, 'At last Monsieur Necker is King of France' but if this was true, he had no policies. Temporary loans enabled the government to limp along but all eyes now turned to the Estates-General. Everyone shared the view that this was the assembly that would regenerate the nation.

The Paris Parlement (the voice of the nobles) is often credited with organising and focusing the opposition. It was seen as the powerhouse of demands for an Estates-General. It was very popular – for the moment. However, the *noblesse* was about to become the object of abuse – the victim rather than the perpetrator. Why?

Attention turned to the control of the Estates-General. In September 1788, the Paris Parlement registered their intention that the Estates-General should meet 'in accordance with the forms observed in 1614'. The kindest interpretation was that 'there is no evidence that the magistrates had thought deeply about the implications of this, or even that all of them knew for certain what the forms of 1614 were' (William Doyle).

The issue here was how the three estates would vote and meet. In 1614, the three estates had met separately – hence the Third Estate would always be outvoted by the other two privileged orders. If they met together and heads were counted, then the Third Estate might well decide the outcome of a vote. This would certainly be true if the Third Estate succeeded in doubling its representation, as it later demanded.

Parlement's decision to separate the Estates had grave consequences. The mood changed. Revolutionary forces regrouped. It is generally accepted that *parlement* was now seen as the selfish defender of privilege instead of the interests of the Nation. The nature of pre-Revolutionary antagonisms changed, according to historian D.G. Wright, in *Revolution and Terror in France* (1974), from being 'a clash between the monarchy and aristocracy' to 'a broad conflict between the privileged and the unprivileged'.

There was, indeed, a reaction against the privileged groups who had given the initial impetus in this pre-Revolutionary period. It was a backlash as the Third Estate turned from being the sleeping partner of privilege to being its enemy. The Third Estate took over the cause and became known as the party of patriots. Pamphlets poured out from the radical clubs and societies. They claimed the right to form an assembly and to discuss a new constitution to safeguard the national interest. In December 1788, Necker persuaded the royal council to grant double representation to the Third Estate but, crucially, it made no decision about voting by head.

It would be tempting to see all this as the time when the bourgeoisie assumed leadership of the revolution. This does not bear close analysis – not yet. Much of the agitation during the winter was the responsibility of liberal nobles. In particular, the **Society of Thirty** was prominent in leading the campaign on behalf of the Third Estate – but not many of them were bourgeois at all.

Society of Thirty: This probably consisted in fact of about 60; only 5 of whom were commoners. Most were liberal nobles but it also included magistrates, financiers, lawyers, journalists and some clergy. They attacked absolutist government and what they regarded as the tyranny of the King. It included some famous names such as Charles Talleyrand-Périgord, Bishop of Autun, and the Marquis de Lafayette, who had fought with George Washington in the American War of Independence.

How important was the Tennis Court Oath (20 June 1789) in bringing revolution?

Against this political background was a deepening economic crisis. Its motive power was bread. When it was in short supply, it tipped the fragile subsistence of peasants from starvation level into famine. If bread prices rocketed, the whole economy was badly affected. Peasants and workers, who made up the largest sector of the population, would find the major part of their income spent on bread. Following the catastrophic harvest of 1788 the price of bread rose, and by the following spring, consumed anything up to 88% of a Parisian worker's wages. As there was little money to spend on other goods, it didn't take long for manufacturing to begin to suffer. Textile production was cut by 50% in 1789 and unemployment rose by a similar amount. Shortages were apparent and *intendants* frantically sent out instructions to try to maintain grain supplies.

Rumours that grain was being stored only to be sold at inflated prices led to grain riots. Grain convoys were attacked on the assumption that supplies were being earmarked for Paris, or for export.

All this coincided with the meeting of the Estates-General on 4 May 1789. As the delegates gathered, Necker seemed unwilling to seize the initiative.

Meanwhile, the Society of Thirty was responsible for raising the political stakes – its pamphlets poured from the presses and, in this explosive situation, their ideas spread like wildfire.

In January 1789, Abbé Sieyès continued the campaign against privileged groups in his pamphlet 'What is the Third Estate?' The bourgeiosie's awareness of the interests of the nation was increasing. Sieyès argued: 'What has it (the Third Estate) been until the present time? Nothing. What does it ask? To become something.' Bourgeois indifference was evaporating. The idea of representative assemblies to introduce reforms, both financial and political, was a new feature of their demands. They expected a voice for themselves. As William Doyle argues in *Origins of the French Revolution*, 'the difference, in 1788/9, was that now the bourgeoisie was well educated', literacy levels were improving and it was the bourgeoisie who were eager to join in the debate.

Before the Estates-General met, each estate had contributed to *cahiers* (lists of complaints and proposals for reforms). It would be wrong to argue that the privileged orders were stubbornly blocking all attempts at reform. The *cahiers* from each Estate favoured a new constitutional arrangement that would give an assembly powers to pass laws and to control taxation. There was universal condemnation of absolute rule and, most remarkably, large sections of the nobility and the clergy agreed that they were willing to abandon financial privileges. Given the personal loyalty to Louis that most people continued to feel, it was still possible for the King to win backing for a programme of reform. The matter of voting in the Estates-General remained unresolved.

The Estates-General met on 4 May 1789. Hopes were quickly dashed. The first two estates were divided in membership. Over 200 out of the 291 clergy represented the poor clergy, the village *curés*, who had more sympathy with the Third Estate than with privileged bishops. *Curés* had used the *cahiers* to signal their grievances about the pluralism and opulence of the upper clergy. There were a similar number of nobles and, of these, about 90 might be identified with the 'patriots' party – liberals who wanted changed and reform. Most of the Third Estate, around 400 out of 578, were *officiers*. About 13% were lawyers – representatives of capitalism who, Marxists claimed, were the power-house of revolution.

Necker opened the session by talking at length about taxation but offering no lead on the crucial matter of voting. Indeed the decision about voting was left to each of the three estates. Both the clergy (narrowly) and nobles decided to meet separately. On 17 June, a confident and expectant Third Estate gave itself the title 'National Assembly' and claimed to represent the true interests of the Nation. Two days later, the clergy decided to join the National Assembly. A joint session with the King was called, to be attended by all three Estates.

On 20 June 1789, members of the Third Estate turned up to find the

Emmanuel-Joseph Sieyès (1748–1836)

Catholic churchman (*Abbé* = abbot) who led the bourgeois attack on royal and aristocratic privilege in the Estates-General (1788–9). Active in the early years of the French Revolution, he gained power under the Directory (see page 112). He later retired from politics, but re-emerged as an organiser of the coup that brought Napoleon I to power in 1799.

Use details from the painting to explain how the painter shows support for the actions taken by the Third Estate in June 1789.

building closed for alterations so the Royal Session could not take place. Nobody had told them of the closure. An indignant mob gathered in the pouring rain and followed their leaders to the nearest building that could offer shelter, an indoor tennis court. Here they took an oath – the Tennis Court Oath – that sealed the Revolution. They voted never to dissolve as an assembly until a new constitution had been established.

'The Tennis Court Oath', painting by Jacques-Louis David in 1789

The Royal Session took place on 23 June. It was too late to offer reforms such as no taxation without representation and abolition of *lettres de cachet*. The Third Estate deputies had become more radical – neither were they impressed by the King's declaration that the National Assembly was null and void. As more clergy and nobles joined the Third Estate, Louis took the decision that he should have taken weeks before: all three estates would join and sit together. Voting would be by head. Once again he had proved fatally indecisive in face of the Third Estate and of the people of Paris. The city witnessed daily demonstrations. The atmosphere was highly charged, with rumours about plots to hoard grain, starve Paris, destroy the National Assembly and dissolve the Estates-General.

News of the arrival of royal troops did nothing to settle the Parisian mob. From 22 June onwards, the increase in military strength round the capital must have appeared menacing. By 4 July, just under 30,000 soldiers had been called up. If the King had decided to force the dismissal of the National Assembly, he had not counted on the revolt that now gripped Paris.

1. Why did the Third Estate turn against the nobility and clergy?

2. Does the evidence support the view that by July 1789 there was 'a broad conflict between the privileged and the unprivileged'? Explain your answer.

Cahiers de Doléances

Over two-thirds of nobles and the Third Estate agreed that:

- the Estates-General should meet regularly and should control taxation;
- there should be more financial equality;
- *lettres de cachet* should be abolished.

3.8 Why have historians differed in their view of why the French Revolution began in 1789?
A CASE STUDY IN HISTORICAL INTERPRETATION

The Marxist view

The origins of the French Revolution have given rise to furious debate, which continues unabated. Georges Lefebvre's book *Quatre-Vingt-Neuf* (*Eighty-Nine*), written in 1939, set out the Marxist interpretation which for many years was the accepted view of the origins of the French Revolution. What is the Marxist interpretation of the Revolution? It claims that, in 1789, the class struggle between the clergy and nobles on the one hand, and the bourgeoisie on the other, exploded into violence.

● The clergy and nobility were set apart from the rest of society by their prestige, privileges and high status.

● Aristocratic families measured their wealth in land – this for centuries had been the key to their importance.

● These groups desperately clung on to their power and influence within the *ancien régime*. They conspired to prevent the King's ministers from carrying out reforms that might undermine their privileged position in society. Their days were numbered. Why?

● A new class, the bourgeoisie, was growing in wealth, confidence and expectations.

● Their fortunes were being made in commerce and industry – in other words, they were capitalists, not landed proprietors.

There is evidence of wealth creation by the bourgeoisie. France had the largest population of any country in Europe – 26 million by 1800. Western ports such as Bordeaux and Nantes bustled with overseas trade that had grown fourfold since the death of Louis XIV. Ships left for the Levant, Africa and the Caribbean in ever-increasing numbers. Not only did this line the pockets of colonial merchants, but also of entrepreneurs who were following England's lead in industrialisation. Coal and iron production were forging ahead, as was cloth-making through the domestic system. However, the bourgeoisie may have advanced in prosperity, but they were apparently unable to advance their status in society.

Here is the central trend in Marxist thinking – the revolution from below. Power based on land in feudal society was in decline; its showdown with the bourgeoisie and its wealth based on industry and commerce would mark the transition to capitalism.

How did the bourgeoisie take control of the revolutionary chaos of 1789?

The Marxist interpretation put forward by Georges Lefebvre explains how this happened during the four revolutions, not one, of 1789. The four revolutions of 1787–79 are shown in the diagram:

Georges Lefebvre
Professor of the History of the French Revolution at the Sorbonne (Paris). He was acclaimed as the greatest authority on the subject. Although many copies of *Quatre-Vingt-Neuf* were deliberately destroyed during the Second World War, Lefebvre's *The Coming of the French Revolution* was translated into English (1947) and became a bestseller.

> **1 The aristocratic revolt**
> The nobles established a stranglehold on the monarchy and stifled reform. The bourgeoisie supported the nobles against what they claimed was the despotic power of the King.

> **2 The bourgeois revolt**
> An angry bourgeoisie and Third Estate changed from the ally to the enemy of the aristocracy. The crucial moment was when the nobles decided that, when the Estates-General met in 1789, the system of voting adopted would always mean aristocratic dominance at the expense of the bourgeoisie who would always be outvoted. The Third Estate had turned against the nobility and formed themselves into a National Assembly.

> **3 Population of Paris revolt**
> In the third revolution, the population of Paris fought to prevent the King and nobles from using the army to recover their lost power.

> **4 Peasant revolution**
> Finally, the peasant revolution pushed events to a conclusion, with the attack on landlords and the end of feudal control, as the peasants seized land and swept away ancient rights and dues once claimed by the rural aristocracy.

With what justification can it be claimed that there was a 'revolution from below' in France, 1787–1789?

In dramatic fashion, feudal society was trampled underfoot by pressure from the lower orders in society. This, essentially, was the orthodox Marxist case, although students of this period would do well to acknowledge the dangers of over-simplifying many great works of Marxist historiography. Albert Soboul, for instance, only identified one revolution, led by the bourgeoisie and supported by the peasants.

However, as the Marxists were refining their arguments, alternative views were appearing in print.

How have revisionist historians attacked the Marxist interpretation?

The opening shots against the Marxist view were fired in 1954 by Alfred Cobban in a lecture called 'The Myth of the French Revolution'. Research into the bourgeoisie and nobility was beginning to raise awkward questions. What Cobban started, others followed. Indeed, just as Marxist views accommodate a range of ideas, so it was that **revisionist** arguments too would advance along several lines of attack. The first brought the bourgeoisie under the spotlight of research.

Initially, Cobban undermined the idea of a single bourgeoisie, dominated by capitalists such as merchants, all intent on overthrowing the old feudal order of privileged, exclusive, noble landowners. His analysis of bourgeois members of the Estates-General found that two-thirds of them were lawyers and minor government office-holders. Only slightly over 10% were involved in commerce, which hardly accords with a revolutionary bourgeoisie overthrowing an outdated feudal system. Cobban's case was that the bourgeoisie who drove France towards revolution were officers in lowly government positions, who were making little progress up the social

Revisionist: Historical writing which challenges and revises the Marxist view of the Revolution.

ladder. Their way was blocked by wealthy merchants who were purchasing prestigious titles, and by the upper reaches of the *noblesse*. If the bourgeoisie did not strike the blow that brought feudalism to its knees, then it was almost certainly struck by the peasants who pursued the revolution against their landlords in rural France.

Cobban's ideas found support from historians who cast doubt on the bourgeoisie as a unified, mature, capitalist class. George V. Taylor had already commented, in 1951, on the diversity of the bourgeoisie and the difficulty of identifying similarities of occupation, wealth and cultural background. Lawyers, *rentiers* and government officials may have been interested in affairs of state, but the artisans, shopkeepers, merchants and manufacturers among them shared little of their enthusiasm. Taylor and others were not slow in pointing out that far from the bourgeoisie being capitalist manufacturers and merchants, they were more likely to have their wealth in land. A central fact is that the wealthier bourgeoisie had only one aim in mind – to abandon their capitalist roots (if they had any) and secure social prestige, by purchasing a noble title. They longed for the life of a noble gentleman, owning property and land (France's traditional source of wealth), and enjoying the status which went with it.

Far from being engaged in a class war against the nobles, the bourgeois were keen to join them. Between 1774 and 1789, 2,477 did so and many of them were merchants, financiers and manufacturers. Such enthusiasm was evident throughout the 18th century. Later Marxist historians have acknowledged that the strict division between bourgeois and nobles distorts what really appeared to be happening – that is, the mixing of the wealthiest, most cultured and liberal members of the two groups into one landed and privileged elite, called 'the notables'.

Neither was this one-way traffic. It is worth turning to the traditional view of the nobility as a greedy, closed caste who used *parlements* to protect these privileges against the reforming tendencies of the king's ministers. Cobban and Lefebvre may well have agreed on this orthodox interpretation.

Revisionists, however, are able to draw historians' attention to two questions:

● Could the nobles have been a closed, exclusive class when so many of the bourgeoisie were able to join them?

● How could there be such a clear-cut class war between feudal landowning nobles and capitalist bourgeoisie when so many aristocrats were energetically involved in capitalist ventures?

Both George V. Taylor (1967) and a French revisionist, Guy Chaussinand-Nogaret (in *The French Nobility in the Eighteenth Century*, 1976), found large numbers of nobles investing heavily in industry, particularly coal and textiles. The newer forms of wealth creation in the state were still dominated by land ownership. Even at this early stage of industrial capitalist development, the nobles were behaving like the bourgeoisie. In some manufacturing towns like Lyons, nobles were being modestly successful in industrial development.

Other French historians, such as François Furet and Denis Richet, also began to argue that the upper reaches of the bourgeoisie and nobles had much in common, and that the crude Marxist language of class war was no help at all in grappling with the origins of the revolution. However, was there conflict *within* each class? There emerged a strong case for concluding that many bourgeois merchants and manufacturers did not see eye to eye with other bourgeois members of the legal profession or government service. Nor did the rich nobles, who groomed themselves in the salons of Paris and Versailles, have much in common with the poor nobles rooted in their estates in an effort to maintain a dwindling income. Hostilities between 'robe' and 'sword' nobles were never far from the surface. Older aristocratic families welcomed efforts to push aside those who had more recently bought themselves into aristocratic circles. The 1781 'Ségur Ordinance' only allowed fourth-generation nobles into a career in the officer corps of the army.

If the Marxists consider that their revolution was about liberty and equality, when the crisis came to a head in 1789, *officiers*, lawyers and nobles alike showed no signs of agreeing on what should be done. When the *cahiers* were submitted for the Estates-General in 1789, radical ideas for reform were not on the agenda.

So, did the revolution represent a victory for capitalism? Economically, the Revolution was a disaster for France. Indeed, little changed. Ten, or even 20, years later, agriculture was at a subsistence level and manufacturing took place in small workshops. War had undermined trade and weakened fledgling industries.

Few now subscribe to the social and economic arguments at the core of the Marxist interpretation. However, other explanations will come and go and may themselves incorporate aspects of previous theories. Have the revisionists themselves constructed an interpretation of the origins of the revolution that will stand analysis?

Summary

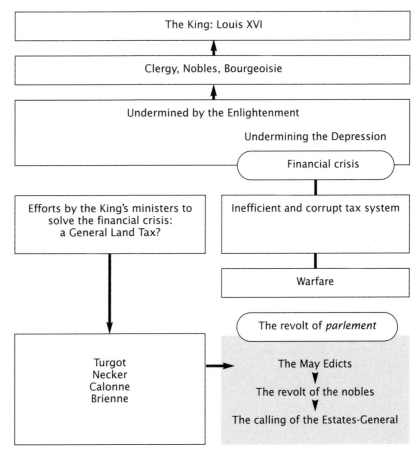

1. Why have historians differed on the reasons for the outbreak of the French Revolution in 1789?

2. To what extent were the bourgeoisie (middle class) responsible for the outbreak of Revolution in 1789?

Source-based questions: Louis XVI, Marie Antoinette and the Monarchy

SOURCE A

He [Louis XVI] had not the willpower to over-ride the opposition to measures which he thought were right; he too easily succumbed to the various pressure-groups at Versailles, not least that led by his headstrong wife, Marie Antoinette. When her brother Joseph II of Austria visited her in 1777, he was not impressed by the way the government was run. 'The Court at Versailles is different; here rules an aristocratic despotism', he wrote. 'The King can change his ministers, but he can never become master of his business … Petty intrigues are treated with the greatest care and attention, but important affairs, those which concern the state, are completely neglected.

Caught in the contradictions of the *Ancien Régime*, Louis XVI backed reform and the opposition to reform at one and the same time.

From E.N. Williams, The Ancien Régime in Europe, *published in 1970.*

SOURCE B

Louis XVI was lazy and of such a conventional and conservative disposition that it was difficult to persuade him to take any decisive action. Royal failures of will and character are not to be dismissed, though they are of only limited significance when weighed against the enormous pressures which eventually destroyed the *ancien régime*. Paradoxically, the Kings' chief contribution to the crises was their insistence that nothing had changed in the personal nature of their authority. It was the fate of the French monarchy to be overthrown not because it had become despotic but because it had become irrelevant. The summoning of the Estates-General indicated that fact.

From France Before the Revolution *by J.H. Shennan, published in 1983.*

SOURCE C

As the mid-18th century chancellor, Lamoignon, declared, the King of France was a sovereign to whom everything was not permitted, but everything was possible. In this sense the King bore the final responsibility for everything the state did – or failed to reform itself, this was in large measure the fault of Louis XIV, Louis XV and Louis XVI, for they alone had the power, the authority and the right to authorise necessary reforms.

From Origins of the French Revolution *by William Doyle, published in 1980.*

---

1. Study Source A.

How useful is this source to a historian studying the weaknesses of Louis XVI?

2. Study Sources B and C.

To what extent do these sources disagree about Louis XVI's role in the origins of the French Revolution?

3. Use all the sources and your own knowledge.

'The financial crises rather than the absolutism of the French monarchy caused Revolution in 1789.' Explain whether you agree or disagree with this statement.

4 The French Revolution

Key Issues

- *What attempts were made to establish a new political system to replace absolute monarchy?*

- *How did foreign wars affect the course of the Revolution, 1789–1799?*

- *How far did the Revolution and Terror change France up to 1799?*

Framework of Events

1789	11 July: Necker is dismissed
	14 July: The fall of the Bastille
	17 July: Louis XVI recognises the National Assembly, Commune and National Guard
	20 July–6 August: The Great Fear
	August: The August decrees
	26 August: The Declaration of the Rights of Man and the Citizen
	October: October Days: the King is forced back to Paris
	November: Church property is sold
1789–1791	The Constituent Assembly
1790	July: Civil Constitution of the Clergy
	November: The clergy take the oath to the constitution
1791	Spring: Fraternal and popular societies in Paris join the Cordeliers Club in a federation
	20/21 June: The flight to Varennes
	16 July: The King is 'suspended'
	17 July: The Champ de Mars attack
	1 October: The first meeting of the Legislative Assembly
1792	20 April: War is declared on Austria
	May: Prussia declares war on Austria
	20 June: The march on the Tuileries
	1 August: The Brunswick Manifesto
	9 August: new revolutionary Commune is set up
	10 August: the violent *journée* to the Tuileries. The King taken into custody
	20 September: The National Convention meets
	22 September: a new Republic is set up
	The September Massacres
	Battle of Valmy – the Prussians are defeated
	November: Savoy is annexed

1793	January: Nice is annexed
	15 January: Louis XVI is found guilty
	21 January: Louis XVI is executed
	February: war is declared on Britain and Holland – the Vendée revolts
	March: war is declared on Spain
	Neerwinden – French forces defeated by the Austrians. Dumouriéz defects
	March–May: measures taken to enforce control of the state
	June: fall of the Girondins. The Jacobins dominant
	Summer: revolts in Normandy, Bordeaux, Lyon, Marseilles and Toulon. Paris under threat from Austrian and Spanish forces
	August: *Levée en masse*
	4/5 September: *Journée*: 'Terror the order of the day'
	Armées revolutionnaires set up
	Law of suspects passed
	August–December: the federal revolt is crushed
1794	January–May: Vendée revolt is crushed

The Dictatorship of the Committee of Public Safety

1793	December: the Law of 14 Frimaire
1794	March: Hébert is guillotined
	April: Danton is guillotined
	June: Law of Prairial

Summer – The Great Terror

1794	28 July: Robespierre is executed
	The Thermidorian reaction
1795	April: The Germinal rising
	May: The rising of Prairial

1795 – The White Terror

	October: The Rising of Vendémiaire
	The Constitution of the Year III
	The Directory
	The Babeuf Plot
1797	September: Coup of Fructidor
	October: Treaty of Campo Formio
	British naval victories
1798	May: The Law of Floréal
1799	November: Coup of Brumaire. The end of the Directory.

Overview

THE course of the Revolution can appear to be a complex chain of events. As France searched for a new constitution against the background of economic crisis, efforts were made to turn it into a limited monarchy. The Constituent Assembly introduced important reforms in finance, government, the law and religion. Paris fought to defend the Declaration of Rights issued in August 1789 – that 'men are born free and equal in their rights'. As fears of foreign armies (Austria and Prussia) and counter-revolution grew, revolutionary extremism gained ground and radical measures were taken to root out those who threatened the Revolution. The fatherland was in danger – *la patrie en danger* – while the King seemed determined not to co-operate with elected deputies. Violence against the enemies of the state became commonplace. It seemed to Paris that even Louis XVI himself was willing to turn to foreign armies to restore his absolutism.

Republican movement:
Those citizens who
supported the abolition of
the monarchy.

A **Republican movement**, linked with mob violence, sent Louis XVI to the guillotine in 1793. To the list of enemies of France in 1792 can be added Britain, Holland and Spain. Civil war broke out in the Vendée (see map on page 106) as Catholic priests and aristocrats organised a popular counter-revolution which spread to other parts of France. In response, constitutional government broke down and the dictatorship of the Committee of Public Safety escalated 'the Terror'

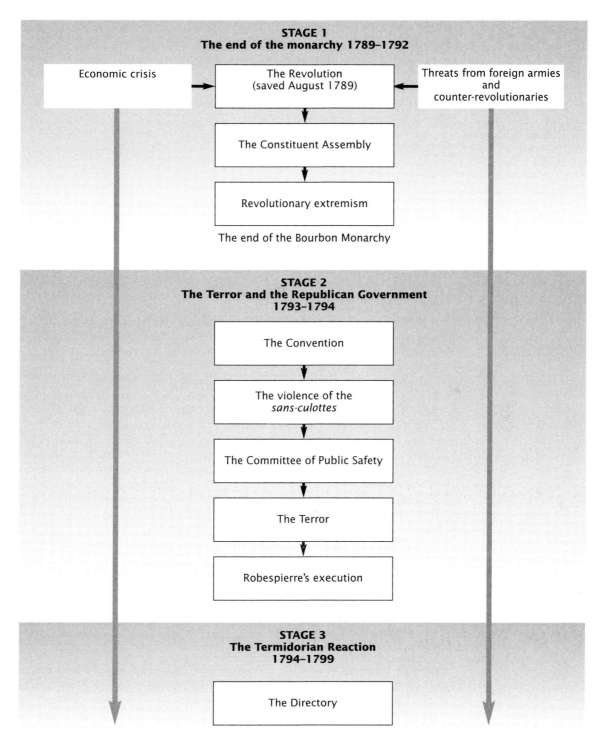

– a fierce repression of those who were seen as threats to the Revolution. The *sans-culottes* (see below) were responsible for driving France into the chaos of the Great Terror (1794) and the dominance of Maximilien Robespierre. However, a reaction against the Terror from those who felt threatened by it not only took Robespierre to the guillotine but also brought to an end the instability caused by the *sans-culottes*. The Thermidorian Reaction broke the *sans-culottes* and brought to power the five-man Directory. As the Directors struggled to govern a country that had become used to bloodshed and administrative breakdown, it relied on the army for support. It was a reliance which eventually backfired – when a young army officer, Napoleon Bonaparte, seized the opportunity to take over.

France's search for a new constitution to replace Bourbon absolutism ended in the dictatorship of Napoleon Bonaparte.

Maximilien Robespierre (1758–1794)
Educated at a Jesuit College in Paris. Elected as a deputy in the Estates-General (which became the National Assembly and then the Constituent Assembly). His defence of democratic principles made him popular in Paris. Robespierre was leader of the Jacobins (see page 92) in the National Convention. He supported the execution of Louis XVI and the overthrow of the republican Girondins. He has been associated with the guillotine and Terror. He became a dictator through the skilful manipulation of events, choosing his moment, via the Jacobin Club and the Commune, to secure power once he was established. The Terror kept him there. He was elected to the Committee of Public Safety in July 1793. He made lots of enemies and, in July 1794, he was overthrown and executed.

Who were the sans-culottes?

Most were shopkeepers, craftsmen, traders, small-scale masters, clerks and wage-earners with some factory owners, wine merchants and better-off professionals. They controlled the Sections, the 48 voting districts of Paris. Many of these 'passive' citizens had also joined the National Guard. They had enormous influence in Paris. They were proud, conscientious and modest – the honest artisan. Their political base was secure and they used it to bully the government. As they wore their redcaps they stood for liberty, equality and the right to carry out armed risings or *journées* in defence of the Revolution. For them, 'aristocrat', 'the wealthy', 'hoarders', 'royalists', 'traitors', 'counter-revolutionaries', and even 'moderate', were terms of abuse. A good revolutionary was not proud, finely dressed or snobbish. He called you 'citizen', he defended the revolution and showed respect to no one who claimed social status. The *sans-culottes* became the driving force behind events in Paris until early 1794.

[*Sans-culottes* means 'without knee-breeches', i.e. without the dress code of the aristocracy.]

4.1 How did revolution develop in France in July 1789?

The atmosphere in Paris had reached boiling point. Up to the return of Parlement in September 1788, Paris had not played a significant role in the political crisis. The arrival of the deputies who were attending the Estates-General raised the political temperature. Expectations were that they would act on the grievances, listed in the *cahiers*.

Philippe, duc d'Orléans (1700–1700)
The King's cousin. Despite this, he had been a prominent liberal and had joined the National Assembly in June 1789. People spoke freely at the Palais Royal and Philippe's support for the Third Estate led to him becoming known as 'Philippe-Egalité'.

The mansion of the duc d'Orléans, the Palais Royal, became the focus of popular radicalism. Its salons, gardens and coffee-houses attracted the crowds who came to listen to agitators or the latest rumours. Underlying everything was the continued rise in bread prices, despite Necker's attempts to bolster supplies from abroad. The King's claims that the military build-up was merely to 'protect' the National Assembly from further riots seemed more threatening than reassuring.

At least Necker was still in government. As popular as ever, there was a touching faith in his ability to maintain bread supplies and to defend the Third Estate. However, Louis XVI had decided on a remarkably assertive course of action. He had come to dislike Necker's sermons about what needed to be done and had resolved to dismiss his minister and then challenge the National Assembly.

On 11 July, Necker was dismissed and ordered to return to Switzerland. As the news spread, a complex and dramatic chain of events would take the King as well as the Assembly by surprise. The *ancien régime*'s days were numbered. The appearance of German cavalry regiments in the streets to quell disorder confirmed the threat from the King. In the Palais Royal, rumours spread that the King would soon attack the Assembly.

On the night of 12/13 July the alarm was raised. Bells rang out to warn Parisians who began to search the city for weapons and gunpowder.

The *gardes-françaises* (French Guards), a well-organised crack corps of troops, were beginning to question where their loyalties lay. Many were drifting to the Palais Royal; others forced royal troops to retreat from the centre of Paris. Order was lost. Gunsmiths' shops were raided, prisons attacked and the property of anyone suspected of hoarding grain was ransacked. Forty out of 54 customs posts, which had ringed the city since 1785, were destroyed – a clear signal of disapproval of the extra duties levied on certain types of food.

The monastery of Saint-Lazare, supposedly the residence of well-fed monks with ample supplies of grain, was taken over. Neither the King nor the National Assembly could have felt comfortable about these developments. Louis was told by Baron de Besenval, the military commander of the region, that royal troops could not be relied upon to remain in the city and suppress the people. Over the next few days, the King's troops stood by and took no action. Nor, meanwhile, did the worthy citizens of Paris approve of the threat to property and order posed by the mob.

At the Hôtel de Ville (town hall) there was an emergency session of the electors who had chosen the city's representatives for the Estates-General. Paris had to be protected from chaos as well as from the King. Their answer was to set up a **paramilitary force**, the National Guard, as well as a committee, called the **Commune**, to run the city.

Paramilitary force: An organisation similar to an army but not the official army of the country.

Commune: In Paris, this revolutionary committee was set up by electors (many of whom owned property) to run the city. It was to become a very powerful body.

Les Invalides: Louis XIV's hospital for old soldiers.

Journée: Crowds which took to the streets; they were often armed and well organised. They played a decisive role in the Revolution.

The Fall of the Bastille

Paris was taken even further out of the King's grasp on 14 July. *Les Invalides* was occupied by a crowd of some 8,000 people and its entire stock of 30,000 muskets, its gunpowder and cartridges were distributed. It was not enough. The *journée* moved on to the Bastille where there was sufficient gunpowder to supply the citizens. The old fortress may well have been the symbol of tyranny and oppression. However, the attackers' aims were much more limited – take the powder and remove the cannon. Two representatives from the Hôtel de Ville went out to see the governor, the Marquis de Launay, at 10.00 a.m. But the crowd was kept waiting until the afternoon and became impatient.

When the crowd managed to reach the inner courtyard, firing started. It was presumed that de Launay's soldiers had been ordered to defend the

Bastille. On the arrival of *gardes-françaises*, the crowd broke in, freed the seven prisoners and took the gunpowder. Ninety-eight of the citizen's army had been killed – far more than the defenders. De Launay was arrested and, before they could decide what to do with him, he was bayoneted and shot after a scuffle with his captors. His head appeared on the end of a pike, much to the crowd's amusement. Royalists were quick to accuse criminals, **vagabonds** and a paid rabble for the attack. Historians have shown that those responsible were *sans-culottes*.

Vagabonds: Homeless and unemployed people who tended to roam in search of casual labour, but could resort to crime and begging in order to survive.

What were the results of the events of July 1789?

Paris had armed itself purely in a reaction to rumours that the King would use troops against the Assembly. Louis XVI had never tested the loyalty of his army. It meant that he had lost control of Paris and he had to admit, according to William Doyle in *Origins of the French Revolution*, 'that he had no means of enforcing his will against Paris, or indeed against anybody. All hope of stopping the course of the Revolution had now gone.'

Troops were pulled back and Necker was recalled. News of the fall of the Bastille filtered through to rural France, where peasants responded by staging a wave of risings against their landlords.

The story, often repeated since, tells how Louis XVI reacted to the news of the fall of the Bastille. 'Is it a revolt?' he is supposed to have asked; to which he received the reply, 'No, Sire, it is a revolution.' There was nothing for it but to return to Paris and accept the inevitable. Absolutism was finished. Power was passing to the National Assembly – or the National Constituent Assembly, as it now called itself. This was indicative of the brief it had set itself – to devise a new constitution for France.

On 17 July, Louis XVI appeared on the steps of the Hôtel de Ville in Paris wearing a red, white and blue cockade (rosette worn in the hat). He had to concede defeat, declaring himself: 'Louis XVI, Father of the French, The King of a Free People'.

Louis recognised the authority of the National Assembly, the Commune and the National Guard. It seemed as if the revolution might have been successfully concluded in a 'triumph of justice and liberty', as a Parisian newspaper trumpeted. There was general agreement that the Constituent Assembly should establish a representative government that would defend liberty and the law. Paris had saved the Assembly and the Revolution. Historians comment that the emigration of many prominent nobles now began in earnest. The King's youngest brother, Artois, and the royal princes, de Conti and Condé, could stand things no longer.

In all only around 8% of nobles left – a surprising number were determined to stay and support the revolution. They would face some difficult times, particularly outside Paris. What was happening in the provinces?

1. What impact did Paris have on the Revolution in July 1789?

2. To what extent did Paris 'save' the Revolution?

How significant on the course of the Revolution were the peasants risings in the provinces?

If the King had lost Paris, he was also losing authority over provincial towns. Shockwaves from the fall of the Bastille were widely felt as power became decentralised. Most serious, however, were the peasants revolts. It was the same mix of rising bread prices, rural unemployment (there was less demand for the peasants' woven cloth) and hope of better things to come. The King had retained some popularity. There was a belief that peasant grievances would be acted upon, bread prices and grain supplies would be regulated and feudal and seigneurial dues would be abolished.

Many peasants, by the summer of 1789, had stopped paying taxes and dues, which were seen as completely unreasonable given the price of bread. Grain convoys had been regularly attacked throughout the year. What started as a tax revolt against tithes, feudal dues and indirect taxes in areas such as Burgundy, Normandy, Picardy and Franche-Comté, became more widespread.

Estates suspected of hoarding grain were attacked and **châteaux** were broken into. Where the *terriers* could be found, they would be burnt. If the *terriers* were not located, the châteaux would be burnt so as to prevent any return to feudalism.

The attackers were not a lawless horde. The peasants did not intend indiscriminate violence. Much of it was conducted in an orderly fashion, in the King's name and (it was assumed) with his approval.

But there were other fears, such as rumours of aristocratic conspiracies. Rural France was regularly gripped by stories of groups of vagabonds moving round the countryside terrorising village after village. This time, these vagabonds were supposed to be in the pay of aristocrats who were intent on burning the harvest and destroying farm animals. Such was the heightened state of anxiety that, in Champagne on 24 July, 3,000 men took up arms to fight a gang of vagabonds only to find that they were a large herd of cows.

The vagabonds never appeared. What became known as the 'Great Fear' (20 July – 6 August), however, had a remarkable effect on the National Assembly, which had been taken aback by these events. The deputies had not only failed to address peasant grievances but also lacked a sense of purpose or direction. According to historian Tim Blanning, in *The French Revolution: Class War or Culture Clash?* (1986):

'Unfortunately, it seems clear – to revisionist historians, at least – that the ideology of the revolutionaries was actually forged during the revolutionary crisis itself and that a sharp break occurred in 1789. The evidence of the *cahiers de doléances* suggests that the Enlightenment had not created a revolutionary mentality, that most people wanted moderate reform and that very few had any idea just how radical the Revolution would turn out to be.'

Indeed, the events of early August prove the point – events were driving the revolutionaries into unexpected territory. The National Assembly faced a dilemma. Peasant support was important, but the threat to property was too much for the bourgeois deputies, many of whom had acquired seigneurial rights of their own.

The August Decrees and the Declaration of Rights

It was idle to talk of using troops to suppress the peasants – it was never an option, given the size of the task. Hence, on the 14 August, a plan was hatched. Liberal nobles, many of them extremely rich like the duc de Châtelet, spoke in favour of ending feudal dues and labour services.

However, the debate in the Assembly took a remarkable turn. The Vicomte de Noailles (Lafayette's brother-in-law) started an attack on the feudal system. The duc d'Aiguillon pointed out that 'feudal barbarism' served to spread inequalities in society. What followed was a night of 'patriotic drunkenness', as one noble called it. All tithes and privileges were renounced. As historian Simon Schama states, in *A Chronicle of the French Revolution* (1989), it was '... like nervous acolytes [devoted followers] made giggly with the thrill of initiation, successive ducs, marquis, vicomtes, bishops and archbishops stripped themselves down to the happy nakedness of citizenship'.

In the August Decrees, the feudal system and the *ancien régime* were swept aside. Equality as a principle was established – equality of taxation, status and entry into the professions.

Châteaux: Mansions or large country-houses.

Terriers: These listed feudal obligations owed by peasants to landowners.

Cahiers de Doléances

In these, over two-thirds of nobles and the Third Estate agreed that:

- the Estates-General should meet regularly and should control taxation;
- there should be more financial equality;
- *lettres de cachet* should be abolished.

Painting of 1792 by Louis Boilly showing a *sans-culotte*, Chenard, carrying the revolutionary *tricolor*. His dress reflects the poverty of the new state.

Inviolable: Nobody could deprive another person of their property.

Arbitrary arrest: Being detained for no particular reason. See **martial law** below.

Martial law: Military law when applied to civilians. Normal civil rights are suspended, allowing the government to arrest individuals and detain them without trial. Suspects could be tried by military court (without a jury) and given the death penalty if found guilty.

Insurrection: Violent action taken by a large group of people against the rulers of their country, usually in order to change the system of government.

Militias: Organisations that operate like an army but whose members are not professional soldiers.

The peasants were freed of feudal obligations and it bound them closely, for the time being, to the Assembly. Fears of conspiracies, hatched by nobles who might seek to overturn these decrees, rallied the mass of the population to the Assembly.

The speed at which principles which had divided French society for centuries were dismantled, must have been breathtaking. An administration had to be reconstructed because provincial estates and *pays d'état* had gone. Offices could not be bought and were now open to anyone of merit. The bourgeoisie and nobles asserted the right to receive compensation for offices or feudal dues lost. Peasants, in theory, would have to redeem some contractual dues by paying sums to their landlords. In reality, peasants did not pay and all debts were cancelled anyway in 1793.

The excitement within the Assembly was amazing. More was to come on the 26 August 1789. The Declaration of the Rights of Man and the Citizen brought the *ancien régime* to an end. It powerfully served the interests of the bourgeoisie because Article 17 spoke of the **inviolable** right to property.

Other articles struck directly at abuse of taxation and of the law, laying down citizens' rights to equality of treatment. **Arbitrary arrest** and torture were over and all had the right to representation in law-making.

How would the King react?

Louis XVI refused to accept both the August Decrees and the Declaration of Rights. For over a month, there was intense debate about the King's power to either delay or veto the Assembly's decrees. His position as an important player in the constitution was never questioned. He was still on the stage and no one suggested expelling him from it.

Incidents at the beginning of October brought matters to a head. With the price of bread rising, the Flanders regiment of the King's Guard was recalled to Versailles. News of their banquet on arrival travelled fast – apparently the revolutionary *tricolor* (see picture) was trampled into the ground, to be replaced by the white Bourbon cockade. Paris took this as incitement.

On 5 October, 7,000 women marched to Versailles followed by 20,000 of the Paris National Guard under Lafayette's command. On arrival, the Assembly was invaded. Representations were made to the King who, it was intended, should accompany the people back to Paris.

Louis XVI did not argue. He accepted both the August Decrees and the Declaration of Rights. The next day, the royal family and the Assembly made the five-hour journey back to the city.

The strains were showing. The King had made it difficult to arrive at a constitutional agreement. The Assembly had seen the mob in action and was uncomfortable. They feared disorder, the threat to property and the distinct possibility that the Assembly might become the victim of **insurrection**.

Martial law was imposed as the Assembly tried to clamp down. Had the revolution run its course? Was now the time to draw up a constitution and reform the government? The Assembly thought so. Much of value would be achieved in the coming months.

As *intendants* fled, the bourgeoisie took over existing councils or set up new committees once the old corrupt town councils had been forced from office. **Militias**, along the lines of the National Guard, were set up to protect the revolution.

August Decrees 1789

The following were abolished:

- tithes
- financial privileges
- tax exemptions
- seigneurial courts
- the feudal system
- venality
- guild restrictions
- personal subjection to a lord
- corporate and provincial privileges.

Why was it proving difficult to establish a monarchy with limited political power from July 1789?

Extracts from the Declaration of Rights, August 1789

1 'Men are born and remain free and equal in right.'

2 'These rights, are those of liberty, property, security and resistance to oppression.'

3 'All sovereignty resides essentially in the nation.'

7 'No man may be accused, arrested or detained except in cases determined by the law.'

8 'Only strictly necessary punishments may be established.'

9 Every man must 'be presumed innocent until judged guilty'.

11 'Free expression of thought and opinions is one of the most precious rights of man. Accordingly, every citizen, may … speak, write and print freely.'

13 '[Taxation] should be borne equally by all citizens in proportion to their means.'

17 ' … the right to property is inviolable and sacred.'

How did the Declaration of Rights of August 1789 bring about major change in France?

4.2 How important was the work of the Constituent Assembly?

There is a case, put most strongly by François Furet and Denis Richet, that the reforms of the Constituent Assembly laid lasting foundations for a new governmental and administrative structure. Also, subsequent events, such as the Terror, never really destroyed those foundations.

The Assembly faced many difficult tasks:

- to transform France into a limited monarchy from an absolutist one;
- to decide on a new constitution;
- to rebuild the economy and decide how the government should be financed;

- to decentralise the administration by giving more power to local authorities;

- to develop a more efficient, uniform and humane system of laws and justice;

- to agree a new relationship between Church and State.

Of course, much would be asked of Louis XVI. He would be abandoning age-old assumptions about the privileges and status of the monarch, nobility and Church. Did he have the ability to guide the Crown into giving up many of its powers? 'How could this poor ... King, with his gift for stubbornness and docility at just the wrong times, comprehend so demanding an assignment?' (Schama) The monarchy would be preserved – but, while the King kept 'supreme power', he could only veto laws for up to four years. He was not to be trusted, but there was little serious talk of getting rid of the monarch – for the moment.

Départements: Largest local government units in France.

Local administration

- The August Decrees had swept away provincial estates and municipal corporations.

- A local structure of government was vital to maintain food supplies, law and order, and taxation.

- France was divided into:

83 ***départements***
↓
which were divided
into 547 districts
↓
which were further divided
into 43,360 communes

- Officials were elected according to voting qualifications, partly based on wealth but also on their merits.

- It involved thousands of new participants in the administrative system.

- Results were patchy – some areas had educated bourgeoisie to fill the posts. However, 'it soon became apparent that merely establishing such institutions did not make skilful men out of often illiterate farmers and previously inexperienced townsmen' (Franklin Ford).

- Nevertheless, the structure survived to be developed later.

- These changes reflected the decentralisation that had happened in 1789. Control from the centre was loosened, which would certainly be an obstacle if the King or aristocracy tried to regain power.

Voting rights

Tier 1 – for elections to the councils which ran local government:

- only males over 25 could vote, as long as they were 'active' citizens.

- An 'active' citizen was one who had resided in one place for a year and paid taxes to the equivalent value of three days' wages.

Tier 2 – for elections to a higher assembly (districts and *départements*):

- an active citizen could become an elector on a higher assembly – this would choose national deputies.

- to be an elector would require paying taxes equivalent to 10 days' wages.

Tier 3 – for election as a national deputy:

- to qualify as a national deputy, that person would be paying a silver mark (52 livres) or 50 days (about) in taxes. Wealth was clearly important in qualifying for voting.

Around a quarter of adult males were unable to vote at all – they were 'passive' citizens. Certainly the numbers who qualified, particularly at municipal level, stood at over four million – the highest proportion in Europe.

The law

- Some Enlightened principles were put into practice.

- In keeping with the Declaration of Rights, 'men are born equal in their rights'.

- The law was to be fairer, accountable and open to all.

- A jumble of different laws (Roman law in the south, customary law in the north) and courts were to be replaced by a single legal system.

- *Parlements*, seigneurial and church courts were abolished.

- *Lettres de cachet* were abolished.

- New courts were introduced, run by elected and experienced magistrates and judges.

- Cases had to be brought to court within 24 hours.

- Appeal courts were introduced.

- Serious criminal cases were heard in front of a jury.

- Barbaric practices – torture, branding and hanging – were outlawed.

- Fewer crimes were punishable by death, which was to be by the guillotine.

These reforms were a remarkable step forward and they formed an enlightened basis for France's legal system. They were a step forward for a legal system which previously had a reputation for cruelty, inefficiency and corruption.

Assignats: Paper money originally printed by the Government; bonds to be exchanged for Church lands.

Inflation: An increase, sustained over time, in the general level of prices. The annual increase may be small (creeping inflation) or large and accelerating (hyper-inflation). Inflation can be caused by an increase in the cost of raw materials which is then passed on to the consumer, or by a shortage of goods the demand for which pushes prices up.

Finance and the economy

● National finances were in crisis. Attempts to maintain the tax system of the *ancien régime* led to rioting in heavily taxed areas as well as widespread tax avoidance – perhaps up to 66% of what might be expected.

● Many people assumed that the revolution would bring the whole practice of privilege crashing down and the tax system with it.

● In November 1789, the Constituent Assembly took a huge step – it decided that Church property would be sold for the nation.

● *Assignats* (government bonds which were bought and exchanged for Church lands) were issued. By 1790, the *assignats* were worth millions of livres. They became a form of paper currency.

● Nobles who emigrated would have their property confiscated and sold.

● The more *assignats* that were printed, the more this currency lost value through **inflation**.

● Many bourgeois bought Church lands, but historians now understand that many peasants also became smallholders because the land was cheap.

● Those who purchased *assignats* now had interest in maintaining the post-Revolutionary situation as they had no wish to have their land confiscated and returned to the Church.

● In return, the state took over many Church responsibilities. It paid clerical salaries, financed education and looked after poor relief.

● New taxes on land and property were introduced.

● The *gabelle* and other indirect taxes were abolished.

● While there were unfair variations in the taxes paid by different parts of France, the poor paid less and exemptions had been removed – hence most peasants agreed that this was a more equitable system.

● Unfortunately, poverty was such a widespread problem that it was unlikely to be dealt with effectively.

● The Constituent Assembly's economic reforms were a mixture of enlightened ideas and suppression.

On the one hand:

– free trade was introduced, particularly in grain;

– guilds and internal tariffs were abolished;

– a uniform system of weights and measures was introduced.

On the other hand:

– Le Chapelier law prevented the formation of trade unions;

– strikes were made illegal.

● Despite these reforms, France's finances remained in crisis.

1. What do you regard as the most important reform of the Constituent Assembly? Explain your answer.

2. To what extent did the reforms of the Constituent Assembly benefit only the propertied bourgeoisie?

Who benefited?

Most of the reforms promoted bourgeois interests:

- Le Chapelier law
- the abolition of guilds
- the voting qualification based on increasing wealth
- the way the bourgeoisie came to dominate local administration
- the abolition of noble titles in favour of 'citizen' as the revolutionary mode of address also emphasised the new status of the bourgeoisie.

How did the Civil Constitution of the Clergy deepen the split in French society?

As the section on finance and economy above shows, the financial crisis led to the sale of Church lands and helped to forge a link between the class of landed proprietors and the revolution. By purchasing church lands, the bourgeoisie had invested in the revolution and would directly oppose a royalist reaction in which they would lose their newly acquired lands.

The Assembly would take matters much further. Their belief in liberty, equality and popular sovereignty stimulated a range of reforms which were never anti-Catholic, nor would there be any change in the status of the Catholic Church as the official or State Church. Indeed, many of the reforms had tacit clerical support. As the *cahiers* showed, abuses were to be swept away.

Church reform

Between August 1789 and February 1790, the following abuses or special privileges were abolished:

- tithes
- pluralism
- *don gratuit* (the 'free gift' of taxation decided by the clergy)
- annates (payments to the Pope)
- contemplative, monastic orders – those which did little 'good' work to help the poor.

Protestants were to receive equal civil rights and toleration.

The Civil Constitution of the Clergy

Church and local administration were brought together.

- Each *département* would have a bishop (83 in all, instead of 135).
- Clergy were to be elected in future.
- The Pope would no longer have any say in accepting or rejecting bishops.

Even the Civil Constitution of the Clergy (July 1790) didn't provoke overwhelming opposition. The clergy would certainly lose out – fewer would be required and those who remained would have to submit themselves to election.

Conflict could have been avoided. However, the next step was unnecessary and dangerously divisive. The Clergy wanted a **synod** of the Church to discuss the Civil Constitution and agree on a way forward. The Assembly refused – it saw no reason why the clergy should see itself as a special case. What authority did the Church have to challenge the sovereign power of the Assembly? None, concluded the Assembly. The Pope was also taking his time to comment on this matter.

Synod: A special council of members of the Church, which meets regularly to discuss religious issues.

The Assembly made a rash move – it wanted to have its way, so the clergy would be forced to take an oath to the Constitution and the nation. The results of this tactic were catastrophic. France divided into those who were for or against the oath. This went far beyond what had been intended. The Pope and most of the clergy rejected the oath. Those who accepted the oath and a 'Constitutional' Church amounted to only a handful of bishops and just over half the other clergy. They were associated with the nation and revolution. Those who rejected it were called 'non-jurors' or refractory priests. They became associated with royalists, *émigré* nobles – counter-revolutionaries, particularly in the west and south. Many peasants in these areas were devoted to refractory priests and they formed the raw material for revolts against the revolution.

1. How serious was the quarrel over the Civil Constitution of the Clergy?

2. To what extent did the Civil Constitution of the Clergy bring about lasting problems in France?

The Civil Constitution, then, had a lasting impact in splitting France and it gave the counter-revolutionaries a large base of support. If the Assembly had handled things better, these hostilities could have been avoided.

4.3 Why did the monarchy come to an end in 1792?

The development of revolutionary discontent

In 1791 and 1792, France lurched towards a more radical and extreme solution. Despite the work of moderates in the Assembly to complete the constitution and draw a line under the 1789 Revolution, thereby bringing it to a close, France was about to embark on what Marcel Reinhard and Albert Soboul, 20th-century French historians, both referred to as a 'second revolution'. It would bring an end to the monarchy in September 1792 and a bloody foretaste of the Terror. What had happened to cause this?

Louis XVI was increasingly unwilling to go along with the Constituent Assembly's wishes. Honoré Mirabeau, perhaps, might have succeeded in convincing all parties that a limited monarchy was possible. Although this liberal noble had been a president of the Assembly, he seemed to enjoy the confidence of the King, speaking up (with not inconsiderable ability) on his behalf. Mirabeau's death, which stunned the political nation in April 1791, was a setback.

In seemed to many contemporaries that whatever constitutional experiment was introduced, Louis would treat it as a temporary nuisance until a time came when he was better able to renegotiate. The King was also sorely troubled by the Civil Constitution of the Clergy. He wished he had never signed it. Moderate deputies found themselves in a dilemma. Some nobles and clergy thought things had gone too far. However, there were groups who thought that things had not gone far enough. These radicals were working in a frenzied atmosphere.

Jacobin clubs: The original club of 1789 met at the convent of the Jacobins (see page 94) and was called the 'Society of the Friends of the Constitution'. The first club allowed the Breton deputies to meet and plan strategy. Membership swelled but with an annual subscription of 24 livres it was confined to better-off citizens.

Networks of political clubs had sprung up since 1789 to act as pressure groups on the Assembly. They organised political dissent. The **Jacobin clubs**

Benjamin Franklin (1706–1790)
American scientist, statesman, writer, printer and publisher. He was the first US ambassador to Europe (1776–85). In this capacity, he enlisted French help for the American Revolution. Franklin wrote and published *Poor Richard's Almanac* (1733–58), as well as inventing such things as the lightning conductor and bifocal spectacles.

Georges Danton (1759–1794)
Lawyer who practised in the appeal courts. Possibly the most honest of the revolutionary leaders. In 1792, his stirring speeches inspired the resistance which made victory at Valmy possible. Since he was Minister of Justice in September 1792 he must take much of the blame for the terrible prison massacres (see page 97). Danton tried to retire from politics in 1793, but returned to plea for calm in the Terror. On 5 April 1794, he died as recklessly as he had lived: 'Show my head to the people. It is worth the trouble.'

took their lead from people such as Mirabeau and Benjamin Franklin. Their members were well off moderates. Even the presence of radicals such as Robespierre amidst their ranks could not stifle the messages which emerged from their endless revolutionary debates – their belief in limited, constitutional monarchy.

However the **Cordeliers Club** was a different matter. A cheap admission fee brought in the *sans-culottes* (see page 82), the working class. They favoured radical, direct action, insurrections and violent attacks on all forms of privilege. Their leaders – Georges Danton, Camille Desmoulins and Jean Paul Marat – were responsible for politicising 'the menu people' (lower groups in society). In the spring of 1791, the fraternal (brotherly) and popular societies in Paris joined the Cordeliers club in a federation. The next action of the King played into their hands.

On the night of 20/21 June 1791, Louis XVI decided to abandon the Tuileries with his family. His coachman had orders to drive east towards the border. The King reached Varennes where he was recognised and returned to Paris.

The 'flight to Varennes' had catastrophic consequences for the King. It was assumed that Louis had planned either to join royalist soldiers in Lorraine or to appeal to his brother-in-law, the Emperor Leopold II of Austria. Paris and the Assembly were anxious about the threat from foreign monarchies and about the King. The flight confirmed the impression that Louis was a traitor and was encouraging intervention from across the borders. Moderate deputies disliked the idea of a republic but now faced growing pressure to dethrone the King. Radicals demanded that Paris should be armed in case of attack and that counter-revolutionaries, **refractory priests** and monarchists should be rooted out.

On 16 July, the Assembly managed to 'suspend' the King until he had agreed to the constitutional proposals which were being drawn up. Divisions deepened – within the Assembly and within the Jacobin Club too. Some felt the suspension of the King was a step too far, while others felt that this would remain unfinished business until dethronement was achieved. For the time being, though, those who wished to include Louis in a constitutional monarchy controlled the Assembly – men like Adrien Duport who had helped to form the **Feuillant Club** when they left the

Cordeliers Club: A revolutionary club that represented radical and *sans-culottes* opinion.

Refractory priests: Otherwise known as non-jurors. They had refused to take the oath to the Constitution.

Feuillant Club: Moderate revolutionaries who reacted against the republicans in the Jacobin Club and formed their own society with the aim of coming to a constitutional agreement with the King.

Camille Desmoulins (1760–1794)
French revolutionary who summoned the mob to arms in Paris on 12 July 1789, thus starting the revolt that ended in the storming of the Bastille. He was sent to the guillotine for being too moderate!

Jean Paul Marat (1744–1793)
Doctor to the Guards of the Count of Artois until the Revolution. His newspaper, the *Friend of the People*, made him the leader of the *sans-culottes*. His outbursts were a major factor in provoking the prison massacres of September 1792. He was also largely responsible for the Jacobin coup of 2 June 1793, and the arrest of Girondins. Marat was murdered on 13 July 1793 by Charlotte Corday, a member of the Girondins. His death, if anything, hastened the Terror.

Jacobins. The Jacobins wanted dethronement. The survival of the Feuillants, who were moderate, depended on winning the King over.

> ### The 1791 Constitution
>
> ● An elected assembly, called a legislative assembly, would pass laws and would determine foreign policy and war.
>
> ● The King had a veto, but this excluded anything relating to the constitution or finance.
>
> ● The King could appoint his own ministers.

The Assembly tried to clamp down and martial law was introduced. On 17 July, however, a peaceful Republican demonstration by 50,000 people on the Champ de Mars was attacked by Lafayette and the National Guard, under orders from the Commune and, presumably, the Assembly. Fifty demonstrators were killed. It was time for others to flee – such as Marat and Danton, leaders of the Cordeliers Club, who were clamouring for dethronement. In the short term, the radicals had suffered a setback. But the Feuillants had to make the new constitution of September 1791 work, and the signs were not hopeful. Marie Antoinette referred to the constitution as 'monstrous'. There was a noticeable increase in the numbers of nobles emigrating, including over half of the army officers by the end of the year. When the new, and ultimately doomed, Legislative Assembly met on 1 October 1791, it was dominated by the bourgeoisie, who had probably been elected by only 10% of citizens. The King wasted no time using his veto in November. He prevented the passage of two laws – one which would have declared *émigré* nobles as traitors and their property forfeit if they failed to return to France; and another which declared that refractory priests were to lose their income and be treated as conspiring against the nation. The latter was a response to unrest in the south of France, where camps of royalist Catholics could not be seen to go unpunished. The King would never agree to such punitive measures against loyal priests. Was the veto the last straw for the constitution? The answer probably doesn't matter as the foreign situation signalled the death-knell of the monarchy.

How did war affect the course of the Revolution?

King Frederick William II of Prussia and the Emperor Leopold II of Austria had already met, at Pillnitz in August. They expressed concern about the safety of Louis XVI, but their undertaking not to attack France without the agreement of England and the other powers sounded threatening. Foreign powers looked as if they were planning to interfere in French politics. Nevertheless, war was distant. Leopold welcomed the 1791 constitution, despite Marie Antoinette's letters inciting him to armed intervention. England was not prepared to act, and Russia's attention was focused on Poland.

How did attitudes change? Following Leopold's death early in 1792, the Austrian Emperor Francis II took a more aggressive view of foreign policy. He signed an alliance with Prussia (February 1792). Formally, here was a cause on which many French leaders could agree – the desirability of war – but they agreed for different reasons.

Louis might seize the opportunity to regain absolute power. In the Assembly, the **Girondins** were keen to use war to unite France in defence of the nation and to expose treacherous priests and monarchist counter-revolutionaries once and for all.

Jacques Brissot, the leader of this group of Girondin deputies, spoke of

Jacques Pierre Brissot (1754–1793)
French revolutionary leader. He became a member of the Legislative Assembly and the National Convention, but his party of moderate republicans (Girondins or Brissotins) fell foul of Robespierre. Brissot was guillotined.

Charles François Dumouriéz (1739–1823)
French general during the Revolution. In 1792 he was appointed Foreign Minister, supported the declaration of war against Austria, and after the fall of the monarchy was given command of the army defending Paris. After plotting with the royalists he had to flee for his life, and from 1804 he lived in England.

putting the King on trial and stories circulated that France's foreign policy was being run by the 'Austrian Committee' led by Marie Antoinette and counter-revolutionaries. Headstrong radicals spoke of sealing the Revolution with blood and sacrifice – *'vaincre ou mourir'* – and the orators got their wish. When the King appointed a new government, including Girondins, the mood changed. The Foreign Minister, Charles Dumouriéz, loathed Austria and saw a chance to further his ambitions. War was declared on the Emperor Francis II on 20 April 1792.

The French were ill-advised to embark on war. Not only had they lost many officers, but also the entire military organisation was confused. Training and discipline had been eroded. Inevitably, the French armies suffered defeat after defeat, leaving the country open to invasion.

To make matters worse, Prussia joined Austria in May and declared war on France. In this hothouse atmosphere, scapegoats were quickly sought. As fear and panic set in, politicians looked for more extreme solutions.

What impact did the creation of a Republic have on the Revolution?

In Paris the tension increased.

- Revolutionary clubs were organising discontent
- Could the demands of the *sans-culottes* be ignored?
- Could the Legislative Assembly decide the fate of the King?
- Would the Girondins get their way and dethrone the King?
- How might the French armies cope against the Austro-Prussians?
- Could radical elements in Paris be controlled?
- What should be done about refractory priests and counter-revolutionaries?

Some of these questions were soon answered.

On 29 April, defeats in the Austrian Netherlands (Belgium) caused a retreat by French Armies and opened the borders to invasion. The King not only vetoed two laws but also dismissed Girondins ministers. They had tried to:

- deport refractory priests
- set up a camp for 20,000 *fédérés* in Paris. Both laws were stopped.

Fédérés: National Guards from the provinces. They were known to be militant revolutionaries who wanted to destroy the monarchy; unlike the Paris National Guard which tended to be royalist.

These followed two violent *journées* that sealed the fate of the King. The first was 20 June. The Cordeliers Club organised 8,000 demonstrators to march on the Tuileries. The King stood his ground. Wearing the red revolutionary cap, he drank the health of the nation. He did his best, in the face of the armed mob, to convince them that he would support the Constitution. He got away with it – for the time being.

Meanwhile, the Assembly's decree – *'la patrié en danger'* – asked all Frenchmen to defend the fatherland. However, the Sections, the *fédérés* and the *sans-culottes* were clearly gaining the upper hand.

The King's future took another turn for the worse when the Commander of the Austro-Prussian army announced the **Brunswick Manifesto** (1 August).

Brunswick Manifesto: This warned Paris that the city would suffer a 'military execution' if the royal family was harmed.

Paris was in uproar. It was only a matter of time before another violent rising took place. Robespierre demanded, in front of the Jacobin Club, an end to the monarchy. The *fédérés* petitioned for the same thing.

On 9 August, a new revolutionary commune was set up when the *sans-culottes* occupied the Hôtel de Ville.

On 10 August, there was the second and decisive *journée*. The Tuileries was attacked by *fédérés*, *sans-culottes* and other National Guards who had joined the insurrection. The numbers in the National Guard had been swelled by 'passive' citizens who had been allowed to join their ranks – hence their militancy. Six hundred of the King's Swiss Guards were massacred at the cost of 300 *sans-culottes* and 90 *fédérés*.

The Legislative Assembly was also occupied and the King was taken into custody. The revolutionary Commune was in control. Moderate deputies (monarchists), shaken by all this, kept away. A committee of ministers under Danton was able to pass some important measures – the most important of which was to set up a National Convention. Its task was to decide on a new constitution. Would it be Republican or would it include the King?

The Second Revolution was about to take place. The monarchy would soon be at an end.

1. In what ways did Louis XVI and his family cause their own downfall?

2. To what extent did the threat from abroad lead to the fall of the French monarchy?

4.4 Why did the Terror develop?
A CASE STUDY IN HISTORICAL INTERPRETATION

Was the Terror an immediate reaction to the emergency facing France or did it arise out of the revolutionary struggle?

On 20 September 1792, the National Convention met. All men over 21 had voted for it. Its members were republicans, Jacobins, Girondins and supporters of the Commune.

The next day they voted to end the monarchy and, on 22 September, the new Republic was proclaimed. Amid great excitement, the Convention declared its Revolutionary principles – 'Liberty, Equality, Fraternity'. The new spirit was captured in the birth of a new calendar – Year 1 Day 1 was to begin from the first day of the Republic. Each revolutionary month was renamed, in accordance with the weather and seasonal life in the country.

The French Republican Calendar

Revolutionary month	Reference	Gregorian calendar
Vendémiaire	Vintage	22 September – 21 October
Brumaire	Fog	22 October – 20 November
Frimaire	Frost	21 November – 20 December
Nivôse	Snow	21 December – 19 January
Pluviôse	Rain	20 January – 18 February
Ventôse	Wind	19 February – 20 March
Germinal	Buds	21 March – 19 April
Floréal	Flowers	20 April – 19 May
Prairial	Meadows	20 May – 18 June
Messidor	Reaping	19 June – 18 July
Thermidor	Heat	19 July – 17 August
Fructidor	Fruit	18 August – 16 September
Sans-culottides	National Holidays	17 September – 21 September

Despite the general air of excitement, several matters overshadowed the Convention:

● the September Massacres

● deep rifts in the Convention itself

● threats from foreign armies.

September Massacres

The September Massacres were a response to military defeats. The Prussians were already on French soil and Lafayette had defected to the Austrians. The news was greeted with alarm in Paris. The Commune raised thousands of volunteers to defend the Revolution. They began to look round for spies and royalists. Rumours were flying that nobles, royalists and priests, who were packed into Parisian prisons, would escape and help the Prussians to invade the city. In an orgy of violence that lasted several days, starting on 2 September, prisons were opened and suspects put to death. Probably over 2,000 were killed. Most of these were criminals. The *sans-culottes* were responsible for the massacres. It seemed that no one was in a position to challenge them.

Rifts in the Convention

When the 782 members of the Convention met, a rift between the 200 Girondins and 100 Jacobins was immediately apparent. Between these two extremes was the 'Plain' – a large, unattached group. In September 1792, the Girondins had most support.

There was better news from the war at the end of 1792. In September at Valmy, the Prussians were thrown back which removed the threat from Paris. General Dumouriéz occupied Belgium after defeating the Austrians at Jemappes. Nice, Savoy and Avignon were all annexed – the French wasted no time exporting the benefits of the Revolution to these three small states by abolishing feudal dues.

Meanwhile, the problem of what to do with the King still needed a solution. The Girondins favoured imprisonment of the King; the Jacobins wanted a trial and execution. But when Marat called for deputies to announce their verdict in public, Louis XVI's fate was a foregone conclusion. Marat was ready to expose anyone who defended the King.

On 15 January 1793, the King was unanimously found guilty, but his execution was only narrowly secured: 361 voted for execution, 319 for imprisonment. On 21 January 1793, Louis XVI went to the guillotine in the Place de la Concorde, in Paris. The Girondins suffered too – their 'softer' line had lost them support – the 'Plain' was drifting towards the Jacobins who were gaining ground.

In the hall, the moderate Girondins faced the Jacobins who sat on the upper benches and became known as the 'Montagnards' (the mountain people). Amongst the Jacobins were Robespierre, Marat and Danton.

Why had it proved impossible to save the King and the monarchy

Print of the execution of Louis XVI, 21 January 1793

The war and beginnings of the Terror

In 1793, the shedding of blood became so commonplace that it was accepted as the 'norm'. The Terror is associated with the guillotine – and Frenchmen just became accustomed to it. They were used to the ease with which people could be accused as traitors and sent to their death. The hunt for enemies inside France followed in the wake of a war that had gone badly.

The Convention wished to offer other Europeans the chance to gain their liberty. It also aimed to expand France to its 'natural frontiers' – the Rhine, the Alps and the Pyrenees. This would anger Britain – its trade would be threatened by French expansion into Belgium and the area surrounding the river Scheldt.

In February and March, France declared war on Britain, Holland and then Spain. In March, at Neerwinden and following Dumouriéz's defection to the Austrians (there were rumours that he was going to march on Paris), France was pushed onto the defensive. The Austrian Netherlands was lost and invasion loomed. In the summer, Paris was threatened by Austrian and Spanish forces. But quarrels between the Allies meant that their campaigns were uncoordinated. France was saved from external threats partly because of Allied disunity and partly because it mobilised the resources of the whole state behind the Revolutionary wars in August 1793. Half a million soldiers were to be equipped and trained.

If external dangers were pressing enough, the Republic also faced internal dangers. These were:

- the possibility of economic collapse
- risings and federal revolts
- struggles for power inside the Convention, leading to the fall of the Girondins
- the problem of how to ensure that the government maintained control of the country.

The government faced a number of risings against its authority – the most persistent of which was in the Vendée (February 1793 onwards).

> In August 1793, France began military and economic planning on a scale never known before:
>
> - Half a million men were to be conscripted in a *levée en masse*.
> - State-run factories would produce weapons and ammunition.
> - The government would ensure that arms factories had sufficient raw materials to equip the armies.

How did the Convention enforce control?

Measures taken by the Convention, March to May 1793

By far the most important group was the **Committee of Public Safety (CPS)**. The first was formed in April and a new one (which Robespierre sat on) was agreed in July. This 12-man committee had the authority to check on the work of ministers; in fact, real executive authority was exercised by the CPS.

A revolutionary tribunal: it had judicial powers to try counter-revolutionaries. It was a major group which carried out the Terror.

Representatives-on-mission: These were the agents of Centralised government sent out to the provinces. They ruthlessly took over local government and enforced decrees. They spied on generals and made sure conscription was taking place fast enough.

Comités de Surveillance: Watch committees who spied on foreigners and suspected traitors. They could execute rebels without either appeal or referring cases to a jury.

The **Committee of General Security** was another major agent of the Terror. This 12-man committee controlled spies and ran a secret, revolutionary police.

The *armées révolutionnaires* carried out tasks for the authorities – such as seizing grain, attacking hoarders and helping to root out counter-revolutionaries.

The Convention faced serious economic problems. The war had to be paid for, prices were rising and the *assignats* were losing their value. Food shortages were occurring partly because the army was seizing supplies and partly because farmers were not keen to sell their produce if all they received were *assignats*, which had been badly hit by inflation.

Several measures were taken to help the situation, including raising prices and wages, confiscating property and introducing rationing.

● On 4 May, a maximum price was fixed for grain, and the rich had to make a loan to the government.

● Rationing cards made sure meat and bread were fairly distributed.

● Hoarders would receive the death penalty. In September the Law of the Maximum fixed prices at the 1790 level plus one-third, and fixed wages at the 1790 level plus a half. In general, this was unpopular with peasants and clashes took place between peasants and the *armée révolutionnaire*. Prices were increased further in 1794 which helped the peasants and the Law of the Maximum did prevent food riots. As a result, the *assignat* also increased in value.

The CPS had to deal with a series of risings throughout France. The Vendée revolt started as a protest against conscription in February 1793. While it had some economic causes, such as rising land taxes and rents, this was also about their support for refractory priests and aristocrats who had been hit by the Revolution. Both these royalist and clerical elements were behind a revolt which, by May, had drawn 30,000 troops away from the war into the Vendée to suppress the rebels.

Why did the Girondins fall from power in June 1793?

Power within the Convention was moving towards the Montagnards, as more of the Plain supported them. The Girondins were being blamed for all France's problems. They had not been helped by Dumouriéz's defection (he was a Girondin). The *sans-culottes*, whose backing was essential in Paris, were firmly behind the Jacobins. In fact, they were calling the tune. Most of the events of the Terror were a response to their demands. It was the *sans-culottes* who provoked the collapse of Girondin power. Robespierre knew this and he encouraged the people of Paris to rise up against the Girondins, whom he accused of treachery and corruption. There was no love lost between them. The Girondins repeatedly accused the *sans-culottes* of being 'buveurs de sang' (drinkers of blood).

The Girondins had become the enemy of the Revolution. On 2 June, 80,000 National Guards surrounded the Convention and pointed their cannon at the building. The Girondins were finished. Their leaders were arrested and the remainder expelled. Jacobin dominance was assured, as long as they were backed by the *sans-culottes*. The *sans-culottes* placed their mark on a new Constitution, passed in June, which gave the vote to all adult males and which granted the right to use insurrection as a legitimate tool to carry out their wishes. Indeed, the wishes of Paris, and therefore of the Jacobin-dominated Convention, were identified with the wishes of the *sans-culottes*. The results of this were quickly felt outside Paris.

The Federal revolt and the Terror

Federalism: A movement which would mean different areas of France keeping some independence from the government in Paris.

The provinces hated interference from Paris, conscription and the Civil Constitution of the Clergy. But the fall of the Girondins also sparked off risings all over France. The new Committee of Public Safety, on which Robespierre sat, would need all its resolve to fight what it referred to as the forces of **federalism**.

Throughout mid-1793, France was threatened by Allied armies. But Allied disunity and quarrels over the partition of Poland meant that the danger passed.

Trouble broke out in Normandy, Bordeaux and Lyon. In Marseilles, Jacobins were executed and the city had to be taken back by force. In Toulon, the city was opened to British and Spanish troops and control was only restored in December, after an attack by forces led by the young Napoleon Bonaparte. Lyon was held out to siege for two months, until October 1793.

In the autumn, the revolutionary armies retook each area of revolt, bit by bit. This was accompanied by the Terror. The *journée* of the 4/5 September 1793 was sparked off by grain shortages, starvation and unemployment in Paris. As the crowd gathered outside the Hôtel de Ville, the Convention was sufficiently intimidated to take action. 'Terror is the order of the day' was announced – *les armée révolutionnaires* would requisition grain supplies for Paris and assist in the suppression of federal revolts. Between September and December 1793, 56 other *armées* were sent to the provinces. Robespierre was not in favour of them. Peasants would be angry at grain seizures and there was a loss of central control over the agencies of the Terror, which went on a violent rampage throughout France. Officially, the Committees of Public Safety and of General Security would bring the accused before the Revolutionary Tribunal (see insert on page 98). But it was in areas of federal revolt where the worst acts of savagery were committed.

The Law of Suspects (September 1793) gave powers to new revolutionary committees. Mass arrests took place; over-enthusiastic watch committees, *armées révolutionnaires* and representatives-on-mission condemned thousands. There was usually only one verdict – death. Seventy per cent of these executions took place in the south and west. The Vendée suffered most. About half the victims of the Terror came from here. Indiscriminate savagery reduced the Vendée to a ghostly shell. Farms were destroyed and famine forced many to flee. Carrier, the Representative-on-Mission from Nantes, was responsible for the mass drowning of 1,800 people. In all, 17,000 were probably executed – another 30,000 died either in prison or without trial.

What was Robespierre's role?

Marxist historians such as Albert Soboul and G. Rudé accuse him of starting to follow socialist principles but eventually turning against the people by turning popular sovereignty into the dictatorship of the CPS. Lacking humour and warmth, and puritanical he may have been, but Robespierre had a highly developed ethical and moral code that translated itself into a strict political programme. His dream was based on the 'Republic of Virtue', in which Frenchmen would be free, equal and devoted to 'la patrie' (fatherland). He was a tolerant defender of the people – he disliked the rich and the differences of wealth as well as the labelling of people as 'passive' citizens. Democracy and liberty were worth saving – and if it was necessary to root out the enemies of the Revolution then so be it. Terror would be the instrument to suppress treachery and counter-revolutionary plots within France and from outside. Terror would guarantee virtue. Robespierre called it the 'despotism of liberty'. If he followed the beliefs of Rousseau and 'the general will', it was to impose Revolutionary principles on the people. There was no time for the common good to evolve and be recognised by the Community.

'The Incorruptible', as Robespierre was known, had to defend liberty justice and treachery by whatever means were available. He disliked the masses, although he cleverly used the support of the *sans-culottes* to establish his position on the CPS. It is likely that the people he fully understood and represented were bourgeois property-owners, or independent masters – in other words, men of modest substance. Robespierre was

1. How important was war in causing the Terror?

2. In what ways were the **sans-culottes** *driving events in France at this time?*

Dechristianisation campaign: This was a determined effort to close all the churches (by Spring 1794), to destroy religious artefacts and force priests to marry. The Convention and many revolutionaries still associated the Constitutional Church and Catholicism with plots against the Revolution. A new calendar (see page 96) undermined its Christian basis and substituted days associated with the Republic and seasonal features. In rural areas, this attack on Christianity was met with anger and suspicion.

Jacques Hébert
Journalist and leading member of the revolutionary Commune. He tried to take charge of the violent factions among the *sans-culottes* and revolutionary armies in order to further his personal ambitions for power. His faction (called *Hébertists*) supported the right of insurrection, dechristianisation and the death sentence for those who hoarded food. Hébert had a particular skill in stirring up the *sans-culottes*.

certainly popular in Paris but his power was wielded through a committee, which included other prominent figures. His influence was there but was exercised alongside others in the CPS. It seems that he may have seen the Terror as a temporary measure and that he had no liking for the most extreme excesses of revolutionaries. For Robespierre, the safeguarding of the Revolution was everything.

Why did the Committee of Public Safety become a dictatorship?

While there were counter-revolutionaries to be crushed, the Committee of Public Safety let the Terror run its course. But so much authority had been decentralised to representatives, revolutionary committees, the *armées* and so on that central government was functioning in a chaotic situation. The *sans-culottes* were the force behind the Terror, and the Convention had gone along with their demands. The Declaration of Rights (June 1793) recognised their belief in the right to work, to be educated and to defend equality by insurrection.

The *sans-culottes* had also pushed the **dechristianisation campaign**. At some point, though, they would have to be reined in.

In late 1793, internal revolts were being crushed and French armies were on the offensive. In late 1793, the CPS began to put the Revolution into reverse. Several things had to go: decentralisation, elections to posts, as well as safeguards against the concentration of power in the hands of a few.

By the Law of 14 Frimaire (December 1793):

● *armées revolutionnaires* in the provinces were disbanded

● the Committee of Public Safety was given huge powers over ministers, generals, local government and representatives-on-mission

● the Committee of General Security was given powers over the police and the Revolutionary Tribunal.

Both committees, then, had complete power, while the *sans-culottes* were on the wane. Dangerous opponents had to be dealt with. The Terror was about to reach another climax as the Revolution began to devour its own at a bewildering rate.

Girondin leaders went to the guillotine in October. Jacques Hébert, who called for insurrection against 'those who oppress us' through the pages of his popular newspaper *Le Père Duchesne*, went too far when he attacked Robespierre for setting up a 'dictatorship'. He was arrested, accused of being in the pay of foreign monarchists and guillotined in March 1794.

Danton was next. He, too, was opposed to the concentration of power in the CPS. He wanted to end the war and the Terror. Probably because he had followers in the Convention, Danton had to be removed. Danton was accused of plotting against the Republic and no time was wasted in sending him to the guillotine in April. The signs were obvious. Criticism of the CPS, or even a word, a glance, a nod of the head, could send anyone to the guillotine. Fear induced silence. In the summer of 1794, over 1,000 a month were being executed. It seemed that an appearance in front of the Paris Revolutionary Tribunal was enough to bring the death sentence.

Robespierre's Law of Prairial (June 1794) opened the floodgates. Anyone accused of trying 'to mislead opinion' could be tried, without recourse to a defence or the bringing forward of witnesses. Four panels were set up to try cases – and anyone could be brought before them. The Great Terror was on, and the guillotine was not short of victims. However, even at the height of the CPS's dictatorship, the seeds of Robespierre's downfall were being sown. The *sans-culottes* could see their position being reduced – the popular societies had gone and so had the revolutionary armies. They were hit by bread shortages and rising prices, as well as by the fact that the Law of Maximum was now placed on wages, causing them to fall. There were even jealousies between the two committees running the Jacobin dictatorship.

Rivalry between the CPS and CGS

The Committee of General Security (CGS) was supposed to have full police powers. Its working relationship with the Committee of Public Safety was breaking down in April 1794. Robespierre had set up his own network of police. And when the law of 22 Prairial was introduced, the CGS had known nothing about it. Fears that Robespierre's dictatorship threatened everybody's safety were rife. The Plain felt particularly vulnerable.

People were apathetic and fearful. Local government had been paralysed by lawlessness, fear and administrative overload. It was impossible to keep up with the twists and turns of policy in Paris. Robespierre decreed that a new religion, the Cult of the Supreme Being, would be set up to heal France's spiritual divisions. The opposite happened: Catholic priests attacked it as false, and Robespierre was accused of assuming God's full support for the Revolution, which some regarded as blasphemy.

---

1. To what extent did the Committee of Public Safety reverse the revolution at the end of 1793 and beginning of 1794?

2. How was the dominance of the sans-culottes ended?

What changes inside France is this print meant to represent?

Interpreting the Terror

Historians have argued about the Terror. Marxist historians, such as Albert Soboul, see it as one of the final parts of the class struggle – the *sans-culottes* (lower orders) were rising up to drive the Revolution forward and destroy what was left of the feudal system and the aristocracy. At the other extreme, the Terror was seen as a temporary reaction to root out counter-revolutionaries, because of the fear of military defeat, invasion and revolts throughout France. The historian Tim Blanning (who discusses this debate in *The French Revolution, Class War or Culture Clash?*) refers to this as a 'knee-jerk' reaction to an emergency. F. Furet, in *Revolutionary France* (1992), takes a third position. This recognises the immediate dangers posed by counter-revolutionaries, but claims that the Terror was developing from 1789 throughout the revolutionary period. Those in power had to claim that they were the *only* ones who knew what the popular will was and who represented the revolution. So political enemies had to be destroyed. During the Terror, this reached its peak. The debate will, no doubt, continue.

Vive le Roi,Vive la Nation.

This print shows how the tables had turned in France. There is a message of peace in the peasant's pocket; the sword is to protect the nation and the priest carries the scales of justice to balance equality and liberty.

4.5 How did the Thermidorian Reaction affect the Terror?

The Terror would consume Robespierre himself. Exhausted from overwork, two speeches proved crucial. On 26 July (8 Thermidor), he attacked other members of the CPS, such as Lazare Carnot, Joseph Fouché and Collot (see Chapter 5). On the next day, Antoine Saint-Just (sometimes known as the 'Angel of the Terror') produced a list of accused citizens in front of the Convention. Not surprisingly, its members feared the worst, and voted to arrest both Robespierre and Saint-Just. The Paris Commune could not raise enough soldiers or a *journée* to support them. Robespierre hesitated. In the meantime, the Convention passed a decree to outlaw him – Robespierre could be executed without trial. Following his arrest, he was guillotined along with Saint-Just and 20 others on 28 July 1794 (10 Thermidor). No popular rising took place to save him. The Plain, like many others, recognised that the Terror had become unnecessary.

The Austrians had been defeated at Fleurus in June 1794, and French armies were advancing into the Austrian Netherlands, the Rhineland and across its 'natural frontiers'. The threat had gone for the time being. It would be a mistake to think that a new era was beginning which turned its back on the guillotine, judicial execution or plain murder. It is true that the structures associated with the Great Terror were removed. The government of Thermidorians, as the moderate deputies who took control were called, quickly reduced the number of executions. The Jacobin Club and Paris Commune were closed down and the Committee of Public Safety lost its say in domestic affairs. The Revolutionary Tribunal was to survive for less than a year. Paris relaxed. Theatres, press, even wigs and fashionable dress began to appear again.

However, a new phase of terror was about to begin. Events did not favour the Convention and protests forced it to rely on the army for survival. France had become used to a certain scale of violence – it was not going to subside as quickly as the moderate Thermidorians would have wanted.

Free market: Access by buyers and sellers if unrestricted by government.

In an effort to go back to a **free market**, the Law of Maximum was swept aside. Without any control on wages and prices, *assignats* fell in value to less than 10% of their original value, and inflation took hold. Bad harvests not only made bread prices rocket, but also the spectre of famine had appeared again by the spring of 1795. The protest of Germinal (1 April), when 10,000 people surrounded the Convention about bread shortages, was easily dealt with by the National Guard. The leaders of the demonstration, who had once been on the CPS, were deported.

However, the bread riot of 1/2 Prairial (20/21 May 1795) was a different matter. Part of the National Guard joined a huge demonstration and marched on the Convention, which was suitably intimidated. The President of the Convention received the protesters' demands and peace was maintained. Two days later, the army was called out to suppress the rebels. Arrests took place and large areas of Paris, particularly where the *sans-culottes* lived, were disarmed. With no army and no one to organise them, the *sans-culottes* were finished. Forty-two National Guard leaders and some Montagnard deputies were executed.

White Terror: Movement that took its name from the colour of the Bourbon flag. But only some of its members were royalist *émigrés*. Most of them wanted to settle old scores against revolutionary extremists.

Émigrés: Political refugees who have left their own country, usually for political reasons, to live and work abroad.

The **White Terror**, as it has come to be known, now took hold. It continued, in some parts of France, until 1797. Those responsible for the White Terror wanted revenge on those who had participated in the revolution. Their targets were *sans-culottes*, government officials, constitutional priests and particularly those had rounded up people for the Revolutionary Tribunals. It was the backlash against the Jacobins who had fed the guillotine. In Paris, the violence was limited to gangs of middle-class youths (*la jeunesse dorée*) beating up victims. However in the Vendée and Brittany, thousands of former terrorists were murdered.

In Brittany, the **guerrillas** were called Chouans and they had not only British support but also that of 3,000 *émigré* troops who landed in June 1795. Once again, it was the regular army under General Hoche which spent over 12 months suppressing the guerrillas and restoring order.

The Republican government's troubles were not over. Work had begun on a new Constitution. The Thermidorians went to great lengths to ensure that no dictatorship like the CPS could ever return to French politics and to ensure that people should be given back their voting rights.

Guerrillas: People who fights as part of an unofficial army, usually against an official army.

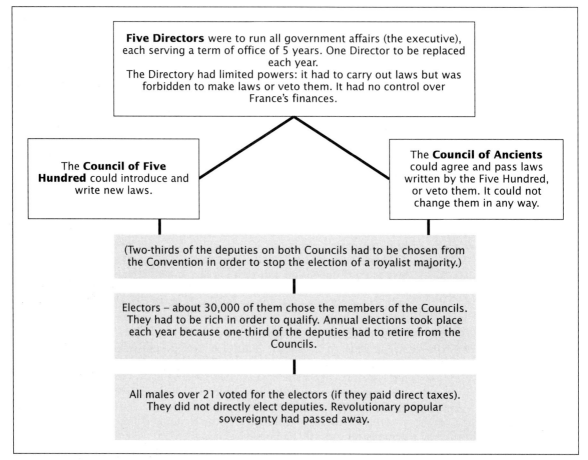

Five Directors were to run all government affairs (the executive), each serving a term of office of 5 years. One Director to be replaced each year.
The Directory had limited powers: it had to carry out laws but was forbidden to make laws or veto them. It had no control over France's finances.

The **Council of Five Hundred** could introduce and write new laws.

The **Council of Ancients** could agree and pass laws written by the Five Hundred, or veto them. It could not change them in any way.

(Two-thirds of the deputies on both Councils had to be chosen from the Convention in order to stop the election of a royalist majority.)

Electors – about 30,000 of them chose the members of the Councils. They had to be rich in order to qualify. Annual elections took place each year because one-third of the deputies had to retire from the Councils.

All males over 21 voted for the electors (if they paid direct taxes). They did not directly elect deputies. Revolutionary popular sovereignty had passed away.

Did the system work? If it was intended, through these checks and balances, to prevent the concentration of power in one group, it worked perfectly. However, if the Directory and council were in disagreement, then paralysis of government was a possibility. The Directory could neither introduce its own laws nor change those made by the Council of Five Hundred. If the councils did not co-operate, then it was difficult to get things done. Elections also tended to be won by royalists, which disturbed the Directors, who were appointed in the first instance because they were Republican and regicides (king-killers). As the constitution was fixed for nine years, the Directory was to turn to the army if urgent action was required.

Just before the new Constitution came into being, the rising of 13 Vendémiaire (5 October 1795) took place. Twenty-five thousand armed protesters set out to besiege the Convention. They were an assortment of

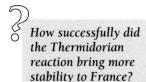

How successfully did the Thermidorian reaction bring more stability to France?

workers, wage-earners, factory and property owners, and civil servants. There were some royalists present but not as many as has been claimed. A young general, Napoleon Bonaparte, trained his cannon on the rebels and treated them to a 'whiff of grapeshot'. If the protesters had meant to force something to be done about low wages, inflation and their desperate poverty, they failed. Three hundred were killed. It was the final armed rising for many years.

In October, the new Directory took over.

4.6 Was the Directory a complete failure?

It is tempting to write off the Directory – even the Directors plotted its eventual downfall with the support of the army. The system of separation of powers led to dissatisfaction. The stability, which the Directory was supposed to restore, could not be guaranteed. It is fair to point out that the Directory's problems were daunting: war, debt, inflation, lack of order but, most of all, the scars left by the Terror.

Throughout the Revolution, events had been driven by the military situation. The Directory relied on the army's success. Not only did the army support the Directory, but some talented generals disposed of France's enemies one by one. By early 1798, the army had ensured that only Britain was left as France's sole enemy and that foreign conquests were at their peak.

1795:

● By the time of the Directory, the Batavian Republic had been set up, consisting of Belgium and the United Provinces.

● Prussia had made peace with France so she could pay some attention to the partition of Poland. Spain made peace with the French and they became allies in 1796.

● Austria was to be defeated by two advancing French armies: one across Bavaria and one, under Napoleon, would march across the Alps into Italy and on to Vienna. Napoleon's campaign was incisive and brilliant – he took Piedmont and defeated the Austrians, taking Milan and Mantua in the Process. When the Austrians pushed the Army of the Rhine back, Napoleon ignored the Directory and concluded the Treaty of Campo Formio in October 1797 with Austria (see page 113). Britain remained stubbornly undefeated. In 1797 the British navy destroyed the fleets of France's allies – the Spanish at Cape St Vincent and the Dutch at Camperdown.

Regardless of these setbacks, the Directory needed to support itself and its army with foreign conquests. Switzerland and Geneva were invaded. In Italy, the Papal States fell and France was able to surround itself with friendly republics – the Batavian, Helvetic, Cisalpine, Ligurian and Roman. By 1798, even the left bank of the Rhine had been handed over to France. Even though Napoleon's campaign against the British in Egypt (see page 113) went badly, warfare under the Directory had been largely one of advances, right up to the end of 1798.

1799:

This year, however, was a different matter. The Second Coalition brought renewed warfare against Austria and Russia. After initially taking all of Italy, France's armies were driven out of Switzerland and Italy and back to the Rhine. Arguments between Austria and Russia saved France from invasion and enabled French soldiers to turn Russia out of Switzerland. Napoleon (see Chapter 5) would smash the second Coalition.

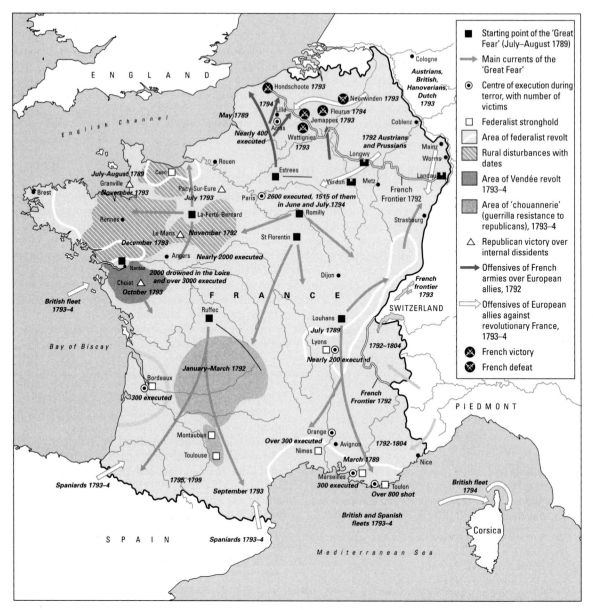

Legend:

- ■ Starting point of the 'Great Fear' (July–August 1789)
- → Main currents of the 'Great Fear'
- ⊙ Centre of execution during terror, with number of victims
- □ Federalist stronghold
- Area of federalist revolt
- Rural disturbances with dates
- Area of Vendée revolt 1793–4
- Area of 'chouannerie' (guerrilla resistance to republicans), 1793–4
- △ Republican victory over internal dissidents
- → Offensives of French armies over European allies, 1792
- ⇨ Offensives of European allies against revolutionary France, 1793–4
- ⊗ French victory
- ⊗ French defeat

The revolution in France

Desperate measures were taken to restore the Treasury's finances. At least it can be said that complete financial collapse was avoided. Loot from abroad was helpful but the collapse in the value of the *assignat* was disastrous. A new currency was introduced and that, too, became worthless. Coins became the sole legal tender but there were not enough of them in circulation. Those who owned government investments (*rentes*) were given bonds. These suffered the same fate, although the Directory was pleased to see the *rentes* reduced so much in value that much of their debt disappeared. New taxes were introduced and commissars (working directly for the Directory) were put in charge of tax collection. Bourgeois investors and property-owners suffered accordingly. Those who had gained by the Revolution were now losing out.

It was not the only threat the Directory faced. A series of plots denied it the stability it was trying to maintain. In May 1796, Gracchus Babeuf planned a Conspiracy of Equals. This was a rising by a small group of well-disciplined *révolutionaires* against the wealthy on behalf of all the people. Babeuf went to the guillotine in 1797.

More serious were two occasions when the Directors themselves used the army to deal with what they thought were threats from the right and from the left.

In 1797, apathy with the war and the Directory resulted in the election of large numbers of monarchists to the Councils. Such was their advance that, by 1798, royalists might have a majority. Hence two Republican Directors used troops under the command of Napoleon (September 1797, or Fructidor year V) to round up Directors and deputies suspected of being sympathetic to the royalist cause. Election results were quashed and Directors Carnot and Barthélemy were exiled. *Émigrés* were forced to leave and hundreds of refractory priests were deported.

The troubles of Floréal (May 1798) show how little the Directory now commanded respect, or interest. This time, the Jacobins won about one-third of all the seats – not enough for a serious threat, but again the Directors overturned their election. The fact that the government found it difficult to ensure the re-election of its candidates indicates the public mood.

In 1799:

- The war against the Second Coalition was going badly.

- Conscription in 1798 and a *levée en masse* in 1799 were widely evaded and caused huge resentment.

- The Law of Hostages (July 1799) enabled the government to arrest and seize the property of nobles and their *émigré* relatives, in rebellious areas.

- Forced loans, to pay for the war, added to the unpopularity of a government which had already lost the sympathies of the bourgeois.

- Order and local government were disintegrating. Some areas were completely lawless and government tax commissioners were lucky to escape with their lives.

- The Directory had lost its backing, and was twice guilty (Fructidor and Floreal) of suspending the Constitution to suit itself.

What were the main problems faced by the Directory? Was the army responsible for its downfall? Explain your answer.

Directors Emmanuel-Joseph Sieyès and Roger-Ducos plotted to cut through the chaos and use the army to overturn the constitution, while imposing a three-man Directorship with wide powers.

So it was on 19 Brumaire (10 November 1799) that Napoleon Bonaparte was enlisted to bring the Directory to an end and forcibly introduce the rule of the Consuls (see Chapter 5). A new era had begun – the Napoleonic. It closed the page on the Revolution. In the end, the Directory had ended with a whimper.

Source-based questions: The downfall of the French monarchy

SOURCE A

However unbelievable the Revolution may appear, it is none the less absolutely certain that from now on the city of Paris has assumed the role of a King in France and that it can, if it pleases, send an army of 40 to 50 thousand citizens to surround the Assembly and dictate laws to it.

Mercy Argentau, the Austrian Ambassador to France in 1789, after the fall of the Bastille

The Jacobin Society is truly the committee of inquiry of the nation ... because it covers by its correspondence with other societies all the nooks and crannies of the 83 *départements*. Not only is it the great instigator which terrifies the aristocrats, it is also the great instigator which redresses all abuses and comes to the aid of all citizens. The club acts as a public ministry alongside the National Assembly.

Desmoulin, himself a member of the Jacobin Club, writing about its influence in 1791.

SOURCE B

At a window, I saw the King wearing a red cap. The people had entered his apartment in considerable numbers, shouting 'Down with the Veto! Ratify the decrees! Long live the nation!

The King was wearing the cap of liberty on his head and was drinking from a bottle. He was unable to make himself heard and several times he rang a little bell to get them to listen. When he finally got their attention he told them that he was in favour of the Constitution and swore to uphold it. The people shouted that it wasn't true, that he had already deceived them and would do so again, shouting 'Bring back the patriot ministers!'.

A member of the Jacobin Club reporting on the journée of June 1792, to the Tuileries

SOURCE C

All the clubs and assemblies and churches of patriots demand correspondence with the Jacobin Club and write to it as a sign of fraternity.

---

1 Study Sources A and B.

How far did the events described in Source B prove the writer of Source A correct?

2 Study Source B.

Explain what was meant by 'he had already deceived them and would do so again'.

Use the source and your knowledge to help you answer the question.

3 Study Source C.

How useful is this source to a historian studying the importance of the Jacobins?

4 Study Sources A, B and C and use information contained within this chapter.

'Do these sources fully explain the downfall of the French monarchy?' Explain your answer.

5

Napoleon, France and Europe

Key Issues

- *What was the nature of Napoleon's personal rule?*

- *How did he attempt to create a Napoleonic Empire in Europe?*

- *To what extent did Napoleon build on the French Revolution?*

Framework of Events

Early campaigns: Italy and Egypt (1796–1799)

1797	Treaty of Campo Formio
1798	Second Coalition
1799	Coup of Brumaire
	Napoleon named as First Consul

The Consulate and early Empire

1800	Bank of France is set up
	Battles of Marengo and Hohenlinden
1801	Concordat with the Pope
1802	Peace of Amiens
1803	Failed invasion of England
1804	Code Napoleon
	Napoleon is crowned Emperor
1805	Battles of Ulm, Trafalgar and Austerlitz
	Napoleon is crowned King of Italy
1806	Confederation of the Rhine set up
	Battle of Jena
	Continental Blockade (until 1813)
1807	Treaty of Tilsit

Decline and defeat

1808	Spanish Campaign (until 1814)
1809	Battle of Wagram
	The Pope captured
1810	Holland annexed
1812	Russian campaign
1813	Battle of Leipzig
1814	Fall of Paris; Napoleon abdicates
1815	The Hundred Days
	Napoleon in exile
1821	Death of Napoleon.

'Napoleon crossing the Alps' – a painting by Jacques-Louis David

How does this painting help historians to understand the 'Napoleonic legend'?

Napoleon Bonaparte (1769–1821)

- Born in Corsica, an island which had only become French the year before he was born.
- His cultural heritage was more Italian than French.
- Napoleon received an excellent education at the expense of the French by attending the École Militaire in Paris. Here he trained as an artillery officer.
- He supported the French Revolution and saw the chances that the emigration of so many noble officers would offer him. He saw the opportunity to advance his career and did so.
- Napoleon was deeply hostile towards the Paris mob and the scale of violence associated with *journées*.
- In 1793 he seized an opportunity to make a name for himself. Toulon had revolted against the Revolution. British and Spanish fleets had been allowed into the port. Napoleon organised the French troops besieging the town and, with the clever use of artillery, forced the enemy fleets to quit.

- Following this, his fame spread quickly. At 24 he was already a Brigadier General.
- After writing a pro-Jacobin pamphlet, he entered the Robespierre circle of radical politicians and was appointed an Army planner.
- Robespierre's downfall threatened to cut Napoleon's career short. He spent a month in jail but was saved from the guillotine by Saliceti, a Corsican himself, who investigated Napoleon's case.
- Following this escape, Napoleon's career resumed its amazing climb. He planned an invasion of Italy, provided cannon fire to disperse royalist rioters (the 'whiff of grapeshot'), became Major-General and married the 32-year-old Josephine de Beauharnais.
- By 1796, Napoleon had not only survived but also had achieved a meteoric rise in military and revolutionary society. The scene was set for military glory.

Overview

I n May 1821, Napoleon was buried in an unmarked grave on St Helena, 1,000 miles from Africa in the South Atlantic. If the intention was to place Napoleon in a remote backwater, then it failed. His body was brought back to *Les Invalides* in Paris, in 1840. As a result, his reputation and legendary status continued to grow. Even today interest in Napoleon is strong. Few historical figures have made such a remarkable impact – to the extent that historians still refer to the first half of the 19th century as the 'Napoleonic' and 'post-Napoleonic' eras. The wars against France bear his name and the years following the French Revolution are known as the 'Napoleonic period'.

As historical research continues, interpretations of Napoleon continue to be revised. He remains a complex figure; perhaps he was a 'great bad man' but the task of arriving at an historical judgement of him is daunting. Napoleon's career was astonishing and dazzling. His rise to power, his military conquests, his domestic reforms, his fashioning of an Empire, his eventual decline and fall, and the remarkable impact he had on Europe were all dramatic.

But his character was many-sided. His career was on a vast scale. His motives and actions are often hidden behind contradictory evidence. Napoleon was a great propagandist. He had a huge capacity for deceit and for massaging the truth. As soon as he came to prominence in the 1790s, propagandists were hard at work. The Napoleonic legend developed during his lifetime and continued to do so after his death.

Military victories became epic deeds. He claimed to be the 'son of the French Revolution', Enlightened, devoted to the common good. He also claimed to be maintaining liberty and equality, and to be embarking on radical reform. Here was the strong ruler, France's 'saviour'. In the same way the Roman Emperor Julius Caesar did, Napoleon committed the nation to building a grand empire with the army at his back. One of the greatest military leaders, he came to be regarded as the all-conquering hero.

On the other hand, opponents saw him as the evil dictator, a self-seeking 'little corporal' who took advantage of every situation for his own ends. For instance, his qualities as a military tactician have been admired but it did not stop him from making blunders, over-reaching himself or being able to profit from the incompetence of his enemies.

As a man, Napoleon's personality has given rise to fierce debate. He could inspire his men with his leadership. He had energy, vision, intelligence and the ability to organise and single-mindedly pursue his aims. His violent temper and willpower would persuade others not to get in his way.

Charismatic: Able to attract, influence and inspire people by your personal attributes.

His darker side has been widely analysed. **Charismatic** he may have been, but he was also hard-hearted, arrogant and ruthless. Such were his feelings of self-importance that he exploited others when they were of value and blamed others when things went wrong. He fitted the **stereotype** of a self-important Machiavellian rather too well. Napoleon has been accused of being a schemer who had little grasp of moral values. On occasions he could be merciless, and at all times demanding and ambitious.

Stereotype: Fixed general image that a lot of people believe represents a particular type of person.

Humanitarian concerns rarely troubled him, despite his acquaintance with the works of the *philosophes*.

5.1 How important to his rise to power were Napoleon's military campaigns in Italy and Egypt?

The Directory: A five-man executive government chosen by the Ancients (see page 104).

Indemnity: Insurance or protection against damage or loss, especially in the form of financial compensation.

Napoleon's over-developed sense of his own destiny – the belief that fate had chosen him for greatness – was soon confirmed by his exploits in Italy. As commander of the French Army in Italy, he had glorious plans to invade it, plunder it and push France's conquests beyond its 'natural' frontiers – the Rhine, Alps and Pyrenees. The Directors (see page 104) were glad to be rid of the young Napoleon who combined flair, fame and ambition. A glorious interlude might not do **the Directory**'s reputation any harm.

In March 1796, Napoleon set out with 35,000 troops who were experienced and in good spirits but terribly short of equipment, clothing, food and, most of all, pay.

The Army welcomed its talented new commander. They would be paid in silver not paper money. First of all, the army of Piedmont was brushed aside and Napoleon turned his attention to the Austrians. He pursued them into Lombardy and after beating them at the Battle of Lodi, Napoleon entered Milan in May 1796.

Napoleon realised that he was not ready for an Alpine crossing so he turned South into Bologna and Tuscany. The Pope and the Kingdom of Naples felt sufficiently threatened that they signed an alliance with the French and paid an **indemnity**. Napoleon faced renewed threats from the

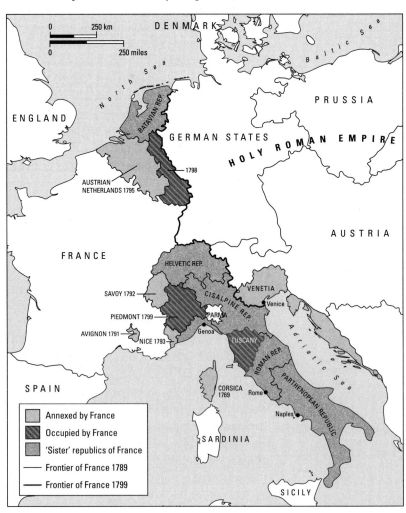

France and Italy – the early campaigns

Austrians. Four separate armies were sent against him and each was defeated. In early 1797, Napoleon entered Mantua – he now dominated Italy. Treasures were sent to Paris, along with his version of events. Not content, and utterly convinced of his invincibility and powers of leadership, Napoleon pushed north into the underbelly of the Austrian Empire. He reached within 60 miles (96 kilometres) of Vienna before his armies ran out of steam. Supplies were difficult and his men tired. Napoleon may have appeared vulnerable, but he dictated terms to the Austrians. He offered them the **Treaty of Campo Formio**.

Treaty of Campo Formio, 1797: France gained Belgium, parts of the Venetian Republic and large areas of Italy. The map opposite shows the new French republics formed in Italy and Switzerland.

Napoleon returned to Paris in triumph and formally presented the treaty. He was soon to be consigned elsewhere in case he became too dangerous. In May 1798, in command of the Army of the Orient, he set off to strike a blow against the British. Malta was taken on the way to Aboukir Bay, in Egypt. From here the army marched first to Alexandria and then to Cairo. This time, things did not go according to plan. Horatio Nelson arrived and his British fleet destroyed the French in Aboukir Bay. Cut off, Napoleon nevertheless scored a victory at the Battle of the Pyramids, but then faced an Egyptian revolt against him. The British blockade of Egypt tightened. Napoleon invaded Syria. He took Jaffa and then shot 2,000 prisoners whom he couldn't feed. Napoleon was successful here but failed completely to take Acre from the British. He returned to Cairo with only half his men.

By now, other events were pulling Napoleon back to France. He abandoned the army and made his way to Paris at the Directory's request.

The Revolt of Brumaire – how did Napoleon seize power?

In November 1799 (Year VIII of the Revolution in the month of Brumaire), Napoleon seized power. How much credit can he take for this? The Directory faced what it thought was a severe challenge. It thought Napoleon might help.

Council of Ancients: A council of 250 who could accept or reject laws referred to it by the Council of Five Hundred.

The Directory was not providing strong government or stability. If the separation of powers into the **Council of Ancients** and the Council of Five Hundred (see diagram on page 104) was meant to avoid any person or group gaining dictatorial powers, then it was succeeding. It was difficult to get things done.

Emmanuel-Joseph Sieyès, one of the Directors, was considering using the army to change the constitution so that firm decisions could be taken. Others were approached first, but it fell to Napoleon to take centre stage. He met Sieyès and others who were in agreement with their plans. Napoleon was to take control of the Paris **garrison** (around 100,000 men), while the two Councils were to move to the Paris suburbs at St Cloud. Napoleon's brother Lucien, president of the Five Hundred, played an important part in this decision and in what was to follow. The Councils were in a nervous mood. There was talk of plots against the Republic.

Garrison: Group of soldiers whose job is to guard the town or building in which they live.

Napoleon tried to seize the initiative. On 10 November he spoke first to the Ancients. Napoleon was acknowledged to be a poor speaker and, although he claimed to have made an impassioned speech defending liberty and equality, it is more likely that he rambled on without making much sense. He then spoke to the Five Hundred. The mood changed. Napoleon may have tried to sound like a defender of the Revolution but they thought he was plotting to seize power with Army support. Amid angry scenes, Napoleon narrowly avoided being taken out and shot when accusations were made that he was an 'outlaw'. He had to be pulled from the chamber and led to safety by four soldiers. Lucien informed troops outside that **assassins** with daggers had attacked his brother and that the whole Council should be forcibly expelled from the building. This was

Assassins: People who murder someone for political reasons.

done. When the Five Hundred met for the last time that evening, there were in fact only about a hundred left.

Lucien saw to it that these were entirely in agreement with what he wanted. They approved a plan put forward by the Ancients to get rid of the Directory and to appoint three Consuls instead: Napoleon, Sieyès and Ducos. This was the Law of Brumaire. It also provided for two committees to ensure power was not abused – but they didn't last long. At the time, these events did not make much of a stir. People were apathetic. No doubt Napoleonic propaganda might have sought to portray him as the saviour of France, responding to the needs of the nation. Not so. If Marxist historians think that Napoleon was popular with the bourgeoisie because he would defend their newly-acquired investments (*biens nationaux*) and stimulate commerce through warfare, then it is an unlikely argument. No one at the time could predict how Napoleon would turn out. No doubt the army was central to his success – he was, after all, the hero of Italy. But the key to success had been Lucien. It was he who engineered the move to St Cloud and the termination of the Five Hundred. His appeal to the troops probably saved his brother, although he got little in the way of thanks for it. Lucien's 'reward' was to be sent well out of the way. Meanwhile, the three Consuls set about rewriting the Constitution.

1. What different interpretations of the Revolt of Brumaire are shown in these pictures?

2. Why are the interpretations so different?

A British cartoon of the Revolt of Brumaire, November 1799

Napoleon and the Council of Five Hundred at St Cloud – painting by François Bouchot

5.2 *How far did Napoleon establish a dictatorship in France?*

Consuls: Supreme magistrates with semi-regal authority over the state.

In Year VIII of the Republic, the new constitution took shape. It was authoritarian. Napoleon would concentrate power in his own hands in a centralised and dictatorial system. His ambitions were clear from the start. If Sieyès imagined that Napoleon would retire quietly to Versailles, then he was disappointed. The two legislative councils were set aside. When the three **Consuls** met to decide the constitution, Napoleon's views dominated. He would become First Consul, while Ducos and Sieyès would act only in an advisory capacity. There would be no going back to the political chaos and arguments of the 1790s. Napoleon's system would be decisive and efficient. He, alone, would control ministers, introduce legislation and decide foreign policy. State officials were answerable to him, including appointments and dismissals.

At grass roots level, there were six million male voters. On the face of it, such a wide suffrage gave the constitution a 'democratic' appearance. Nothing could be further from reality. Six million voters were only voting for men to be placed on lists of those fit for public service. Only 6,000 men were on this national list. From these, 400 would be chosen who would sit on the Tribunate or the Legislature.

The chart shows how Napoleon stopped authority passing down to the four groups at the top: the Senate, the Tribunate, the Legislature and the *conseil d'état* (Council of State).

The 40 men on the *conseil d'état* were chosen by Napoleon. It suggested legislation only on his instructions. The Senate of 60 men would be consulted about legislation but were unlikely to defy the First Consul. Senators were given social status, large estates, and considerable salaries (25,000 livres). They did not turn against such generosity. The Tribunate dared to criticise Napoleon in 1802 over the Civil Code, but like the Legislature, never repeated the exercise. Napoleon ensured that both groups were supportive.

Constitution: A legal statement of limitations upon the power of the government, and of the rights and freedoms of the governed.

Plebiscite: A direct vote of all the electors of a state to decide a question of public importance. Otherwise known as a referendum.

It will be clear from the chart that this was a complex constitution. It proved so difficult to draw up the lists that the Consulate **constitution** never operated properly. A **plebiscite**, held in 1800, reflected the general lack of interest in the constitution. People apparently voted by 3 million for to 1,500 against in a corrupt exercise. It is likely that only 20% of voters actually approved of the Consulate's constitution.

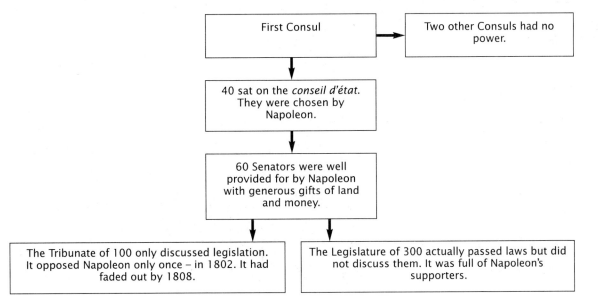

First Consul → Two other Consuls had no power.

40 sat on the *conseil d'état*. They were chosen by Napoleon.

60 Senators were well provided for by Napoleon with generous gifts of land and money.

The Tribunate of 100 only discussed legislation. It opposed Napoleon only once – in 1802. It had faded out by 1808.

The Legislature of 300 actually passed laws but did not discuss them. It was full of Napoleon's supporters.

What was the significance of this event in the development of Napoleon's power?

By 1802, the system had been abandoned. Adult males elected rich tax-payers to a department board. Men were then elected from these boards to the central government. The people who benefited most from Napoleon – **bourgeois property-owners** – were being drawn into the administration. Napoleon made sure that the interest on their investments was paid promptly and that reassurances were given that 'biens' would never be restored to *émigrés*, nobles or the Church. It was just what the propertied classes wanted to hear. Their investments at home were protected and France's honour on the battlefield was being enhanced. Their loyalty against a **Bourbon** backlash was assured.

Napoleon was offered the position of Consul for life in 1802. And another plebiscite showed overwhelming support for this. However, Napoleon faced opposition. There were royalists, *émigrés* and a revolt in the Vendée. There were even assassination plots. The government wasted no time in taking action. Executions were swift. The leaders of the Vendée were executed. Rumours circulated that the duc d'Enghièn was plotting against Napoleon. He was kidnapped and murdered. No evidence against him was presented. It served as a lesson to others and Napoleon faced few other serious threats. In May 1804, the Consulate came to an end – Napoleon became Emperor.

Napoleon's personal rule – honours, prefects and control

Napoleon had been adopting what appeared to be all the trappings of court life. His liking for ceremonial was illustrated when he took the new Imperial Crown off the Pope in **Notre Dame** and placed it on his own head as Emperor of France (see painting). Josephine became his Empress and the title was made hereditary in Napoleon's family. Josephine failed to

Napoleon crowning himself Emperor in 1804 – detail from a painting by Jacques-Louis David

---

Main elements of Napoleon's system of patronage

1802	Legion of Honour, awarded mainly for distinguished military service, although a small number were given to civilians.
1804	*Sénatoreries* (regional estates) were granted to senators. They carried large salaries, palaces and huge lands.
1804–1808	Imperial nobility and Court positions. Again four-fifths of the new titles rewarded the military: 18 generals became marshals or 'Grand officers of the Empire'. Others became 'Grand Dignatories'. Such titles also carried large estates and salaries (some in excess of half a million livres).
After 1808	A new Imperial nobility, consisting of about 3,600 people, was created. Lands in the Grand Duchy of Warsaw, Italy and Germany were granted to a whole range of titles. They included:

- princes (Grand Dignatories)
- counts (senators and archbishops)
- barons (bishops and mayors).

Given that their estates were often situated in conquered territories, they were inextricably linked to the fate of the Empire.

Josephine de la Pagerie 1763–1814)

Born in Martinique in the Caribbean, she was Empress of France (1804–09). She married Alexandre, Vicomte de Beauharnais in 1779. Their daughter, Hortense, married Louis, Napoleon's brother, and their son became Napoleon III. Beauharnais was guillotined during the Terror for his alleged lack of zeal for the revolutionary cause, and for his lack of success as Commander of the Republican Army of the North. In 1796, Josephine married Napoleon I, who divorced her in 1809 because she had not produced children.

Catechism: A series of questions and answers about the religious beliefs of a particular church, which is learned by people before they become full members of that church.

bear him a son. Their marriage ended in divorce in 1809. A year later, Napoleon married Marie-Louise of Austria (the niece of Marie Antoinette) and in 1811 a son was born. He became the King of Rome and an Imperial dynasty was founded – or so Napoleon hoped at the time. If the aim was to encourage loyalty and widespread acceptance of Napoleon's family as a legitimate alternative to the Bourbons, then he failed. In 1814 and 1815, military defeat caused Napoleon's position to evaporate quickly. Ultimately, there was no strong support either to save Napoleon or to accept his son as second Emperor.

In the meantime, though, Napoleon took whatever measures he needed to secure power. The Senate and the *Conseil d'ètat* were controlled by the Emperor and became the means by which laws were passed. The Tribunate and Legislature fell silent. Their rare efforts at criticising Napoleon led to them both being made powerless. The Tribunate was dissolved in 1808 and the Legislature limped on, doing what it was told.

Napoleon knew the power of patronage. A new honours system was set up over a period of time to reward those in state service, to ensure loyalty and to draw the sting from any potential opposition – either radical or royalist (see panel).

Education

The Imperial **catechism** for French children made Napoleon's priorities in education clear.

Q: 'What are our duties towards the Emperor, Napoleon?'

Notables: Bourgeois and noble property owners who were promoted in the service of the state.

Civil servants: People who work in the Civil Service (all the government departments that administer the affairs of a country).

1. *In what ways did Napoleon take on the trappings of a monarchy?*

2. *Was France ruled by an absolutist ruler by 1804?*

A: 'We owe him love, respect, obedience, fidelity, military service, all the contributions ordered for the defence of the Empire and Throne ...'

For the children of ordinary people, Napoleon demanded obedience – a simple 'moral' education would do. For the sons of **notables**, he had state service in mind – hence advancement was not open to all. State service was primarily military, although there were a few opportunities for boys to become **civil servants**. Nevertheless, the emphasis was clear. In 1802, the *lycées* (schools) selected the best boys for a military education. Approved teachers, who had taken an oath to obey those in charge, would teach everyone identical lessons.

Only the better-off could afford it. Free education was only for the sons of officers. After 1806, the Imperial University supervised teachers and examinations. It acted as a ministry overseeing all education. Research for its own sake, particularly in Science, was not given enough attention. It seemed not to serve a useful enough purpose. Centralised control was set up. Napoleon's firm control of the teachers enabled him to have 'the means of directing the political and moral opinions of the country'. It was a formula that didn't appeal to the property-owning classes. They still sent their sons to private church schools beyond the regimented state system.

5.3 How effective were Napoleon's financial and economic polices?

There are three strands to this question:

1. Was Napoleon successful in financing his armies?

2. Did the French economy enter a period of sustained growth under Napoleon?

3. Was the Continental System a success?

The evidence is unclear and economic conditions differed from one part of France to another. However, general trends are as follows.

Was Napoleon successful in financing his armies?

To 1806, Napoleon financed his armies without resorting to crippling taxation and without suffering from excessive debt and inflation. There was confidence in Napoleon's system, which was more efficient at harvesting France's wealth for the Treasury.

- A Central Treasury administered and supervised tax officials and prefects.

- Expenditure and income were carefully monitored and recorded.

- A Bank of France, which was eventually taken into state control, regulated the money supply.

- Paper money was abandoned in favour of metal currency (e.g. the silver franc).

- Indirect taxes and customs dues were increased to inject money into the Treasury. Tobacco, alcohol and salt taxes quadrupled.

- The bourgeoisie supported the government because land taxes remained static and interest was paid on the National Debt.

- Plunder from foreign conquests financed the armies, kept prices low and provided employment. This enabled Napoleon to balance the budget.

When the plunder from abroad was less plentiful after 1806, the army began to drain the financial system heavily of funds and taxes rose significantly. By 1810, debt was at an intolerable level and financial ruin threatened the regime. Inflation took hold, banks collapsed, firms went bankrupt and unemployment rose. Taxes doubled and a bad harvest, in 1811, sent bread prices into an upward spiral. The whole country suffered, but particularly the landed bourgeoisie – they had been Napoleon's mainstay. As confidence waned, they deserted him.

Did the French economy enter a period of sustained growth under Napoleon?

Generally speaking, the economy did not grow. There were exceptions, but the sustained growth in the economy, which is associated with the agricultural, industrial and transport revolutions taking place in Britain did not happen in France until the middle of the 19th century. The population, again unlike in Britain, only grew slowly. The **birth rate** was falling, as people had smaller families. More research is needed to explain this. Economic trends in the late 1780s and 1790s were certainly unhelpful to population growth. The effects of birth control and warfare are often exaggerated, but the latter certainly robbed France of young men who were at the age when they might marry. High casualties, after the start of the Russian campaign, robbed the country of about one-third of that generation who were in their early 20s. Without population growth, agriculture and industry changed very little. **Capital** was in short supply; the technology was backward. Food production increased up to about 1811 – there were good harvests and strong prices – but farming techniques remained old-fashioned. Increases in output were caused by more acreage being used for growing food.

Poor communications meant that the huge market for French goods created by the **Continental System** could not be tapped. France remained largely in a 'pre-industrial state' – small scale and cottage based. Although 12,000 workers were employed in cotton spinning in Paris in 1807, few of them worked in factories. Mechanisation had a long way to go. There were technical advances in the chemical industry, but this was the exception. Napoleonic warfare did stimulate iron production, but techniques were out of date, with charcoal still used for **smelting**. This was the more typical picture of French industry. Industrial wages declined and usually fell below rising prices and taxes.

What effect did the Continental System have on France?

The Continental System caused economic disruption, not only to its intended victim but also to France. It proved impossible to enforce and smuggling was commonplace. The French navy had been fatally weakened after the battle of Trafalgar (1805) and, as French troops were required elsewhere, the ban on British goods was continually being breached.

While Britain's economy was able to withstand the strain, there is no doubt that considerable distress was caused. By 1810, Britain's balance of payments was suffering. Exports had declined and Britain was short of gold to pay for imports.

In France, the Atlantic trading areas, as well as the shipbuilding industries, were badly hit. The linen industry of the north and west was ruined. However, other areas benefited. Strasbourg and Marseilles developed their trade with Germany, Italy and the east. Luxury goods developed in Paris and Lyons.

The System and its extension throughout the Empire gave French industrialists a huge, protected market. Conquered peoples were forced to

Birth rate: Number of births. This is usually measured by recording the number of births among every thousand of the population.

Capital: Wealth used to invest in business, so stimulating production and output.

Continental System: After 1793 British goods were prohibited from French territories. Napoleon expanded this as a way of weakening Britain and protecting the Napoleonic Empire, which now became a huge market for French goods. After that, the economic campaign against Britain intensified. As First Consul in 1803, Napoleon banned British goods from north-western Europe. The ban had only limited success. The Berlin Decrees of 1806 had more bite – the blockade of Britain would now mean that goods coming from British (and colonial) parts would be excluded and seized.

As the Empire expanded, so Napoleon's hopes of success rose. By 1807, the Treaty of Tilsit brought Austria, Russia, Denmark, Sweden and Portugal into the blockade. In December 1807, the Milan Decrees turned the screw still tighter – if any neutral ship had called at a British port, its cargo could be confiscated.

Smelting: The process of heating metals until they melt, so that the metal can be extracted and changed chemically.

buy French goods at inflated prices. Nevertheless, demand did not increase significantly. Alsace and Belgium did well, but elsewhere the advantages were insignificant.

In the final analysis, Napoleon's attempts to extend the Continental System proved catastrophic. This was partly the motive behind the invasions of Spain and Russia – two campaigns which cost France dear. Furthermore, the resentment which it caused throughout the Empire contributed to the growth of **Nationalism** and opposition. Little wonder that the Empire collapsed so rapidly. The Continental System had proved to be a liability.

Nationalism: The growth and spread of loyalty towards a nation, rather than an individual ruler.

5.4 How important were Napoleon's religious policies to his rule in France?

Concordat: A treaty made between the Papacy and a state government.

In 1801, Napoleon signed a **Concordat** with Pope Pius VII. The Concordat said that:

- the state would pay the clergy a salary and make appointments to senior positions, such as bishops and archbishops. The position of the Pope as Head of the Catholic Church was agreed and recognised.

- the Catholic clergy would obey the state and promised on oath to do so. The Church would not try to regain the lands confiscated by the Revolution. It agreed that services would be supervised under police powers.

It was agreed, then, that Catholicism regained its place as the official religion of most Frenchmen. This suited Napoleon. The Revolution had split the Church. The Civil Constitution of the Clergy (see page 91) had forced a hard core of clergy into opposition. They were all the more dangerous because they were identified with royalists. What better opportunity for Napoleon to gain Catholic support for his dynasty rather than the royalist cause? It might bring the country behind the Empire, heal old wounds and make it easier to control the people.

Meanwhile, the Catholic Church – a conservative force right across Europe, with an interest in maintaining the *status quo* – could help Napoleon to spread the virtues of obedience and loyalty. Refractory priests had played their part in stoking resistance, such as in the Vendée. Winning those priests back to the State would help subdue unruly areas.

Enlisting the Pope's help in restoring the unity of France would be even more effective if it could be made to appear as a 'grand gesture of reconciliation', a planned attempt to restore the place of the Catholic Church in the State. It was an opportunity not to be missed – to sap the support of the royalists and to underpin the stability of Napoleon's government, and at no cost. Church lands would never be restored. That made property-owners content, and they were the mainstay of the State. It went further though. Napoleon understood that the Church remained a powerful institution – better for it then to be controlled by the government. In the Organic Articles of 1802, he ensured that the clergy, in particular the bishops, were controlled by the government. This was at the Pope's expense. Once Napoleon knew he could appoint bishops, then they could become an arm of the State, encouraging conscription or relaying government propaganda and decrees, and could be used to reinforce its authority.

In 1806, however, this went beyond political control. Changes were made to the Catholic catechism, much to the Pope's anger. Napoleon was made a saint. August 16 became St Napoleon's Day, replacing the festival of the Assumption of the Virgin. It was a Christian's duty to obey Napoleon. If God was respected and honoured, then so was Napoleon.

Napoleon's lack of genuine interest in promoting Catholicism was made clear when he took a tolerant attitude to not only Protestants but also Jews who served France well.

How far was the clergy won over? At first, the clergy supported the state and army. To avoid conscription was equated with opposing the will of God. Deserters were condemned and confession was denied them. However, the Pope must have been less than happy with the Concordat and, if Napoleon thought he could guarantee the clergy's loyalty, he was wrong. They never accepted being civil servants. Many remained stubbornly royalist and it was not long before the Church began to recover lost ground. It had always been a force to be reckoned with in education and private church schools became very popular. The clergy never completely abandoned the Bourbon cause. Their annoyance was made more obvious when Napoleon annexed the Papal States and arrested the Pope. Not for the first time, the institution of the Church was proving troublesome to the Head of State.

1. Why was the Concordat of 1801 important for Napoleon I?

2. How successful were Napoleon's religious policies?

5.5 How successful was Napoleon in enforcing centralised control of France?

A powerful state apparatus developed to maintain control over France. First of all, a police state was established.

Prefects were the key to the administration in the provinces. Apart from ensuring that the taxes were being collected efficiently and that conscription was being enforced properly, they were the eyes, ears and voice of central government. They reported on opposition to Napoleon, as well as keeping a tight grip on public opinion through censorship and propaganda.

Prefects: Each *département* had one. Napoleon himself nominated these powerful and usually competent officials, who reported directly to the Ministries of the Interior and Police. See panel below for a list of the prefects' duties.

Prefects' duties

● To enforce the system of conscription and to pursue deserters

● To supervise the collection of taxes

● To oversee food supplies and prices

● To ensure the smooth running of the local administration, check the work of sub-prefects and magistrates, and appoint mayors and town councils

● To obtain information about the *département*, particularly if there was discontent among the population

● To spy on people who might be politically dangerous and submit reports about them

● To spread propaganda issued by Napoleon and help his ministries

● To help to increase commerce and trade.

The prefects were loyal administrators who were expected to carry out government wishes to the letter. Napoleon took a personal interest in these appointments, advancing men of talent who had proved themselves capable administrators. It was a good way to heal divisions. As the historian D.G. Wright notes, in *Napoleon and Europe* (1984), prefects were 'from all shades of the political spectrum' – the pre-1789 nobility, middle class or the military.

Joseph Fouché
French politician, who was elected to the National Convention (the post-Revolutionary legislature) and organised the conspiracy that overthrew the Jacobin leader Robespierre. Napoleon employed Fouché as Minister of Police.

Napoleon did not rely only on prefects to maintain a firm grip on France. Under Joseph Fouché, the police had formidable powers. They spied on individuals who were regarded as rebellious, searched for deserters, supervised prisons, acted as censors and provided constant intelligence about the public. Militant Jacobin and royalist elements would find fewer opportunities for stirring up trouble. Fouché was required to send daily reports directly to Napoleon. Not that Napoleon relied exclusively on these – he had the prefects and his own network of spies, too.

Anyone caught could expect strict treatment from a reorganised legal system. Special new courts were set up. Tribunals for political crimes met, on which 'magistrates for public security' sat. Military courts dealt with terrorists. In 1810, the government increased its powers still further by re-introducing imprisonment without trial. The government's preference was for house arrest which was used regularly, although figures tend to suggest that surveillance produced the desired results. Opposition had been quietened. In 1814, only 2,500 people were in prison for political offences.

Napoleon's hand was clearly seen in the task of law reform. Judges may well have been appointed for life but they were closely supervised. The Civil Code of 1804 (or the Code Napoleon) attempted to unravel the confusions of French law, which differed significantly in the north and south. Napoleon's more unified system was more repressive and certainly less liberal.

Equality, particularly that of women, took a severe knock. Legal codes asserted male rights, particularly in marriage and property. Husbands and fathers had their control over their families enshrined in law – 'a wife owes obedience to her husband', it said. Wives who strayed faced jail. Family life was centred on the father's dominance and women's status suffered for it. Workmen needed a *livret* (permit) to obtain work. It enabled the police to supervise workers closely.

In these ways, Napoleon attempted to build stability and a strict framework of order, obedience and social control. The work of **codifying laws** came to its conclusion when the Commercial, Criminal and Penal Codes were published. Napoleon knew his main supporters were property-owners. This was acknowledged by the codes that legally and finally transferred property titles to those who had bought '*biens nationaux*'. They turned the clock back to the pre-Revolutionary days of hard labour, and harsh punishment. The message was that the liberal days of Revolution were over.

Codifying laws: To bring different laws into one coherent, systematic collection.

These signals were reinforced by the use of strict **censorship**. The government kept a firm hold on papers, books, theatres, artists and information. The government controlled the issuing of news by trying to ensure that only its own version was published. Its official bulletins, many written by Napoleon and his ministers, came out in *Le Moniteur*. The news was deliberately rewritten (see details of the Battle of Marengo). The 73 political journals that existed at the time of the Directory, were cut to nine. By 1809 each paper had its own censor. Reports were compiled on books, plays and lectures. As early as 1803, publishers had to have official permission if books were to be published. Booksellers, publishers and editors all faced grim punishment if they attempted to slip unapproved material past the censor. Theatres had to have a licence. Artists, architects and sculptors were employed to celebrate the achievements of Napoleon and the Imperial armies. Jacques-Louis David's official portraits of the Emperor contributed to the Napoleonic legend (see page 110). Napoleon, then, was able to seize huge personal power in his own hands. This was a highly centralised system. Ministers were not required to think for themselves either.

Censorship: The practice or policy of censoring books, plays, films, reports etc., especially by government officials.

Independent ideas that failed to conform to those of Napoleon were not encouraged. The police state did its job effectively.

Opposition was limited. Patronage, honours, police control and 'packing' such groups as the legislature with supporters, were all methods which largely succeeded. The network of spies made sure that its enemies rarely troubled the regime. Only two problems persisted:

1. *What were the most important measures taken by Napoleon to ensure his firm control of France?*

2. *How successful were these measures?*

● desertions and avoidance of conscription reached alarming proportions by 1813, and punishments included forced labour or lengthy terms of imprisonment;

● gangs of vagabonds who terrorised rural areas during periods of economic depression.

5.6 Why was Napoleon so successful in military affairs before 1808?

Napoleon was a remarkably successful military leader. The scale of his victories up to 1808 gave him an enviable reputation – that of a young, invincible commander at the height of his powers, brushing aside the armies of the great powers of Europe.

His success was based on:

● the armies he inherited;

● his own abilities in the art of warfare;

● financial and domestic reform;

● the weakness of his enemies.

How effective were the French Armed Forces when Napoleon took power?

The historian G. Best, in *War and Society in Revolutionary Europe* (1982), shows how much the French Army had changed since the onset of the Revolutionary Wars in 1793. Napoleon would reap the benefit. France had become a 'nation in arms'. The *levée en masse* (conscription on a large scale) had produced a citizen army of unprecedented size. By the end of 1793, one million men had been drafted into the army to defend the nation – '*la patrie*' – and the Revolution, from foreign invaders. With such superior numbers, the French had a crucial lead over its rivals.

The motivation of these patriots, it is argued, also made a real impact. Gone were the small mercenary armies of the 18th century – men who fought with little concern except for the size of their purse, sometimes made for a poor fighting force. Gone were the manoeuvrings of slow, lumbering armies which sacrificed themselves for the personal dynastic aims of their rulers. French armies fought to defend the liberties won during the Revolution. As D.G. Wright notes in *Napoleon and Europe* (1984):

'War between Revolutionary France and the Austrians and Prussians from 1792 marked a transition from the limited conflicts of the earlier 18th century – motivated neither by ideology nor by aggressive nationalism and aiming to gain mere slivers of territory or to bring about a dynastic reshuffle – to "people's wars", based on the concept of "the nation in arms".'

In addition, France's population of 28 million, the largest in Europe, gave Napoleon reserves which would sustain years of warfare. That figure was

Satellite states: Countries that are under the influence of a larger and more powerful neighbouring country.

Infantry: Soldiers in an army who fight on foot rather than on horses.

Amalgamé: Amalgamation. New recruits were brought together with seasoned troops so that discipline could be maintained and effective training undertaken after the initial basic instruction had taken place.

Lazare Carnot (1753–1823)
French general and politician. Member of the National Convention in the French Revolution, he organised the armies of the Republic. After the *coup d'état* of 1797 he went abroad, but returned when Napoleon seized power (1799). War Minister (1800–01) and Minister of the Interior 1815) under Napoleon. His work on fortification, published in 1810, became a military textbook. Carnot's transformation of French military techniques in the Revolutionary period earned him the title 'Organiser of Victory'.

Jacques, the Comte de Guibert
A military writer who wrote about the 18th century. He argued that an army could campaign more quickly if it lived off the countryside instead of waiting for slow-moving supply trains. Guibert wrote that swiftly executed cavalry charges at an enemy's rear or flanks would have the element of surprise and force the opposition into chaotic retreats. Napoleon followed many of Guibert's ideas.

---

even larger when recruits from annexed and **satellite states** are included. By 1813, Napoleon's army numbered in excess of 300,000.

This then amounted to a revolution in warfare. In comparison, changes in weaponry, training and tactics were minor. **Infantry** continued to rely on the old muzzle-loading muskets, which were slow to fire and not very accurate. Artillery tended to miss the target beyond half a mile and took ages to reload. But there were some improvements which Napoleon would use to good effect later – lighter fieldpieces were deployed by the horse artillery, while heavy cannon were given to special regiments, allowing them to concentrate their firepower.

As a young cadet, Napoleon also learned about changes in tactics dating back to 1791. France's enemies, such as the Prussians, persisted in deploying their infantrymen in long lines, with each line firing volleys of shot according to strict orders. They relied on frontal assaults in open ground and had difficulty in manoeuvring quickly if the lines were attacked in the rear or flanks. They were almost immobile. French drill had perfected what became known as the 'mixed order'. Revolutionary armies could use the line if need be, but could also advance in long columns or files, using their bayonets instead. They moved round the battlefield quickly. Revolutionary armies relied not only on speed, but also on shock tactics. The mass bayonet charge with the cavalry following up became their trademark.

French Revolutionary armies had been reorganised into *Corps d'armée* (Army corps). The French army rarely marched as one huge body of men. Each corps of 15,000–30,000 men moved independently and quickly – probably at 15 miles a day. The corps spread out. They could reinforce each other if attacked, but the clear advantage was that they no longer relied on slow, lumbering columns of supply waggons, nor were they tied down to using pre-arranged supply depots. As the corps advanced, lines of communication to the baggage train or supply dumps were often stretched. Instead, Revolutionary armies were ordered to 'live off the land'. They requisitioned food from the neighbouring area as required.

It would be wrong to assume that the citizen army had undergone lengthy training. After a week's basic training and a forced march to the site of each campaign, the conscript may well see military action. From the outset in 1793, the '*amalgamé*' brought raw recruits together with veterans. These experienced men could amount to half the size of the army. They provided the backbone of, as well as further training for, inexperienced troops.

Such was the Revolutionary Army left to Napoleon by Lazare Carnot. However, Napoleon did have exceptional skills, which he used to good effect with the army he had inherited.

How effective was Napoleon as a military leader?

Apart from making a few changes to the armies themselves, Napoleon also owed many of his strategic ideas to Jacques, the Comte de Guibert. What marks Napoleon apart was the talented application of old ideas and strategies to the problems he faced, and the bonds of loyalty and genuine admiration that he forged with his men. The Revolutionary armies, which became his Grande Armée, were used with great success up to 1808.

The Duke of Wellington, Napoleon's opponent for so many years, admired his qualities as a general. In terms of command, Napoleon took sole control of military affairs. Divided orders, with the commanders of different French armies pursuing their own strategies had no place in Napoleon's Grande Armée. The historian D. Chandler, in *Napoleon* (1973), remarks on Napoleon's insistence on complete personal oversight of every detail. But there was more to it than that. Napoleon had the ability to gain the respect, confidence and loyalty of his men. This derived partly from the aura surrounding the figure who was First Consul, then Emperor and Commander-in-Chief of the armies. It was also partly due to his reputation as an heroic general who brought glorious victories – part of his legend of invincibility. The Army enjoyed its special status. Napoleon used propaganda to encourage his men to regard themselves as gallant warriors, whose dashing exploits would be celebrated in **Bulletins**. Great stress was placed on Napoleon's leadership and the way he took part in campaigns. It was 'we' – Napoleon and his men – who would overcome the enemy. While he never ignored the lure of plunder to ensure the obedience of his troops, there is plenty of evidence of soldiers holding him in high esteem. Even during the darkest days of the Russian campaign, with disaster staring them in the face, one sergeant who marched with him said 'Always the genius … with him we were always sure of victory in the end'.

Bulletins: Regular reports of Napoleon's heroic deeds, which were carefully edited and sent back to France.

There is more controversy about Napoleon's reputation as one of the greatest military commanders of history.

Was Napoleon a military genius? It appeared to be so – particularly if one takes a casual look at his victories up to 1807. He seemed able to apply strategy brilliantly. Napoleon claimed that he could prepare for battles well in advance. He was certainly able to bring his forces together just at the right time, concentrating them in readiness for an offensive. Napoleon could see how a battle might develop over a large area. His strategies have been celebrated.

● The swift movement round the battlefield, using infantry, sharpshooters and light cavalry to make the pretence of an attack.

● Luring the enemy out into the open.

He tried to keep the opposition guessing and confused. Once the enemy was committed to a position, he would use his reserves to make swift attacks either on the enemy's flank or rear. They would be completely wrong footed. Their slow, lumbering lines would be outmanoeuvred and often surrounded. Once Napoleon knew that he had part of the enemy in the wrong position and outnumbered, he would use mass artillery, and the cavalry and bayonet charge to break up their lines and relentlessly pursue them. Casualty rates were often much heavier among Napoleon's enemies, because of the pursuit during their retreat.

However historians such as O. Connelly, in *Blundering to Glory* (1987), and Correlli Barnett, in *Bonaparte* (1997), point out that Napoleon's reputation as a tactician and general is not entirely deserved. It has already been noted that he was not an innovator. He inherited an army and tactics dating from the Revolution.

Napoleon made numerous errors. Often it was his planning which was inadequate. As Correlli Barnett explains, off the battlefield the 'Bonapartian army lacked system and discipline; it pillaged and struggled'. He refers to the establishment, at this time, of *'le systèm D'*, where D stood for *débrouiller* (muddle through). On countless occasions, 'living off the land', especially in the depths of Eastern Europe, left the army badly supplied.

Some of Napoleon's victories were close-run things. He sometimes failed to bring sufficient men together just before battle, or threw exhausted, hungry men into campaigns. Training and weaponry developed very little. He made mistakes because of inadequate understanding of geography or weather. His grasp of naval matters, such as the effects of tides or winds, was pitiful.

If he did plan carefully prior to engagements, then it was his ability to abandon the pre-arranged plan and adapt it as the battle progressed which set him apart as a skilled tactician. He drew on the *règlement* of 1791 which instructed on the use of mixed order as the changing conditions dictated – line for defence, columns for attack. Napoleon was good at improvising, and his men's flexibility and mobility meant that he could get away with it. He was undoubtedly assisted by the incompetent generals he faced. They were fighting semi-static battles in the past, such as the Austrians who were rooted to the ground at Ulm.

Napoleon had superior numbers, incompetent enemies and the ability to decide tactics and alter them in an instant. Up to 1807, he was unstoppable. But his enemies would learn and would, themselves, adapt. Until that happened, Napoleon's blunders would go unpunished.

How did the domestic situation help Napoleon?

Napoleon's absolute powers gave him not only unique control over military matters, but also over the whole resources of the state, which could be thrown into the war effort. Domestic reform strengthened his control. There was no room for dissent between military and civil authorities.

Military expenditure was enormous. Conquered territories were exploited to make the army self-sufficient. Troops were quartered on annexed or occupied lands. Huge indemnities were demanded from defeated countries as part of the price of peace. As mentioned earlier, this worked only up to a point – foraging for supplies during an eastern European winter was a desperate matter. Worse still, what might happen if the Empire began to contract?

To what extent did the weakness of Napoleon's enemies contribute to his success?

It is clear from the arguments already presented that, while Napoleon may not have been responsible for the revolution in warfare that took place at the end of the *ancien régime*, he certainly used the new arts successfully. His troops were more numerous, flexible and mobile than the static armies he faced.

Britain, Russia, Austria and Prussia were all his enemies at some time during this period. They attempted to form **coalitions** against Napoleon. In this time of French victories, it is hardly a surprise that these powers were incapable of united, concerted actions. They quarrelled about strategy. When things went wrong, they blamed each other. Napoleon was not slow at causing division. He knew that if it suited them, each would make peace and abandon their allies. He was skilled at forcing these coalitions apart.

Mutual suspicions were never far from the surface. Allied disunity was one constant on which Napoleon could rely.

What conquest took place under the Consulate?

At the end of 1799, Austria, the Ottoman Empire and Britain were at war with France. Russia had been the other partner in this Second Coalition but, after his defeat in September 1799, the Tsar had abandoned the coalition. Despite this good news, Napoleon was short of money and reserves, and the Austrians were a real threat in Italy. He talked of peace – appeals were made to both England and Austria. On the other hand, he knew that military glory would strengthen his power as First Consul. Napoleon told his foreign minister, Charles Talleyrand, 'in order to speed the coming of peace, we must simultaneously carry on the war and the negotiations'.

Forced loans were raised from Holland, Genoa and France's satellite state, Switzerland (called the Helvetic Republic). Two armies were prepared – one would attack the Austrians on the river Rhine and the other would brave the ice of the Alps and relieve André Masséna's French Army of Italy (which was outnumbered and partly besieged in Genoa).

In June 1800, Napoleon met the Austrian forces at the battle of Marengo. He found himself faced by a larger force on ground, which he had not properly studied. Napoleon had dispatched three divisions to try to outflank the Austrians and he was only saved when one of them turned up late in the day. Napoleon's bulletins, however, spoke of an amazing victory. Lombardy was captured, but it took another defeat of the Austrians, in December at Hohenlinden, to convince them to come to the peace table. The Treaty of Lunéville was signed in February 1801. Austria was humbled – it lost all its Italian lands except Venice.

England was left isolated and was likely to remain so. Napoleon was doing his best to entice Russia and Tsar Paul into a Franco–Russian Alliance.

Malta had become the focus of worsening relations between England and Russia. The former had occupied it much to the anger of the latter who wanted it. Despite this, Napoleon never quite managed to secure the alliance with Russia.

However, the Russians who, once again, set up the Armed Neutrality of the North (Russia, Sweden, Prussia and Denmark) aggrieved England. The aim was to unite against England in the Baltic. When Horatio Nelson led the Royal Navy and destroyed the Danish fleet at Copenhagen in 1801, and when Tsar Paul was killed, Napoleon's plans against England appeared to be collapsing. England's economy was being badly affected by warfare. Both sides saw the advantage of coming to a settlement. In 1802, the Peace of Amiens was signed.

The Peace of Amiens, 1802

- England agreed to hand Egypt back to the Ottoman Empire.

- England agreed to hand the Cape of Good Hope back to Holland.

- England agreed to hand Malta back to the Knights of St John.

- France agreed to independence of Naples and Portugal.

Why did Britain go to war with France after the Peace of Amiens?

Despite the Peace of Amiens, it was not long before war broke out again. In May 1803, Britain declared war on France. Why?

Amiens had solved nothing. A 'cold war' existed and it was only a matter of time before fighting restarted. Britain was still prevented from selling its goods to French territories, and Napoleon had not yet evacuated Holland. Britain was also not convinced (rightly) that Napoleon had given up plans to retake Egypt – hence the British government kept hold of Malta.

Could Britain create a Third Coalition against Napoleon? Not yet. Russia and Britain were at odds over Malta; Austria resented being abandoned by Russia before the Battle of Marengo. Napoleon profited from these rifts. In the meantime, he prepared his invasion plans of Britain. A massive programme of shipbuilding had to be undertaken to transport the 150,000-strong Army across the Channel. The project was doomed.

The Royal Navy had massive superiority and Napoleon had little understanding of tides or the logistics of fighting at sea. Neither could Napoleon lure the Royal Navy across the Atlantic to the West Indies. In 1805, Napoleon gave up. His Grande Armée was to march back to the Danube in October. Nelson destroyed the joint Franco–Spanish fleet at Trafalgar, and Napoleon's chance to invade Britain had gone.

The coalitions against Napoleon

The Second Coalition, 1798–1802

- Britain, Russia, Austria and the Ottoman Empire
- Russia defeated at Zurich (September 1799)
- Austria defeated at Marengo (June 1800) and Hohenlinden (December 1800)

The Third Coalition, 1805

- Russia, Austria and Britain
- Austria defeated at Ulm (October 1805)
- Austria and Russia defeated at Austerlitz (December 1805)
- Prussia declared war on France in 1806
- Prussia defeated at Jena (October 1806)
- Prussia and Russia defeated at Eylau (February 1807)
- Russia defeated at Friedland (June 1807)

The Fourth Coalition, 1813–1815

- Russia, Prussia and Britain from February 1813
- Austria joined the Coalition in August
- France defeated at 'Battle of the Nations', Leipzig (October 1813)
- The Allies entered Paris (March 1814)
- The Battle of Waterloo (June 1815)

Why did the Third Coalition fail?

Why did Napoleon set out for the Danube? He did so because, at last, the allies had managed to form the Third Coalition in 1805 – consisting of Austria, Russia and Britain.

- Austria was still angry that it was being excluded from Italy – Napoleon had been crowned King of Italy in Milan.

- Alexander I, a young Russian **Tsar** who also dreamt of military glory, felt threatened by Napoleon in those areas where Russia wished to expand – France had taken Hanover and had considerable influence in Germany. Napoleon may also have wished to expand towards Turkey – an area where Russia traditionally looked for **warm-water ports**.

These resentments brought the three powers together. They could equally force them apart, because clearly they were fighting for completely different

Tsar: Title of the emperor of Russia. Also spelled Czar and Tzar. Believed to be a shorted form of Caesar (Roman emperor).

Warm-water ports: Accessible ice-free ports which Russia needed for all the year round trade and military use.

aims. Prussia, for the moment, stood aloof from the conflict, bought off by Napoleon's promise of Hanover (territory belonging to King George III of Britain).

Napoleon knew he had to break this coalition. In October, he had a huge army, superb artillery and a well-planned strategy for mobility. He caught the Austrians on the Danube at Ulm, outflanking and surrounding them. The result was never in doubt and the Austrians surrendered. In an even finer display of strategy in December, Napoleon caught up with an Austro–Russian force at Austerlitz. Here, he cut the enemy in two and inflicted a crushing defeat – with minimal casualties to the French.

Napoleon appeared unbeatable. At the Treaty of Pressburg, Austria was left with no lands in Italy and Germany at all. What action did Prussia then take? Neutral so far, but resentful of Napoleon, Frederick William of Prussia now joined Britain's coalition, or what was left of it. The Prussians were finding it difficult to stand by while Napoleon set up and dominated the Confederation of the Rhine in central Germany. Napoleon was insisting that trade with Britain should be cut off.

Prussia embarked on an ill-fated military campaign against Napoleon with an army which was big enough but which had learned nothing from either the recent military revolution or from Napoleon's victories.

When the Prussians and French met at the Battle of Jena in October 1806, the Prussian forces were shattered. Historian D. Chandler comments that this took place so swiftly and decisively that Europe was stunned. Napoleon entered Berlin, occupied Prussia and another great power had been humbled.

Napoleon was not content. He knew that Tsar Alexander I of Russia would feel threatened by the French occupation of Prussia.

French plans were prepared for the next onslaught. The Grande Armée would march across Poland and inflict defeat on the Tsar, who was joining forces with Frederick William's remaining Prussians. It was not plain sailing for Napoleon. In February 1807 at Eylau, the French were surprised by a larger Prusso–Russian force and escaped only with considerable casualties.

Napoleon at the height of his powers, 1808

But the members of the coalition were arguing – either over strategy or accusing each other of not doing enough to help.

The French regrouped and enlarged their army. In June 1807, the Russians were defeated at Friedland. The Tsar asked for peace and Alexander met Napoleon at Tilsit.

The Emperor charmed the young Tsar. They became allies and the Third Coalition was shattered. Prussia was abandoned and left powerless.

Only Britain remained at war – impregnable and defended by the sea. Napoleon became obsessed with strangling Britain economically. He extended the Continental System. This policy would draw him into further damaging conflicts. At the time, however, Napoleon was at the height of his powers (see map on page 129). This was confirmed in 1808 when Napoleon took over the Papal States to strengthen the Continental Blockade.

5.7 Why did French power decline from 1808?

1 The Spanish ulcer

Should Napoleon ever have become involved in Spain? On the face of it, there were good reasons for doing so. He wanted to extend the Continental System and to plug a gap to stop British trade. Portugal remained out of Napoleon's grasp. Not only were its ports being used by the Royal Navy, but also just under a million pounds worth of British exports passed through there.

Perhaps Napoleon saw Spain as another country that could be added to his empire. Spain was in the hands of the weak Charles IV and the Queen's favourite Chief Minister, Godoy. In 1795, Spain had been forced to make peace with France. It was a dishonourable settlement to many Spanish. Their country was compelled to become France's ally and a supplier of men and resources. Napoleon was not satisfied. Despite the effort of a Franco–Spanish force to overrun Portugal in 1807, the conquest had not gone smoothly. Napoleon insisted on the abdication of Charles IV and, for good measure, made the Spanish heir, Ferdinand (who had no liking for the French) renounce his claim to the throne. Instead Joseph, Napoleon's brother, was to be crowned in Madrid. The signs for Joseph were not encouraging.

In May 1808, the ordinary people of Madrid started an insurrection against Joachim Murat, who had been sent there with the French army. The French suppressed the revolt and carried out horrifying reprisals. Joseph found himself in a largely hostile land, as Spain divided for and against the French. There were groups of Spanish people, many of them from the educated and middle class, who wanted to reform their country and to draw on the French example to bring about change. However, the overwhelming impression is that Spain was willing to take up arms to liberate itself. The Spanish clergy stirred up opinion against the French, who were identified with dechristianisation and attacks on the Catholic Church. Property-owners were equally suspicious. Hence the forces of tradition rose in defence of Ferdinand's cause.

Juntas (local resistance committees) were formed and Spanish partisans armed themselves. At Baylen, in July 1808, a French division was defeated by Spanish forces. News of the first defeat of Napoleon's forces shot round Europe. Bonaparte called it a 'horrible catastrophe' and, in his anger, ordered two corps of the Grande Armée to Spain. These 100,000 troops were intended to do the trick. The Spanish *junta* appealed to England for assistance. It arrived in the shape of Sir Arthur Wellesley (later the Duke of Wellington) in August 1808, with 10,000 men. At Vimiero, the French Army of Portugal was defeated. Portugal was reclaimed.

Despite always having numerically smaller forces, the English had already realised two major advantages. Firstly, their Portuguese bases meant that they would be supplied constantly by the Royal Navy. Secondly, and this was to be repeated later, well-trained English musketeers standing in lines had blasted the French columns with devastating effect. When Sir John Moore arrived to take over the English force, even the presence of Napoleon himself (in November) could not prevent French plans being wrecked.

Moore paid particular attention to two important matters. Napoleon didn't. Napoleon failed to grasp the geography of Spain and its sheer size. He did not give enough thought to supplies. Living off the land would prove problematic, given the hostile population and their **'scorched earth' policy**.

'Scorched earth' policy: The destruction of crops and shelter, removing support from the land for soldiers.

Moore also played Napoleon at his own game. He manoeuvred to try to cut Napoleon's only line of communication back to France. The English forces never quite achieved the blow they wanted to strike – and were forced to retreat to Corunna in the west. Here they were evacuated by the British Navy, but not before they had inflicted significant damage on the French forces and drawn them away from their objectives – to retake Portugal and subdue the south of Spain. In January 1809, Napoleon was forced to leave Spain. He never returned. The Austrians were planning an attack on the Danube so he left Spain to French Marshals who disliked each other and who had never been used to doing anything apart from obeying Napoleon's orders. Given the job of subduing the Spanish, they seemed incapable of devising plans of their own to do this. Instead they quarrelled. Spain became, to the French, an 'ulcer' right up to 1814. It sucked in a quarter of a million French troops and enormous amounts of gold. French invincibility and pride were dented, and the Peninsular War became more and more unpopular in France.

Sir Arthur Wellesley, with only 30,000 men, was well supplied. He guarded Lisbon behind the huge fortifications known as the Lines of the Torres Vedras. The Spanish employed 'hit and run' guerrilla tactics – hitting French columns and supply lines before disappearing back into the landscape. Napoleon tried to conduct the war from Paris, but he was out of touch. The French starved, while the Emperor scoffed at the English and the Spanish. He never understood how to counter guerrilla warfare, how to keep his men supplied or how to give the war some realistic, unified direction. In the end, Joseph was giving overall charge. This was not a wise move. He had no grasp of military strategy. Wellesley broke out of the Torres Vedras and, by 1813, he had defeated the French at Vitoria and entered Madrid. Joseph, who had never effectively ruled Spain, turned on his heels. Wellesley pursued his campaign and invaded France, defeating the French at Toulouse in 1814.

The war had crippled France. Napoleon's plans elsewhere were left in tatters. For example, there would be no Middle East campaign. If the Peninsular campaign was meant to tighten the Continental Blockade, it had proved an expensive failure. British goods poured through Portugal and trade increased sixfold.

2 What French weaknesses did the Wagram campaign of 1809 expose?

In 1808, Austria planned to recover lost pride – it wanted to reclaim its status and assert its old influence over Germany and Italy. War began in February 1809. The narrative is straightforward enough. Napoleon clashed with the Austrians in Bavaria. Although battered, the Austrians retreated and regrouped. By May, Napoleon had entered Vienna but he then had to march against further enemy forces to the north of the Danube. Napoleon only narrowly averted disaster. At Essling, he was outnumbered and forced to retreat onto an island in the Danube. He lost 20,000 men in a bloody exchange which again sapped French prestige.

By July, with preparations complete, Napoleon met the Austrians again – this time at Wagram. Napoleon was victorious in this epic, two-day clash of artillery. Casualties on both sides were enormous. Napoleon lost at least 32,000 men, while the Austrians retreated with 80,000 survivors.

Peace was dictated to Austria at Schönbrunn. It was Napoleon's last great victory. The signs of French problems were disturbing.

1 Napoleon's troops were of poorer quality – he had fewer veterans and more raw recruits and foreigners (from satellite states) in the army. At Wagram, some of these had deserted in the face of the enemy onslaught. Ill-discipline and terror had run through the ranks.

2 Austria had been copying the French. Archduke Charles had more men at his disposal, they were more mobile and supplies were more than adequate. Their artillery had performed well but the French had lost their lead.

3 Not for the first time, Napoleon's arrogance had led him to prepare inadequately. Hence the defeat at Essling when he was faced with superior numbers.

4 The Spanish campaign and risings in Germany and the Alps also diverted French troops from their main objectives. Once again, Napoleon's infallibility had been challenged. This served only to encourage the spirit of resistance and to demoralise the French.

3 Why was the Russian campaign of 1812 such a disaster?

In June 1812, the French campaign against Russia began when the river Niemen was crossed. Why did Napoleon order the attack on Russia?

1 Tsar Alexander I was angry with Napoleon's marriage alliance with Austria (he married Marie-Louise in 1810). No attempt had been made by the French to support Russia's policy of expanding into the eastern Mediterranean and taking Constantinople. French troops were stationed in the east on the river Oder and in the Duchy of Oldenburg. Russia felt endangered by the close proximity of French troops. The fact that the Duke of Oldenburg was married to the Tsar's sister did not help either. The Tsar was also concerned that France might wish to put Poland back on the map, in which case Napoleon might want back Polish land which Russia had taken in 1793 and 1795 when Poland was partitioned.

2 Napoleon, however, nursed the most serious grievance. Russian trade had been badly affected by the Continental System. At the end of 1810, Alexander wrecked Napoleon's trade embargo. He put tariffs on French imports and let neutral ships (no doubt carrying British goods) into Russian ports. Napoleon could not let this go unpunished. Both Alexander I and Napoleon had an inflated sense of their own importance. In this trial of strength, Napoleon was determined to strike the first blow.

Napoleon always claimed that this catastrophic campaign could be blamed on the weather – freezing temperatures, ice and frostbite. Not so.

The campaign faced other problems that would be most difficult to overcome.

- Russia was too large – if Napoleon could not lure them into an open, pitched battle quickly, then he might have to march hundreds of kilometres in pursuit.

- If that happened, 600,000 troops would be impossible to supply. Many men were untrained and badly disciplined. They were a varied rabble drawn from all over the Empire. Long supply lines would be prey to enemy attack.

- The soldiers had only four days' rations – it was planned that the whole campaign would last only nine weeks. In the meantime, could 600,000 men 'live off the land'? Unlikely, particularly since the Russians were setting fire to supply dumps as they fell back.

- The French had inadequate maps, poor clothing and few medical supplies. Before they crossed into Russia, 60,000 men had fallen because of disease.

The omens did not look favourable. Once, Napoleon's Grande Armée had relied on speed and mobility. With no roads and with supply routes blocked by deserters and corpses, the French lines were quickly stretched.

1 Hunger and disease slowed the army, which already had to forage for supplies.

2 Vilna's supply dumps were set on fire by the Russians who were falling back rather than giving battle.

3 The French had suffered huge casualties mainly through starvation and diseases, as well as through the raids by bands of **Cossacks**.

4 The Russian armies fell back from Smolensk. A new commander, Mikhail Kutuzov, was appointed. He was careful, cunning and skilful.

5 Borodino – it was here that the open battle took place.

Napoleon did not have good enough troops to outflank Kutuzov. So he decided on a head-on attack. The battle lasted 10 hours. Casualties were huge on each side: the Russians lost 40,000 and the French 28,000.

Napoleon could claim a win because the Russians retreated. Kutuzov also claimed a victory because he was able to escape with only 700 taken prisoner. He regrouped, south of Moscow, to protect rich farmlands there.

6 On 14 September, Napoleon entered Moscow. His troops looted the city while the Russian governor set fire to it. With supplies being constantly attacked by Cossacks, Napoleon decided to retreat – it was either that or starve. More than half of his army was already dead.

7 On 19 October the retreat from Moscow began. Kutuzov harassed the Grande Armée the whole way. The French were starving, ill and moving desperately slowly. They lost 35,000 men in one week alone.

8 The winter was just beginning. As the temperature dropped, the Russians decided to block Napoleon's escape at the river Beresina. Only the superhuman efforts of General Eblé and his teams of engineers saved what was left of the Grande Armée. **Pontoon bridges** were built to replace the ones destroyed by the Russians and the main force got across in time.

9 By December, in freezing temperatures, Napoleon left for Paris. His departure almost led to the disintegration of the army. He had been

---

Size of the armies

French: 130,000 men
          587 guns

Russian: 120,000 men
          640 guns

Cossacks: Peoples of southern USSR, noted as horsemen from early times.

Mikhail Kutuzov (1745–1813)
Prince of Smolensk. Commander of Russian forces in the Napoleonic Wars. Commanded an army corps at Austerlitz and the army in its retreat (1812). After the burning of Moscow (1812), he harried the French throughout their retreat and later took command of the united Prussian armies.

Pontoon bridges: Floating bridges supported on flat-bottomed boats.

1. How did the war in Spain and the Russian campaign contribute to the French decline?

2. 'French decline at this time was caused by stronger enemies rather than French weakness.' Do you agree? Explain your answer.

forced to leave because of news of a plot, led by the royalist Malet, against him. Malet tried to set up a provisional government before he was dealt with.

10 As the French regained order in the retreat, only 25,000 of the Grande Armée had survived. Poor discipline, poor planning, lack of supplies and weak command had done the damage long before winter had arrived.

5.8 Why was Napoleon eventually defeated in the years 1812–1815?

In the final campaign against Napoleon, France's military difficulties were exposed. What were the reasons?

- Morale had been sapped by the Spanish and Russian 'disasters'.

- Armies had become too large for Napoleon either to control effectively or to ensure that they were properly supplied and fully trained.

- Napoleon's early campaigns had relied on mobility. Given, for example, that he had 600,000 men at the start of the Russian campaign, speed and flexibility were lost. His opponents' armies also tended to be as large. Hence battles became more setpiece artillery clashes, followed up by frontal assaults. The mass charge was used for battering through the enemy centre.

- Casualties increased as a result – only 25,000 of the Grand Armée survived Russia. This increased the reliance on raw recruits and non-French conscripts. They were less reliable.

- Opponents had copied Napoleon's tactics. They used artillery and speed, and were careful not to be lured into open battle.

- Napoleon's generals lacked experience of taking the initiative. There was no army staff to assist Napoleon, who often refused to share tactics, ideas or details of the battle.

- Napoleon's arrogance meant that he failed to grasp how dangerous his opponents were becoming. This was particularly true of the Fourth Coalition.

How important was the creation of the Fourth Coalition to the defeat of Napoleon?

Tsar Alexander I now set about forming the Fourth Coalition. He was determined to rid Europe of Napoleon, but his efforts to persuade all his potential allies to sign a single united treaty failed.

As a result, in 1812, the following alliances were forged:

- Russian and Prussia

- Britain and Russia

- Britain and Prussia.

Napoleon was not ready for a campaign so soon after the terrible Russian mauling.

In May 1813, at Bautzen near Dresden, Napoleon beat off the allies but agreed to an armistice. He was wrong to think he would have the time to rebuild his forces. Austria had decided to join the Fourth Coalition. Metternich was willing to suspend his suspicions about the Tsar (who he thought wanted to dominate Germany) enough to abandon France and attack it instead.

When fighting got under way, the two sides met at the Battle of the Nations, at Leipzig in October 1813. France was outnumbered and outgunned by three to two. After two days in the field, Napoleon had to retreat. He lost many men – either as casualties or under siege in Germany.

For Napoleon, it now became a desperate struggle to defend 'natural frontiers' and the Empire fell apart with staggering speed. Within weeks, he was left with only Italy, Belgium and Switzerland, and an army of 60,000 laid low by **typhus**.

Typhus: A contagious disease associated with poor levels of hygiene and diet.

The Allies might have quarrelled at this crucial time. Napoleon wanted victory and, despite everything, he tried to raise another army. But France had been bled dry by years of taxation and conscription. The Allies stuck together and for the first time all signed a single treaty, at Chaumont in March 1814. They even agreed to maintain the alliance while the future of Europe was settled. And so it was that, in March 1814, the Allies entered Paris. Napoleon abdicated as Emperor and the Treaty of Paris, in May, took France back to its 1792 borders. He was sent into exile to Elba. He would be there for less than a year before returning.

How important were the '100 Days' of 1815 in Napoleon's career?

Napoleon returned from exile on Elba in March 1815. He landed in the south of France with only 1,000 men. He was going to have to rely on rallying support, drawing on the unpopularity of the Bourbons. Louis XVIII had been restored to the throne under the Charter of 1814. But as taxes remained high and there was no sign of an end to conscription, Louis XVIII was regarded with suspicion. Army officers were unimpressed by being on half-pay, while rumours spread about the seizure of '*biens*' so that they could be returned to their pre-Revolutionary owners.

Workers and peasants flocked to support Napoleon. So did Marshal Ney, who had been despatched to arrest Napoleon. As Louis XVIII left Paris, Napoleon entered the city. It was a calculated risk. He talked about a new constitution – *Acte Additionel* (Additional Act) – which would win over liberals by promising free elections, a free press and a constitutional monarchy with two powerful Chambers or Assemblies. No doubt he would re-establish his personal dictatorship, once his power was assured. Support for Napoleon appeared encouraging, as crowds urged him on from Lyons to Paris. Reality was different. A plebiscite about the new constitution was marked by apathy – people could not be bothered to turn out and vote.

The second risk concerned the allies. They had, once again, being arguing and there were concerns about the growing power of Russia (which wanted Poland) and Prussia (which wanted Saxony). If Napoleon thought he could exploit divisions between the allies, and persuade Britain and Austria to sign a separate peace, he would be proved wrong.

As Napoleon began to raise an army of 300,000, the Fourth Coalition (Russia, Prussia, Austria and Britain) came together to remove him.

Napoleon, short of commanders and men, needed a victorious military campaign against each ally independently. If troops from the coalition did unite, he would be finished.

Indeed, Napoleon's strategy almost worked. In Belgium, he prevented Wellington's British forces and General Blücher's Prussians from joining up. But the French did not press home their advantage. Wellington had time to choose his ground and, although the Battle of Waterloo (1815) started without them, Wellington knew that 81,000 of Blücher's Prussians were on their way.

British musket fire destroyed the French lines of infantry and, as the Prussians arrived late in the day, the Imperial Guard collapsed. It was, in Wellington's words, 'a damned close thing'.

As the allies moved towards Paris, the Senate and Legislature knew it was all over. Napoleon abdicated. His son was denied the Imperial throne. The ex-Emperor was taken to St Helena, to be guarded by the British until his death in 1821.

The Second Treaty of Paris reinstated France's borders as they had stood in 1790, and the allies took steps to ring France with more powerful states.

5.9 What impact did Napoleon have on Europe?

Why did Napoleon create his Empire?

The reasons for the creation of the Napoleonic Empire have been the subject of controversy. Once again, Napoleon himself contributed to the mythology. His exaggerated, and sometimes fanciful, claims have served to confuse rather than to clarify. Many of these claims were written while he was on St Helena at the end of his life. Napoleon sought to deflect those attacks which portrayed him as a dictator who exploited other states to serve the wartime demands of France.

Instead, Napoleon argued that he wished to bring the peoples of Europe together (*'l'agglomeration'* he called it) to form their own national countries. He would help to unify each national group in their own country so they could share their common language, culture and traditions. He would say, then, that he was exporting the virtues of the French experience to the rest of Europe. What did he mean by this? He meant sweeping away the *ancien régime*, attacking tradition and privilege, and concentrating power in the hands of a more efficient, centralising administration. In an effort to 'modernise' the state, serfdom and feudalism would be abolished, and the law would be reformed to guarantee liberty and equality. Only in these ways could the happiness of the greatest number be secured. So much of this became part of the Napoleonic legend.

At the opposite extreme is the view that reduces everything Napoleon did to cynical self-glorification. This is the side of his character that emphasises his ambitions, his desire for personal glory, his obsession with power to ensure that his name should live on after his death – his 'place in history'. These aspects of his character were always likely to play their part at some time during Napoleon's long career.

However, there is more to it than this. Napoleon aimed to establish a dynasty for his family and relatives. Presumably, he assumed that they would form a loyal base of support across Europe, although Napoleon's letters at the time complained that they were not fulfilling their obligations either to France or to him.

Given the trouble Napoleon went to over his divorce, the birth of a son was an important milestone. It may have contributed to his decision to annex and absorb into France a number of territories after 1810.

Lands allocated to Napoleon's relatives

Holland: Louis Bonaparte up to 1810
Italy: Eugène Beauharnais as **Viceroy**
Naples: Joseph Bonaparte up to 1808, then Marshal Murat (his brother-in-law)
Westphalia: Jérôme Bonaparte
Spain: Joseph Bonaparte

Viceroy: Governor of a country or province acting in the name and authority of the ruler; a vice-king from 'roi', French for king).

Apart from lands for his family (see insert), the growth of the Empire also provided estates for those who were due to receive Imperial honours. As there was little land left to bestow in France, territories such as the Grand Duchy of Warsaw could be used to reward the new Imperial nobility.

As Napoleon achieved victory after victory, and as he became more convinced about his own sense of destiny, so his vision of empire knew almost no bounds. His letters reflected an obsession with the idea that he was the new **Charlemagne**, that he had inherited his mantle and that he wished to expand on Charlemagne's authority.

Charlemagne: Charles I the Great (742–814), King of the Franks from 768 and Holy Roman Emperor from 800. By inheritance and extensive campaigns of conquest, he united most of western Europe by 804. A cycle of heroic legends and romances developed around him.

On a more practical basis, satellite states supported France's military conquests. They sustained campaigns for even more conquest. Satellite states were expected to send men (eventually they provided one-third of the Grande Armée), supplies, cash as well as quarters for those parts of the army stationed there. Strategically, they provided a buffer zone around France, thereby protecting the motherland's frontiers.

Satellite states were also a crucial part of the Continental Blockade against Britain. This was a powerful factor in expanding the Empire and annexing land more completely into France. The more complete the blockade, the better the chances of bringing Britain to its knees.

The expansion of the Empire was crucial to the effectiveness of this 'Continental System'.

How effectively did Napoleon control and exploit his Empire?

In terms of military supplies, the Empire supplied the Grande Armée with men, resources and money throughout Napoleon's campaigns. Taxation and conscription were despised and maintained by force. Small groups of people, probably urban and bourgeois, were content to back the French but they were the exceptions to the rule. Annexed territories did adopt French law and administration. Elsewhere, among satellite states, the picture was more patchy. Napoleon found that he could not rely on his relatives to carry out his wishes to the letter.

● Louis, in Holland, resisted all attempts to be ruthless with the Dutch. Conscription was not introduced. Some self-government was allowed and the Continental Blockade was never fully imposed. Dutch trade was particularly badly hit by the Continental System and the authorities took a relaxed attitude to any trade with Britain which did take place. Hence, in 1810, Louis was forced to abdicate.

● In Spain, Joseph was never in control and he proved incapable of overcoming Spanish opposition and the British military. No reforms were put in place. Joseph was a figure of contempt. For many Spanish, the Peninsular adventure had a significant impact in draining Napoleon of valuable men and gold.

● In Naples, there was persistent resistance and this undermined reform. The administration could not introduce the Code Napoleon and the Continental Blockade was totally ineffective.

● In other areas, French reforms were carried through. In Italy at least feudal dues were abolished and the Code Napoleon introduced. Education improved and French law and administration functioned reasonably well. Eugène Beauharnis proved an able viceroy.

● In Westphalia, Jérôme Bonaparte was also able to abolish the feudal system, reform the law, and introduce the Code Napoleon and religious toleration. In return, Westphalia provided or supported nearly 50,000 troops. Despite this, Jérôme's refusal to carry through the Continental Blockade – a cause so close to Napoleon's heart – placed him in a vulnerable position. He, too, may well have been forced to abdicate.

If Napoleon aimed to introduce liberty and equality before the law, as well as abolish feudalism, he succeeded in some corners of the Empire, but failed in others. Generally speaking, those who won liberties and privileges under Napoleon continued to hold them in the post-Napoleonic Europe. There was more continuity than change.

In other dimensions, Napoleon's activities had unintended consequences. In parts of the Empire, the same spirit of national resistance which galvanised France after 1793, in defence of '*la patrie*', began to spark into life. This time it was aimed against the French. This was particularly so in Germany. It was here that a united nationalism against the enemy was strongest.

Napoleon had encouraged a form of Polish nationalism when he formed the Grand Duchy of Warsaw in 1807 and when he hinted at the recreation of the Polish State (which had been partitioned between 1772–95) in order to raise troops for the Russian campaign. This was probably rhetoric – Napoleon clearly had little interest in encouraging nationalism. For him, 'France first' summed up the aim and purpose of the Empire. Indeed Poland received nothing in the post-war settlement. Italian nationalism, against the trend, came later – in the post-Napoleonic era.

Perhaps it was in the accidental stimulus that Napoleon gave to nationalism that his impact was strongest.

These annexed territories included:

- German territories to the west of the river Rhine
- Nice
- Savoy
- Belgium
- Piedmont
- The Ligurian Republic.

1. What were Napoleon's real motives for creating the Empire?

2. How far is it true that Napoleon's Empire was destroyed by nationalism?

5.10 Was Napoleon a reactionary, a reformer or a revolutionary?
A CASE STUDY IN HISTORICAL INTERPRETATION

This historical controversy has its origins in Napoleon's own writings. At different times and depending on circumstances, he claimed to be the 'heir of the Revolution', the defender of what it stood for. 'The French Revolution need fear nothing,' he wrote. At other times, he spoke of the 'evils of revolution', the anarchy and chaos which it causes. In 1814, when facing defeat he even admitted that 'I myself have destroyed the Revolution'.

Did he, then, keep to the ideals which the Revolution stood for or did he drift back to aspects of the *ancien régime*? Between these two extreme interpretations, Napoleon also made the case that it was he who had brought the two together and restored unity. 'I became the arch of the alliance between the old and the new, the natural mediator between the old and new orders.' Then, in a crucial phrase, he wrote 'I belonged to them both'.

Where does the truth lie – was he revolutionary or did he react against it and restore pre-1789 France? The claim, firstly, that he was the 'heir of the revolution' rests on what he preserved from the 1790s – liberty, equality, popular sovereignty and the support given to property-owners. Feudalism, that key feature of the *ancien régime*, would remain a thing of the past. Its abolition was written into the law. The *biens nationaux*, the Church and aristocratic land sold during the Revolution, were to remain in the hands of those who had purchased them. The law granted (theoretical) equality and religious toleration. These measures amounted to real and significant consolidations of the Revolution.

Napoleon's claim to have opened up positions to those with talent and ability is less secure. Peasants could only rise so far. Most important military and administrative posts were occupied by nobles, and many more by the bourgeoisie. Indeed the bourgeoisie dominated. Industry and trade were run by a small handful of old families, while money was still needed to buy into a profession or the civil service. A full and deep purse could (indeed was required to) purchase the route to the top of the ladder. It could even buy a substitute, so that conscription could be avoided. As education was very expensive, the well-off always had the advantage. There was continuity of personnel from the Directory into Napoleon's Consulate. The great majority of Prefects, or members of the Tribunate and Legislature, had taken part in Revolutionary assemblies or had held senior administrative positions before Napoleon's coup. Half the Council of State had done so. They provided stability in a changing administration. It is here that similarities with the Revolution fade, and where more features of the pre-1789 *ancien régime* can be identified

Libertarian freedom: Those liberties and rights (such as freedom of expression) which had been claimed during the Revolution.

Libertarian freedom was no longer in fashion, neither was popular sovereignty. Censors and spies were out in force, and government became centralised and increasingly authoritarian. Napoleon argued that people wanted firm leadership. It suited him to provide it and it gave him a hold over his growing Empire. France took steps towards absolute government which would owe more to the *ancien régime* than to the less centralised, more devolved power exercised by the Directory. People had less freedom. The new Constitution of 1799 may appear to have granted the vote to millions, but the reality was that power was concentrated at the top. Most voting was indirect. They were choosing people to go onto a list from which those fit for government service would then be chosen (see page 115).

In any event, Napoleon kept control. He may have chosen to be called the Emperor, and not the King, but even that was hereditary in his family after 1804. In the traditions of the Kings of France, the Pope was invited to the coronation to show the Church's favour, and to give the Napoleonic dynasty more esteem. Indeed, the concentration of powers in the hands of one man went far beyond anything even Louis XIV could have dreamed of. There were few of the checks and balances that had limited Louis XIV's absolutism. Napoleon's Council of State, very much under his control to carry out business, appeared to be similar to the old Bourbon Royal Council. If the old royal provincial administrators (*intendants*) had wide powers in pre-revolutionary France, the use of prefects in centralising the government again, went much further. Local councils were nominated by the prefect and crucial functions, such as tax collection and conscription, were run by them. When Napoleon referred to people as 'subjects' not 'citizens' in Imperial decrees, it sums up the way liberty was undermined and the way that the law, the promotion of titles, the invention of an Imperial nobility and the energetic use of police powers harked back to a time before 1789. Even the Church, through the 1801 Concordat, managed some form of restoration when Catholicism was recognised as the official religion of the majority of French people. However, with the clergy carefully supervised and since Church lands sold off during the Revolution would not be returned, the rehabilitation was less than complete.

Napoleon was neither a revolutionary nor a reactionary. There is a case that, according to his needs, he maintained the principles of the Revolution but he also abandoned them when it was necessary to impose his authority at home in order that he could pursue the growth of the Empire and military conquest. The balance of the argument, however, does point to Napoleon as less the 'heir of the Revolution' and more to a man who borrowed what he could to maintain his power. Just as his rhetoric and tone changed, both pro and anti the Revolution, so he changed according to circumstances. As Franklin Ford argues, in *Europe 1780–1830* (1989), there is no evidence that Napoleon was determined to maintain all the trends of the 1790s, or that he intended to reverse them all. He was too pragmatic for that. 'Whether he revived a specific feature of the old regime or embraced some characteristic of the Republic he had overthrown, he acted without admiration of the devolved principles of either. He, after all, was now the System.'

Why are there different views on Napoleon and his achievements?

What would Napoleon have us believe? That he was the heroic leader and military genius. He bestrode Europe like a colossus – 'the Lord's Anointed'. A peace-loving ruler who was forced into patriotic wars in order to save the French Revolution from the oppressive monarchs of Europe.

He claimed to be the Emperor who tried to liberate the peoples of Europe from feudalism and bring them together into nationalist groups. In order to do this he had to adopt autocratic or dictatorial methods – here was the nationalistic Frenchman who served his country so gloriously. The 'people's Emperor' had to use whatever strategies were necessary to defend, and spread, the progress which the Revolution symbolised. If that meant concentrating power in his own hands, then so be it. As the '100 Days' showed, Napoleon would much rather have defended people's rights within a constitutional monarchy guaranteeing liberty and free elections – in other words, popular sovereignty.

This was the version of history that he himself created.

As there has been so much written about him, there is a wide range of interpretations of his career. He has been viewed as:

● a liberal reformer or dictator;

● the radical 'heir of the revolution' or a reactionary despot;

● a guardian of liberty and progress or as a self-seeking tyrant who trampled over people's rights;

● as a nationalist, fighting to free people from semi-feudal monarchists, or as a greedy conqueror, determined to create an Empire for himself and his personal dynasty;

● a man of principle or an arrogant, selfish 'Corsican ogre' (as the contemporary writer Benjamin Constant described him).

Probably none of these extremes will do.

Different versions of history are often determined by their historical context:

1. the motives of the author or historical figure;

2. the time they were written;

3. how selectively the achievements of the individual are emphasised.

The motives of the historical figure

There is little doubt that Napoleon carefully prepared his own propaganda. During the Egyptian and Italian campaigns, regular reports were sent back to the Directory which hailed Napoleon as the conquering hero. The Treaty of Campo Formio was returned and handed over personally by Napoleon to reinforce what he claimed to be a 'master stroke' of diplomacy over the Austrians. The Imperial Coronation of 1804 in Notre Dame (see page 116) was such a stage-managed spectacle that it could not fail to advertise the epic proportion of Napoleon's new status, as well as the Concordat with the Pope.

Painters were used in order to romanticise the view of Napoleon as the victorious young Caesar, conquering all and following in the footsteps of

Charlemagne. Jacques-Louis David produced some of the most well-known images. For example, when showing Napoleon crossing the Alps was he on a mule, struggling against the odds across a desolate landscape? No. Look again at the image of a dashing, brilliant general, as portrayed by David (page 110). Napoleon was adept at rewriting history to suit himself. The battle of Eylau became a great victory. The retreat from Moscow was blamed on the weather. Relays of messengers from the front fed the doctored versions of what happened to the only news source in Paris after 1806 – *Le Moniteur*. Exile on St Helena afforded more opportunities for Napoleon to leave for posterity an image that played down his role as dictator or military adventurer, and emphasised his patriotic, liberal side.

His doctor, O'Meara, and the Comte de Las Casas both committed their discussions with Napoleon to paper. The Comte's 'Mémoriale de Ste Helénè', which clearly bears Napoleon's handprint, contributed heavily to the adoration of the ex-Emperor following his death.

The time when it was written
Subsequent generations re-invented the Napoleonic era as a mythical golden age. A succession of artists looked back to a glorious time of French ascendancy and heroism, which contrasted sharply with the tedium and lacklustre days of the Bourbons and Orleanists that followed. Honoré de Balzac, Lord Byron, Victor Hugo and 'Stendhal' reflected the nostalgia and desire for excitement of what Lamartime called 'a bored generation'. The return of Napoleon's body to Les Invalides, in Paris in 1840, took place with such ceremony and splendour that Napoleon's legend was secure. It was a legend that Napoleon had done much to create. When France suffered reversals in war, such as in 1870 at the hands of Prussia, the strength of the Napoleonic legend – that of a glorious, all-conquering warrior – would redouble.

How selectively the achievements of the individual are emphasised
The debate about Napoleon's 'greatness' will continue as subsequent generations rediscover him, reinterpret him in their own context or choose which aspects of his career deserve attention. Aspects of his life are indeed worthy: the Code Napoleon, his assertion of religious toleration and equality before the law, the abolition of feudalism, the energy and the brilliance of some of his early military campaigns.

On the other hand, it is difficult to ignore the criticisms levelled by one notable contemporary, the Catholic nobleman François Chateaubriand who, in 1807, dismissed Napoleon as a tyrant. Critics such as the historian

---

Honoré de Balzac (1799–1850)
One of the major French novelists of the 19th century. He studied law and worked as a notary's clerk in Paris. His patroness was Madame de Berny. He intended his major work, *La Comédie Humaine* (The Human Comedy) to comprise 145 volumes, depicting every aspect of 19th-century France. He completed 80 volumes.

Victor Hugo (1802–1885)
French poet, novelist and dramatist. Hugo was the son of one of Napoleon's generals. His first book of poems appeared in 1822. *Notre Dame de Paris* was published in 1831. It was later filmed as 'The Hunchback of Notre Dame' (1924 and 1939). *Les Miserables* (1862) was adapted as a musical in 1980. Originally a monarchist, Hugo's support of republican ideals in the 1840s led to his banishment (1851) for opposing Louis Napoleon's *coup* d'état. Lived in exile in Guernsey until the fall of the Empire (1870), later becoming a senator under the Third Republic. Died a national hero.

'Stendhal' (1783–1842)
Pen name of Marie Henri Beyle. French novelist. Served in Napoleon's armies and took part in the ill-fated Russian campaign. Failing in his hopes of becoming a prefect, he lived in Italy from 1814 until suspicion of spying drove him back to Paris (1821) where he lived by writing. From 1830 he was a member of the consular service, spending his leaves in Paris. *Le Rouge et le Noir* (The Red and the Black, 1830) and *La Chartreuse de Parme* (The Charterhouse of Parma, 1839) were pioneering works in their treatment of disguise and hypocrisy.

1. Why has the Napoleonic legend had such a powerful effect on later generations of people?

2. 'Napoleon Bonaparte: "son of the Revolution". In reality there is no justification for this interpretation.' Do you agree? Explain your answer.

Correlli Barnett cannot overlook the darker side of his career. For example, the censorship and control, secret police, conscription, taxation, and the use of colonial slaves, the lust for power, the abandonment of popular sovereignty, the exploitation of French blood to create an Empire which flowered only briefly and failed to survive him. Even the brilliance of his military exploits has been called into question.

Napoleon may have been a 'great, bad man' (Chandler), but the scale of his efforts impressed and dazzled contemporaries and later generations. In that sense, his career was remarkable.

Source-based questions: Napoleon's rule in France

SOURCE A

He was a dictator who attempted to break with new legislation what resistance was left in the old society; who intensified his power in the state by means of a centralised administration; who suppressed, not only all organised influence or control and expression of opinion, but free thought itself; who hated the intellect, and who thought that the censorship, police and propaganda, he would be able to fashion the mind to his wish.

From Napoleon: For and Against *by Pieter Geyl, published in 1958*

SOURCE B

I can understand how it was that men worn out by the turmoil of the Revolution, and afraid of that liberty which had long been associated with death, looked for the domination of an able ruler. The slightest disturbance terrified the French people. The belief, or rather the error, that only despotism could maintain order in France was very widespread. He had some grounds for his belief that he was necessary; France believed it, too. People believed quite sincerely that Bonaparte, whether as consul or emperor, would exert his authority and save us from the perils of anarchy.

From Claire, Comtesse de Rémusat, Memoirs, *published in translation 1880*

SOURCE C

One may wonder by what magic spell Bonaparte, so aristocratic and so hostile to the mob, came to win the popularity which he enjoyed. Daily experience shows that the French are instinctively attracted by power; they have no love for liberty; equality is their idol. Now equality and tyranny are connected. In these two respects Napoleon won the hearts of the French.

From the memoirs of François Chateaubriand, a 19th-century writer and critic of Napoleon

SOURCE D

In 1799 Napoleon proclaimed that his new constitution was 'based on the true principles of representative government and on the sacred rights of property, equality and liberty. The powers it sets up will be strong and lasting.'

---

1. Study Sources B and C.

In what ways do these sources agree about Napoleon's appeal to the French people?

2. Study Source B.

How useful in this source to a historian studying how Napoleon was able to establish his authority over France? Explain your answer.

3. Use all the sources and the information contained in this chapter.

To what extent did Napoleon defend 'the sacred rights of property, equality and liberty'? Explain your answer.

International relations from the Congress of Vienna to 1848

Key Issues

- *How successful were the European Congresses of 1814–1822?*

- *How and why did relations between the European Powers change 1815–1848?*

- *How successful were the powers of Europe in their handling of the 'Eastern Question' 1822–1841?*

Framework of Events

1813	October: Battle of Leipzig
1814	1 March: Treaty of Chaumont
	31 March: Tsar Alexander I of Russia and Friedrich Wilhelm III of Prussia enter Paris
	April: Napoleon abdicates and is exiled to Elba
	30 May: Louis XVIII is restored to the French throne
	First Treaty of Paris
	1 November: Congress of Vienna
1815	1 March: Napoleon lands in southern France. The '100 Days' begins
	18 June: Napoleon is defeated at Waterloo and exiled to St Helena
	26 September: The Holy Alliance is produced
	20 November: Second Treaty of Paris
	Quadruple Alliance is signed by Austria, Prussia, Britain and Russia
1818	September–November: Congress of Aix-la-Chapelle
1820	May: Castlereagh's State Paper states the principle of British non-intervention
	October–December: Congress of Troppau
1821	January–May: Congress of Laibach continues the work of the Troppau Congress
	April: Greek War of Independence begins (lasts until 1829)
1822	October–December: Congress of Verona considers the Spanish revolt
1823	The French intervene in Spain
1826	Convention of Akkerman is signed between Russia and Turkey
1827	Battle of Navarino
1828	Russia intervenes on behalf of the Greeks, beginning a Russo–Turkish war
1829	Treaty of Adrianople ends the Russo–Turkish war
1830	Greece is declared independent under protection of Britain, Russia and France
	July: Louis-Philippe becomes king following a revolution in France

1830	August: Belgium proclaims its independence from the Kingdom of the Netherlands
	November: a rising begins in Poland against Russian control
1831	The Polish revolution is suppressed. Leopold of Saxe-Coburg becomes King of the Belgians
1832	Otto of Bavaria becomes King of Greece
	Turkey declares war on Egypt
1833	Treaty of Unkiar Skelessi, Turkey recognises independence of Egypt. Treaty of Münchengratz is signed by Austria, Russia and Prussia
1834	Quadruple Alliance of France, Great Britain, Spain and Portugal
1839	Treaty of London. Renewed fighting between Turkey and Egypt
1841	Straits Convention
1848	Revolutions break out in Italy, France, the Austrian Empire, Poland and Germany.

Overview

B ETWEEN 1815 and 1848, the affairs of Europe were dominated by the activities of five great powers – Austria, Russia, Prussia, Great Britain and France (see chart and map on page 147). At the beginning of this period, a war lasting almost continuously for 23 years had just come to an end. During the war, the French, under the Emperor Napoleon from 1804, had succeeded in extending their Empire far beyond the original borders of France. However, in 1814, the 'Grand Alliance' powers of Austria, Prussia, Russia and Britain had finally succeeded in defeating Napoleon. With the return of peace, the victors of 1814–15 had met to arrange a settlement, designed to prevent such wars from ever recurring. Their decisions, which became known as the Vienna Settlement, were influenced by their belief that future peace could only be assured if there was a 'balance of power' in Europe. This meant that territory and influence in Europe would be shared between the great powers, in a way that would prevent domination by any one country. From 1818, the great powers included France as an equal partner.

Having made what they saw as the best possible settlement in the circumstances, these powers spent the next 40 years attempting to maintain it. They all wanted to preserve it, but, as we shall see, they differed in their views as to how far it should be adapted according to changing circumstances. These differences of opinion were to shape the pattern of international relations between 1815 and 1848.

The means by which the powers tried to uphold the settlement varied throughout the period. From 1815 to 1822, congresses were favoured. These were large, important affairs, usually attended by Heads of State or principal ministers, at which a variety of issues was discussed. However, these proved unworkable as the attitudes of the powers began to differ and clash, once they no longer had a common enemy. After 1822, therefore, problems tended to be addressed as they arose, at conferences set up to deal with particular issues.

The division that developed in the Congress period, between the 'repressive' powers of the east (Russia, Austria and Prussia) and the more 'liberal' western powers (Great Britain and France) gradually changed. (The chart of political views on page 155 explains these terms.) New issues, in particular that of the weak Turkish Empire, posed different problems. The division of East and West, which was briefly revived by the revolutions in Europe 1830–31, broke down as the powers showed an increasing concern for individual interests. England co-operated with Russia in the near east, while Austria and Russia grew increasingly suspicious of one another's intentions. Britain and France nearly found themselves at war over the second Mehemet Ali Affair in 1839–40.

By 1848 international relations had become more flexible, but there was still an over-riding concern not to upset the principles established in 1815. The Great Powers' determination to work together to decide matters of international importance could still be seen over issues such as the Straits Convention of 1841.

6.1 How did the Congress of Vienna deal with the problems it faced?

Why was a congress necessary?

The long wars against France from 1792 to 1814 had affected most of Europe. There had been many political and territorial changes as rulers and regimes had been overthrown and property had changed hands. By 1812, the French Empire (see map on page 146) included Belgium (the former Austrian Netherlands), Holland (the former United Provinces), the left bank of the Rhine, the coast of North Germany, as well as parts of Italy and the Adriatic coast (known as the Illyrian provinces). French influence had also been extended into a number of dependent states, such as Spain, the rest of Italy, the Confederation of the Rhine and the Grand Duchy of Warsaw. In these, members of Napoleon's family or loyal **marshals** had taken control.

Marshals: Important and trusted military commanders.

With the conquests had come new patterns of administration and new ways of life. The French soldiers had fought and conquered in the name of the French Revolution (see Chapter 4) and had carried with them liberal ideas, such as the abolition of serfdom and guarantees of personal rights. Even countries that had not been conquered were affected by some of the revolutionary changes, as their soldiers serving away from home encountered these different ways of thinking. Politically, economically and socially, the wars had ensured that Europe could never be quite the same again.

The peace settlement was being planned even before the wars ended. In February 1813, during negotiations for the Treaty of Kalisch, Russia and Prussia compiled their own scheme for the future of Europe. This involved Russia taking almost all of Poland and Prussia taking the rest, together with Saxony the only German state to have remained loyal to Napoleon. After Napoleon's defeat at **Leipzig** in October 1813, the allies became even busier with their negotiations and plans. In January 1814, Viscount Castlereagh, the British Foreign Secretary (whose details appear on page 149), went to Europe to add his ideas. The following month, Prince von Metternich, the Foreign Minister of the Austrian Empire (see page 147), arranged the Congress of Chatillon between Russia, Austria, Great Britain and Prussia. From this came the Treaty of Chaumont, signed in March 1814. The powers agreed to continue the war until Napoleon had accepted their terms. The treaty also confirmed decisions already taken on the future of Holland, Spain, Italy, Germany and Switzerland. The allies also promised to work together for 20 years to prevent any further French disturbances, and to meet from time to time to deal with any international crises.

Battle of Leipzig (16–19 October 1813): This battle freed Germany from Napoleonic control. Napoleon was defeated by a larger force of Austrians, Prussians and Russians, joined by the Saxons who deserted Napoleon on 18 October. It is sometimes known as 'The Battle of the Nations'.

By April 1814, the armies of the Grand Alliance had taken Paris. Napoleon was forced to abdicate and was exiled to the island of Elba, off the Tuscan coast of Italy. In May 1814 the First Treaty of Paris was drawn up, to establish the position of France. Although this forced France to accept the restoration of the Bourbon monarchy, in other respects, France was treated leniently. (For details see the map opposite.) Appreciating that a harsh treaty would only cause trouble in the future, the allies allowed France to retain its borders of 1792 and its art treasures looted from conquered lands. It was agreed that this treaty should be confirmed at a congress (meeting) of all the powers. So it was arranged that the allies would meet in the Austrian capital, Vienna, in November 1814.

How did the Congress go about its business?

Metternich of Austria, as a staunch supporter of the idea of a peace congress, and a man who enjoyed grand social occasions, was more than happy to organise the Vienna Congress. His master, the Emperor Francis I, played the host. He entertained in his own palace the Tsar of Russia, four Kings, two Crown Princes, three Grand Duchesses and 32 German royals, in addition to all their servants. Elsewhere in the city were

> *Compare this map with that of 1789 (page 15) and that of 1815 (page 147). What changes can you find to (a) France (b) Prussia (c) Germany (d) Italy?*

The French Empire in 1812

to be found 215 Princes and their families, together with ministers and representatives from all the European States. A special committee had to be set up to cater for these guests and no expense was spared in providing suitable entertainment. There were balls, banquets, concerts, theatre, ballet, hunting parties and sleigh rides. Francis I bore the costs of all this hospitality, estimated at £7 million, despite the dire financial straits of his Empire at the end of the wars. The social activities were an integral part of the whole affair, and provided an arena in which the diplomats could

From the information given here, assess the strengths of the great powers of Europe in 1815.

Europe after the Congress of Vienna, 1815

What were the great powers of Europe like in 1815?

Great Britain
Population:
13 million
(25% rural)
The most economically advanced and a trading nation with an overseas empire protected by a powerful navy. It had a parliamentary system of government in which the monarch had limited political influence. Freedom of speech and of the press were well-established 'rights'.

Prussia
Population:
about 10.5 million
(70% rural)
The weakest of the 'great five'. Traditionally agricultural, but enlarged by the acquisition of the industrialised Rhineland in 1815. A military power. The king ruled, in conjunction with his ministers, council of state and civil service.

Russia
Population:
about 48 million (95% rural)
A backward economy. Over half the rural population were serfs, owned by the nobles. Most of the rest were state peasants. The size of the country and its huge armies accounted for its power. The ruler, the Tsar, made all the decisions.

France
Population:
about 29 million (75% rural)
Still primarily agricultural, but with some industrial growth especially in the north. It had a powerful army. Was Britain's main rival at sea. A constitutional monarchy from 1815, although the King retained a good deal of power, and the right to vote was very limited. Defeated in 1815, but still regarded as powerful.

Austria
Population:
about 25 million (80% rural)
In area, the second largest state after Russia. Largely agricultural, but industrial growth in Italy and Bohemia. Its army had drained its finances in the war years, leaving severe debts. Ruled by an emperor, who had absolute power over his subjects, who were made up of many different races.

meet. It is often said that the best deals are made over dinner or in quiet corners of parties.

Originally the Congress was seen as a ratification of the decisions of the first Treaty of Paris, but it actually turned into something rather more. It not only settled the fate of France, it also attempted to establish a balance of power in Europe – rewarding the victors, punishing the vanquished and providing for future security. It lasted eight months until the final agreement was signed in June 1815. During this time, the representatives of the great powers repeatedly met with one another, both formally and informally. Ten special committees concentrated on particular questions. When appropriate, other nations were invited to join the great powers in their discussions. Unlike more recent international meetings, there were no full sessions around a conference table. Indeed the participants never all met together until the signing of the final Act.

What were the attitudes and interests of the main statesmen at the Congress of Vienna?

Alexander I (1777–1825), Tsar of Russia (1801–1825)
Tsar Alexander I had personally led Russia in the war against Napoleon and had then had been the first to reach Paris in March 1814. He was a powerful figure at the Congress of Vienna, but the other powers were never quite certain of his intentions. Alexander appeared torn between **conservatism** and **liberalism** (see panel on page 155). Although he was an autocratic ruler (see panel on page 150), he was attended by a group of liberal advisers. He was also deeply religious and his views were liable to be influenced by the mystic, Madame Krudener. Finally, it was known that Russia was keen to expand into south-east Asia, at the expense of Turkey, which made the other powers wary of Russian ambitions. This also explains why, in the early stages of the talks, Alexander I had little time for the 'balance of power' idea. Instead, he favoured:

● a Polish State under Russian control, which would provide greater security for Russia;

● a divided Germany that would pose no threat to Russia;

● Prussian control of Saxony, which would keep it away from Poland.

Friedrich Wilhelm III (1770–1840), King of Prussia (1797–1840)
The contribution of Prussia to the final stages of the Napoleonic wars earned Friedrich Wilhelm a seat at the Congress of Vienna, although Prussia was regarded as a junior partner by the other powers. Friedrich Wilhelm had entered Paris behind Tsar Alexander I, and accompanied him on the journey to Vienna. Throughout the Congress he appeared anxious not to offend this powerful neighbour, and to follow Russia's lead. Because of the King's timidity and indecision, his Chancellor, Karl Hardenberg, did most of the negotiating. Friedrich Wilhelm favoured:

● a harsh settlement for the French, for whom most Prussians had 'an undying hatred' (according to historian C. Webster);

● the expansion of Prussian territory, preferably by expanding into North Germany, and absorbing Saxony.

Prince Klemens von Metternich (1773–1859)
Metternich was the Austrian Foreign Minister who presided over the Congress, with his master Emperor Francis I. Although he was an extremely able diplomat, his position was not an easy one. Austria itself

was a large, unwieldy central European Empire composed of many different nationalities. It felt threatened by Russia to the east, France to the west and by the ambitions of its peoples from within. It is no wonder, therefore, that much of Metternich's attention at the Congress was taken up in minimising the spread of liberal and nationalistic ideas and working for a balance of power. Metternich favoured:

- a strong central Europe, under the influence of Austria, to balance Russia and France;

- restraining Russian and Prussian ambitions;

- the continuance of monarchical government and aristocratic leadership.

Viscount Robert Stewart Castlereagh (1769–1822), British Foreign Secretary (1812–1822)

Castlereagh led the British delegation, representing Lord Liverpool's Tory government. He had been central to the organisation of Napoleon's defeat and shared Metternich's belief in the need to stabilise Europe by creating a 'balance' among the powers. However, the British position was slightly different from that of the other powers. Britain already had a liberal political system. Castlereagh was far too realistic, however, to force political change on other nations. Britain was also interested in its growing colonial empire and trading links, not in the acquisition of territory in Europe. Castlereagh favoured:

- peace and stability;

- moves towards liberalism, where possible (e.g. in France and Poland);

- the retention of Britain's wartime gains overseas;

Humanitarian liberalism: For example, the abolition of the slave trade, which Britain had already abandoned voluntarily in 1807.

- **humanitarian liberalism**.

Charles Talleyrand-Périgord (1754–1838)

Talleyrand represented the defeated France, on behalf of the newly restored Louis XVIII. Crippled as a child, he had entered the Church, becoming a bishop in 1789. However, he had still supported the Revolution and worked for the French Republic in the 1790s, and for Napoleon until 1807. Then he had schemed for the restoration of the Bourbons and was chief negotiator with the allies in Louis XVIII's cause. His position at the Vienna Congress was not easy, but he was ready to exploit any differences of opinion between the other nations in order to assert French power. He was careful to stress that he spoke for the restored Bourbon monarchy and not the defeated Napoleon. Talleyrand favoured:

1. Which of the statesmen at Vienna shared similar attitudes and which possessed differing views? Give examples to support your answer.

2. What were likely to be the most important shared aims? Over what issues might conflicts of opinion be expected to occur? Explain your answer.

- legitimacy (the right of a ruler to hold power by strict hereditary law), as established in France;

- restrictions on Prussian expansion, so that Prussia did not impose a direct threat to France;

- asserting France's claim to be regarded as a major power.

> ### Types of monarchy in the early 19th century
>
> **Autocratic/absolute monarchy**: all power in the hands of the ruler (e.g. Tsar of Russia).
> **Constitutional monarchy**: the ruler's power slightly limited by a written constitution (e.g. the Bourbon monarchy in France).
> **Parliamentary monarchy**: the ruler's power considerably limited by the power of an elected parliament (e.g. King of Great Britain).

How were the main problems dealt with?

You should look at the maps on pages 146, 147 and 151 for details of the territorial changes. Further information can also be found in the relevant chapters on individual countries.

How was France to be controlled?

One of the biggest problems facing the peacemakers was that of ensuring France could never expand again in the way it had during the wars. For this reason, the allies tried to create strong **buffer states** on the boundaries of France. These are sometimes referred to as the *Cordon Sanitaire* (see map).

Buffer states/*Cordon Sanitaire*: States that separate ambitious powers from one another and protect them from each other's aggression. The *Cordon Sanitaire* was the name given to the 'wholesome', uninterrupted border of buffer states surrounding France from 1815.

- Belgium (the old Austrian Netherlands) and Holland (the old United Provinces) were to become the United Kingdom of the Netherlands. They were joined together under the Dutch King. The frontier would be reinforced by the restoration of the old 'barrier' fortresses. Luxembourg – part of this new kingdom – was to have a Prussian garrison.

- Prussian territory was to be extended on the left bank of the Rhine and in the old Napoleonic Kingdom of Westphalia, along the lower and middle Rhine. Bavaria and Baden were strengthened. This placed Prussia in the position of protector of Germany, and left it able to provide to support to the King of the Netherlands if necessary.

- The independence and neutrality of the Swiss Confederation of 22 **cantons** was recognised by all the Great Powers, including France.

Cantons: The regions of Switzerland that were largely self-governing. The cantons were groups of small states ruled almost entirely by small merchant elites. They were traditionally left alone by the Popes and other surrounding rulers.

- The formerly independent Republic of Genoa was to be incorporated into the Kingdom of Piedmont-Sardinia to strengthen this border. Being given Nice and most of Savoy from France also strengthened Piedmont. East of Piedmont, Italian Lombardy was to be controlled by Austria, so offering a military back-up.

How was the security of Italy and Germany to be assured?

The powers were determined to break the strong French influence that Napoleon had imposed on Italy. Consequently, Italy was divided up in a similar way to that which it had enjoyed before the French conquests, with separate states, for most part under their old ruling dynasties.

- Austria acquired the northern and eastern Italian states of Lombardy and Venetia to make up for the loss of the Austrian Netherlands. This provided a strong Austrian influence behind the enlarged state of Piedmont-Sardinia.

Habsburgs: The Imperial family of Austria since 1282. The dynasty was officially the House of Habsburg-Lorraine after 1745.

- Austrian influence was also established through the restoration of rulers related to the Austrian royal house, the **Habsburgs**, in the central Italian duchies of Parma, Modena, and Tuscany.

1. **How effectively did the allies succeed in 'containing' France in 1814–15?**

2. **Which boundaries were (a) strongest, (b) weakest?**

3. **Can you foresee any problems with these arrangements?**

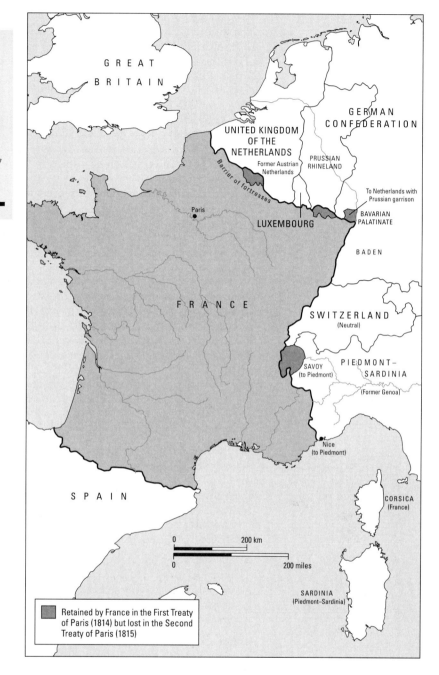

The *Cordon Sanitaire* around France, 1814–15

Pope: Head of the Roman Catholic Church. The Pope was a spiritual leader to Catholics (see page 154) everywhere but he was also an earthly ruler with his own territory, known as the Papal States, with Rome as its capital.

Diet: The governing council of the German Confederation. It consisted of representatives chosen by the rulers of the various states of Germany.

● The **Pope** was returned to the Papal States, with Austrian troops, and Ferdinand I was returned to Naples.

● The old Holy Roman Empire, which had been made up of 360 separate states in Germany, was not re-established. Already destroyed by the French conquests, it was replaced by a loose union of 38 (from 1817, when Hesse Homburg joined, 39) states which formed the German Confederation. It was hoped that such a union would be able to resist attack more effectively. The Confederation (*Bund*) included most of Prussia, German Austria and the Kingdom of Bohemia. It had a central **diet** at Frankfurt, under an Austrian President.

How did the powers resolve the issue of Poland and Saxony?

The future of Poland and Saxony was the hardest issue the Congress had to resolve, and it nearly brought them to war. Metternich was unhappy about the Russo–Prussian deal made at the Treaty of Kalisch in 1813. He feared Russian expansion and wanted the Austrians to have some control over the German States. However, since there were Russian troops in both Saxony and Poland at the end of the wars there was little he could do. Castlereagh was also suspicious of Russia, and tried to persuade Prussia to oppose the Tsar's plans for Poland. However, the Prussian King was too weak to cope with Tsar Alexander's anger. Instead, he ordered his chief minister, Hardenberg, to stop negotiating with Castlereagh.

It was Talleyrand of France who saw the chance to gain from the dispute. He provided the third ally Metternich needed in his stand against Russia and Prussia. On 3 January 1815, Austria, Britain and France joined in an alliance to resist the other two powers. Alexander realised he must compromise to avoid conflict and, in January 1815, Castlereagh negotiated a compromise solution.

Russia gained most of Poland, which became known as 'Congress Poland', and was granted its own constitution. A large section of Galicia, however, was retained by Austria and Prussia got Posen. Prussia only received two-fifths of Saxony (40% of the population, 60% of the land), but it was also given a large section of the Rhineland and Pomerania. The historian A.J.P. Taylor, in *The Course of German History* (1945), referred to the Rhineland settlement as 'a practical joke played by the Great Powers on the weakest of their number'. Prussia was far from convinced that the industrially advanced but liberal, Catholic areas of the Rhineland were worth having. Little did the Powers realise that this union was to provide the foundation stone for the powerful German Empire.

What other decisions were made at the Congress?

Many of the decisions mentioned above went some way towards rewarding the victors and penalising the losers. Further agreements carried this one stage further, and recognised changes that had come about in wartime. Some decisions of a more general nature were also made, largely at Great Britain's request. Here is a summary of the remaining terms of the Treaty of Paris, 1814:

- The Habsburg Empire was expanded by the absorption of territories that had been independent before the wars, such as the Archbishopric of Salzburg. Bavaria restored land to Austria in return for the Palatinate and other German territory. Austria also acquired the Illyrian provinces, which had formerly belonged to the Venetian Republic.

- Great Britain was able to expand its overseas Empire. The Ionian Islands in the Adriatic, formerly belonging to the Venetian republic, were placed under British protection. Britain also acquired Malta from France. In the Caribbean, Britain retained Tobago and St Lucia from France, and Trinidad from Spain. Three former Dutch colonies in South America were combined to form British Guiana. In Africa, Britain took Cape Colony from the Dutch and Mauritius, a naval base in the Indian Ocean, from France. In the Far East, it kept the former Dutch Ceylon (Sri Lanka). Heligoland, a North Sea island, was taken from Denmark. Britain paid financial compensation to Holland for Ceylon (6 million pounds) and the Cape (2 million pounds), but the money was earmarked for the construction of the barrier fortresses on the Belgian/French border.

- Sweden acquired Norway from Denmark, which had remained loyal to

Napoleon. This confirmed an agreement of 1812 and compensated Sweden for the loss of Finland to Russia.

- The navigation of rivers flowing through several countries was declared open to commerce of all nations, without any increase in duties.

- France promised to prohibit the slave trade, and Spain and Portugal accepted cash sums to abandon it by 1820. The Dutch agreed to end the trade in return for keeping colonies, such as Java (in the East Indies), which Britain had taken during the wars.

Why was a Second Treaty of Paris necessary?

The First Treaty of Paris was approved by the Congress, and the debates had moved on to other matters when proceedings were interrupted in March 1815 by another Napoleonic bid for power. Escaping from Elba, Napoleon landed on the south coast of France and marched triumphantly to Paris, and on into the southern part of the new Kingdom of the Netherlands (present-day Belgium). Not until Wellington, aided by the timely arrival of a Prussian force under Blücher, had checked his advance at Waterloo, in June 1815, was he finally removed from the political scene. With his exile to the island of St Helena, 5,000 miles away in the mid-Atlantic, Europe was at last rid of the Napoleonic threat.

However, the substantial French support for Napoleon's final campaign, dubbed the '100 Days', caused the allies to rethink their generous treatment of France in the first Treaty of Paris. The Second Treaty of Paris was signed, in November 1815, after the Vienna Congress had dispersed. This imposed harsher terms on France, although it was still not as punishing as Prussia and the Netherlands had wanted. French frontiers were reduced to those of 1790, and an indemnity of 700 million francs was imposed. Furthermore, France was to return all looted art treasures and to bear the costs of an army of occupation, which was to remain until the indemnity was paid off.

What was the Concert of Europe?

Having produced such a carefully planned settlement, the next problem was how to preserve it. At the Treaty of Chaumont in 1814, the allies had already agreed to work together for 20 years, and to hold meetings to deal with any problems that might arise in Europe. These pledges were renewed with the signing of the Second Treaty of Paris in November 1815, when the Quadruple Alliance of the wartime allies was re-established. In this alliance, each power promised it would resist any further attempt by Napoleon or his family to return to France and would contribute 60,000 men should there be any attempt to overturn the peace settlement and thus threaten the other nations of Europe.

By the terms of Article VI of the Treaty, the idea of continuing their meetings was laid down. The powers agreed 'to renew their meetings at fixed periods ... for the purpose of consulting upon their common interests and for the consideration of the measures which ... shall be considered the most salutary for the repose and prosperity of nations and for the maintenance of the peace of Europe.' This agreement provided the basis for what became known as, the 'Concert of Europe'. This is the term given to the habit of the great powers, which included France from 1818, of consulting and working together. No permanent structure for meetings was laid down, but the idea survived well into the second half of the century and may be deemed one of the most lasting achievements of the Vienna statesmen.

Arthur Wellesley (1769–1852), Duke of Wellington

Wellington joined the British army in 1785, at the age of 16. From 1796–1805 he served in India as an administrator and soldier. He was knighted in 1805, before gaining a seat in the House of Commons (1805–08). He was involved in the Peninsular War against the French (1808–14). Became Earl of Wellington (February 1812); Marquis (October 1812) and Duke (1814). He attended the Congress of Vienna, and commanded the British forces at Waterloo. In January 1819, he joined Lord Liverpool's Cabinet as 'Master-General of the Ordinance' and, in this position, he attended the Congresses of Aiz-la-Chapelle and Verona. Became Tory Prime Minister (January 1828–November 1830). He was a strong opponent of parliamentary reform and lost some popularity as a result. He was known as 'The Iron Duke'.

Prince Regent: A person ruling a country when the king or queen is unable to rule because they are too ill. George IV of Great Britain was named Prince Regent in 1811 (at the age of 49) when his father, George III, was declared too insane to rule. George IV did not attend the Congress of Vienna. His refusal to sign the Holy Alliance of 1815 helped to emphasise the difference between the King of Great Britain, whose position was limited by parliament, and the constitutional monarchs. George IV became king in his own right (1820–30).

Catholic/Orthodox/Protestant: These represent different groups within the Christian faith. Roman Catholics believe the Pope to be God's representative on earth, while Orthodox Christians regarded the Tsar of Russia as their earthly leader. The Protestants, who broke away from the Catholic Church in the 16th century, believe in direct individual communication with God.

There was also a second agreement, which provided for regular consultation between powers, but this was of a rather different kind. Tsar Alexander I, much influenced by the Christian mysticism that had particularly affected him in the later years of war, believed it was his duty to unite his fellow Monarchs in a 'holy alliance'. By this alliance, signed in September 1815, the monarchs of Europe undertook to work together and act in accordance with 'the sublime truths which the Holy religion of our Saviour teaches'. They would watch over their respective peoples 'as fathers of families'. Although many privately agreed with Metternich that it was a 'loud sounding nothing', virtually all the rulers of Europe in 1815 were prepared to sign it. The **Prince Regent** of Great Britain stayed out, however, because he claimed that his country's constitution forbade him to enter into such personal agreements. He was joined by the Sultan of Turkey, a non-Christian, and the Pope who, as head of the Roman **Catholic** Church, would not join with **Orthodox** and **Protestant** monarchs.

Although it appeared a fairly harmless agreement at the time, this alliance was to prove troublesome, for a number of reasons.

1. It was an agreement between rulers, not nations or peoples. The Prince Regent's abstention hinted at a division between the autocratic and constitutional monarchs (see chart of political views) that was to grow wider with time.

2. The alliance spoke of maintaining 'decent Christian order'. This was later to become an excuse for repressing liberal movements, although it was Metternich, rather than the Tsar, who was principally responsible for using the alliance in this way.

3. The very existence of a second alliance, in addition to the Quadruple Alliance, was to prove confusing. The powers were now uncertain of the basis of any future meetings. Were they to be in accordance with the principles of the Quadruple or the Holy Alliance?

Britain's gesture, in staying out of the Holy Alliance, revealed the fundamental weakness of the whole Vienna Settlement. The attitude of a country with a parliament and a limited monarchy was likely to be very different from that of an autocratic Empire, such as Russia or Austria. Once the common enemy, France, had gone, it was going to be increasingly difficult for such countries to work in harmony together. Castlereagh, and later his successor, George Canning, kept to a fairly strict legal definition of the Quadruple Alliance. They claimed that they were only required to act if a change in the settlement threatened other nations and the general peace of Europe. Austria, Prussia and Russia, however, were increasingly to base their actions on the principles of the Holy Alliance. They stressed, in particular, the need to retain 'decent Christian Order' in the face of growing liberalism and nationalism.

George Canning (1770–1827)

Canning began his political career as a Whig, but supported Pitt's Tory government during the period of the French wars. He remained out of the Cabinet (1809–16) because of a quarrel with Castlereagh which ended in a duel. With Castlereagh's suicide in 1822, Canning became Foreign Minister, a post he held until 1827. Although his policies were broadly similar, he gave a very different impression from his predecessor, since he knew how to capture public opinion with patriotic speeches. Canning abandoned involvement in the Congress System, recognised the independence of the former Spanish and Portuguese colonies in South America, and sent troops to Lisbon (to safeguard the constitution) and to Greece (to support the Greek revolt against Turkey). His policy of co-operating with Russia in order to restrain it was working well at the time of his death, but shortly afterwards it ended in disaster with the Battle of Navarino. Canning was Prime Minister for the last five months of his life, favouring moderate Tory reform.

Terms commonly used to describe political views

Conservatives dislike too much change. They like to keep things as they are, or even to go back to things as they had been (**reactionary**). They might try to suppress those who want change (**repressive**).

Liberals want to change things so that there is greater freedom for the individual. In theory, **radicals** and **revolutionaries** are more extreme but the terms often meant the same in the early 19th century.

Liberals generally favour **constitutional** or **republican** government. Constitutionalists want the monarchs' power limited by a written document guaranteeing rights and giving the people some say in the running of the country. Republicans want to dispense with a monarch and give the people a lot of influence in government.

Nationalists believe that all those of the same race or background should be united in a single country. Some liberals were also nationalists. The feeling was influential in Italy, Germany, Belgium, Poland and Hungary.

6.2 Was the Vienna Settlement a success or a failure?
A CASE STUDY IN HISTORICAL INTERPRETATION

In assessing the relative merits of the Vienna Settlement, it must be remembered that this settlement was made up of not one, but three sets of negotiations. These were:

● the First Treaty of Paris (May 1814)

● the Congress of Vienna itself (November 1814–June 1815)

● the Second Treaty of Paris (November 1815).

Taken together, the provisions of the settlement have often been condemned. It has been alleged that it was an attempt to 'turn the clock back', that no notice was taken of liberal and nationalist sentiments, and that it ignored issues such as those of Turkey and the near east, which were to become major sources of tension in the ensuing years. The settlement received a lot of condemnation later on in the 19th century, and still has its critics today. However, on the whole, modern historians have been more enthusiastic, regarding the settlement as a triumph in its achievement of peace, stability and a balance of power in Europe.

What is the case for failure?

According to E.V. Gulick – a modern American historian who has given the agreements only guarded praise – the Vienna Settlement was 'unfair in many respects, incomplete in numerous details, (and) destined to be endlessly revised' (The New Cambridge Modern History Volume IX, 1965).

Was it unfair?
During the later 19th century, when both liberalism and nationalism became powerful and successful political forces, historians looked

Legitimacy: The belief that members of the same royal family had a God-given or 'divine' right to rule their nation. At Vienna (1814–15), this meant the restoration of rulers to their pre-Napoleonic positions of power by strict hereditary right.

Karl Marx (1818–1883)
Marx was a writer and thinker from the Rhineland of Prussia. He developed a theory of history in which economic and social conditions were held to be the cause of all change. In his most famous book, *The Communist Manifesto* (1848), he explained his theories and in particular his views of the continuing struggle between different economic classes of people. His 'socialist' ideas made him antagonistic towards the backward-looking, aristocratic statesmen at Vienna. He blamed them for holding back the progress of Europe.

unfavourably on the arrangements made in 1814–15. They claimed that the diplomats at Vienna were too backward-looking and 'out of touch' with the changes brought about by the French Revolution. These criticisms were not new. No sooner had Castlereagh returned home to report on events, than the complaints had started in Great Britain. A fellow member of his Cabinet, Lord Greville, declared that he must have been 'seduced by his vanity' and had 'his head turned by Emperors, Kings and Congresses' to have agreed to such an arrangement. In 1817, the English Radical newspaper, *Black Dwarf*, had complained of the 'accursed principle of **legitimacy**' upheld by the Congress of Vienna. In 1821, a pamphlet entitled 'The Declaration of England against the Acts and Projects of the Holy Alliance' voiced the criticism often repeated by later historians: 'Public opinion was disregarded. National feeling was despised and the expression of it harshly repulsed. Whole countries were transferred from one prince to another, without any consideration of their wishes or habits.'

French historians were particularly hostile. They blamed the Vienna Settlement for provoking the 1830 and 1848 revolutions in France and felt that Louis XVIII, the restored Bourbon monarch, was unduly punished for the crimes of Napoleon. The Frenchman, Antonin Debidour wrote in the 1890s that the allies 'consulted only their own convenience and interest and took no account of the aspirations of the people'. Such a view has lasted to our own day and can be found, for example, in the works of J. Droz in the 1960s and 1970s.

On the whole, British and American historians have been more favourable, but Norman Davies, writing in *Europe – A History* (1997), was still highly critical. 'The spirit of the settlement was more than conservative: it actually put the clock back. It was designed to prevent change in a world where the forces of change had only been contained by a whisker. The victors were terrified of the least concession.'

It is easy to find examples to support these views. Norway was transferred to Sweden, Belgium to Holland, Poland to Russia, Nice and Savoy to Piedmont, the Rhineland to Prussia, Lombardy and Venetia to Austria and numerous colonies to Great Britain, without any attempt to consider the wishes of their inhabitants. 'Legitimate' monarchs, often of the most despotic kind, were restored to many of the Italian states and were imposed on France, despite the experience of the revolution. Nationalism was ignored, and disturbances and revolutions were to break out in Europe in the 1820s, 1830–31 and again in 1848, which could only be controlled by the use of force.

Was it incomplete?

Karl Marx, in a letter of 1853, wrote:

'Napoleon could dispose of a whole continent at a moment's notice, aye and dispose of it too in a manner that showed both genius and fixedness of purpose. The entire "collective wisdom" of European legitimacy (princes and monarchs) assembled in Congress at Vienna took a couple of years to do the same job; got at loggerheads over it, made a very sad mess indeed of it, … without ideas, without initiative, they adore the *status quo* they themselves have bungled together.'

It would seem that, in many respects, the Congress of Vienna was something of a wasted opportunity. Only in some general agreements on the abolition of slavery and the navigation of rivers (which actually made little difference in practice) was there any attempt to 'reform'. The diplomats were too frightened of what the Duke of Wellington put into words in 1830: 'Beginning reform is beginning revolution'. Speaking of the diplomatic representatives, E.V. Gulick wrote that, 'with the exception of Tsar Alexander, their minds did not lift above the orthodox (meaning normal or ordinary). There was no stunning act of leadership and no lasting or creative advance towards the future.'

It has also been argued that the Vienna Settlement was 'incomplete' in so far as it relied very heavily on the Great Powers to enforce it and assumed their continuing desire to work together. Austria, for example, was left with commitments that were far beyond its financial and military resources. Britain, on the other hand, having avoided any continental entanglements in 1814–15, was to grow increasingly independent over the following years and less inclined to co-operate with the other European powers unless its own interests were at stake.

Finally, it must be remembered that the problems of the declining Turkish Empire were entirely ignored at the Congress. It was over this issue that the powers were to become more divided in the future. The Near East was to become the most important area of conflict in the 19th century, and yet it was not even discussed.

Destined to be endlessly revised?

No one can deny that many of the terms of the Vienna Settlement were short-lived. In a little over 15 years, the newly created Kingdom of Holland was broken up, the Bourbon restoration in France had ended, and Tsar Nicholas I had revoked the constitution granted to Poland. During the second half of the 19th century, Austria was thrown out of Italy, the German Confederation was dissolved and French boundaries were altered.

Peninsula: A body of land surrounded on three sides by water.

Although it is sometimes alleged that the Vienna Settlement preserved the peace of Europe until the Crimean War of 1854, this argument breaks down when the number of 'near-misses' are considered (such as in the disputes over the Iberian **peninsula**, Belgium and the Near East). There were plenty of incidents in Europe, as differences of opinion emerged over revisions to the settlement. It would seem that the appearance of unanimity at Vienna was deceptive. In any case, the absence of a general European war can hardly be attributed to the arrangements of 1814–15 when so many significant parts of the settlement were soon changed.

What is the case for success?

R. Albrecht-Carrié wrote, in his review of the Vienna Settlement in 1958, 'History is forever rewritten'. Reacting against 19th-century hostility, 20th-century historians – with experience of one or two world wars, and in some cases a 'cold war' too – have tended to regard the first half of the 19th century as a period of relative stability. Charles Mowat, in *Britain between the wars, 1918–1940* (published in 1958), and Harold Nicolson, in *The Congress of Vienna* (1946), praised the peacemaking at Vienna which, to them, contrasted favourably with that of Versailles in 1918. The Americans E.V. Gulick and Henry Kissinger have also stressed the stability which the settlement provided. To them, it was a rather more successful arrangement than that which followed the Second World War. E.V. Gulick wrote that the Settlement was 'remarkably consistent with the ideal of re-establishing in Europe a balanced state system'.

These historians would argue that success and failure could only be measured against the aims of those involved. At Vienna, the two principal aims – the restoration of peace and the establishment of a balance of power – were achieved. The Vienna Settlement was successful in so far as it placed a *Cordon Sanitaire* around France, which contained it without being too punitive. This did ensure that France caused no further trouble for the next half century. The Settlement rewarded the victors and re-established peace, while ensuring that no single nation dominated, or was left feeling aggrieved. France was even re-admitted to the alliance in 1818.

The settlement restrained some of the Russian ambitions in the east, and Prussian greed in the North. Also, by giving Austria a strong hand in central Europe, it achieved what it set out to do. Rather than condemn the diplomats for their failure to prevent the outbreak of revolution in Europe in subsequent years, modern British and American commentaries on the period have applauded the diplomats for producing a settlement, the essentials of which could be maintained throughout these times. When criticism has been handed out, it has tended to be directed against the later inflexibility of the powers involved, rather than the Vienna statesmen themselves. According to Sir Charles Webster, 'The primary need of Europe, once the Napoleonic tyranny was overthrown, was a period of peace; and this the statesmen of Vienna undoubtedly secured in a far greater degree than the publicists of the time dared to hope.'

Historians in favour of the Settlement have argued that it has been unfairly condemned for ignoring liberal principles and promoting reactionary ideas. They have pointed out, for example, that the principle of legitimacy, which involved the restoration of rightful rulers to their thrones, was far from universally applied. Legitimacy was, at best, used only selectively. It played no part in Western Germany, Poland, Saxony, Norway, the Austrian Netherlands and Northern Italy. It was applied to the French Bourbons but, as L.C.B. Seaman reminds us in *From Vienna to Versailles* (1955), 'it was almost exclusively in their interest that the slogan was invented'. Furthermore, some Liberal ideas were present in the settlement. The French monarchy was restored with a charter, which made it more liberal than any other major country of Continental Europe. Russia gave a constitution to Poland, the Netherlands also had one, while the terms of the German Confederation made provision for states to grant individual constitutions to their subjects. Norway, which had not been a separate country since 1397 anyway, kept its own parliament, government, army and navy.

Even nationalism, although hardly a powerful force in 1815, received some token of acceptance in the reduction of the number of German states and in the recreation of Poland. Indeed, the fact that the powers were prepared to consider Poland as a separate state is remarkable, given its history of division and its position between other major powers. According to L.C.B. Seaman, 'diplomats cannot be criticised for not wanting to negotiate their countries out of existence and the creation of a unitary Germany would have involved the representatives of Austria and Prussia in doing precisely that'. We should also remember that the representatives at Vienna did rid Europe of French domination. As L.C.B. Seaman reminds us, 'there were far fewer people being ruled and despoiled by foreigners by the end of 1815 than there were at the end of 1810'.

There were clearly gestures towards liberalism and nationalism, but the case for the success of the settlement is largely based on the appreciation that neither liberalism nor nationalism in their later, popular form was particularly widespread in 1815. The representatives of the Great Powers did not ignore a universal clamour for more liberal institutions, since there was none. Republicanism, as a product of the French revolution, had led to the longest period of war in living memory. So, it is argued, it was entirely natural for the Vienna statesmen to try to recreate the political conditions of the mid-18th century, which had provided relative stability. It could not be argued that the smaller powers would have made the settlement any more liberal. Some of the German States and Holland, for example, would have liked to see France treated far more harshly.

The Great Powers did show some consideration for the lesser ones. For example, guarantees of religious toleration and commercial equality were given to the Belgians, and promises of national rights were accorded to the Norwegians and Poles. In any case, practicalities demanded that smaller states be 'protected' by larger ones. An independent Belgium could not have survived in the circumstances of 1815, when it would have been left defenceless in the shadow of France, and an independent Poland would have been equally vulnerable. Since French influence had been strong in Northern Italy, it was felt that an absence of Austrian control was likely to result, not in Italian freedom, but in subjection to France. In any case, the lesser powers were represented at the Congress and signed the final treaty.

Finally, some historians have argued that, had nationalist ideas been heeded, it would only have encouraged aggressive expansion, as happened later in the century. Then there would have been even greater disruption to the settlement.

So, to conclude with a quotation from E.V. Gulick, the Vienna Settlement, 'performed a series of skilled operations, and made solid contributions in ending the Napoleonic tyranny, granting Europe a breathing spell and giving France sound frontiers. They also made a noteworthy advance in the creation of a system of diplomacy by conference.'

1. Why have historians disagreed about the success of the Vienna Settlement?

2. Which of the two cases presented here do you find more convincing? Give reasons for your answer.

6.3 What was the Congress System and how effective was it?

From 1818 to 1822, the Concert of Europe worked through a series of congresses at which the great powers tried to resolve the problems that occurred. These meetings are sometimes referred to as 'the Congress System', although the use of this term can be misleading for a number of reasons.

- There was no agreement between the powers as to what the congresses were for.

- There was no regular basis for the holding of congresses.

- There was no procedure for where congresses were to take place.

- There was no continuity between congresses (although the Congress of Troppau, 1820, did reconvene at Laibach, 1821, after a Christmas break).

- There were no permanent staff, civil servants or **secretariat**.

- There were other meetings, such as conferences of ambassadors and more informal discussions, in the same period.

- The congresses were never 'Congresses of Europe' as the smaller powers were excluded from the most important decision making.

- Key individuals were absent from some of the congresses.

Secretariat: Department or office responsible for the administration of an international political organisation.

However, congresses were the dominant form of co-operation between the powers, and it was at these that major European decisions were taken and major disagreements emerged between 1815 and 1822.

How successful was the Congress of Aix-la-Chapelle (September–November 1818)?

The Congress of Aix-la-Chapelle (modern-day Aachen) was attended by all the rulers or Foreign Secretaries of the great powers and met to consider the position of France. Wellington argued that maintaining troops in France was more likely to disturb the peace than maintain it. In any case, a council of ambassadors in Paris had already prepared the ground for the withdrawal of troops as France made its last indemnity payments. All that was needed was for the congress to agree to end the military occupation and to sort out the final details of payment. This done, France was a free country once more.

The next question was whether or not France should be re-admitted to the Concert of Europe and attend future congresses as an equal partner. The Tsar was in favour of this and wanted to turn the Quadruple Alliance into a Quintuple Alliance, 'to protect the arts of peace' and in the interests of monarchical solidarity. In fact, his reasons were really more selfish. He disliked the way Austria and Britain had worked together and, he suspected, against him at Vienna. Furthermore, Prussia's allegiance had switched from Russia to Austria after 1815, as it believed Austria could provide greater support for its vulnerable frontiers. Consequently, Russia was feeling isolated in 1818 and wanted France's support to balance the alliance. Castlereagh and Metternich naturally opposed the Tsar's suggestion, but proposed a compromise. France was to be admitted to The Congress System, but the allies also renewed their promises to one another as stated in the Quadruple Alliance.

The Tsar also had another proposal. His idea was for an '*Alliance Solidaire*', or Universal Union, to guarantee monarchs' thrones and lands. He spoke once again of 'sacred principles of order' and of the need for regular congresses and an international army that could be used to restore deposed monarchs. However, he also urged all monarchs to grant constitutions for the well-being and peace of their peoples in an 'Empire of Christian Morality'.

Naturally enough, the proposal was far from welcome to Castlereagh, who announced that his government would oppose any attempt 'to provide the transparent soul of the Holy Alliance with a body'. He argued that intervention in the affairs of other countries could only be justified if disorders threatened the peace of Europe. Metternich was also hostile, fearing the expansion of Russian influence into western Europe. The idea therefore came to nothing, but the division it caused did not bode well for future harmony.

The Congress of Aix-la-Chapelle was, therefore, broadly successfully in so far as it dealt effectively with France. It also produced some other general agreements:

● a definition of Jewish rights

● the abolition of the slave trade

● the improvement of relations between Sweden and Denmark.

However, it also saw some keen disputes, not only between Russia and Great Britain but also between Britain and France.

What changes affected the attitude of the European powers before the next congress (1818–1820)?

The next congress did not meet until October 1820, even though there were several outbursts of liberal activity in Europe before this. Metternich, in conjunction with Prussia, dealt with the student-led, liberal disorder in Germany, and they were able to suppress it without consultation with the other powers. However, matters grew more alarming when the assassination of the duc de Berri, in France in 1820, was followed by a military-led revolution in Spain, against King Ferdinand VII, in January 1820. There was also a revolution in Naples in July and in Portugal in August.

As soon as news reached Alexander I of an outbreak of revolution in Spain, he was keen to hold a second congress. He wanted immediate

---

Ferdinand VII (1784–1833)
A member of the Spanish royal house of Bourbon. He became king in 1808 when his father, Charles IV, abdicated amid popular discontent. Shortly afterwards, Ferdinand was forced to give up his crown to Napoleon, and was kept under guard in France. He returned to Spain in March 1814, abolished the liberal constitution that had been granted in 1812, and tried to impose autocratic rule. By 1820, he faced a new rebellion and only held on to his throne with military help from Louis XVIII. His harsh treatment of the liberals, and his attempt to break tradition by ensuring the succession of his daughter, Isabella (aged 3 on his death), meant that Ferdinand left his country in a start of near anarchy.

action to deal with this threat to the monarchy and was prepared to march Russian troops across Europe to help Ferdinand VII, although he accepted that a French force might be able to do the job more easily. Metternich, however, held back. While he did not approve of revolution, he remained suspicious of both Russia's and France's intentions. Britain, too, was hostile to any form of intervention, for various reasons.

- Britain had a particular interest in the affairs of Spain and the Spanish South American colonies with which Britain had forged important trading links. Those had developed during the period of war when the colonies had begun to act independently. Britain did not want a strong government restored in Spain, which might reassert control of these colonies.

- Britain also had interests in Portugal, and its colony of Brazil, which had also claimed independence. Britain had long-standing ties with Portugal and regarded this country as within its sphere of influence. It kept a naval squadron in the river Tagus and was in a position to dominate the capital, Lisbon, should there be any interference from another power.

State Paper: An official statement of policy.

- On 5 May 1820 Castlereagh issued a **State Paper** in which he repeated that Great Britain did not approve of intervention by an outside power in the internal affairs of a country.

The Quadruple Alliance, he pointed out, 'never was intended as a union for the government of the world, or for the superintendence of the internal affairs of other states'. Castlereagh argued that Spain presented no threat to the general peace of Europe nor was the principle of monarchy threatened. Spain should therefore be left to its own devices.

Consequently, it was not until Naples was affected by revolution, and Austrian interests were directly threatened, that Metternich agreed to a congress. The British attitude to the revolution in Naples was made clear before the congress met. Great Britain was, rather conveniently as regards its own interests, happy to view the revolt in Italy rather differently from that in Spain. While the British could not agree to any general plan of intervention in the affairs of other nations, they accepted that Italy had quite clearly been put under Austrian 'protection' in 1815. They therefore agreed that action might be undertaken, but it would have to be by Austria alone, not the Quadruple Alliance. The British, therefore, did not regard the proposed congress as essential for deliberation and the Foreign Minister did not attend. However, the Government sent Lord Stewart and a British delegation, instructed to oppose any project to send foreign troops into either Italy or Spain. The French also sent only two observers, Caraman and La Ferronay. They had favoured the idea of a congress, and hoped to persuade the other powers to support the institution of a charter, modelled on that of France. This would have given France prestige as the model for constitutional government and given it cause to rival Austria's influence in Italy.

What differences of opinion emerged at the Congress of Troppau (October–December 1820)?

Since the Congress of Troppau (in Silesia, modern-day Poland) only attracted the rulers and ministers of Austria, Prussia and Russia, it is not surprising that most of the decisions followed the 'Holy Alliance' principles. However, the French observers and the British delegation certainly contributed to some animated discussion.

The Spanish question promoted a good deal of debate. Metternich was not particularly concerned by the affairs of the Iberian Peninsula, which did not threaten Austrian interests. He had no wish to provoke the antagonism of the British and adopted the view that the Madrid revolution was likely to burn itself out anyway. Largely thanks to his persuasion, the issue was put to one side for the time being, and the powers also contented themselves with sending protests to Portugal.

However, Metternich did want the support of the Russians for the idea of intervention in Naples. This was particularly important to him after the new government there declared, on 1 October 1820, that it would respect the boundaries of bordering states. According to the British, this meant that there was no threat to other countries and outside intervention was not justified.

Metternich had to be sure of Russia before he could risk offending his British friends. It was essential for Austria to be in a group of three within the concert of the five great powers and at the outset he could only be sure of Prussian support. Metternich had to work hard to win over the Tsar.

Alexander I had arrived at the congress with his liberal adviser, Capodistrias, torn between support for the French idea of promoting reform in Naples to satisfy the opposition, and the Austrian desire to reassert monarchical authority. Metternich had to play on Alexander's fear of revolution. He fed him endless stories of revolutionary conspiracies master-minded from Paris, and pointed to the assassination of Kotzbue, the Russian agent in Germany, in March 1819 as an example of the threat they posed.

Protocol: System of rules about the correct way to act on important formal occasions (e.g. at meetings between the governments of different countries).

On 19 November 1820, a preliminary **protocol** was drawn up, which was to become known as the Troppau Protocol. It declared that:

> 'States that have undergone a change of government due to revolution cease to be members of the European Alliance. If, owing to such situations, immediate danger threatens other States, the Powers bind themselves by peaceful means, or if need be by arms, to bring back the guilty State into the bosom of the Great Alliance.'

This was signed by Russia, Austria and Prussia. Interestingly, its provisions were very like those Metternich had imposed in Germany in the Karlsbad decrees. The British and French could only protest. The Troppau Protocol, which was opposed to Castlereagh's State Paper of May 1820, was adopted as the Charter of the Holy Alliance. It thus introduced an idea that was not contained in the original alliance, whose principles had been wide and liberal rather than narrow and reactionary. From this point the 'Holy Alliance Powers' were Austria, Prussia and Russia alone.

What decisions were taken at the Congress of Laibach (January–May 1821)?

The Congress of Laibach (modern-day Ljubljana in Slovenia) was really a continuation of the Troppau meeting, which had adjourned for Christmas. The Holy Alliance powers attended it, along with observers from Britain and France. A mutiny among Tsar Alexander I's Semenovsky Guards in St Petersburg in December 1820 had provided the final straw that won him over to Metternich's way of thinking. His words, 'under no circumstances would I do in 1820 what I did in 1812. You (Metternich) have not changed, but I', must have been music to the Austrian minister's ears. Ferdinand of Naples was also present, having received the permission of the rebels in Naples to go to the congress to make a case for the changes there. The new regime had rejected the idea of a French-style charter, and before Ferdinand left for Laibach they had made him swear to uphold the liberal constitution the rebels sought. However, the King now pleaded for intervention.

The Holy Alliance duly stressed their determination to help and the British spokesman, Lord Stewart, once more declared that intervention was unjustified since there was no direct threat to international peace. However, there was no real effort to reach a compromise. Austria was given Holy Alliance support to send in the army. On 19 January 1821, Britain made a formal public protest against this action. By 24 March 1821, the Austrian army and local royalist troops had succeeded in crushing the Naples rebellion at Rieti. The short-lived Piedmontese rising of March 1821 was also suppressed by Austrian troops, although there was less excuse for this action in a country outside the immediate Austrian area of influence.

In theory, the campaigns were the work of the Holy Alliance powers, acting under the terms of the Troppau Protocol. However, Austria was anxious to avoid the Tsar's offer of troops entering western Europe both on its own account and in the hope of retaining some favour with Great Britain. Nevertheless, the action was of great importance internationally in that a precedent had been set for intervention in the internal affairs of states. It was now going to be much harder for Austria to resist the Russian desire to intervene in Spain. However, no decisions were taken on this at Laibach and it was only just as the congress was breaking up that news reached the diplomats of a new revolt. On 2 April 1821, Greek unrest had developed into a war of independence against Turkish rule. No decisions were taken on the issue, but it must have filled the diplomats with a sense of foreboding as they returned home.

Why was the Congress of Verona (October–December 1822) the last great congress?

By the time of the Congress of Verona (Austrian Venetia) in 1822, the unanimity which had brought Russia, Prussia, Austria and Great Britain together in the Quadruple Alliance, had been virtually destroyed. The historian Franklin Ford, in *Europe 1780–1830* (1970), refers to the Verona Congress as 'a funeral service for earlier hopes of co-operation between Great Britain and the Continent'. Austria and Russia, who viewed one another suspiciously, dominated it. Metternich had originally hoped that he and Castlereagh would be able to work together to restrain Alexander. They had held preliminary meetings in Hanover in 1821 to this end. However, Metternich's plans were thwarted when, in August 1822, after a long physical and nervous decline, Castlereagh committed suicide. His successor, George Canning, refused to attend the Congress at all. Consequently, the British sent Wellington, as an observer. The French also sent representatives in the same role.

Metternich feared Tsar Alexander's intentions in the Greek affair. He suspected that he might use the excuse of Greece and Russia's shared Orthodox religion to intervene on behalf of the Greeks and increase Russian influence at the expense of Turkey (see section 6.5). However, he managed, with some difficulty, to persuade Alexander to stay out of Greece, and they made a joint declaration that the revolt was 'a rash and criminal enterprise'.

The Spanish question was again fiercely debated. The situation there had grown worse, with extremists gaining influence on both sides, plunging the country into a state of near civil war. In May, King Ferdinand VII appealed to the monarchs of Europe for help, which the French, under the Comte de Villèle, and the **Ultras** hoped to supply. They had no sympathy for the rebels and saw this as a way of regaining some influence in European affairs, thereby distracting the critics of the government. France had always regarded Spain as within its sphere of influence, and this seemed an opportunity to show its strength. An army was built up in the

---

> **Comte Jean Baptiste de Villèle (1773–1854)**
> Villèle was Louis XVIII and Charles X's chief minister (1821–1828). He led the 'Ultra' faction in the French Chamber, which favoured conservative policies. They believed in French greatness, and had no more sympathy for the liberal rebels in Spain than they did for liberal political opinion at home.

Ultras: The Ultra royalists were strong supporters of traditional monarchical control. They wanted the king to recreate, as far as was possible, the position of the monarch ruling with the support of the aristocracy – as before the Revolution. Led by the Comte d'Artois, the Ultras included powerful men such as Polignac, Montmorency, Chateaubriand and Villèle. They came to dominate the new Chambers of Deputies and Peers.

south of France on the pretext that it was necessary to stop the anarchy spreading to France itself. This alarmed Metternich, who feared France would try to set up a French-style constitutional monarchy in Spain. The British too, and particularly Wellington, who had fought to rid the peninsula of French influence, were hostile to the French stance. The Tsar, meantime, grew increasingly impatient. He was totally committed to action and, to Metternich's horror, repeatedly offered troops to join an international force.

In this atmosphere of suspicion, little was achieved at the Verona Congress. In the end, Metternich proposed that all the powers should send diplomatic notes to Spain at the same time, and that only if these were rejected would they have a reason to justify intervention. The British would have none of this, and on 30 November 1822 Wellington left Verona, refusing to be associated with their plans. By the time the congress broke up a month later, there was little unity left.

Was 'the Congress System' a failure?

What happened after 1822?

After Verona, there were no more comparable meetings. There was an attempt to deal with the Greek rebellion at St Petersburg in 1825, but the meeting was not attended by all the powers and reached no decisions. There were congresses later in the century, but these dealt with individual issues, usually in the aftermath of war, as in the Congress of Berlin in 1878. Whereas the period of the great Congresses (1815–22) had tried to bring all the powers together to work in the interests of peace, later meetings were rather different. They were more like those of the past, with individual countries often trying to steal an advantage over each other. Franklin Ford wrote, 'after Verona now one and then another major state took the initiative, employing means and encountering responses, most of which would have been familiar to 18th century statesmen'.

1. Why did the French intervene in Spain?

2. Why were the British concerned by this attack on Cadiz?

This print shows the French attack on the Trocadero Fort at Cadiz, August 1823

If we accept that it is possible to talk of a 'congress system' between 1815 and 1822, the problems of the Verona Congress and its aftermath would suggest that the system proved a failure. In 1823, despite the Verona agreements, France took independent action. It did not abide by the Verona promise to send a diplomatic note to Spain at the same time as the other powers. Instead, it sent an army of 100,000 men, under the duc d'Angoulême, across the Pyrenees on 6 April 1823 to restore the authority of the Spanish king. The forces were victorious in August–September 1823, much to the relief of the Tsar. However, this was achieved by one nation acting alone, in defiance of another great power, Britain, and independently from any Congress decisions.

What is the case for calling the system a failure?

It could be argued that, in themselves, the congresses achieved nothing. There was, in reality, little link between the congresses and the actions taken. For example, the ending of the military occupation of France would have happened, under the terms of the Vienna agreement, without the congress held at Aix-La-Chappelle. It is also likely that Austria would have intervened to suppress the Italian revolts, regardless of the decisions at Laibach and Troppau. Since meetings of ambassadors and diplomats continued to take place, as in the past, the congresses were really unnecessary.

Only the simplest problems were sorted out at the congresses, such as the issue of the reintegration of France into Europe and the suppression of the revolts in Italy. Rulers were happy to deal with problems, such as the troubles in Germany, without reference to the Congresses when they could. What is more, the most difficult international problems were left untouched. The congresses produced no solution to the problems of the Spanish civil war, the rebellious colonies, or the Greek revolt.

By bringing the powers together, the congresses also forced them apart. Historian E.L. Woodward, in *War and Peace in Europe 1815–1870* (1931) wrote, 'The Great Powers were united by their fear of Napoleon. They were divided upon almost every issue of importance after 1815.' Constant meetings forced them to air their differing views on topics such as intervention and the balance of power. In some ways, this made their positions look more fundamentally opposed than they really were. Britain and Austria, for example, really had a good deal in common in their attitude to Russia and French ambition. However, the Troppau Protocol – accepted by Prussia, Austria and Russia, but rejected by France and Britain – seemed to create two different camps. Howard Nicolson wrote of the years after Laibach, 'The Great Coalition was thus finally dissolved; the Concert of Europe had disintegrated; the Holy Alliance had succeeded in destroying the Quadruple Alliance; the conference system had failed.'

How might failure be explained?

The problem with 'The Congress System' was that the principles upon which it was based were never clearly defined. Castlereagh continually argued that the Congresses tried to alter the principle of the Quadruple Alliance. As the British saw it, changes could be made to the 1815 settlement provided the essential balance of power in Europe remained. However, the Tsar acted on the assumption that the Holy Alliance was part of the general alliance and that the job of the congresses was to carry out its principles. This, as later defined even more clearly in the Troppau Protocol, implied a rigid support of the 1815 settlement, with action to be taken against any disruption. The problem was that the Great Powers all had their own interests. In a system with no means of compulsion, they were free to pursue these interests as they saw fit. They interpreted 'principles' in accordance with their own national interests. They attended and used congresses when it was to their advantage to do so.

Above all, neither of the two strongest powers in Europe at this time, Britain or Russia, were prepared to be flexible. They could not see any reason why they should be so. The British position became even more anti-compromise after Canning replaced Castlereagh as Foreign Minister. Although the basis of British policy was made clear by Castlereagh, Canning was much happier than his predecessor to reject the whole Congress idea. He declared that things were returning 'to a wholesome state again' and 'every country for himself and God help us all'.

What is the case against calling the system a failure?
Even if it is accepted that 'The Congress System' had its faults, it should be remembered that there had been effective diplomacy in these years without recourse to war. France had recovered its international standing without destroying the Quadruple Alliance. Revolutions had been quelled and Russian ambitions had been held in check. Congresses may have been unnecessary, given that the other diplomatic channels remained open, but they must have helped speed up decision making in these years. In the days when a journey from London to Vienna might take a fortnight, and to St Petersburg four weeks, the advantages of assembling the European statesmen together for the purposes of discussion were enormous. The period of the congresses had therefore laid the basis for a stable international order in a difficult period. It must be remembered that this was a unique experiment in co-operation and, since there was no real 'system' behind it anyway, it is probably unfair to have expected it to do more than it did.

1. What were the main European issues discussed in the period of the Congresses? Which were resolved successfully and which were not?

2. What differences of opinion made agreement between the powers difficult?

3. Was The Congress System a failure? Give reasons for your answer.

6.4 How did the affairs of Spain, Portugal and their former colonies affect international relations, 1822–1830?

After 1822, their own interests increasingly guided the Great Powers. This was particularly apparent in the affairs of the Iberian peninsula. The French acted independently by sending troops and temporarily occupying Spain, while the British ignored their earlier anti-interventionist stance by sending aid to Portugal and by adopting an independent line over the former Spanish and Portuguese colonies in America.

How did the affairs of the Iberian peninsula affect France and Great Britain?

The French-aided restoration of Ferdinand VII in Spain briefly linked the French and Russians. Russia had been the chief supporter of intervention against the liberals and was delighted by the French success. The French had ignored the despatch sent by Canning, the British Foreign Secretary, demanding no permanent French military occupation of Spain and no interference with the Spanish colonies or Portugal. Although they had not, in practice, acted contrary to these demands, tension with Great Britain had run high. The restoration was a clear demonstration of the French military recovery. It was with dismay, however, that Louis XVIII watched Ferdinand re-establish his rule by executing hundreds of liberals and imprisoning or exiling thousands more. He denounced these events as a betrayal of the honour of the French soldiers but, to critics at home and abroad, it seemed as though France had placed itself on the side of reaction.

Developments in Portugal, after 1822, added to the British unease and led to independent action, which appeared contrary to the anti-interventionist stance the British had always adopted at the congresses. In 1821 John VI had returned to Portugal from Brazil, where he had fled during the Napoleonic wars. He had accepted a constitution, only to abandon it in 1822, but he had continued to believe in some form of parliamentary rule. However, his death in 1826 left a difficult situation. His son, Dom Pedro, introduced a charter of liberties, but then abdicated in favour of his young daughter, Maria. While a regency council on her behalf tried to rule constitutionally, John's second son, Dom Miguel, tried to establish traditional, **absolutist rule**. He was encouraged by the powers of the Holy Alliance. In December 1826, Canning sent 4,000 troops in response to pleas from the legal government. Not until reassured by Dom Miguel's promises in 1827, did the British withdraw. However, Dom Miguel's subsequent attacks on the liberals sparked off a civil war.

Absolutist rule: Power that is not restricted by a constitution, meaning a set of rules or laws. This was the 'traditional' means of rule in Europe before the French Revolution and, in many places, long after it.

How successful was Great Britain in defending its interests in the former colonies, and how did this affect the Concert of Europe?

The issue of the former colonies in America was directly related to the Spanish and Portuguese problems. There had been a rebellion in the Spanish colonies of Latin America against Spanish rule in 1810, when the colonists had taken advantage of Spain's involvement in the French wars in Europe. After 1815, as Spain was again preoccupied with revolt at home, they had continued their struggle for independence. Britain had taken advantage of Spain's weak control in wartime, expanding its trade to the Spanish colonies when European markets were closed to it. The French invasion of Spain in 1823 was therefore a double threat, in that it threatened Portugal, and could lead to the French helping Ferdinand to reimpose control on his colonies, to Britain's loss.

When the French proved successful in Spain, Canning was determined to defend British interests. He held a series of meetings with the French ambassador in London, the Prince of Polignac. The Polignac Memorandum of 9–12 October 1823 was a record of their conversations, in which the British appeared to have secured what they wanted. The French declared that they had no intention of intervening by force in the colonies, while Canning disclaimed any intention of recognising the colonies while there was a possibility of Spain coming to some agreement with them. The memorandum was published in March 1824, and came to be recognised as a statement that Britain would not tolerate interference from another power when its own interests were at stake.

In December 1823, the American President, James Monroe, appeared to support Britain's attitude to the colonies in the declaration made in his annual message to **Congress**. This was later known as the Monroe Doctrine. It made two clear points.

Congress: In this instance, it means the elected group of politicians that is responsible for making the law in the USA. The alternative meaning used in this chapter refers to a large meeting of representatives of different countries.

● 'The American continents are henceforth not to be considered as subject to future colonisation by any European power.'

● 'We owe it to … the amicable relations existing between the United States and those (European) powers, to declare that we should consider any attempt on their part to extend their political system to any portion of this hemisphere as dangerous to our peace and security.'

This was not, in fact, quite what Canning had hoped for. The British had settlements along the Canadian border and Canning would have preferred a joint declaration on the issue of the Spanish and Portuguese colonies only. However, the American declaration did broadly fit with Canning's policies and it helped to justify Britain's refusal to participate in a proposed congress to discuss the affairs of the colonies in 1824.

1. How successfully did Canning uphold British interests in the Iberian peninsula and the Americas? What was the effect of this on international relations?

2. Using the information Sections 6.3 and 6.4, would you agree that Canning's policies continued the course adopted by Castlereagh during the Congress period? Explain your answer.

In 1824, without waiting for a statement from any other government, Britain recognised several former colonies – Argentina, Mexico and Colombia – as independent republics. The same year the independence of Brazil was accepted, under its constitutional emperor, Pedro I, eldest son of John VI of Portugal. These were all relatively stable states. Canning did not recognise those where fighting was still in progress. He told the House of Commons, in December 1826, 'I have called the new world into existence to redress the balance of the old ... I resolved that, if France had Spain, it should not be Spain with the Indies.' He was, of course, able to act as he did because of the power of the Royal Navy, but he liked to play on the 'morality' of his actions.

A conference in Paris 1826, which Canning again refused to attend, could do little more than criticise the British action. Canning had certainly been successful in upholding British interests, but this was clearly at the expense of the 'Concert of Europe'.

6.5 How, and why, did the Greek struggle for independence affect the powers of Europe?

What sort of character is shown in the centre of the picture? What influence might he have had?

The Greeks were just one national group within the vast Turkish or Ottoman Empire, which had been built up by Turkey's once formidable military strength. As can be seen from the map opposite, it stretched from the borders of Austria and Russia, through the Balkans and Asia Minor to Persia, Syria and parts of Arabia, Egypt and the coast of north Africa. Since it contained many nationalities and religions, government had never been easy. It had only survived by allowing a certain amount of local rule. By

Riots at the beginning of the Greek War of Independence

Janissaries: Special high-ranking Turkish soldiers who had helped Turkey to carve out an empire from the 14th century. By the 19th century, however, they had become an independent force. Their oppressive behaviour in the provinces, had led to resentment and rebellion. They could no longer be relied upon militarily and were disbanded in 1826.

the 19th century, Turkey's army of **Janissaries** was in decline and Russia had defeated Turkey in war in 1768–74. The bureaucracy was inefficient, privileged groups – especially religious ones – opposed all suggestion of reform, and the Empire appeared unable to halt developing unrest.

From the beginning of the century, the Turks' control of south-east Europe had been under attack in Greece and Serbia. The inspiration of the French Revolution, a growing awareness of nationalist ideas and a developing middle class of Greek merchants who had benefited from the wars in Europe to extend their control of trade in the eastern Mediterranean, had helped to inspire resistance to their inefficient masters. In 1814, the Philiké Hetairia had been founded, to campaign for the liberation of Greece. It was, however, the outright demand for independence, made by the Greeks in April 1821, that brought matters to a head. It turned the issue into one affecting the other powers of Europe. It was generally accepted that Turkey could not survive as an empire without some change, but each power had its own particular view of what should happen.

The Ottoman Empire in 1815; (inset) Greece in 1830

What were the attitudes of the powers to the weakness of Turkey in 1822?

Russia

Russia had a particular interest in Turkey as its neighbour to the south. It had fought several successful wars against the Turks (1768–1812), which had brought the Russians to the north of the Black Sea and the northern Caucasus. By the Treaty of Kutchuk-Kainardji in 1774, the Russians had established three important rights:

● Freedom of navigation for Russian merchant shipping on the Black Sea.

● The right of passage for merchants through the Black Sea Straits, the Bosphorus and the Dardanelles, into the Mediterranean.

● The right of protection for Orthodox Christians in the Turkish Empire.

Russia's chief concern was to keep the crucial Black Sea Straits in Turkish, or Russian, hands. This was vital for the export of Russian grain. However, its views on the future of Turkey were not fixed and were to vary through the century. Russia had three potential courses of action:

1. To look for further Russian expansion in Asia Minor or the Balkans, at Turkey's expense.

2. To support nationalist movements against Turkey, in the hope of creating states that would be dependent on Russia

3. To send aid to Turkey against its rebels, so maintaining it as a weak neighbour and therefore subject to Russian influence.

Muslims: People who believe in Islam and live according to its rules.

Religion also played a part in Alexander's reaction to the issue of the Greeks. They were fellow Orthodox Christians (see page 154), while their masters were **Muslims**. The Tsar believed himself God's representative of the Orthodox religion and had promised to protect all Orthodox Christians. In the course of the century, Russia was to adopt or neglect this promise, according to how it best suited the policy of the moment. However, it must be remembered that, at the time of the Greek revolt, Alexander was going through a spiritual phase of his life, and this may well have been an important consideration for him, if not for all his advisers.

Great Britain

The policies of the British towards the decaying Turkish Empire were not clear-cut either. Although generally anti-interventionist, British sympathies were on the side of the Greeks in their struggle for independence in the 1820s. There was a somewhat irrational sympathy for the Greeks from the English upper classes, reared as they were on the history and literature of classical civilisation. They believed they were heroes, fighting for the re-establishment of the great Greek civilisation.

There had also been growing trade and investment in Turkey after 1815. Britain had acquired the Ionian Islands and Malta in 1815 (shown on page 169) and had trading links in the area, as well as important communication links through the Eastern Mediterranean and overland to India. It feared any increase of Russian control in this area and so was, in general, committed to the preservation of the Ottoman Empire. It was, at times, difficult to reconcile this belief with the anti-Turkish, anti-Russian mood at home. Initially, however, Castleregh, and Canning after him, took the view that any aid to the Greeks could only increase Turkish weakness and Russian power.

British cartoon entitled 'Turkey in danger'

1. Who do you think the bear represents?

2. What does this cartoon tell us about British views?

Austria

Austrian interests, at this time, lay in Italy and central Europe. So, although Austria shared a border, it had no plans to expand in the direction of Turkey in the first half of the 19th century. However, Austria did fear an expansion of the influence of Russia in that area and believed it preferable to help, and so preserve, the Ottoman Empire, in order to stop Russia growing stronger. Austria was also anxious about the spread of nationalism, which could cause the break up of its own multinational Empire.

France

France enjoyed well-established political and commercial links with Turkey. The French had even negotiated special privileges for European traders in the Empire, including immunity from Turkish law. The King of France had been recognised as protector of the Roman Catholics in the Empire, and had influence in Constantinople. Napoleon's expedition to Egypt, 1798–99, had temporarily upset this good relationship, but links between Egypt and France survived the war. Mehemet Ali, the Pasha of Egypt, a local ruler under the Sultan, was regarded as a French *protégé*. France was always looking for ways to expand its influence in the Mediterranean. Nevertheless, although its connections might seem to have favoured co-operation with Turkey, the French upper classes, like the British, were also infected by 'Philhellenism' (love of the Greeks), which made its policies uncertain.

Protégé: Person who is under the protection or patronage of another (usually someone older, or of greater experience).

Prussia

Prussia was the Great Power least interested in the affairs of a distant country like Turkey. Nevertheless, it was a committed member of the Holy Alliance and looked to Austria and Russia for leadership. Since these two powerful nations could not agree over the Greek affair, the Prussian position was difficult. Prussia lacked the strength to act as a mediator. Instead, Prussia tended to follow Austria, whose backing it most needed, but it remained very cautious of offending Russia.

What was the initial reaction to the Greek Revolt, 1821–1824?

Prince Alexander Ypsilanti, a Greek but also a Tsarist army officer, first raised the revolt in Moldavia in April 1821. He was aiming to win freedom for the Greek and Romanian Christians. This rebellion collapsed in June, since the Romanians hated the Greeks even more than the Turks! However, a sympathetic Greek revolt broke out on Morea (see map of Greece on page 169). It then spread to all of Greece and the Greek Islands. As the Turks tried to enforce control, both Christians and Muslims slaughtered their enemies in a bloodbath. By the summer of 1821, Morea had been freed from the Turks. The success of the Greeks made all too clear the weakness of the corrupt Turkish Janissaries.

Russia felt compelled to intervene. In July 1821, the Russian ambassador, Stroganoff, presented a four-point ultimatum to Turkey demanding that it fulfil its treaty obligations, one of these being to allow the Christian and Islamic religions to co-exist peacefully. On 18 July, Turkey rejected these demands and the ambassador was withdrawn, making war look inevitable. Metternich was fearful of the Tsar's intentions, and met informally with Castlereagh in Hanover. Here they decided to work for the maintenance of peace between Turkey and Russia, as well as to press Turkey to moderate behaviour.

Throughout 1821 and 1822, the Tsar wavered from one course to another, torn between the policy of caution advocated by his Foreign Minister, Nesselrode, and the interventionist pro-Greek policy of his friend and adviser, Capodistrias. The matter was, of course, complicated by the agreement entered into at Troppau. According to the Troppau Protocol, he should not assist the Greeks since they were engaged in rebellion, which had been declared a crime.

The Greeks continued to have the upper hand, although the Turks took bouts of vengeance: for example, the massacre of 25,000 and enslavement of 47,000 inhabitants of the Island of Chios in 1822.

'Belligerent rights': The recognition that a race or group is entitled to the claims it is fighting for. The British were saying that they would treat the Greeks as an independent nation, even though they were still fighting to establish this.

In March 1823, Canning granted the Greeks **'belligerent rights'**, to the annoyance of Russia and Austria. Canning's motive was to protect British shipping from Greek piracy and to please the upper classes. In January 1824, Alexander sent a note to the powers, proposing the creation of three Greek principalities owing allegiance to Turkey and garrisoned by Turkish troops. It satisfied neither side, as it involved more territory than the Greeks actually controlled but not as much as they claimed. A conference of the representatives of the powers in St Petersburg failed to come to any conclusions, as Metternich repeatedly tried to block any suggestions of pro-Greek intervention.

How did the situation change 1824–1827?

Vassal: A ruler who acknowledges the overlordship of another.

In December 1824, the situation was transformed. The sultan appealed to his **vassal**, Mehemet Ali, Pasha of Egypt, for aid. He possessed the most efficient army in the Turkish Empire. Bribed with the promise of rewards for his aid, including Morea if he could reconquer it, Mehemet Ali sent his son, Ibrahim Pasha, with 10,000 men to Crete and then to Morea where they landed in February 1825. The Greeks, weakened by internal rivalries, now began to suffer defeats (1824–25).

It was clear that, unless the other powers intervened, the revolt would be suppressed. Public opinion in France and Britain was inflamed. Lord Byron contributed thousands of pounds to the Greek cause, organising military contingents, before dying of disease at Missolonghi in 1824. Writers and poets such as Percy Shelley inspired the view that this was a war for civilisation. Meanwhile, the Russians focused on the fact that Greeks were members of the same Orthodox Church and the Tsar was subject to increasing pressure in Russia to help the Greeks. He was angered at the failure of the other powers to support his attempts at a solution at the St Petersburg Conference. In August 1825, Nesselrode asserted that Russia would follow its own views. This was a rejection of the Concert of Europe and the stage seemed set for war. However, a number of agreements and incidents took place before the Russians finally intervened.

In 1825, Tsar Alexander, whom Metternich had managed to persuade to his point of view, was succeeded by Nicholas I who was determined on a more independent policy for Russia. Charles X of France, while no friend of liberals, was affected by the pro-Greek fervour that was sweeping his country. He was also anxious to restore French influence in the eastern Mediterranean. George Canning, also influenced by public opinion, became convinced of the need to co-operate with Russia to prevent it acting alone.

An Anglo–Russian agreement to grant Greek independence, the St Petersburg Protocol, was signed in April 1826. This committed the Russians and British to work together to make a settlement with Turkey. They planned to establish a self-governing Greek state under the rule of the Sultan, and with some Turkish control over the choice of ruler.

In the Treaty of London (6 July 1827), France joined the Anglo–Russian agreement. An extra clause was inserted which stated that, if either Greece or Turkey rejected the proposals, all three powers would give naval support to the other side. Austria and Prussia refused to join this agreement, which was contrary to all Metternich had worked for. 'The Continental alliance on which our peace and prosperity rests has ceased to exist', he moaned. The Great Powers were quite openly following their own interests.

Russia, pursuing its own dispute with Turkey, persuaded the Turks to sign the Convention of Akkerman in 1826. By this, the Turks promised that they would respect the earlier treaties made between Russia and Turkey, with their promises regarding the rights of the Christians in the Empire. This encouraged Nicholas I and revived Greek hopes.

Hopes of a peaceful settlement were dashed by Ibrahim Pasha's continuing success. He recaptured Navarino in 1825, Missolonghi in 1826 and Athens a year later. Although the Greeks had reunited and elected Capodistria, Alexander's old adviser, as their President, their chances of survival without outside aid were looking slim. The Sultan, encouraged by this success, rejected the offer of mediation.

A British, French and Russian squadron was therefore given instructions to blockade Morea. The English Admiral Codrington carried out some quite extraordinary orders: 'to block all Turkish and Egyptian supplies without letting the operation "degenerate into hostilities"'. Canning died on 8 August 1827 and did not live to see the consequences of his policy.

The allied force located the Turkish–Egyptian fleet at harbour in Navarino bay in September and maintained a watchful eye on events from the sea. Ibrahim Pasha did suspend his operations for several weeks awaiting discussions but, on 20 October 1827, Codrington received news that Muslim armies had restarted hostilities on shore. He sailed his fleet to

Navarino to intimidate the Muslims by entering the bay as if prepared for battle. As they entered, an Egyptian boat fired upon a ship, even though it flew a flag of truce. Admiral Codrington returned fire and, amid some confusion, sunk the greater part of Turkish–Egyptian fleet in a little under three hours. It had been British policy only to compel the Turks to accept mediation. Their action now weakened Turkey and made the crisis worse.

Why did the Russians intervene?

The Navarino incident had several disastrous consequences and opened the way to Russian intervention.

● The Sultan blamed Russia. He repudiated the Akkerman Convention and declared a *jihad* (holy war) against Russia.

● The Turks totally rejected any mediation from the three powers.

● The forces of Ibrahim Pasha were now stuck in Greece, which clearly stood no chance against them.

● The British government was embarrassed by the whole affair. The Duke of Wellington, who had been unsympathetic to Canning's policy, became Prime Minister in January 1828, and had to deal with the consequences of the British action.

● In March 1828, Russia announced its intention to go to war in the Balkan area because of the Turkish repudiation of the Convention of Akkerman. Despite the efforts of Wellington and his Foreign Secretary, Lord Aberdeen, Russia declared war on Turkey on 24 April 1828, with French, but not British approval.

What were the consequences of Russian intervention?

As the Russians fought and encountered stiff resistance in the Romanian principalities, Wellington tried to find a way out of the tangle by negotiation. In July it was agreed that France should send troops to evict the Egyptians from Morea. While the French attacked and concluded their own armistice, Admiral Codrington drew up the Convention of Alexandria with Mehemet Ali in August. By this agreement he would withdraw his forces, leaving only a token force of 1,200 men. In December 1828, ambassadors met at Constantinople to draw up recommendations for a new Greek State.

By June 1829 the war had turned in favour of the Russians and, in August, they took Adrianople. This was the nearest that Russian troops had ever come to the capital, Constantinople. With another Russian army advancing, the Sultan sued for peace. Weakened by disease and the long marches, the Russians agreed to negotiate with the Turks.

On 14 September 1829, the Treaty of Adrianople was signed. The Russians made substantial gains in Asia Minor. These included the entire Danube delta on the Black Sea, with two Black Sea ports, and recognition of their claims to Georgia and Armenia. Other gains were a large cash indemnity and a safeguard of Christian rights in the Romanian principalities of Moldavia and Wallachia. In return, Russia evacuated their recent conquests. This suited the Tsar, whose attitude to Turkey was already changing. The Kochubei Committee, one of Tsar Nichols I's many secret committees (see Chapter 10), produced a report on 16 September 1829. This concluded that it was in Russia's interests to keep Turkey weak rather than destroying or reducing it. The destruction of Turkey, it argued, would only lead to other powers claiming influence in this area, while a reduction in the size of Turkey would allow change

George Hamilton Gordon (1784–1860), Earl of Aberdeen
Aberdeen entered the House of Lords in 1806 and enjoyed a long political career. He was Ambassador in Vienna in 1813 and served as Tory Foreign Secretary under Wellington (1828–30). He took this position again, under Peel, in 1841 and, adopting a less aggressive approach than Palmerston, spent the next five years pursuing the difficult policy of co-operation with France. He was Prime Minister (1852–55).

that might make it more vigorous and keen to win back land in the Caucasus. So, it concluded, 'the advantages of maintaining the Ottoman Empire are greater than the inconvenience it causes'. Consequently, Russian policy became more subject to national interests than to any abstract religious views or principles.

At Adrianople, the Turks accepted the terms of the Treaty of London, which had offered Greek independence under Turkish rule. However, before the final terms were signed on 30 November 1829, the British, Russian and French representatives increased their demands to include absolute independence for Greece (minus Crete, which would go to the Egyptians). Matters were not finally settled until 1832. By an agreement in 1830, Greece was declared independent under the protection of Britain, Russia and France, and the boundaries were established. However, the first ruler, President Capodistrias, was assassinated in October 1831. He was replaced by the Bavarian, Prince Otto, who became King of Greece. In the Treaty of London of 1832, the five Great Powers finally accepted Greece as an independent kingdom.

What was the impact of the Greek Revolt on international relations?

1. Explain why the powers of Europe viewed the Greek rebellion in a different way from rebellions elsewhere in Europe.

2. Was the policy of (a) Britain and (b) Russia, towards the issue of Greek independence, successful? Give reasons to support your answer.

3. How, and why, did the Greek Revolt affect international relations?

The success of the Greeks represented a crushing defeat for Metternich. The negotiations in St Petersburg in 1824–25 had failed because of the opposition of Austria and Prussia. Consequently, Austria had found itself virtually excluded from the Great Power negotiations during the last years of the crisis. It was unwilling to support the decisions already taken but was also unable to prevent them. This defeat was doubly frightening from Metternich's point of view. Not only did it show the weakness of Austria as an influential power in Europe, but it also showed the potential force of revolutionaries. He was horrified by what Franklin Ford has called 'the emergence of an international public opinion endorsing the national and constitutional goals of the Greek rebels'. Most of all, he feared that the success of the Greeks would inspire liberal ideas elsewhere and, to some extent, he was to be proved correct.

The breakdown of the Holy Alliance and the alignment of Britain and France with Russia did not, however, survive the impact of revolution nearer home in 1830. It could be argued that the affairs of Greece and Turkey had been viewed in quite a different way, and for very different reasons, from those of the rest of Europe. In any case, Russian policy changed after the war of 1827–28. Its failure to make substantial gains, the findings of the Kochubei Committee, and the fright of the 1830 revolutions in Europe meant that Nicholas became less self-interested after 1830.

6.6 What was the effect of the 1830 Revolutions and the continuing struggles in Spain and Portugal on the relationship between the powers, 1830–1840?

In 1830, there was another revolution in France. The 'legitimate' Bourbon monarchy, which had been established in 1814–15, was overthrown, and Louis-Philippe came to power. He was regarded as a 'middle-class' king, and he ruled with a more restricted constitution. (See Chapter 7.) The revolution soon spread to Belgium, Poland and Italy, while troubles continued in Spain and Portugal. Once again, the major powers were faced with important decisions regarding the future stability of Europe.

How did the Great Powers react to the troubles of 1830?

What was the impact of the Revolution in France?

The eastern powers were naturally alarmed as the French Revolution revived memories of the earlier troubles in France. They still regarded France as the main danger in Europe, and feared that the new France might wish to expand as the old revolutionary France had done. Metternich wanted to intervene. However, the other European powers would not agree to send troops to France. Britain disapproved of intervention and the new Whig government of November 1830, which included Viscount Palmerston as its Foreign Secretary, welcomed the change in France. Russia and Prussia might have given Austria support, but they had their own problems in Poland and Germany respectively. Metternich even considered a single-handed Austrian invasion, but was told by the Austrian High Command that they could not afford a war.

When Metternich met Nesselrode of Russia at Carlsbad in August, they agreed that there should be no interference in France provided the troubles did not affect 'the material interests of Europe or the internal peace of the various States composing it'. However, Tsar Nicholas refused to recognise Louis-Philippe until January 1831. This destroyed the co-operation between France and Russia that had come about from their shared interests of intervention in Spain and in support of the Greeks.

Why did the Belgian revolt create problems for the powers?

The Kingdom of the Netherlands, created in 1815, had not worked. By the 1820s, there was considerable discontent among the Belgians who resented the enforced use of the Dutch language and submission to Dutch officials. They also protested over what they considered to be unfair taxation, and the whole issue was made worse by the fact that the southern Belgians were Catholic while the Dutch were Calvinists. In August 1830, a riot in Brussels turned into a full-scale revolt when Dutch troops tried to restore order. By September, most of Belgium was in revolt and a provisional government was set up. The King of the Netherlands' appeal for aid was quite legitimate as the rebellion was undermining one of the provisions of 1815. However, conditions in 1830 were rather different from those in 1815. The rebellion caused the Duke of Wellington to remark that it was 'a devilish bad business'.

The gravest fear of the other powers was of intervention by the new 'liberal' French government in support of fellow Catholic Belgians. The eastern powers were horrified at this upset to the settlement and the effect of revolution generally. Since the Napoleonic wars had partly been fought to drive the French from this area, the prospect of armies once more travelling north was most alarming. Although their reasoning might be different, the British were just as concerned as the eastern powers. They did not want the Belgian ports falling into French hands. There was also the complication that Prussia might, based on the terms of the Vienna Settlement, feel obliged to go to the aid of the King of the Netherlands.

In August 1830, the French declared that they would intervene in Belgium if Prussia were to send troops to help the King of the Netherlands. The crisis the other powers so desperately wanted to avoid looked imminent.

How were the problems resolved?

By October 1830, the Belgians claimed their independence. To diffuse the situation, the Prussians and French agreed to a policy of non-intervention. In November, a conference of ambassadors took place in London, between

British, French and Dutch representatives. They advised that the old frontiers of the United Provinces (Holland) and the Austrian Netherlands (Belgium) be re-established, but they could not agree on three issues:

- The position of Luxembourg, which was part of the Kingdom of Holland but also within the German Confederation.

- Exactly where the boundaries should be drawn.

- What type of government the new Belgian State should have.

The Dutch were, in any case, still hopeful of restoring control, while Russia, hostile to the revolution, was threatening to send an army to crush it. Matters grew tense in the spring of 1831, when the French called up 80,000 men. However, Russia's inclination to act was curbed by the revolution in Poland from November 1830 to October 1831. Once again, Austria could not act alone, and Prussia was anxious to avoid confrontation with Britain.

Meanwhile, the arguments continued. It was obvious that the union could not be maintained, but the French argued that Belgium should not have a settlement it disliked forced upon it. Britain, for its part, was horrified by a French proposal that the Duke de Nemours, Louis-Philippe's second son, should be made king. Fortunately for international peace, Louis-Philippe chose to decline the offer and by April 1831 agreed to accept Leopold of Saxe-Coburg-Gotha, uncle of the future Queen Victoria and a neutral candidate. By June 1831, Talleyrand-Périgord, now French ambassador to London, had agreed to terms of Belgian independence with the British, leaving the issue of Luxembourg for separate negotiations.

However, Europe's fears were still to come about. The Dutch chose to reject the terms and abandoned the **armistice** in August 1831. The Dutch promptly defeated the Belgians, so the French army marched north and by 20 August had driven the Dutch from Belgium. This led to new articles of separation in October 1831.

The Dutch still remained hostile and another French force had to be sent, with consent of powers in December 1832, to evict them from Antwerp. Not until May 1833 did the King of the Netherlands accept a truce, and even then he withheld his signature from the final treaty until May 1839 when the financial pressure grew too great. In this, a smaller Luxembourg was given to Holland and the neutrality of Belgium was guaranteed as permanent by the Great Powers. This was an important revision of the 1815 settlement, and remarkably was solved without a major war.

Why was no one prepared to help the Poles in their rebellion?

Events in Poland followed a very different path from those in Belgium or Greece. In November 1830, following the events in France, the Tsar prepared for intervention there by ordering a **mobilisation** in Poland. However, the Warsaw garrison, whose young officers and cadets had been attracted by liberal, nationalist ideas, was sympathetic to the changes in France. Joined by students from Warsaw and Vilna, they disobeyed Russian orders and rose in revolt against Russian rule. By January 1831 the Polish Diet had proclaimed the deposition of Nicholas I and had, in effect, declared war on Russia.

The rebels enjoyed some early successes because the Polish army outnumbered the Russian forces in Poland, but they failed to attract the peasants. These were more hostile to the Polish landowners who now led the rebellion, than to the Russians, who had treated them relatively leniently. Division in the rebel faction also weakened the opposition.

Armistice: Agreement between countries who are at war with one another, to stop fighting for a time and discuss ways of making a peaceful settlement.

Mobilisation: The preparation of troops for war.

So by late Spring 1831, the Russians had begun to restore control. By September, they retook Warsaw, and Poland was placed under military rule. The use of the Russian language was imposed and the separate Polish Diet, the army and universities were abolished.

The Poles had expected support from the west, particularly as their claims to independence had greater historical backing than those of the Greeks or Belgians, whose wishes had been granted. However, their position in the east of Europe, away from British and French influence and where British sea power was of no relevance, meant they were deserted. The French felt some obligation, but the new regime could not afford to take risks. The Russian army was too formidable, so the French merely condemned the action and proposed a conference of powers to urge Russia to make concessions. Viscount Palmerston was sympathetic to the Poles, but Britain was too committed to the events in western Europe. So the Poles were, therefore, left to their own devices.

What was the part played by France and Austria in the Italian revolts of 1831?

It was the French example, again, which inspired the 1831 risings in Modena, Parma and the Papal States. In the expectation of French help against Austria, liberals in Modena pressed for constitutional reform and some form of Italian union in February 1831. The revolt spread to nearby Parma, while a provisional liberal government established itself in the Papal States. However, the risings were unco-ordinated and France showed caution. When Metternich tried to find out the French position, he received a message suggesting that France was only prepared to defend its immediate neighbours, Belgium, Piedmont, the Rhineland and Spain, from intervention by other powers. In fact, the French were looking for an honourable way out of a clash with the Austrians.

This was taken one step further in March 1831, when Casimir Périer announced that, as long as French honour was not harmed, the French would stay out of Italy. Reassured by these promises, Metternich felt safe enough to send in Austrian troops. They successfully occupied Modena on 4 March 1831, and Bologna on 21 March. This was a test case for Austrian intervention as, although Modena was firmly within the Austrian sphere of influence, Bologna was in Papal territory. Casimir Périer salvaged French honour by declaring that they would be prepared to support the Pope if reforms were made in the Papal States.

On 21 May 1831, a five-power conference of ambassadors took place in Rome and produced a list of proposals for the reform of the Papal States. The Pope agreed to the suggestions, and the Austrian army subsequently withdrew on 17 July. However, not all the suggestions were put into effect, and there was rioting in the province. The Austrian troops returned and occupied Bologna in January 1832. France reacted promptly. Feeling obliged to fulfil its declaration and to match Austrian intervention with its own, French troops were sent to Ancona in the Papal States, in the same month, even though the Pope had not granted authority for this. The newly-elected Pope Gregory XVI looked to Austria for support, but the French remained until 1838, when Austrian troops left Bologna. It was a symbolic gesture only, but there was clearly little goodwill between France and Austria during this period.

How did events in Spain and Portugal affect Anglo–French relations in the 1830s?

After Britain had withdrawn its troops from Portugal in 1827, the absolutist supporters of Dom Miguel had been able to make him King, forcing

Constitutionalism: The practice of governing or organising a particular country according to a constitution.

1. To what extent did the reactions of the powers to the Belgian revolt show that there was still a 'Concert of Europe'?

2. In what ways does the attitude of the Great Powers explain why the Belgian and Greek revolutions succeeded, but the Polish one did not?

3. How successful was the British handling of the affairs of Spain and Portugal in this period? You should consider Britain's own interests, and its relationship with other powers.

the nine-year-old Queen Maria II to flee to Brazil in 1828. In 1832, her father Dom Pedro appealed for British aid and in 1833 he entered Lisbon, with the support of British troops.

However, in September 1833, a further crisis occurred in Spain. Ferdinand, who had for so long struggled to maintain his absolutist control, died. His brother Don Carlos, supported by absolutists, claimed the throne. The legitimate heir was Ferdinand's daughter, the three-year-old Queen Isabella II, whom the liberals supported with her mother acting as regent.

The French now adopted the role of supporters of **constitutionalism**, and offered Great Britain an alliance early in 1834. They wanted the two countries to work together in support of the constitutional governments of Spain and Portugal.

Palmerston was still suspicious of French motives. He rejected the French offer but, in April 1834, he was prepared to accept a wider Quadruple Alliance of Britain, France and the constitutional monarchies of Portugal and Spain. This was pledged to defend liberal institutions and to exclude Miguel from Portugal and Carlos from Spain. However, by the terms of the treaty, whereas Britain might intervene alone in Portugal, in defence of its measures, France was specifically forbidden from doing so in Spain.

In accordance with the Treaty, a combination of the Spanish Army and the British navy destroyed the absolutist forces of King Miguel and Don Carlos in the spring of 1834. This allowed Palmerston to boast that he had created an alliance of constitutional states as an answer to the close association of Austria, Russia and Prussia, which had been re-affirmed in a treaty at Münchengrätz in 1833.

Miguel fled, but Carlos presented more of a problem. He renewed his claim and raised more troops, joining forces with the **Basques** in their fight for independence. Neither Britain nor France was prepared for guerrilla warfare. Furthermore, Britain was frightened of allowing a French army into Spain, so they ignored the legitimate government's appeals for aid in 1835, and only permitted volunteers to go and fight. By 1836, Anglo–French co-operation had broken down.

6.7 How did the powers react to the Mehemet Ali Affairs?

What was the reaction of the Great Powers to the first crisis of 1831–1832?

Basques: These were the people of the relatively prosperous area in the north-west of Spain, who were hostile to the central control of the government in Madrid and resented economic changes. They had developed a tradition of banditry and guerrilla warfare during the Peninsular War against the French. They were only too happy to join the 'Carlists', as the supporters of Don Carlos were known, in their fight for the throne.

The outbreak of troubles in the Near East in 1831 stemmed from the determination of Mehemet Ali, the Pasha of Egypt, to exact the rewards he had been promised by Turkey in return for his aid against the Greeks. In 1831–32, his son invaded and occupied Syria, driving out the Turks. As his forces advanced further into Turkish territory, the Turks were defeated at the Battle of Koneih in December 1832, and the Pasha's forces came to within 150 miles of Constantinople. In February 1833, the Sultan appealed to the other powers for help. He was hoping for aid from Britain, France or even Austria but, when none was forthcoming, turned to Russia. Each power viewed the events differently.

Palmerston wanted to give support but was overruled by the Cabinet, who argued that the British fleet was fully committed off Portugal and Holland. Assistance to Turkey would have involved raising extra funds and risking unpopularity at a time when an election was due. There was still a good deal of anti-Turkish feeling among the general public and, even in Parliament, there were those who felt that the Ottoman Empire was not worth preserving anyway.

The French wanted to keep Mehemet Ali as a French agent in the Mediterranean, and preferred to work for a compromise.

The Austrians supported joint action in favour of Turkey to settle the troubles as quickly as possible. Their main concern was over Russian policy, and the possibility of independent Russian intervention.

The incident alarmed the Russians since they feared that, if Mehemet Ali were successful against his master, he could revitalise the Turkish Empire and place a far stronger, and perhaps more aggressive, power on the Russian border. Warnings against such a situation had been given by the Kochubei committee. Furthermore, Mehemet Ali was a rebel, acting against his legitimate master, the Sultan, and Russia feared his French connections might lead to undue French influence in the area.

What was the result of Russian intervention?

As Austria feared, Russia chose to act independently. In February 1833, a Russian squadron was sent to the Bosphorus, followed by several thousand Russian troops. Mehemet Ali backed down and, by the peace of Kutiah (April/May 1833), he was given recognition of his claim to Syria for his lifetime and to the northern district of Adana for his son, Ibrahim. The first crisis had been brought to a successful conclusion, as far as Russia was concerned.

In return for its help, Russia was granted the Treaty of Unkiar-Skelessi in July 1833. This was officially a treaty of mutual assistance, but it contained a secret clause by which Turkey agreed to close the Black Sea Straits to warships of all nations. This only repeated what was an ancient tradition, but the implication was that Turkey would close the Straits at Russia's demand. It also suggested that in any future crisis Turkey would approach Russia for help, giving a legal basis for Russian intervention in near-eastern affairs. The secret clause was soon known in Great Britain, thanks to a Turk who disliked his country's 'surrender' to the Russians. Palmerston was determined to change the treaty at the earliest opportunity.

How did the Russian actions affect its relationship with the other European powers?

Austria was determined to prevent Russia continuing its independent line and was pleased to make an agreement with it at Münchengrätz in September 1833. This is sometimes described as another 'Holy Alliance'.

Prussia was to join it, a month later, at the Convention of Berlin. By this agreement, Austria and Russia agreed to maintain the Ottoman Empire, to defend the Sultan from any further activities by Mehemet Ali, and only to act after consultation should further trouble occur. It also reasserted the solidarity of the eastern powers that promised:

● to help each other in the suppression of rebellions;

● to prevent counter-intervention by a fourth power, such as France, whose occupation of Ancona since 1832 had annoyed Austria.

This was a triumph for Metternich who had been trying to gain such an agreement since the days of the Greek Revolt.

Britain was very suspicious of the Treaty of Unkiar-Skelessi. The mistaken belief that Russia had gained the exclusive right of passage for its warships through the Black Sea Straits, caused alarm. Indeed, in March 1834, in a note to the British Ambassador in Constantinople, the

Commander-in-Chief of the British Mediterranean fleet was ordered to support any Turkish request for help against a threatened attack by the Russians.

The crisis increased British and French mistrust of Russia's policy in the Near East. Although Palmerston claimed that the Quadruple Alliance of 1834 – Britain, France, Spain and Portugal – was a liberal counterbalance to the powers of the Holy Alliance, the allies had very different purposes. What Palmerston really wanted was an agreement involving all the powers over the Eastern Question. This was best achieved by working with, and not against, the Holy Alliance powers.

This was made easier with the outbreak of a second crisis in 1839. The chief threat to peace this time came from the French.

What was the reaction of the Great Powers to the second crisis of 1838–1840?

In May 1838, Mehemet Ali announced his intention to declare the independence of Egypt and Syria. By January 1839, the Sultan was making military preparations. He invaded Syria in May 1839. The campaign was not a success for Turkey. The newly-reorganised army was defeated at the Battle of Nezib in June, the Turkish fleet deserted to the Egyptians, and the Sultan died. Initially, the European Powers acted together and assured the new Sultan of their support. However, a conference of powers in Vienna broke down in the Spring of 1840 when Adolphe Thiers, the French Prime Minister, declared French support for Mehemet Ali (see Chapter 7).

The other powers ignored the French protests and devised their own settlement. By the Treaty of London, July 1840, they issued Mehemet Ali with an ultimatum. He might have hereditary rule over Egypt and rule for life in southern Syria, but they threatened force if he rejected these.

The French were furious. There was talk of war, and even of an invasion along the Rhine, as a sign of their strength and anger. However, the tension passed when, in October, Thiers was dismissed. Louis-Philippe refused to allow his country to follow a policy that might bring about a war in which France would be isolated.

How was the crisis resolved?

The French, consequently, agreed to support the joint action. When Mehemet Ali rejected the ultimatum, the British bombarded Beirut in September and landed Turkish troops there. In November, they captured Acre and by February 1841 Syria had been cleared of Egyptian troops. Mehemet Ali was forced to agree to restore the Turkish fleet, and thanks to the intervention of the powers, was allowed to retain his hereditary rights in Egypt only.

The outcome of this co-operation was the Straits Convention of 13 July 1841, which included France again. This stated the old principle that no warships should pass through the Straits while Turkey was at peace. The agreement of Unkiar-Skelessi, with its implications of preferential treatment for Russia, then lapsed. Once more the Powers had shown that they could work together to resolve a difficult situation, although the strained relationship of the western powers, Britain and France, over Spanish/Portuguese affairs, was made worse by the events of 1839–41.

1. How successfully did (a) Russia, (b) France and (c) Britain uphold their interests in the Near East between 1831 and 1841?

2. How, and why, did Britain's relationship with France and Russia change in this period?

Source-based questions: The Great Powers and the Mehemet Ali Crisis, 1839–1840

SOURCE A

The real danger for Europe at large is not in a combat carried on in Syria between the troops of the Sultan and those of the Pasha of Egypt.

Neither would there be a danger to Europe if the Sultan succeeded in reconquering Syria, as he wishes and hopes to do. The danger would not become serious until, in the event of the fate of arms declaring against the Sultan, the Pasha of Egypt should profit by this advantage to place the safety of Constantinople and the existence of the Ottoman Empire in peril ...

To prevent things reaching such a point, it is of consequence to take measures in time to confine the struggle between the Sultan and Mehemet Ali within certain limits ...

With this in view, it has appeared essential to us to come to some understanding, frankly, with the great powers of Europe who, equally with us, have at heart to prevent the danger which we have just pointed out.

A despatch from Nesselrode, the Russian Foreign Minister to Count Pozzo di Borgo, the Russian Ambassador in Paris, 15 June 1839

SOURCE B

... the Emperor (of Russia) will entirely agree to our views as to the affairs of Turkey and Egypt and will join in whatever measures may be necessary to carry those views into effect. He will unite with us, Austria and Prussia, either with France, or without her, and although, politically speaking, he sees the advantage of having France of the party, personally he would be better pleased that she should be left out ...

Nothing can be more miserable than the shifts and changes in the opinions and schemes of the French government, and it is evident that they have wishes and objects at bottom which they are ashamed of confessing. In short their great and only aim is to do as much as they possibly can for Mehemet Ali, without caring a pin for the Sultan, or having the least regard for their declarations and pledges.

I wish you to see Soult [French Prime Minister May 1839 – February 1840] and to ascertain from him ... what the French government mean to do. If Soult should hint that France would oppose the four powers, you might suggest that ... it could not be worthwhile for France to make war with the four powers ... that no French interest could be promoted thereby.

Adapted from a private letter from Lord Palmerston (British Foreign Secretary) to Sir Henry Lytton Bulwer (Secretary of the British Embassy in Paris), 1 September 1839

SOURCE C

ARTICLE 1 His highness the Sultan, having come to an agreement with their majesties (of Great Britain, Austria, Prussia, and Russia as to the arrangement to be offered to Mehemet Ali), their Majesties engage to act in perfect accord, and to unite their efforts in order to determine Mehemet Ali to conform to that arrangement ...

ARTICLE 2 If the Pasha of Egypt should refuse to accept the above mentioned arrangement ... their Majesties engage to take, at the request of the Sultan, measures concerted and settled between them, in order to carry that arrangement into effect ...

Separate Act
1. His Highness promises to grant Mehemet Ali, for himself and for his descendants in the direct line, the administration of the Pashalic of Egypt; and his highness promises moreover to grant to Mehemet Ali for his life ... the administration of the southern part of Syria ...

From the Convention for the Pacification of the Levant, 15 July 1840

SOURCE D

The day the Sultan's throne collapses, the empire itself will break up into several parts, some of which will pass into the hands of Christian Powers, while others will endeavour to set themselves up as more or less independent States, offering the unedifying spectacle of Moslem anarchy, such as characterised the regencies in Africa for centuries. As for Europe, her fate when this heavy blow falls will be wars of political rivalry.

The views of Prince von Metternich on the consequences of the collapse of the Ottoman Empire, from a circular of 11 October 1840

Source-based questions: The Great Powers and the Mehemet Ali Crisis, 1839–1840

1. Study Source A.

According to this source, what was 'the real danger for Europe' in 1839?

2. Study Source B.

What do the language and tone of the source tell us about Palmerston, and the British attitude to France in 1839?

3. Study Sources A and C.

To what extent does the agreement made in Source C support the views expressed in Source A?

4. Study Source D.

How useful and reliable would this source be to a historian studying the attitude of Austria to the decline of the Ottoman Empire?

5. Use the information given in all these sources and in this chapter.

How far would you agree that 'The Eastern Question was the most severe threat to peaceful co-operation between the Great Powers between 1822 and 1841'?

6.8 How, and why, had the relationship between the powers changed by 1848?

By the 1840s, the old division between the 'liberal powers', Great Britain and France, and the 'reactionary powers', Austria, Russia and Prussia, had broken down completely. France had drawn closer to Austria, sharing a similar anxiety over Russia's policy in the Near East, while the settlement of affairs there, culminating in the Straits Convention of 1841, had helped to bring Britain and Russia closer together than they had ever been since the days of the Napoleonic wars. However, Britain's relationship with France had greatly deteriorated by the beginning of the 1840s following clashes over Spain, Portugal, the colonies and the position of Mehemet Ali.

In the period to 1848, these relationships remained much the same.

Relations between France and Great Britain

France and Great Britain improved their relationship a little, while Robert Peel was Prime Minister, and Lord Aberdeen, Foreign Secretary (1841–46). Aberdeen got on well with François Guizot, the leading French minister. Despite this, there were still constant sources of tension. There was, for example, trouble over Tahiti in 1842, which had been claimed by both British and French missionaries. The French increasingly distanced themselves from the British. Oddly enough, the French King, Louis-Philippe, himself a product of 'revolution', complained to the Austrian ambassador in Paris of 'the unfortunate tendency of the British government at all times to support revolutions and thus disturb the peace of Europe'.

Relations between Spain and Great Britain

The question of Spain also caused continuing problems. The British feared the French would try to gain influence in Spain, by arranging a marriage between the young Queen Isabella and a French Prince. In 1843, Guizot assured the British that this would not happen and that Isabella would marry into the Spanish or Neapolitan (from Naples) branches of the

Robert Peel (1788–1850)
Peel was the son of a Lancashire cotton manufacturer. He became a Tory MP at the age of 21. He held office under Lord Liverpool from 1812 and became Home Secretary in 1822 and 1828–30. He was Prime Minister for four months from 1834–35 and again from 1841–46. He was known for his belief in moderate reform, which created a new type of Conservatism.

House of Bourbon. He also promised that her younger sister, Luisa Fernanda, would not marry until Isabella had children, so ensuring the succession.

However, by 1846, Aberdeen, had been persuaded to agree to new proposals. Although he continued to reject a French marriage for Isabella, he was prepared to accept a compromise whereby she would marry her cousin Francisco of Cadiz, even though he was reputed to be **impotent**.

Impotent: Unable to father children.

Crucially, her sister would marry the duc de Montpensier, younger son of Louis-Philippe. Of course, if Isabella failed to produce an heir, the children of this marriage would inherit the throne. Palmerston, who returned to office in 1846, was furious. He would accept no compromise and produced his own plan by which Isabella would be married to Francisco's brother Enrique of Seville, and her sister Luisa to Leopold of Saxe-Coburg-Gotha, so excluding any possibility of a French prince or heir. This merely provoked Louis-Philippe, who was under considerable pressure from Guizot, to act independently from Great Britain. Without further ado, on 10 October 1846, Isabella was married to her cousin and Luisa to Louis-Philippe's son. Tension ran high, and Franco–British relations were at a low ebb.

They were not helped by the continuing troubles in Portugal. There, Queen Maria, whom the liberals had attempted to guide as a child, had thrown their views aside and introduced unconstitutional measures. Faced with opposition, she requested help from Spain, Britain and France, under the terms of the Quadruple Alliance of April 1834. This placed Great Britain in a very difficult position. Great Britain had always regarded Portugal as its own sphere of influence, and it did not like what Queen Maria was doing. However, as it had agreed to the Quadruple Alliance, and when Spain and France announced that they intended to send aid to the Queen, Britain could hardly stay out. In July 1847, an Anglo–French naval force and Spanish troops destroyed the opposition forces. This preserved British influence but at the expense of its own principles, and Britain blamed the French for forcing the issue.

Relations between Austria and France

Austria and France continued to maintain cordial relations until 1848. Both feared isolation, and the French made a great effort to woo the Austrians. In May 1847, Guizot sent a letter to Metternich in which he claimed, 'France is now disposed and suited to a policy of Conservatism'. Metternich was never entirely convinced of the genuineness of the French attitude, but nevertheless welcomed France's willingness to adopt a conservative policy in Europe.

Relations between Great Britain and Russia

British relations with Russia were the best they had been since the time of the Napoleonic wars. In 1844, the Tsar visited England for talks at Windsor with Peel and Aberdeen.. It was a great success. The Tsar even told Peel, 'Years ago Lord Durham was sent to me, a man full of prejudices against me. Merely by contact with me, his prejudices were all driven to the winds, and that is what I hope to bring about with you and generally in England.'

This was the position of the powers when, in 1848, Europe was again engulfed in revolution, which was to test the Concert of Europe severely.

1. What was the relationship between the powers like in 1848? How had it changed since 1823?

2. Using information from the whole of this chapter, explain why the Great Powers were successful in maintaining peace in Europe 1815–1848.

France 1814–1848

Key Issues

- **What problems faced the Kings of France after 1814?**

- **Why was the restored Bourbon Monarchy of 1814–1815 overthrown in 1830?**

- **To what extent was Louis-Philippe the cause of his own downfall?**

Framework of Events

1814	March: Fall of Paris. Napoleon exiled to Elba
	April: Louis XVIII accepts the Charter
	May–June: First Peace of Paris returns France to frontiers of 1792
1815	March: Napoleon lands in southern France. Louis flees, as Napoleon begins his '100 days' as Emperor
	June: Napoleon is defeated at Waterloo and exiled to St Helena; Louis XVIII returns as King
	November: Second Peace of Paris
1816	The White Terror of revenge on Napoleonic supporters
1818	Indemnity is paid off, army of occupation leaves and France is readmitted to the Concert of Europe
1820	Murder of the duc de Berri
1823	French intervention in Spain restores Ferdinand VII to his throne
1824	Death of Louis XVIII; accession of Charles X
1825	Law provides compensation to former *émigrés*
1827	The National Guard is disbanded
1830	9 July: French army under Bourmont captures Algiers
	25 July: Ordinances of St Cloud (July Ordinances)
	Fighting in streets of Paris. Charles X abdicates. Louis-Philippe becomes 'King of the French'
1831	The National Guard is reconstituted. Revolt of Lyons silk weavers
1834	Further rioting in Lyons crushed by the army; revolt in Paris crushed by the army
	Quadruple Alliance – France, Britain, Spain and Portugal – in favour of liberal governments in the Iberian Peninsula
1836	Louis Napoleon attempts a *coup d'état*
1840	Louis Napoleon's second attempt at a *coup d'état*
	Thiers brings country to brink of war over second Mehemet Ali Affair (1839–40), but is dismissed
1846	Louis-Philippe forces through his own candidates for the Spanish marriages, despite Britain's hostility
1847	Reform banquets held throughout France
1848	Revolution in Paris; Louis-Philippe abdicates.

Overview

Liberty and Equality:
These were two of the
themes of the French
Revolution. 'Liberty' implies
personal freedom, the right
to property, freedom of
speech, worship and the
freedom to participate in
politics. By the 1820s, it had
become more widely used to
imply resistance to
autocratic rule. 'Equality'
implies the rights of all to be
treated in the same way, and
subject to the same laws.

Republicanism: The belief
that a state should be ruled
without a king. Republicans
also believe in a wide
franchise (right to vote) to
give ordinary people more
say in their own
government.

Peasantry: Rural labourers.
As a result of the
Revolution, the peasants
were no longer owned by
the great landlords, and
many had benefited from
the opportunity to acquire
their own land.

Propertied interests: Those
whose wealth derived from
land. These were mainly of
noble birth, aristocrats; but
there were also those who
had made money elsewhere
(e.g. by trade), and then
invested it in land. Such
men tended to oppose
changes that might affect
their status.

Bourbon monarchy: The
Royal House of France since
1610. The French King,
Louis XVI, who had been
guillotined in 1793, came
from this house. So did his
brothers, Louis XVIII
(1814/15–1824) and
Charles X (1824–1830).

Constitutional monarchy:
A king whose power is
limited by a written
document that provides for
an elected assembly
(parliament) and gives
guarantees of basic rights,
such as freedom of speech.

Franchise: The right to vote
in an election.

REVOLUTION in France in 1789 had unleashed a series of forces that were not only to transform Europe, but were also to play a significant part in the internal history of France itself in the first half of the 19th century. Before 1789, France had been the leading power of Europe under a powerful, unrestricted monarchy. With the biggest population of the western world (second only to Russia in Europe), and a rate of economic growth as rapid as those of its main rival, Great Britain (at least to 1780), France had appeared a stable and prosperous power. However, by 1814, the experience of Revolution and war transformed France. Its whole political and social system was changed by the spread of revolutionary ideas of **Liberty and Equality**. Its king had lost his head, many of the nobility fled or were guillotined and land passed into new ownership. The status of the Catholic Church was undermined, its property taken away, new law codes produced, and new systems of government – such as **Republicanism** – were tried out. On top of all this had come a long period of warfare – 1792–1814. During this time, France, ruled from 1804 by the Emperor Napoleon, achieved unprecedented glory, only to be followed by miserable defeat.

It is little wonder that these momentous changes and events created an uncertainty and instability in France that was to plague French politics throughout the first half of the 19th century. Some of the changes proved irreversible, as subsequent French rulers were to find to their cost. After 1815, French governments could no longer ignore the bourgeoisie and **peasantry** who had benefited from the revolutionary changes. Their problem was in meeting the demands of these groups of society, without harming the **propertied interests** on which the rulers relied.

The restoration of the **Bourbon monarchy** did not suit all Frenchmen. Their reigns were troubled by plots, assassinations and riots, but they did at least provide 15 years of relative peace, which is what most Frenchman wanted. The *émigrés,* who had been forced to flee France at the time of the Revolution, and the clergy, who had lost so much of their influence in the troubles, were natural supporters of the return to a traditional style of government. Less convinced but fairly supportive, were the peasants. They were anxious not to lose the land they had recently acquired. The bourgeoisie, who had gained in status from the Revolution, were prepared to accept any government that would uphold law and order.

The Bourbon Monarchy was a **constitutional monarchy**, but it failed to live up to its early promise. By the end of the reign of Louis XVIII and throughout that of Charles X, it was clear that the pendulum was swinging in favour of the 'propertied' classes, the *émigrés* and the Church. In a revolution in 1830, which at one point looked as though it might threaten the whole institution of monarchy, 'Paris again gave France a government', as the historian John Roberts puts it in *The Nineteenth Century* (1970). The dynasty was changed. Louis-Philippe of the House of Orléans, was brought to the throne in an attempt to create a 'bourgeois' monarchy. The **franchise** was slightly widened, the king's powers were slightly restricted, but at the end of the day the change was limited and it did not work. Although Louis-Philippe tried to rule in a moderate way, there were always those who wanted more. They were increasingly driven to pursue the old methods of revolutionaries – secret societies, plots and the distribution of literature and newspapers. Louis-Philippe's reign was also to end in revolution. This time the Republicans, who believed that a better, fairer society could only be created by removing the King, were to triumph, although their victory was short-lived. Perhaps the rulers of France in the period 1814–1848 had failed to absorb the lessons of 1789–1814. Or maybe there were just too many alternatives to traditional government around, so that opponents could always press for something different. Whatever the reasons, this period of French history was one of constant unease, dissatisfaction and political conflict, despite some steady economic progress.

7.1 What was France like in 1814–1815?

Why was Louis XVIII made King?

The wars against Napoleon had not yet come to an end when debate began over how France should be governed on its defeat. Republican government was deemed responsible for provoking war in the first place. It was also regarded with too much hostility, both within France and elsewhere, for it to be considered a practical possibility. The question was therefore not *whether* France should have a king, but *who* that king should be. The best claim to the throne came from the brother of the guillotined Louis XVI. (See the Bourbon/Orléans family tree.) Louis XVIII, as he

The French monarchy – the Bourbon/Orléans family tree

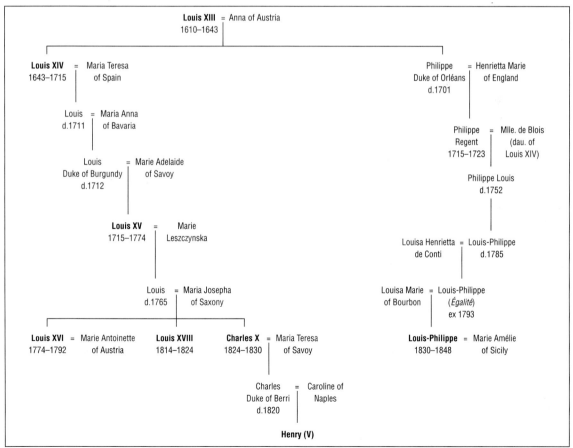

styled himself, was the only 'legitimate' heir, but he was not a popular choice. Louis was not a particularly attractive figure. He was 59, fat, suffered from **gout**, and looked and behaved as though he was even older. He was not an unpleasant or stupid man. On the contrary, he was regarded as sensible and easy-going but, after 20 years in exile, it is not really surprising that there were those who doubted whether he was the right man for France. However, Charles Talleyrand-Périgord took up Louis' claim, on the grounds that he would divide France the least. Talleyrand played on the principle of legitimacy, and his intrigues were helped by spontaneous action on the part of the citizens of Bordeaux. When the British freed the city on 22 March 1814, the citizens declared themselves in favour of a Bourbon restoration. This was enough to convince the British and its allies – Austria, Prussia and Russia – to return France, as far as was possible, to its pre-revolutionary state. Consequently, with the fall of Paris at the end of March, Louis XVIII was asked to resume the throne – an offer he accepted.

What were the conditions of Louis XVIII's return in 1814?

Louis XVIII's return was not entirely unconditional. He was asked to sign a charter, drawn up by a committee consisting of his own advisers, Talleyrand-Périgord and other leading Napoleonic figures. This charter contained 74 articles and was designed to ensure that the new King would obey some of the fundamental changes of the Revolutionary and Napoleonic period. These included:

- equality before the law

- fair taxation

- careers open to all

- freedom of the individual

- religious toleration (freedom), although Catholicism was to be the State Religion

- freedom of the press 'as long as they conform to the laws which must check the abuse of this liberty'

- protection for property owners, although property might be 'given up for the public good with prior compensation'

- a pardon to former revolutionaries

- the abolition of conscription.

The Charter also made clear Louis XVII's position as a constitutional monarch. France was to have a parliamentary system of government, on the British model. There would be two Houses, or Chambers. Members of the Chamber of Peers, or 'upper' house, would be nominated by the King; while those in the Chamber of Deputies, or 'lower' house, would be elected. The franchise was to be restricted to those property owners over the age of 30 who paid over 300 francs a year in direct taxation. There would be a two-tier system of voting. The voters would choose represen-tatives for electoral colleges, and the colleges would then vote for the deputies (see chart on page 201).

The King retained certain important rights. He could choose his own ministers, introduce legislation into the Chambers, veto (refuse) any amendments the deputies might make to his bills, dissolve Parliament when he chose, and control all military and civil appointments.

What was the effect of the Charter?

The Charter certainly made Louis XVIII's return less unpopular. By preventing the possibility of any return to the absolute monarchy of the past, and by giving guarantees of basic liberties and property rights, it helped to make the restoration acceptable. However, despite all the changes of the revolutionary era, the type of government it set up in France was still extremely undemocratic. From a population of 29 million only about 88,000 had the right to vote, and some 15,000 had the right to stand as deputies.

Furthermore, Louis XVIII was determined that the Charter should not undermine his royal status. He had insisted on adding a preamble (introduction), in which he made it clear that the freedoms granted by the Charter were a personal gift to his people, not their basic right. He strongly believed in his own divine right to rule and in the legitimacy of his position. He accepted no responsibility to Parliament.

Louis XVIII therefore remained a powerful figure, although there was no escaping the fact that he had relied on others to put him on the throne. This fact became even more apparent in the period of Napoleon's '100 days'.

What were the consequences of Napoleon's '100 days', March–June 1815?

Louis XVIII's position as King of France would have been much easier had it not been for the continuing ambitions of Napoleon I. When Napoleon had departed for exile on Elba, an island off the Italian coast, in March 1814, it was assumed that France had seen the last of its former Emperor. Louis XVIII returned to Paris in April and, by the first Peace of Paris, drawn up the following month, accepted lenient peace terms on behalf of the French. France was returned to its frontiers of 1792, allowed to keep the art treasures that it had looted from all over Europe, and no indemnity payment was demanded. This moderate settlement seemed to offer the best possible start for Louis' new regime.

Louis XVIII tried to rule in the spirit of the Charter and avoided taking revenge on those he replaced. However, the many years in exile made it hard, for both Louis XVIII and those royalists who returned with him, to understand the changed situation in France. Even in the earliest days, he made mistakes. The replacement of the *tricolor* (French national flag, symbol of the Revolution) with a white flag adorned with the Bourbon family emblem, seemed provocative. When the household guard was reformed under several thousand noble officers, there were murmurings of a return of aristocratic influence.

Consequently, when Napoleon chose to return from Elba, in March 1815, he found plenty of Frenchmen, and in particular former soldiers, who were prepared to accept him back. As he advanced northwards from the south coast, Louis XVIII fled to Ghent (in present-day Belgium). He was forced to put himself under the protection of Britain and Austria, as France increasingly fell under Napoleon's spell. Marshal Ney, who had promised Louis XVIII that he would bring the Emperor back in a cage, rejoined his old master after an emotional reconciliation in Lyons. Before the month was out, Napoleon had been carried up the steps of the Tuileries Palace by a vast, cheering crowd. Napoleon's '100 days' ended in defeat at Waterloo on 18 June 1815, when the British, commanded by the Duke of Wellington and reinforced by the timely arrival of the Prussians under Gebhrad von Blücher, narrowly gained the victory.

Napoleon's final bid for power, which was to end with his exile to the Atlantic island of St Helena, was a severe blow to the success of Louis XVIII's reign. The King had fled. His regime had crumbled and, to

Marshal Ney Michel (1769–1815)
Came from a working-class background, but rose quickly though the ranks to become a commander under Napoleon. He was created a Marshal in 1804, and impressed Napoleon by his contribution to the defeat of the Austrians at Ulm in 1805. His courage at the Battle of Borodino led Napoleon to create him 'Prince of the Moskowa' and to award him the honour of being known as 'bravest of the brave'. In 1814, Louis XVIII allowed him to remain as Commander-in-Chief of the Cavalry, but his desertion to Napoleon during the '100 days' cost him his life. Ney fought at Waterloo but was captured, court martialled and shot in Paris on 7 December 1815. His execution, which Louis XVIII personally opposed, aroused resentment throughout France.

the French, he was now firmly associated with the enemies of France, on whom he had relied. Furthermore, a Second Peace of Paris was drawn up in November 1815 to punish France for this additional interruption to European peace. Although still not as harsh as some nations would have liked, the treaty reduced France to its borders of 1789, imposed a war indemnity of 700 million francs, and left it with an army of occupation that would remain until the indemnity was paid.

What was the economic and social condition of France in 1815?

In 1815 France had a population of around 29 million, around 75% of which lived and worked in the countryside. There was plenty of productive land, and France itself had escaped much of the devastation that its wars had brought elsewhere. Agriculture was thriving, along with small-scale domestic industry, maintained by the hard-working peasantry. There was, however, comparatively little large-scale industrial development. Although France had enjoyed strong economic growth in the 18th century, from 1780 it was eclipsed by Great Britain and Belgium. War had widened the gap, removing France's colonial markets and encouraging the protection of industry, which therefore had little incentive to change or adapt to new technology.

The most significantly developed area was in the north-east, around the textile towns of Lille and Roubaix, but the country as a whole suffered from poor transport links. Although coalmining was growing, France still had to import from Great Britain and Belgium. The same was true of pig iron and textiles. Consequently, its towns remained quite small and only seven had a population of over 50,000. (The maps and figures on page 213 give more precise details about the state of the French economy.)

Paris was, nevertheless, a large city. It was quite different from most of France in that the pressures of industrial change had begun to make themselves felt there. A recognisable working class, for example, solely reliant on their wages for their livelihood, could already be found in Paris. Here, too, a 'bourgeois' middle class of industrialists had begun to develop. However, although France was changing slowly, industry had made little impact on society outside Paris.

The social elite in France was made up of rich landowners, bankers, merchants and lawyers. These men might not all have possessed the aristocratic titles of the past century, but in their outlook they were much the same. It was this group which received political influence in the new constitutional regime of Louis XVIII. They exercised an influence out of proportion to their numbers, which amounted to under half of 1% of the population. They were known as the 'Pays Légal'.

What was the attitude to the Church in France in 1815?

France was a Catholic nation and, before the Revolution, the Catholic Church in France had great wealth and influence. Indeed, its attitude had been one of the factors leading to revolt. Developments after 1789 had increased **anti-clericalism** still further. Under Napoleon, Church land had been confiscated and sold, monasteries and nunneries disbanded, and priests made salaried officials of the state. So, although in 1815 most of the population claimed to be Catholic, at least in name, many of the more educated were openly irreligious. They associated the Church with the horrors of the pre-Revolutionary era. Those who had benefited from the Revolution, and in particular the *Pays Légal*, possessed a genuine fear of the restoration of its influence.

Pays Légal: This was the group that had the franchise (right to vote). In France in 1815 this depended on wealth, so it mainly represented the large landowners and a smaller group of senior government officials. Trade, finance, industry and the professions were under-represented.

Anti-clericalism: Hostility to the clergy, who were the representatives of the Catholic Church.

Why did Louis XVIII find it difficult to establish his royal authority in France in 1814/1815?

The French people oppressed by Absolute Monarchy – a contemporary French **caricature** on the re-establishment of the monarchy under Louis XVIII, 1814.

Caricature: A drawing or description of someone that exaggerates parts of their physical features or personality so much that they appear ridiculous.

Can you explain the characters represented in it? Do you think it is a fair representation of what French people might expect from Louis XVIII?

7.2 How successful was Louis XVIII as King of France 1815–1824?

What were Louis XVIII's successes?

In many respects, Louis XVIII handled France well. He pursued fairly moderate policies and was helped by capable ministers such as the duc de Richelieu and, later the duc de Decazes. Although he preferred to keep out of party politics, he tried to work with his Parliament. He chose ministers who could command reasonable support in the Chambers. Louis tried to resist the demands of his more extreme supporters and, at least in the early years of his reign, he was supported by most of those that mattered – the voters who made up the *Pays Légal*.

He was assisted by a general economic recovery, after 1815, in which French industry prospered. By accepting tighter controls on government spending, the war indemnity was soon paid off and, by 1818, the foreign troops had left France. At the Congress of Aix-la-Chapelle that year, Louis achieved another success when France was readmitted to the **Concert of Europe**, regaining some of its international prestige. Following this, the French Army was reformed, and Louis put it to good use in 1823.

France had traditionally regarded Spain, to the south, as its sphere of influence. When in May 1822, the Spanish King, Ferdinand VII, had appealed to the monarchs of Europe for help against liberal rebels, Louis XVIII responded. Using the excuse that trouble might otherwise spread to France, an army was prepared in the south of France. The French refused to co-operate with the other powers at the Congress of Verona in 1822 to reach a joint decision on the question of intervention in Spain. They also ignored British demands for a guarantee that their intentions were limited to the restoration of Ferdinand VII.

Concert of Europe: The great powers of Europe working together to try to settle international problems. In the period 1815–22, the powers – Great Britain, Austria, Prussia, Russia and France – met in congresses. After that date they held special meetings as problems arose.

An army of 100,000 men under the duc d'Angoulême crossed the Pyrenees on 6 April 1823. They were victorious in August–September 1823, and Louis XVIII was able to boast that he had achieved something even Napoleon had failed to do: establish control in Spain. Although, in the Polignac Memorandum of 1824, the French did promise the British that they would not overstep the mark and interfere to help the Spaniards regain their former colonies in America, their actions in Spain were a sign of growing confidence and recovery. (See Chapter 6 for details of Spanish affairs and Anglo/French relations.)

Who were the Ultras and what problems did they pose for Louis XVIII?

Despite his successes, Louis' reign was constantly unsettled by the demands of the Ultras, many of them former émigrés, who used their power and influence to gain positions in the new Chamber of Deputies. In 1815, they came to dominate the newly elected Chamber. Louis referred to it as 'La Chambre introuvable' ('the impossible-to-find Chamber') because it was more Royalist than he was himself – something he had not deemed possible! Its members were led by the King's younger brother and heir, the Comte d'Artois. They hoped to do away with the Charter and with Parliament. They wanted the return of the lands lost by aristocrats and the Church in the Revolution. They constantly tried to push Louis XVIII further than he was prepared to go.

For example, they encouraged the 'White Terror', especially in the south of France in 1816, in revenge for Napoleon's '100 days'. Harsh punishments were handed out to the 57 leaders who had rallied to Napoleon, and some 7,000 supporters of Napoleon were imprisoned or executed. Louis XVIII could see the folly of such revenge but, given the Ultras' strength in the Chamber, he was powerless to do much about it. Although some of the condemned were encouraged to escape to exile, the execution of men like Marshal Ney, created a public outcry and provided the Bourbons' enemies with a future **martyr**. Similarly, it was the Ultras who successfully pressed Louis XVIII for a purge of the civil service and local government, replacing Napoleonic officials with their own nominees. Despite Louis XVIII's promises of 'freedom of the press' in the Charter, they insisted on the censorship of political news and comment. Furthermore, they were continually asking for a return of their estates, a demand regarded with horror by those who had bought that land and were now thriving on the income from it.

Martyr: Person who suffers or is killed because of their religious or political beliefs, and who therefore gives strength to people who share those beliefs.

How did Louis XVIII deal with the threat of the Ultras?

Louis was far from happy with his first 'Ultra' Chamber and his chief ministers, Charles Talleyrand and Joseph Fouché, who he felt had let him down by failing to exercise sufficient control over the elections. They were dismissed, and the Duc de Richelieu was made President of the Council of Ministers. Richelieu changed the electoral system, in September 1818, in order to create a new Chamber, more favourable to Louis' views. By these changes, there would be annual elections by which a fifth of the Chamber would be replaced regularly. This was expected to increase the number of independents who could be influenced by ministerial pressure, and to reduce the numbers of Ultras. It succeeded in the short term and in December 1818, Élie duc de Decazes, a man of more reformist views, was able to command sufficient support to take control. He pursued a moderately liberal policy and, in 1819–20, he tried to do away with press censorship altogether. However, an assassination presented the Ultras with the perfect excuse to press their demands.

What was the effect of the duc de Berri's murder in 1820?

Louis' nephew, the duc de Berri, son of the Comte d'Artois, was murdered outside the Paris opera house in 1820. The murder was highly significant since the duc de Berri was the only male member of the Bourbon royal family capable of providing an heir to ensure the succession. This unexpected act played into the Ultras' hands. They forced a shift in government policy and secured the dismissal of the moderate Decazes.

Richelieu returned to office and carried through the Ultras' demands for further electoral change in favour of the wealthy. The number of seats in the Chamber of Deputies was increased to 430 (see the table on page 201), but the additional 172 deputies were to be elected by a small group of the highest taxpayers. Around 15,000 of the richest men in France would now be responsible for choosing over a third of the deputies. In addition, more press censorship was introduced in 1821, the clergy were given greater influence in education and plans were drawn up to compensate the many *émigrés* who had lost land during the Revolution.

This was a turning point for the monarchy. Louis XVIII, racked by disease, lacked the physical strength to resist the Comte d'Artois and the Ultras. Disillusionment with the Bourbon government began to extend to those who had previously been prepared to tolerate, if not support, it. To make matters worse, in September 1820, the wife of the duc de Berri gave birth to a son, some months after her husband's death. This assured the future of the dynasty, and was not welcome news to those who feared the way the government was heading. Richelieu again resigned (1822), and the pro-Ultra Chamber was led by the Comte de Villèle, who remained as Chief Minister from 1822 to 1827.

In many respects, Villèle was a successful minister. He carried through important financial reforms which helped him to balance the budgets, for example. However, his support for the Ultras made him unpopular. There was an outcry when he persuaded the ageing Louis XVIII to dismiss the Vicomte de Chateaubriand. Even French intervention in Spain in 1823 was interpreted by the doubters as a sign of support for a despotic king, rather than an assertion of France's international prestige. So it was that when Louis XVIII died in 1824, he left a well-established pro-Ultra parliament and a good deal of underlying discontent in the country.

How widespread was opposition to the Monarchy by 1824?

Although there was friction between the moderates and the Ultras during the reign of Louis XVIII, they both accepted the idea of monarchy. However, there were some extremists within France who would have liked to see the monarchy disappear altogether. Some of these were members of secret societies, based on the Italian **Carbonari**. They favoured republican government and a wide franchise, which would give ordinary working men some say in the running of their country.

Carbonari: Literally, the 'Charcoal burners'. This began as an Italian movement that wanted liberal reform. Members met in secret to avoid persecution, usually with elaborate rituals, special passwords and handshakes. They planned risings but were not very successful as their numbers were small and the groups unco-ordinated. Rituals were based on the practices of the freemasons and there were seven grades of initiation. The Carbonari was strongest in Naples but spread elsewhere in Europe, notably France.

François René, Vicomte de Chateaubriand (1768–1848) From an old aristocratic family. He was a great speaker and well-respected literary figure. He fled to the USA in 1791 and remained in exile, both in America and fighting in the counter-revolutionary armies until 1799. He returned to France to serve under Napoleon, but resigned in 1804. He supported the Bourbon Restoration and became Ambassador and Foreign Minister to Louis XVIII, but he was regarded as too moderate by the ultra-royalists who forced him out of office. Nevertheless, he refused to serve Louis-Philippe in 1830 and spent his later years writing.

Socialism: A set of political beliefs and principles whose general aim is to create a system in which everyone has an equal opportunity to benefit from the country's wealth.

1. *Why were Louis XVIII's domestic policies influenced by the demands of the Ultras during the period 1815–1824?*

2. *Did Louis XVIII's intervention in Spain in 1823 show his strength or his weakness? Give reasons for your answer.*

3. *'The tragedy of Louis' reign was that his good sense was shared by so few of his supporters.' Would you agree with this view of Louis XVIII's reign? Give reasons for your answer.*

Claude Henri, Comte de Saint-Simon (1760–1825)
An aristocrat who developed a clear socialist programme. He had fought in the American War of Independence and became enormously rich, buying land during the French Revolutionary period. However, he was later to lose much of this, suffer imprisonment and be forced to live off his friends. He had little influence in his own lifetime, but his writings were a great inspiration to later socialists. He argued that the army, Church, Kings and Princes were all out of date. The men that mattered were bankers, industrialists, scientists and engineers. Scientists were to be the new priests. He believed that, in a successful state, poverty would disappear, there would be no more war and there would be justice and equality.

The French Carbonarist movement had developed under the guidance of exiles fleeing persecution in Italy, who had made contact with student and intellectual groups. At its height, in the early 1820s, it could claim around 40,000 members, and it had even managed to attract some dissatisfied upper-class followers, such as the marquis de Lafayette. However, the numbers had fallen as government spies uncovered the activities, and a planned rising in 1822 failed when the army did not give its support.

By 1824, this type of 'radical' opposition to the monarchy had become less organised, but it had not disappeared. With the collapse of the Carbonarist movement, some students began to take an interest in the writings of socialists such as Claude de Saint-Simon whose last book, *Le nouveau Christianisme* ('The new Christinity'), was published in 1825. **Socialism** encouraged its supporters to challenge traditional government and to establish a new type of society that favoured the working class.

Opposition to the Constitutional Monarchy, established in 1814–15, was still quite limited in 1824, but the stirrings of socialism were already present. Left-wing intellectuals were beginning to spread the word among the growing numbers of working men in Paris, whose conditions made them willing to support any movement that promised a better future. Although few realised it at the time, such developments were far more dangerous to the monarchy than the dispute between the moderates and Ultras in the Chamber of Deputies.

7.3 Why did the reign of Charles X (1824–1830) end in revolution?

What sort of King was Charles X?

Formerly the Comte d'Artois, Charles X, Louis XVIII's brother, had led the Ultra-royalists since his return to France in 1814. In 1824 he was an energetic 67-year-old with firm convictions. 'I had rather chop wood than reign after the fashion of the King of England', he declared, showing his intention to play an active role in government. Since he inherited Villèle as his chief minister, supported by a Chamber that was already firmly Ultra in attitude, he had high hopes of carrying out the policies he had believed in for so long.

However, many members of the *Pays Légal* viewed him suspiciously. His stubbornness and determination not to show any sign of weakness, made him appear aloof and disinterested in the views of his people. He was also deeply religious, and insisted on a pompous coronation at Rheims surrounded by medieval pageantry (see opposite). The revival of customs such as visiting hospitals to cure those inflicted with **scrofula** by his **Holy Touch** frightened the anti-clerical *Pays Légal*.

Scrofula/Holy Touch: Charles X revived the medieval practice whereby it was believed that French (and English) Kings could cure scrofula, a disease which caused the glands to swell and was sometimes known as 'the King's Evil'.

The coronation of Charles X in Rheims Cathedral

Why was this coronation a significant event in the reign of Charles X?

How did Charles X's policies increase opposition to the Bourbon Monarchy?

Charles X managed to alienate all shades of political opinion with his policies. One of his first actions was to abolish the annual elections introduced by Richelieu in 1818, which had created a sizeable moderate faction in the Chamber of Deputies. He showed his intention of maintaining the rule of the Ultras by increasing the term deputies were elected for from five to seven years.

In accordance with the wishes of the Ultras, a law was passed in 1825 to compensate the *émigrés*. In many respects it was a fair measure. There was no return of land, for even Charles X saw this as potentially revolutionary. Instead, the Act confirmed present ownership, so making landowners more secure, while providing an annual grant of money as compensation to the former holders. It aimed to provide the financial security that many ex-*émigrés* had sought, and it seemed a reasonable reward for their loyalty. However, opposition centred not only on the measure itself, but also on the way the compensation money was raised. The scheme involved reducing the interest payable on the **national debt**. This meant that the value of government bonds, many of which were held by the *Pays Légal*, fell. In reality, the sums involved were not as large as were made out. They were insufficient to satisfy many *émigrés*, but it was the principle that caused trouble.

Charles X's association with the Catholic Church also caused resentment. He took steps to promote Catholicism. For example, religious orders, although theoretically disbanded at the Revolution, were encouraged to return. The influence of the restored **Jesuit order** was particularly resented. All sorts of rumours circulated about the plans of Charles X and the Jesuits to undermine the provisions of the Charter. Charles also made

National debt: The amount of money 'owed' by a country – the difference between its income (from the sale of goods elsewhere) and its expenditure (purchasing goods and materials from other nations).

Jesuit order: These were members of the Society of Jesus, a powerful Catholic Order which concentrated on education and conversion to the faith. They had been banned during the revolutionary period.

Heresy: The open denial of the teaching of the Catholic Church.

Sacrilege: The destruction or abuse of sacred objects.

Capital offences: Crimes that were punishable by death.

Lay teachers: These were teachers who were not ordained as priests or monks and who therefore provided an education uninfluenced by religious views.

heresy and sacrilege capital offences and continued to extend the control of the Church over education. In 1821 bishops had been made responsible for secondary education and in 1824 they were given the right to nominate primary school teachers. **Lay teachers** at universities were replaced by clerics. In 1827, 66 out of 80 philosophy teachers in the colleges were priests and, by 1830, this amounted to about a third of all teachers.

Charles X tried a variety of ways of curbing the press. Louis XVIII had had to resort to some controls despite the promises of the Charter, but Charles X went further. Newspapers did not have a wide readership. About half the population was illiterate anyway, and many others were unable to afford newspapers. Nevertheless, press control was important because a significant number of the 20,000 or so readers were members of the *Pays Légal*. The press could be an effective weapon in the hands of the opposition, as Charles X's ministers were well aware. Various schemes were tried. There was an expensive attempt to buy up opposition newspapers. Another scheme was to price newspapers out of the market by increasing postage rates and the stamp duty on paper. Ministers also threatened legal action against printers who produced material contrary to regulations, as opposed to the writers, but none of these measures met with much success. By 1827, censorship was being applied to all books and journals. When, in 1828, the Minister, Vicomte de Martignac, tried to relax this, there was an outpouring of criticism in the press.

Charles X added to his enemies by purging the army of 56 Bonapartist officers, although he did manage one successful foreign venture. Unfortunately for him, rather like Louis XVIII, he gained little popularity for what he did. In 1830, an expedition against the **Barbary pirates** led to the capture of the pirates' base in Algiers. However, for the *Pays Légal*, hostility to domestic policies had, by this date, reached a crisis point and far overshadowed any pride in Charles X's daring.

Charles X refused to consider any political reform. He had his own view of the Charter and the Chamber. Whilst not seeking to act illegally, he refused to be told what to do by his deputies.

The policies of Charles X split the Chamber of Deputies far more than the policies of Louis XVIII. The moderate, middle group of men who believed in the Charter and had held the balance in Louis XVIII's Chamber dwindled as these men increasingly formed the 'liberal' opposition. They were firmly opposed to the Ultras, with whom the King was clearly identified.

Barbary pirates: Superb seamen, based in Algiers in northern Africa, who tended to make their living from piracy. They often attacked shipping in the Mediterranean.

Why was there a revolution in France in 1830?

What were the short-term causes?
By 1827, there were many signs of widespread discontent in France:

- In March, the middle-class Parisian **National Guard** was disbanded when some members shouted '*à bas les ministres*' ('down with ministers') during a review by the King.

- There was mounting criticism of Villèle's unpopular ministry. Chateaubriand, still smarting from his dismissal, led a campaign against Villèle, both in the press and from the Chamber of Peers.

- A liberal political society, *Aide toi, le ciel t'aidera* (God helps those who help themselves) was founded in 1827 by François Guizot. It was backed by the banker, Jacques Laffitte. It helped to increase opposition to the type of government Charles X had created.

- Charles X again attempted to alter the Chambers to win back support. He created 76 new Peers in the upper Chamber, and announced new

National Guard: First set up at the beginning of the French Revolution, this was a middle-class citizens' military force. It was regarded as a sign of the people's power that they should maintain their own order, rather than being subject to the regular army forces commanded by the king.

elections to the Chamber of Deputies. However, despite the use of much government influence, the move failed. Guizot's society successfully encouraged as many as possible of those eligible, to turn out to vote, and the elections of November 1827 consequently increased the liberal opposition in the Chamber of Deputies. There was a liberal majority of 60, and even some former Ultras began to waver as they became increasingly dissatisfied with Charles X's leadership. Villèle was forced to resign in January 1828.

● Charles X appointed Martignac as his first minister. Martignac had more moderate views, but this only allowed the liberals to increase their demands. By August 1829, Charles X could stand this no longer and created a ministry of close friends. His favourite, Prince Jules de Polignac, an ex-*émigré* who believed he was guided by visions of the Virgin Mary, became his new first minister. His declared aims were 'to reorganise society, to give back to the clergy their weight in state affairs, to create a powerful aristocracy and surround it with privileges'. François Régis, Comte de la Bourbonnaye, who had earned fame as a supporter of the White Terror, became Minister of the Interior. Jean Courvoisier, a cleric, became Minister of Justice. Louis Bourmont, who had deserted Napoleon just before Waterloo, became Minister of War. When the 1829 election returned a large liberal majority, the few remaining moderates joined the opposition.

● On 3 January 1830, *Le National* was founded. This was a liberal, middle-class newspaper. It was again supported financially by Jacques Laffitte, and one of its editors was the politician Adolphe Thiers. It produced many articles attacking the government and its ministers.

● In March 1830, the Chamber passed a vote of 'no confidence' in the government. Charles X responded by dissolving the Chamber and calling elections in June–July 1830. However, yet again the normal workings of government pressure failed to produce the support the King's Ministers needed. The liberal opposition grew stronger, but there was no talk of removing Charles X at this stage. The deputies merely wanted the dismissal of his unpopular ministers, and their most revolutionary idea was a refusal to pay taxes.

● Encouraged by Bourmont's success in capturing Algiers on 9 July 1830, which he thought would win over public opinion, Polignac prepared a further change in the franchise. This was a last resort. Charles X planned to use a clause in the Charter that permitted him to change the voting system by royal edict, without going through the Chambers.

● On 25 July 1830, the Government published the new edicts, known as the four Ordinances of St Cloud, in its official newspaper, *Le Moniteur.* The New Chamber of Deputies was dissolved before it had even met, and fresh elections were called, with an electorate that had been reduced from 100,000 men to the 25,000 richest members of the *Pays Légal*. Furthermore, the edicts forbade the publication of any unauthorised newspaper or pamphlet of less than 20 pages. All of this was legal within the terms of the Charter, but to Charles X's opponents it seemed like a *coup d'état*.

Coup d'état: An illegal attempt to seize power. In this case, the issue of the July Ordinances was (wrongly) regarded as an illegal action by Charles X, designed to overthrow the Charter and give the monarchy more power.

What were the results of Charles X's actions?

Charles X had over-estimated the loyalty he commanded. The best of his troops were still in Algiers, Bourmont (the Minister of War) was absent, Jean-Baptiste de Champagny (his deputy minister) was not informed and

Auguste Marmont (in charge of the Parisian garrison) knew nothing of the Ordinances until he read *Le Moniteur*. There had been no attempt to round up opposition leaders before the July Ordinances were published, and Charles X was, apparently, so unconcerned that he went hunting. Even at this stage, most deputies were fearful of violence, but the republicans and the Marquis de Lafayette began mobilising support. Displeased printers (the very men asked to print the ordinances), journalists who were threatened by the curbs on the press, students who believed in radical change and discontented working men all joined in the protests. By 28–29 July, there was severe rioting and barricades started to go up in the streets of Paris. What troops there were, were forced out of Paris. Charles X, now 73, swiftly decided that abdication was the only course of action open to him. On 1 August 1830, he announced his departure in the mistaken belief that it might save the throne for his grandson, son of the assassinated duc de Berri. On 17 August, Charles fled to England to avoid arrest, as France reorganised its government once more.

What were the long-term causes of revolution?

To some extent, both Louis XVIII and Charles X can be held personally responsible for the collapse of the Bourbon Monarchy in 1830.

Neither Louis XVIII nor Charles X was ideally suited to be King. Both had been *émigrés*, and long exile had left them out of touch with the changes brought by the French Revolution. They were elderly monarchs and, although Louis XVIII was negative and uninspiring, Charles X lacked commonsense and showed an inability to compromise. They both shared grand hopes of reasserting France's power and strength in Europe, but they seemed dull after the glory brought by Napoleon. Furthermore, they showed their insensitivity by stressing their divine right to rule and insisting on using the Bourbon flag.

The Bourbons brought back the *émigrés* and reasserted the influence of the Catholic Church. This was seen as a threat to the changes brought by the Revolution and was particularly resented by those property owners and office holders who had benefited from it.

Both monarchs increased the opposition they faced. Louis XVIII allowed the 'White Terror' and repeatedly gave in to the Ultras' demands as his reign progressed. Charles X pursued his own personal views regardless of those around him, taking actions such as disbanding the National Guard, and announcing the July Ordinances with little thought for the consequences.

Their policies offended the very group that the monarchs most needed for support, the *Pays Légal*. Charles X, even more than Louis XVIII, refused to listen to public opinion as expressed through the Chamber and his failure to win over this powerful and influential group in society sealed the fate of the dynasty.

However, it would be unfair to suggest that the Bourbons were solely to blame for their fate. The circumstances under which they took the throne

Marquis de Lafayette, Marie Joseph Motier (1757–1834)
An aristocrat who became attracted by the idea of 'liberty' while fighting as a volunteer in the American War of Independence in 1776. He returned to France determined to spread his views and he helped to draft the 'Declaration of the Rights of Man' (August 1789) – a statement of people's basic rights and freedom. Lafayette was made the first commander of the new National Guard, but events turned against him and he was forced to flee from France (1792–99). By 1815 he was highly regarded as a symbol of liberty. He helped to overthrow Napoleon's government and was later involved in a military conspiracy against the Bourbons in 1821. Lafayette attached himself to the Orléanist opposition and was one of Louis-Philippe's supporters in 1830. He was keen to extend the principles of 1830 abroad, but died before he could do this.

1. *With reference to (a) The Ultras, (b) The Catholic Church and (c) The Liberals, explain who gained and who lost the most from the reign of Charles X.*

2. *Using the factors given in this section, rate, in order of importance, the reasons that you think provide the most convincing explanation for the overthrow of the Bourbons in 1830.*

3. *Do you think it is fair to say that 'neither Louis XVIII nor Charles X learnt anything from the French Revolutionary and Napoleonic period'? Give reasons for your answer.*

were not ideal. They had, to some extent, been imposed on France by its enemies and life was never going to be easy for them, particularly after the difficult times France had been through. France's recent past had shown that there were plenty of alternative schemes of government, and these increased in appeal when things began to go wrong.

In some respects, they were unlucky. Unfortunate incidents such as the '100 days', which set Louis' reign off to a bad start, the assassination of de Berri, which gave the Ultras the upper hand, and Louis XVIII's poor health, were all factors beyond their personal control.

The growth of the Carbonarist secret societies and the influence of the socialists provided the intellectual leaders who were ready to seize any opportunity to put their views into practice.

The gradual spread of industrialisation, especially in Paris, also contributed to the unrest. Slumps, unemployment and high food prices, particularly after 1826 when an economic depression hit France along with the rest of western European, created a willing Parisian 'mob', prepared to follow those who promised them a better future. A 30% wage fall in the building trades of Paris, a 40% fall for the textile workers, together with poor harvests which raised the price of food, meant that those workers who had migrated to Paris in search of jobs were particularly badly hit. It was these men who had manned the barricades and provided the forces that so frightened Charles X.

7.4 How successful was Louis-Philippe as King of France (1830–1848)?

Why did Louis-Philippe become King in 1830?

In July 1830, the opponents of Charles X were divided about who or what should replace him. Many of the popular Parisian leaders, supported by the workers and students, favoured a republic under the presidency of Lafayette. However, the lawyers, bankers and members of the bourgeoisie who had spoken out so strongly against the Bourbon Monarchy, feared revolutionary activity even more. They were hostile to the idea of a republic and were determined to avoid any form of government that threatened their status and power.

While the liberal deputies were debating their course of action in the final week of July 1830, the republicans and working men seized the initiative. By the 28 and 29 July the barricades had gone up and the *tricolor* flew over Notre Dame. If the bourgeoisie were to benefit from the revolution they had provoked, they had to act quickly. It was Adolphe Thiers who provided the leadership. He had the walls of Paris covered with posters in favour of Louis-Philippe, duc d'Orléans, on 29–30 July. He calculated that Louis-Philippe, who had a royal claim to the throne and yet was known to have fought for the French Revolution, could maintain the monarchy in France as well as win the support of both the middle and lower classes. Louis-Philippe's cause was also promoted by Thiers' newspaper, *Le National*. Although Charles X had abdicated in favour of his nine-year-old grandson on 1 August, the child, Henry (V), was to 'rule' for only one week. The banker Lafitte, who also favoured a constitutional monarchy, persuaded the deputies to offer Louis-Philippe the position of 'Lieutenant General of the Kingdom'. Thiers approached Louis-Philippe in person and, after much negotiation with the republicans, Louis-Philippe received their backing and entered Paris. He met and embraced Lafayette in the Hôtel de Ville (Town Hall). To the cheers of a large crowd, Lafayette and Louis-Philippe appeared at the window, wrapped in a *tricolor*. On 9 August, Henry V was deposed, and Louis-Philippe was recognised as 'King of the French by the grace of God and the will of the nation'.

What sort of person was Louis-Philippe?

Louis-Philippe was a direct descendant of Louis XIII, and the eldest son of Philippe, duc d'Orléans. His father had supported the Revolution and favoured the execution of Louis XVI. This had earned him the nickname *'Égalité'* (equality), although it had not saved him from the guillotine. Louis-Philippe was the next in line to the throne after the family of Charles X, and so had a fair claim to the inheritance (see family tree on page 187). He had served as a military commander in the Revolutionary armies of 1792 and although he had fled to Austria in 1793, as the revolution grew more extreme, he had never supported the enemies of France. He had remained in exile in Switzerland, the USA and England, returning at the restoration. During the years of Bourbon rule, his home, the Palais Royal in Paris, had been a focus for middle-class opposition to the monarchy. By 1830, it was the bourgeoisie, with whom he associated, who were determined to see him as King.

Louis-Philippe could not have been more different from the pompous and aloof Charles X. His revolutionary parentage and years of poverty had made him thrifty in his habits, and he liked to think of himself as one of the bourgeoisie. He even dressed like them, complete with his trademark umbrella and tailcoat. He is sometimes called the 'citizen king' as he enjoyed a simple and unaffected way of life. Louis-Philippe rose early. He liked to light his own study fire, to shave himself and to lunch on soup. He led an exemplary life, was a happy family man and, to the horror of his guards, liked to stroll through the streets of Paris unattended. In many ways, he was the perfect gentleman. However, as the years wore on, the working men who had helped to bring him to power found him increasingly dull and boring. Finding nothing else to accuse him of, the Parisian press and other journals regularly caricatured him as an overweight and uninspiring pear-shaped character. (See cartoon in Source D on page 209.)

In 1830, aged 57, Louis-Philippe appeared comparatively young after the Bourbons and it looked as though he had the ideal qualities needed in a constitutional King. The French historian, Bertier de Sauvigny, wrote that 'in many respects he was one of the most capable men who have ever occupied the throne'. He had received a good education, had a widely cultivated mind and spoke four languages fluently. He had a pleasant manner, enjoyed the company of others, and was both well meaning and hard working. It was only as he grew older that those around him grew less sure. One unfortunate personality trait, that grew worse with his advancing years, was his anxiety to please everyone he met. He found it increasingly hard to make decisions which avoided giving offence and became so talkative that his listeners sometimes feared that he paid little attention to them. What he said, thought and did were not always the same thing and by deceiving some of his closest advisers, he eventually lost their respect and confidence.

How bourgeois was Louis-Philippe's monarchy?

The case for the bourgeois monarchy

In July 1830, Laffitte declared, 'from now on bankers will rule'. The changes of 1830 and Louis-Philippe's personal lifestyle helped to create the impression that his reign was a 'bourgeois' monarchy, favouring the middle classes. Membership of the National Guard, reconstituted under Louis-Philippe's own elected officers in 1831, was restricted to members of the middle class. The qualification for the vote was extended to include wealthy, middle-class men. The age for election to the lower Chamber fell to 30, instead of 40 years, and the franchise was widened to include all those who paid 200 francs or more in direct taxation, as opposed to the 300 francs minimum demanded in the Bourbon period.

Financial bourgeoisie: Members of the upper middle class who had made large sums of money through industry, trade or investment and were therefore eligible to vote (members of the *Pays Légal*) in Louis-Philippe's reign.

Historians influenced by the Marxist interpretation of history believe that the 1830 revolution was a triumph for the **financial bourgeoisie**, the upper middle classes of industrialists, bankers and merchants, who had made their money through trade and industry. They argue that this group of people consolidated their control, after 1830, at the expense of the workers. However, there were other middle-class men at the top in Louis-Philippe's reign. One influential group was that of the journalists and lawyers, such as Thiers. They worked closely with the business classes, and spoke up for their interests in the Chamber of Deputies. Also prominent were university professors such as Francis Guizot. The old aristocracy, barred from the Chamber of Peers by a decree repressing hereditary peerage in December 1831, was forced to retire to their country estates. In 1827, 44% of the deputies had been nobles; by 1836 it was only 14%.

The French electoral system, 1816–1848

The Chamber of Deputies

Year	Number of seats	Deputies' qualifications Tax	Age	Electors' qualifications Tax	Age	Size of electorate	Additional points
1816	258	1000 fr	40	300 fr	30	88,000–110,000 (1814–1830)	Members elected for 5 years
1817					25		
1818							One-fifth of members to be elected annually
1820	430						The additional 172 deputies to be elected by the chief taxpayers
1824							End of annual elections. Members elected for 7 years
1830/1	459	500 fr	30	200 fr*	25	166,000–241,000 (1830–1848)	* Also members of the Institut de France and retired army officers paying 100 francs in tax. Members elected for 5 years

The case against the bourgeois monarchy

Those who argue that the monarchy of Louis-Philippe was not bourgeois, usually point to the fact that many who considered themselves 'bourgeois', and in particular the less wealthy industrialists, traders and students whose income failed to qualify them for the vote, were excluded from active participation in the reign. Although the electorate rose from around 166,000 in 1830 to 241,000 in 1848, because growing economic prosperity increased the numbers of those eligible to vote, this was still not enough to give the vote to the 'lower' middle classes. Indeed, some historians, notably D. Pinkney, have argued that the governmental changes after 1830 were a change of personnel rather than of class. The upper middle class was every bit as wealthy and remote from the lower shopkeepers and students as the landowning nobles of Charles X's time had been.

Furthermore, it can be argued that the regime never really lived up to bourgeois expectations. The government showed little interest in the economic problems of the lesser bourgeoisie. A notable example of this came, in the 1840s, when Guizot completely mismanaged a plan to extend railway building in France. By passing a law for the compulsory purchase of land for railway construction in 1841, the government appeared to be supporting middle-class speculators and providing government backing for railway development. As more companies were set up and money poured into both the railways and their feeder industries, such as iron, there was a crisis of over-production. Share prices suddenly fell. As always, the crisis hit hardest at the lower middle class, many of which had limited facilities for borrowing money and, therefore, faced bankruptcy. The government did nothing to ease their lot, and they became some of Louis-Philippe's harshest critics.

Similarly, middle-class interest in reform, be it political, social or economic, met with little response from the so-called bourgeois monarchy. It is not surprising, therefore, that it was the bourgeoisie who led the mounting barrage of criticism in the 1840s. The historian Theodore Zeldin claims that the frustration felt among students, in particular, helped to create the 1848 revolution.

In what respects did Louis-Philippe's position differ from that of his predecessors?

In addition to the increase in the bourgeois elements in government, and the reduction of the old aristocratic influence of the Bourbon era, Louis-Philippe's accession brought a number of other changes both to the position of the monarchy and the style of government:

- Louis-Philippe accepted the *tricolor*, symbolic of the French Revolution, instead of the white flag of the Bourbons.

- Louis-Philippe was deemed *roi des Français* (King of the French), not *roi de France* (King of France). The new title was meant to reinforce the fact that he had accepted his crown from the French people. The old-style title had implied that the King had a divine right to rule the country.

Disestablished: This meant removing the special status of the Catholic Church, which had formerly been regarded as part of the State, and received financial support from it. Those who did not support the Catholic Church would no longer be treated as second-class citizens.

- The Catholic Church was **disestablished**. The Catholic faith now became the 'religion of the majority of Frenchmen' rather than the State religion. The Church lost its control of education, bishops' incomes were reduced and the Jesuits were forced to leave France.

- Press censorship was relaxed.

However, the extent of change must not be exaggerated. There were still similarities with what had gone before.

1832 Reform Act: By 1832, there was much popular demand for the extension of the narrow, propertied franchise in Great Britain. The general effect of this Act was to give the middle class, but not the working class, the vote. The franchise in France, however, although widened in 1830, was still narrower than in the unreformed British system.

- The right to vote was still very restricted, and based on wealth. More than 97% of men over 21 years of age were still excluded from the vote. This meant that the electorate formed a smaller proportion of the population than that in Great Britain before the **1832 Reform Act**.

- The new Chamber of Peers still consisted of those nominated by the king, although those with hereditary titles were excluded.

- Although more locally elected councils were established, the Mayor was chosen by the government, maintaining central influence in the localities.

- Many of those who had served under Charles X retained their places under Louis-Philippe.

- The regime remained firmly opposed to the demands of the working class. The National Guard was used as an internal security force against workers in the towns and the authorities were not afraid to use the regular army to break up strikes and to suppress trade unions and political clubs. There was no interest in social reform and the government saw its main task as the preservation of law and order.

How extensive was the opposition to the new regime?

Louis-Philippe's monarchy was, in many respects, a compromise. So, despite the new King's friendliness, it is not surprising that he attracted limited loyalty.

Most monarchists supported the new King, although the old-style royalists were unimpressed by his personal way of life. A few remained in opposition and the 'legitimist' cause even attracted some younger men as memories of Charles X faded and the idea of the 'divine right' of kings developed a new type of romantic fascination.

The clergy were disappointed with Louis-Philippe, after Charles X. He appeared to be working against the Catholic Church, reducing its status and undermining its control of education. When a law of 1833 set up secular (state) training colleges for teachers, the Catholic newspaper, *L'Univers*, began a campaign to fight for Church education. In fact, Louis-Philippe did attempt to gain some concessions for the Church in a law of 1844, but this was rejected by the Chamber. By this stage, however, there was little clerical support for the regime.

Bonapartists: Supporters of Napoleon Bonaparte, his descendants, and his style of government. Broadly in favour of stable, prosperous government, preserving the moderate reforms of the French Revolution, but resisting the dangers of more radical social reconstruction.

A new and growing opposition force was that of the **Bonapartists**. They disliked Louis-Philippe and felt France needed a strong man, like Napoleon, to reassert French greatness and power. The first hints of trouble were at the funeral in June 1832 of the old Napoleonic soldier, General Lamarque, when riots broke out on the streets of Paris. The publication of Thiers' *History of the Consulate and Empire* and the raising of Napoleon's statue to the top of the column in the Place Vendôme in 1833, all helped to create a somewhat idealistic picture of the glorious Emperor and of what France might have become. Louis Napoleon, nephew of the Emperor, made his first attempt at a *coup d'état* in 1836, when he tried to bribe the garrison at Strasbourg to mutiny in favour of the Bonapartist cause. This was a fiasco. His second attempt to seize power, in an uprising at Boulogne in 1840, was no more successful. However, the completion of the Arc de Triomphe in 1836 and the burying of Napoleon's remains at Les Invalides in 1840 were reminders of Napoleonic days. They unwittingly helped the growing appeal of the Napoleonic legend.

Left: This refers to those who hold reformist views – the more extreme, the more 'left'. In 1830, they included liberals, radicals, republicans and socialists. The term itself derives from the position of the seats in the semi-circular French Chamber of Deputies, where the conservatives sat on the right, the moderates in the centre and the radicals on the left.

By far the largest group of opponents to Louis Philippe came from the **left**. This widespread group included both working-class radicals and middle-, and even upper-, class socialists. Among those members of the Parisian working class who had manned the barricades in 1830, were republicans who felt cheated that they had merely exchanged one monarch for another. In the fluctuating economic circumstances of the 1830s and 1840s, the idea of republicanism, which was believed to mean a government in the interests of ordinary, working people, had a great deal of appeal. It is impossible to be precise about the numbers involved. Many of those with republican sympathies were not involved in any type of active republican organisation, but it would seem that in the cities many of the lower classes regarded republicanism as a remedy for poverty and unemployment. There were also middle- and upper-class republicans. These educated men were attracted by the ideas of the French socialists and their enthusiasm was fuelled by a number of histories of the French Revolution published about this time. These idealised the first French Republic. By the 1840s, there were few who could remember the Revolution itself, and republicanism had lost some of its former horror.

There were a number of prominent political figures who became increasingly disillusioned with the sort of leadership Louis-Philippe provided. These men were not against the monarchy as such, but they saw the need for social and political reform. They despaired of Louis-Philippe's disinterest. Some, such as Thiers, also longed for Louis-Philippe to exert a more positive influence abroad. They disliked his caution and apparent willingness to follow Great Britain's lead. (See details on foreign policy below and in Chapter 6.)

How did Louis-Philippe govern France?

Louis-Philippe pursued a cautious line. His natural inclination was to be moderate and, for most of his reign, he relied on ministers of similar views. He used traditional means of influence to ensure that the Chamber of Deputies supported his chosen leaders. Between 1830 and 1847, he was able to increase the number of royal officials who sat as deputies from 142 to 193, out of a total of 459 seats.

In the early years of his reign, when many ministers and deputies had high hopes of change, control was not easy. His first ministerial team was led by Jacques Laffitte. It regarded the July revolution as a beginning only and favoured further reform. However, continued rioting and disorder, particularly in Paris, soon persuaded Louis-Philippe that he needed a firmer and more conservative hand at the top. Therefore, in March 1831, Lafitte was replaced by Casimir Périer.

Périer was quite a different type. As a traditional liberal, he regarded the July revolution as nothing more than a change of monarch, bringing a more sincere application of the Charter. According to the French historian Bertier de Sauvigny, Périer 'typified the monied bourgeoisie, loathing disorder and he brought to the task of governing a force of willpower and energy that was almost wildly passionate'. The elections of July 1831 were very carefully managed, in order to return a Chamber prepared to use force, if necessary, to curb unrest. Casimir Périer demanded unquestioning obedience from his colleagues, and even Louis-Philippe was persuaded to stand aside and let him command. When the Chamber met, he announced his programme. 'At home order, without calling on liberty to make any sacrifices; abroad, peace with no cost to honour.' He was remarkably successful. The army was used against demonstrators in Lyons (October 1831). In a little over a year, before he was tragically struck down by **cholera** in Paris, Périer had managed to quell the unrest and set the regime on firm foundations.

Cholera: A serious and often fatal disease that affects the digestive organs. It is caused by drinking infected water or eating infected food. There was a cholera epidemic in France in 1832.

François Guizot (1787–1874)
A protestant (Huguenot) from Nîmes in southern France. He became Professor of History in Paris in 1812 and did not enter politics until he was 43, in 1830. He became a minister (1832) and Foreign Minister (1840–47). He was the most influential figure in Louis-Philippe's government during this time. The King liked his conservative attitude and relied on him. As Prime Minister from 1847 to February 1848, his failure to respond to demands for the extension of the franchise helped cause the 1848 revolution. Guizot fled into exile and his last years were spent writing history books.

Adolphe Thiers (1797–1877)
Thiers was a lawyer, journalist, writer and politician. In 1830 he was among those who persuaded Louis-Philippe to accept the throne. Became Minister of the Interior in 1834, and was responsible for the repression of the riots in Lyons and Paris in 1834. He became Prime Minister, briefly (1836 and 1840), but Louis-Philippe did not like Thiers' attitude, which was to keep the King out of politics as much as possible. When he nearly brought France to war in 1840, Louis-Philippe was pleased to have an excuse to dismiss him. Thiers became a focus for opposition to Guizot in the Chamber of Deputies in the 1840s, and constantly pressed for an extension of the franchise. However, when trouble broke out in 1848, he tried to persuade Louis-Philippe to leave Paris and repress the revolution with support from the provinces. Thiers' advice went unheeded. Nevertheless, he survived to enjoy a long political career under Napoleon III and the Republic of 1871.

Close season: A hunting term that refers to the time of year when it is forbidden to shoot certain game birds or animals.

After Périer's death, in May 1832, Louis-Philippe experienced difficulty in finding a new ministry that would carry out his wishes. Between May 1832 and October 1840, there were no less than 10 ministries in all. During this period, Adolphe Thiers, François Guizot and the duc de Broglie were the most influential spokespeople in the Chamber. Although Thiers had helped to bring Louis-Philippe to power, their attitudes to the King's position were quite different. Thiers believed that the King should act as a figurehead, whereas Louis-Philippe wanted a real say in government through a 'puppet' Prime Minister. De Broglie and Guizot, on the other hand, were content with the constitutional system of government that gave the King an active say in affairs.

Following the dismissal of Thiers in 1840, which was the result of the foreign policy crisis of that year (see foreign policy section below), Louis-Philippe eventually came to rely on Guizot. Marshal Soult was nominally in charge, but as Minister of Foreign Affairs, and Chief Minister from September 1847 when Soult retired, Guizot dominated politics. At last the king had found a minister on whom he could rely, and who was prepared to let him exercise some influence in government. In any case, as Louis-Philippe grew older he became less energetic and was happy to leave decision making to Guizot.

Guizot controlled the government through extensive manipulation of the electoral system. He gave government posts, business contracts and pensions to members of the government, and thus secured a majority in the Chamber of Deputies even though he was increasingly opposed by those outside the Chamber. He was a talented speaker, but had little time for 'public opinion'. He preferred to keep things as they were and declared that 'the duty of the government is to go slowly and wisely; to maintain and to set bounds'. Such views coincided perfectly with Louis-Philippe's. Thiers and Odillon Barrot led the opposition to Guizot in the Chamber, regarding him as a barrier to reform but, while the vote was so restricted and Guizot could maintain his position by bribery, there was very little they could do.

How did Louis-Philippe deal with the unrest between 1830 and 1847?

Louis-Philippe was well aware of the undercurrent of unrest throughout his reign but, rather than address its causes, he tended to accept it as something beyond his control. He spent a good deal of time personally reviewing and boosting the morale of his revived National Guard, which was responsible for maintaining order, and he showed remarkable resilience in the face of six assassination attempts. In 1835, a machine comprising 24 muskets killed 41 people but left the King with only a grazed chin. On another occasion, when a bullet found its way into his hair, he remarked, 'it is only in hunting me that there is no **close season**'.

Signs of discontent fluctuated along with economic circumstances, but they were never far below the surface. The government tried to take a firm stance when troubles broke out and the use of the army by Casimir Périer in 1831 to quell the revolt of the Lyons silk weavers, set the pattern of the reign. In Paris, in June 1832, the army was again used to restrain the rioters at Lamarque's funeral, and 800 were killed or wounded. A further strike in Lyons (13 February 1834) was followed by a rising in April that took four days to crush. A law of 16 March 1834 stated the government's intention of dealing harshly with members of secret societies but, in April, there was an open protest led by members of such groups. Angry students and workers in Paris were savagely dealt with in 'the massacre of Rue Transnonain', and their leaders arrested. Socialists, such as Louis-Auguste

Louis Auguste Blanqui (1805–1881)
A professional revolutionary who spent 33 years in prison for his part in conspiracies and unrest. He joined a Carbonari society at 17 and fought against the Bourbon monarchy in 1830. However, after the failure of the Lyons silk weavers' riots in 1834, he rejected the old ways. He believed in the power of the workers, who would eventually overthrow the other classes. He set up the 'Society of the Seasons' to train a professional minority of working men who would seize power directly. He tried to put his ideas into practice in 1848.

Blanqui and Armand Barbès were involved in many plots, but only after an attempted *coup d'état* in May 1839 were they imprisoned for life.

Throughout his reign, Louis Philippe resisted pressure from both inside and outside the Chamber, to widen the franchise and to address issues of social reform. He believed the political system was working well and required no changes. To him, the poor were poor because of factors beyond the government's control. To interfere, he believed, would probably make things worse. Guizot was also disinterested in social matters. The government's message to '*enrichissez-vous*' ('go and make yourself rich') was not much comfort to the Parisian poor. So, despite the worsening economic climate after 1840, the government did nothing to tackle the growing problems that were becoming particularly acute in Paris, where poor living conditions and unemployment left many dependent on charity. It is hardly surprising that these people were ready to turn against Louis-Philippe.

How successful was the July Monarchy in foreign affairs?

Louis-Philippe's policies abroad were moderate and realistic, but they were seen at home as rather dull and cowardly. They contrasted unfavourably with the traditional role of France as a powerful and respected nation in Europe. This was a role which many politicians, as well as ordinary Frenchmen, had been hoping France would resume after 1830. Louis-Philippe's reasoning was, however, quite sound. He knew that any attempt at French expansion would be strongly resisted by the other powers of Europe. What is more, he feared for his own throne, if France were to antagonise powers such as Russia and Austria. They had committed themselves to the prevention of revolutionary change in the Troppau Protocol of 1820, and yet his own position had been dependent on a revolution. For this reason, he was anxious to maintain British friendship. Since Britain had opposed the Troppau agreement, it seemed an obvious ally. With Britain's support, Louis-Philippe felt the other powers would not act against him.

Louis-Philippe displayed his moderation almost as soon as he came to power. The area we now know as Belgium had been incorporated into the Kingdom of the Netherlands, and placed under Dutch control in 1815. However, inspired by the example of the French, there was a Belgian rebellion against Dutch rule in August 1830 (see Chapter 6). The French saw this as an opportunity to display their power. France had long claimed that its 'natural frontier' in the north should be the river Rhine (see maps on pages 146 and 147). The frontier chosen to divide the Kingdom of the Netherlands from France was completely artificial. In the eyes of many Frenchmen it was quite unjustifiable since French was spoken on both sides of the border. However, Louis-Philippe ignored the clamour to intervene. He favoured Belgian independence, and certainly did not want Russia or Austria taking steps to crush the revolt, but he was not prepared to risk **annexation**. Instead, he adopted a policy of co-operation with the British. He also ignored suggestions in France that he should put forward his second son, the duc de Nemours, as a candidate for the throne of a newly independent Belgium. Once again, Louis-Philippe did not want to upset the British. The French glimpsed two brief moments of potential glory when their troops were compelled to enter Belgium, with British approval, to force the Dutch to accept terms in 1831 and again in 1833. However, it was all too clear to his subjects that Louis-Philippe had allowed the British to assume the driving seat in this affair.

In Spain, Louis-Philippe was also cautious. There had long been a tradition of French influence there, and in 1821 Louis XVIII had helped

Annexation: The act of incorporating new territory into a state.

restore the rightful King Ferdinand VII (Section 7.2). However, Ferdinand VII had struggled to retain his throne and, on his death in September 1833, there was another crisis. The dispute was between his brother Don Carlos, whom the absolutists favoured, and his young daughter, Isabella, supported by the liberals. This seemed to offer a new opportunity for French intervention. However, Louis-Philippe once again chose to work with the British, who were determined to keep the French out. Lord Palmerston, the British Prime Minister, rejected the French suggestion of an alliance with Great Britain in support of the constitutional governments in Spain and Portugal. Instead, in April 1834, he proposed his own Quadruple Alliance of Britain and France, together with the constitutional monarchies of Portugal and Spain. Crucially, this prevented independent French action in Spain, while permitting the British to act independently in Portugal.

Louis-Philippe eventually showed a streak of independence over the question of the Spanish marriages. It was proposed that one of his sons marry the young Queen Isabella or, failing that, her sister. With some deference to the British, then represented by the Foreign Secretary Lord Aberdeen, it was settled that Queen Isabella would marry an impotent Spanish nobleman, Francisco of Cadiz, while her sister would marry de Montpensier, a younger son of Louis-Philippe. Palmerston, returning to office in 1846, tried to overthrow this agreement, but the French pressed ahead regardless. This uncharacteristic move was probably an attempt to avoid another humiliation at the hands of the British, although cynics said it was simply because Louis-Philippe wanted to benefit his own family. This was the one instance of Louis-Philippe's independence in Spanish affairs. Although France was quick to join Spain in promising aid to the Queen of Portugal in 1847, no action was taken until the co-operation and support of the British had been secured.

Another area of foreign policy which made Louis-Philippe unpopular was his part in the Mehemet Ali affair of 1839–41. France had long-standing economic links with Egypt and, in the 1830s, the Pasha (ruler) of Egypt, Mehemet Ali, was regarded as a French *protégé*. Mehemet Ali had become a very powerful ruler and resented the fact that he owed allegiance to Turkey for his lands. He tried to declare the independence of Egypt and Syria in 1839. This aroused the concern of the European powers who feared the consequences of the break-up of the Turkish Empire. A conference was held in Vienna in the spring of 1840. At this time, Louis-Philippe had reluctantly accepted Thiers as his Prime Minister. However, he was far from happy with the stance Thiers took at the conference. Thiers had declared French support for Mehemet Ali and refused to endorse any action, arguing that the Pasha should be left to pursue his own affairs. He even threatened war should the other powers act against him.

Ignoring the French protests, and encouraged by Palmerston, they did just that. An ultimatum, drawn up in The Treaty of London, July 1840, threatened Mehemet Ali with force if he did not accept their terms. The French were furious, and there was an outcry for war. Thiers threatened an invasion along the Rhine, which caused considerable alarm in Prussia and the German Confederation (see Chapter 8), but Louis-Philippe could not risk a single-handed contest. He had no alternative but to dismiss Thiers in October and accept the humiliation the event had caused. Although, by joining the joint action against Mehemet Ali and signing the Straits Convention in 1841, the French were soon back in co-operation with the other powers, Louis-Philippe's reputation had suffered another blow.

In 1844, Louis-Philippe again seemed to back down to British demands. Faced with a dispute over influence in Tahiti, he disowned the agent who had tried to annex the island in the name of the French. Instead, he agreed to pay £1000 to a British missionary who had been arrested by the French.

To the dismay of the 'left', Louis-Philippe showed no interest in supporting fellow revolutionaries abroad in 1830–31. The Poles looked in vain for French help in their rebellion against the Russians, while in Italy, the pronouncement of the new French Foreign Minister, Horace Sébastiani in September 1830, that France would oppose any intervention by Austria outside its own frontiers, raised false hopes. Louis-Philippe informed Metternich privately that he would not oppose Austrian intervention to crush the Italian rebellions. The only action taken by the French was to send troops to Ancona in the Papal States (February 1832–38), to match the Austrian troops who had gone to curb disorder at the request of the Pope, and had remained stationed in Bologna. (For full details, see Chapter 9.)

Louis-Philippe did have one successful military venture. The conquest of Algeria, begun by Charles X in 1830, was achieved in 1847 after a long drawn-out campaign. However, this success brought no honour to the King. The expense, the vicious fighting, the disease and the part played by five of Louis-Philippe's own sons, attracted only criticism. In any case, events outside Europe were regarded as only second best to those within it.

According to historian Anthony Wood, in *Europe 1815–1945* (1964), 'caution and commonsense were hallmarks of the reign of Louis Philippe' and nowhere is this seen more clearly than in his foreign policy. However, a policy that avoided confrontation and often seemed to be tailored to suit British demands, was not what most Frenchmen wanted. They were not prepared to accept that France was in no position to do more, and instead began to wonder whether a different regime might not do better.

1. To what extent, and why, did the monarchy of Louis-Philippe differ from that of his Bourbon predecessors?

2. How, and with what success, did Louis-Philippe address the problems that he faced up to 1848?

3. How successfully did Louis-Philippe uphold French interests abroad?

Source-based questions: The July Monarchy

SOURCE A

Louis-Philippe leaving the Royal Palace on his way to the Hôtel de Ville in Paris on 30 July 1830.

Source-based questions: The July Monarchy

SOURCE B

It was not the French bourgeoisie that ruled under Louis-Philippe, but one faction of it: bankers, stock-exchange kings, owners of coal and iron mines and forests, a part of the landed proprietors – the so-called finance aristocracy. The industrial bourgeoisie proper … was represented only as a minority in the Chambers. Since the finance aristocracy made the laws, (and) was at the head of the administration of the State … the same mania to get rich quick was repeated in every sphere … to get rich, not by production, but by pocketing the already available wealth of others.

From The Class Struggle in France, *written by Karl Marx, the great communist thinker after the revolution of 1848–50. His assessment of the July Monarchy was shared by many Socialists and radicals.*

SOURCE C

In theory the France of Louis-Philippe should have shared the political flexibility of Britain. In practice it did not. For though it was clear that the ruling class of France represented only a section of the middle-class interest, the memory of the revolution of 1789 stood in the way of reform. For the opposition consisted not merely of the discontented bourgeoisie, but of the politically decisive lower middle class, especially of Paris. To widen the franchise might thus let in the Radicals … who would be republicans.

From The Age of Revolution *by Eric Hobsbawm (1962) – a secondary source from a Marxist historian*

SOURCE D

'Punch' cartoon – Louis-Philippe's candle is snuffed out by the 1848 revolutionaries.

1. Explain the following details of the illustrations:

(a) The tricolor in Source A.

(b) Louis-Philippe's caricature in Source D.

2. Study Sources B and C.

In what ways do these sources present a similar picture of French government in the reign of Louis-Philippe?

3. In what respects do Sources A and D present opposing views of the July Monarchy?

4. 'The Bourgeois Monarchy was bourgeois in name only'.

Using the information in Sources B and C and in Section 7.4, would you agree with this statement? Give reasons for your answer.

5. By studying all the sources and the information in Section 7.4, can you explain why the July Monarchy ended in failure?

7.5 Why did revolution break out in France in 1848?
A CASE STUDY IN HISTORICAL INTERPRETATION

Alphonse de Lamartine (1790–1869)
An aristocrat who became a poet and a politician. He was regarded as the most outstanding French romantic poet of the 1820s. He became a deputy in 1833 and was an opposition figure during the Orléans monarchy. He supported the 1848 revolution, but was discredited after June 1848 and devoted the rest of his life to his literary work.

Anti-Corn Law League: A middle-class organisation set up in Great Britain to campaign for the repeal of the Corn Laws. By a combination of public meetings and parliamentary pressure, it was successful in 1846.

Manhood suffrage: The right of males over the age of consent to vote for a government or a national leader.

Alexandre Auguste Ledru-Rollin (1807–1874)
A radical and a contributor to the socialist journal, *La Réforme*. He believed in Republican government and manhood suffrage, and he soon became a prominent speaker at the political banquets of 1847. He helped to create the Revolution of 1848 and became Minister of Home Affairs in the provisional Government of 1848.

What were the short-term causes?

The short-term causes of revolution are relatively simple and easily explained.

By 1848, as Alphonse de Lamartine noted at the time, 'La France s'ennuie' (France was bored). Louis-Philippe's reign had grown stale and, with Guizot at the helm, no change looked possible. It seemed essential to force a widening of the franchise, if the Chamber was to reflect the true wishes of the French people. Since Thiers and Barrot's campaigns to extend the vote were making little headway within the Chamber, pressure for reform moved outside.

It was Laurent-Antoine Paguerre, a publisher, who first suggested a committee to organise opposition candidates to Guizot. From this, in May 1847, came the idea of a series of banquets in favour of electoral reform. Banquets were chosen as this got round the law against political meetings. The organisers copied the methods of the successful **Anti-Corn Law League** in England, and hoped to demonstrate support for their cause through local meetings. The first was held on 9 July 1847 and was addressed by Paguerre. Thiers, fearing the effects of involving the lower classes in their campaign, did not approve. His predictions proved correct. Around 70 banquets were held but, after the Lille banquet of November 1847, they became increasingly radical. Leadership fell to more extreme republicans such as Ledru-Rollin, who demanded **manhood suffrage**, while the popular press stirred up public opposition.

The banquet campaign was planned to culminate in a mass banquet in Paris on 22 February 1848. The government, fearing disorder, banned the banquet. Moderate and liberal politicians accepted this move with some relief. However, more radical politicians and republicans called for a protest demonstration. On 22 February, as crowds of students and workers gathered, there was some violence as attempts were made to disperse them. The following day, Louis-Philippe called out the National Guard, which had not met since 1840, hoping to intimidate the demonstrators. However, they made their support for reform clear, and several units handed their weapons to the rioters. The mob demanded the resignation of Guizot and, on 23 February, Louis-Philippe complied and appointed the more liberal Louis Mathieu Molé.

Guizot's dismissal led the opposition to believe that they had forced Louis-Philippe onto the defensive. When troops guarding the Ministry of Foreign Affairs fired on a fairly obedient crowd, wounding 80, the Republicans mobilised support. Barricades went up, the mob seized the Hôtel de Ville and street fighting followed. Although the army was still loyal, Louis-Philippe did not call it out.

Disillusioned by the lack of support from the National Guard, Louis-Philippe abdicated in favour of his grandson, the nine-year-old Comte de Paris, on 24 February. He departed, in disguise, for exile in England. The Chamber was invaded by the mob and, amid disorder, it reluctantly declared a Republican government.

What were the long-term causes?

Historians have tried to explain the long-term causes of the 1848 revolution in France in a number of different ways. Marxist historians have placed an emphasis on economic factors. They believe the revolution was the result of the developing economy in France, which brought about a clash between

Ideological: Believing in a particular set of ideas. Socialism was an ideology which said that the State, not private individuals, should control enterprises such as big industry, railways and banks.

Real wages: What can be bought with money taking into account inflation (see page 90).

the working and middle classes. Others have produced an **ideological** explanation, linking the outbreak of revolution to the growth of socialism and republicanism. Finally, some historians have been dismissive of these elaborate theories. Instead, they have tended to view events as a simple reaction to the incompetent rule of Louis Philippe and his ministers.

Marxist interpretation: the case in favour
Karl Marx argued that industrialisation had helped to create a greater awareness of class differences. While the middle class, or bourgeoisie, owned the factories and mines, and grew rich on the profits, the working class, which he called the proletariat, relied on inadequate wages. There was, Marx believed, a direct link between the effect of industrialisation and revolutionary activity. Once the workers realised that the bourgeoisie's wealth depended on their work, they became revolutionary in order to destroy this class. This is what Marxist historians believe happened in France in 1848.

The growth of industrialisation and urbanisation, while slower in France than in Britain, had changed the position of the working classes. There were 400,000 factory workers in France by 1848 and many of these, newcomers to the towns, were male, young, ill-educated and easily persuaded to join in any revolutionary protest. Evidence on standards of living varies, but some historians have suggested that **real wages** fell more or less continually between 1817 and 1848. This would make working men prepared to support any cause that might improve their lot.

Their position was aggravated by the financial and food crises of 1846–47. The industrial crisis decreased confidence and raised unemployment, while agricultural troubles brought rapid increases in the price of bread, grain and potatoes. This hit working-class standards of living further. With rural distress came yet more migration to the towns, particularly Paris which had risen from just over 70,000 inhabitants in 1817 to over a million by 1846.

So, it is argued, in 1848 there was a spontaneous rising of the working class against the bourgeois middle class that held the reins of power. It was, we are reminded, the working classes that manned the barricades. 'It was their hunger that powered the demonstrations that turned into revolutions', wrote the Marxist historian Eric Hobsbawm, in *The Age of Revolution* (1962).

Marxist interpretation: the case against
Since the most industrialised nations of Europe, Belgium and Britain did not undergo revolution in the 1840s, and since French industry was still underdeveloped, the Marxist explanation seems too simple. (See chart of the French economy on page 213.) There is no doubt that economic factors played a part in the events of 1848, but economic crises do not always cause political revolution. In any case, many of the food riots were localised and disorganised affairs, often in rural areas and places far from political power. Furthermore, there was a slightly better harvest in 1847 and food prices were beginning to fall in 1848, when the political troubles began.

There is just as much evidence that it was the discontent of the bourgeoisie itself that led to revolution, as that of the working classes. There was growing disappointment with their 'bourgeois' monarch. The frustration of the lesser bourgeoisie, who failed to qualify for the vote and the economic problems of the 1840s, made the lower middle classes highly critical of the regime. The collapse of the stock exchange, following Guizot's ill-fated attempt to sponsor the railways, a banking crisis and tax revenue failure, all combined to create conditions for revolt. It was the middle classes that provided the ranks of the National Guard that so crucially defected. They were also avid readers of the critical popular press and were the leaders of the banqueteers' campaign, being well placed to voice their discontent.

Ideological interpretation: the case in favour

Historian Charles Pouthas claimed, in Volume X of *The New Cambridge Modern History* (1960), that 'The 1848 revolutions were not revolutions of the masses; their leaders and instigators were intellectuals.' While the 'masses' in France, at least in Paris, did turn out to fight in the streets, it seems unlikely that they would have done so without the intellectual leadership of men such as Alphonse de Lamartine and Louis Blanc. The Marxist/economic interpretation of events ignores the ideological forces that had already led to a questioning of traditional means of government well before 1848. The French Revolution had challenged the rule of Kings and the French attempt to create a constitutional monarchy under the Bourbons, Louis XVIII and Charles X, had already failed. The events of the year 1848 can, therefore, be seen as the logical outcome of the various political experiments that had taken place since 1789 and the result of developing political ideas spread by the increase in educational opportunities. By 1846–47 certain positive programmes of reform had replaced the disorganised revolutionary violence of earlier years. They offered an attractive alternative to the stagnation of Louis-Philippe's reign. The part of the 'educated' students in the revolution adds weight to this theory.

The republican idea that a government without a king would represent the views of the people much better, and the socialist theory that everyone should share in the economic wealth of the country, clearly had considerable appeal for those who had been excluded from Louis-Philippe's political regime. 'Socialism' embraced a wide number of theories, some more extreme than others. However, there is little question that socialist ideas in their various forms had already demonstrated their appeal in intellectual circles. Supporters of the pro-socialist argument claim that, as confidence in the political leadership of the King, and of the liberal moderates, disappeared, it was inevitable that socialism would widen its appeal to provide the revolutionaries of 1848.

Ideological interpretation: the case against

To quote Charles Pouthas again, 'never was an event more unavoidable nor yet more accidental'. Although the first part of this quotation supports the idea of an inevitable challenge to a regime that depended on limited support, the second part challenges it. The revolution was accidental, Pouthas claims, insofar as those who led the protests in the Chamber, and the majority of those who organised the reform banquets outside it, were working for change within the system and never wished for the monarchy to be overthrown. Socialism may have been present, but it is almost impossible to prove that it was the decisive force in 1848. Nor, of course, did all Socialist leaders want the same thing. There is some evidence to suggest that the educated artisans were attracted to socialist ideas but, despite the spread of schooling, education was still limited. Furthermore, ideas of socialism and republicanism were not new. They had been debated for a considerable amount of time without causing a revolution. The socialist theory of revolution is also challenged by the knowledge that France, in 1848, was not actually highly industrialised. (See the chart of the French economy.) According to the historian John Roberts, in *The Nineteenth Century* (1970), the 1848 revolution in France was 'the revolution of a pre-industrial society, and not the one prophesied by those early socialists'. Finally, it should be remembered that those who took to the barricades, the working classes, were the very people least likely to understand abstract socialist ideas.

Louis Blanc (1811–1882)
Developed his socialist ideas as a law student in Paris. In 1839 he published *L'Organisation du travail* ('The Organisation of Work'), in which he explained his theories. This was followed in 1841 by *Histoire des dix Ans* ('History of the Last 10 Years') in which he criticised the monarchy of Louis-Philippe. He provided leadership in the troubles of 1848 and was a member of the French Provisional Government that took control after the revolution. During this time he tried to put some of his theories into practice and established National Workshops to relieve unemployment. With the collapse of the revolution in June 1848 he was forced to flee to England, where he remained until 1871.

The French economy 1815–1850

(statistics for Great Britain are given for comparison)

	France		Great Britain	
Population	**1815**: 29 million	**1850**: 35.8 million	**1815**: 18 million	**1850**: 27.6 million
Output of coal (metric tonnes)	**1815**: 882,000	**1850**: 4,434,000	**1815**: 16,200,000	**1850**: 50,200,000
Output of pig iron (metric tonnes)	**1815**: Negligible	**1850**: 406,000	**1815**: 310,000	**1850**: 2,285,000
Railways (km)	**1835**: 141	**1855**: 5,037	**1835**: 544	**1855**: 11,744
Numbers employed in agriculture	**1840**: 6,940,000		**1840**: 3,400,000	
Value of output in agriculture	**1840**: £269,000,000		**1840**: £218,000,000	

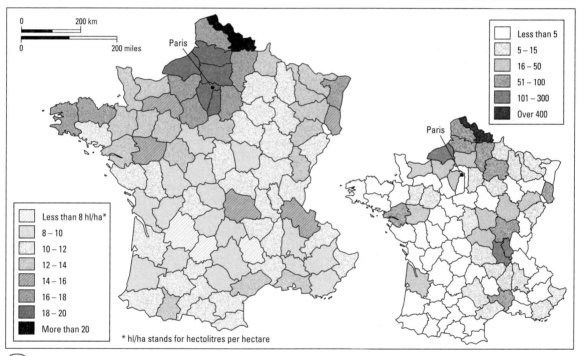

(Left) Wheat yields in 1840; (right) numbers of steam engines in each *département*, 1841.

1. What do these maps and statistics tell us about the development of the French economy 1815–1850?

2. In 1848 the banquet campaign was strongest in the areas to the north and east of Paris. Is there any connection between economic development and political opposition?

Reaction interpretation: the case in favour

By 1848, Louis-Philippe had very few supporters left. Lamartine's comment on French boredom certainly contains some truth. His government had done nothing for the working class, had failed to live up to the expectations of many of the middle class and had turned its back on the upper classes. Abroad he appeared happy to take second place to Great Britain, while at home his reliance on Guizot had become a liability.

Historian P. Stearns has written that, 'weakness and confusion at the top were vital to the causation of the revolution'. The government faced powerful critics. Thiers and Barrot maintained a tireless campaign for reform, although they never sought to depose the King. More extreme leaders, such as Ledru-Rollin, were prepared to go further and were not afraid to speak

Anti-establishment propaganda:
The 'establishment' refers to the group of people in a country who have power and influence, especially politicians, civil servants and businessmen. It is generally opposed to making changes to the existing political and social order.
Propaganda is information, often exaggerated or false, which is spread in order to influence general opinion. In this instance, the false information was against the 'establishment'.

Alexis de Tocqueville (1805–1859)
Historian and politician. He entered the Chamber of Deputies in 1839, supported the 1848 revolution and became Foreign Minister for a brief period in 1849. He is best known for his writings, in which he examined the cause and effect of the French revolution.

1. Using the information in this section, to what extent can the revolution of 1848 in France be explained in economic terms?

2. How convincing do you find the explanations of revolution given in this section? Explain your answer.

3. Using the information given in the whole of this chapter, why do you think that France experienced a revolution in 1830 and again in 1848?

directly to the masses. There was plenty of **anti-establishment propaganda**, particularly in the form of newspapers and journals, such as *L'Avenir*, *Le National* and *La Réforme*. However, there was no single revolutionary leader who could be held responsible for creating the revolution. Louis-Philippe had all the advantages on his side, but he failed to make use of them.

By 1848, Louis-Philippe was old, insecure and easily frightened. He seemed to have little idea of the reality of the situation and he became an object of ridicule and contempt. 'In God's name', implored the French writer Alexis de Tocqueville in January 1848, 'change the spirit of the government, for that spirit will lead you to the abyss.' Louis-Philippe took no notice. Guizot was unpopular, inflexible and complacent. 'I cannot find among us today, in the actual state of society, any real and serious motive, any motive worthy of a free and sensible country, to justify the proposed electoral reform,' Guizot had declared. Louis-Philippe failed to see the approaching storm, took no notice of the warnings of the prefects and, despite the loyalty of the army, made no attempt to prepare for the reaction to the July Ordinances.

Reaction interpretation: the case against
Those who think an explanation based on the failings of those involved is inadequate, have asked why it was that this regime fell, when equally incompetent regimes had survived in the past. They argue that boredom alone cannot make a revolution and that, whatever the failings of Guizot and Louis-Philippe, other forces were necessary to turn the discontent into a revolution. According to the historian M. Agulhon, in *The Republican Experiment 1848–1852* (1983), it was not so much the personalities that were at fault, but the fact that they occupied positions that were not clearly defined in 1830. He describes Louis-Philippe as a 'makeshift monarch' and, since his regime lacked 'a true system of principles and convictions', it 'could hardly arouse any fanatical defenders'.

Many historians believe that the revolution can only be explained by looking at a large number of factors. This is what Alexis de Tocqueville, writing two years after the events of 1848, attempted to do. He said that government was not overthrown but allowed to fall. Perhaps the many crises of the period – agricultural, industrial and intellectual – produced a mood of defeatism. There was a sense of fear at the top – a fear of the new industrial changes, the new ideologies and a fear of violence. Louis-Philippe gave in to the pressures with little fight and so, in the words of Louis Blanc, allowed the 'sceptre to slip from his hand'.

The German Confederation and the Austrian Empire, 1815–1848

Key Issues

● *What was the role of Metternich in the German Confederation and Austrian Empire, 1815–1848?*

● *How great a threat did liberalism and nationalism pose to the German Confederation and Austrian Empire, 1815–1848?*

● *In what respects, and for what reasons, did the relationship between the German Confederation and Austrian Empire change, 1815–1848?*

Framework of Events

1815	Congress of Vienna. Germany is formed into a Confederation
1816	Diet of the German Confederation meets
1817	Festival of Wartburg provokes student demonstrations
1819	Murder of Kotzbue by German students
	Karlsbad Decrees suppress revolutionary activity
	Prussian trade treaty with Schwarzburg-Sonderhausen lays foundation for *Zollverein*
1821	Austrians reimpose control in Italy. Metternich is appointed Chancellor of the Austrian Empire
1823	Establishment of provincial diets in Prussia
1830	Revolts in Hesse, Brunswick and Saxony
1831	Hesse-Cassel and Saxony granted a constitution
1831–32	Austrian troops suppress troubles in Papal States and Piedmont
1832	Hambach Festival advocates revolt against Austrian Rule
1834	Establishment of the *Zollverein* (excluding Austria)
	Metternich issues the Six Articles in the German Confederation, extending the Karlsbad decrees
1835	Baden joins the *Zollverein*
	Death of Francis I of Austria; accession of Ferdinand I
1837	Augustus suppresses the Hanoverian Constitution
1838	Austria evacuates the Papal States apart from Ferrara
1840	Friedrich-Wilhelm IV is crowned King of Prussia
1847	Friedrich-Wilhelm IV summons a united Diet
1848	Revolution in France sparks revolutions in the German Confederation and Austrian Empire.

Overview

German Confederation:
Also known as the *Bund*.
The alliance of German
states, under the presidency
of the Austrian Emperor,
established in 1815 to
guarantee the security of its
members in the aftermath
of the Napoleonic Wars.

French Revolution/
'liberal' ideas: The French
Revolution, which had
broken out in 1789, had
challenged the idea of
monarchy and traditional
ways of governing. It had
spread the message of
liberty, meaning personal
freedom and equality – the
right of all to be subject to
the same laws. Nationalism
– the belief that those of the
same race should form a
single nation – was not a
direct theme of the
revolution, but became
associated with the idea of
liberty. (For further details
of differing political views
in early 19th century see
chart in Chapter 6.)

Diet: A council
representing all the
different States of Germany.
Its members were chosen
by the rulers of the States.

Court intrigue: Underhand
plotting or scheming by
those close to the Emperor.

FROM the Congress of Vienna to the revolutions of 1848, the history of the **German Confederation** and the Austrian Empire was dominated by Prince Klemens von Metternich (see Chapter 6). He was the Austrian Foreign Minister from 1809 and its Chancellor from 1821. Metternich was also to play a decisive role in the internal history of both Germany and Italy in this period. He was no friend of the **French Revolution** with its **liberal ideas**. From 1809 to 1815, he led Austria in the Fourth Coalition against Napoleon and he looked forward to the day when Europe could be restored to its pre-revolutionary condition. Metternich's views, largely shared by the rulers of the other major European powers, influenced the work of the Congress of Vienna.

This meeting in 1814–15, at the end of the French wars, provided a peace settlement for Europe. Its decisions were based on the need for peace and stability. In order to provide this, the powers tried to create a balance of power in Europe. Consequently, Metternich's own country, Austria, was confirmed as a strong central European State. Its role was to balance the vast power of Russia to the east and the former aggressor, France, to the west. Austria had an empire in its own right, but its influence was to extend far beyond its own boundaries. To the north and west, the newly created German Confederation was to be controlled by a central **diet** with an Austrian President. To the south and west, a mixture of direct rule and royal family connections was to ensure that Austria also had considerable influence in Italy.

Austria emerged from the 1815 settlement with a huge responsibility. Its empire was peopled by many races, not all of whom were happy with this condition. Austria had a commitment to maintaining order in Italy and Germany, and a sense of responsibility to Europe as a whole. It is hardly surprising, therefore, that Metternich did not always find it easy to pursue his anti-liberal views. He tried to maintain a tight control using spies and censors but he did not get his own way entirely. Within the Confederation were many German princes and rulers, some of which had their own, rather different, ideas about how their states should be run. There was also a developing middle class and an intellectual movement within both Germany and the Austrian Empire which constantly forced Metternich on to the defensive. Furthermore, in Austria itself, Metternich's position was never more than that of a minister of the Emperor which made him subject to the Emperor's whims and to **Court intrigue**.

Nevertheless, Metternich's strategies did help to prevent any major outbreak of trouble in the Austrian Empire, Italy or the German Confederation before 1848. As far as the future of Austria was concerned though, this was done at a price. Austria was forced to maintain the bulk of its army in Italy until 1848, to curb the growing nationalist feeling there. Meanwhile, Germany was undergoing a major transformation. There was considerable modernisation in the more progressive German states, in particular in the largest, Prussia. A huge population growth, agricultural improvements, industrial development and the spread of education that brought the highest level of literacy in Europe, transformed Prussia in this period. By 1848, German nationalist feeling was growing and this served to erode Austria's position in Germany.

Foreign preoccupations also prevented Metternich from giving his full attention to the rise of Nationalism in his own Empire. By 1848, the Hungarians, Czechs and Croats (see map) were all demanding national rights. The future of the Empire was threatened, but it was still far from obvious, that within 20 years, the Empire would be divided and Prussia would eject Austria from its dominant place in Germany. So, in the period 1815–1848, despite several worrying incidents, **liberalism** and nationalism scored no permanent victories.

8.1 *What were the Austrian Empire and the German Confederation like in 1815?*

Liberalism: This idea, spread by the French Revolution, encouraged personal and economic freedom. Personal freedom included the right to property, freedom of speech and worship, and the freedom to participate in politics. The term came to imply resistance to autocratic rule and liberals favoured government by an elected, representative assembly.

Slav: The peoples of eastern Europe who speak a Slavonic language.

What was the Austrian Empire?

The Austrian Empire was a vast stretch of territory of around 250,000 square miles, dominating central Europe. By the Vienna Settlement of 1815, Austria had given up lands in southern Germany and Belgium. Instead, it acquired Dalmatia to the south, Lombardy and Venetia in Italy, and had indirect influence over a number of Italian states (such as Tuscany). The historian A.J.P. Taylor has pointed out that 'the Habsburg lands were not bound together either by geography or by nationality'. In fact, the Empire contained 11 different racial groups and comprised many different geographical regions, each of which might be peopled by a variety of different races (see map).

The Germans (43%) were the dominant race in the Empire, followed by the Magyars (20%), the natives of Hungary. There were also a large number of different **Slav** races (45%) – the Czechs, the Poles, the Ruthenians, the Croats, the Serbs, the Slovenes and the Slovaks. Finally, there were two major non-Slav groups, the Italians (7%) and the Romanians (6%).

The Austrian Empire in 1815

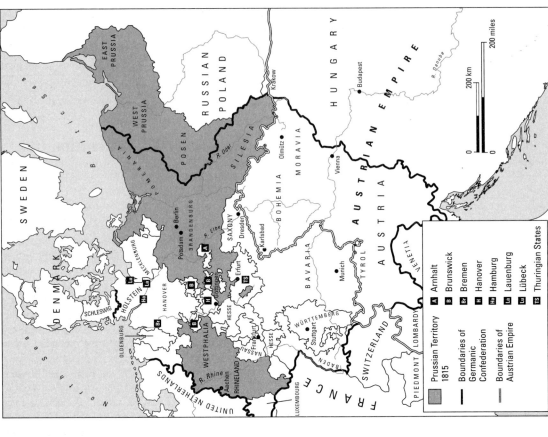

Germany in 1815 – the German Confederation

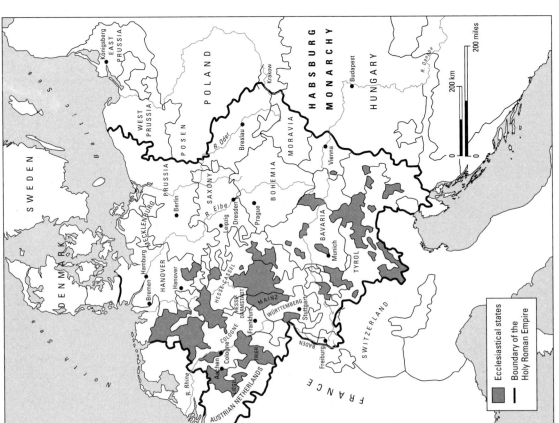

Germany in 1780 – the Holy Roman Empire

The map of the nationalities within the Austrian Empire shows where most of these different nationalities lived. Austria itself was principally German. Bohemia and Moravia contained a mixture of Czechs, Slovaks and Germans. Hungary was mainly Magyar, but there were many minority groups there too, particularly Serbs and Croats. Galicia was Ruthenian and Polish, Transylvania was peopled by the Romans, of Latin descent, while Illyria and Dalmatia contained Serbs and Croats. The new acquisition of Lombardy and Venetia also brought Italians into the Empire.

The potential for discord in such a multinational empire is obvious but, in 1815, only the Italians, and possibly the Germans of Austria itself, were much affected by ideas of nationalism and liberalism, so there was no immediate threat to the government. Indeed the Austrian Emperor, Francis I, saw some virtue in the diversity of his subjects. He observed, 'my peoples are strangers … of their dislike, order is born; and of their mutual hatred, universal peace'.

What was the German Confederation?

In 1815, the German Confederation was a loose association of a number of separate states. Before the French wars there had been 360 different states in the area known as Germany (see map of Germany in 1780). These had been loosely held together by the authority of the **Holy Roman Emperor** who, since 1438, had been a Habsburg, with the result that the position always fell to the Habsburg Emperor of Austria. This ancient empire had been broken up during the Napoleonic wars and Francis I had renounced his title in 1806 (see map of Europe in 1812 on page 146). In 1815, at the Congress of Vienna, a new German Confederation, or *Bund*, had come into being. This consisted of 38 states (39 from 1817 when Hesse Homburg joined) combined together in a confederation. (See map of the German Confederation in 1815.)

Holy Roman Emperor: In the Middle Ages, the Holy Roman Emperor was regarded as having authority from God to rule over large parts of Europe. However, by the 15th century, the Empire had been reduced to the States of Germany and the ruler was always a member of the powerful Habsburg family (see below). Napoleon abolished the Empire in 1806.

Each state had its own ruler, but there was also to be a central diet at Frankfurt, under Austrian Presidency. The boundaries of the new Confederation were modelled on those of the old Holy Roman Empire. While not as diverse as the Austrian Empire, it did include a number of different races in addition to the Germans. There were Poles, Czechs, Danes and French within the Empire, although some German-speaking areas were excluded. Luxembourg, Holstein and Hanover, all ruled over by foreign monarchs in their capacity as German Princes, were within the Confederation, as were Prussia (the largest of the states), the Austrian (German) part of the Austrian Empire and the Kingdom of Bohemia.

Prussia had played a significant part in the defeat of the French at the Battle of Leipzig in January 1813 and was therefore able to exert its claim to be treated as a major power at Vienna. As a reward for its efforts, and in return for giving most of its Polish lands to Russia, Prussia duly received the Rhineland and Westphalia, half of Saxony and Pomerania (see map of Europe 1815).

These acquisitions brought problems as well as advantages. The Rhinelanders resented their annexation by a country with which they had little in common and which lay 80 kilometres away. The Rhinelanders were mainly Catholic, whereas the Prussians themselves were Protestant. The Rhineland was industrialised and urban, whereas Prussia was rural. Furthermore, the Rhineland had come under French influence as the 'Confederation of the Rhine' and the inhabitants regarded themselves as western Europeans with a totally different culture from the eastern Prussians.

However, although no one appreciated it at the time, these changes had

What were the main differences between Germany 1780 and Germany 1815?

considerable significance for the future. Prussia was suddenly transformed from a north-eastern to a central German power. What is more, its economic potential was increased and its population was doubled, to more than 10 million.

In 1815, these developments did not appear to threaten the dominance of the Austrian Empire. Indeed, Austria had favoured a settlement whereby Prussia's possessions were split and the *Bund* kept relatively weak. There were more individual states in Germany than in the whole of the rest of Europe put together. It looked, therefore, as though the Austrians would still be in a position to dominate the area.

How was the Austrian Empire governed?

The Austrian Empire was ruled, from Vienna, by the Emperor Francis I. He assumed this title in 1804, and was to rule Austria until his death in 1835. He was a member of the ancient, powerful dynasty of the Habsburgs. He was an autocrat, although imperial rule in Austria had been reformed in the 18th century by the **enlightened despots** – the Empress Maria Theresa (1740–80) and her son, the Emperor Joseph II (1780–90). Metternich, working in close co-operation with the head of the police force, Count Sedlnitzky, maintained a high degree of censorship and a network of spies and informers throughout the Empire. However government was, on the whole, reasonably just and fair. Local government was in the hands of the **provincial diets**. Hungary, whose history gave it certain separate privileges, had its own Diet, which was meant to meet every three years.

Central government, however, was slow and inefficient. Major policy decisions were taken in Vienna, by the Emperor, assisted by his chosen ministers and a huge Council of State. There was no provision for the Emperor's ministers to meet together to co-ordinate policy, while the Council of State consisted of many sections and sub-sections. All changes demanded a mountain of paperwork and an army of civil servants to put them into effect. This made government cumbersome. Francis I was not an inspiring man. He worked hard. So long as there was good order and the government ran smoothly, he was uninterested in grand policies. Hartig, a colleague of Metternich, wrote that 'administration had taken the place of government'.

Francis I was well aware of the problems of his Empire. He once said, 'My realm is like a worm-eaten house – if one part is removed one cannot tell how much will fall.' However, he resented too much advice and, on the whole, preferred to leave things as they were. According to the historian C.A. Macartney, Francis I was 'mentally near-sighted and unimaginative, mistrustful and timid of the unknown'. Historian H. Kohn refers to this period of the Empire's history as 'an era of stagnation'. Francis I developed a strong relationship with Metternich, whose political beliefs he shared, but even this great Chancellor could not persuade Francis to undertake major reform. Metternich tried in 1811, and again in 1817, to persuade the Emperor to reform his administration, but with little success. Emperor Francis I (1792–1835) stood by his motto, 'rule and change nothing'.

To make matters worse, the Empire had been forced to declare itself bankrupt in 1811, following massive expenditure in the campaigns against Napoleon. After 1815, 39% of revenue went to paying back loans. The unenviable task of trying to improve Austria's chaotic finances in 1814 fell to the imperial Minister of Finance, Philip von Stadion. He made some progress. By the imperial edicts of 1816 and 1818, a national bank was established, the issue of paper money was brought under control and a **sinking fund** was set up. However, by the time of Stadion's death in 1824, the budget still failed to balance. The situation had, in fact, grown

Enlightened despots: These were rulers who maintained their complete power in theory, but in practice allowed some liberal reforms.

Provincial diets: Local representative councils. These usually consisted of, and were chosen by, members of the nobility.

Sinking fund: The 'national debt' was the money which the government had been forced to borrow to pay for war. Interest had also to be paid to the people who had loaned the money. The sinking fund was a way of reducing that debt by setting up an independent body. This would use government money to buy back government stock that had been issued when the government had borrowed money. They would hold the stock, collect interest on it, then use that interest to buy back more stock.

worse because of the costs of maintaining an army to keep order against the revolutionary outbreaks in Italy.

The fundamental problem was that the resources of the Austrian Empire were not being tapped fully. As Metternich himself put it, 'Hungary and its dependent territories enjoy privileges that paralyse the machinery of State'. The tradition of local government meant that taxation was not fairly distributed throughout the Empire and no minister felt brave enough to do anything about this.

Count Franz Kolowrat, a Bohemian nobleman, became a minister in 1826 and took a dominant role in internal affairs. However, even he only operated a policy of short-term remedies. He sometimes managed to balance the books but, more often than not, Austria's **budgets** were in **deficit**. Kolowrat was forced to rely on massive borrowing from the **Rothschilds** and elsewhere.

Metternich clashed with Kolowrat over a number of issues. In particular, Kolowrat resented Metternich's heavy commitment to military spending, which accounted for 40% of State revenues. They also disagreed over government reform and, with the Emperor's preference for doing nothing, Kolowrat won the day. In the 1820s, Metternich produced new plans to improve efficiency by co-ordinating the various departments of state under a small central council, while maintaining the diets of the individual provinces. Francis I considered the reform when he was ill in 1826 but, when he recovered, he went back on his word. He agreed during another bout of illness in 1834 but, by the time of his death in 1835, nothing had been done.

In 1835, Francis was succeeded by his son, Ferdinand I (1835–1848). Ferdinand suffered from **rickets** and **epilepsy** and was described by Lord Palmerston as 'the next thing to an idiot'. He was incapable of ruling personally, so that task was taken over by a Council of State, presided over by Archduke Ludwig, Ferdinand's uncle. Consequently, Metternich found himself less able to influence affairs of state. Francis' three brothers and Kolowrat were all keen to curb Metternich's power. His proposed central council was again rejected in 1836, and Metternich was virtually excluded from all say in the domestic affairs of the Empire. It is hardly surprising that Metternich was to remark, 'I have sometimes ruled Europe, but I have never governed Austria'.

How was the German Confederation governed?

The *Bund* was set up in June 1815. It was not intended to promote unity in Germany, but to offer a means whereby the 38 (and shortly 39) separate German States could provide for their joint defence and discuss matters of common interest.

The terms of the **Federal Act** made it clear that 'the independence and integrity of the individual states' was to be maintained.

● There was to be a diet known as the *Bundesrat*. This would meet permanently in Frankfurt. It would have 17 members, one each from the 11 largest states and six representing various groups of smaller states.

● The members of the *Bundesrat* were to be chosen by the rulers of the various states and the president would be an Austrian nominee.

● The President was to be responsible for deciding the business to be discussed and the procedure to be adopted.

● The Confederation could appoint ambassadors and make foreign treaties on behalf of its members.

Budgets – deficit: Budgets were intended to ensure that income matched, or exceeded, expenditure. If there was a deficit, income was less than expenditure, so the national debt increased.

Rothschilds: Baron James de Rothschild (1792–1868 was the founder of the Rothschild banking house in Paris. His father, Meyer Amschel Rothchild (1743–1836), supervised the family business in Frankfurt while his brother, Nathan, ran a branch in London. They grew very wealthy during the Napoleonic wars as they began to specialise in lending money to princes and governments. A branch was also set up in Vienna, which developed close ties with the Habsburg monarchy.

Rickets: A disease that children sometimes get when their food does not contain enough Vitamin D. It makes their bones soft, and causes their liver and spleen to become too large.

Epilepsy: A disease that causes a person to suddenly lose consciousness and have violent fits.

Federal Act: This act created a federation of states in which decisions about foreign policy and defence would be taken by the central government, while the individual states had complete control over internal policies.

- Members were not to declare war on one another and could, if necessary, organise a federal army and federal defences.

- Members could develop commercial and economic co-operation between the states.

- Individual states were to establish constitutions within their own domains.

- Any fundamental change in the laws of the Confederation was to be considered by a General Assembly of 69 members so as to have the full agreement of all member states for the proposal.

It is clear that a number of these terms placed limits on the powers of the Federal Diet. It represented the princes, not the people. It was subject to an Austrian presidency. Furthermore, the need for a general assembly for any 'fundamental change' made the possibility of radical reform virtually nil. Together with the powerful Austria, several other foreign countries – England, which controlled Hanover, Denmark, ruler of Holstein, and Holland, which owned Luxembourg – would be present at such a gathering. They were unlikely to support any major disruption to the Vienna settlement.

Initially, little came of the more progressive clauses of the Federal Act either. Commercial co-operation was discussed in 1816, but local jealousies meant that nothing significant was done. Similarly, a scheme to build federal fortresses for the defence of Germany was soon abandoned.

Prussia and Austria also ignored the demand that the States provide constitutions. Friedrich-Wilhelm III of Prussia was solidly conservative. He ruled in conjunction with the **Junker class**. He enjoyed close ties with Austria and was a personal friend of Metternich. He was fearful of disorder. Hampered by a huge debt of 217 million thalers (Prussian currency), he tried to avoid too much change. Although, in his enthusiasm before Waterloo, Friedrich-Wilhelm had promised his people a constitution, his only reform was the creation of eight provincial assemblies, or Landtags, in 1823. These, like the Austrian provincial diets, provided the nobility with a small say in government. They could make suggestions, but not decide on policy.

In the rest of Germany, some Princes did introduce more liberal forms of government. In Bavaria in 1818, for example, a parliament was set up representing the peasants, townsfolk and nobles. Baden, Würtemberg, Saxe-Weimar and Hesse-Darmstadt all introduced constitutions modelled on the French Charter of 1814, but the majority of states maintained traditional forms of government. They were ruled by Princes aided by ministers drawn from the aristocracy, with no representation of the educated middle class or peasant classes.

In many ways, the German Confederation reflected the views of the time. Although ideas of liberalism and nationalism had begun to develop in Germany, there was still a strong degree of state loyalty. There was a traditional respect for the rulers of the individual states and men thought of themselves as Bavarians or Prussians, rather than Germans. Furthermore, although the Germans shared a common language and cultural heritage, there were other divisions within the Confederation. For example, in the north and east the people were predominantly Lutheran Protestant and, in the south and west, Catholic. Such divisions put a brake on national developments.

Junker class: The landowning aristocracy which also controlled the Prussian army and provided the Emperor with a host of able officials.

1. What were the main problems facing the Austrian Empire in 1815?

2. How, and why, had the decisions made at Vienna in 1815 transformed the State of Prussia?

3. To what extent, and why, did the constitution of the German Confederation limit the likelihood of political change in Germany?

8.2 How were the Austrian Empire and the German Confederation influenced by economic developments, 1815–1848?

In 1815, both the German Confederation and the Austrian Empire were overwhelmingly rural. In Austria, 80% of the population lived and worked on the land. In Germany, the rural population was around 73.5%, and this figure did not fall much before 1848. In most of this central European area, society followed the traditional pattern. At the top were the landowning aristocracy and below them the mass of landless peasants who worked the soil. There was also a small 'middling class' divided between the shopkeepers and merchants at the lower end, and lawyers, bankers and professionals at the top.

Tenant farmers: People who each rent a plot of land from a landowner.

There was, of course, considerable variation. In some places, peasants had become **tenant farmers**, and some areas were economically and socially more advanced than others. Nevertheless there were places, notably in central Germany and in Hungary, where traditional feudal practices were retained. These included an aristocracy that was exempt from taxation, peasants compelled to work for their landowners and, in the towns, trades controlled by restrictive **guilds**. At the other extreme, the most progressive area was the Rhineland area of Prussia. Here these practices had been abandoned, and plentiful natural resources together with social advances following the occupation by the French, had increased prosperity.

Guilds: In medieval times these controlled the various trades in towns, providing rules for apprenticeship and establishing standards of quality. By the 19th century, their practices had become restrictive and damaging to the growth of industry.

In the years after 1815, there were certain important developments, particularly in Prussia, which had experienced a powerful economic growth. The population of the German Confederation as a whole grew from 23.5 million to 34.5 million between 1800 and 1850 and, in Prussia, the population doubled. This growth was most marked in the rural areas (increasing by 75%), leading many to drift to the towns in search of work. Berlin, the capital of Prussia, grew from 172,000 in 1800 to 419,000 in 1850.

Following its defeat by the French at Jena in 1805, Prussia had undertaken a considerable modernisation of its government and economy. **Serfdom** was abolished, the old restrictive trade guilds lost some of their power and the education system was improved. After 1815, with the acquisition of the Rhineland areas, these economic changes began to bear fruit. In 1821, the Gewerbe Institute was set up to encourage industry. With the help of British technicians, more machinery was introduced in Prussian factories.

Serfdom: Serfs were peasants who were allowed to farm land for themselves in return for work for their lords or, in some cases, a money payment. Whatever the nature of their dues, the personal freedom of serfs was restricted. They could not leave their village, marry or inherit, without their lord's consent.

This growth was mirrored all over the Confederation, making it the next major area to be affected by the industrial revolution, after Britain and Belgium. Saxony, Silesia, the Prussian Rhineland and Brandenburg all developed as centres of coal extraction and iron production. Between 1815 and 1850, coal output in Silesia increased almost 10 times. In the 1820s, the first steam engine was built in Berlin. By 1838 Prussia had its first railway, running from Berlin to Potsdam. The textile industry developed in Saxony. By 1848, there were almost 600,000 industrial workers in the German states.

Compared with the German Confederation, economic growth in the Austrian Empire was very slow. There was some development in Bohemia and in Austria itself. Indeed, Austria led the way in railway construction with a line from Linz to Budweis in 1828, and the port of Trieste was developed to provide an outlet to the Mediterranean. However, strict State control stifled initiative and the Hungarian part of the Empire remained almost exclusively agricultural until after 1848.

Zollverein: An area in which no customs duties (taxes) were charged on the movement of goods.

Whereas German economic growth owed a good deal to the development of the ***Zollverein***, Austria retained its customs barriers and controls.

1. With reference to economic and social developments, what were (a) the similarities (b) the differences between the Austrian Empire and the German Confederation after 1815?

2. How important do you think these economic and social factors were for the subsequent development of the German Confederation and the Austrian Empire? Explain your reasoning.

Whereas the member states of the German *Zollverein* produced 5.6 million tons of coal in 1845, the whole of the Austrian Empire produced only 710,000 tons. Nevertheless, there was some growth of towns and Vienna doubled in size from 247,000 to 444,000 between 1815 and 1848.

The extent of the economic changes must not be exaggerated. The number and size of factories before 1848 was small. In Prussia factory workers represented only 4% of the population while, in Hungary, only 1% was engaged in any form of industry. Railway development was slow. There were only 549 kilometres of line in the German Confederation by 1840 and despite its early start Austria still had only a few, fragmented lines linking major cities. In 1846 the total output of coal from Prussia was 3,200,000 tons, much less than that from Belgium.

A modern class society was beginning to evolve in parts of the Confederation, but the nobility remained powerful and there was little 'working-class consciousness'. In the Austrian Empire, there was even less. Metternich remarked to Karl von Kübeck in 1841, 'I have just been to Germany in the midst of the industrial developments there; I have observed the forces which are stirring everywhere and the tendencies which they follow, and it has induced in me an acute feeling of inferiority.'

Look at the map of the European railways in 1848. What can we learn from this map about the economic state of the German Confederation and Austrian Empire before 1848? Can you explain any differences between German and Austrian development?

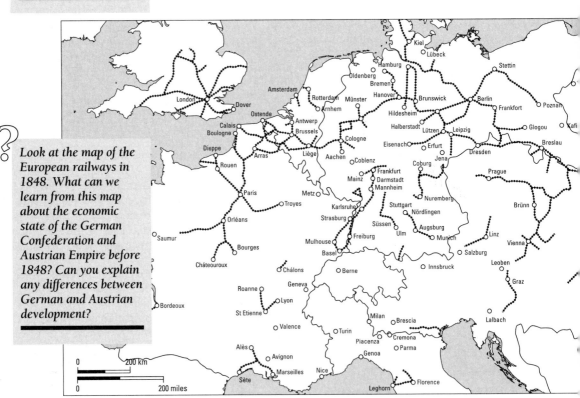

European railways in 1848

8.3 *How extensive was the threat posed by liberalism and nationalism within the Austrian Empire, 1815–1846?*

Along with the rest of Europe after 1815, the Austrian Empire could not escape the impact of the liberal and nationalist feeling that had been encouraged by the French Revolution. Indeed, as a multinational empire, Austria might have been expected to suffer more than most countries from the spread of nationalist ideas. However, this was not entirely the case. Although there was a growth in nationalist attitudes, only the Italians, and possibly some of the Austrian Germans, showed any desire to break up the Empire. As far as the other races were concerned, they were more interested in improving their status within the Empire. Their nationalism, therefore, had a strong 'liberal' side to it.

How were the Germans affected?

For the Austrian Germans, the patriotic fight against the French, in which they had united with their fellow German speakers to the north, had encouraged them to widen their horizons. Although German was established as the language and culture of the Empire in the 18th century, they had always thought of themselves as Austrians not Germans. However, after 1815, with the creation of the German Confederation, there was renewed interest in what constituted 'Germany'. The German Austrians were part of the Confederation and the growth of nationalism within many German States heightened the conflict of loyalties. This worried, but did not threaten, the Empire in the years to 1848. Perhaps more important than the nationalist threat was the growth of liberal thinking in the Germanic part of the Empire. The Diets of the German-speaking provinces increasingly began to voice their discontent with the lethargy of the central government and became the centres of liberal ideas.

How were the Italians affected?

Nationalism and liberalism posed a much greater threat to the Austrians in Italy than elsewhere. Lombardy and Venetia, the only states of Italy directly ruled by the Austrian Empire, were generally less troublesome than those in the rest of the peninsula. Nevertheless, Metternich spent a good deal of time and money trying to stamp out these ideas wherever they occurred. He organised a system of spies, imposed censorship and when required sent in the army, as in 1821 and 1831 (see Chapter 9). He certainly frustrated the hopes of the radicals up to 1848, but he never succeeded in removing their threat. Italy remained a constant drain on Austria's resources.

How were the Hungarians affected?

For the Hungarians, the growth of liberalism and nationalism largely derived from two experiences. One was exposure to the superior economic and social conditions of western Europe during the time of the French wars, and the other was a dispute with the Austrians.

In 1811, Francis I had tried to persuade the Hungarian Diet to bring the Hungarian currency into line with Austrian values and to grant him a loan to help him to finance the wars. When they had refused, he dismissed the Diet. Ignoring the promise to call a Hungarian Diet every three years, he then ruled Hungary by decree for 13 years. Naturally enough, this caused a good deal of resentment among the Hungarian nobility, who were used to a certain amount of control over their own affairs. Interestingly, it was the landowning class and the gentry that led the nationalist revival in Hungary.

Count Istvan Széchényi (1791–1860) Hungarian writer and statesman. Author of many works advocating economic and social modernisation as a route to Hungarian progress. His writings helped to reinforce the idea of Hungary's natural development being restricted by the other nationalities in the Empire. Active in Hungarian affairs in 1848–50, he became mentally ill and eventually committed suicide. **Magyar**: The Hungarian language and culture. **Lajos Kossuth (1802–1894)** From a Protestant family of the poorer Hungarian gentry, he became well known in the 1820s and 1830s as a prominent liberal nationalist. He was a lawyer, and wrote patriotic pamphlets and newspaper articles campaigning for national political and economic freedom. Kossuth was imprisoned for treason (1837–40) but on his release became editor of the nationalistic newspaper, the *Pesti Hirlap*. In 1847, he was elected as a member of the Hungarian Diet. He was a good speaker and demanded Hungarian independence from Austria (although he accepted the Habsburg monarchy until 1849). He was fiercely patriotic, and opposed the demands of the other races within the Hungarian part of the Austrian Empire. His speech to the Hungarian Diet on 3 March 1848 sparked off the revolution in Hungary that year, and he became leader of the Hungarian revolutionary government. On its defeat in 1849, Kossuth was exiled and never returned to Hungary.	There were very few that could be classified as middle class here, so the movement was slightly different from that in the rest of Europe. Count Széchényi led the moderates. His family had a long record of service to the Habsburgs, and he always maintained his own loyalty. However, he was equally determined that his countrymen not be held back by their membership of the Empire. He published a series of works (1828–33) advocating economic reform. He wanted an end to the nobles' immunity from taxation, the abolition of feudal peasant dues, and agricultural improvements in order to increase the economic output of his country. Széchényi scored one major victory at a time when Metternich was pre-occupied with the 1830 revolution in France. This was to persuade Francis I that Hungarian or **Magyar**, not Latin, should be recognised as the language of government in that section of the Empire. This came into effect from 1836 and stimulated the teaching of Hungarian in schools. This, in turn, brought a revival of interest in national history and culture, which further intensified nationalist feelings. However, virtually all Széchényi's other proposals were blocked by Metternich who worked in alliance with the conservative Hungarian Chancellor, Count Apponyi. Metternich was also concerned about a second, and rather more threatening, side of Hungarian nationalism. While Széchényi was a politician of the old school, Lajos Kossuth was a fiery, nationalist liberal who represented the lesser nobility or gentry. His demands were far more extreme. Like Széchényi he wanted the abolition of serfdom but he also had democratic aims. He called for an independent Hungarian Parliament, freedom of speech, freedom of the press and right to fair trial. He believed that Hungary was being exploited by Austria. Kossuth wanted tariffs (customs duties) on goods entering Hungary from other parts of the Empire, to encourage its economic growth. This was too much for the Austrian authorities, who imprisoned Kossuth (1837–40) for daring to print such ideas. The action backfired. On his release, Kossuth found himself a national hero. He was able to spread his ideas further, as the editor of *Pesti Hirlap* ('The Pest Herald'). This Magyar journal soon reached a circulation of 10,000. ### How were the other races affected? The Hungarian nationalist movement helped to spark off other nationalist movements within the Empire in the 1820s and 1830s. No sooner had language concessions been granted to the Hungarians, than the Croats started to advance their own claims. In 1835, Ljudevt Gaj founded the *Croat News* in Zagreb, to influence opinion against what was seen as Hungary's bid for independence. By 1844, the Croat deputies were refusing to accept the use of Magyar as the official language of the Hungarian Diet. In Transylvania, Romanian nationalism also developed as a reaction to the demands being made by the Hungarian Magyars. Elsewhere, however, nationalism was a more intellectual movement. Traditionally, German had been the official written language of the Czech lands but Josef Jungmann produced a Czech dictionary and Frantšek Palacky set up the Czech Foundation in 1831 to encourage the publication of books in Czech. In Prague, events were promoted where only Czech was spoken, such as the Czech ball of February 1840. The Slovaks, too, had their nationalist poet, Jan Kollar, who inspired a consciousness of Slavic traditions in 1820s. The growth of Slavic nationalism was also given a boost by by the Polish rising of 1830.

How extensive were the demands by the 1840s?

By the 1840s, despite Metternich's best endeavours, the Empire had certainly been infected with liberal and nationalist ideas. The accession of Ferdinand I, in 1835, had brought no change to the traditional means of rule. Throughout the Empire, there were increasing demands for governmental reform. In Austria itself, political clubs were set up in the cities, and middle-class intellectuals such as Alexander Bach in Vienna became involved in the drawing up of programmes of reform.

The discussion of liberalism was also advanced in Hungary, where Kossuth was elected to the Hungarian Diet in 1847. Everywhere, the provincial Diets began to express their discontent. The Bohemian Diet demanded the right to vote its own taxes. The Diets of Lower Austria wanted agrarian reform. The Hungarians demanded equality for Protestants and the use of Hungarian at all meetings.

In 1846, the Poles within the Empire broke into revolt, with the landowners joining the middle-class intellectuals. To suppress this rebellion, the Austrians promised the peasants that the '*Robot*' (labour rent) would be abolished if they rose against their masters. The move proved successful, but only in the short term. The Austrian concession helped to inflame peasant demands throughout the Empire.

Before 1846, the slow growth of liberalism and nationalism had never caused undue alarm to the rulers of the Austrian Empire. Indeed, the concept of nationalism had never even seemed to sink into the brain of Ferdinand I. He once commented, 'Peoples? What is that? I know nothing of peoples, I only know of subjects.' Metternich was far more aware of the dangers but, thanks to his vigilance, all had remained superficially calm. According to the historian C.A. Macartney (1965), 'It was the remarkable destiny of the Habsburg Monarchy, after passing between 1780 and 1792 through the most changeful 12 years in all its history, to pass the next 56 years in a condition of **suspended animation**, as near complete as the considerable ingenuity of its rulers could contrive.' By 1846, however, things were set to change.

Suspended animation: A period of time during which people appear to be expecting something to happen, but it never does.

1. Which racial group posed the greatest threat to the authority of the Austrian Empire after 1815? Give reasons for your answer.

2. Can you explain the second part of the quotation from C.A. Macartney? ('It was the remarkable destiny of the Habsburg Monarchy ..., to pass ... 56 years [1792–1848] in a condition of suspended animation, as near complete as the considerable ingenuity of its rulers could contrive.') What evidence supports this view?

8.4 How was the growth of liberal and nationalist ideas in the German Confederation controlled, 1815–1840?

Why were liberalism and nationalism affecting the German Confederation in 1815?

Many of the German States had experienced considerable change during the period of the French wars, when the French had reduced the number of states and brought the Confederation of the Rhine under direct French rule. The amalgamation of states had helped to improve administration and to topple outdated laws. The growing middle classes had been particularly influenced by the French model of **representative government** and had benefited from the increased use of **French Legal Codes**. Alongside these 'liberal' ideas, nationalism had also made some limited progress during the period of French domination, particularly in the universities.

Some of the views that helped to create a belief in German nationalism, particularly among intellectuals and students, are shown in the insert. The German philosophers, Johann von Herder, Johann Fichte and Georg Hegel, all contributed theories which supported the ideas that Prussia and Germany were destined to create a great Germanic nation.

Representative government: A form of government in which an assembly elected by the people makes decisions.

French Legal Codes: French law was rewritten in the time of Napoleon, to take account of the changes made during the Revolution. This was the law applied in the states controlled by France as a result of the Napoleonic conquests. It included the right of everyone to fair trial and justice. It included personal freedoms such as free speech and freedom of the press and it abolished feudal practices such as serfdom.

> ### Some influential German philosophers
>
> ### Johann Gottfried von Herder (1744–1803)
>
> Came from Prussia and studied under the German philosopher Immanuel Kant. He became a teacher and a Protestant pastor (preacher) and travelled extensively in France before the Revolution. Herder was interested in the cultural development of peoples. He developed the idea of a *Volkgeist*, or national soul. He believed that all peoples, or races, sharing the same language, customs and culture, had their own unique spirit that distinguished them from their neighbours. Each nation, he argued, was quite unique. However, he showed no interest in the idea of a united Germany.
>
> ### Johann Gottlieb Fichte (1762–1814)
>
> Developed many of Herder's ideas during the Napoleonic era. He was particularly interested in the German peoples whom, he believed, enjoyed a superior culture to those around them. Fichte was accused of atheism (not believing in God), in 1799, and was forced to resign his post as Professor of Philosophy at Jena University. He then went to Berlin, where he gave a series of lectures developing the idea of liberal nationalism.
>
> ### Georg Wilhelm Friedrich Hegel (1770–1831)
>
> Professor of Philosophy, first at Heidelberg (1817–18) and then at Berlin University (1818–31). Although he favoured the Prussian State and the existing order of things, he did argue that a man could only truly fulfil himself as a member of a **nation state**. From this grew the idea that Prussia and Germany had a special destiny.

Nation state: A state formed from a distinctive racial group with a shared language or culture.

German student groups had certainly taken the lead in local risings to expel the French, although Friedrich von Gentz, writing shortly after the events, claimed that 'peoples, youth and volunteers contributed hardly anything (to the defeat of Napoleon)'. Furthermore, the historian A.J.P. Taylor has dismissed the extent of active nationalist involvement in 1813–15. He wrote, 'the myth of the German national uprising against Napoleon was … fostered by the German intellectuals'.

How were the ideas of liberalism and nationalism spread?

The years 1815 to 1848 have been referred to by German historians as the *Vormärz* years (literally, 'pre-March', the month when revolution broke out in Vienna in 1848). They are traditionally regarded as a time of political debate, when the new liberal and nationalistic ideas were spread through books, pamphlets, and lectures. It is difficult to know how true this picture is.

There are instances of the message being carried to the workers in the cities. Study groups, either set up by well-intentioned Liberals, or sometimes formed by workers such as printers, appeared in some major centres. In Hamburg, for example, there were some quite large groups, with several hundred members. They discussed politics and expressed radical views, in favour of republican rather than of monarchical government. They also believed in strikes and, if necessary, violence, to achieve their aims. However, only a small proportion of workers was involved in this sort of activity, and rural workers and peasants were scarcely affected at all.

The evidence would suggest that political debate was mainly confined to the young and educated, particularly university students and professors, together with some of the middle and upper classes. Poetry, music, history and philosophy – based on a hatred of France and the greatness of Germany – all encouraged the growth of nationalism in the 1820s and 1830s. In the universities a number of student societies advocating liberal reform developed. These included the Gymnastic clubs for patriots (*Turnvater*) and the students' drinking clubs with vaguely patriotic aims (*Burschenschaften*), inspired by the ideas of Friedrich Jahn. They spread rapidly, helped by the German system whereby students moved from one university to another in the course of their studies. However, there was little real challenge to authority in the immediate post-1815 years, and it was only when the societies were threatened by Metternich's suppression that their fame spread.

How did the authorities react to the spread of liberal and nationalist thinking?

What was the effect of the Wartburg festival in 1817?

On 18 October 1817, a festival took place in the castle at Wartburg in Saxony. It was organised by the students of Jena University and brought together several hundred members of the *Burschenschaften*. They assembled to hear speeches and to sing songs. It was officially a celebration of the anniversary of **Luther's 95 theses**, which had led to the Protestant Reformation in Europe. Martin Luther had sheltered in this same castle. It was also the 4th anniversary of the Battle of Leipzig (1813), when the Germans had defeated the French. So the rally had a part religious and part nationalist significance.

Luther's 95 theses: The Protestant Reformation was a breakaway movement from the Catholic Church in Europe in the 16th century. It is said to have begun when Martin Luther nailed 95 theses, or protests, to the door of Wittenberg Castle Church in 1517.

In the evening there was a torchlight parade. A minority of excited students built a bonfire and threw anti-liberal books, journals and pamphlets (or pieces of paper bearing their titles) on it. They burned effigies, including one of Metternich himself, and emblems of the Prussian army which had adopted French fashions – jackboots, the corporal's cane, a pig-tailed military wig and leather corsets. It was only a student demonstration, but Metternich was concerned. At that time he was suspicious of the 'liberal' Tsar Alexander I of Russia (see Chapters 6 and 10), whom he suspected of trying to stir up trouble in Europe. He also believed in taking firm action at the first sign of unrest. He won the

---

Friedrich Ludwig Jahn (1778–1852)
A German nationalist who tried to put his ideas into practice by organising youth movements. He has been referred to as a 'crude peasant'. Jahn dressed in German costume, with an unbleached cloth gown and flowing hair and beard. He supported the idea of national festivals to commemorate the great events of Prussian history and he wanted to reform education along nationalist lines. He hoped to abolish the regular Prussian army and replace it with a national militia. In 1810, he founded his first gymnastic society and these soon spread throughout Germany. On his suggestion, the *Burchenschaften*, founded in June 1815, adopted the colours black, red and gold. By 1832, its flags had become a national symbol. Black symbolised the night of servitude, from which Germany had to emerge, red the blood which would have to be shed, and gold the day of liberty. Jahn proposed that a future German state should include Switzerland, the Netherlands and Denmark, as well as Prussia and Austria. He wanted a new capital – Teutonia. His followers included Karl Sand.

sympathy of the German Princes. The students were made to promise to stay out of secret societies.

Through the winter of 1817–18, the students continued to push their liberal ideas. They met in secret to draw up a manifesto (formal statement) demanding free speech, trial by jury, a free press, the abolition of the secret police and of censorship, and the establishment of a federal state ruled by a German Emperor. However, only seven students were prepared to sign their final document as the rest were too frightened for their future careers.

How did the student unrest provoke repressive measures?

In the grand Duchy of Hesse-Darmstadt, Karl Fallen emerged as the leader of the radicals. His followers, numbering a few hundred, formed the *Schwarzen Umbedingten*. They demanded the unification of all Germans, including the Swiss and Dutch. There were also peasant disturbances in Hesse in the winter of 1818, following a drought and heavy taxation, but few students were prepared to join the peasant unrest.

On 23 March 1819, students were again at the centre of trouble when August von Kotzbue was stabbed to death at his home in Minim. Kotzbue was an unpopular, anti-liberal German journalist, playwright and Russian spy, who was regarded as trying to influence Alexander I against liberal ideas. His assassin was Karl Ludwig Sand, a theology student from the University of Jena and a follower of the writings of Karl Fallen. Sand acted without the knowledge or support of his comrades, but Metternich seized the opportunity to challenge these nationalist ideas. Sand was beheaded, but the repercussions of his actions went much further.

Metternich acted quickly. He won over Tsar Alexander I who was to say in 1820, 'Today I deplore all that I said and did between 1815 and 1818. I regret the time lost; we must study to retrieve it. You have correctly judged the condition of things. Tell me what you want and what you want of me, and I will do it.' Metternich also met with the King of Prussia, Friedrich-Wilhelm III, in July 1819, and convinced him that a dangerous situation was developing. Friedrich-Wilhelm III was persuaded, with little difficulty, to forget the constitution he had once promised his people and to support Austrian action. The chief ministers of the nine largest German states were summoned to meet Metternich at Karlsbad, in Bohemia. This group appointed a joint commission to investigate the recent activities and the agitation all over Germany. On the basis of their findings, they drew up a series of decrees, which were presented to the Federal Diet at Frankfurt. They accepted the decrees on 20 September 1819.

What were the Karlsbad Decrees?

These decrees were designed to crush agitation and to deliver a clear message to any would-be revolutionaries. Demands for reform would be treated as **treason**, in future.

Treason: To commit treason is to take action against your own country. This is traditionally regarded as one of the worst crimes that a person can commit.

● All universities were to have a government supervisor.

● Any professor found to be spreading 'unsound' ideas was to be removed from his university and forbidden from teaching anywhere in the Confederation.

● Any student expelled from one university for his political opinions was forbidden from studying at another.

● Student societies, such as the *Burschenschaften* and the *Turnvater*, were to be suppressed and political meetings forbidden.

- Strict censorship was to be imposed.

- A permanent committee was to be set up at Mainz to see the rules were applied and to collect evidence against liberals and other revolutionaries.

What were the results of these decrees?

Extensive repression followed. Some Princes carried matters to extremes and suppressed the mildest discontent. A number of university professors were dismissed, and those branded as leaders in the troubles, were imprisoned. Some chose exile. Hermann von Boyen, the army reformer, and Alexander von Humboldt, the University of Berlin's founder, both tendered their resignations in protest against such action, only to find their resignations accepted.

There were protests from some of the more liberal states such as Baden, Bavaria, Würtemberg and Saxe-Weimar but, from Metternich's point of view, the decrees were remarkably effective. They checked the development of liberalism and nationalism, and made the Princes more watchful. In 1820, further measures were passed by which the Federal Diet was given powers to use armed force to suppress revolution in any of the states of Germany.

Metternich was by now suspicious of even the limited constitutions granted by the south German states. He tried to abolish them at the Congress of Troppau in 1821. He did not succeed, but he did persuade the states to restrict the topics their assemblies could discuss in an attempt to halt the spread of dangerous liberal ideas.

The flag in the foreground has black, red and gold stripes. Why is this significant to liberal and nationalist Germans?

The Hambach Festival, 27–30 May 1832

Why was further repression necessary in the 1830s?

? *Can you explain what the German caricature depicts? Is it a fair representation of conditions in Germany in 1819?*

In 1830, it looked as though Metternich's prompt action in the Karlsbad Decrees had successfully halted German demands. When the July revolution against Charles X broke out in France in 1830, and was followed by revolutions in Belgium, Poland and Italy, it provoked only localised protests in Germany. The liberal poet, Heinrich Heine, remarked sarcastically, 'When I was at the top of the St Gotthard Pass, I heard Germany snoring.'

German caricature of 1819. 'The Thinkers' Club. The important question to be deduced today: How long shall we go on being allowed to think?'

The only significant repercussions were in the south German States. Here, where constitutions had not been granted, there was considerable resentment and, where they did exist, there was pressure to extend them. Consequently, new constitutions were gained in revolts in Hesse, Brunswick and Saxony; while in Bavaria, Baden and Würtemberg, liberals pressed for further reform. There was also trouble in Luxemburg, a member of the *Bund*. In Hanover a constitution was granted in 1832, but it was abolished in 1837 by the new King, Ernest Augustus, uncle of Queen Victoria. This resulted in further trouble.

Although the troubled years of 1830–31 passed without major incident, the nationalist cause had not been abandoned. Two further incidents provoked further reaction from Metternich and the Princes shortly afterwards.

'Young Germany': After the failure of an attempted revolution in Italy in 1830, the Italian liberal champion, Giuseppe Mazzini (see Chapter 9) was forced into exile in Marseilles. Here, he founded a new society, 'Young Italy'. This society developed various offshoots, including 'Young Germany'. They all supported the idea of young, liberal, nationalist movements to free their countries.

- In May 1832, around 30,000 nationalists from a number of different German States, as well as liberals and republicans from Poland and France, gathered at the Hambach Festival. This was organised by the 'German Patriotic Association for the Support of the Free Press', set up the same year. The flag of the *Burschenschaften* was flown and revolutionary speeches were made demanding more liberal forms of government and the unification of Germany.

- In April 1833, a group of armed German students, members of the **'Young Germany'** movement, supported by a group of Polish *émigrés*,

1. How extensive were liberal and nationalist ideas in the German Confederation, 1815–1840?

2. Did Metternich's handling of the affairs of the German Confederation do more to advance or to retard the development of liberal and nationalist ideas? Explain your answer

tried to enter the Diet at Frankfurt to voice their views. They were easily defeated, but their action prompted further repression.

What were the 'Six Articles'?

In June 1834, Metternich enlisted Prussian support to persuade the Diet to pass the 'Six Articles'. These reinforced and added to the Karlsbad Decrees. They declared all political meetings illegal. Even to wear the colours (red, black and gold) of the *Burschenschaften* was made a crime. Over the following years, there were further dismissals of professors. These included the **Brothers Grimm** (writers of the fairy tales) who, along with seven other professors, had dared to criticise Ernest Augustus' suppression of the Hanoverian constitution in 1837. The Diet, which was responsible for overseeing these measures and was under Austrian control, came to be regarded as a symbol of repression. There seemed to be nothing the liberals could do.

8.5 How was the German Confederation altered by the development of the Zollverein?

What was the Zollverein?

Brothers Grimm: Jakob Ludwig Karl (1785–1863) and Wilhelm (1786–1859)
The brothers were interested in German language and culture. Jakob was professor of philology (the structure and development of languages) at Göttingen University and his *Deutsche Grammatik* of 1819 was the first attempt to explain the historical development of the Germanic languages. Together, they collected folk tales, such as Hansel and Gretel and Rumpelstiltskin. They published *Kinder und Hausmärchen* (1812–15) and *Deutsche Sagen* (1816–18). They were nationalists in so far as they were interested in anything German, but they were intellectuals, not politicians. So, for example, when the Elector (ruler) of Hesse-Cassel was returned to his throne in 1815, the two brothers ran alongside his coach cheering. Their dismissal from their university posts in 1837 was more because of what others might make of their works, than their own active political involvement in the growing nationalist movement. Their reinstatement by Friedrich-Wilhelm IV, helped to arouse liberal hopes.

In 1818, 70 Rhineland manufacturers complained to the Prussian authorities about the competition they faced from foreign imports, particularly from Britain, many of which entered their country freely. 'All states favour home industries by tariffs; Germany alone fails to protect her children,' they wrote. As a result, Prussia carried out a review of its chaotic internal and external trading system.

Prussia had nearly 4,000 customs duties of various kinds on goods entering Prussia, and 67 different tariffs within its territories. Clearly reform was overdue and the enquiry led to Maassen's Tariff Reform Act of 26 May 1818, which created the Prussian Customs Union.

● Prussia abandoned its internal customs duties. The movement of goods from one district of Prussia to another was now free of tolls and delays.

● A low duty was placed on goods entering Prussia from elsewhere. There was no tariff on raw materials, which were needed to boost Prussian industry, but a charge of about 10% on manufactured goods and 20% on luxury 'colonial' goods such as tea and sugar was made.

● A heavy tax was placed on any foreign manufactured goods passing through Prussian territory.

● The tariffs were kept low, at first, to discourage smuggling and to prevent other nations levying high duties on Prussian corn and linen in retaliation. In time they were raised, and raw materials such as English cotton and iron were included. Initially, the industrialists benefited less than the farmers. The tariff on manufactured goods was still low enough for British competition to continue, but the general advantage was soon apparent.

In 1819, the tiny state of Schwarzburg-Sonderhausen in Thuringia, with a population 45,000, signed a treaty which brought it into the Prussian customs system. Between 1819 and 1826, the small non-Prussian States within Prussian territory sought to enter the scheme.

The advantages of the scheme were soon seen by other states. The map

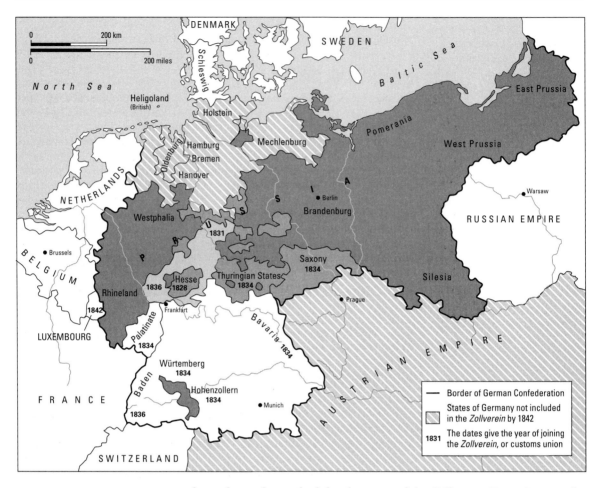

The development of the *Zollverein*, 1818–1842

above shows the gradual development of the *Zollverein*. Hesse-Darmstadt, a larger neighbouring state, which was experiencing difficulties because it was cut off from the Prussian market, joined on 14 February 1828. However, some States feared domination by Prussia and so chose to create their own groups.

In 1828, two rival unions came into being. Bavaria made a commercial treaty with Württemberg (18 January 1828). Hanover, Hesse-Cassel, Brunswick, Saxony, Nassau, Frankfurt-on-the-Main, Bremen and the Thuringian states formed the 'Middle German Commercial Union', on 24 September 1828.

For a while there was intense rivalry as Prussia controlled the north–south routes through northern Germany while the 'Middle Union' tried to keep open the roads from the North Sea ports to the central German cities of Frankfurt and Leipzig. They even built new roads to go round the Prussian customs union. The Prussian Finance Minister thwarted this by building roads joining Prussia directly with Bavaria, Württemberg and Frankfurt. He also extended Prussian trade along the Rhine, through an agreement with the Dutch.

The economic pressure was such that this situation could not continue. In 1830–31, financial difficulties and revolutionary upheavals drove Hesse-Cassel to join the Prussian group, so providing a link between the eastern and western parts of Prussia. The 'Middle Union' collapsed. In August 1832, Hanover proposed to the Diet that a general customs union should be created to include all the German states, but negotiations broke down. Prussia was happy for states to form trade treaties with it, but it did not want to come into some general system. In the course of 1833, Bavaria, Würtemberg, the Thuringian states and Saxony joined Prussia. From 1 January 1834, the *Zollverein* came into being, covering 18 states. Other states, including Baden and Nassau, joined in 1835. Frankfurt-on-the-Main joined in 1836. By then, it covered 25 states and some 26 million people.

The *Zollverein* was therefore a group of states that had agreed to abolish all customs duties between themselves. It was supervised by a specially appointed body, the Zollverein Congress, which could negotiate with other European states on matters of trade. Its status was confirmed in 1844 when it successfully negotiated a trade treaty with Belgium on its members' behalf. It took the lead in other matters of common interest, such as the unification of the currency, weights and measures. Roads, railways and postal systems were also extended and adapted to improve communications between the member states.

By 1844, the *Zollverein* covered virtually all of Germany, although Hanover did not join until 1854, and the cities of Bremen and Hamburg stayed out. As well as these, the other excluded party was Austria. It had refused to join at the beginning, as it preferred **protectionism** to free trade. Austria had large markets within its own Empire for its manufactured goods and it wanted high import duties to protect its industries from foreign competition. Since Prussia refused to raise the general level of duty, Austria preferred to act independently. By the time it realised its mistake, it was too late.

Protectionism: Tariff or customs barriers to prevent or reduce foreign goods entering the country. This allows native producers to sell their products without competition.

What was the significance of the Zollverein?

By 1844, thanks to the *Zollverein*, the German Confederation enjoyed virtual economic union under Prussian leadership. Although this was not the same as political union, it bred the habit of the states working together. This example of co-operation encouraged nationalist thinking. Its practical success gave weight to arguments for political unity, which pointed out the savings to be made from a reduction in the number of different administrations.

It also encouraged the states to look to Prussia for leadership. As Prussia itself developed economically and administratively, it was increasingly capable of fulfilling this role. Austria's absence and Prussia's control were to be of great significance for the future of Germany. In some ways, it seems odd that Austria allowed this to happen. Probably, Metternich did not foresee its consequences and, in any case, his attention was focused elsewhere. The Italian troubles, the question of Spain and the Greek Revolt from 1821 (see Chapter 6) absorbed much of Metternich's energy at the time of the first treaties, leaving Prussia with the freedom to do as it wished. On the occasion of the trade agreement with Hesse-Darmstadt, Metternich had declared, 'The point will eventually arrive when we will have to assert ourselves, but that time has not come, and I especially do not want our higher political relationships with the court of Prussia to be spoiled by a bit of true political rubbish.'

Whether Prussia had intentionally set out to extend its leadership at the expense of Austria is a matter of speculation. As early as 1830, the Prussian Finance Minister had pointed out to the King that a free trade league would not only bring prosperity to Prussia and its associates, but would also isolate Austria. Many modern historians agree with the view that this was indeed Prussia's intention, at least from 1830, and that those who benefited financially from the *Zollverein* were won over to support Prussian-led political union. Certainly, despite its **reactionary** politics, Prussia was seen by many as the potential leader of a united Germany by the 1840s.

Reactionary: This literally means reacting against new ideas. It refers to those who are backward looking and hostile to change.

1. How and why did the Zollverein develop in Germany between 1818 and 1840?

2. Explain the significance of the development of the Zollverein for the future of Prussia and Germany.

8.6 How did liberalism and nationalism develop in the German Confederation in the 1840s?

By the 1840s, German nationalism had grown considerably. In the panic of 1840, when it was believed France might invade along the Rhine to force the other powers to agree to its demands over the Mehemet Ali affair (see Chapter 6), it received a new boost. The publication of various histories helped to build up a picture of Germany's role in Europe. Songs, such as 'Deutschland über alles' and 'Die Wacht am Rhein' ('The Watch on the Rhine') by Max Schneckenburger, reinforced the patriotic message. Many German towns established choral societies promoting German music and songs. The universities continued to turn out works on nationalism and liberalism, and the German philosopher, Ernst Moritz Arndt (1769–1860), gave German nationalism a further racist twist. He wrote, 'the Germans have remained more than other peoples in their original purity'. Nationalist societies spread and, in 1847, *Die Deutsche Zeitung* ('The German Newspaper') was founded in Heidelberg to spread liberal and nationalist ideas.

Another threat, in 1846, raised an enormous outcry. The King of Denmark was hoping to incorporate Holstein (the German-speaking state which he ruled but which was part of the Confederation), and Sleswig (another separated duchy, part-Danish, part-German speaking) into his kingdom proper.

Anti-semitism: Against Jews or the Jewish religion (Judaism).

This excitement reflected the heightened emotions throughout Germany. Working-class unrest in the new industrial areas of Saxony, antagonism between Protestants and Catholics in the Rhineland, and **anti-semitism** among the radicals of the southern states formed a background of latent violence.

Throughout the German Confederation, there were gradual moves to greater liberalism, particularly in the States of the south-west. Grand Duke Leopold was persuaded to appoint a liberal ministry in Baden at the end of 1846. This led, in 1847, to the relaxation of press censorship, reform of the police and of the judicial system. In Hesse-Darmstadt, the liberal movement was strong and demanded changes in electoral rules and a free press. There was an unsuccessful attempt, on the part of the Elector of Hesse-Cassel, to restrict the local constitution in 1847. In Bavaria, under the half-mad King Ludwig, more liberal ministers were appointed. This was not, however, a move of conviction. The previous Conservative ministers had refused to grant Ludwig's lady friend, a dancer of British extraction, a title and land.

What was the position of Prussia in the 1840s?

Friedrich-Wilhelmm IV (1795–1861), King of Prussia (1840–1861)
Friedrich-Wilhelm IV was the eldest son of Friedrich-Wilhelm III. The German liberals welcomed his accession, but hopes of a new era were disappointed when he turned out to be fundamentally conservative. He had a romantic idea of German nationalism, but was opposed to liberal, constitutional government. In the revolution of 1848, he initially showed some sympathy to the views of the liberals, but he refused to become the Emperor of a united Germany. His later years as king were characterised by repression and censorship.

Friedrich-Wilhelm III of Prussia died in 1840 and was succeeded by his son Friedrich-Wilhelm IV. Friedrich-Wilhelm IV was known to be religious, humane and anxious to avoid all forms of persecution, so his accession raised liberal hopes. He began by releasing political prisoners. He appointed liberals as ministers and reinstated liberal academics, including the brothers Grimm in Berlin. In 1842, he arranged for the provincial diets of Prussia to send representatives to meet in Berlin as an advisory body, on a temporary basis. He also extended the powers of the provincial diets and allowed them to publish reports of their debates.

However, his well-meaning gestures were wrongly interpreted by radicals anxious for more. There was agitation for a constitution in the Rhineland. In 1841, in Cologne, Karl Marx attacked the existing government and social system in the 'Rheinische Zeitung'. Demands for a single, elected diet representing all the Prussian lands frightened the Junkers

1. *How extensive was nationalism in Germany by the 1840s?*

2. *Using the information in this chapter, can you explain why liberals and nationalists looked to Prussia for leadership in the 1840s?*

3. *'Prussia was prepared to offer economic, but not political, leadership, 1815–1847.' How far would you agree with this statement? Give reasons for your answer.*

who even considered a *coup d'état* to replace the King with his brother, Wilhelm. Friedrich-Wilhelm IV reacted promptly. The *Rheinische Zeitung* was suppressed and press censorship reimposed in 1843. Liberals were banished and, by 1845, the King was even requesting the French government to expel subversive German writers from France.

When Friedrich-Wilhelm IV announced the summoning of a United Diet to Berlin in 1847, the liberals believed their hopes were about to be realised. They were bitterly disappointed. The Diet was divided into two houses – one for the peasants and middle classes, and another for the nobility. It was granted little more than debating rights. It could vote taxation and could present petitions to the King, but had no law-making powers. It had been summoned solely for the purpose of voting a loan for the building of a railway to link East Prussia with Berlin. When it refused, it was dispersed in June 1847.

Friedrich-Wilhelm IV vowed, 'Never will I permit a written sheet of paper … to come between our Lord God in Heaven and this country, to govern us through its paragraphs and replace the old sacred loyalty.' In his opinion, he had a divine right to rule, and no constitution (sheet of paper) should detract from this.

8.7 What was the condition of the German Confederation and Austrian Empire on the eve of revolution, 1846–1848?

Potato blight: A disease caused by parasites, which destroys the crop.

While peasant unrest was not uncommon in either the Austrian Empire or the lands of the German Confederation, by the late 1840s the situation had grown worse. The 1840s saw problems throughout Europe and the predominantly rural populations of those central European countries were particularly badly hit. In 1845, the potato crop failed. A serious outbreak of **potato blight** followed in 1846. By July 1847, prices in central Europe had as much as quadrupled. There were disastrous corn harvests in 1845–47 and the price of cereals rocketed. The year 1847 saw bread riots in Stuttgart and Ulm, and violence in Berlin, sparked by the shortage of potatoes. In Hungary, there was an outbreak of cattle plague. As thousands died from hunger and typhus, unrest grew.

Many people left the countryside and made their way to the towns in search of work. Here, they added to the problems of the growing population. Townsfolk were, in any case, little better off. They were also hit by rising prices as a result of dwindling food supplies. In Germany, there was a depression in the textile trade in 1847. The amount of spun yarn exported by the member states of the *Zollverein* fell by 40%. There was a cut in wages, and the standards of living for workers in the towns fell. The *Zollverein* tariffs did not protect native industry from British and Belgian competition, and there was the added problem of the old handicraft industries which could not compete with the new factories. Early 1848 saw the burning of mills in Düsseldorf, demonstrations by weavers in Chemnitz and attacks on the new railways from waggoners in Nassau. In Austria, the slow rate of industrialisation meant that there was insufficient work to absorb the rapid influx of labour. There were around 10,000 unemployed in Vienna by 1848, for example. However, the working classes and peasantry did not create revolution on their own.

It was the middle and upper classes – those most affected by the

Swiss cantons: Switzerland was made up of 22 independent regions, known as cantons, with a central diet (government), similar to that in Germany. In 1845, seven of the Catholic cantons formed a league to protect their interests against the liberals in the central diet. This was called the *Sonderbund*. There was brief civil war in 1847, after which it was disbanded.

1. What do you consider to be the most important changes that had taken place in (a) the German Confederation and (b) the Austrian Empire between 1815 and 1848? You should refer to economic, political and intellectual changes in your answer.

2. Make a list of the factors that you feel were contributing to German unity, 1815–1848, and another of those that were holding it back. You should include economic factors such as the spread of railways and the Zollverein, political factors such as the Bund, and intellectual factors, such as the contribution of the German philosophers and the growth of liberalism. You should also mention the position of Prussia and Austria and, if you have studied Chapter 6, the attitude of the other nations of Europe. Explain the points you make.

growing liberal and nationalist feeling of the 1830s and 1840s – who provided the revolutionary leaders in 1848. In Germany, Austria and Czechoslovakia, it was mainly the middle classes and the intellectuals who led the demands for change. In Hungary and the Italian territories of the Habsburgs, the landed classes were the leading element. Demand for more representative government, in both the German Confederation and within the Austrian Empire, entered a new phase. This was partly inspired by events elsewhere. In 1846, there was the Polish rebellion in Galicia. In 1847, the more democratic **Swiss cantons** overthrew the conservative, autocratic ones (the *Sonderbund*) which had been formed under Austrian patronage. According to historian C.A. Macartney, by 1847–48 'almost every social class and almost every nationality in the monarchy was chafing under the system and demanding change'.

In the German Confederation, the catalyst for revolution came from Baden which, in October 1847, put forward plans to an assembly of liberals from all the south-west German states for a united Germany. This inspired radical demands throughout south-west Germany for fairer taxation, education, a people's army, improved employment laws and, above all, a united Germany.

In February 1848, the French King Louis-Philippe was overthrown and a republic was established. This was the spark that was needed to ignite the revolutionary discontent. Within a fortnight, there were revolutions in Bavaria, Prussia, Italy and throughout the Austrian Empire. By March, Metternich and the system he had tried to uphold for so long, had been overthrown.

8.8 Is it fair to describe the period 1815–1848 as the 'Age of Metternich' in Central Europe?

A CASE STUDY IN HISTORICAL INTERPRETATION

The period 1815–1848 has often been referred to as 'The Age of Metternich'. This is sometimes meant as a reflection of his dominance in European politics (see Chapter 6) and, sometimes, as a comment on his control over the affairs of the German Confederation and the Austrian Empire. It is the latter we are concerned with here.

What was Metternich's personal contribution to the development of these countries, 1815–1848?

Traditionally, historians and writers have condemned Metternich for his excessive zeal in upholding Conservative policies in the face of European change. Indeed, the Austrian Chancellor inspired a good deal of hatred in his own lifetime, from those of liberal opinions. The English romantic poet, Robert Browning (1812–1899), relating the dearest wishes of an Italian Liberal, had him say,

'I would grasp Metternich until
I felt his red wet throat distil
In blood through these two hands.'

Naturally enough, by the end of the 19th century, when those very ideas Metternich had most condemned – nationalism and liberalism – were successful throughout Europe, he received a 'bad press'. Metternich was regarded as an out-of-date reactionary and, what is more, a failure. These views have continued to our own day. In the 1930s, historian Viktor Bibl condemned Metternich's hostility to reform and, more recently, the historian Paul Schroeder has argued that he had few original ideas and stood in the path of progress.

Norman Davies, in *Europe* (1997), refers to Metternich as the 'embodiment' of the most extreme form of reaction. Franklin Ford, in *A General History of Europe 1780–1830* (1970), comments that 'the Austrian Minister seemed to many observers at the time, as he has to many since, the evil genius of tyranny and reaction'. In both Austria and the German Confederation, it is argued, Metternich ruled with an iron hand. The secret police rooted out all sources of discontent. Censorship prevented the spread of all ideas that were reckoned to be in any way subversive. By means of diplomatic negotiations and the occasional threat of force, the German States were hounded into obedience. The Karlsbad Decrees (1819) and the Six Articles (1834) ensured that discontent was kept firmly under control. The historian, Agatha Ramm, has presented the view of Germany before 1848 as 'a country where to have a political opinion was difficult, to express it almost impossible, and to join with others to promote it, conspiracy punishable by the heaviest prison sentences'. Whether supervising Germany, Austria or Europe as a whole, A.J.P. Taylor has referred to Metternich's attitude as that of 'the policeman on duty'.

Were Metternich's ideas reactionary?

To some extent, Metternich contributed to his own damning reputation by his many anti-liberal pronouncements. In 1832 he declared:

'There is only one serious problem in Europe and that is Revolution ... Two words are enough to create evil: two words which, because they are empty of all real meaning, enchant the dreamers by their emptiness. These words are Liberty and Equality.'

Metaphors: Imaginative ways of describing something by referring to something else which has the qualities that you are trying to express. For example, if you wanted to describe King Friedrich-Wilhelm IV you might say that he was 'ditch-water' (i.e. dull and dreary).

Metternich is said to have used only eight **metaphors** to talk about society, 'volcano, plague, cancer, deluge, conflagration, powder magazines, influenza and cholera'. He referred to revolts as 'earthquakes, conflagrations and torrents'. He left a clear statement of his 'principles' in his memoirs, written after his dismissal in 1848. He explained how the French Revolution and wars had brought about a new conflict in Europe, creating a clash between the forces of 'stability' and 'movement'. His duty, as he saw it, had been to uphold the principles of 'stability', and to preserve government and law against the ideas of 'movement', revolution and anarchy. Metternich believed that monarchical government, together with the aristocracy, was the only security against revolution. Liberalism and nationalism, those products of the French Revolution, were merely the selfish interests of the 'agitated' middle and lower classes. They had to be resisted by censorship, spying and, when necessary, force. He described his role as 'a rock of order' in Europe.

However, some recent historians have taken issue with Metternich's 'reactionary' reputation. The historian Carsten Holbraad wrote, in *The Concert of Europe* (1970), 'till the year of his resignation (1848) the policy of Metternich was to maintain peace and security by preserving the settlement of Vienna'. This, he argued, was not foolish, but appropriate to the period in which he was living. His concern for stability was both wise and successfully carried out, so, despite the multi-national state of the Austrian Empire and the problems of the divided German Confederation, there were no major upheavals in the areas under his immediate influence before 1848.

Heinrich von Srbik (in 1925) and Henry Kissinger (1973) both found cause to praise Metternich's principles and policies. More recently, Alan Sked (1989) emphasised Metternich's sincerity and tried to set his actions in context. Some historians have even questioned whether the principles Metternich spoke of in his memoirs really meant a great deal to him. A.J.P. Taylor reckoned they were just clichés, which sounded good but meant little. Paul Schroeder has written that Metternich never really had 'European principles', but that everything he did was with Austrian interests at heart. Since Austria had the most to lose from instability and nationalist thinking, Metternich 'stuck to the principle that all (liberal) movements must be immediately and automatically put down in the interests of the social order', wrote A.J.P. Taylor. By behaving in this way, Metternich was surely fulfilling the role of a good Austrian statesman.

How much influence did Metternich have?

Apart from the nature of his ideas, historians have also questioned the extent of his influence. As Austrian Foreign Minister from 1809 and Chancellor from 1821 to 1848, Metternich certainly had a good deal of power in the Austrian Empire and its dependencies but, to suggest that he was single-handedly able to assert his own reactionary policies in the Empire, is wide of the mark. For a start, Metternich was never more than a minister of the Emperor. He did have a certain amount of influence over Francis I but that disappeared when Ferdinand I came to the throne and Kolowrat was able to challenge his power. Furthermore, far from being entirely reactionary, Metternich had definite proposals for domestic reform, but his policies for reform within Austria were regularly overruled.

As for the allegation that he turned Austria into a police state, it must be remembered that the Austrian police force was run as a separate ministry under Count Sedlnitzky from 1816 to 1848. Once again, co-operation was dependent on personal friendship, but Sedlnitzky was never subservient to Metternich. The police force was comparatively small and dependent on the support of leading nobles in local areas. There was, of course, a secret police force too, and a network of spies and informers, but this was no more than most European countries had at this time. Direct and indirect censorship, the opening of mail, the editing of news from abroad, random house-checks and secret arrests were more widely practised in Austria than in, for example, the constitutional states of Great Britain and France. However, the evidence would suggest that the system was never as extensive or as efficient as some later historians have made out. **Subversive literature** did find its way into Austria and, provided its readers stayed out of trouble, was largely ignored.

The situation in the German Confederation left Metternich with even less control. Admittedly, Austria dominated the central diet, and Metternich appeared able to impose his will through measures such as the Carlsbad Decrees. However, this would not have been possible without the co-operation of the Princes and, more importantly, Prussia. Metternich could not prevent the granting of liberal reforms in the German Confederation and he was unsuccessful in halting the spread of liberal and nationalist ideas. What is more, as Prussia grew economically stronger and politically less timid, even Metternich could see that the days of Austrian domination were numbered. Speaking of the *Zollverein* in 1834, he predicted 'the links that bind Austria to the other states of the German Confederation' would 'gradually become loosened, and in the end break entirely, thanks to this barrier'.

Was this an 'Age of Metternich'?

Metternich's 'system' may not have been as extensive or as thorough as some have believed, but it would do him a disfavour to dismiss the idea of an 'Age of Metternich' altogether. His basic principles, shared by the Austrian Emperors and Prussian Kings, were dominant in Austria, Italy and Germany. Metternich's influence did cover a vast area and, what is surprising, is not that he was unable to defeat nationalism in Hungary, Italy or Germany but that he was successful in silencing major constitutional demands and preventing significant progress until the outburst of 1848. Furthermore, he was responsible for the governmental stability of central Europe, which served as a barrier to the ambitions of France and Russia in these years. The historian, Alan Sked, has suggested that Metternich genuinely believed that what Austria and central Europe most needed was indeed what was best for Europe as a whole. So Metternich exerted a powerful influence over diplomacy and worked successfully in the cause of peace and conservatism. Although he never ruled supreme in Europe, Austria or the German Confederation, his beliefs underpinned much of what occurred in these years.

Subversive literature: Pamphlets, leaflets and newspaper articles designed to undermine the ruling authority, or to bring about the overthrow or the ruin of a country.

1. Why has Metternich's influence in these years provoked debate between historians?

2. Using the information given in this chapter, explain where Metternich's influence was strongest, and why.

3. What evidence would you use to counter the idea that there was an 'Age of Metternich', 1815–1848?

Source-based questions: The development of Prussia

SOURCE A

(We must) tempt Prussia to put herself forward on the left bank of the Rhine, more in military contact with France. I know there may be objections to this, as placing a power so peculiarly military, and consequently somewhat encroaching, so extensively in contact with Holland and the Low Countries. But as this is only a secondary danger, we should not sacrifice it to our first object, which is to provide effectually against the systematic views of France to possess herself of the Low Countries and the territories on the left bank of the Rhine.

Castlereagh's view on the future role of Prussia as expressed at the time of the Vienna Settlement, 1814–15

SOURCE B

Germany must be mighty and strong if it is to uphold Prussian and German independence, for we have dangerous neighbours to the east and west. In the east lies the most consistently expansionist state since Roman times, Tsarist Russia. This state has already taken up a threatening position in Poland, the heart of Prussia. In the west there is a state that is dangerous because of its internal cohesion, and because of its tenacious[determined and stubborn] and unhappy belief in the need to control the Rhine border sooner or later.

Adapted from David Hansemann, a liberal thinker, writing in August/September 1840

SOURCE C

The Prussian State lies in the midst of all the European great powers, as Germany lies in the middle of Europe. In terms of population and material wealth (however) we are far behind our powerful neighbours. The state is stretched out in a narrow 200-mile strip, from the border of one large empire to the border of another ... What kind of means do we possess to counter these disadvantages? No other than the old Prussian spirit, speed and decisiveness in execution ... We have at times been hailed the champion of Germany, and I believe that we can accept this title without immodesty. We are not the most powerful state in Germany but the more powerful state which borders us is not called by its geographical location to be the champion of Germany as we are.

We, however, have this destiny because our lands everywhere comprise the vanguard of Germany and enemies first have to step over our bodies before they can penetrate further into Germany.

From an address by Ludwig von Thile, a nationalist, to the German Diet in June 1847

SOURCE D

Prussia has risen through circumstances into the ranks of the European pentarchy [the five great powers]. But no matter how militarised and powerful it might be, it cannot be denied that on its own, it does not enjoy the same weight in the great affairs of the world as the other four states. Only in the closest connection with Germany can it find the additional strength it needs. That Germany should be mighty and united is a crucial precondition of Prussia's existence.

From a memorandum by Josef Maria von Radowitz, a Prussian Statesman, 20 November 1847

---

1. Study Source A.

What decision affecting the future of Prussia was Castlereagh referring to here?

2. Study Sources B and C.

To what extent do these two sources agree on the dangers facing the Prussian State after 1815?

3. Study Source C.

How might the tone and language of the source be used to support the view that nationalism in the 1840s appealed mainly to middle-class intellectuals?

4. *In what respects do Sources C and D present a similar view of Prussia's future role in Germany?*

5. *'Prussia's acquisitions in 1815 were crucial to its future development as a leader of Germany.' With reference to all these sources and to the information given in this chapter, explain how far you agree with this statement.*

Italy, 1815–1848

9.1 What was Italy like, 1815–1820?

9.2 What were the causes and results of the revolutions of 1820–1821?

9.3 Why, and with what results, was there further unrest in Italy in 1831?

9.4 What was the contribution of Mazzini to the movement for change in Italy after 1831?

9.5 What influences were promoting nationalism in Italy, 1831–1846?

9.6 What was the effect of Pope Pius IX's election on Italy in 1846?

9.7 Historical interpretation: How widespread was nationalism in Italy before 1848?

Key Issues

● *How widespread was unrest in Italy 1815–1848?*

● *Why did attempts at revolution before 1848 fail?*

● *How extensive were liberalism and nationalism in Italy in this period?*

Framework of Events

1814–15	The Vienna Settlement. A system of separate states, mostly controlled by their former ruling houses, is re-established in Italy
1820	Revolution breaks out in Kingdom of Naples
1821	Revolution begins in Kingdom of Piedmont-Sardinia. Austrian troops are used to destroy both revolutions
1824	Charles Albert becomes King of Piedmont-Sardinia
1831	Revolutions in Modena, Parma and the Papal States are crushed by Austrian troops. Mazzini founds 'Young Italy' (a nationalist society) in Marseilles
1843	Publication of Gioberti's *Primato* arguing for a federation of Italian States under the Pope
1844	Publication of Balbo's *Delle Speranze d'Italia* arguing for national leadership by the Kingdom of Piedmont-Sardinia. Attempted revolution in Calabria (Naples) by Bandiera brothers
1846	Election of Pope Pius IX, widely regarded as a reformer, rouses liberal hopes
1847	Cavour and Balbo found *Il Risorgimento* ('The Resurrection'), a nationalist newspaper
1848	Revolutions occur in many Italian States.

Overview

DURING the period 1815–1848, Italy was not a unified country (see map on page 245). Prince Metternich, the Austrian Chancellor, once referred to the area as 'a geographical expression'. This was nothing new. Italy had been disunited since the fall of the Roman Empire in the 6th century although, during the Napoleonic period, the number of States had been reduced. However,

Vienna Settlement: A peace settlement for Europe after the French wars and Napoleonic domination, 1814–15. Details of this settlement are given in Chapter 6.

Conservative: This implies keeping things as they are.

Illiterate: Unable to read or write.

in accordance with the principles of the **Vienna Settlement** – to reduce French influence and to recreate, as far as possible, the stability of the 18th century – the settlement of 1815 returned Italy to a system of separate states, each under its own ruler and system of government. This arrangement suited the Austrians as it kept the area relatively weak. It also enabled it to exercise a good deal of influence over the peninsula and to control the spread of revolutionary ideas. In its **conservative** aims, Austria was helped by most of the Italian rulers, who were noted for their resistance to change, and by the undeveloped economic state of most of Italy at this time.

The peninsula suffered from long-standing economic backwardness, made worse by its geography and climate. Ninety per cent of the population was dependent on some type of farming, many were **illiterate** and the power of the Roman Catholic Church was strong. By the 1840s, both economic and political progress was being made in some states, notably Piedmont-Sardinia, but most Italians in this period accepted their lot.

For the educated minority, a society in which they had no say in political affairs, no legal means of influencing the decisions of their governors, and little, if any, freedom to express themselves in speech or writing was less acceptable. Consequently, it was this middle-class group that led the movement for change. Working in the utmost secrecy because of the strict censorship, the Carbonari and other societies, inspired a number of risings in the 1820s and 1830s. By the 1840s, the activities and writings of Giuseppe Mazzini, a cultural revival, scientific congresses, as well as the publication of a number of progressive books and journals, in the freer atmosphere of this decade, encouraged the literate to consider what Italy's future path should be.

The desire for political freedom became entwined with a desire for independence from Austria and, in some cases, with a desire for a unified Italy. However, none of these wishes was crowned with success in this period. Although the various risings of the 1815–1848 period brought some minor victories, as rulers fled or were compelled to grant reforms, most were reversed in the reaction that followed. The only lasting improvements were those granted freely by reforming monarchs such as Charles Albert of Piedmont-Sardinia. This was a time of frustrated hopes for the leaders of the insurrections, but some of the ideas that were to form the basis of the later unification of Italy were laid down in this period.

9.1 What was Italy like, 1815–1820?

1. Compare the map of Napoleonic Italy (left) with that of Italy in 1815.

2. Which areas of Italy have changed the most?

Feudal taxes: The dues which peasants owed to their Lords for the right to farm their plots.

What ideas influenced the Italian Settlement at Vienna in 1815?

During the years of French rule, 1796–1814, there had been considerable political and social change in Italy. Not only had the number of states been reduced, the French legal code had been introduced and communications had been improved. Many Italians benefited from wider economic and social contacts both within the peninsula and outside. The position of the old aristocracy had been weakened, the peasants' burden was eased by the abolition of **feudal taxes**, and the educated middle classes enjoyed positions of responsibility in administration and law. Consequently, this 'middling' group of people, in particular, benefited considerably from French rule. They saw the advantages of the greater freedom and unity that it brought to the peninsula.

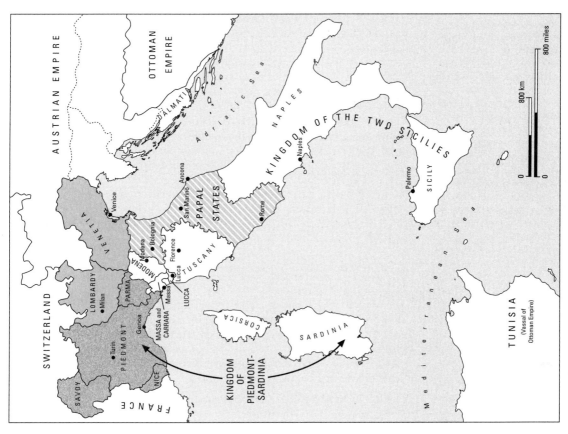

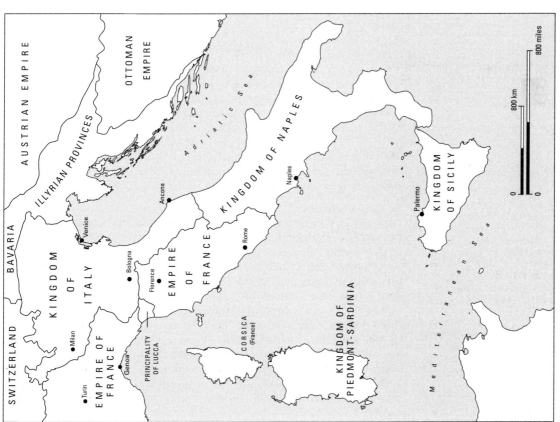

(Left) Italy in 1810; (right) Italy in 1815

Charles Albert I (Carlo Alberto) (1798–1849), King (1831–1849)
He became the great hope of the liberals after 1821 when he was unexpectedly thrust into power as a regent for his uncle Charles Felix. He made vague liberal pronouncements, which were interpreted as a sign of liberal sympathy, although he never really made it clear whether he supported the revolutionaries or not. This flaw was to make him a poor leader after his accession in 1831. He was so hesitant, he became known as *'il re Tentenna'* ('King Wobble'). In 1833 he had 12 men killed following a conspiracy, but after 1837 he carried out extensive reforms in Piedmont-Sardinia, including the reform of the army. He was ambitious and devious. He was certainly not a liberal and, despite several nationalist speeches, his main interest was to extend the power of Piedmont-Sardinia at the expense of the Austrians. Only in 1848 did he finally grant a constitution to his Kingdom.

Domains: Areas over which someone or something has control or influence.

Pope: The head of the Catholic Church. In the 19th century the Pope fulfilled two roles. He was both a spiritual (religious) leader, God's representative on earth, in the eyes of all Roman Catholics throughout the Christian world, and a temporal (earthly) ruler with control over the Papal States.

Papal legations: Areas in which the Pope's officials were in control.

Papal legates/priest-delegates: These were offices held by those who represented the Pope in the different areas of the Papal States.

However, the victors – Russia, Austria, Prussia and Great Britain, who met at Vienna in 1815 – regarded some of these changes as highly dangerous. They believed Italy needed protection, not only from French ambition, but also from such dangerous, modern ideas as liberalism and nationalism. Metternich feared disruption within his own multi-national Empire, should such ideas make headway in Italy. He believed it was his job to 'extinguish the spirit of Italian unity and ideas about constitutions'. The Vienna Settlement, therefore, involved removing French influence, restoring legitimate rulers where possible, and placing Austria in a position of control. The Italian nationalist, Mazzini, was to write later, 'throughout Italy, one stroke of the pen erased all our liberties, all our reform, all our hope'. It is true that many of the more progressive French reforms were swept away with the restorations of 1815. However, to be fair to the Vienna statesmen, even among those Italians who had benefited from Napoleonic rule, there were very few people who even thought in terms of Italian unity in 1815.

What territorial and governmental changes were made in Italy in 1815?

The Vienna Settlement created five main groups of states in Italy (see the map on page 245). Of the four republics that had existed in Italy before the Napoleonic wars – Venetia, Genoa, Lucca and San Marino (a tiny city state) – only the latter survived. The other areas were returned to strong personal rule. (A table of the Italian rulers of this period, beginning with those mentioned below, is on page 250.)

The Kingdom of the Two Sicilies (sometimes known as the Kingdom of Naples and Sicily)

The most southerly Kingdom was restored to Ferdinand I, a member of the royal line of Spanish Bourbons. He had spent the war years in his island province of Sicily, protected by the British navy. In 1815, he was restored to the mainland part of his Kingdom, Naples, and received the title 'King of the Two Sicilies'. His **domains** which were dry, hot and malarial, were the most economically undeveloped in Italy. His subjects were mainly poverty-stricken and highly superstitious peasants. Ferdinand abolished the constitution granted to the area in 1812, and set himself up as an absolute ruler, supported by the higher clergy. His rule was unenlightened. One of his own ministers referred to the executioner as 'the Crown's first servant'. Court and government were corrupt, there was strict censorship, expenditure on social projects such as schools and communications was reduced in an effort to meet financial difficulties, and nothing was done to counter the underlying economic problems.

The Papal States

Pope Pius VII, who had been held as a prisoner by Napoleon, returned from exile in France to recover his former possessions. He was reinstalled in the Vatican Palace in Rome, and enjoyed direct rule over the province of Rome and the two **Papal legations**, Romagna and Umbria. This area was collectively known as the Papal States. Initially, the French greeted Pius' return with some enthusiasm and sympathy, after his harsh imprisonment. He was certainly respected for his spiritual leadership throughout the peninsula. However, his return also meant the return of the power of the clergy. Under his guidance, the Catholic Church became an instrument of conservative and oppressive government. The French system of centralised administration was retained, but priests regained authority. Five **Papal legates** and 12 **priest-delegates** ran the 17 provinces that made up the Papal States. There were a few lay members on local advisory councils, known as 'congregations' (abolished in 1824), but otherwise control was firmly back in the hands of the clergy, most of whom were firmly against any changes brought by the French and any measure of reform. French law was abolished; those who had worked with the French were removed. Laws, which had introduced uniform weights and measures, street lighting and vaccination against smallpox, were cancelled. The Jews were confined to a **ghetto**. The **Inquisition** was reintroduced and torture was used to extract confessions from any whose ideas were viewed as subversive. The 'Zelanti', a powerful Catholic group, blocked virtually all suggestions of reform whether concerning justice, education or economic affairs.

Ghetto: An area, usually on the outskirts of a city, where Jews were forced to live.

Inquisition: A committee that investigated peoples' private lives. Its job was to discover those who denied the teachings of the Church and, traditionally, it used torture and underhand methods to extract confessions. It was hated as a symbol of repression and an infringement of personal liberty.

The Central Duchies

In the central north were a number of duchies controlled by dukes or duchesses. The Vienna Settlement made some complicated provisions for the smaller duchies, which gradually fell under the rule of the larger ones (as can be seen from the map of Italy in 1815 on page 245). The major duchies of the period 1815–1847 were Tuscany, Modena, Parma and Lucca. These were generally better governed than the states of the south although, even here, the historian Franklin Ford commented that 'autocracy and extortion were the twin principles of government'. Duke Ferdinand III of Tuscany, a cousin of the Austrian Emperor, was never excessively heavy-handed. However, another cousin, Duke Francis IV of Modena, was far more oppressive. They both ruled their duchies with the help of an extensive secret police network modelled on that of Austria. In Parma, Marie-Louise, daughter of the Austrian Emperor and former wife of Napoleon, was regarded as more liberal in attitude. French law was retained, judges were permitted independence and this was the only state in Europe where Jews were able to enter the civil service. However, Marie-Louise, who was later to marry the Austrian General, Count Neipperg, never escaped her Austrian connections. The tiny state of Lucca, which had formerly been a republic, became a duchy under the rule of Maria Louisa of the House of Bourbon. However, when the Bourbons retook Parma on the death of Duchess Marie-Louise in 1847, Lucca reverted to Ferdinand III of Tuscany (see table of Italian rulers on page 250).

The Austrian Empire in Lombardy and Venetia

Francis I, Emperor of Austria, assumed direct control of Lombardy and Venetia, the two richest Italian provinces. The administration here was far better than in Naples or the Papal States, and opportunities were wider too. Education was compulsory to the age of 12 and to some extent trade and communications benefited from the Habsburg connection. However, improvements were also offset by conscription and heavy taxation. Although they formed only an eighth of the population of the Empire, they contributed one-quarter of the imperial revenues. Furthermore, direct Austrian rule meant a loss of jobs for those lawyers and administrators who had enjoyed positions of responsibility under the French. Whereas, formerly, the language of administration had been Italian, after 1815 it became German, and the new government only employed Austrian judges, civil servants, police and army officers. Freedom of speech and the press were curtailed and students were forbidden to read such dangerous subjects as 'Modern History' at university. Although the surveillance and censorship was not as oppressive as has sometimes been suggested, there was an intense resentment of the Austrians among those most affected by the changes.

Customs duties: Taxes charged on goods entering a country. Also known as tariffs.

Mass/confession: Two sacraments, or acts, which are essential for true Catholics. Mass involves participation in the religious service commemorating Jesus' Last Supper, at which bread and wine are turned into the body and blood of Christ. Catholics are also required to confess (tell) their sins (misdeeds) to a priest in order to receive forgiveness. Without this, they cannot enter the kingdom of Heaven.

The Kingdom of Piedmont-Sardinia (also known as 'Sardinia', 'the Kingdom of Sardinia' or 'Piedmont')

In the north-west, Victor Emmanuel I of the House of Savoy headed the Kingdom of Piedmont-Sardinia. He had continued to rule the island part of his kingdom, Sardinia, throughout the Napoleonic period. However, in 1815, he regained his mainland possessions, which were considerably increased in size. The two provinces of Savoy and Nice were confirmed as part of his possessions and the former republic of Genoa was added. The King ruled from his capital, Turin (in Piedmont), which was the most economically developed part of his kingdom. His government was reasonably honest and taxation was not too oppressive, thanks to a fair trading revenue. However, one of the King's first actions was to abolish the French legal system and to return lands, tax exemptions and privileges to the nobility and Church. He was fanatically anti-French, removing French 'improvements', such as roads and lighting, and dismissing all those civil servants who wrote an 'R' in the French manner. He also imposed censorship, and a permit was needed to read foreign newspapers. The King brought back internal **customs duties**, reinstated the religious orders, and confined Jews to ghettos. His subjects were obliged to attend **mass** and **confession** at least once a month. Beards and long hair, considered revolutionary, were forbidden.

What was the social and economic state of Italy in 1815?

Compared with Britain and France, Italy was economically backward in 1815. Although it had been a wealthy trading nation in the 15th and 16th centuries, commerce had since lost favour with the nobility. With 90% of the population still working the land, the economy was almost entirely based on agriculture. To make matters worse, the population growth – from 13 million in 1700 to around 18 million in 1800 – had left many peasants short of land. Farming methods were primitive and inefficient, and the fields were cultivated under semi-feudal conditions. Although Napoleon had abolished feudal taxes, some were revived in 1815 and around half the peasantry still had to work for their landlords in the north, and an even greater proportion in the south. There was little industry, and virtually none in the undeveloped southern states. Industrial development was hindered by, among other things, poor transport. Geographically, the mountains of the Apennines cut Italy in two from north to south, and there were few good roads. The King of Piedmont-Sardinia even closed the road over Mount Cenis because the French had built it. Travel between states was not encouraged either. The Duke of Modena once declared 'travellers are Jacobins' and he would not allow stage coaches to cross his territories.

The new rulers restored the customs barriers that had been swept away in Napoleonic times, making commerce between states difficult and costly. The river Po, Italy's main navigable river, was divided into 22 sections by customs points.

In the towns, society was divided between the professional middle classes (lawyers, civil servants, writers, intellectuals and students), the 'financial' middle classes (bankers, merchants, industrialists and engineers), the workers (skilled craftsmen and manual workers) and the unproductive classes (beggars, road sweepers, petty criminals and the like). Few of these were better off after 1815 although, for most of the towns' workers, life did not change a great deal. They continued to live and work in crowded and unhealthy conditions. It was the small but influential middle class that was most obviously affected. Censorship and surveillance caused a good deal of resentment, while many lawyers and administrators lost work with the abolition of French law codes and practices.

What factors were preventing political progress in Italy after 1815?

Apart from the conservative rulers and the economic constraints, there were a number of other factors hampering progress in Italy in these years.

- There was a good deal of political apathy. Every day living was far more important for most Italians than political affairs, and they were resigned to their lot. There was widespread illiteracy and in the south, in particular, much poverty, ignorance and superstition. For the majority of people, 'patriotism' meant loyalty to a state, not to Italy as a whole. Men would describe themselves as, for example, Neapolitans or Tuscans rather than Italians,

- Even language differed between states and this hindered communication. French was spoken in Piedmont-Sardinia, Latin was the official language of the Papal States, while the Austrian rulers used German. The ordinary people also spoke in quite different dialects, often incomprehensible outside their own region.

- Although it had lost power under Napoleon, the Roman Catholic Church regained its influence after 1815. This was particularly marked in the 'Kingdom of the Two Sicilies', Piedmont-Sardinia and the Papal States. Superstition and fear of the Church were rife in the south, where the clergy enjoyed a great deal of local power. In the Papal States, Church law was state law and impinged on every subject. In Piedmont-Sardinia, the Catholic Church was freed from taxation, had full control over education and ran its own law courts. Throughout Italy, Church teaching stifled economic, political and intellectual developments. Preaching a message of conservatism and acceptance, the teachings of the Church reached far more ears than the words of the liberal reformers.

- The influence of Austria was felt everywhere. Apart from its direct control in Lombardy and Venetia, Austrian influence in Italy was maintained through its network of family alliances and military dependence. The Dukes of Tuscany and Modena and the King of Piedmont-Sardinia were all cousins of the Emperor. The Duchess of Parma and the Queen of Naples were both his aunts. The Pope also looked to Austria for support, as it was the most important of the Catholic states of Europe. Naples and Tuscany entered into direct alliance with Austria, promising not to alter their forms of government without consultation. Although the Papal States, Tuscany and Piedmont-Sardinia refused to do this, Metternich set up a 'postal convention', whereby the foreign correspondence of each state had to pass through Austria and was thus subject to Austrian scrutiny and control. Metternich's highly-organised police system and the Austrian spy network ensured widespread surveillance. He maintained an Austrian minister at each court, with agents and informers reporting private conversations and gossip, as well as infiltrating suspected revolutionary groups.

- Since the major powers of Europe had drawn up the 1815 settlement, they had a vested interest in maintaining it, and were not interested in the injustices of the petty rulers. Russia and Prussia were united in the **'Holy Alliance'** of 1815 with Austria, and hated anything which hinted at revolution. Britain and France were slightly more sympathetic but, in the immediate aftermath of 1815, were in no position to help even if they had wanted to.

'Holy Alliance': This came to represent an alliance in favour of the suppression of revolution.

What new attitudes and ideas were influencing Italy from 1815?

Although the vast majority of Italians had little concern for wider issues of government and reform, new political ideas did begin to spread among the educated middle classes after 1815. This was partly a result of the experiences of the Napoleonic period and partly a reaction to the conditions imposed on Italy after 1815. The idea of a *Risorgimento* of the Italian nation had first been suggested in the 18th century. It implied that a 'reborn', unified Italy might once again become great and powerful, as it had in the glorious years of Ancient Rome. Supporters of this idea shared two different beliefs.

Risorgimento: Literally meaning 'rebirth'. This was the term given to the growth in Italian patriotic and nationalistic feeling during the 19th century.

- Nationalism was a sense of loyalty to the State. This included a pride in its shared background and a belief that, only in a united country, could the people truly flourish. In the liberal revolutionary, Mazzini's view the nation was 'the God-appointed instrument for the welfare of the human race'.

- Liberalism was the belief that personal freedoms, such as freedom of thought and speech, as well as freedom from arrest and imprisonment without trial, were among the most important rights of man. Liberals believed only representative government could preserve these. The more extreme liberals were sometimes known as radicals. They favoured republicanism, a form of government with no monarch at its head.

Both of these beliefs clearly appealed to those who had tasted unified and representative government in Napoleonic times. However, those of sufficient education, wealth and ambition to seek change, were still small in number. The keenest supporters came from the professional middle classes, university students, lawyers, teachers and doctors. A number of civil servants and disgruntled army officers left unemployed with the ending of the Napoleonic era, were also attracted to the cause.

The main rulers of Italy, 1815–1848

Kingdom of the Two Sicilies
House of Bourbon
Kings:
Ferdinand I 1759/re-established
1816–1825
Francis I 1825–1830
Ferdinand II 1830–1859

Kingdom of Piedmont-Sardinia
House of Savoy
Kings:
Victor Emmanuel
Charles Felix 1821–1831
Charles Albert 1831–1849
Grand Duchy of Tuscany
House of Habsburg
Dukes:
Ferdinand III 1814–1824
Leopold II 1824–1859

Duchy of Modena
House of Habsburg
Dukes:
Francis IV 1814–1846
Francis V 1846–1860

Duchy of Parma
House of Habsburg
Duchess:
Marie-Louise 1814–1847
House of Bourbon
Duke:
Charles II 1847–1849 (formerly Duke of Lucca)

Duchy of Lucca
House of Bourbon
Duchess:
Maria Luisa 1817–1824
Duke:
Charles Ludwig 1824–1847
(Charles became Duke of Parma in 1847 and Lucca became part of the Grand Duchy of Tuscany)

Papal States
Pope:
Pius VII 1800–1823
Leo XII 1823–1829
Pius VIII 1829–1830
Gregory XVI 1831–1846
Pius IX 1846–1878

Lombardy and Venetia
Directly ruled by Austrian Emperor from 1814
House of Habsburg
Emperor:
Francis I 1804–1835
Ferdinand I 1835–1848

Freemasons: A secretive society, with special ceremonies, which provided benefits to its members

1. *Why was Italy divided into a number of separate states in 1815?*

2. *Who suffered most from this arrangement? Explain your answer.*

3. *Make a list of the factors that were (a) preventing (b) encouraging political change in Italy after 1815. Which do you consider were the most influential? Give reasons for your answer.*

How were the new ideas and attitudes spread?

Liberal and Nationalist ideas were spread through a number of secret societies. These adopted the practices of the **freemasons**, with elaborate rituals, passwords, coded messages and special handshakes. Because of the secrecy surrounding these organisations, it is difficult to estimate the numbers involved, but they were probably small. Membership seems to have been mainly middle class, although they did attract a few nobles with liberal ideas. They had scarcely any working class or peasant following, however.

In the north were the Federati and the Adelfi. In the Papal States were the Spillo Negro ('Black Pin'), the Latinisti and the Bersaglieri. The best known group, however, was the Carbonari. This organisation was quite strong in the south, where it represented around 5% of the adult male population of Naples. It also spread to the Papal States and Piedmont-Sardinia, but was never as powerful in these areas. There was little co-ordination between the groups, scattered as they were in different parts of Italy, and their aims were never clearly defined. Although there was talk of the overthrow of the restored Italian rulers and the expulsion of Austria from Italy, most members seemed to have had more limited aims. They hoped for little more than the establishment of constitutional monarchies within the various states and, in general, seemed happier discussing what they were against, rather than what they were for.

9.2 What were the causes and results of the revolutions of 1820–1821?

How did resistance develop 1815–1820?

Opposition to the 1815 settlement was mainly a secretive, underground movement between 1815 and 1820. With the restrictions that were in place on freedom of discussion and of the press, it was very hard for would-be revolutionaries to spread and co-ordinate the discontent. There were sporadic troubles like, for example, a rising at Macerata in the Papal States in 1817. However, disturbances were rarely well planned enough to escape detection and repression by the diligent secret police. Punishments for subversive activities could be severe. In the Papal States there was an endless struggle between liberal secret societies and the *Sanfedisti*, who supported the Pope. However, with the Pope's blessing, Cardinal Rivarola rooted out the troublemakers, condemned hundreds to exile or 'forced work' schemes and placed many more under police surveillance. He imposed compulsory monthly confession and annual attendance at a chosen **retreat**.

In two states, however, the troubles did pose a real threat to the rulers in the 1820s. These were the Kingdom of the Two Sicilies and the Kingdom of Piedmont-Sardinia.

Sanfedisti: The 'Holy Faithful' was a society set up in opposition to the Carbonari. Members took an oath to 'show no pity for the wailing of children or the old, and to spill the blood of the infamous liberals to the last drop, regardless of sex or rank'.

Retreat: To go into retreat was a Catholic practice involving a period of quiet meditation and prayer at a holy place, such as a monastery.

Why was there an outbreak of revolution in the Kingdom of the Two Sicilies in 1820?

There were two strands to the opposition to Ferdinand's rule in the south. The Carbonari hated the influence of Austria and Ferdinand's autocratic style of government. The Sicilians resented their union with the mainland and felt, with some justification, that little attention had been paid to their needs since 1815. A fall in agricultural prices had hit the Sicilian peasants

The arrest of four members of the Carbonari in 1821.

? *What does this picture tell you about membership of the Carbonari?*

particularly badly and the departure of the court from Palermo to Naples had also caused unemployment in that city.

In 1817, the Austrian garrisons had been withdrawn from Naples and the maintenance of law and order was entrusted to a militia of volunteers under local officers. Unfortunately for the rulers, however, some of these militia were among those most hostile to Ferdinand's style of government. News of revolution in Spain encouraged the dissatisfied, who had long nurtured hopes of changing the regime and the Carbonari led a series of riots and demonstrations.

Ferdinand I's government made a few arrests, but these only fuelled the discontent. In July 1820, the garrison at Nola, a few miles east of Naples, broke into revolt. General Guglielmo Pepe, one of a number of officers made responsible for organising the new militia system, assumed control of the 'revolution'. He extended his forces by enrolling members of the Carbonari, even though he was not a member himself. When he led one infantry and two cavalry units in a march on Naples, the terrified King took to his bed.

How successful was the revolution?

At first, the 'revolution' looked as though it would easily succeed. King Ferdinand I promised freedom of the press and a constitution based on that granted to Spain in 1812. This was very liberal. It involved the abolition of the special privileges of the nobility and clergy, the destruction of the power of the Inquisition, and an elected parliament with a vote for all adult males. Ferdinand even took an elaborate oath to honour his word. 'Omnipotent God – if I do lie, do thou at this moment annihilate me.' Since the all-powerful Lord did not strike him down, his superstitious subjects were foolish enough to believe his promises.

Ferdinand's actions also encouraged further troubles in Sicily. Here, the revolution was led by the trade guilds, the Maestranze, who wanted the separation of Sicily from Naples. The Neapolitan Governor was forced to flee, as riots broke out in Palermo. Government offices were burned down and prisoners released from gaols, amidst demands for a separate Sicilian constitution.

The new Neapolitan Parliament, which met in Naples in October 1820, was made up of professional middle-class men, a few noblemen and priests. The King swore to defend the new constitution and Pepe was put in charge of the army. There was talk of the redistribution of land to the peasants and a reform of the Church. The parliament had no sympathy, however, for the Sicilian revolt and voted to send troops to restore Neapolitan domination.

Why did the revolution fail?

The Naples revolution was clearly a middle-class affair. Although the peasants provided a strong following in Sicily, the mainland leaders had no intention of including the lower classes in their new system of government. Although events had certainly frightened the ruler, Ferdinand I, and the other powers of Europe, the division of the revolt, the lack of popular support and the limited political experience of its leaders, meant that it soon collapsed. Metternich easily won Russia and Prussia over to his way of thinking at the **Troppau** Congress (October 1820), when he voiced his belief that revolution in one country could have an unsettling effect upon others and should therefore be put down.

Troppau/Laibach Congresses: See Chapter 6. At the Troppau Congress, the Troppau Protocol agreed on the principle of intervention against revolutions within states. The second congress (at Laibach) was a continuation of the first, at which it was resolved to put this principle into action in Naples.

In January 1821, Metternich invited Ferdinand to attend another congress, in **Laibach**, to discuss the developments in his kingdom. Ferdinand was granted permission from his new Parliament to attend. They believed naively that he was going to gain international recognition for their new constitution – 'the sanction of the powers for our newly acquired liberties', as they put it. Instead, he sought Austrian support to restore his former powers. Once the Austrian army marched south, the revolution was fated. Despite an attempt at resistance from Pepe and his men, the rebels were defeated at Rieti on 7 March 1821. By 24 March, Austrian troops occupied Naples and the old regime was restored.

What was the result of the revolution in Piedmont-Sardinia in 1821?

News of the revolution in Naples had encouraged the secret societies of the north, who hoped to force Victor Emmanuel I to grant a constitution. Membership rose markedly in 1820–21 and there were a number of incidents. The first, a 'sit-in' of students at the University of Turin in January 1821, followed the pattern of earlier troubles and was violently broken up by the police. However, in March, events took a more serious turn. Undaunted by the depressing news from Naples, a group of aristocratic army officers, led by Count Santorre di Santarosa, showed their determination to press for change in Piedmont-Sardinia. Joined by a few liberal nobles, and a larger body of middle-class liberal revolutionaries, they took over the fortress of Alessandria. They set up a revolutionary government, proclaimed an independent 'Kingdom of Italy', and declared war against Austria.

Once again, despite their relatively small numbers, the revolutionaries had managed to strike fear into their ruler. Following another army mutiny in Vercelli, near Turin, Victor Emmanuel I chose to abdicate in favour of his brother, Charles Felix. He preferred this course of action to that of meeting the liberal demands for a constitution and of war against Austria.

Since Charles Felix was on a visit to Modena at this time, Charles Albert, the King's nephew, was made regent. Under pressure from the liberals, he issued a vague proclamation referring to the Spanish Constitution of 1812 as 'a law of the State'. The liberals believed they had triumphed, but Charles Albert's announcement was, of course, subject to the approval of Charles Felix.

Why did the revolution fail?

The return of Charles Felix brought the collapse of the liberal hopes. Having declared Charles Albert a rebel and exiled him to Tuscany, Charles Felix appealed to Metternich for military aid. Knowing he had the full support of his Holy Alliance allies, Metternich was not afraid to send Austrian troops to restore order. They joined forces loyal to Charles Felix and crushed the revolutionary armies at Novara, on the route from Milan to Turin, on 8 April 1821. By September, Charles Felix was in full possession of his kingdom.

What was the result of the failure of the revolutions of 1820–1821?

In the Kingdom of the Two Sicilies, the reprisals on those who had supported the revolution were swift and harsh. Pepe escaped to London and many fled the country or were exiled. Imprisonment, flogging, hanging and executions ensured there was no further trouble. Indeed, the reprisals were so severe that even Metternich intervened and sacked the Chief of Police.

In Piedmont-Sardinia, too, rebel leaders and thousands of revolutionaries were forced to flee abroad or risk harsh punishment. Many found themselves transported to Austrian prisons, although in contrast with the south, there were only two executions. The Austrians remained in Piedmont-Sardinia, with a 12,000-strong occupying army, until 1823, to prevent any further recurrence of trouble.

All over Italy, and even in areas such as Lombardy and the Papal States where there had been no revolution, liberals were hunted down and heavy sentences passed. It is estimated that around 2,000 were forced to leave the peninsula at this time. The experiences of 1820–21 made liberalism appear a lost cause in Italy.

1. Where and why did revolution break out in Italy in 1820–1821?

2. Why did the revolutions fail? Give reasons to support your answer.

3. Metternich described the troubles in Italy in 1820–1821 as 'earthquakes' and 'torrents'. Do you think he was correct? Explain your answer.

9.3 Why, and with what results, was there further unrest in Italy in 1831?

Although it became even more difficult to organise political opposition within Italy after 1821, those committed to change continued to scheme from abroad, particularly from Paris and London. The outbreak of liberal revolution in France, in July 1830, raised hopes once more. It seemed that the French might be willing to support revolutions elsewhere (see Chapter 7), and this inspired unrest in Modena, Parma and the Papal States.

How were the disturbances in Modena and Parma similar to those of 1820–1821?

The disturbances in Modena and Parma followed a similar pattern to those of earlier years. They were led by the middle classes. In Modena, it was Enrico Misley, son of a university professor and a practising lawyer, who inspired the troubles. In nearby Parma, it was students who began rioting. The aim – constitutional reform – was also similar, although Misley took this a little further, with plans for the establishment of a central Italian Kingdom under Duke Francis IV of Modena.

Even the duplicity of a ruler who appeared to support the liberals' aims, but then took action against them, mirrored the events of Naples in 1821. Although Duke Francis IV was not a liberal, he was pompous enough to show an interest in Misley's plans and to receive Camillo Manzini, a condemned revolutionary who had managed to escape to London. Duke Francis IV waited until two days before the 'revolution' was due to be launched and, in February 1831, had its leaders arrested. Misley's supporters were limited in number and, had Francis IV not made the mistake of travelling to Vienna to seek Austrian support, the revolution would probably have collapsed.

The liberals once again enjoyed a brief moment of glory, as their rulers panicked. Duchess Marie-Louise of Parma followed Francis IV and provisional governments were established in the two states. However, events followed a familiar pattern and, although they set up a joint army to protect their fragile regimes, they had little time to prepare before Duke Francis IV returned, with Austrian support, to defeat them in March.

The disturbances had proved fruitless. The old rulers were restored. The Duke denied any sympathy and resumed his role as absolute monarch, exacting vengeance on those implicated in the troubles.

What was the result of the disturbances in the Papal States?

It was again the middle-class professionals who led the protests in the Papal States, and in particular in the Papal Legations (Bologna, Ferrara and Ravenna), who resented their loss of independence in 1815. The protests were similar to those elsewhere, although here the issue of Church domination of government was the major complaint. Early success led to the establishment of 'The Government of the Italian Provinces, in Bologna in February 1831, which deposed the Pope as ruler. However, the expected support from neighbouring states and from the French did not materialise. Without this, the provisional liberal government had little hope of surviving.

The disturbances in the Papal States demonstrated to would-be revolutionaries that France was to be of little help to them. Louis-Philippe had refrained from supporting the rebels in Modena, which was regarded as being within Austria's sphere of influence, but he might have been expected to intervene in Bologna, which was part of Papal territory. However, he was cautious, and the French Foreign Minister declared, 'the blood of Frenchmen belongs to France alone'.

When Austrian troops went to the Pope's aid and took Bologna on 21 March, Louis-Philippe declared that, if the Pope were to carry through some governmental reform, the French would support him. A five-power conference of ambassadors met in Rome, in May, and drew up a reform programme, which included the secularisation of the administration. When the Austrian army withdrew on 17 July, it looked as though the trouble was over. The Pope was restored, but with promises of reform.

However, the liberals had again been too easily appeased. The agreed changes were not fully carried out, but attempted uprisings were fruitless. The Austrian forces returned in January 1832 and occupied Bologna. France, who was not prepared to let Austria have a completely free hand, responded with the occupation of Ancona in January 1832, but this did little for the liberal cause. Although France remained in occupation of Ancona until 1838, Pope Gregory XVI, who was elected at the height of the crisis, relied on Austrian support. Papal administration, with all its faults, continued.

Why did the revolutions of the 1820s and of the 1830s fail?

The revolutions and disturbances of the 1820s and of the 1830s had much in common. Their failure can be attributed to a number of shared factors.

● The revolutions were all localised. In each case, local grievances or plans were the foremost concerns. Communication and co-operation were limited. The revolutionaries in Bologna, for example, refused to deplete their resources by sending help to Modena in 1831.

● The revolutions were led by the middle classes, who were not naturally inclined to violence. Most had fairly moderate aims and were easily satisfied, and even tricked, by their rulers.

● None of the revolutions, with the exception of that in Sicily, gained much support from the workers or peasants. The middle-class leaders did not even seek it. They would have been horrified by the prospect of the 'ordinary' people playing a part in government. When rulers fled, it was usually out of panic rather than because of the strength of the revolutionaries. The peasants did not understand the demands being made anyway and most were happy to cheer the returning rulers once the troubles were over.

● The revolutionaries were often ill-equipped. Even when army officers or militiamen were involved, their equipment could not match that of the professional armies of the Austrians. Those fighting in the Papal States, for example, carried little more than hunting guns, pikes and scythes.

● The failure of the French to intervene on the side of the revolutionaries after 1830 also allowed the absolutist regimes to survive. In both 1820–21 and 1830–31, there was no outside power prepared to intervene on the liberals' behalf.

● The revolutions were defeated by the power of Austria. Once assured of support at Troppau, Austria showed no hesitation in using its army to support the rulers. By 1831, five of the six main rulers in Italy (Piedmont-Sardinia was the exception) had called in Austrian troops to help them.

How far had Italy changed by 1831?

Italy, in 1831, was much like Italy in 1815. None of the revolutions had been successful and in the Kingdom of Piedmont-Sardinia, Naples and the Papal States, the traditional rulers were actually stronger than they had been before the revolutions. Sicily had been placed firmly under the grip of Naples. The trade guilds, that had been at the forefront of the troubles of 1821, had been abolished. Autocracy was re-established everywhere and those who had dared to challenge their states were either in prison or in exile.

However, there had been some changes.

● There were a number of new rulers. (See the table of Italian rulers on page 250.) Ferdinand I of Naples died in 1825, and was succeeded by his son, Francis I (1825–1830) and then his grandson, Ferdinand II (1830–1859). There was also a new Pope, Gregory XVI, who ruled from 1831 to 1846. There was a new King in Piedmont-Sardinia when Charles Albert, who had given hope to the rebels of 1821, came to power (1824–1849). All of these men were less marked by the conservative attitudes that had accompanied the rulers of the immediate post-1815 period. While they were not excessively 'liberal', they were nevertheless more receptive to ideas of change.

1. In what respects were the revolutions of 1831 similar to those of 1821?

2. How important was the part played by foreign countries in the disturbances in Italy 1820–1831?

3. Which of the various revolutions of the period 1820–1831 do you think came nearest to success? Give reasons for your answer.

- By 1831, the great powers of Europe were no longer as unanimous about the need to keep things as they had been in 1815. Although Prussia and Russia had declared their support for Austria and for a policy of intervention against revolution in 1821, their interest in Italian affairs waned over the following years. Prussia had problems of its own in Germany, and Russia, in Poland. Britain and France had never supported the Troppau agreement anyway, and the troubles in Greece weakened the Austro–Russian alliance, while the revival of French power in Europe acted as a check on Austrian influence. (See Chapter 6 for details of changing international relations.)

- The failure of the old-style secret societies, such as the Carbonari and Federati, meant that a new style of revolutionary politics was able to attract support. The chief protagonist of the new thinking was Giuseppe Mazzini.

9.4 What was the contribution of Mazzini to the movement for change in Italy after 1831?

What were Mazzini's ideas?

The new 'Young Italy' society, launched by the 26-year-old Giuseppe Mazzini in Marseilles in 1831, was based on Mazzini's own views of how revolution was to succeed in Italy.

Mazzini believed that the aims of earlier revolutionaries – constitutional monarchy within the various states – were too moderate. He argued that true liberty would only be possible when Italy was united as a single nation. His society was, therefore, committed to nationalism – 'the universality of citizens speaking the same tongue', as he put it.

The methods of the early revolutionaries were also criticised. Mazzini believed they had been insufficiently committed and had expected countries, such as France, to do their work for them. Mazzini called on the Italian people and, in particular, the young people, to prove themselves worthy of their destiny, to educate themselves and to fight.

He also believed in a republican form of government. The new Italy was to be ruled by a central government, democratically elected. Members of his society took an oath to devote themselves to the creation of a 'free independent republican nation'.

Giuseppe Mazzini (1805–1872)
Son of a doctor from Genoa, he was highly intelligent and joined the Carbonari in 1827. He was arrested in November 1830 and forced into exile. He settled in Marseilles in France and, despairing of the unsuccessful conspiracies of the Carbonari, founded his own movement, 'Young Italy', in March 1831. Mazzini was a republican and spread a nationalist message. He hoped to increase patriotism so that Italians could expel the Austrians and bring about the unification of Italy. Although his planned risings were unsuccessful, he provided an inspiration to nationalists everywhere. Mazzini was a romantic figure. He always dressed in black, in mourning for Italy, and lived in rooms full of cigar smoke and canaries. He was forced to direct his movement in exile, firstly from Marseilles, and later from London (after 1837). Here, he amalgamated 'Young Italy' with similar movements abroad and created 'Young Europe'. He kept up a constant stream of letters and writings. Works such as *Duties of Man* and *Thoughts upon Democracy* were enthusiastically received in European radical circles and Mazzini's name became well known to the literate and politically aware classes of Italy. In 1848, he returned briefly to liberate Milan.

How did 'Young Italy' differ from earlier revolutionary societies?

In some ways Mazzini's new society looked like those of the past. It had the old-fashioned ritual of secret passwords and handshakes. It was also supported by the educated middle classes and was never very successful with the peasantry. However, there were differences.

● 'Young Italy' was a youth movement. The upper age limit was 40 (later raised), but most members were much younger. Their motto was 'thought and action'. They wore a uniform of the national colours – green shirt, red belt, white trousers and a beret. They equipped themselves with weapons – a rifle and 50 rounds of ammunition per member.

● 'Young Italy' was not a localised affair. Its aims were for the whole of Italy, and its contacts international. Mazzini had grand plans for liberal change throughout Europe, and soon groups such as 'Young Germany', 'Young Ireland' and 'Young Europe' followed similar patterns.

How successful was Mazzini as a revolutionary?

In practical terms, Mazzini was spectacularly unsuccessful. Although a convinced republican, he wrote to Charles Albert, the new King of Piedmont-Sardinia, in 1824, asking him to 'Put yourself at the head of the nation; write on your banner "Union Liberty and Independence"'. The gesture achieved nothing, except possibly to encourage the severity with which the King crushed Mazzini's attempts to encourage a mutiny in the Piedmontese army in 1833.

Mazzini's attempt to invade Savoy from Switzerland in 1834 was a fiasco. The Genoan general placed in charge proved incompetent. He squandered the funds given to him to raise an army, allowed his Polish and German volunteers to be seized by the Swiss authorities, and lost the rest of his men while disagreeing with Mazzini over tactics.

There were many bungled attempts at insurrection. Giuseppe Garibaldi, who later became one of the leaders of Italian unification, was condemned to death for his part in the failed Mazzinian conspiracy in Genoa, although he managed to escape. In 1844 the Bandiera brothers, Emilio and Attilo, inspired by Mazzini's ideas, although against his advice, tried to raise a revolution in Naples. They sailed from Venice to the coast of Naples with 19 followers, but were attacked by the local peasants and townspeople. They were captured and nine of them, including the two brothers, were shot.

The martyrdom of the Bandiera brothers is a sign of one of the greatest weaknesses of 'Young Italy'. It never managed to appeal to the peasantry, and never attracted very large numbers. Mazzini estimated its following at about 50,000 at its greatest extent, but it is likely that he exaggerated. Furthermore, it was difficult for him to remain in control, when he spent his life in exile. Mazzini had been banished from France and Switzerland by 1837 and had to live in London until 1848.

What was Mazzini's contribution to the Italian cause?

Although Mazzini's conspiracies all ended in failure, he was very successful as a publiciser of ideas. He wrote thousands of letters and endless articles, which were smuggled into Italy and appeared in his society's newspapers and elsewhere. According to the historian Denis Mack Smith, Mazzini succeeded in 'defining the goal and arousing enthusiasm among practised soldiers and statesmen'. He is therefore important, not so much for what he did, but for the way he inspired many young radicals in this period. He gave their liberalism a new fervour and optimism which kept the cause alive in the face of adverse circumstances.

Giuseppe Garibaldi (1807–1882)
Son of a fisherman from Nice (Nizza), part of the kingdom of Piedmont-Sardinia. At 15, he ran away to sea and joined Mazzini's 'Young Italy' movement. Garibaldi was sentenced to death for taking part in Mazzini's planned invasion of Piedmont-Sardinia in 1833, but escaped to South America where he spent many years of exile. He fought in the civil wars in Argentina and gained a reputation as a guerrilla leader. He returned home in 1848 and devoted himself to the nationalist cause.

'Mazzini's ideas and inspiration transformed attitudes to change in Italy in the 1830s.' Do you agree or disagree with this statement? Give reasons for your answer.

9.5 What influences were promoting nationalism in Italy, 1831–1846?

What were the cultural influences?

In the 1830s and 1840s a new form of literature also began to rouse nationalist ideas. Romantic novels, such as *I Promessi Sposi* ('The Betrothed') by Alessandro Manzoni (published in Milan 1825–27), were popular among the reading classes. Based on past glories, they encouraged patriotic feeling. The arts were frequently used to deliver an anti-Austrian message. To avoid censorship, they would portray another foreign nation as the wicked oppressor. When 'John of Procida' by Giovanni Niccolini was performed in Florence in front of the French Minister, he was annoyed when the audience cheered the lines directed against the French. However the Austrian Minister sitting next to him is said to have observed, 'Don't take it badly. The envelope is addressed to you but the contents are for me!'

Even music was used as a vehicle for patriotic themes, as in Gioacchino Rossini's 'William Tell' and the early Giuseppe Verdi opera, 'The Lombards of the First Crusade'. Verdi was a close friend of Manzoni and he went on to compose many operas with similar themes, again using stories from other countries, such as 'Nabucco' and 'Macbeth', to evade censorship. Painters, too, depicted great battles, while poets such as Giacomo Leopardi glorified liberty.

What was the influence of the Riformisti?

Although, politically, Italy appeared to be standing still, there was a growing interest in social and economic reform after 1830. The *Riformisti* ('the reformers') was the name given to those who believed that economic reform was the key to Italy's future. They believed that, freed from Austria's restrictive influence, Italy could flourish again.

Their ideas were spread in journals, such as Gian Domenico Romagnosi's *Gli Annali* ('The Annals'), produced in Lombardy in the early 1830s, and Carlo Cattaneo's *Politecnico*. These stressed the importance of industrial growth to the future of Italy and put forward plans for savings banks, schools, and a common monetary system which would encompass several states. Scientific congresses, agricultural societies and the construction of the first railway in Italy (in Naples), in 1839, all helped to spread the progressive message. The cheese industry at Gorgonzola and the Chianti wine industry were examples of this concern for economic growth, and a belief that the future of Italy depended on its economic development.

The *Riformisti* opposed the republican, conspiratorial ideas of Mazzini and wanted co-operation between rulers and people in some sort of Italian federation. There was, however, a contradiction in their views. Many of their schemes, such as those for railways and banks, would cut across state boundaries and would inevitably undermine the power of individual rulers.

What were the ideas of the Albertisti?

As Charles Albert showed a greater willingness to reform in the 1830s, a 'monarchist' group, sometimes known as the *Albertisti*, developed. The Piedmontese part of Piedmont-Sardinia was the most economically developed part of Italy. From 1837, Charles Albert introduced extensive legal, administrative, financial and military reforms in his Kingdom. Commerce was encouraged with a reduction in tariffs, the University of Turin was expanded, and extensive plans for the development of railways were drawn up. This made Piedmont-Sardinia the only state capable of leading a national crusade against the Austrians, and some monarchists adopted the idea of Charles Albert as a future King of Italy.

The idea of the supremacy of Piedmont-Sardinia was reinforced by some of the political writings of the 1840s. Cesare Balbo wrote *Delle Speranze d'Italia* ('The Hopes of Italy') in 1844. He favoured a federal Italy under Charles Albert's leadership. Massimo D'Azeglio wrote *Degli Ultimi Casi di Romagna* ('Of the recent events in the Romagna') in 1846. He argued that the recent events in the chaotic Papal States proved that leadership in Italy would have to be granted to Charles Albert.

Most of Charles Albert's supporters favoured a north Italian kingdom, complete with a constitutional government and freedom of the press. However, no specific plans were put forward as to how this might be carried out, and the attitude of Charles Albert himself remained ambiguous. Historian Derek Beales refers to him as an opportunist who was merely interested in increasing the power of Piedmont-Sardinia. However, Charles Albert told D'Azeglio in 1845, 'at present there is nothing to be done, but rest assured that when the opportunity comes, my life, the life of my sons, my treasure and my army will all be spent in the cause of Italy'.

What other political views developed after 1831?

Outside Piedmont-Sardinia, Charles Albert was a less popular choice to lead a national revival, but the political writers everywhere shared a single belief. They paid no heed to the idea of a popular revolution, or democracy. Federalism was often seen as the best way forward. In Lombardy, for example, the writer Carlo Cattaneo's ideas were welcomed by the middle classes. He favoured an independent Lombard Republic that would eventually become a member of a federal republican Italian state. He argued that 'Italy is physically and historically federalist' and had too many differences in its laws, languages and customs for a united Italy to be successful.

Another influential writer was Abbé Gioberti, an exiled Piedmontese theologian and philosopher who wrote *Del Primato Morale e Civile degli Italiani* ('Of The Moral and Civil Primacy of the Italians'), popularly known as *The Primato*, in 1843. He believed that the Pope and the Catholic Church should lead the Italian national revival. Gioberti favoured a federation of states aided by a 'cabinet' of ruling princes, with the Pope as president. He made no specific mention of the expulsion of Austria, and condemned revolutionary means to unity. Although Gioberti's works attracted a fair amount of support, the reputation of the Papal States and Church as reactionary and oppressive stood in the way of his ideas.

How did economic and social developments affect Italy by the 1840s?

Throughout the first half of the 19th century, Italy's economy continued to be based on agriculture. However, Italian farming was inefficient, and vulnerable to foreign competition. This meant that the peasantry was badly affected by the long agricultural crisis, which began in the 1820s and reached its peak in the 1840s. Although the political ideas of the liberal reformers had little appeal for this class, their depressed condition nevertheless encouraged them to participate in acts of disorder, riot and arson. Agricultural prices were subject to fluctuations and this affected the town dwellers too. There were a number of city riots caused by the price of foodstuffs in the 1840s.

1. In what ways, and to what extent, did literature and the arts spread new ideas in Italy in this period?

2. In what ways were the different schemes for liberal and nationalist change in Italy after 1831 similar, and it what ways did they differ?

Italy had begun to move forwards economically in this period, but industrial development was largely confined to the north, where it inspired the *Riformisti*. Furthermore, economic growth had its downside. Workers in cities such as Milan and Turin, which had expanded rapidly in the first half of the 19th century, suffered from overcrowding, poor housing and intolerable working conditions. Elsewhere, towns were often decaying economically, and the populations of Venice and Palermo had fallen since 1815. Living standards in towns declined after 1810 and urban sanitary conditions in Italy were some of the worst in Europe. In Naples in the 1840s, life expectancy was just 24 years.

Source-based questions: Ideas for the future of Italy

SOURCE A

Aims: The independence of Italy, our Country. To give her a single government based on a constitution, freedom of the press and of worship, the same laws, currency and measures.

Methods: To spread liberal ideas and to communicate them to friends, by firmly convincing them of the unfortunate state of affairs of our Mother country. The press, gatherings and private conversations are opportune [suitable] means. Cunning and perseverance are needed, and, above all, the eradication [removal] of all kinds of prejudice.

From the aims of the Order of the Carbonari, the Italian secret society, which had branches in a number of States in the 1820s and 1830s.

SOURCE B

Young Italy is Republican and Unitarian.

Republican:
- because every nation is destined by the law of God and humanity to form a free and equal community of brothers, and the republican is the only form of government that ensures this future;
- because the monarchy necessarily involves the existence of an aristocracy, the source of inequality and corruption to the whole nation;
- because both history and the nature of things teach us that elective monarchy tends to generate anarchy and hereditary monarchy tends to generate despotism;
- because our Italian tradition is essentially republican; the whole history of our national progress is republican.

Unitarian:
- because without unity there is no true nation;
- because without unity there is no real strength and Italy, surrounded as she is by powerful, united and jealous nations, has need of strength before all things;
- because federalism would necessarily place her under the influence of one of the neighbouring nations;
- because by reviving local rivalries, it would throw Italy back on the middle ages.

Adapted from Mazzini's beliefs for 'Young Italy', the society he founded from Marseilles in 1831

Unitarian: This refers to the creation of a single state (united or unified).

Anarchy: Without any organised authority. Anarchists regard all forms of government as oppressive.

Despotism: A despot is a monarch with absolute power who uses that power to oppress his/her people.

Source-based questions: Ideas for the future of Italy

SOURCE C

Italy has within herself all the conditions of her national and political *Risorgimento*, without internal upheavals or foreign invasions. Italian union cannot be obtained by revolutions. The principle source of Italian Union is the Pope who can unify the peninsula by means of a confederation of its princes. Federal government is natural to Italy and the most natural of all governments. The security and prosperity of Italy cannot be achieved otherwise than by an Italian alliance. Foreigners cannot prevent this alliance and far from opposing it they ought to desire it. Two provinces above all ought to co-operate to foster the opinion, which favours Italian unity, Rome and Piedmont.

Adapted from Gioberti's The Primato, *an influential book of 1843*

SOURCE D

The unitary solution is childish, no more than the fantasy of schoolboys. Confederations are the type of constitution most suited to Italy's nature and history. The only obstacle to confederation – a most serious obstacle – is foreign rule, which penetrates deep into the peninsula. An Italian confederation is neither desirable nor possible if a foreign power forms part of it. A democratic insurrection may continue for some time to be the hope of secret societies, but it cannot be an event to be reckoned on as part of any major undertaking.

From The Hopes of Italy *by C. Balbo, the Piedmontese writer in 1844*

---

1. Study Source D. Explain the reference to 'foreign rule which penetrates deep into the peninsula'.

2. In what respects do these four extracts agree with one another?

3. Study all of the sources. To what extent do Sources A and B differ from Sources C and D in their views of how Italy should be governed in the future?

4. Using the information given in this chapter and in these sources, why do you think that the views of the different societies and writers in Italy after 1821 had only a limited impact before 1846?

9.6 What was the effect of Pope Pius IX's election in 1846?

> **Pius IX, Giovanni Mastai-Ferretti 1792–1878, Pope (1846–1878)**
> As a Cardinal, he had gained the reputation of being 'progressive'. He was a kind-hearted man who genuinely wished to improve conditions in the Papal States. He was never the 'liberal Pope' that some Italians, such as Gioberti, had believed on his election.
> Pius IX had no experience of politics and was surprised by the reaction to his liberalism. After the events of 1848, he adopted a far more traditional and conservative position.

Pontificate: Period of time during which a pope is in power.

When Pope Gregory XVI died, in June 1846, and Pius IX was elected, liberals everywhere grew hopeful. 'Pio Nono', as he became known, had a reputation for reforming ideas, and was familiar with Gioberti's writings. Furthermore, he began his **pontificate** by instituting a much-needed plan of reform in the Papal States. He appointed the liberal-minded Cardinal Gizzi as Secretary of State and issued a political amnesty allowing around 2,000 political prisoners, mainly ex-revolutionaries, to be released from gaol. He proposed legal and judicial reforms, and appointed commissions to investigate education and administration. He gave lay people a greater say in government and announced that gasworks and railways might be built in the Papal States, something that Gregory XVI had rigorously opposed. In 1847, he put forward the suggestion of an Italian customs union and he granted three major reforms:

● freedom of the press

● setting up of a Consulta (an advisory body with laity among the elected representatives)

● appointment of a civic guard.

Count Camillo Cavour (1810–1861)
Member of the Piedmontese aristocracy. After a brief spell in the army, he became interested in scientific farming. He visited Great Britain, where he made himself a fortune by farming using machinery and scientific methods on his family estates. He also showed an interest in the parliamentary system in Britain. Cavour invested in the developing industries of northern Italy, and did not begin an active political career until his late 30s when he founded, and became editor of, a new political journal, *Il Risorgimento*. This was first published in Turin in 1847 with the purpose of gaining support for a liberal, monarchical Italy. Cavour joined the Piedmontese parliament in 1850, and thereafter showed himself a capable politician, Prime Minister and one of the architects of Italian unification. Although sympathetic to liberal attitudes, he was more concerned to extend the power of Piedmont-Sardinia.

What can you learn about these revolts from this illustration?

Although many of the Pope's plans were quite cautious, the liberals and radicals seized their chance. Freedom from censorship led to an outpouring of independent, free-thinking journals. Political clubs were set up throughout the Papal domains, and membership grew rapidly. The civic guard, intended to protect property and to curb violence, swiftly became an 'organisation of the people' and provided them with weapons.

There was excitement elsewhere too. In Venice, a speaker at the ninth congress of Italian scientists received rapturous applause every time he mentioned Pio Nono's name. The arrival of a new archbishop in the city of Milan provoked hymn singing to Pio Nono in the streets. Such was the popular hysteria that Metternich made it treason to shout 'Vivo Pio Nono' in Lombardy and Venetia. In the Kingdom of the Two Sicilies, King Ferdinand II also forbade cheers, and complained of 'the wretched little priest'.

Demands for reform elsewhere followed the Papal lead. Genoa sent a series of requests for change to the King in Piedmont. In October 1846, Charles Albert responded with a long list of reforming measures including freedom of the press. This enabled Italo Balbo and Camillo Cavour to found the newspaper *Il Risorgimento*. In Tuscany, Grand Duke Leopold II was forced to abolish the secret police and, in Lucca, a civic guard was formed.

The agitation caused great alarm in the Austrian-controlled states. Metternich was to remark, 'we expected everything except a liberal Pope'. He quickly made treaties with Modena and Parma. In July 1847, he increased Austrian troops in Ferrara, which lay inside the Papal States, to protect the border with Lombardy. The action was a political error. It roused a storm of protests, uniting liberals and Papalists. The Pope appealed to the powers of Europe. Charles Albert offered to put the Piedmontese army at his disposal and began to talk of a war for the independence of Italy. In the face of all this, Metternich was forced to withdraw his garrisons, which added to Pius IX's reputation as a national hero.

Pope Pius IX had raised many hopes but, when his new Council finally met in October–November 1847, it was clear that he did not intend to go too far too quickly. He informed the new body that it would not 'detract

Rioting in Palermo in January 1848. Typical of many of the disturbances which took place in rural areas of Italy, 1815–1848.

Sovereignty of the pontificate: The complete power of the Pope to rule his states as he saw fit.

minimally from the **sovereignty of the pontificate**'. Furthermore, although he might wish to see the Austrians driven out of Italy, as a Pope he could never be the one to declare war. In the event, that honour was left to Charles Albert.

On 3 January 1848, there were clashes in Lombardy between the people of Milan and the Austrian garrison stationed in the town. In Tuscany, after a long period of social unrest that had been building up since September 1847, there was a rising at Leghorn on 6 January. The troubles in Milan grew worse over the following weeks as the patriotic middle-class Italians staged tobacco strikes, symbolically giving up smoking to deprive the Austrians of the tobacco duty which they collected. The riots became serious, and an Austrian cavalry charge through the city killed several people.

Why did the election of Pope Pius IX cause such excitement in Italy?

Between 12 and 27 January, Palermo, in Sicily, rose in revolt and drove out the Neapolitan forces. The movement spread to the mainland. On 29 January, Ferdinand II granted a constitution. Piedmont-Sardinia and Tuscany followed suit in February and the Pope in March. The same month, Austrian troops were forced out of Milan and Venice after several days of street fighting. Charles Albert seized the lead, declaring war on the Austrians in March. It looked as though Italy's moment of glory had arrived but, within a year, those hopes had been shattered.

9.7 How widespread was nationalism in Italy before 1848?
A CASE STUDY IN HISTORICAL INTERPRETATION

The historian H. Hearder, in *Italy in the Age of the Risorgimento* (1983), comments that 'history is to a great extent written by the victors'. He is referring to the tendency of Italian historians, writing after unification in 1861, to regard the events of the early 19th century as a natural prelude to *Il Risorgimento*, the 'national revival' and Italian unification.

Perhaps the most famous of this school of writing was the Italian, Benedetto Croce, who produced, among other books, *History as the Story of Liberty*. In the 1920s and 1930s, when the Fascists were in power in Italy, an emphasis on the 19th-century rebirth of Italy became even more fashionable. Fascist historians tried to glorify the role of Italian nationalism. They wrote of its power in encouraging the people to resist foreign oppression and in unifying their nation. Similarly, in the 20th century, Italian Socialist historians have glorified those who led the secret societies and the rebellions of the 1820s, 1830s and of 1848. English liberal historians, such as George Macaulay Trevelyan, writing at the beginning of the 20th century, also saw the history of Italy as part of the steady growth of liberalism and nationalism, with the rebels fighting the conservative prejudices of their oppressive rulers.

The case for

● The writings and cultural changes that were taking place in Italy in the first half of the century might be considered part of a national revival. Developments in literature, music, poetry and painting encouraged a feeling of unity, a pride in being Italian and an hostility to the idea of separate regional states.

● The cultural revival spread a national language and encouraged people to think of themselves as Italians. It helped to break down the regional barriers.

● Nationalism grew stronger in the face of foreign rule in Lombardy and Venetia, and oppression elsewhere. The attitudes of rulers encouraged the secret societies, rebellions and mutinies. Although these were unsuccessful, they helped to spread patriotism, and their martyrs helped to win more converts to the cause.

● Many, especially the young, were encouraged to take direct action as a result of the teachings of Mazzini, who specifically preached the nationalist message.

Consequently, it is argued, the constant unrest throughout Italy in the early 19th century gradually converted the masses to nationalism. By 1848, there were many prepared to fight for the Italian cause. Italian nationalism had become a popular movement and only needed leaders to carry it to success.

The case against

Historian Derek Beales, in *Risorgimento and the Unification of Italy* (1981), refers to the nationalist arguments as 'the patriotic myth'. Most modern historians, even in Italy, which became a republic after World War II, have questioned the romantic view of Italy's 'rebirth', with its idea of a gradual growth of nationalism after 1815. Denis Mack Smith, Hugh Seton-Watson and Derek Beales all favour the view that nationalism made little progress in Italy before 1848, and that Italy's eventual unification was quite a chancy affair. Without knowing what was to follow, they argue, the troubles in Italy prior to 1848 could easily have been dismissed as minor upsets with little long-term impact.

● Rebels were often uncertain in their aims and the revolts were certainly not all inspired by nationalist motives. Some merely sought constitutional or liberal concessions from rulers, while the Sicilians, for example, sought separation from mainland Italy.

● The rebellions failed, partly because of their localism and the lack of co-ordination and co-operation between the different groups and states. Traditions of local allegiance went deep. Some of the north Italian states, in particular, had a long history of self-government and some saw little point in expelling Austria, only to replace its domination with that of Piedmont-Sardinia. These were hardly nationalist attitudes.

● National unity was rarely considered before the 1840s, and was not the only view put forward for the future development of Italy even then. Federalism, which emphasised the 'separateness' of the different states, was considered an equal possibility.

● Nationalism never affected the mass of Italian people. The peasants were never much involved in the troubles. Only a small minority ever participated in the liberal movements before 1848 and, when they did rebel, it was usually for economic reasons. Barriers of dialect, custom, prejudice and the lack of a formal education system meant that the vast majority of Italians probably had little genuine understanding of what nationalism meant, or what inspired the revolutionaries' activities.

● The supporters of the unrest were drawn from a narrow circle of the middle classes, mainly professionals, intellectuals and army men who were joined by a few liberal aristocrats. They were also mainly from the north of Italy. It was this narrow group of people who were most affected by the cultural revival, but their actions must have owed at least as much to their desire for advancement as to their commitment to nationalism. They shunned the support of the illiterate peasantry, and concentrated on the type of political and economic reform that would most benefit their own type.

- Not until the 1840s did the Italians share a national language. French was the language of government in Piedmont-Sardinia and the 'Kingdom of the Two Sicilies', Latin in the Papal States, and German in the Austrian areas. Ordinary people used local dialects. Even Mazzini spoke a dialect as his first language, French as his second. Such divisions were bound to prevent the growth of nationalism.

- Membership of the Italian societies and involvement in rebellions was small. Garibaldi listed those who took part in the rising in Piedmont-Sardinia, in 1821, as 'in all six superior officers, 30 secondary officers, five physicians, 10 lawyers and one Prince'. The rebellions were too weak and badly organised to have much impact and may well have increased opposition to, rather than encouraged support for, nationalist change.

1. What evidence suggests that nationalism was steadily growing in Italy from 1815 to 1848?

2. Why have historians disagreed over the extent of nationalism in Italy before 1848?

3. Using the evidence of this Chapter, to what extent do you feel that Nationalism had taken hold in Italy before 1848? Give reasons for your answer.

Historian Denis Mack Smith has made an intensive study of this period of Italian history. He points out that the areas where nationalism might have been expected to make the most headway – Lombardy and Venetia – were reasonably content and loyal, at least until 1840. In that year, the Milan Chamber of Commerce even voted in favour of joining the German *Zollverein,* so remote were its feelings from those of Italian nationalism. Although the Austrian taxation policy caused dissatisfaction, these areas were generally the most prosperous in Italy. What is more, censorship and police methods did not press unduly harshly. Massimo d'Azeglio was to write, in his *Recollections* (published in 1867), 'it was essential not to shout too loud, with prudence one could say anything'. Consequently, there was no nationalist upsurge in these areas before the 1840s.

Elsewhere too, historians have shown that the Italian rulers were not the oppressive autocrats that some liberal historians have made them out to be. Rulers, such as Charles Albert and Pope Pius IX, in particular, were willing and capable of transforming their states. Since Italy was making progress anyway, it is argued, nationalist ideas were not only confined to a minority they were also irrelevant.

Russia, 1801–1871

10.1 What was Russia like in the 19th century?

10.2 How successful was Alexander I in the first 14 years of his reign (1801–1815)?

10.3 To what extent, and with what results, did the rule of Alexander I change after 1815?

10.4 What were the main features of the reign of Nicholas I (1825–1855)?

10.5 For what reasons, and in what ways, did the Intelligentsia challenge the autocracy from the 1840s?

10.6 What changes did Alexander II bring about in Russia from 1855?

10.7 To what extent, and why, did Alexander II's reign change direction in the 1860s?

10.8 Historical interpretation: Why have historians differed in their views of Tsar Nicholas I and Tsar Alexander II?

10.9 How successful was Tsar Alexander II in foreign affairs, 1855–1871?

Key Issues

● Why was an autocratic monarchy able to survive in Russia, 1801–1871?

● Why was opposition to the autocracy so ineffective?

● In what ways, and to what extent, did Russia change, 1801–1871?

Framework of Events

1801	Assassination of Tsar Paul I; Alexander I succeeds to the throne
1807	Speransky is appointed to draw up a system of constitutional reform
1815	Treaty of Vienna. Formation of Holy Alliance
	Poland is placed under Russian control, and given a constitution
1825	Death of Alexander I; accession of Nicholas I
	Decembrist Revolt
1826	Nicholas I sets up the Third Section
1830–31	First Polish revolt is suppressed
1848–49	Revolution in Europe. Russia intervenes to defeat revolt in Hungary
	Nicholas's rule becomes more repressive
1853–56	Crimean War
1855	Death of Nicholas I; accession of Alexander II
1861	Emancipation of the serfs
1861–62	Increasing numbers of student demonstrations. Emergence of Nihilism and Populism
1863	Second Polish Revolt
1864	Creation of the zemstva. Legal reform takes place
1866	Assassination attempt on Tsar. Move to more reactionary policies
1874	Students, influenced by Populism, try to incite the peasantry
	Statute on Universal Military Service
1876	Formation of Land and Liberty, a revolutionary society
1881	Assassination of Alexander II.

Overview

THE political development of Russia in the 19th century was quite unlike that of any of the other European countries. In 1801, the ever-expanding Russian Empire had still not reached its full extent, although it was already huge (22 million square kilometres) and contained a wide range of different races. It was held together by the rule of a Tsar, Alexander I, from 1801. He was a member of the **Romanov dynasty**, which had ruled Russia since 1613. His royal authority was the most absolute of any European ruler and, throughout this period, Russia continued to have an autocratic system of government. The Tsar, supported by the powerful Orthodox Church, headed a well-defined social structure. The nobility helped the Tsar run the Empire and provided the officers for his large armies. They were also the landowners who, in turn, had absolute power over their serfs. The serfs, who made up the majority (around 83%) of the population, worked the land, served their masters and provided the military rank and file. (See the panel on page 274.)

Romanov dynasty: The Imperial crown of Russia had been passed from generation to generation of the Romanov family ever since Michael Romanov had been proclaimed Tsar in 1613.

In 1801, western influences had only just touched the surface of Russian society and politics. While western Europe was developing agriculturally, launching into industrial revolution and being exposed to liberal ideas, Russia was standing still. The reigns of the Tsars Alexander I (1801–1825), Nicholas I (1825–1855) and Alexander II (1855–1881) were to witness the results of increasing western influence.

The conflicting problems of leading Russia forward from its backward political, social and economic state without causing chaos and the breakdown of law and order, was a continual worry to the rulers of 19th-century Russia. The conflict between the need to modernise and yet to preserve control, together with the sub-theme of *how* change could be brought about and *how far* it should go, occupied the minds of the Tsars, ministers and intellectuals of the period. The same patterns constantly recurred. Hints of reform raised expectations, while limits to reform brought disappointment. Efforts to bring about change were all too often followed by reaction as the results of reforms created fear of disorder.

This period saw the development of political opposition to autocracy, but it made little progress. The Decembrist revolt of 1825, the radical thinkers of the 1850s–1860s and the revolutionaries of 1860 onwards, all tried unsuccessfully to destroy Tsarist power, or to gain concessions. By 1871, the autocratic monarchy was still in place, although its foundations were far less secure than they had been at the beginning of the century.

Russian terms

An understanding of the following terms is essential for the study of 19th-century Russian history. Those marked with an asterisk (*) are explained in greater detail in box inserts in this chapter.

Autocracy*: System of government whereby all power was in the hands of the Tsar.

Barschina: The work a serf was obliged to perform on his master's land.

Decembrists*: Participants in the failed rising of 1825.

Duma: Elected Town Councils set up in 1870.

Russian terms

Intelligentsia*: A wide group of educated thinkers whose artistic works, or social and political comment set them apart as critical of the Tsarist regime in early 19th-century Russia.

Mir: The village community or peasant commune run by a council of elders.

Nobility: Those of high birth whose families held land. From 1762, they were exempt from service to the state.

Obrok: A rent paid annually by serfs instead of performing work for their master.

Rouble: Russian unit of currency.

Serf*: A person owned by a master who provided him with land in return for service or rent. Freed in 1861.

Slavophiles*: A group who believed that the future development of Russia should be based on its own traditions.

State peasant*: A person working land directly for the state. Enjoyed slightly better terms than serfs, but not entirely free until 1866.

Synod: The governing body of the Russian Orthodox Church. It was controlled by the Tsar through his representative, the Procurator.

Westernisers*: Those who believed that Russia should develop along western lines.

Zemstvo (pl. *Zemstva*): Elected district and provincial council for local self-government set up in 1864.

10.1 What was Russia like in the 19th century?

What was Russia like geographically?

The map of Russia's expansion into Europe gives some idea of how the Russian Empire had grown from the its beginnings around Moscow in the 13th century, while the map of Russian Asia shows the vast stretch of land Russia commanded to the east. This Empire was still growing. The first map shows the territories Russia annexed as it expanded to the west and south in the first 15 years of the 19th century: Georgia (1801–06), Azerbaijan (1805–13), Finland (1809), Bessarabia (1812) and Poland (1815). These borders were to be pushed still further in the course of the 19th century. To the east (see the second map), the Russian Empire absorbed Alaska (1789–1867), territory around the Amur river, the east coast of Manchuria and a large area to the east of the Caspian Sea. It has been calculated that during the period 1683–1694, Russia expanded at a rate of 55 square miles a day, on average.

According to the historian Norman Davies, in *Europe – a History* (1997), 'a country that already possessed more land than it could usefully exploit kept on indulging its gargantuan [huge] appetite'. In 1800, European Russia contained around 35–40 million people; by 1815, around 52 million. These numbers increased, as a result of conquest and population growth, to 56.1 million by 1831 and 97.7 million by 1880. By 1815, Russia covered almost a sixth of the total land surface of the world.

Although vast in extent, much of the Empire was of limited productive use because of its geography and climate. As can be seen on the map, Russia's Empire can be divided into a series of zones of vegetation running east–west, broken in part by mountains. The main zones are:

● the Tundra in the very north around the Arctic Ocean;

● the *taiga* – vast areas of coniferous forest covering the northerly parts of Russia and Siberia;

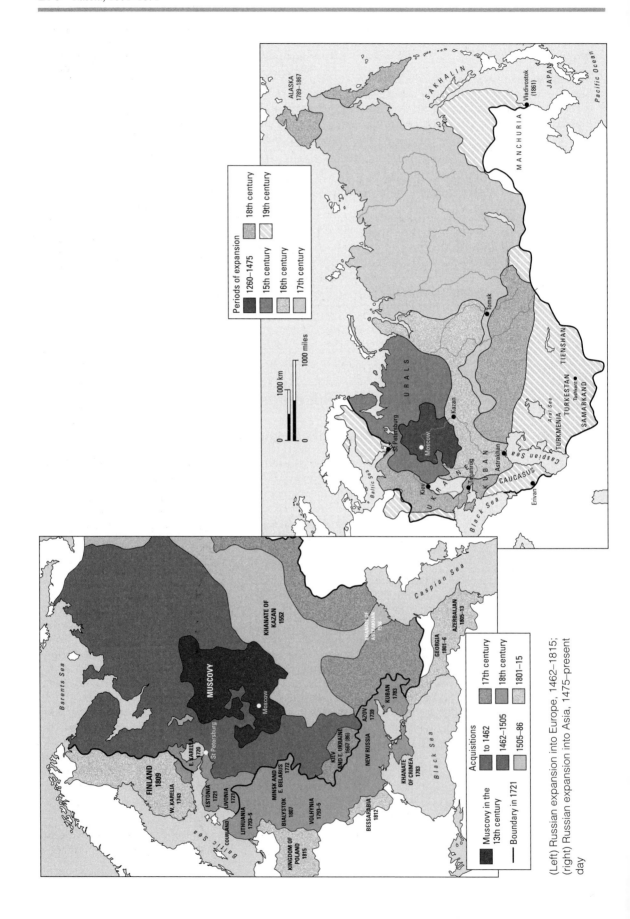

(Left) Russian expansion into Europe, 1462–1815;
(right) Russian expansion into Asia, 1475–present day

Periods of expansion

- 1260–1475
- 15th century
- 16th century
- 17th century
- 18th century
- 19th century

Acquisitions

- Muscovy in the 13th century
- to 1462
- 1462–1505
- 1505–86
- 17th century
- 18th century
- 1801–15
- Boundary in 1721

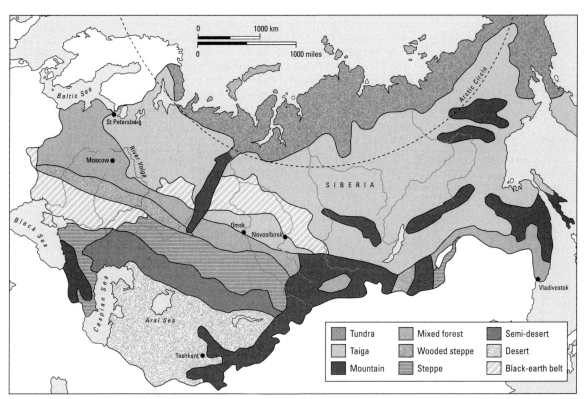

Physical map of Russia showing belts of vegetation

- mixed coniferous/deciduous forest in a thin strip which broadens to the west to include the Baltic region;

- another thin strip of wooded steppe (treeless open grassland), mainly found along a line from the Ural mountains westwards to Kiev;

- the steppe extending from the Black Sea to the central Asian area (the Caucasus). This turns into semi-desert and desert proper further east. (As Russia expanded into the area to the east of the Caspian Sea, it acquired yet more desert land.)

The tundra, desert and mountainous regions could sustain little human activity. However, the *taiga* offered potential for hunting and timber while, beneath the thick grass roots of the steppe, the 'black earth' was rich and fertile. Within both these areas, the main settlements were along the river valleys.

The northerly situation and continental climate of Russia also caused difficulties. Although warm in the *taiga* in summer, the season was too short to ripen crops reliably. Also, the soil was poor and often swampy. The steppe, on the other hand, with a low rainfall, risked drought. The 'black earth' was extensively ploughed, and could dry out disastrously.

The two thin belts between these major Russian zones were much easier to exploit. The mixed forest was easier to clear than the *taiga*, the soils were better and the climate more temperate. The wooded steppe was better watered and easier to cultivate than the main steppe area further south. Consequently, the most developed part of the Russian state – between Kiev, Moscow and St Petersburg – lay within these areas.

What was Russia like economically?

Russia was an overwhelmingly rural country, and agriculture was the mainstay of the economy. As well as feeding its vast population, the grain, grown primarily in the south and west, was Russia's most valuable export. Although Russia had immense natural resources, such as iron ore in the Ural mountains and coal in the Donetz basin (around Taganrog, north of the Black Sea), industry was limited. Russia did produce a fair amount of iron. In fact, it provided a third of the world's iron production in 1800. But as the century wore on, Russia increasingly fell behind in comparison with the western European powers, as the following table shows:

Output of pig iron in metric tonnes

	Austria	France	Germany	Great Britain	Sweden	Russian Empire
1815				310,000		123,000
1850	155,000	406,000	210,000	2,285,000	142,000	228,000
1875	303,000	1,448,000	1,759,000	6,467,000	351,000	428,000

The same was true of Russia's woollen, coal and chemical industries, although the cotton industry fared rather better, using new technology from England. By 1850, it was the fifth largest in the world. The success of cotton, in comparison with the other industries, gives one indicator as to why the Russian economy failed to grow as fast as that in much of western Europe. The cotton industry was a relatively new industry and was free from stifling restrictions. Most of the traditional industries were hampered by controls and were too established in their practices to institute significant change.

A variety of factors was holding Russian industry back:

● Russian industry was 'protected' by duties on foreign imports and, therefore, felt little pressure from its overseas' competitors.

● Government 'monopolies' controlled trade and industry. They hedged them round with complex restrictions thus preventing those outside the monopoly from challenging it.

Joint stock companies: 17th-century forerunner of the present 'limited company'. These grew out of ventures entered into by several people, usually on the agreement that the profits would be shared out in relation to each person's original investment.

● **Joint stock companies** were restricted by state legislation, so that it was impossible to finance large enterprise by raising money in 'shares' and by giving these shareholders a stake in the success of the business.

● State and private banks were unstable, making it difficult for anyone who wished to raise capital to do so in the form of bank loans.

● Reliance on plentiful serf labour meant that there was little incentive to invest in machinery to reduce labour costs.

● The absence of a strong middle class, and the aristocratic distaste for trade and industry, meant that there was no group interested in enriching itself through business enterprises. This meant that capital was tied up in land and not available for industrial development.

● The costs of transporting goods in the huge empire were very high. Resources, such as the coal and iron ore, were often a long way from the centres of population. Communications were poor and transport slow.

Although the Russian economy did grow in the 19th century, in relation to other European economies its record was poor, as the following statistics confirm:

Output of coal in metric tonnes

	Austria	France	Germany	Great Britain	Sweden	Russian Empire
1815	95,000	882,000	1,300,000	16,200,000		
1850	77,000	4,434,000	5,100,000	50,200,000	26,000	300,000
1875	4,471,000	16,957,000	47,800,000	135,400,000	64,000	1,700,000

Length of railway in kilometres

	Austria	France	Germany	Great Britain	Sweden	Russian Empire
1835		141	6	544		
1855	1,588	5,037	7,826	11,744		1,049
1875	4,471,000	10,331	19,357	27,970	23,365	19,029

What was Russia like socially?

Census: Official survey of the population of a country. It is carried out by the government in order to get details of the number of people living in the country, their ages and occupations, where they live etc.

The structure of society in Russia in 1900 (see poster) was no different from that of a century earlier. The percentages of the total population given for each group are based on a table of statistics produced by K. Arseniev, who used the **census** returns of 1812 and 1816.

- At the top, beneath the imperial eagle, sits the Tsar and his wife. The Tsar holds autocratic power and his word is law.

- Beneath the Tsar stands the court, ministers and civil servants appointed by the Tsar to carry out his policies. (All officials: 3.7%)

- The Greek Orthodox Church supports the Tsarist autocracy. (Clergy: 1.1%)

Poster of a cartoon put out by Russian socialists in Geneva, showing a representation of the structure of Russian society in the 19th and early 20th centuries. From the bottom: the workers; capitalists, saying 'We do the eating'; the army, 'We shoot you'; the clergy, 'We mislead you'; and the royal family, 'We rule you'.

- The Army was large and powerful and could be used to crush internal unrest, as well as for expansion elsewhere. (Military: 5%)

- The nobility was an established hereditary class of wealthy landowners who frequently enjoyed a life of idleness. (Nobility: 1.1%)

- The 'workers' at the bottom supported the rest. The only difference between this illustration and conditions in the early 19th century is that a few industrial workers are portrayed here. In the first half of the 19th century, this group was virtually non-existent. (According to Arseniev, this group consisted of 4.2% merchants, shopkeepers and artisans, 32.7% state peasants, 50.7% serfs and 1.5% 'others' – mainly more peasants.)

While the top four tiers of society formed the 'unproductive' classes and comprised 10.9% of the population, the lowest tier of 'productive' classes made up 89.1% (83% of these were state peasants or serfs).

Serfdom

Serfdom had developed in Russia in the 15th and 16th centuries and had been legitimised by Alexis I in 1649. Serfs were essential to the Russian idea of the 'service state', which had been established in this period. The nobility held land in return for 'service' to the Tsar, government and the army, while peasants worked their land. To ensure the nobles' income, these peasants were legally 'fixed' to it, and so became serfs, subject to some state protection. Peter the Great (1682–1725) strengthened the service state and in the 18th century serfdom was more efficiently enforced. However, the serfs' position worsened as they were increasingly regarded as their master's possessions.

Serfs fulfilled their obligations by working a number of days, often three a week (*barschina*) for their landlord, or by paying a rent (*obrok*). The *obrok* was more usual where the land was poor. It meant the serfs could take up other jobs, perhaps in the towns, with their master's permission. A landlord was responsible for his serfs' **poll tax**, while the village commune (*mir*), run by the most senior members of each serf family, distributed land and tasks. Serfdom was not slavery, but there were many restrictions on the lives of serfs, and state peasants were slightly better off.

State peasants were mainly either those working on the crown estates, or non-Russians. They were tied to their villages. They were also liable to conscription, like the serfs, but they were able to engage in any activity so long as they paid their taxes. Their greatest fear, however, was that they could be, and often were, sold into private ownership, at any time.

Serfs were the property of the landowners, who might do whatever they wished with them. They could sell serfs in the market place, sell the serfs' land, sell the serfs without land, split up families, take them into domestic service, arrange marriages and administer justice as they saw fit. Only **capital punishment** was forbidden. A nobleman's status depended on the number of 'souls' he owned and the stability of Russia was felt to depend upon the allegiance of serf to landowner.

The nobles were freed from their service to the state in 1762, but it was not until 1861 that the serfs were legally freed. Even then, although their legal status altered, their conditions of work had not changed greatly by 1870 (see section 10.8).

Poll tax: A sum of money which had to be paid to the state for every serf (a poll is literally a head).

Capital punishment: Execution. This should not be confused with corporal punishment or beatings, which were permitted.

The structure of society, as shown in the poster on page 273, is also interesting in that it reveals the absence of any 'middle class'. Arseniev's figures show a small number of tradesmen, but there was no powerful 'factory owning' or business class, such as had already emerged in Great Britain and was developing in most of western Europe in the early 19th century.

Finally, the poster emphasises the static nature of Russian society. Men were born into a class, and there they remained. There was comparatively little movement between ranks.

What was the effect of the Russian social structure on the country's development?

The hierarchical and hereditary structure of society was one of the causes of Russia's political and economic backwardness in the 19th century.

The structure stifled ambition. The nobility grew used to depending on their serfs for everything. They were increasingly discouraged from exerting themselves and showing any initiative. Many of them continued to serve the Tsar, if only to give themselves some purpose in life. However, the general picture of the nobility, as often portrayed in Russian novels of the 19th century, is of a bored class, which did little more than provide corrupt administrators and incompetent army officers.

The structure restricted the development of industry. The 'unproductive classes' were not prepared to involve themselves in business and trade, which was considered beneath them, whilst most of the 'productive classes' were tied to the land. While the ratio of town to country dwellers in the 1840s was one to two in Great Britain and one to five in France, in

---

Autocracy, Orthodoxy and Nationality

Autocracy

This was the Russian system of government by which the Tsar had no limits on his power and was accountable to no one but God. It was believed that he was divinely appointed and that God supported his actions. The Tsar had advisers but he was not bound to listen to their advice, nor was he obliged to take it. Laws were made by a decree from the Tsar and his will was supreme. This made the authority of the Romanov Tsars the 'most absolute' in Europe. One of the Tsar's strongest supports came from the Orthodox Church.

Orthodoxy

In the 11th century, the Christian Church had split into the western 'Roman Catholic' and eastern 'Orthodox' branches. In 1453, the centre of the Orthodox Church moved from Constantinople (which fell to the Turks) to Moscow. Here, the Orthodox Church developed its own rituals and beliefs, and became quite separate from western influences. By the 19th century, it still enforced superstitious practices that had scarcely changed since the Middle Ages.

The Orthodox Church supported the Russian monarchy as the representative of God on earth and, in return, received state protection. Authority within the Church rested with the Patriarch of Moscow who worked closely with the Tsar. Beneath him were the metropolitans, archbishops and bishops. These were followed by the archpriests and archdeacons, who were known as the 'black' or monastic clergy, and mainly lived in monasteries, under an 'archimandrite'. At the lowest level, the 'white' clergy of priests and deacons served the parishes. They married, and their sons generally continued their way of life.

Orthodoxy taught its followers to accept that conditions on earth were God's will. Good Orthodox Christians should never question their earthly lot, but trust to God's goodness in the world to come. Such teaching, coupled with ancient traditions and a reluctance to embrace change, helped make the Orthodox Church a symbol of the isolation and backwardness of Russia.

Nationality

Many of the people who lived in Russia were of non-Russian nationality. There were the Finns, Poles and Germans in the western part of the Empire. Between the Black and Caspian Seas lived Georgians and Armenians with their distinctive non-Slavic languages, and the Azerbaijanis, who were among the many Turks absorbed into the Empire as it had expanded in the 19th century. In central Asia there were Kazakhs, Bashkirs, Turkomens, Uzbeks, Kalmuks and Kirghiz. There were other races living in eastern Siberia, including Eskimos (now referred to as Inuits).

Altogether there were around 170 different ethnic groups, with the Russians or East Slavs comprising just under half the total population. However, together with the Ukrainians and Belorussians, who were closely related, they were a clear majority and the regime tended to favour them over the non-Russians in the same way that it favoured the Orthodox Church over other religions. Although 'Russification' (a policy of the later 19th century by which non-Russian peoples were forced to accept the Russian language and culture) was not official policy in the time of Nicholas I, the Tsar's clear preference for the Russian nationality was.

Russia it was one to over 11. Such enterprise as there was remained in the hands of the small group of town dwellers. Many of the poorer labourers, artisans and shopkeepers engaged in business within strictly defined rules about how much they might buy and sell. A few managed to gain acceptance into a merchants' guild, which enhanced their status, but left them hampered by restrictions. Furthermore, since vast numbers of serfs and peasants were tied to the land (and even after 1861 it was near impossible for rural peasants to leave their farms), it was hard to attract a labour force to support any industrial development in towns.

The system acted as a brake on the development of efficient agriculture. Reliance on the plentiful labour of the serfs and peasants discouraged labour-saving practices and innovation. Farming continued from generation to generation with the same primitive methods. The controlling elders of the *mir* were usually the very men most committed to the traditional practices of their younger days, and were hostile to change. The strip system, once common in medieval England, was used to allocate land, so fallow land was wasted and holdings were usually scattered and difficult to farm efficiently.

On the whole, the class structure was regarded as 'normal', and ordained by the will of God and the Tsar. Since everyone had a place in life, there was no incentive to improve one's lot and few possessed the power to do so. The nobles remained isolated from the people that served them. Many lived at Court and spoke French rather than Russian, which they regarded as fit only for the use of the lower classes. The serfs (and from 1861 'peasants'), busy providing for their families and masters, had little time to consider their position. If they complained, it was usually about some local injustice rather than about the system as a whole. In any case, they could hardly be expected to have any understanding of 'rights', given their illiterate state.

What was Russia like politically?

All decision making in Russia was in the hands of the autocratic Tsar. He was regarded by his people as the 'little father' and was responsible only to God, a belief reinforced by the powerful Orthodox Church. In theory, at least, he protected and cared for his subjects, as a parent looks after their children – guiding, helping and punishing when necessary. This was a role which the Tsar's subjects, with few exceptions, accepted without question.

However, in a country of the size and complexity of Russia, the Tsar obviously needed help not only in reaching his decisions, but also in ensuring that they were carried out. Consequently, a small band of chosen ministers and a huge army of civil servants, known as the 'bureaucracy' assisted him. The country was divided into provinces, the provinces into districts and the districts into villages. Since communication was slow, local governors were relied on to make decisions, and some wielded a good deal of power. Their corruption was often a focus of 19th-century protests, although these men were sometimes made scapegoats for the Tsar, who was remote from everyday life. There was little encouragement for initiative in a system where length of service counted for more than efficiency.

1. Why might the geography of 19th-century Russia be important to a historical understanding of this period?

2. With reference to Russia's economic development in the 19th century, explain the statistics given in the tables.

3. Which were the more important barriers to progress, Russia's climate and landscape or her social and political institutions?

10.2 How successful was Alexander I in the first 14 years of his reign (1801–1815)?

What sort of Tsar was Alexander I?

Tsar Alexander I was the grandson of Catherine the Great and the eldest son of Tsar Paul I. As a child his time had been divided between his

Tsars of Russia, 1801–1881

Alexander I (1777–1825), reigned 1801–1825. Eldest son of Tsar Paul I.

Nicholas I (1796–1855), reigned 1825–1855. Third son of Paul I.

Alexander II (1818–1881), reigned 1855–1881. Eldest son of Nicholas I.

Alexander I

Nicholas I

Enlightenment: In the second half of the 18th century, writers began to develop a more critical approach to what they saw around them. Traditional styles of rule were questioned, and the idea that government should be devoted to the wellbeing of the people and interfere as little as possible with personal liberty, developed. The Church was subject to fierce criticism, and science and 'reason' were regarded as better guides than religion. Catherine II of Russia claimed to be an 'enlightened despot' – a ruler who followed 'reason', while maintaining her autocratic powers.

Schizophrenic: A mental state in which the mind is split between two contrasting desires.

Jean-Jacques Rousseau (1712–1778)

Born in Switzerland. Became famous for philosophical writings in which he criticised the existing social order. *The Social Contract*, published in 1762, described his political views. He claimed that governments could only be acceptable when the people they ruled supported them. This view is known as the 'sovereignty of the people' and it became extremely influential during and after the French Revolution.

grandmother's Court, a centre for the **Enlightenment** where Catherine had done her best to prepare him as a future ruler, and his father's traditional and regimented soldier's life at Gatchina, a country estate around 30 miles south of St Petersburg.

Catherine had entrusted Alexander's education, between the ages of seven and 17, to the Swiss republican, Frédéric de La Harpe. La Harpe was a follower of Jean-Jacques Rousseau and his teaching was to play a major part in the development of Alexander's thinking. In contrast, at Gatchina, Paul took a different approach to education. He tried, with some success, to instil the virtues of military life, discipline, obedience and order into the young Alexander. These contrasts in his upbringing are sometimes blamed for making him excessively secretive, and possibly even **schizophrenic** in his later years. It may be too easy to blame Alexander's childhood for some of his later problems, but there is no doubt that he displayed increasing uncertainty as his reign progressed. He did not know whether to follow the path of Enlightenment and reform, or whether to adopt the more traditional approach of preventing trouble through control and repression.

How did Alexander I rule Russia?

After the troubles of his father's reign, Alexander I's accession to power as a result of the palace coup led to high hopes, from its supporters, that Russia might enjoy a more enlightened ruler. There was no demand for radical change. Indeed, Tsar Paul's assassins were army officers who had no desire to see the existing structure of Russian society overturned. They, like Alexander I, recognised that Russian development compared poorly with that of western Europe and accepted the need for some change. The dilemma was what that change should be, and how far it should go.

The reign began promisingly. Alexander I freed political prisoners, permitted exiles to return and abolished the use of torture. Most of his father's repressive legislation was repealed. The special, secret police force was disbanded and a commission was appointed to continue the work of codifying the law, as begun in the reign of Catherine the Great. Three new universities were founded, as well as over 40 primary and secondary schools. Censorship was also relaxed and foreign books allowed to enter the Empire.

However, Alexander I showed his determination to be his own master, by detaching himself from his father's assassins. In July 1801, he set up an informal council of young, liberal noblemen to act as his advisers in both domestic and foreign policy. The committee, known as the Secret

The Secret Committee

Alexander I established this informal council of advisers in July 1801. It held regular meetings until June 1802, and the Tsar continued to consult its members until 1806. It was responsible for improvements in administration, education and in conditions for the sale of serfs, but the Tsar's reluctance to consider serf emancipation and more far-reaching reform of government caused it to break up.

Prince Adam Jerzy Czartoryski (1770–1861)

Born in Warsaw. From an ancient Polish aristocratic family. Held as a virtual hostage in St Petersburg (1795–99), following the third partition of Poland. While there, he became a personal friend of the future Tsar Alexander I. Consequently, as well as placing him on the Secret Committee, Alexander I relied on him as his chief foreign adviser for the first five years of his reign. Became assistant Foreign Minister (1802), and acting Foreign Minister (1804–6), since his Polish origins prevented his appointment to the full rank of Minister. He helped draft plans for 'Congress Poland' at the Vienna Congress (1814–15), and became the first President of the Senate in Poland. He gradually became disillusioned with the 1815 settlement and headed the provisional government which was established in Warsaw during the 1830–31 revolution. With its failure, he was forced to flee to Paris. He spent the last 30 years of his life in exile, campaigning for the full independence of Poland.

Nikolai Novosiltsov (1761–1836)

A liberal aristocrat from Moscow, who became friendly with the future Tsar Alexander I in 1797. He became a member of the Secret Committee and, in 1804, was sent as the Tsar's personal envoy (representative) to London, to discuss war aims with the British Prime Minister, William Pitt. Novosiltsov resigned from government office in 1806, when he grew disillusioned with the government's failure to carry through major liberal reforms. However, he returned to favour in 1814 and became the Tsar's first commissioner in Warsaw (Poland). In 1819–20, he was given the task of drawing up a constitution for the Russian Empire with elected advisory committees, but Alexander I soon lost interest in the project and it was abandoned.

Paul Stroganov (1772–1817)

Novosiltov's cousin, and like him, first met the future Tsar Alexander I at Tsar Paul's coronation in Moscow (1797). He was invited to join the Secret Committee and became deputy to Kochubei at the Ministry of the Interior (1802–6). He went with the Tsar in the Austerlitz campaign against Napoleon and undertook a special mission to London on Alexander I's behalf. Although he did not hold office after 1807, he remained an important figure at Court.

Victor Pavlovich Kochubei (1768–1834)

His uncle (Count Bezborodko) had been adviser on foreign affairs to Catherine the Great. The young Kochubei travelled and studied in Sweden, London, Paris and Constantinople, where he became friendly with the future Tsar Alexander I. The latter respected him greatly. Kochubei went into voluntary exile in the reign of Alexander I's father, Tsar Paul, but he returned on his friend's accession and joined his Secret Committee. He became Russian Foreign Minister in October 1801, but his wish to keep Russia free from involvement in the French wars in order to concentrate on internal reform in Russia, conflicted with the views of Alexander I. Kochubei resigned after 11 months. He was Minister of the Interior (1802–7), but he was disappointed with the Tsar's failure to carry out domestic reform. In the crisis caused by the French invasion of 1812 he was frequently consulted by Tsar Alexander I. Minister of the Interior again in 1820. He was a respected adviser on internal affairs in Nicholas I's reign, and headed the Kochubei Committee, set up by Nicholas I in 1829 to advise on Russian policy towards Turkey.

Committee or 'The Committee of Public Salvation', included four close friends of the Tsar from his years as heir to the throne. These were Paul Stroganov, Nikolai Novosiltsev, Victor Kochubei and Adam Czartoryski. The Committee successfully created eight new government ministries to improve administration: the ministries of War, Admiralty, Foreign Affairs, Justice, Internal Affairs, Finance, Commerce and Education. While traditional noblemen of the older generation were appointed to head these ministries, Alexander I's younger colleagues were placed in the position of deputies. In this way, Alexander I planned to get the best of both worlds. The younger liberals provided a check on their older colleagues, while Alexander retained the ultimate power of decision.

Why did Alexander I fail to abolish serfdom?

Alexander I was well aware of the problems posed by serfdom. He once spoke bitterly of 'the state of barbarism to which this country has been reduced by the traffic in men'. However, although some of his liberal advisors urged the emancipation (freeing) of the serfs, Alexander I was more cautious. He was all too aware of his own father's end and feared upsetting the serf-owning nobility. He also feared disorder in the country. Rather than tackling the problem head on, he preferred to pass laws for gradual improvement.

These included a law in 1803 permitting the voluntary emancipation of serfs by their masters. It might have been well intentioned, but in practice it made little difference. Over the next 50 years, fewer than 400 landowners chose to act on it and the numbers made over to private ownership in the same period exceeded the number of serfs freed.

Alexander I did abolish serfdom in some of the non-Russian provinces, such as Estonia and Livonia (see map on page 270). He passed laws to curb some of the worst features of serf discipline, such as punishment with a knotted rope, which was to be limited to 15 strokes. The practice of selling serfs as a substitute for army recruits was also ended, but a proposal to free the state peasants was never carried out.

Alexander I's committee of friends was bitterly disappointed. Alexander was clearly not the liberal Tsar they had hoped for. The committee gradually broke up in the years up to 1806. Alexander I turned to Michael Speransky.

What was the effect of Speransky's work for the reform of government?

Although Michael Speransky had overseen various administrative, judicial and financial reforms at the Ministry of the Interior since 1802, it was not until 1807 that that he became Alexander I's chief adviser on the reform of government. He produced reforms that were designed to strengthen the Tsarist state, not take power away from it. However, recently discovered papers have shown that Speransky did have some quite liberal ideas. He favoured the abolition of serfdom, for example. He believed that a modern, liberal and efficient state was only possible in a society in which everyone was a property owner.

In 1809, he produced some far-ranging proposals. These included a written constitution, an elected national assembly chosen by the property owners, and universal **civil rights**. If Alexander could have brought himself to put these proposals into effect, the subsequent history of Russia would have been very different. Indeed, Speransky himself commented that Alexander was 'too weak to rule'. He bemoaned the fact that although the Tsar had plenty of ideas and good intentions, he did not have the personality to force his reforms into law. However, the proposals would have altered the whole framework of Russian society and Alexander could not

Michael Speransky (1772–1839)
Son of a village priest, Speransky was given an Orthodox education at the Alexander Nevsky seminary in St Petersburg. At only 23, he became Chief Secretary to one of Tsar Paul I's advisers, and in 1802, after Alexander I's accession, he moved to the Ministry of the Interior. He drafted plans for reform and acted as the Tsar's secretary for a congress between Alexander I and Napoleon at Erfurt in 1807. Speransky became State Secretary in 1810 and remained Alexander I's chief political adviser until 1812. He carried through some major reforms, but acquired enemies at court and was dismissed in 1812. He was exiled to Novgorod (now Gorky), returning to provincial office in Penza and Siberia in 1816 and 1819. Speransky returned to favour under Nicholas I, and completed the codification of Russian law in 1832.

Civil rights: These included guarantees of personal freedom. In 1815, Poland was also granted its own administrative and legal system and its own army.

afford to push change too far. This would upset the nobility, the very men on whom he most relied, particularly at a crucial stage in the wars with France. Had the circumstances been different, Alexander I might have been more willing to listen but, even then, it is highly unlikely that he would have voluntarily renounced his God-given autocracy.

Some reform was undertaken in response to Speransky's suggestions. In 1810, a Council of State was set up to advise the Tsar. The first regular system of State budgets was introduced, and the duties of the various government departments were more clearly defined. Examinations, providing promotion by merit, were introduced into the civil service.

However, Speransky faced continual opposition to his proposals from those who felt threatened by these changes. His fate helps to explain why few dared to meddle with suggestions of reform in Russia. When, in March 1812, the nobles were particularly upset by a proposal to introduce a form of income tax to improve Russia's finances, they pressurised Alexander into dismissing his adviser. Speransky was deported to the Russian provinces and put under police guard for some years. He did return to office in 1816, but was kept well away from the front line – first as Governor of Penza (a town 300 miles east of Moscow) and, in 1819, as Governor-General of Siberia. His great task of codifying Russian law was not accomplished until 1832, in the reign of Nicholas I.

How successful was Tsar Alexander I's foreign policy?

Much of Tsar Alexander I's attention, during the early years of his reign (1801–1814), was taken up by the events of the French wars. The hostility towards Britain brought about by his father had caused considerable economic difficulties for Russia. So one of Alexander I's first actions was to make peace with Britain, in June 1801. A treaty with France followed in October 1801, whereby Alexander I supported the French reorganisation of Germany and so gained the right to be consulted in German affairs. He gained a breathing space for Russia, but not for long. In 1805, war with France broke out again and Russia joined the Third Coalition against Napoleon. The Russians put up a good fight, but were defeated at Friedland in June 1807, forcing Alexander I to make peace. In the **Treaty of Tilsit**, Alexander was forced to recognise the French dominance of central and western Europe, but he was able to preserve some vital Russian interests. Napoleon agreed to allow the Russians a free hand to pursue their expansion in Finland and Turkey, and to take part of Prussian Poland.

Treaty of Tilsit, 8 July 1807: Napoleon I and Tsar Alexander I met on a raft in the middle of the river Niemen to agree peace terms to bring the war between France and Russia to a close.

With another much-needed break from the French war, Alexander I's armies campaigned successfully against the Turks in Azerbaijan and Bessarabia, and against the Swedes in Finland (see map on page 270). However, although Alexander I was mesmerised by the force of Napoleon's personality at Tilsit, the two countries had far too many conflicting interests for the peace to last. Alexander I increasingly ignored Napoleon's restrictive economic policies, which prevented Russia from buying much-needed British goods. There was also conflict over Poland, where the French were encouraging a sense of nationalism that ran counter to Russian ambitions. Relations were further strained over Russia's plans for Turkey. Napoleon's second marriage to Marie Louise, daughter of the Emperor of Austria, rather than to a Russian princess, as promised at Tilsit, increased the rift.

In 1812, Napoleon invaded Russia, declaring, 'I have come to finish off once and for all the colossus [giant] of the barbarian north.' The assault on the homeland led to a surge of national feeling within Russia. By avoiding pitched battles until Napoleon's Grand Army had reached Moscow, and then attacking, as the depleted French troops attempted to retreat, the Russians, aided by the winter weather, won the great 'War of

Baroness Julie von Krüdener (1764–1824)
A religious prophetess. She came from Germany but married a Russian diplomat, Alexis von Krüdener, and eventually settled in Paris, where she maintained a 'salon' for like-minded friends. In 1802, following the death of her husband, she published a semi-autobiographical romance, *Valérie*. This brought her to the attention of Tsar Alexander I. She gained considerable influence over him when the national effort to repel the French invasion of 1812 deepened Alexander I's religious convictions. He later wrote of this time, 'through the fires of Moscow my soul has been lightened … I resolved to consecrate myself and my government to God'. As Alexander travelled through Germany in 1813–14, he became interested in the ideas of German mystics. In 1815, he visited Madame Krüdener's salon in Paris in search of religious enlightenment. She is said to have been behind his concept of a 'Holy Alliance', although she may have done no more than approve Alexander I's own views. The baroness personally claimed that the inspiration for the alliance was 'the work of God'. After 1815, her influence waned. She met the Tsar again in 1819 and 1821, but he encouraged her to settle in the Crimea, where she died on Christmas Day 1824.

1. To what extent, and why, did Alexander I attempt to reform Russia politically and socially between 1801 and 1815?

2. Would you agree that 'By 1815 Alexander I had proved himself a practical and successful Tsar of Russia'? You should examine both his domestic and foreign record.

Liberation'. Tsar Alexander I, driven on by a strengthening of his own religious beliefs, personally led his troops in war. His armies successfully crossed Europe, enabling the Prussians and Austrians to rejoin the fight, and the Tsar triumphantly entered Paris in March 1814. He was the first invading monarch to enter that city since Henry V of England in 1420, and was hailed as a great hero, both at home and by all of Napoleon's enemies in Europe.

Alexander I's reputation and decisive contribution to the defeat of Napoleon ensured he was treated with respect by the statesmen who gathered at the Congress of Vienna 1814–15 (see Chapter 6). Here, some of the contradictions in his personality were most in evidence. He fluctuated between liberal and conservative ideas, and his reliance on the mystical Madame Krüdener, under whose religious influence he had fallen, made him far from predictable.

In general, Alexander I supported the re-establishment of traditional monarchies, but he also displayed some liberal sentiments. He insisted, for example, that the restored French monarchy should be established with a constitution. He even offered the services of La Harpe to devise one. Constitutions were granted to the new Russian possessions of Finland, and a reduced-size Poland. Civil rights – such as freedom from arrest and arbitrary imprisonment – as well as freedom of religion and of the press were also guaranteed to the Poles, and far exceeded any concessions made in Russia itself. There was also a broad franchise which gave political rights to a larger group than in either France or Britain at the time.

Fired with religious enthusiasm, Alexander I also proposed an agreement between the Christian monarchs of Europe, by which they would agree to live as brothers, preserving peace 'according to the supreme truths dictated by the eternal law of God'. This Holy Alliance, of September 1815, was signed by virtually all the monarchs of Europe (Great Britain, the Pope and the Sultan of Turkey excepted – see Chapter 6). It seemed, on paper at least, another example of Alexander's liberal-minded concern for both Europe and Russia.

The great victory of 1814 and the Congress of 1815 were regarded as great personal triumphs for Tsar Alexander I. Both at home and abroad, he was hailed as the head of a great and powerful empire. He had defeated the French and, by his schemes of expansion, had added another 12 million people to his empire. However, according to historian Hugh Seton-Watson, in *The Russian Empire 1801–1917* (1988), 'the great victory of 1814 led to a glorification of the regime, the whitewashing of its cruelties and the preservation of its abuses'. This suggests that Alexander I's 'success' actually held back the modernisation of Russia.

10.3   To what extent, and with what results, did the rule of Alexander I change after 1815?

Why is 1815 sometimes seen as a turning point in Alexander I's reign?

By 1815, expectations of reform within Russia were high. Alexander I's early reputation, the growth of patriotism in wartime and the return of peace in 1815, all suggested that the time was ripe for more far-reaching changes. However, after 1815 Alexander I seemed to lose some of his earlier interest. This is partly explained by the increasing influence of religion on his life, which had the effect of instilling a new sense of mission into him. No longer were the 'petty' affairs of Russia of prime importance to him. He had a far greater calling – to ensure the peace of the whole of Europe. His new role, as the upholder of monarchical rule in the face of liberal risings abroad, absorbed much of his energy in the second part of his reign.

From 1816 to 1822, he spent two-thirds of his time abroad, negotiating with the powers of Europe and attending the various European Congresses which attempted to solve the problems that arose. Foreign events, and in particular the popular disturbances of 1820–21, frightened and disillusioned him. His ambitious Holy Alliance became an instrument of **reaction**, as he worked with Metternich to curb threats of revolution. When one of his own elite regiments, the Semyonovsky Guards, mutinied in St Petersburg in November 1820, complaining of their treatment and refusing to disperse, Alexander's alarm reached new heights. He joined Austria and Prussia in the Troppau Protocol of 1820 and became committed to crushing liberalism in Europe.

Alexander I's desire for reform seems to have gradually waned in the years after 1815, becoming even less marked after 1820. His policies in Poland, 1815–20, began promisingly. New law codes were introduced and education was encouraged. The University of Warsaw was founded and communications improved. Indeed, when he opened the Polish Diet in 1818, Alexander I declared that the success of this liberal experiment had encouraged him to extend similar privileges to Russia. However, after 1820, censorship was reintroduced, the Diet was not called for five years, and nothing was done about the promise to the nobility that Poland's ancient possession of Lithuania would, once again, be incorporated into their new Kingdom.

In 1818, a former member of Alexander I's Secret Committee, Nikolai Novosiltsev, was given the task of drawing up a constitution for Russia, based on the Polish model. This would have created a representative council, chosen by regional assemblies, which would meet to assist the sovereign every five years. These plans were presented in 1820, but Alexander I never implemented the scheme. The proposed codification of the law was also abandoned after 1815, only to be resumed in the following reign.

Clearly, Alexander I's views did not change overnight. Records show that he continued to contemplate governmental reform even as late as 1825, the year of his death. That year he was still expressing the hope that he might one day be able to grant Russia a constitution. However, he made few practical moves after 1815–20. It seems that he had grown resigned to leaving things as they were. He commented that to reform Russia was a task 'impossible not only for a man of ordinary powers, like myself, but even for a genius'.

As Alexander I focused his attentions on fulfilling his European mission, the running of the Empire was increasingly left to others. From 1815, two

Reaction: To go back, contrary to modern practices. A reactionary is a traditionalist who opposes new ideas.

Synod: Special council of members of a church, which meets regularly to discuss religious issues.

General Alexis Arakcheyev (1769–1834)
A soldier who had served Alexander I's father, Tsar Paul I. It is said that his influence over Alexander I may have stemmed from the Tsar's uneasy conscience about his father's death. Arakcheyev always appeared humble towards the Tsar, but was regarded as arrogant and dominating by his fellow nobles and ministers. He had a reputation for cruelty (capable of pulling out soldiers' moustaches with his own hand) and for boorish (uncultured) behaviour. After the departure of Michael Speransky, he gradually gathered all the separate branches of government into his own hands. In so doing, he relieved Alexander I of many of the burdens of internal government and allowed him to focus his attentions abroad.

Jesuits: Members of the Catholic Society of Jesus who were active in education and conversions to Catholicism. See also Chapter 7.

ministers in particular dominated the government. One was Prince Alexander Golitsyn, Procurator of the Holy **Synod**, who assumed control of education. The other was Alexis Arakcheyev, a military disciplinarian who believed in dealing harshly with any opposition. The traditional and conservative opinions, which predominated in government under the leadership of these men, did nothing to encourage the few reforming impulses Alexander I might still have possessed.

How were the Russian people affected by changes after 1815?

One of the results of Alexander I's growing fear of militant liberalism was the growth of censorship within his empire. Russia had never been free from censorship, but it was exercised with increasing vigour after 1815. Prince Golitsyn's Ministry of Education was placed in charge. It regarded religious teaching as the only effective remedy for 'liberal freethinkers' who questioned traditional ways. Consequently, literature, poetry, theatre, art and even works of reference and non-fiction were all subjected to the same intensive scrutiny. Works were judged according to the religious prejudices of the members of the Ministry. A work on poisonous mushrooms was disallowed, as mushrooms were the main food for the Orthodox during Lent!

Jesuits were expelled from Russia. The universities were purged of those believed to hold subversive views. The secret police was also expanded after the rebellions of 1820–21 in Europe and the fright of the Semyonovsky mutiny. In the repressive atmosphere of these years even Alexander Golitsyn, who was personally quite tolerant, was dismissed. The new Minister, A.S. Shishkov, believed education was dangerous. He tried to restrict it as much as possible to prevent the spread of unhealthy ideas. Russians were forbidden to study abroad, while economics and controversial subjects like philosophy were withdrawn from the university curriculum.

Another change, which was almost universally resented by those whom it affected, was the setting up of military colonies. This 'reform' was designed to reduce the costs of, and to provide for the continuance of, a large army in Russia. It had already been tried on a small scale but, under the direction of Arakcheyev, it was extended after the Napoleonic wars to provide for a quarter of the army.

Instead of assembling military conscripts in barracks, they were allocated to rural areas. Here, they joined the local peasantry to form a 'military colony'. This enabled the soldiers to continue their familiar rural way of life, and to live with their families when not on active service. It was a move away from serfdom and, in general, the living conditions and standards in these colonies were better than those enjoyed elsewhere. However, those ordered to a military colony became subject to the regimentation of the colony for life. They were required to work, marry and reproduce by command, and failure to comply incurred penalties. Married women, for example, were fined if they did not produce children (to ensure the future of the army) to schedule – initially one, per couple, per year. Not surprisingly, there were revolts, and the brutal suppression of these only added to the colonies' grim reputation.

How extensive was the opposition to Tsar Alexander I?

In fighting Napoleon, many army officers had experienced their first direct contact with the west. What they saw and heard influenced them. Discussions about social and political reform began in the officers' dining clubs. From two of these clubs, the Union of Salvation was founded in 1816. In 1818, the Union of Welfare, which rapidly grew to 200 members,

Paul Pestel (1793–1826)
Son of the Governor-General of Siberia. He was educated in Germany, became a cavalry officer, but was wounded at the Battle of Borodino in 1812. He then travelled in Europe and studied western political philosophy. Pestel became a member of the Union of Salvation (founded 1816), dedicated to the reform of Russia. When sent to fight in Bessarabia against the Turks, he occupied his time developing his ideas for the future of Russia. He believed that Russia should overthrow the Tsar and become a republic ruled by a revolutionary dictatorship. He wanted to see the nobility destroyed as a class, and the land nationalised or redistributed among the peasants. These radical ideas came before the development of Communism in Russia. In 1821, Pestel became leader of the radical Southern Society, based among troops stationed in the Ukraine. He disagreed with the other main opposition group, the Northern Society, over the need to assassinate the Tsar, but they co-operated in preparation for the Decembrist coup (see page 286). After its failure, Pestel was arrested and hanged.

Republic: A country whose system of government is based on the idea that every citizen has equal status, so that there is no king or queen and no aristocracy.

replaced it. These organisations believed reform was essential for the future of Russia but, like the Tsar himself, they were uncertain about the best way to achieve this. Some continued to place their faith in the Tsar. They believed only he could carry out reform. They debated the best means of persuading him. Others took a more radical line. They felt the only way forward was in the abolition of rule by a Tsar and the setting up of a republican-style government.

In the repressive atmosphere of 1821, the Union of Welfare was disbanded, fearing the activity of the Tsar's spies. It re-formed as two separate organisations, with stricter controls over its membership. The Northern Society, led by Nikita Muraviev, believed in a system of government that would maintain a tsar, but as a figurehead with much reduced power. The Southern Society, under Colonel Paul Pestel, was more extreme and favoured a **republic**. This society was joined, in 1825, by the Society of United Slavs. Both societies believed in direct action and plans were made to assassinate Alexander I in the summer of 1826.

The Romanov dynasty, showing the principal rulers from Peter the Great to Alexander II

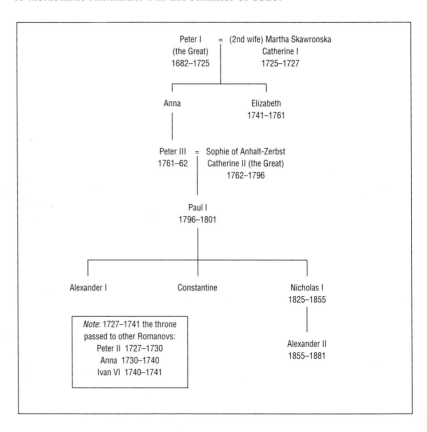

It seems unlikely that either society attracted wide support. The society in the north was dominated by liberal-minded nobles and intellectuals, while the southern society contained a good number of disgruntled army officers, including some of the former Semyonovsky guards regiment which had been disbanded after the 1820 mutiny. As the historian Derek Offord points out, in *Nineteenth Century Russia: Opposition to Autocracy* (1999), 'there was no attempt to couple the reasoned discontentment of sections of the nobility with the rebelliousness of the peasantry which had periodically erupted in large-scale uprisings'. Nevertheless, the class of the men involved in these societies gave them an influence out of proportion to their numbers. The fact that they were able to organise a revolt, in 1825, meant that they were to achieve considerable fame as a source of inspiration to later opponents of the autocracy.

Why did revolt break out in 1825?

The original plans of the two opposition societies were thwarted by Alexander I's sudden death in 1825. Alexander had gone to Tagnarog, on the coast of the Black Sea, for the winter of 1824–25. This was an unusual choice of location, but he may have chosen it in order to help his wife recuperate from illness or to get further away from the depressing troubles of Europe. While there, he fell ill quite suddenly and died on 19 November 1825, at the age of 48. However, there were persistent rumours in Russia that he was not in fact dead, but had disappeared to become a hermit. To disprove this, his coffin was eventually opened in 1865, but was found to be empty! The truth will probably never be known, but Alexander I certainly disappeared from political life in 1825 and left behind him the new problem of a muddled succession.

Alexander I had no legitimate children. Consequently, his brother, the Grand Duke Constantine (see family tree), should have been his heir. However, he was married to a non-royal Polish countess, which meant that his children were unable to succeed him. Alexander I persuaded him, in 1822, to renounce his claim to throne. By a secret decree, Nicholas, a younger brother, who already had a son, was named as Alexander I's heir instead. Only a few close advisers were aware of this – not even Nicholas had been informed.

Alexander I's sudden death meant that there was a gap of nearly a month before the succession issue was resolved. The opposition societies seized upon this as an excuse to take action. Although he had been made aware of the activities of the Southern Society in the last months of his life, Alexander I had taken no action against it. Possibly he had too many personal preoccupations, or perhaps he had grown too used to leaving everything to Alexis Arakcheyev, who had also left St Petersburg, in 1825, to deal with serfs involved in the murder of his mistress. Failure to take action against the Southern Society, and to make clear the provisions for the succession, helped to bring about the army-led Decembrist revolt of 1825.

1. How and why did Tsar Alexander I's attitude to reform change after 1815–20?

2. Why were the educational and military reforms of 1815–25 a cause of particular resentment?

3. What were the main features of the opposition groups of this period?

4. 'Alexander I promised much but achieved little.' Do you agree with this view of Alexander I? Give reasons for your answer.

10.4 What were the main features of the reign of Nicholas I (1825–1855)?

Nicholas is generally painted as a reactionary who shared none of his brother's idealistic aims for Russia and whose only solution to its problems was repression. For those in favour of change, his reign certainly began badly, although the causes of the Decembrist Conspiracy lay in the time of Alexander I.

What was the effect of the Decembrist Revolt?

Plans for revolt were made during the confusion that followed Alexander I's death. Nicholas I learnt of his inheritance for the first time, when news of the sudden death reached St Petersburg. However, on the advice of the city governor, Count Miloradovich, he did not proclaim himself as Tsar immediately. On 27 November, he was persuaded to proclaim his brother Constantine as Tsar and to wait for Constantine to renounce the throne before proceeding further. However, Constantine, at home in Warsaw (Poland), had already received the news of Alexander's death and had written to congratulate Nicholas on his new position. Letters passed to and fro. Not until mid-December did Nicholas proclaim himself Tsar.

The Decembrists are so called because their revolt was planned for 14 December, the day Nicholas I assembled his guards to take an oath of loyalty. Around 3,000 rebels, mainly younger Guards officers, gathered in the Senate Square of St Petersburg, refusing to acknowledge the new Tsar. What they did intend is not altogether clear. The rebels cried for 'Constantine and a Constitution', although it is said that some scarcely understood the liberal implications of this and believed 'Constitution' to be Constantine's wife. They had appointed Prince Sergei Trubetskoi to lead a government on Nicholas's overthrow, but since he took refuge in a foreign embassy and the rebellion came to nothing we shall never know what he might have done.

The army officers, joined by a band of liberal intellectuals, remained in the square for five hours, despite the freezing temperatures. Several attempts were made to persuade them to disperse. A cavalry charge was attempted, but the horses slipped on the icy cobbles. However, the rebels were greatly outnumbered by the 9,000–10,000 troops still loyal to the Tsar. Consequently, when Nicholas ordered the square to be cleared by cannon fire that evening, the rebels could do nothing but flee, leaving around 300 dead.

The Southern Society, based in the Ukraine, did not hear of the events until two weeks later. They decided to press ahead with their own rebellion regardless, but the authorities arrested their leader, Paul Pestel. By January, their troops had been defeated.

In many respects the Decembrist revolt was a mild affair, confined to a minority of the St Petersburg garrison. Like so many earlier aristocratic revolts, the nobility in the army led it. However, in other respects, it broke new ground. The rebels had asked for a new constitution, and there was even talk of the abolition of serfdom. These were major changes. That is why Nicholas I took the whole episode very seriously, starting a thorough enquiry into its causes, and handing out severe punishments to those involved.

After evidence gathering taking six months, severe punishments were imposed as an example to others. The five ringleaders, including Paul Pestel, were hanged even though it was technically illegal and this punishment had not been used in Russia since 1775. The ropes broke for three of the victims, leading one of them to remark that nothing was well done in Russia – not even hanging. A further 116 were sentenced to forced labour in Siberia and, despite the normal tradition of last-minute reprieves, none was given.

The Decembrist revolt did not soften Nicholas's government, but rather the reverse. However, the harsh punishments handed out to the rebels did help their cause in one way, by turning them into martyrs. Later revolutionaries drew inspiration from them and, to quote Derek Offord, 'The Decembrists may, in retrospect, be seen as having taken the first step on the path that led to the revolutionary movement which eventually was to topple autocracy in 1917.'

Was Nicholas I's attitude entirely reactionary?

It is sometimes said that Nicholas I's reaction to the Decembrist revolt set the tone of his reign, showing his belief in repression rather than reform. In some ways this is unfair. Nicholas I had a strong belief in order and discipline. Nevertheless, he was aware of the problems of Russia, and did attempt to address these, even if it was only in a limited way. Unlike Alexander I, he had neither been trained as a future Tsar, nor had he received an enlightened education. Instead, he was brought up as an army officer and he regarded the Empire, which he had so unexpectedly inherited, as a military command. He believed in discipline, obedience, order and efficiency and he tried to maintain these military values in his new position. He liked to be in control of all that went on around him, but he worked hard, sincerely trying to do what he believed to be best for Russia.

Nicholas I saw his task as preserving Russia from the corrupting influence of the west. He adopted the principles of 'Orthodoxy, Autocracy and Nationality' (see panel on page 275) – three concepts which had helped to shape the peculiar character of Russia – as his guide. He was aware that many areas of Russian life needed to be changed. Far from being disinterested in Russia's problems, Nicholas I spent a large amount of time investigating them. However, two personal peculiarities have affected his reputation.

1. He was determined to maintain absolute control over all aspects of government. This had two consequences. He was often unable to complete tasks he set out to do, and he alone was held responsible for all the inadequacies of his government.

2. His preferred method of addressing problems was to set up secret committees, which allowed him to maintain total political control and avoided raising any public expectations. Since he was convinced that any reform should be seen as a gift from himself and not a sign of giving in to outside pressure, he was careful to maintain the utmost secrecy. Naturally enough, this had the effect of leading others to believe that he was doing nothing.

What was Nicholas I's style of government?

How successful were the domestic policies of Tsar Nicholas I?
In many respects, Nicholas I would seem to have been a successful Tsar. When the rest of central and western Europe faced revolution in 1830, Russia had no problems. There was only the 1830–31 rising in Poland, but this was usually regarded as a separate part of the Empire anyway, and it was effectively crushed. When far worse revolutions exploded across Europe in 1848, Russia was relatively unaffected. Centralised control and the powerful Third Section (see chart on page 288) appeared to maintain an order and discipline that rulers elsewhere envied.

After the Decembrist revolt, Nicholas I no longer trusted the Russian nobility. Consequently, he dismissed Arakcheyev and surrounded himself with a new group of advisers, including several non-Russians, such as his Foreign Minister Count Karl von Nesselrode, who was a German. Together with these men, he tackled a number of Russia's problems and carried out some successful reforms and changes.

● A summary of the law was finally compiled in 1832, under the leadership of Michael Speransky. Forty-five volumes were produced. The first 40 contained over 30,000 laws and the remaining five provided the indexes and appendices. A further set of 15 volumes, completed in 1833, listed active (used) laws by subject. From 1835, this new code became the basic reference work for Russian lawyers and was regularly updated. Although it did not live up to Speransky's hopes, it provided the basis for a uniform legal system in Russia.

● A new police body, known as the Corps of Gendarmes, was created under the direct control of the Third Section. It was distinguished from the inefficient, traditional police force by its light blue uniform and white gloves, representing purity. It was well received for its attempts to deal with local corruption and injustice, although in time it became another instrument of repression.

● Extensive enquires were undertaken into the condition of the serfs, and some legislation was passed. From 1826 to 1832 one secret committee examined the condition of Russia, while in the course of the reign nine further committees looked specifically at the serfs. A law of 1827 placed limits on the landowners' rights to send serfs to Siberia. Another law, in 1833, made the splitting of families by selling individuals, and the mortgaging of serfs to obtain loans, illegal. In 1844, serfs in the western provinces were given a written form of their duties to prevent excessive exploitation. Then, in 1847, serfs were given the right to buy their freedom if their village was sold at public auction.

Like Alexander I, Nicholas I believed that serfdom would have to come to an end, but he did not know, any better than his brother had, how to bring this about. His argument against abolition was political. If the power of the landlord over the serf was removed, he feared widespread disorder. However, a major improvement in the status of the state peasants was also carried out when Count Kiselev was placed in charge of the Ministry of

The government of Tsar Nicholas II (1825–1855)

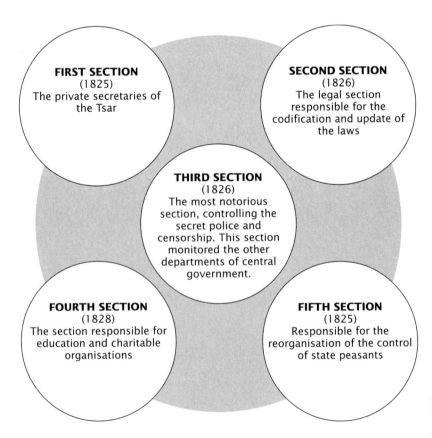

FIRST SECTION
(1825)
The private secretaries of the Tsar

SECOND SECTION
(1826)
The legal section responsible for the codification and update of the laws

THIRD SECTION
(1826)
The most notorious section, controlling the secret police and censorship. This section monitored the other departments of central government.

FOURTH SECTION
(1828)
The section responsible for education and charitable organisations

FIFTH SECTION
(1825)
Responsible for the reorganisation of the control of state peasants

State Domains, created in 1837. Around 20 million state peasants were released from some of the restrictions placed upon them, new land was made available to landless peasants, and hospitals, primary schools and churches were built to support the new developments. Loans enabled peasants to improve their land. New crops, particularly the potato, were encouraged.

Education was encouraged under Count Uvarov, Minister of Education 1833–49. There was a growth in the numbers of both primary and secondary schools, although they were kept under strict government control. Inspectors ensured that schools conformed to rules designed to prevent the spread of improper ideas. Private schools and tutors were made responsible to the state for their teaching. Nevertheless, the numbers receiving some sort of education did increase and the numbers of university students doubled from 1836 to 1848. Scientific and technical research was also encouraged and technical institutes founded. The study of business practices abroad together with the reorganisation of the institutes for mining and forestry, all supported Russia's developing economy.

Some economic advance was made under the German, Count Egor Kankrin, who became Minister of Finance (1823–44). Although he had quite conservative ideas about protecting home industries from foreign competition and balancing the budget, he did help to reduce the national debt and to stabilise the rouble. Business interests were encouraged, and foreign trade increased by 250%. The first Russian Factory Acts were also passed to protect the workers.

In what respects did Nicholas I's policies fail?

Although there were a number of reforms, in many respects there had been very little change in Russia since the reign of Alexander I. Indeed, with the passage of time, some of Russia's problems had actually grown worse.

Few were able to benefit from the measures taken to help the serfs and Kiselev's resettlement ideas for state peasants were not entirely successful. The scheme was not voluntary and some peasants resented the controls over what they could grow. There were, for example, riots (1841–43) when peasants were forced to plant potatoes. In any case, population growth outstripped the benefits of any improved farming that did take place, and the practice of transferring large numbers of peasants from state to private ownership continued. Nicholas I had made it clear that he had no intention of freeing the serfs, in view of the situation in Europe and of his fears for public order. Consequently, the biggest hindrance to Russian progress remained. Furthermore, serfs were becoming more restless. There were around 20 revolts per year in the course of Nicholas I's reign. Serfdom in factories was also increasing and there were undercurrents of unrest in the towns where serfs were paid only half the wages of free men and worked in appalling conditions.

The Third Section attained great notoriety. Censorship was harsh and although only three journals were actually closed down in Nicholas I's reign, punishments for 'subversion' were severe. The section ran its own prisons in St Petersburg and Siberia and victims might be sent to these without trial. During Nicholas's reign, 150,000 from all classes were exiled to Siberia.

Although education was expanded, entry to the new secondary schools was restricted to the sons of gentry and all branches of education were strictly monitored by inspectors and were still influenced by the Orthodox Church.

Following the Polish Revolt of 1830–31 (see Chapter 6), Nicholas withdrew the Polish constitution, closed the universities of Warsaw and

Vilna and, from 1833, kept Poland under martial law and tight Russian control.

Economic advance was slow. Kankrin, the Minister of Finance, opposed the development of the railways, which might spread unhealthy ideas. Although Nicholas I personally intervened to support them, there was no train between St Petersburg and Moscow until 1851. Although its share of world trade remained stable at around 3.7% of the total, Russia fell far behind western Europe, particularly Great Britain, in terms of industrial development. By 1843, the Russian cotton industry had only 350,000 mechanised spindles, compared with 3.5 million in France and 11 million in Great Britain. Its share of world iron production dropped from 12% in 1830 to 4% by 1859. Perhaps the most telling statistic of all is that annual expenditure on the army, which had always consumed a large chunk of the budget, was increased still further to 40% during this period. (The tables on pages 272–3 provide further statistics of economic development.)

Nicholas I's rigid centralised control of government caused administrative inefficiency. Since Nicholas would delegate nothing, all state papers had to pass through the Tsar's own **Chancery**, and government was excessively slow, as the paperwork mounted. Furthermore, since much activity was conducted in secret, civil servants wasted time duplicating tasks, while ministers might reverse decisions taken elsewhere.

Chancery: An office directly under the control of the Tsar and his most trusted ministers – which directed all affairs of state.

What was the impact of the 1848 revolutions in Russia?

After 1848, Nicholas I became even less inclined to consider reform. Before then, he may have appeared fearful to do much, but at least there had been some change. However, the revolutions of 1848 in the rest of Europe seem to have put an end to any reforming ideas he might have had. He believed the revolutions were the result of 'free-thinking', and he wanted to ensure that Russia was kept immune from this. Russia also suffered a severe cholera outbreak in 1848, combined with the worst crop failure for 30 years. Consequently, Nicholas was determined that the economic and social problems which had sparked revolt elsewhere should not lead to similar troubles in Russia.

Censorship reached new heights. Newspapers were prevented from publishing most foreign news. Almost all foreign fiction, including Hans Christian Anderson's fairy tales, was condemned. To ensure that nothing escaped detection, yet another secret committee was set up. Chaired by the reactionary, General D. Buturlin, it was made responsible for supervising and regulating the work of the existing censors. By 1850, there were 12 bodies dealing with censorship.

The universities were threatened with closure. When Count Uvarov resigned in protest, Prince Shirinsky-Shikhmatov, who was happy to admit that he regarded himself as an 'instrument of the Tsar', replaced him. Although they did survive, universities were placed under such strict control that student numbers fell by 25% over the next five years. Theology dominated the curriculum and the study of philosophy and European constitutional law was suppressed.

1. Why did Nicholas I take the Decembrist revolt so seriously? Give reasons to support your answer.

2. In what respects, and why, was Nicholas I's attitude to government different from that of Alexander I?

3. 'Nicholas I achieved nothing of importance. His reign increased rather than solved Russia's problems.' How far do you agree with this view of Nicholas I?

10.5 For what reasons, and in what ways, did the Intelligentsia challenge the autocracy from the 1840s?

The failure of the Decembrist revolt did not mark the end of the liberal opposition. On the contrary, increasing numbers of educated people began to appreciate Russia's backwardness, and to discuss possible remedies. They were known as 'the Intelligentsia'. Despite the activities of

The Intelligentsia

By the early 19th century, it had become common practice for small numbers of young noblemen to travel to western Europe to complete their education. This practice had been encouraged by Peter the Great (1696–1725) and Catherine II (1762–1796) as a means of introducing western administrative, technological and military skills into the Empire. However, it was impossible to ensure that these men only brought back knowledge that was of use to the state. Some developed views which turned them against the Russian autocracy with its rigid social system. Since they were landowning nobles themselves, they developed a sense of guilt and moral responsibility for the social state of Russia and turned to writing, secret meetings and debates in order to spread their views.

The 'Intelligentsia' can be divided broadly into two groups:

1 The Westernisers

For years there had been those who had argued that the way forward for Russia was to learn from the west, just as Peter the Great had tried to do. Some favoured slow, gradual evolution, through reforms, while others believed in revolutionary change. By the 1830s–1840s, the westernisers included a number of influential

thinkers and writers, such as V. Belinsky, Alexander Herzen and Mikhail Bakunin (see page 306). They hated the traditional ways of the Orthodox Church, which preached acceptance of the existing state in Russia.

Although Nicholas revered his great ancestor, Peter the Great, as a soldier and autocrat, he had no sympathy for 'western thinking'. When P. Chadaev wrote a 'Philosophical Letter' in the journal *Telescope* in 1836, arguing that 'the more we try to affiliate ourselves with it (the west), the better off we shall be', the periodical was promptly closed down, and Chadaev was later declared insane.

2 The Slavophiles

This group opposed the imitation of western ideas. In the 1840s they spread their views through the journal *The Muscovite*. They believed that Russian culture and Orthodoxy was superior to that of the west and that progress should be based on Russian traditions. They particularly favoured the development of peasant communes, although not of serfdom. Nevertheless, they were not supporters of Tsar Nicholas I. They were hostile to the intrusion of the state into people's lives and were therefore against Nicholas I's style of rule. They wanted social and legal reform and dreamt of a society in which people were left free, by the absolute monarchy, to pursue their higher spirituality.

Milyutin Brothers – Dmitri (1816–1912) and Nikolai (1818–1872)
The Milyutin brothers are good examples of enlightened thinkers who worked to reform the autocracy. They were aware of the weaknesses of the Russian system and, like other young liberal bureaucrats in the period after the Crimean War, were eager to remedy them. With the support of Alexander II, Nikolai was the outstanding social reformer of the 1860s. In 1858, he became Deputy Minister of the Interior and he did much of the groundwork for the emancipation of the serfs in 1861. He was also responsible for the scheme by which the Polish peasantry was given the freehold to their land in March 1864. His brother, Dmitri, became Minister of War (1861–1881) and carried through extensive reform of the army, despite opposition from senior offices.

---

the Third Section and the practice of censorship, the Intelligentsia became a distinctive opposition force by the 1840s.

The ideas of the intelligentsia took firm root during Nicholas I's reign, and even reached the Court where younger officials, known as the 'enlightened bureaucrats', became aware of the weaknesses of autocracy. Dmitri and Nikolai Milyutin, Count Lev Perovski, the Minister of the Interior, and Nicholas I's younger son, the Grand Duke Constantine Nikolaevich are all examples of members of the government who were influenced by the ideas of the Intelligentsia.

Literature – a social force

From the reign of Nicholas I, Russian literature began to do more than simply entertain. It became a vehicle for comment on the state of Russia and, in particular, Russian society. Russian literature paints vivid pictures of the social circumstances of the time. They show the arrogance, laziness and financial troubles of the nobility. The serfs and peasantry are often depicted as struggling with enormous burdens but entirely resigned to their fate. The administration is revealed as corrupt and aloof from everyday life. Although the Tsar himself was generally spared direct criticism, just about everything that he stood for – the Church, the social hierarchy and the bureaucracy – was subjected to ridicule and contempt. Poets, playwrights and novelists not only pointed to what was wrong, they often made suggestions as to what was needed to remedy the problems. Such activity was, of course, highly dangerous, particularly after 1848. Many writers were punished and persecuted.

Great literary figures of the period include:

Mikhail Lermontov (1814–1841)

A Guards officer, poet and novelist. He expressed his conflict with society in his poetry and prose. However, he was debarred from military honours, and sent to fight against the Turks in the Caucasus after daring to write an ode on the death of Alexander Pushkin.

Alexander Pushkin (1799–1837)

Probably Russia's greatest poet. By the age of 20 he was already being hailed as a genius by the educated, and regarded as a troublemaker with revolutionary sympathies by the Tsarist autocracy. He was well-versed in Classical and European literature and wrote over 800 short poems, 12 long narrative ones, and several prose works. Among the more famous are *Eugene Onegin*, a novel in verse (1823–31) and *The Queen of Spades*, a prose story (1833). In his own words, he 'exalted freedom in an age of cruelty'. Even Tsar Nicholas I recognised his abilities and insisted on censoring his work personally. He was found guilty, in 1826, of involvement in the Decembrist conspiracy, confined to his estate and forbidden to travel abroad. Indeed, his political views may have contributed to his death in a duel in 1837.

Nikolai Gogol (1809–1852)

From a gentry family with a **Cossack** background. His father had written a number of plays based on Ukrainian folk stories. Nikolai went to a provincial school, but managed to obtain a post in a government ministry in St Petersburg in 1829. He began writing novels, mixed in literary circles and met Pushkin. He was Professor of History at St Petersburg (1834–35). From 1835 he travelled in Europe, and spent some time in Rome. He mocked provincial corruption in his play *The Government Inspector* (1836) and criticised serfdom in *Dead Souls* (1842). The censor condemned this on the grounds that souls are immortal.

Fyodor Dostoevsky (1821–1881)

Born in Moscow, the second of a physician's seven children. His mother died when he was 16 and his father was murdered two years later. He studied at the military engineering college in St Petersburg and graduated with an officer's rank. However, he was more interested in writing, and enjoyed a good deal of success with his first novel, *Poor Folk* (published in 1846), which criticised the bureaucratic hierarchy. In April 1849 he was arrested for his involvement with the Petrashevsky Circle, a secret discussion group. After arrest, solitary confinement and mock execution (with a last-minute reprieve), he was sentenced to 10 years of Siberian exile at Omsk penal settlement. His experiences there, mixing with all types of people, including hardened criminals and the deprived, provided him with the inspiration for his later novels. He rejected the optimistic view of the progress of western civilisation which westernisers were arguing should be brought to Russia. Instead, he admired the Christian humility of the simple Russian people. Dostoevsky was saddened by the loss of religious faith and by the growth of selfish and material values, which he believed had spread from the west. He also feared the results of the unchecked growth of **nihilism**. All these beliefs were developed in his great novels *Crime and Punishment* (1860s), *The Idiot* (1868), *The Devils* (1872) and *The Brothers Karamazov* (1879–80).

Ivan Turgenev (1818–1883)

After experimenting with poetry and drama, Turgenev wrote a number of short prose works and rose to fame with *A Huntsman's Sketches* in 1847–52. These were rural sketches that painted a black picture of serfdom. They are said to have helped convince Tsar Alexander II of the need for emancipation. Thereafter, Turgenev's sense of moral duty ensured there was always a political element in his novels, most particularly *Fathers and Sons* (1862), which dramatised the difference between the mild liberals of the 1840s and their successors, the nihilists (believers in nihilism) of the 1860s. Although he was treated relatively leniently for his criticisms, he was arrested for a month and confined to his estate for over a year.

Count Leo Tolstoy (1828–1910)

From an ancient aristocratic family with a history of service to the Tsar, he was educated privately and went on to study Oriental Languages and Law at the University of Kazan. In 1851, he joined an artillery regiment in the Caucasus and took part in the Crimean War. He travelled a good deal but did not begin writing in earnest until after his marriage in 1862. Tolstoy then produced *War and Peace* (1865–69) and *Anna Karenina* (1875–77), which paint a vivid picture of Russian life. He was to become increasingly haunted by ideas of the futility of life and to reject the State, Church and private property. In 1901, he was **excommunicated**.

Cossack: From southern Russia; noted as horsemen from early times.

Nihilism: Belief that rejects all political or religious authority and current ideas, in favour of the individual. From the Latin *nihil* – nothing.

Excommunicated: Expelled from the Church; destined for eternal damnation.

1. In what respects, and for what reasons, did the westernisers and slavophiles differ in their views?

2. To what extent, and why, did the intelligentsia represent a threat to the autocracy of Nicholas I?

3. Why do you think so much great literature was produced during, and shortly after, the reign of Nicholas I?

However, the greatest weakness of the thinkers was that they had no coherent alternative to Tsarist autocracy. They merely sought change and were powerless without the Tsar's support. As we have seen, Nicholas I was not the sort of man to yield to pressure groups and, after the horrors of 1848, he became even more determined to punish troublemakers.

In April 1849, the activities of the Petrashevsky Circle, an 'underground' debating group that discussed contemporary problems in St Petersburg, were uncovered by the Third Section. They were charged with 'impudent criticism of the Church and State'. Although there was no evidence of any conspiracy, 21 were sentenced to death.

However, many writers continued to criticise the autocracy, either directly or by emphasising the corrupt state of Russian society in their works. Indeed, there was a remarkable amount of great literature produced during, and shortly after, Nicholas I's reign.

Source-based questions: Opposition to Nicholas I

SOURCE A

The experience of all nations and all epochs [ages or periods of history] has shown that autocratic power is equally ruinous for both rulers and society. It accords with neither the principles of our holy faith nor those of sound reason. One cannot allow the arbitrary rule of one man to become a principle of government. One cannot accept that all rights belong to one side and all duties to the other. Blind obedience can be based only on fear and is worthy of neither a reasonable ruler nor reasonable ministers. All European nations are securing laws and freedom. More than any other the Russian people deserves both.

From Nikita Muraviev's first draft of the Constitution for the Northern Society 1821–22. In this extract, Muraviev expresses the Decembrists' view on autocracy and reform.

SOURCE B

The Decembrist revolt in St Petersburg, 26 December 1825

Source-based questions: Opposition to Nicholas I

SOURCE C

Nicholas follows the traditions of Peter the Great in his foreign policy but suppresses them at home. Which means that while the territory and importance of the Empire increase, its public life is reduced to less than nothing. Everything is done for the throne, nothing for the people. The Emperor is no more than a military man, and all the attempts at education and culture initiated by Peter are simply thwarted. The Western ideas of human dignity, freedom and justice must be applied to Russian life; serfdom must be abolished, the whole regime transformed into a constitutional, liberal and democratic monarchy or republic. All the talk about Russian humility and orthodoxy is merely helping the reaction; the future of the country lies in free thought, science, individual and collective liberty and the transformation of the social and economic order.

From Alexander Herzen, revolutionary writer and thinker, whose outspoken views forced him to flee to Europe in 1847 to escape the censor.

SOURCE D

The Russian People are not much interested in government. They do not aim to wield power in the state, do not desire political rights for themselves, and do not have within them even the embryo [beginning] of desire for popular rule. Russia's history contains not a single instance of a revolt against authority and in favour of political rights for the people. In the west there is this constant emnity and rivalry between state and people who fail to understand the relationship that exists between them. In Russia we have never had that enmity and rivalry, but the state, in the person of Peter, encroached upon the people, forcibly changing their ways and customs, even their costume. Thus there took place a breach between Tsar and people; thus was destroyed the ancient union between the land and the State. Let us re-establish the ancient union between government and people, state and land, upon the lasting foundation of truly basic Russian principles. To the government, an unrestricted freedom to govern, exclusive to itself. To the people, full freedom to live, under the government's protection. To the government, the right to act and consequently to make laws. To the people the right to have opinions and consequently to voice them. That is the civil structure of Russia! That is the only genuine civil structure!

From Konstantin Aksakov. In this memorandum of 1855, Aksakov argued that it was necessary to understand the nature of the Russian people by studying Russian history, in order to escape the stagnation she was experiencing.

---

1. Study Source A.

What is meant by the highlighted terms:

(a) 'autocratic power'

(b) 'arbitrary rule'?

2. Study Sources A and B.

To what extent does Source B confirm the accusations made in Source A about the misuse of power by the Tsar?

3. Study Sources C and D.

In what ways do these two sources present conflicting views of the state of Russia and the need for change?

4. How reliable is this collection of sources as evidence of dissatisfaction in Russia in this period?

5. Using these sources and the information given in this chapter, would you agree that the opponents of the Tsarist autocracy were too divided to mount any effective challenge in the reign of Tsar Nicholas I?

10.6 How successful was Nicholas I's foreign policy?

Where did the Empire expand?

As can be seen from the map of Russian Asia (page 270), the Russian Empire continued to expand in Nicholas I's reign. During this period, another million square miles of territory was added to the Russian Empire. Land was taken from China along the Amur river, with hardly a fight. In 1849, the mouth of the Amur and the coast of Sakhalin island were reached and small Russian settlements established. The 1860 Treaty of Peking, with China, shortly after Nicholas I's death, confirmed these conquests and added a vast expanse of Pacific coastline to the Russian Empire. Nicholas I's reign, therefore, provided the foundations for the later growth of Russian Pacific naval power, which was to be based on the port of Vladivostok, founded in 1861.

Russian armies also advanced into Armenia, capturing Erivan from the Persians in 1827. War with Turkey, in 1828, began badly but continuing hostilities in the 1830s and 1840s led to the establishment of Russian influence in Dagestan and the Caucasus. Armies also advanced into Turkestan, although this was not completely taken until the 1860s and early 1870s.

Why did Nicholas I revoke the constitution in Poland?

Despite Alexander I's seemingly generous treatment of Poland in 1815, the Poles were far from happy with their situation.

● By 1820, Alexander I had already gone back on the spirit of 1815, reintroducing censorship, and failing to call the Diet regularly.

1. Comment on the way Nicholas and the Russian soldiers are depicted.

2. What methods of dealing with the Polish revolutionaries are shown here?

3. How useful is this cartoon for an understanding of the reputation of Nicholas I as Tsar of Russia?

English cartoon of Nicholas I addressing the Polish revolutionaries of 1830.

- Poles were among those tried and condemned for their part in the Decembrist conspiracy.

- The Poles resented Russian control of the Baltic borderlands. This included Lithuania, which had once been part of their Kingdom and was inhabited by a large number of Poles. Nicholas I made the situation worse by replacing Polish officials in Lithuania with Russian ones.

In 1830, Nicholas I proposed using the Polish army to crush revolts in France and Belgium. As troops were about to be sent westwards from Warsaw, a rebellion broke out, led by the young officer class. The rebels seized control of Warsaw and 10 months of revolution followed. (See Chapter 6 for further details.) Nicholas I was dethroned by the Polish Diet, in January 1831, and Constantine, the Governor, was forced to flee. However, the rebels were never united, the Polish armies wasted their strength on a fruitless mission to Lithuania and, partly thanks to Nicholas I's strategies, the nobility failed to win the support of the peasantry.

Nicholas I reacted to the revolt in predictable fashion. He sent in the Russian armies and, to win the allegiance of the peasantry, issued a promise to reduce the burdens of peasants on lands taken by the Russians. By September 1831, a force of 80,000 Russians had defeated a Polish army half that size and had forced Warsaw to surrender.

Nicholas I immediately withdrew the old Constitution, which he blamed for allowing too much free thinking. Instead he set about imposing tight controls.

- All elections and the Polish Diet were abolished.

- Public meetings and political organisations were banned.

- The University of Warsaw was closed.

- Leading administrative posts were given to Russians.

- The Russian language became compulsory for all government business.

- The Polish army was merged with the Russian.

What part did Russia play in the affairs of the rest of Europe?

There is no doubt that Russia enjoyed a formidable reputation in the rest of Europe in this period, as indeed it had done under Alexander I. A British commentator remarked in 1824, the year before Nicholas I's accession:

'Russia has aspired to and obtained a dictatorship over the states of Europe. She sits like a huge incubus [evil spirit] upon the rest … Russia, in the great struggle that is going on between improvement and **barbarism**, is the commanding champion as well as the efficient representative of the latter.'

Russian territorial expansion, the size of its armies, and the power and splendour of the Russian Court, all confirmed to others that it was a 'Great Power'. However, Russia's part in Europe was, according to this writer, 'a representative of barbarism', by which he meant that Russia used its formidable influence to champion the cause of traditional, monarchical government against the spread of liberal ideas.

Nicholas I was alarmed by the revolutions of 1830 in Europe. He had wanted to intervene in Belgium, but had been distracted by the developments in Poland. With order restored there in 1831, he was desperate to prevent any further European revolts. The Convention of Münchengrätz

Barbarism: Uncivilised, inhuman and uncultured ways of living and behaving.

was signed with Austria in 1833. This partly concerned the preservation of the Turkish Empire, but it also reaffirmed the principles of the Holy Alliance and Troppau Protocol, to intervene wherever and whenever necessary to prevent the spread of revolutionary ideas.

Despite Nicholas I's hopes, trouble did break out again in 1848, over an even wider area and with far greater initial success. Since Russia itself escaped the troubles, Nicholas I was only too happy to re-enter into his role as 'the Gendarme of Europe'. In 1848–49, he co-operated with the Turks against nationalist revolts in Moldavia and Wallachia, and he despatched his loyal troops to Hungary to help restore Austrian authority within its Empire. His intervention allowed Austria to concentrate its forces in Italy and Germany, and was therefore of great value in the suppression of revolution throughout Europe that year.

Why, and with what success, did Nicholas I become involved in the affairs of Turkey?

Much of Nicholas I's attention abroad was taken up with the position of the Turkish Empire – 'the Sick Man of Europe', as he called it. His concerns derived from an odd mixture of motives.

- The need to protect Orthodox Christians from their masters, the Muslim Turks.

- The need to control the Straits leading into the Black Sea, which were essential for national security and the export of grain. (Full details of Nicholas I's involvement in the Turkish question, together with maps of the areas involved, may be found in Chapter 6.)

A Greek rebellion against the Turks broke out in 1821. This posed a problem to the then Tsar, Alexander I. Should Russia intervene on behalf of the Greeks, who were, after all, fellow Orthodox Christians, and try to win gains at the expense of the Turks? Or were the Greeks to be treated as rebels and crushed? Alexander I had never been able to make up his mind but, by the time Nicholas I came to power in 1825, most prominent Russians favoured intervention against Turkey. In response to popular opinion, the British and French also favoured Greek independence, so Nicholas I was able to carry through his policy without opposition.

Russia declared war on Turkey on 24 April 1828. At first, the war went badly, and the Russians met a good deal of resistance in the Romanian principalities of Moldavia and Wallachia. However, by June 1829, the war had turned in favour of the Russians. In August, one Russian army had reached Adrianople, while another was advancing in the Caucasus. Nicholas did not, however, press his gains any further. His armies were already weakened by disease and to continue into the winter might prove disastrous

In September 1829, Nicholas received the report of the secret 'Kochubei Committee', which had been looking into the best policy for Russia with regard to Turkey. Their report concluded that it was in Russia's interests to keep Turkey weak, but to go no further. To destroy Turkey, the report suggested, would only encourage other powers to step into this area. To reduce Turkey might actually make it stronger and more determined to win back lost territory.

Consequently, Nicholas I negotiated the Treaty of Adrianople (1829) with the Turks. Russia made substantial gains in Asia Minor, including the mouth of the Danube on the Black Sea, two Black Sea ports, and Turkey's recognition of its claim to Georgia and Armenia. Russia also received a large cash payment and a safeguard of Christian rights in the Romanian principalities of Moldavia and Wallachia.

Following the warnings of the Kochubei Committee, Nicholas I was alarmed when, in 1833, Mehemet Ali seemed on the point of destroying or reducing Turkey. Nicholas therefore gave the Sultan military aid and, in return, was granted the Treaty of Unkiar-Skelessi in July 1833. A secret clause, which implied that Turkey would close the Black Sea Straits at Russia's demand, alarmed the British who undertook to revise it at the earliest opportunity.

In 1841, having forced Mehemet Ali to terms, the Straits Convention confirmed the old principle that no warships should pass through the Straits while Turkey was at peace. Although this was less favourable to Russia, Russia's cautious policy of action against Turkey appeared to have brought at least some success.

A new crisis, however, was provoked by Louis-Napoleon of France in the 1850s. A dispute between Catholic and Orthodox priests over the care of the Holy Places in Jerusalem provided the French Emperor with an excuse to champion the Catholic cause. Tsar Nicholas I loathed Napoleon III as a **usurper** and a Bonaparte and, in any case, felt that the Russian claim to protect Christians in the Turkish Empire had a firmer foundation than the French one.

The resulting Crimean War (1854–56), fought by an alliance of Britain, France, Turkey and Piedmont-Sardinia against Russia, was a fiasco for all concerned. There was a string of military blunders and administrative inefficiencies on both sides. Of the two, however, Russia fared worst. At the beginning of the war, there was only one musket for every two Russian men and only 4% of Russian troops had the newer, long-range percussion rifle which 33% of the French and 50% of the British had. The army could not be properly supplied and transport arrangements were totally inefficient. Russia had no railway to transport troops or supplies to the scene of war and as many as two-thirds of the men in some battalions died from sickness and hunger before they even reached the Crimea. Indeed, the chaotic administration probably accounted for more deaths than battles.

Usurper: A person who takes a role, title or job from someone else when they have no right to do this.

The Crimean War, 1854–56

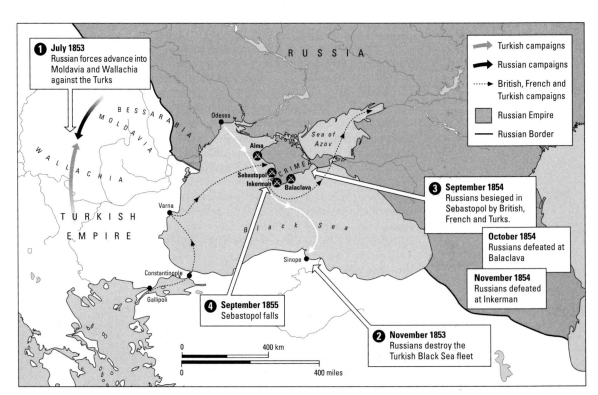

The historian Brian Bond, in *The Nineteenth Century* (1970), claims that 'The Russians, in their weapons and tactics were even more out of date than the allies, moving their troops about the battlefield in dense formations that were suicidal in the face of rifled muskets.' The Russians were defeated at Balaclava (October 1854) and Inkerman (November 1854).

Nicholas I died early in 1855, before the war came to an end. So it was left to his son, Tsar Alexander II, to make a peace treaty. The Peace of Paris in 1856 confirmed the failure of Nicholas I's ambitions.

● Russia lost the territory it had been granted at the mouth of the Danube.

● It was forced to abandon its claims to protect Christians in Turkey (as was France).

● The Black Sea was declared a neutral zone, which could contain no warships in peacetime.

● Russia lost its influence over the Romanian principalities, which, together with Serbia, were given greater independence.

What were the results of the Crimean War for Russia?

As Nicholas was dying, he commented to his son 'I hand over to you my command unfortunately not in as good order as I would have wished'. The failures of the Crimean War meant that, by the end of Nicholas I's reign, Russia was in difficulty.

● The export route for grain through the Black Sea had been closed because of the war causing grave difficulties for the Russian economy.

● The last years of Nicholas I's reign had seen an increase in peasant risings, in particular a rebellion among peasants living by the Black Sea. This focused attention once more on the problems of serfdom, and the old argument that the system was necessary to preserve public order was no longer convincing.

● The war also revealed the inefficiency and corruption of the government. Clearly, some change was needed to the slow, secretive ways maintained by Nicholas I. The 'enlightened bureaucrats', in particular, had come to appreciate this and were pressing for change.

● The war showed the gap between Russia and the west. The western powers had defeated Russia and left it humiliated. Since 1815, Russia had been regarded as the greatest of the European land powers, but the defeat in the Crimea revealed that the 'great colossus (giant)' had feet of clay.

1. What were the main factors to influence Nicholas I's foreign policy? Explain your answer.

2. For what reasons, and to what extent, did Nicholas deserve to be called 'the Gendarme of Europe'?

3. Was Nicholas I's foreign policy a success or a failure? Give reasons to support your answer.

10.6 What changes did Alexander II bring about in Russia from 1855?

Why was change expected after 1855?

Defeat in the Crimea, in 1856, had emphasised some of the problems of the backward Russian State. The growth of the Intelligentsia and the emergence of more enlightened officials, in the reign of Nicholas I, had helped to change the climate of opinion, even within the St Petersburg bureaucracy.

A new Tsar offered the hope of change, particularly since his background seemed to suggest he would be a different man from his father.

Alexander II had already enjoyed considerable governmental experience. He had ruled the country during Nicholas I's absences abroad, had worked for over 10 years on the Council of State, and had served as a member of various committees, including those on serfdom and the railways. Alexander II had been the first member of his family to visit Siberia and had travelled around the Empire. He appeared well aware of the mounting tension within Russia and his first actions as Tsar suggested that he intended to carry out reform.

Alexander II opened his reign with the release of political prisoners and a pardon to all those still held for their part in the Decembrist Conspiracy (1825) and Polish Revolt (1830–31). He relaxed censorship, cancelled the debts of those who owed tax, and restored some of the liberties of Poland and the Catholic Church. Therefore, expectations ran high among those who had opposed the repression of Nicholas I.

A cartoon from the British journal *Punch*, entitled 'The Young Czar [Tsar] coming into Property'.

THE YOUNG CZAR COMING INTO HIS PROPERTY.

1. (a) Who is depicted here?

(b) Comment on the way his throne is illustrated.

2. (a) What is represented by the background (behind the figure's head and shoulders)?

(c) How useful is this cartoon as a piece of historical evidence?

Why did Alexander II grant the serfs their freedom?

During the reign of Nicholas I, attitudes to serfdom had gradually changed. By 1855, there was strong support for abolition within the Ministry of the Interior and a large number of landowners were of the same opinion. The old arguments in favour of serfdom seemed less convincing. Serfdom was no longer fulfilling the function for which it had been introduced. A combination of a rising population and an inefficient agricultural system meant that serfs could no longer produce enough grain to provide for themselves as well as supply their masters with a surplus for sale. The landowning nobility was falling into debt. By 1860, 60% of private serfs were **mortgaged** to the State. As the nobles tried to drive their peasants harder, so the murders of landowners and **bailiffs** grew and serfdom became a source of disorder. Defeat in the Crimean War brought the problem to a critical stage. Minor riots were increasing on an alarming scale. It was clear that the reorganisation of the army required the replacement of conscripted serfs with proper 'citizen soldiers'.

Alexander II hoped that, by emancipating the serfs, he would strengthen the Russian state. It was believed, by those who favoured emancipation, that free peasants would have a greater incentive to work the land effectively. They would therefore provide a grain surplus, and the sale of this grain would provide money for investment. Investment and a more mobile peasantry, some of whom would move to the towns in search of work, would in turn encourage industrialisation and greater prosperity.

In a speech to the Moscow nobility in March 1856, Alexander II declared his intention to 'abolish serfdom from above rather than await the time when it will begin to abolish itself from below'. With this in view, Alexander II had delayed granting freedom, as was normal practice at the end of a war, to those serfs who had served in the Crimea. There was therefore considerable unrest among elements of the serf population, as the nobility tried to delay and weaken the emancipation measure. After 18 months of discussions, Alexander II lost patience and instructed the Ministry of the Interior to produce a plan within a week.

What were the terms of the Emancipation Ukase, 1861?

The plan, which owed a good deal to the efforts of the Deputy Minister of the Interior, the 'enlightened bureaucrat' Nikolai Milyutin, was published in November 1857. After a consideration of comments from the provinces, the work was finished by October 1860 and the edict was published in February 1861. Its terms were proclaimed with much pomp and ceremony from the churches of St Petersburg.

The *Ukase* (decree) was a lengthy and complicated legal document but the most important pronouncement was that **bondage** was 'forever abolished'. Around 21 million serfs became free and a further 20 million state peasants, who had been freed from some of their obligations under Nicholas I, had their remaining restrictions removed in 1866.

The serfs were freed with land, generally that which they had previously worked. The former landowners were compensated by the State in the form of government bonds. To recoup this handout, the government made the peasants pay **redemption** dues. They were required to put down 20%–25% of the purchase price of the land and to pay the rest at 6% interest over 49 years. The *mir* was to hold the land collectively and to be responsible for the payment of taxes. The elders were to take responsibility for the tasks previously performed by the landlord. The decree was designed to come into effect over a two-year period.

Mortgaged: When something is mortgaged, money is borrowed against its value. If the money (and interest) is not repaid, the mortgaged goods (in this case, people) are seized by the lender.

Bailiffs: Law officers who make sure that the decisions of a court are carried out.

Bondage: Serfs were in 'bondage' because they had no civil rights and were owned by others. Once this was abolished they were free men.

Redemption: Paying back. Redemption payments were calculated according to the value of the land each peasant was granted. They included an annual interest charge, and had to be paid every year for a 49-year period.

What were the results of emancipation?

For various reasons, the *Ukase* was not a complete success.

- Not all peasants welcomed freedom. As a class, they tended to be very conservative and hostile to change. It is, perhaps, not surprising that they assumed any change to be for the benefit of others, rather than for themselves. The payment requirements reinforced this view. Many objected to paying for land that their family had farmed for years and which, regardless of legal definitions, they had always regarded as their own. Where peasants were allocated less land than they had farmed before, they were even more aggrieved.

- Land might be shared unfairly. Areas granted were often small, with an average holding of around nine acres. This prevented the intensive farming which the *Ukase* had been expected to promote. By 1878, only 50% of the peasantry farmed large enough areas to enable them to sell surplus goods.

- Personal serfs received no land and, after emancipation, still had to do two years' service. They now became dependent on wage labour and became a new, 'rootless' group in the countryside.

- The *mir* exercised a new control over the peasants that, in many ways, was just as oppressive as that of the former noble landowners. For example, the *mir* was made responsible for assessing taxes according to the income of the peasants in its commune. It could control types and methods of farming in the community and developments might be held back by less progressive neighbours. Where land had been held 'in common', and periodically redistributed, under the old system, a peasant could not leave until the repayments were complete. Any travel required a passport issued by the *mir*. The *mir* also assumed responsibility for settling disputes within its commune. Peasants still lacked full civil rights.

- Redemption payments were often too high, particularly in the less productive areas where landowners tried to push up the estimated value of their land. Many peasants who had received a reasonably-sized holding could only afford to pay for it by returning to work for their old master. Others could only make their farms profitable by renting extra land from him and paying the rent for it with half their crops.

- As peasants bought from one another to try to increase the size of their holdings, some fell into debt, while others became landless and drifted to the towns. Discontent in towns increased as industry was not sufficiently developed to provide employment for all of them.

- In some areas, the terms of the edict took a long time to take effect and, in some cases, 'obligations' carried on until December 1881 when the transfer of lands was finally made compulsory.

- The act failed to encourage rapid industrialisation. Because of the faults explained above, insufficient money was put into the land to develop agriculture to the point at which it might be able to provide capital to finance industrialisation.

- The act failed to save the nobility from bankruptcy. Half the money received by the nobility in the first 10 years after 1861 went to pay off existing debts. By 1905, they had been forced to sell a third of the land they had held in 1861, and over 50% of what was left was mortgaged.

Alexander II has been accused of failing to stem the rising tide of discontent with his emancipation decree. There were 647 serious incidents of riot in the four months after the decree. At Bezdna, in Kazan, 70 peasants were killed by troops in the troubles. In the whole of 1861, 499 cases of unrest had to be quelled by armed troops. Nevertheless, it is difficult to know what else could have been done in the circumstances in Russia at this time. To have had the courage to tackle this issue at all was no mean achievement.

In some respects, the edict was a success. The export trade in grain did increase and, despite passport restrictions, there was a gradual movement to the towns where peasants provided the growing industrial labour force. Wage labour also helped to provide the consumers for Russian industry and, although progress was slow compared with elsewhere, there was a link between the granting of emancipation and the development of industry.

How did Alexander reform local government?

Once emancipation had been granted, further reforms were needed to replace the social system that had accompanied serfdom. Before this period, the government of the localities had been in the hands of the serf-owning landlords. Now their authority had gone, a new system of administration had to be set up. After an enquiry lasting two years, a decree creating the *zemstva* was finally published in January 1864.

Zemstva: Locally elected district and provincial councils with responsibility for primary education, health, poor relief, local economic development, road building and services such as sanitation, fire and water.

The work of the *zemstva* was to be financed from local taxation, which they controlled. Imperial taxation was kept quite separate and was controlled by the central government. The *zemstva* were in two tiers:

- at the lower level were the district *zemstva*, which were divided into 45% nobility, 40% peasantry, and 15% townspeople and clergy.

- Each *zemstvo* elected representatives to the second tier, the provincial *zemstvo*.

Duma: Locally elected town councils set up in 1870.

In 1870, a similar system was set up in the towns, with town councils (known as **Duma**) elected by male property owners over 25 years of age. They had similar rights but no control over the police, which remained under imperial authority.

These assemblies were not allowed to discuss political questions, but they did provide some useful training in self-government for those elected to them. Leading positions naturally fell to the nobles, particularly in the provincial assemblies where the nobility controlled 74 % of all the seats in 1865–67. However, the sort of men who looked for these positions were usually the more progressive members of their class. They were not only able to do some sound work for their localities, they also acquired valuable experience of debating and governing, which they increasingly sought to use on a larger scale.

What legal reforms were carried out?

With the landlord no longer responsible for justice on his estates, a reform of the legal system was also necessary. This took place in 1864. Justices of the Peace, elected by the *zemstva* for three years, took over the petty courts, replacing the landlords as local judges. Local justice was, however, only one part of a very outdated and slow legal system, in which cases were examined in secret and evidence presented on paper. The opportunity was taken to make even more far-reaching reforms.

Trials became public. Juries were introduced and appeal courts set up. Lawyers' salaries were raised to prevent bribery. Judges, although nominated to the regular courts by the Tsar, were to be independent of the government. Although martial law was still retained for political offenders, the new system was generally much fairer and more effective. There was, nevertheless, one side-effect that had not been anticipated. Reform led to the growth of a new type of lawyer. The courts came to provide an excellent training ground in the art of persuasion. The new legal profession, knowledgeable of the law and generally in favour of liberal reform, became a breeding ground for reformers!

How were the armed forces reformed by Alexander II?

Serfdom had formerly provided the conscripts for the army, while the nobility supplied the officers. Again this had to change. In 1859, the 25-year conscription demand had already been reduced to 16 years. In 1875, the Manifesto and Statute on Universal Military Service became law. All classes were deemed liable for conscription, and the hiring of substitutes was forbidden. Service was no longer an optional punishment for criminals. All males had to register at 21 and about a quarter of these were chosen, by lot, to serve. Only the unfit were exempt, although exceptions might be made on compassionate grounds. The length of service, which was established as 15 years with about six or seven years on active service, was reduced for volunteers and those with education. University graduates only had to serve six months and even those with only a primary education had their service reduced to four years. Other reforms included the abolition of the more extreme forms of corporal punishment, in 1863, and a revision of the military code of behaviour and dress.

Under Dmitri Milyutin, Minister of War (1861–81), and Grand Duke Constantine (Alexander II's younger brother), Minister of the Marine, considerable reform took place in the command structure of the armed forces and in the training of recruits. Between 1862 and 1864 new, separate regional commands were established, which helped to decentralise the administration, making it less cumbersome. Special army schools were set up and were open to all classes so that, by 1871, 12% of the junior cadets came from non-noble backgrounds. These reforms met with considerable opposition from the nobility who feared for their loss of influence. However, Milyutin was able to point to the success of the well-organised and well-equipped Prussian army, in its campaign against the French in 1870–71, as evidence of the necessity for reform.

By the time of the Russo–Turkish War of 1877–78, it was clear that the Russian forces, although still wanting in tactics, were at least better organised than those in the inefficient Crimean campaign. Nevertheless, the general staff was still burdened with many tasks and regulations. Its duties were not clearly set down until 1900, and still had not taken effect by 1904. Furthermore, army doctors could be bribed to declare people unfit for service, and the quality of training still lagged behind that of the Germans.

What changes took place in education and freedom of thought?

To educate, and yet stifle criticism, is a hard task for an autocracy, and yet education was essential if Russia was to move forward. While censorship never disappeared in Alexander II's reign, there was a considerable increase in freedom of thought and expression, compared with what had gone before. The number of new books published doubled between 1855 and 1864, and trebled from 1864 to 1881. In the reign of Nicholas I, there had been six newspapers and 19 monthly magazines while, under Alexander II, these rose to 16 and 156 respectively. Even in the later period of his reign, when Alexander is generally seen as having been less tolerant, the press laws of 1865 freed a good deal of material from censorship. This included existing periodicals in Moscow and St Petersburg and all academic publications.

The numbers of university students rose in the early years of the reign and, in 1863, new university regulations reformed the administration and gave the universities greater control over their own affairs. Lectures on European government and philosophy were allowed once more, law was upgraded, outsiders were permitted to attend lectures, and foreign books could be bought for study without censorship. Furthermore, degrees could be awarded to foreigners and needy students could be helped with the deferral or remission of payments.

In the villages and towns, the *zemstva* and Duma were encouraged to expand primary education which, together with secondary education, increased fourfold between 1861 and 1881. From 1862, new schools were placed under the direct control of the Ministry of Education rather than the Church. New schemes of work were devised and prizes given for the best new textbooks. Technical schools and institutes were encouraged. Women's education advanced. In 1872, the first courses for women at Moscow University were introduced and women were also admitted to the Medical Academy in St Petersburg. In 1876, five universities set up courses for women by Imperial statute. By 1881, there were 2,000 women studying at universities in Russia.

What economic reform took place?

Under Reutern, Minister of Finance (1862–78), the treasury was reformed and the administration of finance improved. From 1862, budgets were published and from 1863 a system of duties (taxes) was brought in to replace the old-fashioned licences to sell goods.

Banking and company organisation increased in this period, so that there were 278 municipal banks, 727 loan and savings organisations, 566 joint stock companies and 33 joint stock commercial banks by 1878.

Many of the restrictions that had forced Jews to live in the 'Pale of Settlement' until 1855, were lifted. Jews who paid over a certain amount in taxes, together with foreign Jews, were allowed to live and trade throughout the Empire. This was extended in 1860 to those who had served in certain regiments and in 1867 to all Jews who had been soldiers. The motivation was economic. There was still a good deal of anti-semitism in Russia, but the move helped to inject another source of wealth into the economy.

The output of coal and iron, and the number of railways increased, as can be seen in the earlier tables of economic growth (pages 272–3). Guaranteeing an annual return on investment encouraged railway building. This increased the number of foreign investors. The railways were used to boost grain exports, which increased from 26 million tonnes in 1864 to 86 million tonnes by 1880. However, by 1870, population had grown to 84,500,000, compared with 73,600,000 in 1861. Despite the economic improvements, the growth in production did not match these swelling numbers.

What was the reaction to Alexander II's reforms?

Despite all his good intentions, Alexander II received criticism from all sides. At the lowest level, peasant risings continued and increased. In Court circles, conservatives resented the loss of influence and privilege and accused Alexander of stirring up trouble. Among the Intelligentsia, slavophiles rejected the whole idea of introducing western ways into Russia, while westernisers were frustrated that the reforms did not go further. Writers, thinkers and university students, encouraged by the freer political atmosphere, mocked Russian society, and increasingly questioned the feasibility of propping up the autocratic regime. Deprived of any sort of national assembly in which to air their views, journalists, philosophers, political thinkers, poets, playwrights and novelists, all used their talents to draw attention to Russia's continuing problems.

'Pale of Settlement': A specially designated area in the border regions.

1. What were the chief weaknesses of the various reforms carried out by Alexander II?

2. Who benefited most from Alexander II's reforms: the Tsar, the nobility, or the peasants? Explain your answer.

3. On the basis of the information given here, do you think Tsar Alexander II deserved the title 'Tsar Liberator'?

Populism: Political activities or ideas based on the interests and opinions of the ordinary people. The Populists were groups of revolutionaries in Russia in 1870–81 who emphasised the importance of the peasant problem.

First International: Founded in 1864 by Karl Marx to organise international co-operation between European working-class groups. Karl Marx (1818–1883) produced a scheme of socialist thinking in the 1840s. This was popularised in *The Communist Manifesto* (1848), *Das Kapital* (1867) and in numerous books and articles. His theories stemmed from his belief that economic conditions determined historical change and created class struggles, but which would eventually lead to the dominance of the workers (proletariat).

Anarchist: Someone who seems to pay no attention to rules or laws that everyone else obeys.

Political thinkers

From the 1830s, a number of influential political thinkers began to shape the ideas of the Russian Intelligentsia, and their influence was most marked in the reign of Alexander II. Many were forced to work and write from abroad. However, their articles and books, smuggled back into Russia by their followers, provided a focus for contemporary debate.

V. Belinsky (1811–1848)

Belinsky studied at Moscow University (1829–32), but was expelled before completing his studies for writing a play which criticised serfdom. He worked as a literary critic and journalist (1834–48), before he died of a serious lung disease at the early age of 36. During this time, he became a central figure of the 19th-century Russian intelligentsia. He questioned contemporary Russian society through his articles and encouraged 'social literature' that upheld the rights of the oppressed. He led the westernisers' attack on the slavophiles and adored Peter the Great as the founder of 'modern' Russia.

Alexander Herzen (1812–1870)

Herzen became interested in social and political problems while studying at Moscow University. He was attracted by the westernisers' ideas, but was arrested for his activities and exiled to the provinces in 1834. In 1847, he was granted permission to emigrate and he witnessed the 1848 revolutions in Europe. From 1852, he settled in London where he began publishing an influential journal *Kolokol* ('The Bell') in which he criticised Russia's social structure. The journal spread Herzen's idea of the development of a system of independent, self-governing peasant communes which could transform Russia and lift it out of its backwardness. Herzen was one of the founders of Russian **Populism**, but he opposed any kind of violent revolution.

Mikhail Bakunin (1814–1876)

Well educated and of noble birth. After a brief career in the Imperial Guard, he devoted himself to revolutionary activity. Bakunin took part in the German revolutions of 1848, was arrested, sentenced to death, but then returned to Russia, where he was imprisoned and exiled to Siberia. He then escaped, via Japan and America, to western Europe where he joined the **First International** in 1869. However, he fell out with Karl Marx, and became an **anarchist**. He disliked 'political rules' and believed in the rights of individuals.

N. Chernyshevsky (1828–1889)

Chernyschevsky wrote a series of 'essays' and became a regular contributor to the radical journal *The Contemporary* from 1857. He attacked those who argued for gradual social change. He believed the political and economic basis of Russia needed fundamental change. His hope for the future lay with the *Narod* (the people) and with individual freedom. He was arrested in 1862 and in gaol wrote *What is to be done?* – a title Vladimir Lenin later adopted for one of his books. It contained Chernyschevsky's ideas for a socialist state and became very popular. Chernyshevsky himself was, however, frightened by the increasing violence of those who claimed to be his followers. *The Contemporary* was closed down in 1866 amid the growing unrest.

10.7 To what extent, and why, did Alexander II's reign change direction in the 1860s?

What changes took place within Russia?

Whilst the emancipation *ukaze* was being prepared, the intelligentsia had been reasonably cautious and quiet. As soon as it came into effect, in 1861, and its inadequacies were revealed, there was a growth in radical activity. Pamphlets and leaflets began to spread through the major cities. One, entitled 'The Great Russian', was scattered in St Petersburg and Moscow in July 1861. It called on the educated classes to seize power from the incompetent government.

There was also an increasing number of student protests, including riots in both St Petersburg and Kazan universities in 1861. These were partly a reaction to the plans of the new Minister of Education, Count Putiatin, who wanted to establish stricter control. However, the students also protested about a range of other issues, from the examination system to the problems of emancipation and the Russian social structure. In 1862, there were a number of fires, which destroyed over 2,000 shops in the capital. These were believed to be the work of young radicals.

This new generation of protestors was less disciplined and more outspoken in their criticism of the regime than their fathers had been in the reign of Nicholas I. Turgenev aptly characterised the difference in his novel *Fathers and Sons* (1862). He described both the 'Fathers' – the older generation who hoped Russia could regenerate itself through piecemeal reform – and the 'Sons' – men of action who were impatient for the thoroughgoing transformation of Russia which might, in the last, resort involve revolution. He also pointed to the class difference, the older generation of nobles, and the younger one of lower social status, professionals, students, a growing group of 'middle-class' bourgeoisie and the sons of clergy. These *nihilists* deliberately put on airs, which were aimed at emphasising the hopelessness of the Russian State. They wore floppy hats, long scarves carelessly draped around their necks, and they had long hair and beards. They despised everything and appeared to believe in nothing. They condemned Alexander's reforms and looked for the abolition of the ruling Tsar. They were opposed to the influence of religion and were influenced by Marxist thinking.

In this atmosphere, Alexander tightened control. There were a number of political arrests, including that of Chernyshevsky. The publication of leading radical journals was temporarily suspended in 1862 but a commission, set up to investigate 'revolutionary organisations', only found evidence against the Sunday Schools. These were duly closed down.

What was the effect of the revolt in Poland in 1863?

In the midst of the mounting unrest at home, Alexander II was faced with another threat: a revolt in Poland. Here, as elsewhere, Alexander's reign had begun with a variety of concessions. These included the reopening of Warsaw University, the reinstatement of Polish as the official language, the appointment of a new Catholic Archbishop of Warsaw (1856) and the formation of a new Agricultural Society (1857) to improve the lot of the peasants and to promote new cultivation techniques. However, this was not enough to appease the nationalist nobility and, in the 1860s, their demands for total independence from Russia surfaced once again.

There were nationalist demonstrations in Warsaw in February 1861. When the Agricultural Society was disbanded in April, there were further protests. Not even the Tsar's younger brother, the 'enlightened'

Constantine, who was appointed as Viceroy in May 1862, could calm the situation. The final straw was the proposal to conscript Poles into the Russian army. Open revolt broke out in January 1863 and lasted until August 1864, when it was ruthlessly suppressed. Few peasants gave their support, however, and the loyalty of around 700,000 peasant families was rewarded by the Russian gift of the freehold of half their land with no redemption payments.

The Polish Rising seemed to confirm Alexander II's developing suspicion that reform did more harm than good. The revolt had the effect of whipping up patriotism within Russia, which curbed the radical activity. However, after its suppression, the militancy grew again. In 1865, a group called 'the Organisation' was formed. From this group came the student, D. Karakozov, who attempted to shoot Alexander II in the streets of St Petersburg in 1866. He was unsuccessful and was hanged, but his attempt was symptomatic of the attitude, particularly among students, at that time.

What was Alexander II's reaction to proposals for political reform in 1860s?

In 1865, the St Petersburg *zemstvo* petitioned Alexander II for a central office to which the provincial *zemstva* might send representatives. They were, in effect, asking for a national assembly, although a very limited one. The request was refused. When another petition was sent in 1866, Alexander II dissolved the St Petersburg *zemstvo* and exiled its most prominent figures. The move did not help Alexander II's reputation, or the future of the Tsars. The very men who would probably have been the Tsar's natural allies, had he set up a National Assembly, were now left debating and leading the various provincial *zemstva*, but unable to influence national politics. These men became increasingly frustrated. They were now prepared to support the activities of radical groups.

How did Alexander II attempt to curb the growing unrest, 1866–1871?

In 1866, Count Dmitri Tolstoy, who was regarded as a conservative and a supporter of the Orthodox Church, was appointed Minister of Education. The Scots traveller, Sir Donald Mackenzie Wallace, described how he 'received the mission of protecting the younger generation against pernicious [very harmful] ideas' and 'determined to introduce more discipline into all educational establishments'.

Tolstoy reimposed restrictions on the entry to the universities and placed discipline in the hands of the police. He strengthened governmental control over the appointments of staff in schools, and encouraged the Church to play a dominant role in primary schools. In secondary schools, he stressed the importance of classical discipline. According to Mackenzie Wallace, Tolstoy 'determined to supplant the superficial study of natural science by the thorough study of Latin and Greek'. The crucial final examinations, which provided entrance to the universities from these secondary schools, now became far more dependent on the rote learning of classical grammar, in an attempt to discourage 'free thinking'.

Following another assassination attempt on the Tsar in 1867, controls were tightened further, with an increase in censorship and a reduction in the powers of the *zemstva*. It seemed as though Alexander could do nothing to halt the swelling tide of discontent. The mood among the young in both secondary and university education became more hostile and there were further disorders among the students of St Petersburg and Moscow (1868–69). S. Nechaev helped to organise student circles known as 'Committees of People's Revenge'. He was arrested and imprisoned for involvement in the murder of a fellow student, Ivanov, but his trial generated a good deal of publicity, which only harmed the Tsarist government still further.

The students appeared determined to spread their views regardless of persecution. In 1869, Alexander Herzen appealed for activists to spread the ideas of the nihilists and 'go to the people', by which he meant the peasants who made up the bulk of the Russian population. The 'Chaikovsky Circle', which met in St Petersburg (1869–72), organised the distribution of pamphlets and books that had been banned, to support the idea of bringing the peasants into the students' campaign. This led to the Populist, or Narodonik, movement.

In the summer of 1874, some 2,000 students, dressed as peasants to win support, descended on factories and villages throughout European Russia. They took jobs, and used the access to the common people that this gave them to spread their views and to stir up resentment. The movement was not a success. The combination of educated accents, scruffy clothes and ideas they could not understand merely frightened some peasants into reporting them to the authorities. Many students found themselves deported to Siberia, although their trial once more gave them some useful publicity. They tried again in 1876, with similarly unpromising results. In 1877, these unco-ordinated efforts became a new revolutionary organisation, 'Land and Liberty'.

By the 1870s Alexander II had failed either to appease his subjects by reform, or to curb disturbance by repression. He had, in fact, become increasingly isolated and was to withdraw still further from public life in the last decade of his reign, enjoying a liaison with a much younger woman, Catherine Dolgoruky.

1. Why were university students at the forefront of radical protest in Russia in the 1860s and 1870s?

2. What was the effect of the Polish rebellion of 1863 on Russian internal affairs?

3. Did the radical movements of the 1860s and 1870s pose a significant threat to the autocracy? Give reasons for your answer.

10.8 Why have historians differed in their views of Tsar Nicholas I and Tsar Alexander II?

A CASE STUDY IN HISTORICAL INTERPRETATION

Was Nicholas I a reactionary?

A contemporary critic, Alexander Herzen (1812–1870), referred to the reign of Nicholas I as 'the plague zone of Russian History'. Historians have condemned the reign for its excessive repression, characterised by strict censorship and the use of the secret police. They have also criticised Nicholas I's reign for its failure to tackle administrative and social reform, or to do anything for the ailing Russian economy.

Nicholas has been criticised for his determination to repress liberalism abroad. Historian Derek Offord claims, in *Nineteenth Century Russia* (1999): 'The reign of Nicholas I is among the most repressive periods of 19th-century Russian history. The Tsar himself, more at home on the parade ground … had no interest in or sympathy with liberal or radical ideas.' Another historian, Eric Hobsbawm, in *The Age of Revolution, 1789–1848* (1962), refers to the atmosphere in the reign of Nicholas I as a 'combination of the dungeon and the drill square'.

However, there is some evidence to suggest that such comments are unduly harsh. The historian Hugh Seton-Watson points out that Nicholas I frequently spoke out against the evils of serfdom, and that his fear of social disorder if emancipation were carried out was 'a real problem', not merely an excuse. Anthony Wood, in *Europe 1815–1945* (1964), comments that 'Nicholas was not averse to reform, provided it was imposed from above'.

The codification of the law by Speransky, the attempt to improve the lot of the state peasants, and the laws to help serfs and factory workers were all passed during this reign. Furthermore, it can be argued that the worst of Nicholas I's repression did not really come about until after 1848, when the scale of events in the rest of Europe shook him.

Possibly, Nicholas II tarnished his own reputation with his excessive secrecy. By conducting investigations behind closed doors, no one could ever be sure just what plans he had. He did not wish to appear influenced by outside pressure, nor did he wish to encourage others to think, discuss or proffer advice without his authority. This explains the censorship and the secret police, but it does not mean that Nicholas II was uninterested in reform. According to the historian David Saunders, 'the Tsar knew that changes had to be undertaken but was determined not to allow them to be promoted by any movement or group beyond the control of the government. He believed that reform could be achieved by the government acting alone.' This may have been a mistake, but it does not make Nicholas II a 'reactionary'.

Was Alexander II a 'Tsar Liberator'?

On the whole, Alexander II, Nicholas I's son, has received a much kinder press than Nicholas I. Alexander II is portrayed as a man who tried his best and did great things for Russia, although he could never quite bring himself to go far enough.

In many respects, the title 'Tsar Liberator' seems highly appropriate for him. He carried through the most far-reaching reform in Russia in the 19th century, the emancipation of the serfs. He followed this with reforms in local government, the legal system, finance, education and the army. Even the Russian economy began to pick up a little during this period. Virtually every area of Russian life was affected by Alexander II's changes. Historian Donald Treadgold describes Alexander II as a ruler who did 'more to improve the lot of the Russian people than any other single person in their history'.

However, Alexander II does not escape criticism. There has been disagreement about his intentions. Marxist historians have suggested that Alexander II carried through reform with the sole intention of supporting and strengthening the position of the nobility. There is certainly some evidence in favour of this argument. The landowners received financial compensation under the terms of the serfs' emancipation, and the nobility was to dominate the new councils set up to control local government. It was primarily the nobility and higher ranks of society that benefited from the improvements in education, finance and the organisation of the army.

Non-Marxists have sometimes adopted the same view. For example, the historian Lionel Kochan, in *The Making of Modern Russia* (1973), refers to the emancipation edict as 'a fraud'. Others, such as David Saunders, believe that Alexander II has been credited with ideas and intentions he did not in fact possess. Saunders accepts that Alexander II was aware of the need to do something to reduce the tensions threatening his Empire, but writes that 'the laws which freed the serfs emerged from a process that the Tsar barely understood and over which he had only partial control'. Far from being a convinced reformer, Saunders believes Alexander II merely responded to circumstances. When faced with the Polish rising of 1863–64, Alexander II responded just as Nicholas II had done after 1848, with repression.

The historian Norman Davies refers to the reign of Alexander II as a period of '*liberalisation à la Russe*'. This tongue-in-cheek comment implies that what might have been considered liberal in Russia at that time was certainly not what we would understand by the word today. As he points out, 'progress proved more apparent than real' and Alexander II was unable to sustain the reforming course on which he had set out. Norman Davies believes Alexander II was only driven to social and political reform by the catastrophe of the Crimean War. In the 1860s, he 'back-pedalled' and fierce reaction followed. By the end of the reign, autocracy and the police regime remained in tact.

Some western historians, however, believe Alexander II set out with sincere liberal ideas, but that his plans went sadly wrong. For example, W.E. Mosse, in 'Alexander II and the Modernisation of Russia' (1958), felt that Alexander II made a conscious effort to modernise Russia and reform government and administration. He failed because he could not quite bring himself to abandon the traditional autocracy of his forefathers. Hugh Seton-Watson believes Alexander II's fatal mistake was his refusal to introduce a National Assembly in the 1860s. He wrote, in *The Russian Empire 1801–1917* (1988), 'the chance of introducing the beginnings of parliamentary government in Russia was lost, with fateful results'. If only Alexander II had maintained the reforming impulses of his earlier years, the argument runs, the whole course of Russian history might have been different.

It is therefore generally agreed that the course of Alexander's reign changed in the 1860s. But whether Alexander II had a conscious reforming policy until then or not, remains a matter of debate. Whatever the truth, his attempts at reform are aptly summed up, in Richard Pipe's phrase, as 'too little, too cautious and too late'.

How different were Tsar Nicholas I and Tsar Alexander II as rulers?

The arguments of modern historians have served to improve Nicholas I's reputation a little, while making Alexander II's less praiseworthy. It is the nature of historical enquiry to question traditional assumptions, so it is not perhaps surprising that Nicholas I and Alexander II are now sometimes regarded as not so different. They were both autocrats, patriotic, religious and conservative in outlook. They both believed that the initiative, whether for conservation or change, belonged to the Tsar alone and that reform 'from above' would help to strengthen the autocratic regime, not replace it. They both became more repressive in the later stages of their reigns, Nicholas I after 1848 and Alexander II after 1863. They both drew back from the development of constitutional government and tried to ignore the mounting criticism around them.

It will be left for future generations to debate the motivation behind their actions. Whatever arguments are put forward, it cannot be ignored that, whereas Nicholas II was responsible for few major reforming laws, Alexander II can be credited with many far-reaching changes.

1. What major internal problems confronted both Nicholas I and Alexander II as Tsars of Russia?

2. To what extent, and why, have historians disagreed about the aims and policies of Tsar Nicholas I and Tsar Alexander II, as rulers of Russia?

3. How far would you agree that Tsar Nicholas I and Tsar Alexander II were 'more alike than different' in their attitudes to government in Russia? Explain your answer

10.9 How successful was Alexander II in foreign affairs, 1855–1871?

Alexander II continued the advance into Asia. This was widely supported both by the military and by those determined to find new markets and raw materials to help to improve the Russian economy. There was also an element of **pan-Slavism** in the expansion of this period. This was the belief that it was Russia's duty to carry its superior civilisation to the uncultured tribes of Asia. After the wars in the Caucasus were brought to a successful conclusion in 1864, attention was focused on Turkestan and central Asia. Turkestan and Samarkand were conquered in the 1860s and

Pan-Slavism: This movement, which was to become a major influence on Russian foreign policy after 1871, regarded Russia as the natural protector and supporter of the Slav people.

70s, with little serious fighting, although Turkmenia proved more difficult, and was not taken until 1881.

In the Far East, Alexander II was responsible for the successful acquisition of Sakhalin from Japan, and for drawing up the Treaty of Peking with China (1860). Alaska, however, which in the mid-19th century appeared to be of little economic worth to Russia, was sold to the USA in 1867.

In Europe, Alexander II did not play a large role in affairs until after 1871. Defeat in the Crimea and Alexander's pre-occupation with domestic policy, kept Russia on the sidelines. The Russians had been humiliated by the war. They felt particularly aggrieved by the opposition of the Austrians in 1855, so shortly after Nicholas I had helped them in 1848–49. They also resented the clauses of the Treaty of Paris (1856), which had neutralised the Black Sea. Alexander II's relations with the other European powers were, therefore, shaped by his desire to break the alliance that had fought so successfully against Russia in the Crimea, and to gain a favourable revision of the Treaty of Paris.

Initially, he looked for French friendship, hoping he might be able to separate the French from the Austrians. He was successful in so far as war broke out between France and Austria in 1859. However, his attitude changed when the French showed sympathy for the Polish rebels of 1863. Alexander then considered Prussia as an ally, since it was the only power that did not sympathise with the Poles. Pre-occupations at home meant that Russia remained aloof from the major events of the years 1866–71. As Prussia completed its work of unification, both Austria and France were weakened. Thanks to the Franco–Prussian War of 1870, Alexander II was able to fulfil his wish to revise the Treaty of Paris.

At the Great Power Conference in London in 1871, Alexander Gorchakov, Alexander's foreign minister, announced that Russia intended to reconstruct its Black Sea fleet. The rest of Europe was powerless to do anything to prevent this, and it was agreed that both Turkey and Russia should be allowed to keep naval forces on the Black Sea. By 1871, Alexander could feel well pleased that his cautious policy had enabled Russia to become master in this area once again. He even abandoned his former anti-Austrian prejudices, to join Bismarck's Three Emperors' League, the *Dreikaiserbund*, with Germany and Austria in 1872. This seemed to assure the stability of Europe.

Study the whole of this chapter.

1. To what extent, and why, did Alexander II's foreign policy up to 1871 differ from that of his predecessors, Alexander I and Nicholas II?

2. How successful was Tsar Alexander II as Tsar of Russia, 1855–1870?

3. In what respects, and to what extent, did Russia change politically, socially, economically and geographically between 1815 and 1870?

The Revolutions of 1848 and 1849

Key Issues

● *What were the short-term causes of the revolutions?*

● *What projects for political and social reform were put forward in the major European states?*

● *Why did the revolutions collapse so suddenly in the course of 1848–49?*

Framework of Events

1848	January: Revolt in Palermo, Sicily
	February: Abdication of Louis Philippe and proclamation of the Second Republic in France
	March: Introduction of universal manhood suffrage and the 'right to work' in France. Resignation of Metternich. Violence in Berlin. War between Piedmont and Austria.
	May: First meeting of the Frankfurt Parliament
	June: Meeting of Pan-Slav Congress in Prague. Cavaignac suppresses insurrection in Paris. Windischgrätz bombards Prague
	July: Radetzky defeats Piedmontese at Custoza. Meeting of Constituent Assembly in Vienna
	October: Windischgrätz occupies Vienna
	November: Pope Pius IX abandons Rome
	December: Louis Napoleon is elected President of the French Republic
1849	February: Establishment of the Roman Republic by Mazzini and Garibaldi
	March: Dissolution of the Austrian Constituent Assembly. Defeat of Piedmontese at Novara
	April: Friedrich Wilhelm IV refuses the offer of the German Crown
	July: Suppression of the Roman Republic by French troops
	August: Hungarian rebels surrender to Austrian and Russian troops.

Overview

I N the mid-1840s, the political tensions that beset the governments of Europe were compounded by a complex **socio-economic crisis**. In many parts of Europe these strains, caused by unemployment and high food prices, provoked angry urban demonstrations that added to the intellectual discontent of the middle classes. A combination of various crises led to a temporary conjunction of opposition interests, united in hostility to the governing classes of these states, but for many different reasons. Faced with a groundswell of revolt apparently as broadly based as the one that had brought down the French monarchy in 1789–92, many European governors saw flight, surrender or compromise as the safest course.

In the early months of 1848, it appeared that the politics of western Europe had been transformed by an upheaval that had no precedent in terms of extent or impact. Within a year, however, it was becoming clear that the liberal and radical movements of 1848 had brought about relatively little lasting change. In part, this was due to the incoherence of the 'revolutionary' groups. The political interests of middle-class liberals rarely coincided with the more fundamental, material requirements of unemployed workers. It had often been possible for liberals in one state to establish common ground with those in neighbouring states in terms of their constitutional demands. Yet, in 1848, this community of political interests was often cancelled out by conflicts between the nationalist demands that often accompanied progressive constitutional ideas. The most important element of all in the failure of the revolutions lay in the enduring strength of the governmental systems that they appeared to have overthrown. The economic crises affected the populations of Europe far more seriously than they affected the regimes. These retained the resources, and in particular the military strength, to survive. Above all, while individuals such as Louis-Philippe and Metternich abandoned their posts, the governing classes, in general, still had the will to survive. In such men as Louis Napoleon in France and Franz Josef in Austria, they found new leaders, who were largely willing to preserve the political bases of the pre-1848 regimes.

The revolutions did leave behind certain achievements. Prussia and Piedmont retained constitutions that their rulers could not easily ignore. Feudal obligations were abolished in parts of eastern Europe, never to return. It is tempting to conclude, however, that the main beneficiaries of the 1848 revolutions were, in fact, the governing conservatives. After many years of living in fear of liberal revolt, they had now confronted it and survived. It was they, rather than the liberals, who emerged strengthened by the 'Year of Revolutions'. The next 60 years of European history were to be dominated by conservative governments, confident in their own power, and confident in their ability to harness and control the forces that once seemed such a threat to them.

It is just possible, however, that the confidence of the conservatives was misplaced in the long term. There can be little doubt that the events of 1848–49 brought profound disappointment for liberals and nationalists across Europe, yet their causes did not perish. Within 20 years, the ambitions of moderate nationalists in Italy and Germany had been realised. Conservative leaders – forced to adopt and to adapt the programmes of groups whose ideologies were too popular, and who had too great an economic impetus behind them to be resisted – had unified both states. Hungarian nationalists, also, proved too influential to be ignored by an

Imperial regime that had learned few lessons from the events of 1848. In terms of purely political power, European liberals had less cause for satisfaction 20 or 30 years on. Their economic agenda, however, had proved less easy to ignore. Bismarck's Germany, in the 1870s and the 1880s, provides a prime example of a state embracing many of the economic priorities of the industrial middle classes, even as it strove to exclude them from direct political power. There can be little serious doubt, therefore, that the would-be revolutionaries of 1848 acted prematurely and sought to exploit a 'revolutionary situation' that did not really exist. The events of this 'year of revolutions', on the other hand, provided a clear indication of the evolutionary direction that European politics were following.

11.1 What role was played by economic factors in making 1848 a 'year of revolutions'?

The traditional forms of European society had been under pressure from economic and demographic changes for some time before 1840. The years between 1845 and 1847, however, formed a particularly severe phase of this crisis. Indeed, one of the most helpful contributions to the understanding of the events of 1848 was made by the French historian Ernest Labrousse when he explained, in *How Revolutions are Born* (1948), that the revolts resulted not from one crisis, but from a conjunction of several. A particularly acute agricultural crisis coincided with a newer kind of crisis, an industrial slump. The infant industrial economies of Europe had less experience of this and it gave special urgency to the political problems of the individual European states.

Agricultural crisis

European agriculture entered an acute crisis in 1845. The potato blight of that year had its most dramatic impact in Ireland, where it eventually accounted for the loss of up to a million human lives. The failure of the crop also cut a swathe of hunger and suffering across Europe – in Belgium, Holland, Germany and Poland. The following year, the unusually hot, dry weather caused the failure of the grain harvest. As the failures continued, it became impossible to make good the shortfall from the surplus of the previous harvest. Throughout Europe, there were sudden, steep price rises. In Hamburg the price of wheat rose 51.8% between 1841 and 1847, 70% of that increase occurring in the period 1845–47. In Switzerland, the price of rye doubled in the same two years, and bread prices doubled in the single year 1846/47. Even when imports of foreign grain were feasible, the incomplete state of most European railway systems made its passage to many parts of the continent impossible.

Industrial crisis

The years 1845–47 also saw the most severe of the industrial crises that had hit Europe at intervals of roughly ten years since the end of the Napoleonic wars. Partly, this was a crisis of overproduction, in which manufacturers, finding that they had saturated the markets available to them, cut back production and thus created unemployment or wage reductions. In France, production in the iron and coal industries fell by 30% and 20%, respectively, in 1847. Similarly in Germany, the amount of spun yarn exported by the member states of the *Zollverein* (see Chapter 8) fell by 40% in 1844–47. The crisis was aggravated by the impact of factory production, in some parts of Europe, upon older forms of production in other areas. The hostility shown by skilled craftsmen and artisans to factories, mills, railways and their owners, in 1848, clearly indicated what they thought to be the origins of their suffering.

The industrial crisis was closely linked to the agricultural crisis for, in many localities, the need to use government and bankers' funds to buy large quantities of foreign corn left little or nothing for investment in industry. Bankruptcies multiplied, and business confidence reached a low ebb. The impact of all this upon living conditions was naturally most severe. The coincidence of high food prices with declining wages caused widespread hardship, especially in the towns. Here, three elements of discontent came together: the unemployed and hungry artisans, the peasants fleeing from the rural ills of land-hunger and semi-feudal oppression, and the middle classes with their liberal and nationalist opposition to the existing regimes.

The relationship between crisis and revolt

The violence of 1848 did not occur at the height of the European crisis, but during the steady improvement that followed it. It resulted from the steady accumulation of frustration during the previous two and a half years of hardship. Historian Ernest Labrousse wrote that 'the wave of high prices had spread over the country like a flood, and, like a receding tide, it left behind it a ruined population.' Nevertheless, the increasing prosperity of 1848–49 goes a long way to explain the withering of rebellion in most European states after such promising beginnings. The sparks that set off the outbursts of February and March 1848 must therefore be sought in the political circumstances and disputes of the various European states. In describing these, it is important not to generalise, for the resemblance between the affairs of one state and those of its neighbour was superficial. The views of the revolutionary leaders were usually much more diverse than the common distress that, briefly, provided them with a rank-and-file following. As a whole, wrote French historian C. Pouthas in 1956, of these leaders 'the same vocabulary, the same programme, concealed dissimilar situations'.

1. What kinds of economic crises occurred in Europe in the years leading up to 1848?

2. Why did the agricultural crisis that affected Europe in 1846–48 have a more serious impact than those that had occurred earlier?

3. What evidence is there to support the claim that 'social and economic factors, rather than political ones, were responsible for the outbreak of revolution in 1848'?

11.2 Why did the Provisional Government come to power in France, and why was it unable to implement its radical policies in the long term?

The abdication of Louis-Philippe

For all this accumulation of tension and discontent, the fall of the French government, in February 1848, occurred almost by accident. The degree of political disillusion that surrounded Louis-Philippe's monarchy has already been described (see Chapter 7) but, for all its problems, there seemed little reason to suppose that it was in imminent danger of collapse. There seemed to be little direct danger when a new phase of moderate opposition to the king was launched, in the last months of 1847. In order to stay strictly within the law, at a time when political meetings were banned, the opposition chose the tactic of holding a series of banquets at which after-dinner speakers could put forward their views on political reform. The government's decision (20 February) to ban even this form of protest caused demonstrations in the streets of Paris. Louis-Philippe's nerve was already sufficiently shaken for him to dismiss Guizot, when a clash with troops (23 February) led to the shooting of between 40 and 50 demonstrators. The following day, with much of the population of Paris in outraged rebellion, and with the National Guard refusing to perform its peacekeeping duties, Louis-Philippe abdicated and made his way, in confusion, to exile in England.

Personnel: a compromise solution

A coherent opposition party, or coalition, had not toppled the French monarchy. Indeed, it had not been toppled at all. Its forces had not been defeated, so much as abandoned by their commander. The events in Paris found an echo in a few provincial outbursts, as in Lyon, Limoges and Rouen. In the rest of France, as Roger Price has written, in *1848 in Europe* (1975), 'the revolution must have presented a somewhat artificial and imposed character, accepted because there was no agreed alternative'. The Provisional Government formed on 25 February to fill the vacuum was, like the king it replaced, a compromise. The essentially liberal body envisaged by the poet-cum-politician, Alphonse de Lamartine, was expanded to include more radical elements in order to avoid the risk of the Parisian **insurgents** forming a rival administration. The uneasy coalition between the intellectuals who had spearheaded the ideological struggle and the workers who had risked their lives on the barricades produced an odd mix of a government. Lamartine was its Foreign Minister, with Louis Garnier-Pagès in control of the nation's finances, while radicals such as Adolphe Crémieux and Alexandre Ledru-Rollin held office as Minister of Justice and Minister of the Interior respectively.

Insurgents: People who are fighting against the government or army of their own country, usually because they want a different regime.

Policies: radicalism or reassurance?

In formulating its policies, this administration struggled to reach a compromise between satisfying the radicals' demands and reassuring the bourgeoisie. In foreign policy, its priority was to reassure the powers of Europe that the events of 1848 would not have the international repercussions of 1792. Lamartine's grandiose 'Manifesto to Europe' sought to convince them that they were dealing with a much more peaceful France than that which had given way to the temptations of conquest under Napoleon. All the same, Europe's sense of reassurance must have been undermined by the statement that France no longer felt bound by the treaties that the Bourbons had concluded in 1815. Within a few days, however, revolution had broken out in other European capitals, and most of the powers had more pressing problems on their hands than the question of revolution in France.

The financial policy of the Provisional Government was based upon compromise. In an attempt to maintain business confidence, no attack was made upon the Bank of France and all the debts of the monarchy were officially honoured. This moderate policy represented one of the

Alphonse de Lamartine (1790–1869)	**Louis Garnier-Pagès (1803–1878)**	**Adolphe Crémieux (1796–1880)**	**Alexandre Ledru-Rollin (1807–1874)**
Poet, who entered active politics in the 1830s in opposition to Louis-Philippe. Appointed Foreign Minister in the Provisional Government (1848), his political career ended with the advent of Louis Napoleon to power.	Active in the revolutions of 1830 and 1848. Served in the Provisional Government, and in the parliamentary opposition under Napoleon III. Member of the Government of National Defence (1870).	Part of the parliamentary opposition to Louis-Philippe (1842). Minister of Justice in the Provisional Government (1848). Imprisoned under Napoleon III, he was a member of the left-wing opposition in 1869, and held office in the Government of National Defence (1870).	Member of the left-wing parliamentary opposition to Louis-Philippe (1841). Organiser of the 'banquets' campaign (1846–47). Minister of the Interior in the Provisional Government (1848). In exile from 1849, he was elected to the Assembly at the establishment of the Third Republic (1871–74).

Regency: When a person is given royal authority on behalf of another. It usually applies when the monarch is a minor (under age).

Louis Blanc (1811–1882)
French socialist, influenced by the writing of St Simon. Severely critical of the monarchy of Louis-Philippe in *Histoire de dix ans* (1840). Active member of the Provisional Government (1848) and chairman of the Luxembourg Commission. In exile in England during the Second Empire, but returned to become a socialist deputy under the Third Republic.

---

1. What problems did the Provisional Government face when it came to power in France in 1848?

2. How realistic were the policies that the Provisional Government pursued during its period in power?

administration's greatest failures. It failed to arrest either the slide in share prices or the drain in gold reserves of the previous two years. The government's attempt to strengthen its financial position, by imposing a 45% tax on direct income, caused widespread resentment. It was especially unacceptable to the many small farmers to whom, given that the last remnants of the feudal system had been swept away in France a generation earlier, the government had little to offer.

The Luxembourg Commission and the 'right to work'

The Provisional Government did, however, break radical new ground in terms of domestic political reform. The very decision to found a republic, rather than to accept the **regency** that Louis-Philippe had envisaged, recalled the more extreme phases of the 'Great' revolution. It owed much, like the other domestic reforms, to the pressure of Parisian radicalism. It was followed (2 March) by the introduction of universal manhood suffrage, which instantly raised the electorate from about 240,000 to some nine million.

Most controversial were the measures taken by the administration to alleviate the prevailing social distress. The establishment of the Luxembourg Commission, an assembly of workers' delegates charged with the task of surveying social problems and suggesting solutions, was an eloquent gesture. The establishment of 'National Workshops', to provide work for the substantial number of unemployed, could have been more than a gesture. The workshops were the embodiment of Louis Blanc's theories on state intervention to guarantee the 'right to work', but they turned out to be a poor imitation. Few projects of importance were entrusted to the workshops, for fear of the damage that they might do to private businesses with their cheap labour. They achieved little other than minor public works, such as the levelling of the Champs de Mars in Paris. Nevertheless, they attracted the resentment of middle-class opinion because they represented a dangerous alternative to normal employment relationships and seemed to be using up large amounts of public money without obvious results.

11.3 Why did the events of 1848 in France end in the triumph of conservatism?

Electoral conservatism

The elections to the Constituent Assembly of the Republic, held on 23 April 1848, provided the mass of Frenchmen with their first opportunity to comment upon the events of the previous two months. Their response was unmistakably conservative. Of 880 seats, radical and socialist candidates secured about 100. Candidates supporting the ideal of monarchy secured three times that number. Why was counter-revolution succeeding revolution so rapidly? Certainly, the influence of the conservative clergy was far stronger in the provinces, as the radicals rightly complained, than that of the Provisional Government. However, it is unlikely that they persuaded many to vote against their better judgement.

Karl Marx's classic explanation of the collapse of the revolution was described in terms of class warfare. February 1848, he explained, saw a temporary alliance of middle- and working-class interests against a common enemy, which soon began to disintegrate once that enemy had fled. Although happy to see the back of Louis-Philippe, the bourgeoisie had no desire to see the end of the society that he represented.

More recent writers, although agreeing that the February coalition quickly fell apart, have not seen the causes in such clear-cut terms. Historian Georges Duveau has stressed the diversity that existed in the political views of the Parisian working classes, and has warned against treating them as a single unit. Peter Amann saw the violence of early 1848, not as a statement of coherent class interests, but as a general outburst of anger that had many causes. Common to these interpretations is the picture of the French merchant and the peasant proprietor, aware of the sudden danger to their material interests, salvaging what they could from the wreck of the monarchy.

The 'June Days'

A major clash between radicals and conservatives loomed closer throughout April and May. After a number of demonstrations against the elections to the Assembly, which many of the radicals felt were being held before the electorate was sufficiently 'educated', a mob demanding French support for the rebels in Poland invaded the Assembly on 15 May. The decisive confrontation came with the outbreak of violence in Paris known as the 'June Days'.

The immediate cause of the outburst was the decision of the government (21 June) to expel unmarried men from the National Workshops and to make plans for their closure. In response to a blatant attempt to 'pervert' the revolution, barricades were raised in many parts of Paris. Four days of bitter fighting (23–26 June) raged between insurgents and their opponents before troops, under General Cavaignac, won the first great conservative victory of this French revolution. The rebellious quarters of Paris were reduced, street by street, with the loss of about 1,500 lives. The defeat of the insurgents represented the defeat of the radical element in the revolution. Over 11,000 people were prosecuted, and Paris remained under martial law until mid-October. Much of the work of the February revolution was undone. The National Workshops and all political clubs were dissolved, censorship of the press was reimposed, and clauses such as that concerning the 'right to work' were deleted from the existing draft of the constitution.

General Louis Cavaignac (1802–1857)
Military commander in Algeria (1832) and appointed Governor-General there (1848). Minister of War in the Provisional Government, and crushed the 'June Days' rising in Paris (1848). Arrested in the course of Louis Napoleon's seizure of power (1851).

The election of Louis Napoleon Bonaparte

The triumph of conservatism in France was confirmed in December 1848, in the elections for the Republic's first president. Five of the six candidates had played some role in the events of the year, and their electoral performances clearly showed the limitations of their achievements.

- General Changarnier received 5,000 of the 7.5 million votes cast.

- Alphonse de Lamartine, whose tenure of the Foreign Ministry had lasted little more than a month, achieved 18,000 votes.

- François-Vincent Raspail received 37,000 votes and Alexandre Ledru-Rollin 370,000 votes. They were both too tainted, in the public view by their contact with radicalism, to attract many votes outside Paris.

- General Louis Cavaignac, who was second in the election with 1,448,107 votes, appealed to many as the champion of public order yet, in general, attitudes to the 'butcher of June' varied from one section of the population to another.

Another man, who had not even been present in France for the first four months of the revolution, had the dual advantages of being free from association with either radical or reactionary events earlier in the year. He

1. Which elements within the French population supported the Provisional Government, and which elements were alienated by its policies?

2. Why did the 'June Days' occur, and what effect did the disturbances have upon French politics during 1848?

also bore a name automatically linked in the minds of many Frenchmen with domestic stability and international prestige. Louis Napoleon Bonaparte had already been elected to the Assembly by four *départements* in June upon his return to France. Now he polled an overall majority by receiving 5,434,226 votes, to become the first, and only, President of the Second Republic.

The brief political history of the Second Republic further illustrates the triumph of social conservatism in France. At home, the new elections to the Assembly (May 1849) returned some 500 conservatives against 250 republicans. The most notable domestic legislation of Louis Napoleon's presidency was the so-called Falloux Law (March 1850), giving the Church powers of supervision over education in the localities. This concession to conservative, Catholic opinion had a notable parallel in foreign policy in the military expedition that overthrew the radical Roman Republic, restored the Pope to his capital, and left a French garrison as his guardian. Such measures were merely the prelude to a more lasting form of conservatism, that of the Second Empire.

11.4 Who was Louis Napoleon Bonaparte and what did he offer the French electors?

The most obvious political asset of Louis Napoleon Bonaparte in the presidential elections was his name. Born (20 April 1808) the son of Louis Bonaparte, the Emperor's brother, he was thus a nephew of the great Napoleon. Superficially, there did not seem to be a great deal more to recommend him for the high office that he achieved in 1848. He had lived much of his earlier life in Italy where he was possibly involved in the conspiracies of radical political societies, although this has never been proven. With the death of Napoleon's only legitimate son, the duc de Reichstadt (1832), he assumed the leadership of the Bonaparte dynasty. Attempts to pursue what he clearly believed to be his own and France's destiny ended in humiliating failure. Attempts to raise revolt in Strasbourg (October 1836) and Boulogne (August 1840) led, first to flight, then to imprisonment in the fortress of Ham on the Belgian border and, finally (1846), to further exile in England.

Bonaparte's image, when he returned to his native city upon the fall of Louis-Philippe, was not an attractive one. Yet the unsuccessful nature of his earlier career was one of the factors that aided him at this fateful moment. His success in 1848 owed a great deal to the support of established politicians who felt that they had little to fear from this 'mini-Napoleon', but that they might exploit his name for their own ends. 'He is a cretin,' commented Adolphe Thiers, unkindly and inaccurately, 'whom we will manage.' His very lack of any positive connection with the politics of the mid-1840s was, at this time, a recommendation. Louis Napoleon's hands were clean.

Then again, if he had achieved little in the past by direct action, Louis Napoleon had shown his worth as a propagandist. Two works, written in exile, had already sold half a million copies in France by 1848. *The Napoleonic Ideals* (written in 1839) and *The Extinction of Pauperism* (1844) jointly propounded the theory that the social and political problems of France, its economy, its international status and its domestic divisions, had only been tackled effectively in the last half century by one regime – that of the Emperor. Only he had been able to reconcile the just principles of the Revolution with the national desire for stability and order. The Napoleonic ideal, he proclaimed, was 'to reconstitute French society, overthrown by 50 years of revolution, to conciliate order and liberty, the right of the people, and the principles of law. It replaces the hereditary system of the old aristocracies by a hierarchical system, which, while securing equality, rewards merit and secures order. It disciplines democracy, and renders it an element of strength and stability.'

His electoral manifesto, published in December 1848, pledged Louis Napoleon to the reduction of taxation, the reduction of unemployment, the expansion of private economic enterprise, the freedom of the press, and the protection of the educational rights of the Church. It drew largely upon *The Napoleonic Ideals* and had the widest possible appeal to the new electorate.

An anti-Bonapartist caricature of 1848, showing Louis Napoleon, a donkey dressed in the ill-fitting uniform of the great Napoleon, being presented to the French voters.

Candidat présenté par Nicolas, appuyé par la Presse.

MAIS NON, PUISQUE C'EST LE CHAPEAU   HA ÇA!.... MAIS.... MAIS C'EST

1. Why did Louis Napoleon Bonaparte believe that his rule would benefit the people of France?

2. What elements in the French electorate supported Louis Napoleon Bonaparte, and for what reasons?

3. 'The French began 1848 with a moderate conservative regime, overthrew it, and then elected another one before the end of the year.' Explain why this happened.

11.5 Why did the movement for liberal reform achieve such success in Germany, and then collapse so rapidly?

The combination of crises in Germany

The sensational political events in France, in early 1848, impacted upon German states whose economic and political problems were subtly different. The economic crisis in the German towns displayed two

'Luddism': A form of political protest, specifically against industrial mechanisation and its effect upon employment, which took the form of attacks upon factories and machinery.

distinct characteristics. The first was the material distress that had resulted from the failure of the harvest in the countryside. In 1847, there were bread riots in Stuttgart and in Ulm, and violence in Berlin triggered by the shortage of potatoes. Secondly, German urban revolt was fuelled by the distress of traditional artisans, already under pressure from the growth of mechanised production before the depression of 1846–47 hit them. The early months of 1848 witnessed such acts of **'Luddism'** as the burning of mills in Dusseldorf, demonstrations by weavers in Chemnitz, and assaults by wagoners in Nassau upon the newly constructed railways. Factory production, too, experienced severe difficulties as investment and demand declined, and there were strikes for higher pay and shorter hours in Berlin, Leipzig and Dresden. The combination of all these economic factors was, in some cases, catastrophic.

We have already seen some of the political tensions that existed in the states of the German Confederation before 1848 (see Chapter 8). Much remained to be done in the German states that had been achieved in France a generation earlier, and historians have delivered some damning verdicts. Agatha Ramm wrote, in *Germany 1789–1919: a Political History* (1968), that Germany before 1848 'was a country where to have a political opinion was difficult, to express it almost impossible, and to join with others to promote it, conspiracy punishable by the heaviest prison sentences'. A.J.P. Taylor's view (*The Course of German History*, 1945) of the personal unfitness of the rulers of many of the German principalities is only slightly exaggerated: 'Ceaseless inbreeding, power territorially circumscribed, but within those limits limitless, produced mad princes as a normal event; and of the utterly petty princes hardly one was sane.'

In Prussia, in particular, the solidarity of the governing classes appeared to be weakened by an unusual development. The mainstay of Prussian conservatism, the landowning Junker class, found itself in an unaccustomed position in the years immediately before 1848. Their desire for the construction of an eastern railway (*Ostbahn*), linking their agricultural estates in East Prussia with markets in the major cities, had temporarily placed them in the unusual position of supporting the decision to summon an assembly which alone could grant the necessary funds. Strange and perturbed as the political scene in Prussia seemed in 1846–47, and real as the economic distress was it must be stressed that no genuine governmental crisis existed. The administration was soundly organised and in many cases, in economic matters for instance, it was pursuing far-sighted and logical policies. The finances of the state were sound, far sounder than those of the Austrian Empire. The army was well trained, well equipped and loyal. In the context of the improving harvests and falling food prices in 1848, it was likely to take more than a temporary loss of nerve on the part of the government to achieve any permanent revolution in Prussia.

The first wave of reforms

In the German states, as in much of central Europe, the news of the February revolution in Paris was the trigger that turned long-term resentment into political confrontation. 'It is impossible,' declared a leading Berlin newspaper, 'to describe the amazement, the terror, the confusion aroused here by the latest reports from Paris crowding on each other almost hourly.' And if the political society of Prussia's capital seemed shaken, what hope was there for such minor entities as Mecklenburg-Strelitz?

By the second week of March, the leaders of most German states had despaired of surviving where the King of the French had perished. Instead, they began the wholesale granting of constitutional demands. In Bavaria, King Ludwig abdicated and his successor, Maximilian II, accepted the principles of a constitutional assembly, as well as ministerial responsibility, a jury system and a free press (9 March). In Baden, all feudal obligations were abolished (10 March) and, in Würtemberg, the king renounced his hunting rights. Even Prussia could not escape. At first, Friedrich Wilhelm seemed to preserve his political position by ordering his troops not to fire upon demonstrating crowds, and by putting his name to the usual list of concessions. An outbreak of street fighting on 18 March broke his nerve and he sought to save himself by ordering the withdrawal of the army from Berlin. As a virtual prisoner of his people, he then appointed a liberal ministry led by Rhineland businessmen, Ludolf Camphausen and David Hansemann.

The Frankfurt Parliament

Liberal reforms were only one of the elements in what seemed a remarkable victory for the insurgents. On the face of it, the most spectacular concession of the rulers of Prussia, Bavaria, Baden and Württemberg was their agreement to participate in the organisation of a German national parliament, a vehicle for the unification of the nation. At the height of the liberal success, the first steps towards such a body were already being taken. A group of enthusiasts, mainly academics and predominantly from the southern states, resolved at a meeting in Heidelberg (5 March) to summon a preliminary parliament (*Vorparlament*) which would, in turn, supervise elections to a German representative assembly. Thus this assembly had its origins, not in the exercise of any state's power, but in the absence of power, in a vacuum characteristic of March 1848. The *Vorparlament*, in its five-day session, decided that elections should be by universal male suffrage and **proportional representation**, with one delegate for every 50,000 Germans.

Proportional representation: A system of voting in elections. Each political party is represented in parliament in proportion to the number of people who vote for it.

The assembly that finally gathered in St Paul's Church in Frankfurt (18 May) was predominantly elected by those middle classes preoccupied with constitutions and parliaments. It was a classic illustration of Lewis Namier's description of 1848 as 'the revolution of the intellectuals'. Of 830 delegates who sat there at one time or another, 275 were state officials, 66 were lawyers, 50 were university professors and another 50 were schoolmasters. Only one came from a truly peasant background, and only four from the artisan classes. Relatively united in social origins and in their view of the Germany that they did not want, they were to discover, like most revolutionaries, that the construction of a new state and society is a much more difficult process.

The failure of the Frankfurt Parliament

Historians have dealt more harshly with the German liberals who dominated the Frankfurt Parliament than with any comparable group in the 19th century. Historians of the Left have followed Karl Marx and Friedrich Engels in condemning them for not taking violent action to overthrow existing power structures. In the decades immediately following unification, such 'Prussian' historians as Treitschke blamed them for their opposition to Germany's 'best hope', the Prussian monarchy. Foreign commentators, such as Lewis Namier and A.J.P. Taylor, have seen them as ideological frauds, pretending to favour democratic reform, but ultimately interested only in German power. Indeed, the failure of the Frankfurt Parliament was almost total, not because it failed to use its opportunities, but because the opportunities of 1848 were illusory.

The first set of difficulties faced by the Frankfurt delegates concerned the eventual nature of the state that they hoped to create. What would be the constitutional framework of the united Germany? The majority of deputies felt it was of great importance to recruit the princes as supporters of a monarchical Germany, rather than risk the radical politics that accompanied republicanism. Two other issues followed from this.

● Which of Germany's royal houses should predominate?

● What should be the relationship of the Parliament with the older authorities within Germany?

Conservatives preferred to see the constitutional decisions of the Parliament implemented by the princes in their individual states, while more radical spirits wished to see princely authority overridden by that of the Parliament.

In June, under the influence of its president, Heinrich von Gagern, the Parliament took the decision to claim executive power, superior to that of any state or to that of the Federal Diet. They also decided to entrust the leadership of Germany to the greatest of the German families, the Habsburgs, in the person of the Archduke John. The Parliament was thus moving towards a 'Greater Germany' (*Grossdeutschland*), which included all German speakers, rather than a 'Lesser Germany' (*Kleindeutschland*), which excluded the Germans of the Habsburg territories. That ambition was to be thwarted by the recovery of Habsburg authority in the Austrian Empire, in October and November 1848.

The challenge of non-German nationalism

A second set of problems arose from the fundamental weakness of the Frankfurt Parliament, its total lack of material power. Lacking an army of its own, it was bound to depend upon the goodwill of the major German princes for the most basic functions of government, such as the collection of taxes. Like other constitutional bodies set up in 1848, this assembly was only, ultimately, able to survive if the regimes that it sought to replace voluntarily handed over their power.

In particular, the Parliament faced two challenges that it was powerless to resolve. Firstly, various nationalities had laid claim to territories seen by the Parliament as part of the Fatherland. In March 1848, Denmark occupied Schleswig and Holstein. This was closely followed by Frantšek Palacky's declaration that Bohemia belonged to the Czech nation, and by a rising by Polish nationalists in Posen. The initial sympathy of the assembly for the aspirations of other nationalists evaporated when those aspirations seemed to threaten German power. Seeing no other alternative to the diminution of Germany, the assembly applauded many of the selfish acts of their erstwhile enemies. The victory of the Austrian army in Prague, and the suppression of the Poles by the Prussian army both received widespread approval. When foreign pressure forced the Prussian army, in action against the Danes, to accept a disadvantageous armistice (August 1848), the assembly, for all its harsh words, could only confirm its impotence by accepting the settlement.

The challenge of working-class radicalism

The other challenge came from the undeveloped and incoherent working-class movement. In the last months of 1848, German workers' organisations were beginning to react to the failure of the Frankfurt Parliament to solve working-class problems. While the Frankfurt liberals devoted themselves to the abstract task of drawing up a constitution, separate and independent workers' assemblies met in Hamburg and in Frankfurt itself, making economic demands against the middle-class

---

Frantšek Palacky (1798–1876)
Czech nationalist, and author of *History of Bohemia*. President of the Pan-Slav Congress (1848). Opponent of the Dual Monarchy in Austro-Hungary after 1867.

interests of the delegates in St Paul's Church. They requested the limitation of factory production, restrictions upon free economic and industrial growth, and the protection of the privileges of the old artisan guilds. When barricades went up in Frankfurt (18 September) and disturbances followed in Baden, Hesse-Cassel and Saxony, the Parliament's only recourse was to use Prussian and Austrian troops once more.

The recovery of Prussia

The emergence of the national issue and the growing fear of working-class violence were two of the factors that paved the way for the triumph of conservatism in Germany. The third factor was the steady recovery of nerve by the King of Prussia. By August, Prussia's own parliament had demonstrated its radicalism by seeking to abolish the feudal, legal and financial privileges of the Junker class. This had brought the Junkers into open opposition to the liberals. Encouraged by their support and by increasing evidence of the reliability of the army, Friedrich Wilhelm dismissed his liberal ministers and ordered his troops back into Berlin. In December, he first banished and then dissolved the Prussian parliament. The anti-nationalist stance of the Austrian Habsburgs in March 1849 gave the Frankfurt assembly little alternative but to offer the crown of Germany to the only other German powerful enough to wear it. Friedrich Wilhelm's refusal to 'pick up a crown from the gutter' sealed Frankfurt's failure.

Much has been written about the Prussian king's motives. Certainly, his distaste for constitutional monarchy was genuine, but there is also evidence that he harboured a deeply traditional belief in Austria's divinely ordained leadership of Germany and its princes. With the withdrawal of Prussian and Austrian delegates from Frankfurt, the Parliament was already a shell when it moved to Stuttgart to await its dispersal by Prussian troops (June 1849). Although permanent agrarian reforms survived from the events of 1848–49, the liberal, constitutional revolution had achieved nothing. Indeed, we may even accept the judgement of A.J.P. Taylor that there was, in no realistic sense, a political revolution of any kind in Germany in 1848. 'There was merely a vacuum in which the liberals postured until the vacuum was filled.'

1. What were the main aims of German liberals in 1848?

2. To what extent would you agree with the judgement that German liberals failed in 1848 because their aims were unrealistic, and because the existing German governments were strong and healthy?

11.6 In what respects was the crisis in the Austrian Empire more dangerous than in other parts of Europe?

Political and economic weaknesses within the Empire

Nowhere was the conjunction of different economic and political crises so dangerous as in the Austrian Empire. In 1848–49, the Empire was threatened not merely with radical constitutional change, but with the very collapse of its complex, multinational structure. Historian Hans Kohn has described the period of Austrian history between 1815 and 1848 as 'an era of stagnation'. Those years had witnessed some half-hearted attempts by Metternich at political and fiscal reform, thwarted by the conservatism of the Emperor. Latterly, the political scene had been dominated by rivalry and jealousy, notably between Metternich and his rival, Count Kolowrat. The accession, in 1835, of the Emperor Ferdinand, physically sick and mentally abnormal, merely ensured that the political malaise spread to the pinnacle of the state system.

Economically, the Austrian Empire had produced nothing to rival Prussia's policy of tariff reform and industrial modernisation. Austria and

326 The Revolutions of 1848 and 1849

Hungary together produced 710,000 tons of coal in 1845, compared with the 5.6 million tons produced by the member states of the *Zollverein*. They made only modest and halting progress in railway construction. Although Austrian cities were, as yet, spared the horrors of industrialisation, they had little to offer those peasants driven from the countryside by **agrarian depression**. Urban unrest in Vienna or Budapest owed more to the lack of industrial employment than to the hardships that such employment entailed. Also, the government imposed, or attempted to impose, an intellectual straitjacket upon the Empire. 'I do not need scholars,' an earlier Emperor had informed his schoolteachers in 1821, 'but obedient citizens. Whosoever serves me must teach what I command.'

Agrarian depression: Economic depression (unemployment and falling wages) affecting agricultural production in the countryside.

The challenge of nationalism within the Empire

The rise of nationalism gave the Austrian crisis a distinctive flavour of its own for, in a state with so much racial diversity, such doctrines were always likely to be explosive. Although Germans dominated the politics and commerce of the Empire, they constituted only a little less than a quarter of its population. Of the total, nearly 20% were Hungarians, about 7% were Italians, 6% Romanians, and 45% Slavs. This last section then subdivided into a bewildering variety that included Czechs, Slovaks, Serbs, Ruthenes, Poles and Croats.

The question of national identity and the awareness of national cultures had come to prominence only relatively recently. At the beginning of the century, vernacular languages were largely confined to the peasant populations, with the business of the provincial assemblies, or Diets, conducted in Latin. In 1840, Hungarian nationalists succeeded in replacing Latin by **Magyar** as the official language of their Diet. Over the next four years, Magyar also became established in legal and educational usage. Other languages made headway in literary contexts, as in the publication of Jungmann's Czech dictionary, Palacky's history of the Czechs and Preseren's Slovene poetry. Otherwise, the aims of these national minorities varied. Some, such as the Czechs, aimed for improved status within the Empire. Others, such as the Italian nationalists, hoped to secede from the Empire to form part of a larger, independent nation. In Hungary, there was a significant increase in political tension in the late 1830s and early 1840s with the rise of a radical, nationalist journalist, Lajos Kossuth. Where moderate nationalism, under Count Széchényi, had previously aimed at cultural and economic advance within the Empire, Kossuth demanded far more. His aims were administrative autonomy and parliamentary rule for Hungary. His method was to win the support of the Hungarian gentry for the revival of the old Hungarian state by appealing to their anti-Slav interests and prejudices.

Magyar: Official language of the Hungarians.

The fall of Metternich

As had been the case in Germany, the news of the February revolution in Paris triggered political revolt in Austria. Middle-class liberals, student radicals and elements of the Viennese working class joined together in street demonstrations and in the presentation of petitions to the Emperor in the first weeks of March. On 13 March, clashes with regular troops led to loss of life. The Emperor, who had already lost his wits, now lost his nerve. Later that day, the 1848 revolutionaries gained their most notable 'scalp', with the resignation of the Imperial Chancellor, Klemens von Metternich. Two elements seem to have combined in the fall of the great champion of European conservatism. Some historians, such as the Frenchman M. Pouthas, saw fear as the main motive within the Austrian court. They portray Metternich, like Guizot in Paris, as a victim sacrificed to save the rest of the establishment.

Confrontation across a barricade in the streets of Vienna in May 1848

For the Austrian, G. von Poelnitz, the personal antipathy of such rivals as Kolowrat played a greater role, and the popular disturbances provided an opportunity for the pursuit of personal vendettas. The difference in interpretation is important, for what could be seen as the most sensational event of early 1848, takes on far less significance if it was merely the result of temporary divisions within the governing elite of the Empire.

With the departure of Metternich into exile, Ferdinand, like Friedrich Wilhelm, preferred concessions to flight. In April, he conceded freedom of the press, and gave permission for a constitution for the German-speaking areas of the Empire. The following month, he promised a constituent assembly based upon universal manhood suffrage and accepted the arming of a volunteer National Guard in Vienna.

Reform in Hungary

It was inevitable that the collapse of Imperial willpower would encourage opposition in the provinces of the Empire. Indeed, the Hungarian Diet meeting at Pressburg (Bratislava) had begun the formulation of its demands ten days before the fall of Metternich. These demands crystallised into the so-called March Laws, a mixture of classic liberal demands with more specifically nationalist ones. Freedom of the press, equality of taxation, equality before the law, and freedom of religion stood alongside the demand for the removal of all non-Hungarian troops from Hungarian territory. In the countryside, all remnants of serfdom were to be abolished, as was the practice of *robot*, the compulsory labour owed by many peasants to their landlords. Further, it must be understood that when Kossuth and his supporters spoke of 'Hungary' they envisaged, not merely a state embracing those areas where Magyar was spoken, but all those territories that had been part of the medieval Kingdom of Hungary. Transylvania, Croatia and Ruthenia could thus expect no Hungarian sympathy for their own cultural or national aspirations. On 11 April, Ferdinand conceded all the demands of the Hungarian Diet and effectively accepted the establishment of an independent Hungarian state.

Bohemia and Austro-Slavism

Pan-German: The policy which dictates that all those of German racial origin should be united in a single German state. This naturally involved the union of Germany with those parts of the Austro-Hungarian Empire whose population was ethnically German.

1. Which areas of the Austrian Empire were most affected by the demands of local nationalists?

2. In what ways did the demands and expectations of the revolutionaries in the Austrian Empire differ from one another?

In Prague, the second great centre of nationalist unrest, confidence in national strength was less pronounced. The Pan-Slav Congress which assembled there (2 June) chose, not the path of national independence, but that which became known as 'Austro-Slavism'. This centred upon the view that the best course for the Slav peoples of the Empire lay within a reformed, yet intact, Habsburg Empire. Outside, they would merely fall prey to the selfish desires of the Germans and the Russians. Indeed, Palacky's refusal to accept a seat at the **Pan-German** Frankfurt Parliament was a landmark in the Czechs' claim for the recognition of their own national identity. 'If the Austrian Empire did not exist', he concluded, 'it would be necessary to create it' for the safety of the minor Slav nationalities.

Thus the demands from Prague were that the Czech language should have equal status with German, that the *robot* should be abolished, and that there should be what Palacky called the 'peace, the liberty and the right of my nation'. They did not include the demand for an independent Czech state. Austro-Slavism represented an impossible paradox. It depended upon the weakness of the Viennese government for its success, and upon the voluntary dismantling of absolutism by the Habsburgs. Yet it trusted in Habsburg strength for protection against German or Russian domination. While it illustrates the high hopes of 1848, it also provides a classic example of the chronically weak foundations upon which these hopes rested.

11.7 How was the Austrian government able to re-establish its authority?

Radical defeat in Prague and Vienna

Alfred von Windischgrätz (1787–1862)
Entered Austrian army in 1804. Military commander of Bohemia (1840–48). Successful against insurgents in Prague and Vienna (1848). Captured Budapest (1849) but was unable to crush the Hungarian rising, and was recalled to Vienna in disgrace.

The first major success of the counter-revolution in 1848 occurred in Prague. As even the Czechs seemed convinced of their own weakness it is scarcely surprising that those commanding the undefeated Austrian forces in the north moved towards the same conclusion. In reaction to renewed radical and student violence in the city (13 June), General Windischgrätz took the decision to bombard Prague. Within three days, the city was in his hands. Not only was the resistance of the insurgents ineffectual, but they found themselves largely without sympathy in the outside world. The hostility of the Frankfurt Parliament was repeated in the violent language of radicals in Vienna. 'The victory over the Czech party in Prague,' rejoiced the journal *Friend of the People*, 'is and remains a joyful event.' The events in Prague serve well to illustrate the fatal isolation of each of the 1848 risings from all of the others.

The revolution in Vienna suffered from a steady decline rather than from a sudden collapse. By the time of Windischgrätz's triumph, the Viennese radicals had achieved some notable triumphs of their own. They had formed a constituent assembly and a National Guard, and there was more to come. In September, the assembly struck at the social basis of rural Austria by abolishing the *robot* and the hereditary rights of the nobility in local administration. These should perhaps be seen as the major lasting changes wrought by the 'Year of Revolutions' in the Empire. The end of the practice of *robot* had a ruinous effect on the lesser gentry, who lost a valuable source of cheap labour. This breaking of the power of the local landlords, although it was not the direct aim of the assembly, was to confirm the subsequent dominance of the central authority of the Imperial government.

Johann Radetzky (1766–1858)
Austrian military commander. Commander-in-Chief in Lombardy (1831). Defeated Piedmontese at Custoza and recaptured Milan (1848). Victor at Novara (1849). Military Governor of Lombardy and Venetia (1849–57).

Fatal weaknesses were already becoming evident in the position of the revolutionaries. The dynasty remained in power and continued to be served by ministers of the 'old school'. The Imperial army was not only undefeated, but actually victorious in the provinces. Worse, divisions began to appear in the ranks of the revolutionaries themselves. Some elements among the German-speaking radicals favoured the cutting of links with the non-German provinces of the Empire. They aimed at a form of *grossdeutsch* unity with the other states represented at the Frankfurt Parliament. Others wished to see the territorial preservation of the Empire and applauded the victories of Alfred von Windischgrätz and Johann Radetzky.

Count Josef Jellacic (1801–1859)
Croat soldier and politician. An enthusiastic supporter of Habsburg authority, he played a major role, as Governor of Croatia, in the suppression of the 1848 risings.

The discussion of a constitutional settlement aggravated the divisions. Many liberals remained content with a constitutional monarchy of the sort recently overthrown in Paris, while stricter radicals sought a republic. The emergence of workers' organisations in Vienna revived memories of the 'June Days' in Paris, and in August demonstrations were broken up by the middle-class National Guard. The government's decision (3 October) to declare war on the Hungarian rebels brought matters to a head. Radical demonstrations in favour of Hungary, in which the Minister of War was lynched, emboldened the conservatives to treat Vienna as Prague had been treated. The task was harder and bloodier, but by the end of the month and at a cost of 3,000 to 5,000 lives, Generals Windischgrätz and Jellacic had reconquered Austria's capital.

Count Felix von Schwarzenberg (1800–1852)
Austrian statesman. Ambassador to Naples (1846–48), and active in the re-establishment of Austrian authority in Italy in 1848–49. Appointed chief minister of the Emperor (November 1848), he was active in disbanding the Constituent Assembly and restoring imperial authority. Also active in negotiating Russian intervention against the Hungarian uprising in 1849.

The re-establishment of Imperial government

The regeneration of conservative government was steadily consolidated. In November, a new government, under Count Schwarzenberg, took office. In December, as the living symbol of regeneration, the 18-year-old

Franz Josef ascended the Imperial throne upon his uncle's abdication. The new administration was firmly based upon realism and upon power politics for, in A.J.P. Taylor's words, 'Schwarzenberg was too clever to have principles, Franz Josef too blinkered to understand them.' The fate of the constituent assembly well illustrates the methods of Austria's new masters. Since October, it had lingered in exile in the Moravian town of Kremsier deliberating over an Austrian constitution. By the completion of its task (1 March 1849), Schwarzenberg felt strong enough to do without an assembly, but not without a constitution. Within three days of the formulation of the 'Kremsier Constitution' he had dissolved the assembly and allowed the Minister of the Interior, Count Stadion, to introduce an Imperial constitution of a different kind. While it permitted a parliament based upon universal manhood suffrage, it stressed the indivisible nature of the Empire. Although Hungary received recognition of its linguistic separatism, it, and all other regions of the Empire, could now expect only direct government from Vienna.

Schwarzenberg's reaction to the events of 1848–49 has significance for the history of the Habsburg Empire in the later 19th century. It suggests that he had learned much about the weaknesses of the nationalist movements, but little from the weaknesses of his own state. Therefore, while the 1850s were a decade of economic modernisation and reform in France, in Prussia and Piedmont-Sardinia, they witnessed only the consolidation of political conservatism in Austria. There was to be no Austrian Cavour, and not even an Austrian equivalent of Louis Napoleon. By the end of the century, as historian Peter Jones suggests in *The 1848 Revolutions* (1981), Austria would have paid a heavy price for that fact. 'Austria's revival was illusory. The survival of the Habsburg monarchy owed more to individuals – Radetzky, Windischgrätz, Schwarzenberg, Franz Josef – than to any revitalisation of the system of government.'

The reconquest of Hungary

The most important factor leading the government to grant constitutional concessions was the need to maintain a degree of general support while Hungary remained undefeated. From October 1848, the policy of the Imperial government towards Hungarian autonomy had been one of open hostility. Three methods of attack suggested themselves. Firstly, tacit support for the Slav minorities alienated by Kossuth's 'March Laws' became active and overt. The advance of the Croat General Jellacic into southern Hungary was, however, short-lived (September 1848) and unsuccessful. Secondly, the hope that Windischgrätz might win a third counter-revolutionary success with Austrian troops proved ill-founded. He moved slowly against a divided Hungarian leadership and was eventually defeated at Isaszeg, in early April 1849. A week later, in response to Schwarzenberg's constitution, a Hungarian republic was proclaimed, and the Viennese government was forced into the extreme measure of appealing for foreign aid. Russia's response to the Austrian appeal owed as much to fears that the Hungarian example would be imitated in Poland as it did to conservative principles, but it proved decisive. The three-pronged attack of Jellacic, Windischgrätz and 140,000 Russians ended the life of the Hungarian republic at Vilagos (13 August 1849) and opened a period of bloody repression and retribution. The official annulment of the Hungarian constitution, in 1851, put the final touch to the conservative triumph in the Austrian Empire.

1. What, if anything, had revolutionaries within the Austrian Empire achieved by the end of 1849?

2. Why did the Austrian Empire survive the revolutions of 1848–1849?

3. To what extent was the survival of the Austrian Empire in 1848–1850 due to the weakness of the revolutionaries?

11.8 Why did Italian nationalists consider the prospects of Italian freedom and statehood so promising in 1846–1848?

The economic and political state of Italy: the beginnings of conservative reform?

If the initial outbreak of violence in France came as a surprise, the disturbances in Italy were wholly predictable. The political and economic crises in the Italian states had roots going back to the restoration of 1815 and, in many cases, far beyond. Economic hardship in Italy was the result, not merely of a temporary, cyclical crisis, but of long-standing backwardness.

Radical and nationalist politics also had a long history in Italy (see Chapter 11), yet there were some signs, in the years immediately before 1848, that the time might be ripe for change. Traditionally, Italy's political regimes have been portrayed as reactionary, out of date and as resistant to change as the Italian economy had been. While there is much evidence to support such an image, it is also possible that the years before 1848 witnessed changes that might have offered hope to more moderate Italian reformers. Recent research has suggested that some of Italy's conservative regimes were gradually coming to realise the advantages of modernisation and efficiency, as the mid-century approached. Metternich himself seems to have realised the advantages of combining legitimist principles (see page 341) with the greater efficiency that the Napoleonic administrations had achieved.

Vittorio Fossombroni in Tuscany and Luigi de Medici in Naples provide examples of ministers who attempted to implement such policies. Above all, a revisionist study by Narcisso Nada has emphasised the extent of the legal, administrative, financial and military reforms brought about by Charles Albert in Piedmont long before he placed himself at the head of the national cause. Seen in this light, 1848 does not represent a clean break with past Italian history, and the actions of both Charles Albert and Pope Pius IX may be seen as part of a longer process of 'conservative reform'. The reformist policies of Cavour (see Chapter 9) may be seen to have had a much older pedigree.

For the churchman Vincenzo Gioberti, however, the future of Italy lay not with Piedmont, but with the Papacy. Gioberti, in his work *Of the Moral and Civil Primacy of the Italians* (*Del Primato Morale e Civile degli Italiani*), published in 1843, had portrayed the Papacy and the Catholic Church as the chosen agents of Italian national revival. He condemned revolutionary means towards unity, made no specific mention of the expulsion of the Austrians from the peninsula, and advocated a confederation of Italian states under the presidency of the Pope. The scheme certainly had the merits of preserving the local status of the individual princes and of placing the Austrians in the potentially embarrassing position of opposing the head of their own Church. On the other hand, up to 1846, there had seemed little prospect of finding a Pope willing to play the role designed for him by Gioberti and his **'neo-guelph'** supporters. Abruptly, however, in 1846, it seemed that Gioberti might have hit upon the right path.

'Neo-guelph': In medieval Italy the Guelph faction supported the political claims of the Papacy, as opposed to the Ghibelline faction, which favoured the rival claims of the Holy Roman Empire. Because Vincenzo Gioberti and his followers also placed the Pope in a position of political prominence, they were regarded as the 'new Guelphs'.

The election of Pius IX

It is misleading to refer to the events in Italy as part of 'the revolutions of 1848' for that particular phase of Italian history began in 1846 with the sensational election of Cardinal Giovanni Mastai-Ferretti as Pope. Under his chosen title of 'Pius IX', he was one of the key figures in the events of the next two years.

The election of Pope Pius IX appeared to transform overnight the prospects of success for that form of federal unity envisaged by Gioberti and the neo-guelphs. In his initial burst of political reform Pius **amnestied** political prisoners and accepted a measure of non-clerical participation in government. In 1847 he put forward the suggestion of an Italian customs union. When Austria, thrown off balance by this 'liberal' Pope, dropped the broad hint of establishing a garrison at Ferrara (July 1847) within Papal territory, Pius protested so vigorously that he became a national hero for such an anti-Austrian gesture. For all his subsequent failure to lead the Italian cause to success, the election of Pius had a stimulating effect upon Italian politics. 'It must have seemed,' wrote the historian G. Berkeley, in *Italy in the Making, 1815–1848* (1940), 'as if the chief anti-nationalist stronghold of [the nationalists'] opponents had suddenly hoisted their own *tricolor*.'

Charles Albert and Piedmont

The second key figure of these years in Italy was Charles Albert, King of Piedmont since 1831. Italian nationalist historians in the intervening century have created a 'legend of Charles Albert', gallantly sacrificing his own interests, even his own throne, in the national cause. Today it is more acceptable to view him either as 'a romantic without the willpower to transform his vision into reality' (as did the Italian A. Omodeo) or like Derek Beales, in *The Risorgimento and the Unification of Italy* (1981), as a thorough conservative.

1. What did Italian nationalists hope for in 1848 (a) from Pope Pius IX and (b) from Charles Albert of Piedmont-Sardinia?

2. How convincing is the argument that events in Italy in 1848 owed more to traditional Italian politics than to revolutionary events elsewhere in Europe?

Certainly, Italian conservatism appeared to be in crisis even before the rising in Paris. In January 1848, patriotic middle-class Italians staged a 'tobacco strike', giving up smoking in order to deprive the Austrians of the revenue from their tobacco duty. On 12 January, Palermo, in Sicily, rose in revolt against government from Naples. In February and March, the rash of new constitutions began to affect Italy too. Tuscany received one from its grand duke (11 February), and Naples from its king. Even the Pope could not avoid the fashion (4 March). Also in March, Austrian troops were expelled from Milan and Venice after several days of street fighting. Charles Albert did not stop at the granting of a constitution. Less than three weeks later, he committed Piedmont to war against the apparently disintegrating Austrians, in support of the risings in Lombardy and Venetia. With reluctant initial support from Naples and the Papacy, Charles Albert had at least the superficial appearance of leading the greatest bid in modern Italian history for freedom and nationhood.

11.9 How was Austria able to reassert its conservative influence over Italy?

The defeat of Piedmont

For all the theories and ideologies of the previous decades, the chance for nationalist action in Italy had been provided by the disruption of the European *status quo* and, especially, by the distraction of the Austrian armed forces. The return of European stability, and the recovery of the Austrian government spelled the doom of Italian freedom. A month after the triumph of Windischgrätz in Prague, the Piedmontese army met the forces of Marshal Radetzky at Custoza (25 July 1848). The Papacy and the King of Naples had already withdrawn their troops, and defeat badly undermined Piedmontese morale. Although the army survived largely intact, the pessimism of the generals and Charles Albert's own fear of radical activity at home led to retreat from Lombardy.

Renewed pressures upon the king only led to another defeat at Austrian hands at Novara (23 March 1849). The price paid, this time, was the permanent removal of Charles Albert from political life through his abdication in favour of his son, Victor Emmanuel. In addition, Austria imposed an indemnity of 75 million lire upon Piedmont. That it retained its territorial integrity was due mainly to the European objections that would have been raised to any tampering with this important 'buffer' zone on France's borders. Charles Albert's proud boast that 'Italy will do it herself' (*Italia fara da se*) had proved absolutely empty.

The flight of Pius IX

Confidant: A person with whom people can discuss private problems and other secret matters.

The war had also served to demonstrate the limitations of Pius IX as a leader of the national cause. Leading a confederation of Italian states was one thing. To lead one Catholic state against another was quite a different matter. Pius' **confidant**, G. Montanelli, put the kindest interpretation upon the Pope's motives. 'As an Italian he wanted to see the foreign invaders driven out of the country, but as Pope – as the universal Father – he could never declare a war of independence against Austria.' A more recent historian, E.L. Woodward, has interpreted the whole pretence of liberal-national leadership as a piece of confused thinking. 'How could the **Sovereign Pontiff** become a constitutional ruler? Who could be responsible for the actions of the Vicar of God on earth?' Nevertheless, Pius continued to work with his constitutional government until November. Then he fled Rome for the safety of Naples. With his flight, died the last hope of the Papacy fulfilling the role that Gioberti had mapped out for it.

Sovereign Pontiff: A sovereign is the person who is regarded as having the highest level of authority; the Pontiff is the Pope.

The defeat of radicalism

'The royal war is over, the war of the people begins', declared Mazzini in a national appeal in August 1848. The flight of the Pope paved the way for a second, equally unsuccessful, phase in the struggles of 1848–49, the republican phase. In February 1849, a Roman Republic was proclaimed to fill the vacuum left by Pius. With Mazzini providing its political inspiration, and Giuseppe Garibaldi conducting its military defence, the Republic represented the pinnacle of radical aspirations. Its decrees, calling for the distribution of Church lands to the peasantry and for the public housing of the poor, could not offset its weaknesses. It was ravaged by inflation, starved of support from other quarters of Italy, and subjected to the combined hostility of France and Austria. After a heroic defence, the Republic was defeated, in June 1849, and the presence thereafter of a French garrison in Rome strengthened foreign interest in Italy's future.

Meanwhile, with the defeat of Piedmont, both Venice and Tuscany had gone their respective ways. Under the leadership of Daniele Manin, Venice once more declared itself a Republic, as it had been until the Napoleonic invasion. It resisted Austrian siege warfare, with its horrors of bombardment, cholera and starvation, until late August 1849. Tuscan radicals expelled their Grand Duke, in February 1849, but could not do the same to the Austrian forces that came to restore him in April.

The combination of circumstances in Italy in 1848–49 made those years seem particularly auspicious for the cause of Italian freedom. Yet what did it all achieve? Firstly, we find the famous judgement of G.M. Trevelyan that 1848 was 'the turning point at which modern history failed to turn'. Then we have the judgement of the patriot, Luigi Settembrini, that 'this generation made Italy', and that the example of 1848 was 'the point at which we became Italians, felt ourselves united and gathered together under a single standard'. We must conclude that,

1. *What effect did the events of 1848–49 have on the political credibility of (a) the Papacy and (b) the Piedmontese monarchy?*

2. *To what extent is it true that the balance of power in Italian politics was the same after the revolutions of 1848–49 as it had been before?*

although the rebels of 1848 achieved nothing material in Italy, except for the Piedmontese constitution, the future course of Italian history was significantly altered. The refusal of Pius IX to put himself at the head of the national cause, and his conservative response to the events in Rome, killed the hopes of Gioberti and the neo-guelphs.

The failure of radical republicanism demonstrated once more its various faults: the failure of its various advocates to co-operate with one another, and its impotence in the face of opposition from a major power. Leopold II, Grand Duke of Tuscany, and Ferdinand of Naples had shown their true colours by refusing to co-operate with Charles Albert, and much of northern Italy was more firmly than ever under the control of Austria.

The one exception to this catalogue of gloom was the state of Piedmont-Sardinia, whose king had embraced a constitution and staked his soldiers' lives and his own crown upon the Italian cause. Italian nationalists were not likely to forget those actions. The future of Italy, as the next two decades were to prove, lay with Piedmont-Sardinia.

11.10 Is it true that the European revolutions of 1848 achieved nothing?
A CASE STUDY IN HISTORICAL INTERPRETATION

In the immediate aftermath of the 1848 revolutions and of their suppression, the French socialist Pierre-Joseph Proudhon admitted that his cause had been utterly defeated: 'we have been beaten and humiliated. We have all been scattered, imprisoned, disarmed and gagged. The fate of European democracy has slipped from our grasp.' A century later, the British historian G.M. Trevelyan wrote that '1848 was the turning point at which modern history failed to turn'. Such conclusions, 100 years apart, have helped to establish a strong historical consensus that the 'Year of Revolutions' produced no worthwhile social or political change.

Yet both of these commentators considered the revolts from a specific, ideological viewpoint, and both reached such pessimistic conclusions because the revolts did not produce the results that they hoped for. Proudhon believed and hoped that the time was ripe for the advance of true popular democracy in Europe. Trevelyan, on the other hand, interpreted the history of western Europe largely as a march towards parliamentary democracy. For him, the undermining of the Frankfurt Parliament or of the Second Republic in France were major failures, indicating that 1848 was of little significance in the long-term political development of Europe. In the middle years of the 20th century, many other leading liberal historians, such as the Italian Benedetto Croce and the German Friedrich Meinecke, shared Trevelyan's view that in the crucial question of democratic advance 1848 had proved to be a false start. All looked for a fundamental transfer of power away from traditional, monarchical government and no such transfer had taken place. The decades that followed were the great decades of European conservative government, dominated by Bismarck, Napoleon III and Cavour.

Yet it would be wrong to believe that conservatism survived the events of 1848–49 unscathed or unchanged. European governments did not merely shrug off the events of 1848 as a bad experience that could now be forgotten, and many conservative regimes showed that they had learned valuable lessons. The most important of these was that the revolts had made it possible, even necessary, to construct new, stronger conservative coalitions. The propertied middle classes emerged from the experience of 1848 as the natural allies of the traditional governing classes, tied to them by their common fear of revolution, and by their increased appreciation of strong government. Many historians have seen this as a case of the governing classes fooling the middle classes and, thereby, gaining their support for the continuation of traditional conservatism.

Such an interpretation ignores the fact that conservative government changed significantly in many states in the 1850s and the 1860s. Such states were now governed by a coalition of propertied interests, and within that coalition it was no longer possible for the traditional rulers to ignore the interests of their allies. Thus Prussia could not dispense with its constitution and the Piedmontese constitution survived to become that of a united Italy. In France and in united Germany, it could be argued that the liberals did actually achieve many of the 'freedoms' that they had sought in 1848. There was a parliamentary constitution in both states, and the suffrage was widely available to the middle classes. It may be going too far to claim, as Peter Jones has done, in *The 1848 Revolutions* (1981), that 'the use of a democratic franchise for essentially conservative purposes was in its own way revolutionary'. It would be reasonable to reflect, on the other hand, that in France and in Germany, although the suffrage did not give the middle classes control over the government, it did force the government to pay some attention to the interests of the voters. Neither Napoleon III nor Bismarck could otherwise be certain of obtaining the election results that they desired.

If the traditional elite were the senior members of the partnership immediately after 1848, the increasing prosperity and industrial growth that took place in the subsequent decades of stability caused the initiative to move more and more towards the middle classes. Some economic historians, such as Eric Hobsbawm, in *The Age of Capital: Europe from 1848 to 1875* (1976), have pointed out that this prosperity was stimulated, in part, by the success of conservatism in 1848–49. Increased political confidence did much to restore business confidence, and contributed to the economic growth of the 1850s. At the same time, greater material prosperity reduced the demand for liberal political concessions. It can be argued that, even if this was not all the work of 1848, the conservative victory and the emergence of a new, strengthened conservative coalition were vital links in this chain of development.

This point can be further emphasised by considering the Austrian Empire. Barely surviving the disruption of 1848–50, and relying heavily upon Russian military aid, the Empire stood on the verge of two decades of decline. It did not retain the constitution that the Emperor had granted under extreme pressure, and it did not, could not, embrace the cause of nationalism. Within 20 years, it had lost its control over the affairs of Germany and of Italy, and had been forced to make substantial concessions to its own Hungarian subjects. Such was the fate of unreconstructed conservatism.

Middle-class parliamentarians were not the only beneficiaries of this new form of conservatism. In eastern Europe, labour dues and other signs of feudalism were abolished forever, in the full knowledge that such measures would discourage peasant rebellion in the future. In France, the peasantry became an important element in the new conservative coalition, and even the Kingdom of Naples introduced agricultural reforms as a means of reducing peasant radicalism.

It is hard not to regard 1848 as a significant stage in the development of European nationalism. Apparently defeated in every part of Europe in 1848, the principles of the nationalists were adopted by the existing ruling classes in many cases, and they were adopted with greater enthusiasm and with greater long-term effect. From being the preserve of the urban middle-class intelligentsia, nationalism subsequently became a means by which a state such as Prussia or Piedmont could broaden its base of domestic support and extend its own power and international status. The cause of nationalism now lay in the hands of men who could do something about it. It is also possible to argue, as Roger Price does, that the events of 1848 had done much to heighten ethnic differences and tensions within Europe, between Germans and the inhabitants of neighbouring lands, for instance, or between the racial groups that made up the population of the Habsburg Empire. Historians have interpreted this linking of nationalism with conservative government in two ways. For some, it has seemed that nationalism was taken over by the traditional rulers and that its impetus was thus diverted to serve their interests. Thus Peter Jones concludes that 'after 1848 nationalism became an instrument used by conservative politicians to justify the continuation of monarchical power and to promote war. Above all, nationalism proved a powerful force for reconciling the internal class conflicts of the state.'

Others have argued, however, that the growth of nationalism could not be controlled or diverted, and that it was, therefore, the agendas of conservative governments that had changed, from the aristocratic solidarity of 'Vienna' Europe to the self-seeking expansionism that culminated in the First World War. Clearly, such an interpretation would force us to view the events of 1848–49 as crucial formative factors in European politics in the second half of the 19th century.

It is much more difficult to decide whether 1848 can be regarded as a turning point in the development of European socialism. Certainly, it struck a cruel blow at the hopes and beliefs of most established socialist thinkers. As Peter Jones puts it, 'the 1848 revolutions destroyed the idealistic, almost mystical belief that universal suffrage would bring with it social equality.' It could be argued that these events destroyed belief in revolution, and heralded one of the calmest periods of the century. On the other hand, they convinced Karl Marx (*The Class Struggles in France*, 1850) and Friedrich Engels (*Revolution and Counter Revolution in Germany,* 1851–52) that 1848 heralded the beginning of the great **proletarian** revolution. Both drew attention to social and economic elements that were of far greater importance than the theories of such 'old women' and 'humbugs' as the Frankfurt liberals. We should probably conclude, however, that these elements were confronted by such a strong conservative alliance that several decades were to pass before they could exercise any major influence upon European politics.

Overall, the revolutions of 1848 might appear to have much greater significance if they are considered as an end, rather than as a beginning. The state system and the dominant political doctrines reaffirmed at the Congress of Vienna had frequently been challenged in the intervening 30 years. It was the outburst of 1848, however, that made it clear that the 'Vienna system' no longer served conservative interests. Thus it played a major role in ending, not only the political career of Metternich, but also the political and diplomatic system that he represented. A.J.P. Taylor, in *The Struggle for Mastery of Europe, 1848–1918* (1954), pointed out that the election of Louis Napoleon Bonaparte as President of France in 1848, and the acceptance of his *coup d'état* in 1851, proved that the Vienna Settlement was dead and buried.

Proletarian: Relating to the class of people in a country who are paid wages for work that they do with their hands.

1. Why have so many historians been convinced that nothing was achieved by the revolutions of 1848–49?

2. What arguments might be put forward to support claims that European politics were changed significantly by the events of 1848–49?

Source-based questions: Working-class discontent and the 'June Days' in Paris

SOURCE A

What will the poor man do? He will say to you, 'I have hands, brains, strength, youth. Take them all, and in exchange give me a little bread.' That is what the proletariat does and says today. But at this point you reply to the poor man, 'I have no work to give you.' What would you have him do then? The answer to all of this is very simple. Guarantee work for the poor. You will still have done very little in the cause of justice, and you will still be a long way from the reign of fraternity, but at least you will have warded off the worst perils and prevented revolt.

The government should be considered the supreme regulator of production, and should be invested with large powers in order to accomplish its task. The government should raise a loan, and use the proceeds to create social workshops in the most important branches of the nation's industry. The government being the sole founder of the social workshops, it should be the government that draws up the rules for them. These rules, debated and passed by the nation's representatives, should have the form and force of law. Work in the social workshops should be offered to all workers presenting guarantees of good behaviour.

From Louis Blanc's work, L'Organisation du Travail, *first published in 1839. This passage is taken from the fifth edition and appeared in 1848.*

SOURCE B

I have carefully noted the nature of these gatherings seen in the street over the last fortnight, of the speeches made by the ringleaders, and the fact that the manufacturers can neither get the workers back into their workshops, where there is employment for them, nor even keep those that had remained. This has led me to the conviction that a hostile organisation is behind these disorders. The alliance is organised by the delegates to the Luxembourg.

The delegates to the Luxembourg are represented by an executive committee. Besides this supreme executive council, which represents the combined interests of all the industries, each section has its own committee, which arranges for the supreme committee's decrees to be carried out.

Report of the Paris Prefect of Police, 3 June 1848

SOURCE C

The Paris workers have been overwhelmed by superior forces. They have been beaten, but it is their enemies who have been vanquished. The momentary triumph of brutal violence has been purchased with the destruction of all the deceptions and illusions of the February Revolution, with the dissolution of the whole of the old republican party, and with the fracturing of the French nation into two nations, the nation of the possessors and the nation of the workers. The tricolor republic now bears only one colour, the colour of the defeated, the colour of blood. There was no republican group of repute on the side of the people. Without leaders, without any other means than insurrection itself, the people withstood the united bourgeoisie and soldiery longer than any French dynasty, with all its military apparatus, ever withstood a fraction of the bourgeoisie united with the people.

From an article by Karl Marx in the Neue Rheinische Zeitung, *June 1848*

SOURCE D

In truth it [the violence during the 'June Days'] was not a political struggle, but a class struggle, a sort of 'servile war'. One should not only see it as brutal and blind, but as a powerful effort of the workers to escape from the necessities of their condition, and by the sword to open up a road towards that imaginary well-being that has been shown to them in the distance as a right. It was this mixture of greedy desires and false theories that engendered the insurrection and made it so formidable. These poor people had been assured that the goods of the wealthy were in some way the result of a theft committed against themselves. They had been assured that the inequalities of fortune were as much opposed to morality and the interests of society as to nature. This obscure and mistaken conception of right, combined with brute force, imparted to it an energy it would never have had on its own. One should note, too, that this terrible insurrection was not the work of a number of conspirators, but was the revolt of one whole section of the population against another.

From the Recollections *of Alexis de Tocqueville, a moderate French conservative*

Source-based questions: Working-class discontent and the 'June Days' in Paris

1. Study the Sources. Explain the following highlighted references:

(a) 'the delegates to the Luxembourg' (Source B)

(b) 'the tricolor republic' (Source C)

(c) 'the goods of the wealthy were in some way the result of a theft committed against themselves' (Source D).

2. Compare and contrast the explanations for working class discontent in Paris offered by the authors of Source B and Source D.

3. What common ground do you detect in the analyses of the 'June Days' offered by Marx (Source C) and de Tocqueville (Source D)?

4. The authors of Source A and Source C both regarded themselves as socialists. What differences are demonstrated in these sources between their respective socialist ideas?

5. 'The French radical leaders in 1848 were not primarily concerned with the interests of the urban working classes.' To what extent do these sources lead you to accept or to reject this claim?

12

France: Second Republic and Second Empire, 1848–1870

Key Issues

- *How was Louis Napoleon Bonaparte able to establish his power in France?*

- *Was Napoleon III's rule over France beneficial for most French people?*

- *Why was Napoleon III's foreign policy unsuccessful in restoring France's former greatness?*

12.1 Why did the Second Republic survive for so short a time?

12.2 What was the nature of the regime established by Louis Napoleon in 1851?

12.3 What was the economic achievement of the Second Empire?

12.4 How genuine and how consistent was the liberalisation of the Second Empire?

12.5 To what extent did Napoleon III have coherent and consistent aims in foreign policy?

12.6 To what extent did the colonial policy of the Second Empire make France an effective world power?

12.7 To what extent, and for what reasons, did France's diplomatic position become less secure in the 1860s?

12.8 Why, and with what results, did French relations with Prussia degenerate into war between 1868–70?

12.9 Historical interpretation: Napoleon III: statesman or political adventurer?

Framework of Events

1848	December: Louis Napoleon Bonaparte elected President of the Republic
1851	December: Louis Napoleon overthrows the Republic in a *coup d'état*
1852	December: Louis Napoleon is proclaimed Emperor as Napoleon III
1854	Outbreak of Crimean War
1855	September: Fall of Sevastopol
1856	Treaty of Paris brings Crimean War to an end
1858	July: Franco–Piedmontese agreement at Plombières
1859	May: French troops enter northern Italy. Battle of Magenta
	June: Battle of Solferino
	July: Agreement with Austria at Villafranca
1860	Conclusion of 'Cobden–Chevalier' trade treaty with Great Britain
1862	Beginning of French intervention in Mexico
1865	October: Franco–Prussian agreement at Biarritz
1866	Beginning of French withdrawal from Mexico
1869	Appointment of Ollivier as Prime Minister. Introduction of reform programme establishing the 'Liberal Empire'. Opening of Suez Canal
1870	July: Outbreak of Franco–Prussian War
	September: Battle of Sedan. Collapse of Second Empire and proclamation of Third Republic.

Overview

THE events of 1848 had a complex impact upon France. They were sufficiently powerful to sweep away the government of Louis-Philippe, but were unable to dislodge the conservative interests that had created and supported his government. These political groups – the landowners, the urban propertied classes, the army, the Church – quickly rallied in support of a new conservative icon. They blunted the threat of a republican government by electing Louis Napoleon Bonaparte as its President. By doing so, of course, they added a new element to the normal conservative agenda. The President's dynastic background raised the prospect of a new Napoleonic age, in which domestic stability would be enhanced by the restoration of France's international prestige and authority.

Louis Napoleon thus had a great deal to live up to, and many conflicting expectations to fulfil. Historical evaluation of the Second Empire has been complicated by the fact that historians have disagreed not only about its nature and its achievement, but also about the terms by which it should be judged. Some have argued that the regime was immoral and illegitimate from the outset, because Louis Napoleon betrayed the republican responsibilities to which he was democratically elected in 1848. Others have claimed that there was a strong consensus, in France, for the kind of order and stability that Louis Napoleon represented. They view his two decades in power as an oasis of calm in which both the economic and the political life of the country developed along moderate lines.

Two elements have to be taken into account in reaching a conclusion about the domestic achievement of the Second Empire. There can be little doubt that the French economy developed considerably in the 1850s and the 1860s, although historians have not always agreed about whether this was mainly due to enlightened government policy, or to background circumstances beyond the government's control. More controversy has surrounded the political and constitutional development of France during this period. It is now usual to divide the Second Empire into two sections: one in which government was relatively 'authoritarian' and **repressive**; and another in which greater political freedom was gradually introduced. But which of these represented the Emperor's true inclinations? Did the **liberalisation** of his later years represent a reluctant surrender to the ideals of others, or did it show an enlightened Emperor steadily eroding and modifying the entrenched conservatism that had initially brought him to power? One answer forces the historian to dismiss the Second Empire as a sterile regime, and as a temporary obstacle to the development of political liberty in France. The other allows the Empire to be viewed as an essential element in the political and economic continuity of a major European state.

Unfortunately, attempts to portray the Second Empire as a positive and successful regime are undermined by the undoubted failure of its foreign policy. While Louis Napoleon adapted his uncle's economic and constitutional ideas to suit contemporary circumstances, his vision of Europe remained rooted in the long-standing French desire to revise the Vienna Settlement. Yet the Europe in which he operated was no longer the Europe of 1815. On the one hand, Austria was less capable of playing the crucial conservative role in central Europe that the 1815 settlement had allocated to it. This fact contributed largely to the relative success of

Repressive: A form of government that denies individual freedoms and freedom of political activity, and which takes deliberate action to keep them under control.

Liberalisation: The process by which the politics, economy or society of a state becomes more liberal.

the essentially anti-Austrian policy that France pursued in the 1850s. On the other hand, the French government was no more aware than any other in Europe of Prussia's potential to usurp Austrian authority. In the 1860s, the Second Empire failed to develop either a military capability or a diplomatic system strong enough to resist the advance of Prussia. Thus, if the domestic policies of Napoleon III made an essential contribution to the stability and prosperity of modern France, his foreign policies contributed, similarly, to the isolation and diplomatic weakness that haunted France for the rest of the century.

12.1 Why did the Second Republic survive for so short a time?

The strength of French conservatism and the position of the President

The main weakness of the Second Republic in France lay in the incompatibility of its President and in the constitution by which he was bound to govern. The vast majority of the votes cast for Louis Napoleon Bonaparte in 1848 were votes for permanence, for stability and for order. These were essentially conservative principles and, by 1851, Louis Napoleon had set himself at the centre of a formidable conservative coalition. The elections of May 1849 returned an assembly in which the 'Party of Order' – a coalition of Legitimists, Orleanists and Bonapartists (see panel) – held 64% of the seats. The support of the French Catholics was assured, not only by their fear of the 'Reds', but by their approval of the French military intervention in Italy in support of the Papacy, and of the Falloux Law passed in 1850. The position of this coalition was further consolidated by the introduction of a new Electoral Law (May 1850), which reduced the **electorate** by some three million voters.

Electorate: That part of the state's population which has the right to vote in elections.

Legitimists: French royalists supporting the claim to the throne of the Bourbons, the pre-revolutionary ruling family.

Orleanists: French royalists supporting the claim to the throne of Louis-Philippe and his family.

Bonapartists: Supporters of Napoleon Bonaparte, his descendants, and his style of government. Broadly in favour of stable, prosperous government, preserving the moderate reforms of the French Revolution, but resisting the dangers of more radical social reconstruction.

The position of the President

On the other hand, the President remained saddled with a constitution specifically designed, in 1848, to prevent the emergence of a dominant Imperial figure. The President was limited to a tenure of office of only four years, and he was not eligible for re-election at the end of that period. This arrangement worried a large proportion of the French electorate as much as it concerned Louis Napoleon himself. The strength of the conservative coalition did not necessarily reflect the personal strength of the President himself, and it seemed increasingly likely that the 'Party of Order' would replace him with an Orleanist candidate when the presidency was next contested in 1852. After the experiences of 1848, however, the bulk of the propertied electorate would not necessarily welcome the renewal of such political contests. Both the President and the wealthy property owners who made up the electorate thus approached 1852 with fear – the one facing the prospect of a return to political oblivion, and the other anticipating renewed political battles, and a return to the street fighting of 1848.

The coup d'état of 1851

It is unlikely that Louis Napoleon ever considered giving up power in order to return to obscurity at the end of his four-year term. There is some truth in the charges that his personal debts made it impossible for him to turn his back upon the fruits of office. More important, though, was the mission to restore stability and prosperity in France, clearly set down in the *Napoleonic Ideals*.

'**Operation Rubicon**': The Rubicon is a river to the north of Rome. When Julius Caesar crossed it at the head of his army in 49 BC, it was an indication that he was marching on Rome in order to seize power as Emperor. 'Crossing the Rubicon' has since been taken to mean that someone has taken a decisive action that cannot be reversed.

1. How was the Second Republic transformed into the Second Empire?

2. Why was there so little support for Louis-Philippe as King in 1848 and so much for Louis Napoleon as Emperor in 1852?

There is only rough justice in the view expressed by Victor Hugo (French poet and novelist, 1802–1885) that Louis Napoleon had sworn his oath to the Republican constitution the better to destroy it, and the better to plunder the state. For some time, the President sought to extend his presidency by working within the constitution that he had sworn to implement. Forceful action was very much the last resort of a man who had consistently resisted the temptation to mount a *coup d'état* earlier in his term of office. Besides, Louis Napoleon had no desire to repeat the experience of his earlier coups. Ignoring the advice of bolder spirits such as the duc de Persigny, Louis Napoleon attempted to persuade the Assembly to amend the constitution to allow the re-election of the President. Such a change, however, required a 75% majority – the support of some 540 deputies. By July 1851, it was clear that Louis Napoleon would not overcome this constitutional obstacle and, by the last month of that year, his choice lay between yielding to the letter of the constitution or overthrowing it.

The groundwork for the eventual coup and the preparation of public opinion were thorough. Louis Napoleon had used his presidential powers to remove potential opponents, such as the commander of the Paris garrison, and had replaced them with reliable allies. Marshal Armand Saint Arnaud now commanded the troops in Paris, Charlemagne Maupas was Prefect of Police, and Charles de Morny (the President's illegitimate half-brother) was Minister of the Interior. A series of provincial tours, in the late summer and autumn, allowed Louis Napoleon to gauge public support. The date chosen was 2 December, a great 'Napoleonic' date, for it was the anniversary of the great victory at Austerlitz in 1805. The code-name, '**Operation Rubicon**', also had Imperial overtones. Seventy-eight police officers, unaware that they were part of a concerted plot, each arrested a prominent member of the opposition. The dissolution of the Assembly was announced, and was enforced next day by Saint Arnaud's troops. The casualty list, by 4 December, stood at 215, and 27,000 arrests had been made, of whom some 9,000 were eventually sentenced to deportation, mainly to Algeria.

The effect of the *coup d'état* was twofold. Firstly, in general, it went smoothly and was easily accepted. 'If the *coup d'état* of December 2nd was a crime,' F.A. Simpson concludes, in *Louis Napoleon and the Recovery of France 1848–1856* (1965), 'then France was its accomplice rather than its victim.' This was borne out by the results of the plebiscite held on 21 December, when 7.5 million out of 8 million voters cast a 'Yes' vote in approval of Louis Napoleon's action. The President was delighted and relieved. 'More than 7 million votes have just absolved me,' he told the committee that had organised the plebiscite, 'by justifying an act that had no other aim than to spare our country, and perhaps Europe, from years of trouble and misfortune.' Secondly, in Paris the margin in favour of the President was only 133,000, with 80,000 abstaining. These figures indicated that a centre of opposition had been created there that Louis Napoleon would never overcome.

12.2 What was the nature of the regime established by Louis Napoleon in 1851?

Presidential powers

The first concern of the transformed President, having destroyed the constitution of the Second Republic, was to dictate to the French a new constitution free from the obstructions of 'parliamentarians'. It was an unashamedly Napoleonic constitution. 'I have taken as a model,' Louis Napoleon explained, 'the political institutions which have, since the beginning of the century, consolidated a society which has been disrupted, and raised France to a high degree of prosperity and greatness. Why should we not adopt the political institutions of that period?' The constitution granted the President absolute power for a period of ten years. Although he was 'responsible before the French people', and therefore not 'absolute' in the old monarchical sense, he alone could initiate legislation, or conclude treaties of peace or war. He commanded the armed forces and the **civil service**, and could, if the occasion demanded, govern by decree. He also appointed or dismissed ministers, and these ministers had no collective responsibility to the **legislature**.

Civil service: The body of state officials that is responsible for the organisation and administration of government.

Legislature: The body or institution in a country which holds the power to make laws.

Political institutions

The legislature consisted of three bodies, all effectively subject to the authority of the President.

- The Council of State (*Conseil d'État*) was directly appointed, by the President, from among the ranks of the senior civil servants. Its main task was the drafting of legislation, although it had, of course, no powers to initiate any such legislation.

- The Senate, the upper house of the Assembly, consisted of 'notables', such as generals or retired administrators, appointed for life by the President. They were the prime illustration of Louis Napoleon's claim that he did not 'mind being baptised with the water of universal suffrage', but 'refused to live with his feet in it'.

- The Legislative Body (*Corps Legislatif*) was indeed elected, for a period of six years, by universal male suffrage, but the 260 deputies were limited to the role of accepting or rejecting legislation proposed by the government. They could not initiate their own projects, and could not question ministers on points of their policies. Furthermore, the public could not attend their debates.

This stifling of public political life, a basic principle of the new regime, was further reflected outside the Assembly. Political parties and the political press, already severely handicapped by the deportations and arrests that followed the *coup d'état*, were further shackled. Political meetings could now only be held in the presence of government officials, and the Press Decree of 1852 gave the government extensive powers to suspend and suppress publications. In Paris, for example, only four political journals survived the year.

The establishment of the Empire

The French constitution, at the start of 1852, was Imperial in nature if not in name, and Louis Napoleon made little attempt to conceal the fact. It only needed a short step to transform the authoritarian President into an Emperor. Emboldened by the popularity of his moves in 1851, Louis Napoleon began once more to 'test the water' of popular opinion. He made a series of provincial tours in the autumn of 1852 and, upon his return, the Senate dutifully produced the legislation necessary to create an Empire in name as well as in form. Appealing to the people once again by plebiscite, Louis Napoleon received overwhelming popular support, this time by eight million votes in favour of the Empire, with only 250,000 against. Louis Napoleon claimed to base his Second Empire upon this evidence of popular support. Yet it was noted that he chose as his Imperial title 'Napoleon III', as though the duc de Reichstadt, the only legitimate son of the first Napoleon,

A British image of Napoleon III in 1851 as an irresponsible military adventurer.

A BEGGAR ON HORSEBACK;

Or, the Brummagem Bonaparte out for a Ride.

had succeeded his father in spirit. It is hard to resist the conclusion that he considered his power base to be as much dynastic as democratic.

The new regime acted swiftly to consolidate its power and to remove all alternative sources of influence and authority. The National Guard, for example, was suppressed. It had long been regarded as the safeguard of the bourgeoisie against the military tyranny of the monarchy. A good case could be made for regarding it as redundant, now that the champion of the bourgeoisie was firmly in power. Similarly, in a measure that anticipated the actions of future dictators, the Emperor demanded an oath of allegiance from all government servants and officials. The oath was taken, not to the state or to the nation, but to the head of state in person.

The Emperor and his ministers

Popular though it undoubtedly was at the time of its creation, the strength of the Second Empire lay in the effective administrative machine that it operated. The ministers depended very much upon the approval and support of the Emperor. Napoleon III drew his ministers from three main sources.

- Some were members of the dynasty. Prince Jerome was his cousin, and Morny (Minister of the Interior and later President of the Legislative Body) was his half-brother, the illegitimate offspring of one of his mother's extra-marital relationships. Alexandre Walewski (ambassador to London 1851–55, and Foreign Minister 1855–60) was an illegitimate son of Napoleon I.

- Others, like Persigny (Minister of the Interior, and then ambassador to London) had served the dynasty faithfully in exile.

- Most were survivors of the previous, conservative regimes. Morny himself had served under François Guizot, but without reaching the highest ranks and unduly dirtying his hands. Many others, such as Achille Fould, Pierre Magne, Auguste Billaut and Eugène Rouher, had similar histories.

This helps us to conclude that, although the principles of the regime were Bonapartist, the personnel were not. Nor could it have been, for no Bonapartist party or hierarchy had developed in France during the 1830s and 1840s.

Government authority in the provinces

It was clearly important that the regime should exercise authority in the localities as well as in Paris. Although the Second Empire was a distinctly centralised and authoritarian state, it was not, in any real sense, a military or a police state. This point was stressed by the historian W.H.C. Smith, in *Second Empire and Commune: 1848–1971* (1985), when he wrote that 'to describe the Second Empire as a dictatorship is to miss the point. The government was authoritarian but at no time, except for the immediate aftermath of December 1852, was France without representative institutions or a code of law.' The Emperor made many concessions to the army to retain its support, such as the reconstruction of the **Imperial Guard**, the institution of decorations for gallantry, and of improved pensions. Yet at no stage after the *coup d'état* was it used as an instrument of government. In the country at large, government influence operated through the **prefects** and the mayors, themselves creations of the First Empire. The major tasks of the prefects were to keep the Emperor informed of the state of public opinion in the *départements* and to serve the Emperor's interests in local affairs. At elections, in particular, they were under specific instructions to aid government candidates and to do all that they could to hinder the opposition. Their efficiency in this task is reflected in the fact that only nine opposition candidates were successful in the 1852 elections. The Church was also a close ally. It was able to exercise a more subtle influence over the populace, while gaining further important concessions in return. These included increased government aid towards the repair of churches and the payment of clerical **stipends**, greater control over education, after the precedent of the Falloux Law of 1850, and the acceptance of the religious orders in France.

To gain a clear understanding of the nature of the Second Empire it is also important to understand the precise nature of the Emperor's relationship with his conservative allies. Although Napoleon III stood at the head of a formidable conservative coalition, he was the representative, rather than the absolute master, of those conservative interests. At no time during his tenure of power could he afford to ignore them, or to ignore the possibility that those interests might attempt to replace him with another representative. Such considerations are especially important when seeking to understand the policy changes undertaken during the 1860s.

Eugène Rouher (1814–1884)
Converted from republicanism to support the 'Party of Order' by the events of 1848. Minister of Commerce, Agriculture and Public Works (1855–63). Supporter of the Mexican expedition and opponent of liberalising policies in the 1860s. In the early days of the Third Republic, he was a leading member of the Bonapartists in the Assembly.

Imperial Guard: An elite body of soldiers formed by Napoleon I as his personal guard.

Prefects: The government officials responsible for local government in the *départements* (regions) into which France was divided. Sub-prefects were their closest assistants, while the mayors of the towns within the *départements* were directly responsible to them.

Stipends: Salary paid to a clergyman.

1. By what means did the government of Napoleon III control France?

2. What justification is there for the claim that Napoleon III's rule over France in the 1850s was 'authoritarian'?

12.3 What was the economic achievement of the Second Empire?

The economic policy of the Second Empire

The most important, and lasting, achievements of the Second Empire were those in the related spheres of French commerce and industry. Hostile commentators have tended to claim that these achievements were overshadowed and devalued by the Emperor's destruction of personal freedoms. They agree with historian J.M. Thompson's judgement, in *Louis Napoleon and the Second Empire* (1965), that Napoleon III aimed 'to award economic prosperity as a consolation prize for loss of political liberty'. Others have been more inclined to reverse this judgement, and to see political authoritarianism as a means to the real domestic end of the reign, the drive to realise France's true economic potential.

Much has been made of the similarity between the policy of Napoleon III and the principles of the Saint Simonians. The followers of Comte Henri de Saint Simon (1760–1825) stressed the primary importance of economic production, and the primacy of those involved in this vital area. There is little evidence that the Emperor ever aimed systematically to implement such a philosophy. He was not a sophisticated thinker in either philosophical or economic terms, but the philosophy accorded well enough with the policies of his uncle's regime. If the new Emperor was not a Saint Simonian himself, he was well enough versed in contemporary economic and political thought to give wide freedom to men, such as the Pereire brothers, de Lesseps and Chevalier, who were directly influenced by Saint Simon.

The Second Empire opened under the most favourable economic circumstances. The steady decline in world prices, that had prevailed from 1815 to 1850, and which had exercised a generally depressing effect upon trade, was sharply reversed by a dramatic increase in the gold supply. The major 'strike' in California, in 1849, was followed by the equally spectacular 'gold rush' in Australia two years later. Together, these roughly doubled the world's gold supply. The Emperor's opponents made much of these circumstances to belittle the economic achievement of the Second Empire. Nevertheless, the French derive credit from the fact that no other European country made comparable advances in the 1850s under such favourable circumstances.

Reform of the banking system

The major obstacle to the modernisation of the French economy was the conservatism of the French banking system. Wealthy and highly developed though it was, it lay largely in the hands of such families as the Rothschilds, established bankers with strong links with conservative dynasties, and with equally conservative economic policies. With the aid of the more progressive Pereire family, the government began to outflank these bastions of finance. The *Crédit Foncier*, a mortgage bank, and the *Crédit Mobilier*, an **industrial credit** institution, were both founded in 1852. Both offered shares for sale to the public. They thus tapped the vast private wealth that was, perhaps, France's greatest economic advantage. With these huge funds, they could make loans to finance public works undertaken by private contractors, without placing an undue burden upon government finances. The older establishments had little choice but to extend their own range of investments in order to engage themselves more deeply in industrial finance.

The appearance of the *Société Générale de Crédit Industriel et Commercial* (1859), and of the *Crédit Lyonnais* deposit bank (1863) completed what

---

Ferdinand de Lesseps (1805–1894)
Diplomat and administrator serving in Spain and in Egypt. Formed the Suez Canal Company and was largely responsible for the design and construction of the canal. Disgraced in 1889 over the collapse of a similar company involved in the construction of the Panama Canal.

Michel Chevalier (1806–1879)
French economist and advocate of Saint-Simonianism, and of free trade. Chief French negotiator of the trade treaty with Great Britain in 1860.

Jacob Rothschild (1792–1868)
Founder of the Paris branch of the family's banking empire in 1817. Banker to Louis XVIII, Charles X and Louis-Philippe, and representative of Austrian diplomatic interests in France.

Industrial credit: The process of lending money for the purpose of industrial development.

J.M. Thompson has termed 'a financial revolution'. For all their immediate success, the new institutions were to encounter difficulties in the less favourable climate of the 1860s, and they remained a matter of much dispute between the Emperor and some of his more traditionally conservative backers.

The development and impact of the railway system

'**Infrastructure**': The necessary land on which to build the railway, and the supporting network.

'**Superstructure**': The buildings, rolling-stock and so on.

French industrialisation was a long and continuous process, and its foundations had existed before the advent of the Second Empire. The progress made in the course of the Empire's 20-year life span was, nevertheless, most striking. Communications constituted a priority, for no industry could thrive without ready access to its sources of raw materials and to its markets. Work on French railway construction had begun under Louis-Philippe but, consisting mainly of short stretches of track dictated by local needs, it scarcely formed a viable basis for a national system. Under the Second Empire, public and private finance combined to encourage and to fund more comprehensive development. By 1870, the state had invested some 634 million francs in railways, usually by paying for the '**infrastructure**' and for shares with which to maintain its interest in the companies. The companies themselves paid for the '**superstructure**' and were granted long-term concessions, up to 99 years, for the exploitation of their new investments.

With the consolidation and rationalisation of the system, from 42 smaller enterprises into six main companies, the railways effectively transformed the social and economic life of France. The average cost of transporting a ton of produce dropped from 25 centimes to five in the course of 20 years. Total traffic increased, from 6.2 billion kilometres/tons in 1852 to 11.82 billion in 1869, while prices dropped. By linking the major economic centres of France with Belgium, Spain, Germany and Italy, the railway system was also the key to French international commerce. Lastly, not only did the railway 'boom' provide a new demand for the products of heavy industry, consuming 7.2% of their total production in 1855–64, but it opened the way to new markets and new sources of raw materials. The table illustrates both the growth of the French railways and the related growth of other areas of French heavy industry. The telegraph network, a vital tool of the centralised administration, grew from 2,000 to over 70,000 kilometres, in the course of the reign.

French industrial development, 1845–1870

	1845	1848	1855	1860	1865	1870
Railway track (thousand km)	–	2.2	5.5	10.0	13.6	16.9
Freight carried (million tons)	–	2.9	10.6	27.9	34.0	44.0
Mineral fuels (million tons)	4.2	–	7.5	8.3	11.6	13.3
Miners employed (thousands)	34.8	–	54.3	65.6	77.9	82.7
Iron ore (million tons)	2.5	–	3.9	3.0	3.0	2.6

Agriculture

For all this, France remained the land of the peasant smallholder, and agricultural interests continued to play a major role. In 1866, 51.5% of the population earned its livelihood from the land. The improvement of agricultural production in France was a vital area of government concern.

1. **What evidence is there to support the claim that Napoleon III presided over the emergence of a modern economy in France?**

2. **Is there any justification for the claim that, in the 1850s, Napoleon III 'awarded economic prosperity as a consolation prize for the loss of political freedom'?**

Georges, Baron Haussmann (1809–1891)
Administrator under Louis-Philippe, and supporter of the Bonapartist *coup d'état* in 1851. Served as prefect in several *départements* before his appointment as prefect of the Seine *département* in 1853. In that capacity, he was responsible for the substantial rebuilding of Paris, but was dismissed for financial irregularities by Ollivier's government in 1869. A man of sufficient energy and determination to cut through the web of vested interests and allied complications that stood in the way of the transformation of the medieval city.

Homogeneous: All having the same set of interests; in agreement with one another.

Although similar methods were applied as in other areas of the country's economy, the results were less striking. Some impressive figures, nevertheless, can be quoted. By irrigation and drainage, 1.5 million hectares of new land came under cultivation, making the total area of cultivated land in France at the end of the Second Empire 26.5 million hectares, the highest figure in the country's history. The area given over to the cultivation of wheat was 33% greater in 1862 than in 1840, and the increase in the area of sugar beet production stood at a huge 137%.

Spectacular improvements, however, tended to be local rather than national, and 'success stories' are offset by cases where no substantial change in production or agricultural methods took place at all. Modernisation occurred, but irregularly, and most frequently on the large estates. France boasted 9,000 mechanical harvesters in 1862, but they were spread between 3.6 million cultivators of the land.

Who benefited from the economic and social policies of the Second Empire?

The transformation of Paris

The clearest physical imprint of the Second Empire was that left upon the fabric of its capital city. In the first year of his reign, Napoleon III indicated his concern with the material state of Paris by completing his uncle's avenue – the rue de Rivoli – and by the construction of Les Halles as a central market for the city. The following year, he appointed Baron Haussmann to be Prefect of Paris. Over the years that followed, Haussmann transformed the city into an Imperial showpiece on the scale of London, Vienna or St Petersburg. The process was long and difficult. The debts incurred were not finally paid off until 1929, and Haussmann made many enemies for himself and for the regime through his cavalier attitude to finance. Enemies claimed that the main purpose of the Emperor and his Prefect was to replace the easily barricaded, revolutionary rabbit warren of 1848 with vistas that were as suitable for artillery fire as they were pleasant to the visitor's eye. Doubtless, the strategic advantages were not lost upon Napoleon III, but they do not seem to have been uppermost in his mind. His intense personal interest in the project bears out Persigny's contemporary judgement: 'his main aim throughout was to carry out great works in Paris, and improve the living conditions of the working classes, to destroy unhealthy districts, and to make the capital the most beautiful city in the world'.

The modern boulevards, the railway stations, the open spaces at the Parc Monceau and the Bois de Boulogne, all date from this period. Gas lighting was introduced throughout the city, and a vast new system of sewers was constructed, although these failed to save the city from further outbreaks of cholera in 1866 and 1867. The second stage of the project saw the construction of residential suburbs for those workers displaced from the centre. Numerous other towns – among them Lyon, Rouen, Le Havre, Bordeaux and Marseilles – experienced similar public works schemes on a smaller scale.

Urban poverty and political opposition

By the mid-1860s, however, substantial sections of the French population were indicating that they felt little enthusiasm for the Emperor's reforms. Was this merely ingratitude, or did it reflect a deep-rooted failure on the part of the government to transform society as the Emperor's early writings had promised? Once more the answer is complicated by the vast diversity between region and region, and between industry and industry. It is by no means possible to speak of a **homogeneous** working class in France in the 1850s and the 1860s with a single set of interests and reactions.

The Parisian workers remained opponents of the regime, from the plebiscite of 1851 to the legislative elections of 1863, when the opposition made a clean sweep of the Parisian constituencies, and beyond. The discontent was partly ideological, partly material. The problem of poverty in the first years of the Second Empire was enormous. Research based upon the wills of urban workers suggests that, in 1847, between 70% and 80% of the population of Paris was too poor to bequeath any property. The figure scarcely descended below 70% over the next two decades. The rebuilding of Paris, impressive as it was in the eyes of visitors, in the long run merely changed the location of the slums. The workers found it impossible to return to the rebuilt centre of the city, where rents had advanced far beyond their capacity to pay. They now had to be content with the new suburbs where, in the phrase of L. Lasare, higher rents and immigration from the provinces had created 'a red belt enclosing, besieging the centre of the city'.

Conditions in the textile industry

'**Cotton famine**': Term applied to the shortage of raw cotton that resulted from the disruption, caused by the Civil War, in the cotton-growing southern states of America. It caused unemployment and hardship in the cotton manufacturing regions of Europe.

The French textile industry also provides evidence that causes historians to question the impressive statistics of the Empire's economic growth. Not only did it suffer badly from increased competition from Britain after 1861, but it was then savagely hit by the '**cotton famine**' that resulted from the American Civil War. In 1860, 365,000 bales of cotton entered France through Le Havre, compared with only 31,000 bales in 1862. Thus, although real wages showed a distinct increase under the Second Empire, factors such as those mentioned above meant that in local cases no real improvement in living conditions would be noticed. The situation was further complicated by price fluctuations beyond the control of any government, such as those caused by bad cereal harvests in 1853, 1855, 1861 and 1867.

Consumption and education

Nevertheless, contemporary statistics suggest substantial improvements in the lot of the 'average' French person. Consumption per head of all major foodstuffs was higher in the decade 1865–74 than in the decade 1845–54, as the table shows, sometimes by a large margin.

Consumption per head (in grams per week)

	Bread	Potatoes	Fruit/Veg	Sugar	Meat/Fish	Milk/Cheese	Butter
1845–54	714	107	45	0	78	168	17
1865–74	763	254	265	20	100	208	21

1. In what ways were ordinary Frenchmen better off at the end of the Second Empire than they were at the beginning?

2. Discuss the view that, 'as a result of Napoleon III's policies in the 1850s, most Frenchmen gained more than they lost.'

Perhaps the most spectacular social developments were in education. The work of Gustave Rouland (1856–1863) and Victor Duruy (1863–1869) at the Ministry of Education made great inroads into the problems of illiteracy and lack of instruction. Only 312 French communities were left without a school in 1867, compared with 2,690 in 1850. By 1866, 68% of French children between five and 14 years of age were attending school, compared with 51% in 1851. Between 1856 and 1881, the estimated rate of illiteracy fell from 31% to 15%. J. Rougerie concludes, in *Histoire de la France* (1970), that 'there was still real misery, but there is no doubt that the worker of the 50s and 60s lived better than his predecessor of the 40s.'

12.4 How genuine and how consistent was the liberalisation of the Second Empire?

There is no doubt that, in its last decade, the Second Empire softened its authoritarian nature and adopted a range of more liberal characteristics. Historians have found it hard to agree, however, about the motives behind such changes. To the enemies of the Emperor, including many French republican historians, the explanation is simple. Napoleon III was forced into concessions by mounting opposition, and by mounting difficulties in foreign affairs, in an attempt to retain his power. Yet he had always spoken of authoritarian government as a temporary expedient. In *The Napoleonic Ideals*, he used the comparison that 'liberty is like a river; in order that it may bring fertility and not devastation, its bed must be hollowed out deep and wide'. Indeed, in 1851, he had given himself ten years of absolute power for the accomplishment of this task. More sympathetic commentators have found it reasonable to accept the argument that pressures such as those provided by the economic recession of 1857–58, and by the limited success of the Italian campaign in 1859, did not create the policy of liberalisation, but merely dictated its timing.

Economic liberalism

Legislative Body (*Corps Législatif*): The formal name for the lower (elected) house of the French National Assembly.

A policy of economic liberalisation had been advocated by the Emperor since 1853, but had been resisted by the **Legislative Body**. Napoleon III still had two major reasons to regard the principle of freer trade as essential. Not only was it an essential foundation for the future economic expansion of France, but it also served as the cornerstone of an understanding with Great Britain, which he considered a vital element of foreign policy. British suspicion of French policy in Italy, in 1859, made *rapprochement* more urgent than ever. The free trade treaty, signed with Britain in 1860 and known as the Cobden–Chevalier Treaty, after the chief negotiators, had such distinct political overtones that Cobden described it as 'nine-tenths political rather than politico-economical, with a view to cement the alliance with this country'. All the same, its economic consequences were far reaching. Import duties on British coal, textiles, iron and steel were to be lowered by 25% over five years, and French wines, silks and fancy goods would enter Britain at greatly reduced rates. It was the tip of a *laissez-faire* iceberg, since it was followed by reciprocal trade treaties with Belgium (1861), the *Zollverein* (1862), Italy (1863), Switzerland (1864), Spain and the Netherlands (1865), and Austria and Portugal (1866).

Rapprochement: Establishment of harmonious relations between countries.

This was not, however, a policy guaranteed to bring calm and stability. The beneficial effects of free trade were always envisaged as being in the long term. For the present, the government faced the opposition of conservative businessmen and financiers, as well as the unrest of workers whose industries suffered from immediate competition with the industrial might of Great Britain.

Constitutional reforms and concessions to the working class

The most important factor in reaching a conclusion about the liberalisation of the Second Empire is the interpretation that one gives to the liberalisation of French government in the 1860s. It becomes much easier to understand these reforms if they are viewed in terms of political realism, rather than in terms of ideology. The historian James McMillan takes this view, in *Napoleon III* (1991):

Politique: A politician who is guided by practical considerations, rather than by ideals.

'Napoleon III remained neither a traditional conservative nor an orthodox liberal, but a *politique* who manoeuvred with immense skill to maintain himself in power. Before it was 'authoritarian' or 'liberal', the Empire was a 'personalist' regime. At its centre was a lonely figure, wielding power through men who often did not share his vision of politics.'

There is much evidence to suggest that the main threat to the position of the Emperor, in the late 1850s, came, not from republicans or from political radicals, but rather from Orleanists and other conservatives. Such men saw less need for this Napoleonic figure now that the main work of stabilisation and preservation of property had been completed. McMillan and other recent writers see the liberal reforms of this period, not as a form of surrender to the pressures of French radicalism, but as a piece of inspired *realpolitik*, aimed at the establishment of new political alliances which might thwart conservative designs.

There is little doubt that the Emperor proposed the first package of constitutional reforms himself, and that it met with considerable opposition from the conservative ministers that surrounded him. In 1860, came the grant to the Legislative Body of a package of concessions in the vital area of finance.

Realpolitik: German term indicating an approach to politics that is based upon realism and practicalities, rather than upon abstract principles and ideals.

- The Emperor renounced the right to borrow money from elsewhere when the Legislative Body was in recess (not meeting).

- He agreed that the budget should be voted in sections rather than as a whole, thus giving the deputies more chance to attack any unpopular sections.

- For the first time, parliamentary debates could be observed and reported by journalists.

The first concessions to the **urban proletariat** predated this initial batch of parliamentary reforms by a year, and the pace of such reform increased in the course of the 1860s.

Urban proletariat: Term used by Karl Marx to describe those who lived in towns and cities and who owned no property and had to sell their labour to survive.

Amnesty: Official pardon granted by a state, especially to people being punished for political crimes.

- In 1859, an **amnesty** was offered by the government to all political exiles. Only Ledru-Rollin, the extreme republican, was excluded from the general amnesty, although a number of others refused the conciliatory gesture.

- In 1862, the government subsidised the visit of a workers' delegation to the International Exhibition in London, allowing a degree of contact with foreign workers that would have seemed highly dangerous a few years earlier.

- Peaceful strikes were legalised in 1864.

- The theory of the equality of employer and worker before the law was recognised.

- The legality of trades unions was fully established by 1868.

- Proposals to abolish the *livret* (a form of workers' passport without which a man could not be employed) were before the legislature when war broke out in 1870.

The limits to reform

Important as these measures were, it is hard to maintain an image of an enlightened Imperial government pursuing a consistent policy of liberalisation on all fronts. The ambiguity of the Emperor's attitude was well illustrated during the legislative elections of 1863. These saw the return of 32 opposition candidates – a combination of republicans, Orleanists and others – where there had been only five before. It would have been a compliment to the freer political atmosphere in France had not Napoleon III subsequently dismissed Persigny from his post as Minister of the Interior for his failure to secure better results. Thus the government contradicted itself by granting greater freedoms and then reacting uneasily when those freedoms revealed opposition to the regime. Why? One reason seems to have been that the ministers generally found it hard to accept the new course chosen by the Emperor. The limited political activity of the 1850s left the Emperor with a small range of politically experienced men from which to choose a new generation of ministers. Of the older generation most, like Eugène Rouher, christened the 'Vice-Emperor' for his domination of domestic politics from 1863–69, were bitterly opposed to any relaxation of Imperial control.

The reforming zeal that existed in some quarters, in the 1860s, and the range of interests that opposed reform, may be appreciated by considering two areas in which reform failed.

One was education. Victor Duruy, for all his achievements at the Ministry of Education, attempted a far more radical advance when he proposed free, compulsory, primary education, with a great reduction in clerical control. His statement that 'we have left this education in the hands of people who are neither of their time nor of their country' anticipated the campaigns of Jules Ferry (1832–1893) by two decades. Clerical influence was not yet ready to yield, however, and opposition to these proposed reforms forced Duruy's resignation in July 1869.

A more damaging defeat was that which the government suffered over the army reforms proposed by Marshal Niel, Minister of War, in 1867. Niel aimed to increase the size of the army and to make provision for a substantial reserve force, while overhauling the system of conscription to eliminate the inequalities and injustices in it. A set of proposals that would have left the French army in a far better position to resist the Prussians in 1870, provoked a storm of opposition from a variety of sources. Republicans, with an ideological objection to a standing army, joined with prosperous bourgeoises and with peasants who had no desire to see their sons dragged into the army, when they might earlier have found it easy to avoid conscription. The opposition in the Legislative Body so reduced the effectiveness of the proposals that the measures passed in January 1868 constituted little more than an impotent compromise. This was to serve France badly in the crisis of 1870.

Lastly, no account of the last years of the Second Empire makes consistent sense without the knowledge that, at least from the middle of 1865, the Emperor was acutely ill and often in severe pain. 'I find a sick man,' commented the Empress in 1866, 'irresolute, exhausted. He can no longer walk, no longer sleep, and scarcely eat.'

The emergence of the 'Third Party'

Emile Ollivier (1825–1913)
Entered the Assembly (1857) as a republican, but formed the more moderate Third Party in 1863. An opponent of Rouher, he replaced him as Prime Minister in 1870, but his political career was wrecked by the French defeat in the Franco–Prussian War.

Perhaps the decisive domestic stimulus to reform was the formation, in 1863, of the 'Third Party'. Its origins lay in a group of 40 members of the government majority in the Legislative Body who broke away, not to oppose the government outright, but to press for further reform within a constitutional framework. They were joined by others from different political backgrounds, by Orleanists and by former republicans, such as Emile Ollivier. Adolphe Thiers collaborated with the group, although he was never formally a member. The amendment proposed by Ollivier (March 1866) to the Emperor's address from the throne, summarised the attitude of much of the apparent opposition at this time. 'France, firmly attached to the dynasty that guarantees order, is no less attached to the liberty that she believes to be necessary for the fulfilment of her destinies.' Other pressures for reform were caused by the failure of the Mexican expedition, and by the virtual collapse of the Pereire banking empire.

Mandate: The political authority given by voters to the parliament or to the individual that they have voted into power.

The new elections of 1869 finally pushed the government into action at a realistic pace. To the government's credit these were the freest held under the Second Empire, and they were the closest. The margin in the government's favour was now 1.2 million votes (4.5 million to 3.3 million). The situation seems less dramatic if one considers that of the 270 opposition deputies, 116 belonged to the essentially loyal 'Third Party'.

The completion of the 'Liberal Empire'

The **mandate** for substantial reform was clear, and Napoleon III chose the moment to establish the 'Liberal Empire' at which his policies had been hinting. Accepting the resignation of Rouher, he called to office Emile Ollivier. The Emperor then adopted the reforming programme of the 116 as his own. Under the new laws of September 1869 the Legislative Body could propose legislation, elect its own officers, and debate and vote on the budget. At last, the Emperor had touched the pulse of the nation. Share prices rose and journals, previously hostile to the regime, acclaimed its transformation. The plebiscite held in May 1870 to ratify the measures returned a favourable majority, with 7.3 million saying 'Yes', 1.57 million 'No', with 1.9 million abstentions. The popularity of the Empire seemed to have returned.

It can never be clearly established whether this was a temporary expedient, which the Emperor aimed to reverse at the earliest opportunity or whether, as historian Theodore Zeldin claims, it was a genuine 'attempt to break the vicious circle of revolution and reaction in which France had been caught since Louis XVI'. Before that question could be answered, the Second Empire had been destroyed by quite different factors. What may safely be concluded is that, by May 1870, the Empire was safe from internal disintegration. Perhaps it always had been, for what opposition there was, was much more opposition to the 'authoritarian' Empire than to the idea of Empire itself. So it seems that the causes of its sudden collapse must be sought further afield.

---

1. In what ways did the government of France become less authoritarian in the 1860s?

2. 'A sham aimed at prolonging the life of the regime' or 'a genuine attempt to liberalise the political life of France'. Which of these judgements on the political reforms of the 1860s do you find more convincing?

3. 'In domestic terms, the Second Empire was more secure in 1870 than it had ever been.' Do you agree with this statement?

12.5 To what extent did Napoleon III have coherent and consistent aims in foreign policy?

Eugénie de Montijo (1826–1920)
Born in Spain, she married Napoleon III in 1853, and bore him a son, the Prince Imperial, in 1856. Eugénie was considered by some commentators to exercise considerable influence over her husband, especially in the case of her enthusiastic support of the interests of the Catholic Church. She was also considered a major influence upon Napoleon III's decision to go to war with Prussia in 1870. Eugénie fled into exile in England after the French defeat but, after the death of her husband (1873) and of her son (1879), she returned to France, and died in Paris.

The ideas laid down in Napoleon III's *The Napoleonic Ideals* on the subject of foreign policy were considerably vaguer than those on domestic policy. His uncle, declared Louis Napoleon, had aimed 'to substitute, among the nations of Europe, the social state for the state of nature, to found a solid European association, by resting his system upon completed nationalities and satisfied general interests'. Did this mean that the foreign policy of the Second Empire was to be a pursuit of the romantic doctrine of nationalities, or was that merely a cover for a general attack upon the autocratic interests that upheld the Vienna Settlement?

The limits of Napoleonic expansionism

The best answer is, perhaps, provided by a rare moment of honesty in diplomacy. In February 1863, at the height of the Polish revolt, the Empress Eugénie discussed with the Austrian ambassador a far-reaching plan for the settlement of current European disputes, and for the logical resettlement of the map of Europe. Her aim was, presumably, to test his reactions and those of his government.

● The Polish question would be settled by the creation of an independent state.

- As compensation, Russia would be free to expand into Armenia and the Caucasus at the expense of the Turkish Empire.

- Austria would surrender Venetia to Italy, thus completing the business of 1859, and would find compensation in the annexation of Silesia, and in influence over that part of Germany south of the river Main.

- Prussia would be persuaded to accept this by the acquisition of Hanover, and by **hegemony** over Germany north of the Main.

- Prussia would thus be able to release the Rhineland, which could form an independent 'buffer state' under the rule of the King of the Belgians.

- Belgium itself could then be partitioned between France and the Dutch.

Hegemony: The domination or control of one country or state over a group of others.

Of course, the scheme was far too ambitious, and touched upon far too many sensitive areas, to get further than this theoretical stage. Yet, in the light of previous and of subsequent events it is not fanciful to see it as a statement of the 'ideal' outcome of Second Empire foreign policy. It incorporated the realisation of national ideals, but only to the extent that best served French interests. Thus there would be two Germanys and three Italian states, where full unification would create powerful and dangerous neighbours on France's borders. The plan also betrays the idealistic extent of desired French expansion. France might expand to its 'natural frontiers' of the river Scheldt, the Alps, and perhaps the Rhine, with friendly, and relatively weak, 'client' states beyond those borders. Potential enemies, such as Austria, Russia, and perhaps Prussia, could then be kept at a safe distance.

The place of Britain in French foreign policy

1. What were the main aims of the foreign policy of the Second Empire?

2. Why might the other European powers have regarded the foreign policy of the Second Empire with suspicion?

The one element that is not shown clearly enough in the plan of 1863 is the element that Napoleon III undoubtedly regarded as the cornerstone of his policy. Above all, he felt that it was the opposition of Great Britain that had defeated his uncle. As the 1860 commercial treaty illustrated, the friendship of Britain was to be retained at all costs. Initially, however, the distrust of all the powers, not least that of Great Britain, limited Napoleon III's freedom of diplomatic action. The editor of *The Times* in 1853 was convinced 'that in order to retain his precarious hold upon the French people, and especially upon the army, Louis Napoleon was resolved upon a forward policy'.

To what extent had Napoleon III restored French international prestige by 1860?

One of the most dramatic changes in French policy in the 1850s lay in the fact that, after three and a half decades on the 'sidelines' of European diplomacy, France became once more an interventionist power, directly involved in the major issues of European power politics.

How successful was French participation in the Crimean War?

The Eastern Question: Term applied to the issues raised by the decline and disintegration of the Turkish Empire in the 19th century. The most important of these was the question of which states would fill the power vacuum left by the decline of Turkish power in the Balkans, and what the impact would be upon the balance of power in that part of the world.

For ten years after the foundation of the Second Empire, French foreign policy centred upon the Mediterranean. Firstly, attention was concentrated, as so often in the past, upon the '**Eastern Question**'. The factors that led to this latest revival of an old controversy were ostensibly religious. Having recently (December 1852) secured the restoration of the rights of the Catholic Church in the Holy Places of Palestine, Napoleon III now saw those rights withdrawn again as a result of the mission of the Tsar's envoy, Prince Menshikov, to Constantinople in March 1853. Menshikov demanded a Russo–Turkish defensive alliance, as well as

Turkish recognition of Russia's right to act as the protector of all Orthodox Christians within Turkish territories. Lord Palmerston was absolutely correct, however, in his observation that 'the Greek and Catholic Churches are merely other names for Russian and French influence'.

The contemporary English historian of the Crimean War, A.L. Kinglake, formulated a popular and long-lived interpretation when he claimed that, from this stage, Napoleon III aimed for war with Russia. This reading of events was based on traditional English mistrust of the French in general, and of the Bonapartes in particular. Certainly, Napoleon III had much to gain from such a war:

● the chance to cement his popularity with the Catholic voters in France;

● the chance to erase the 'blot' of 1812 from the Napoleonic record;

● the chance to protect important commercial interests in the Levant;

● the chance to work in harness with Great Britain, and thus to consolidate an important friendship.

Vienna Note: A draft peace plan drawn up by representatives of Britain, France and Austria, in July 1853, to resolve the differences between Russia and Turkey in the Middle East. Although accepted by Russia, it was dismissed by the Turks as it required them to make too many concessions to their rivals.

All of these objectives, however, could equally well be secured by diplomacy. Thus, the Russian occupation of Moldavia and Wallachia in July 1853, to exert a protective influence over the local Christians, was met by the so-called **Vienna Note**, rather than by war. In this initiative, France joined Austria and Britain in attempting to pacify the Tsar by confirming the Treaty of Kutchuk-Kainardji, while the Turks added a guarantee of goodwill towards Christians within their territories. As late as January 1854, Napoleon III was still proposing to reach a peaceful conclusion through a four-power conference. That war ultimately broke out was the responsibility of the Turkish Sultan. Emboldened by this evidence of widespread international support, he decided upon military action against the invaders of his northern territories. His land victory at Oltenitza was offset by the destruction of his fleet at Sinope, which confronted Britain and France with the prospect of Russian naval domination of the Levant.

In a war fought by inexperienced generals and untried troops in unfamiliar terrain, it was difficult for any country to emerge with honour. France, however, probably had more cause for satisfaction than any of the other major powers involved. The campaign centred upon the naval base of Sevastopol, without which the Russians would be unable to maintain a significant fleet in the Black Sea. The Russians finally evacuated their positions there at the end of a year of siege warfare, during which the French contingent had struck the two most important blows. The destruction of the Russian supplies at Kertch, and the successful assault upon the Malakoff fortress in early September 1855, provided the allies with the 'great success' that Napoleon III had promised them. The cost, however, was high. Combined allied casualties totalled 115,000 by the time Sevastopol fell, and the **siege** was estimated, in its last stages, to be costing the equivalent of £2.75 million per week. With all the major French interests already served, and with **Russophobia** never so high in France as it was in Britain, it was time to resort to diplomacy again.

Siege: A military operation in which an army tries to capture a town by surrounding it and preventing food or help from reaching the people inside.

Russophobia: Fear of anything Russian.

What did France gain from this intervention?

There can be little doubt that the Treaty of Paris, which concluded the war in 1856, marked the high point of Napoleon III's diplomacy. It achieved most of the aims that France could ever seriously have hoped for.

● The independence and integrity of the Turkish Empire were guaranteed.

● Russia's influence in the region was restricted by the 'Black Sea Clauses', which forbade it to build fortifications on the shores of the Black Sea, and which reaffirmed the Straits Convention of 1841.

● The Sultan acknowledged that his Muslim and Christian subjects enjoyed equal rights.

● Russia's claim that it would protect Greek Orthodox subjects was rejected.

Arbiter: One who decides a dispute between other parties.

Perhaps most important of all, and in contrast to decades of isolation and diplomatic impotence, Paris had become the centre of the first major resettlement of Europe since 1815, and its Emperor could with justification pose as the **arbiter** of Europe. If anyone could truly claim to have won the Crimean War, it was France.

Why did France intervene in Italy in 1859?

If France had greatest cause for satisfaction, the real loser in the Crimean War was the major non-combatant, Austria. By refusing to extend help, or even sympathy, to Russia so soon after Russia's important intervention in Hungary in 1849, Austria had lost its major ally, and had found no substitute. 'You did not conciliate Russia,' Eugénie criticised the Austrian ambassador to Paris. 'You did not regain your influence over Germany, and you cannot count upon the gratitude of France and England.' The main factor that denied French and British gratitude to Austria was the Italian question. Nevertheless, the Piedmontese delegation to the peace conference had received little support or encouragement, and had left Paris despondent. For all his past experience of Italian romantic conspiracy, it scarcely seemed possible, in 1856, for the French Emperor to free his hands in order to 'do something for Italy'. Many factors seemed to make intervention impossible: the concern of French Catholics for the temporal powers of the Pope; French war-weariness after the Crimean conflict; the dangers of causing further offence to the legitimist powers so soon after the Russian war.

The situation was changed by one of the most bizarre episodes of Napoleon III's colourful administration. In January 1858, an Italian patriot, Felice Orsini, attempted to assassinate the Imperial couple. Innocent bystanders were killed and injured, but Napoleon and Eugénie emerged unharmed. Orsini was captured and condemned to death. Surprisingly, however, the Emperor allowed his would-be murderer to transform his outrage into martyrdom. From the death cell, Orsini was allowed to launch a final appeal to the Emperor to act in support of the Italian cause, his neglect of which had caused Orsini to seek his death. 'The present state of Europe makes you the arbiter of whether Italy is free or the slave of Austria and other foreigners. The happiness or unhappiness of my country depends on you.' Recent writers, such as W.H.C. Smith, have tended to interpret Napoleon III's attitude to Orsini as calculated exploitation of a most welcome opportunity.

Relations between France and Piedmont rapidly became closer and warmer in the course of 1858. The key meeting took place on 20 July between the Emperor and Cavour, at Plombières in the Vosges. Negotiations were secret and personal, and lasted only four hours, but a clear programme for French intervention in Italy emerged.

● A proposed union between the tiny principality of Massa-Carrara and Piedmont would be used as the bait to provoke Austria into a threatening response to Piedmont. Thus France would appear to enter Italy as a protector, rather than as an aggressor.

- A French force of 200,000 men would supplement 100,000 Piedmontese troops.

- This joint force was committed to sweep the Austrians from Lombardy and Venetia, which would be handed over to King Victor Emmanuel of Piedmont.

- The joint Franco–Piedmontese operation would be limited to northern Italy, leaving the Pope undisturbed.

- The result would be an Italy of four separate, independent sections – the enlarged Piedmont-Sardinia, a Kingdom of Central Italy headed by the Duchess of Parma, the Papal territories, and the Kingdom of Naples.

- In return, France would gain Savoy, and perhaps Nice, from Piedmont.

In the first month of 1859, a formal military alliance between France and Piedmont-Sardinia demonstrated to the world the closeness of serious action by the French against Austria.

Nevertheless, war was not inevitable. As late as April 1859 it seemed that British pressure might bring the powers involved to the conference table. The immediate cause of the war was Austria's blunder in presenting Piedmont with an ultimatum (19 April) demanding **unilateral disarmament** or war. This occurred just as international negotiations seemed to be stripping France of any credible pretext for intervention. Austria's declaration of war three days later enabled Cavour and Napoleon III to play precisely the roles that they had envisaged at Plombières.

Unilateral disarmament: When one country, or one side in a dispute, disarms without the other side doing so.

How successful was the French intervention?

The French campaigns of May and June 1859 lacked the dash and romance of those of the first Napoleon, but they achieved results. The battle at Magenta (4 June) was 'a battle without plan or co-ordination' (J.M. Thompson in *Louis Napoleon and the Second Empire*, 1965), but it left the road to Milan open to the French. The Battle of Solferino (24 June) was equally confused and twice as costly. The two engagements cost the French 2,300 casualties to add to the 4,500 who had died of disease. These were considerations serious enough for a humane Emperor reduced by the sight of the Solferino battlefield to 'a half fainting, half vomiting mass of misery' (L.C.B. Seaman in *From Vienna to Versailles*, 1963). Other considerations were more serious still. A further advance into Venetia would involve a campaign against the Quadrilateral, a formidable formation of Austrian fortresses, and Cavour's occupation of Tuscany left many French Catholics concerned about the Pope's prospects in this new Italy. Most serious of all, Prussia's mobilisation in the Rhineland left France exposed and vulnerable with its main forces committed to a lengthy campaign in the south.

It was no surprise that Napoleon III chose this moment to meet the Austrian Emperor at the conference table at Villafranca (11 July 1859). By the armistice concluded there, and ratified at Zurich in November, Austria surrendered Lombardy to France (less embarrassing than surrendering it to Piedmont) and retained Venetia. Only in the short term, and from a strictly French point of view, was Napoleon III's Italian venture a success. The Emperor had shown energy and industry, if little military skill, and had withdrawn when France itself seemed endangered. Eventually, in March 1860, he succeeded in negotiating the acquisition of Nice and Savoy, thus completing the first substantial push towards France's 'natural

1. What did Napoleon III achieve by his intervention in the Crimean War and in Italy?

2. In what ways, if any, was France a more powerful international force in 1860 than it had been in 1848?

frontiers'. He had left many loose ends, however, and these were to form a complex knot. The Italian question remained unresolved, with the Austrians still in possession of Venetia. Villafranca ensured the future suspicion of Italy towards France, without diffusing Austria's resentment. Prussian and British suspicions of Napoleonic ambitions were revived so that, in effect, France was as isolated in 1860 as Austria had been in 1859. Lastly, the continued instability of Italian politics gave Napoleon III no chance to withdraw from the thankless, expensive and dangerous task of protecting the Pope from his radical enemies.

12.6 To what extent did the colonial policy of the Second Empire make France an effective world power?

Imperialism: The policy of building an empire, extending the power of the state by acquiring foreign territories, their resources and their markets.

The Second Empire made a concerted attempt to regenerate French **imperialism**. The colonial empire of 1850 was a scattered and shabby affair. It consisted largely of remnants of the 18th-century empire that had been preserved from British annexation, and its total population amounted to little more than 659,000. The Emperor's motives in encouraging colonial expansion ran, as the historian J.P.T. Bury points out, in *Napoleon III and the Second Empire* (1964), parallel to his motives in domestic politics and economics. Economic concerns held a narrow lead over the hope of gratifying the army by presenting them with easy conquests, and the Catholics by conversions to the faith.

Africa

In keeping with the general Mediterranean orientation of French foreign policy in the 1850s, the most striking colonial efforts were made in North Africa. Building upon foundations laid by the July Monarchy, the development of Algeria was impressive in terms both of physical extent and of modernisation. By 1857, French control extended as far inland as the edge of the Sahara desert. Even the traditionally troublesome Berber tribesmen were effectively tamed. As in **metropolitan** France, political liberties were suppressed, especially in view of the republican exiles deported there in 1851–52, while railways and telegraphs spread rapidly. In contrast to metropolitan France, however, the Emperor's ideal of humane civilian government came to nothing. Partly, this was the result of factors beyond his control, such as the locust plague of 1866, the drought of 1867 and the cholera epidemic of the following year. Partly, it was due to the later apathy of an Emperor increasingly beset by European problems.

Metropolitan: In this case, the term is used to describe mainland France – as distinct from its overseas territories.

French colonialism had its successes in other parts of Africa, too. In Senegal, the appointment of the enlightened General Faidherbe as governor (1854) proved to be a happy decision. Not only did it mark the beginning of systematic penetration inland, but also of successful and peaceful economic development, typified by the creation of the port of Dakar (1857) as a base for the export of local goods.

Informal empire: A form of imperialism in which the imperial power does not directly rule the colonised territory. Instead, it leaves it nominally independent, while pursuing economic penetration and exploitation of the territory.

The Suez Canal

Further east, the French emphasis upon limited 'informal empire' ensured that Egypt would provide one of the great successes of the Second Empire. Ferdinand de Lesseps combined French strategic ambitions in the Mediterranean with Saint-Simonian economic ideals in his project for the

Isthmus: A narrow strip of land connecting two larger land areas. In this case the Isthmus of Suez connects the Sinai peninsula and the mainland of Egypt.

construction of a canal linking the Mediterranean and the Red Sea through the **Isthmus** of Suez. The opening of the Suez Canal in 1869, after ten years' work, was a monument to the vision and industry of the Second Empire. Yet, in practical terms, it badly damaged relations with Turkey and with Great Britain, both of whom naturally saw the project as a serious threat to their interests in a most sensitive area.

The Far East

In eastern Asia, 'formal' and 'informal' empire went hand in hand. In China, there was substantial co-operation with the British to secure further European trading rights, but it was that British presence which frustrated French hopes of the establishment of a major economic base such as the British enjoyed in Hong Kong. In Indo-China, on the other hand, Napoleon III was influenced by the reports of French missionaries, which assured him that direct intervention against the unpopular ruler of Annam, Tu-Duc, would bring rich benefits to the Church and to France alike. As has often proved to be the case since then in Indo-China, the ruler proved to be more popular and able than had been expected. France found itself engaged in a lengthy and distant conflict, between 1857 and 1860, before the capture of Saigon finally wrung concessions from Tu-Duc. By the Treaty of Saigon, France then gained control over the three eastern provinces of Cochin China, and guarantees for the free exercise of the Catholic faith over all Annam.

By that time, however, the French government was becoming far too preoccupied with its involvement in Mexico to be able, effectively, to exploit its advantages on the opposite side of the globe. Only by the energy of local French administrators did French influence penetrate to Cambodia (1863) and to the Mekong Valley (1870). Generally, French colonial expansion demonstrated the same tendencies as her political and economic record in Europe. The dynamism and impressive achievement of the 1850s gave way to a slowing pace, and sometimes to confusion and stagnation in the 1860s.

Mexico

Opportunism: The policy of conducting government by taking advantage of opportunities as they arise, rather than conducting government by a preconceived set of principles.

The limitations on French success in Asia and Africa paled in comparison with the spectacular failure of the Emperor's daring intervention in the New World. In terms of results the Mexican venture was Napoleon III's most disastrous piece of **opportunism**. The original plan, however, was no worse than dozens of 19th- and 20th-century interventions by European countries undertaken in order to protect their threatened financial interests. It could even be seen as a visionary attempt to revise, radically, the balance of power in the Americas in France's favour.

The independence of Spain's South American colonies in the 1820s had benefited two major powers in particular. The United States of America were able to establish a virtual monopoly of political influence in the continent, and Great Britain alone possessed the naval strength to exploit the region's economic potential effectively. Other powers traded with, and invested in, the former colonies, treating them like 'poor relations'. The events of 1856–61 offered a chance to revise this state of affairs. Firstly, Mexican politics plunged into a period of renewed anarchy when civil war broke out between the forces of Benito Juárez (an economic liberal and anti-cleric) and the conservative president Miguel Miramón. Established in office in 1861, Juárez suspended the payment of interest on all Mexico's international debts. At the same time the Civil War in the USA dimmed any prospect of American intervention in Mexican affairs. The dual prospect of bringing relief to the Catholic Church and to French investors was attractive enough to Napoleon III. The additional attraction of breaking the hegemony of the United States in the American continents was perhaps the final factor in persuading the Emperor to launch his scheme for a European expedition to oust Juárez and to restore European interests in Mexico.

However sound in conception, the expedition soon got out of hand. What was to have been an international intervention, became a purely French one in 1862 when Spain and Britain developed severe reservations about the possible American reaction. Then, in May 1863, the defeat of a French column at Puebla stung France into a deeper and more costly commitment involving 30,000 troops.

The true tragedy of the scheme, however, sprang from that part of it which was entirely of the Emperor's conception. Possibly under the influence of the Empress, he proposed cementing Mexican stability by establishing a European dynasty there. The choice fell upon the Archduke Maximilian, brother of the Emperor of Austria, and thus the project had the agreeable side effect of repairing relations between France and Austria. By the Convention of Miramar in 1864, Maximilian accepted the proposal and agreed to pay France 270 million francs once he was established, as repayment of Mexico's original debt and to cover French military expenses.

Maximilian became Emperor of Mexico at a bad time. By 1864, the civil war was drawing to a close and the USA were extending encouragement and aid to Juárez in order to repel the unwelcome European intervention. By 1866, France had far more urgent need in Europe for the forces tied down in Mexico. Long before Maximilian had the time to win the hearts and minds of his new subjects, his French forces began to be evacuated. The process was complete by February 1867 and within four months the capital had fallen to Juárez. Gallantly refusing to flee his adopted country, Maximilian was executed by firing squad (19 June). 'None,' observed Eugéne Rouher to the Legislative Body, 'could calculate the passions of the Mexican nation.' It was a pretty poor excuse for a failure that had cost France 6,000 men and the equivalent of £45 million.

12.7 To what extent, and for what reasons, did France's diplomatic position become less secure in the 1860s?

Between the conception of the Mexican expedition and its final fiasco, a series of events had begun to set in motion a revolution in European diplomacy. For a decade, the Mediterranean had been the focus of diplomatic attention. Now a succession of crises turned this attention towards the north. The details of the Polish revolt, of the Schleswig-Holstein affair and of the general collapse of Austro–Prussian relations are described elsewhere. What concerns us here is their impact upon French diplomacy.

The context of French isolation

No French interests were directly involved, either in Poland or in Schleswig-Holstein. Domestic tension and the diversion of a substantial force to Mexico would have made intervention difficult in any case. Such sympathy as existed in France for the 'underdog' did not go as far – as the Emperor was constantly reminded by his agents in the provinces – as support for a war. Reasonable as such an attitude was, the most ominous feature of the events of 1863 and 1864 was the wall of distrust that met the Emperor's attempts to organise a diplomatic solution to the Polish question. Intervention in Italy and in Mexico had encouraged the conviction that

Napoleon III's diplomacy was designed so that France could pick up further pieces from European collisions. From being the focal point of Europe in 1856, the Emperor found himself isolated and burdened with embarrassing commitments as the greatest threats began to emerge to the interests of his state.

Biarritz and the Austro–Prussian War

The Convention of Gastein (August 1865), that seemed to patch up relations between Austria and Prussia over Schleswig-Holstein, appeared to push France further along the path towards diplomatic isolation (see Chapter 14). It must have been with great relief that Napoleon III heard of Bismarck's willingness to meet him privately at Biarritz in October 1865. The secrecy that surrounded the Biarritz interview makes it impossible, to this day, to state with certainty what took place. It seems probable, however, that Bismarck revealed his plans for an armed confrontation with Austria, and secured French neutrality with vague promises of compensation in the Rhineland. Napoleon III may also have pressed Bismarck on the issue of Venetia, which would, in the event of any future hostility, be prised away from Austria to complete France's 1859 undertaking to Piedmont.

As Austro–Prussian relations deteriorated, French policy was based upon the assumption that any future war between them would be long and evenly matched, leaving France perhaps as arbiter, or as holder of the balance of power in Europe. Perhaps it would even be able to present a bill for its services in either case. France settled its stance by an agreement with Austria (June 1866) that it would maintain its neutrality in return for Austria's promise to surrender Venetia, whatever the outcome of the war. At the beginning of July 1866 it seemed highly unlikely that the German question could be resolved without the co-operation and blessing of France.

The impact of the Battle of Sadowa (Königgrätz)

On 3 July, that view was totally discredited when the Austrian army was routed at Sadowa in Bohemia. In Paris, the initial satisfaction at the discomfiture of autocracy and at the liberation of Venetia was quickly soured by the realisation of the wider implications of Prussia's triumph. 'We felt,' reported Pierre de la Gorce, 'that something in the soil of old Europe had just crumbled. Among the people, uneasiness. In the sovereign's circle, bitter complexity.' The situation might still have been saved, however. It is possible that the real error in French policy was not committed at Biarritz, but at the meeting of the Council of State at St Cloud, on 5 July. At the very last minute, the proposals of the Foreign Minister and of the Minister of War to mobilise 50,000 men with a view to action against the Rhineland were reversed by the Emperor. Why did France remain inactive? The strongest argument against military demonstrations had been that they would imply support for Austria, and would thus ruin France's long-term relations with Italy. Furthermore, the agricultural depression, the policy of greater economy in the military budget, and the knowledge that war was not popular with the people, were all inhibiting factors.

The policy of compensation

Officially, the French government remained calm, stressing that the 1815 settlement had been overturned, Venetia had been liberated, and the cause of national self-determination had been advanced 'without the movement of a single French soldier'. Unofficially, it was clear that French prestige, too, had been mauled at Sadowa and that Prussia could overturn the present balance of power in central Europe whenever it wished to do so. Empress Eugénie spoke for many when she remarked to the Prussian ambassador that 'with such a nation as a neighbour, we run the risk of seeing you at the gates of Paris one fine day before we scarcely realise it. I shall go to bed French and wake up Prussian.'

Napoleon III's government was left with two possible means of redressing the balance. It could accept the growth of Prussian power and use diplomacy to build up a system of alliances that might guarantee French security. On the other hand, it could search, unilaterally, for territorial compensation to re-establish national prestige. The two courses were incompatible yet, in the years that remained to the Second Empire, French policy was to pursue them both.

From July 1866, the French ambassador in Berlin was pressing Bismarck on the subject of compensation, mentioning the frontier of 1814, Luxembourg and the Rhineland. Early the following year the Emperor broached the project that came closest to success. His approach to the King of the Netherlands, with the offer to purchase from him the Grand Duchy of Luxembourg, contained many promising elements. Not least of these, was the financial embarrassment of the Dutch monarch. Dutch agreement to the deal was conditional, however, upon the agreement of Prussia, who maintained a garrison in the Duchy. Bismarck raised no official objection to the transaction but German national reaction to the Luxembourg proposals was predictably hostile. In early April, Bismarck replied to a parliamentary question, saying that he was officially committed to the maintenance of all 'German' territories. The Luxembourg deal was dead. This fact was confirmed in May 1867 when an international conference in London, although depriving Prussia of its rights to garrison the Duchy, declared Luxembourg a neutral and independent state.

The failure of what Bismarck dismissed as a 'policy of tips' increased the pressure on the French government. The icy response of the Legislative Body to the news of the Luxembourg check confirmed that it could ill afford any further loss of face. If the government continued to speak of peace, it showed that it recognised the possibility of war by attempting to construct an anti-Prussian alliance. Austrian and Italian responses, in the course of 1867, were, however, most cautious. Austria was understandably reluctant to suffer further defeats, and the price demanded by Italy, the withdrawal of French troops from Rome, was too high. The year 1868 opened, therefore, with France still in a position of total diplomatic isolation.

> 1. In what ways did French prestige and security decline between 1860 and 1868?
>
> 2. How true is it that Napoleon III handled Austria with skill and vision in the 1850s, but completely failed to appreciate the threat from Prussia in the 1860s?
>
> 3. What contribution did French foreign policy make during the Second Empire to the destruction of the Vienna Settlement?

12.8 Why did French relations with Prussia degenerate into war between 1868–1870, and with what results?

The Hohenzollern candidature and the Ems Telegram

> **Antoine Agénor, duc de Gramont (1819–1880)**
> French diplomat, who served as Ambassador to Turin (1853), Rome (1857) and Vienna (1860). An advocate of French friendship with Austria as a means of protection against Prussia. Appointed Foreign Minister in 1870.

In 1869–70, a new challenge to France's international prestige arose from an unexpected source. The circumstances whereby the throne of Spain came to be offered to a branch of the Hohenzollern family, the ruling house of Prussia, are described elsewhere (see Chapter 14). Our prime concern here is with the French reaction when, on 2 July 1870, the French Foreign Office received official confirmation of the move that would threaten them with diplomatic encirclement. Feeling that justice was wholly on the side of France this time, it was made clear, especially through a fiery speech by the duc de Gramont, the Foreign

Minister, that this was considered sufficient grounds for war with Prussia. In the face of such threats, the Prussians rapidly denied any knowledge of, and of course any support for, the candidature. By 12 July, Hohenzollern hopes of the throne of Spain were as dead as those of Napoleon III for Luxembourg.

No sooner had the French government ensured that the mistake of 1866 would not be repeated than it committed a new one. The day after the withdrawal of the candidature, the French ambassador 'buttonholed' King Wilhelm at the resort of Bad Ems, 'to ask me in an importunate way that I pledge myself never again for the future to give my consent if the Hohenzollern renewed their candidature'. The implied lack of faith in the Prussian monarch and the attempt to rub Prussia's nose in its own diplomatic defeat were ill-timed and far more likely to cause offence in Germany than the remote diplomatic defeat itself. Bismarck's press release of the skilfully edited text of the king's telegram about the incident, the 'Ems Telegram', created the desired uproar in both countries. It acted, as Bismarck had intended it to, as 'a red rag upon the Gallic bull'.

France now had to gauge its reaction to the outcry. At first, a plan was produced for another international conference but, as public opinion in 1864 or 1866 had not been ready for war, so now it was not ready for conciliation. The wife of the Austrian ambassador observed that 'Paris was given over to unrestrained enthusiasm, and cries of "On to Berlin!" Don't let them try to tell me today, as they like to do, that nobody in France wanted war; everybody wanted it.' Just as in domestic policy, the Emperor's 'Napoleonic Ideal' combined with public pressure to produce the 'Liberal Empire', so in foreign policy the same factors combined to produce the Franco–Prussian war. War credits were voted on 15 July, the French ambassador was withdrawn from Berlin the following day, and on 19 July France declared war.

Why did France lose the Franco–Prussian War?

How well was the French army prepared for this, its greatest trial? Some improvements had been made since the 1859 campaigns. Even in its curtailed form, Niel's recruitment law had increased the number of men with military training. By 1870, most of these man were equipped with the Chassepot rifle, a splendid weapon with a range double that of the German Needle Gun. Even so, the weaponry did not necessarily compensate for other defects. 'I am afraid,' commented the writer Prosper Merimée, upon hearing the news of war, 'that the generals are not geniuses.' Nor had they the experience of European wars that the Prussian commanders had recently acquired. General Charles Bourbaki had seen successful action, but only in Algeria. Marshal Bazaine, in Mexico, had not even enjoyed a record of unambiguous success. Edmé de MacMahon and François Canrobert had yet to be weighed in the balance. Most ominously, the French mobilisation was disjointed and, at times, downright chaotic. Finally, the French were outnumbered, with 275,000 troops covering a front of 250 kilometres, while 450,000 Germans held a narrower 160-kilometre line.

Within three weeks, the shape of the war had been established by a series of German attacks in Alsace. At Spicheren (4 August) and at Forbach and Froeschwiller (6 August) the forces of Bazaine and MacMahon were surprised and forced into a retreat. Bazaine's retreat took him towards the fortress town of Metz. His fate was sealed by a major engagement between the villages of Gravelotte and St Privat (18 August). There, from good defensive positions, with their Chassepot rifles, the French inflicted heavy casualties. One Prussian regiment lost 8,000 men

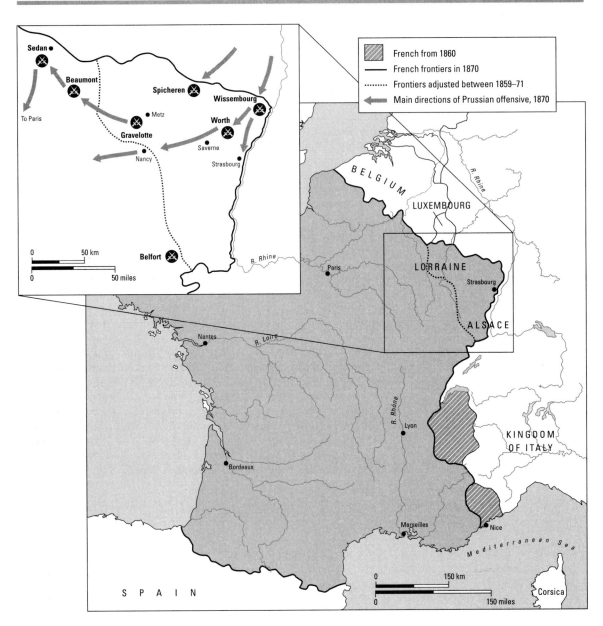

France and the Franco–Prussian War, 1870

in 20 minutes at one point, but Bazaine failed to take advantage of the situation by counter-attacking. Instead, the timid commander chose to fall back on the supposed safety of Metz, where he was besieged by the reinforced enemy, and was able to emerge only at the end of October to surrender.

The collapse of the Second Empire

The second French army, commanded by MacMahon and accompanied by the sick Emperor, moved to the relief of Metz. The slowness of its progress, and the indiscretion of the French press, from whom the enemy learned of the army's whereabouts, allowed the invaders to surprise MacMahon some 25 kilometres from Sedan. The French then fell back upon that town to fight the decisive action of the war. On 3 September, the French were subjected to a murderous bombardment,

1. Why did France go to war with Prussia in 1870?

2. In what ways did Napoleon III's conduct of French foreign policy contribute to Italian and to German unification?

ended only by the Emperor's personal decision to surrender. One hundred and four thousand men, 6,000 horses and 419 guns were handed over to the German forces and, although the war was to continue for some months after Sedan, its outcome was no longer in doubt. Partly in the hope that the war could be passed off as a dynastic struggle, decided by the collapse of one of the warring dynasties, the Legislative Body declared the Second Empire at an end (4 September 1870) and the Republic re-established. For the second time the Bonaparte dynasty, which had offered France glory in many different fields, failed to survive a major reverse on the field of battle.

12.9 *Napoleon III: statesman or political adventurer?*
A CASE STUDY IN HISTORICAL INTERPRETATION

Polemicists: People who are skilled at arguing passionately for or against an opinion or belief.

The collapse of the Second Empire, amid national humiliation, ensured that immediate historical judgements upon Napoleon III would be harsh. Indeed, the tone had been set during his reign by two **polemicists** with fundamental political objections to the Napoleonic regime. Writing in 1852, in protest against the Bonapartist *coup d'état*, Victor Hugo (*The Little Napoleon*) and Karl Marx (*The 18th Brumaire of Louis Napoleon*) both used ridicule as their chief weapon. They claimed that Louis Napoleon was a petty adventurer, rising on the reputation of a man whom he could not hope to emulate. Equally, since the fall of the Second Empire, the judgements of many French commentators have been shaped by political outrage. Given that France had been a parliamentary republic for all but five years since 1870, it is not surprising that Napoleon III's historical reputation has been adversely affected by the 'guilt' of his destruction of the Second Republic. Within France, republican writers such as Taxile Delord and Albert Thomas condemned him, while foreign historians, such as Hermann Oncken (*The Rhine Policy of Napoleon III*, 1926) established the view that the Emperor was an irresponsible and dangerous expansionist in his foreign policy.

To an extent, of course, all of these judgements were based upon the authors' political ideology, or anti-French patriotism, rather than upon objective assessments of Napoleon III's record of achievement. Time and distance have tended to soften judgements on the Second Empire. The major works of the 'revisionist' school have been written by British and American historians, less concerned with the ideological preoccupations of French republican politics. F.A. Simpson, in *Louis Napoleon and the Recovery of France* (1923), stressed that, especially in terms of domestic achievements, the Second Empire was more important than the First. It was certainly more fruitful than the regimes that immediately preceded it in terms of the economic advances that it achieved, and it played a major role in the emergence of France as a modern, commercial and industrial society.

This line of argument was greatly advanced by the work of Théodore Zeldin. His books on *The Political System of Napoleon III* (1958) and on *Emile Ollivier and the Liberal Empire of Napoleon III* (1963) have largely illuminated the internal workings of the French government, and revised views on the nature and origins of the liberal phase of the Empire. Above all, Zeldin emphasises that, in his political liberalisation of the regime in the 1860s, the Emperor genuinely sought to break free from the more reactionary influences that had dogged French politics throughout the century. Among other English writers, the tradition of hostility towards

Napoleon III has been maintained by J.M. Thompson, whose *Louis Napoleon and the Second Empire* (1954) draws parallels between the Emperor and Hamlet, showing both men as not great enough for the tasks that they set themselves. On the other hand, J.P.T. Bury (*Napoleon III and the Second Empire*, 1964) and James McMillan (*Napoleon III*, 1991) both maintain the Anglo-Saxon tradition of greater sympathy for the Emperor, dwelling upon the consistency with which he applied original and imaginative domestic policies.

With the passage of time, French historians, too, have shown a growing appreciation of the long-term achievements of the Second Empire. Recent French authorities, such as A. Plessis (*The Rise and Fall of the Second Empire, 1852–1871*, 1985) and L. Girard (*Napoleon III*, 1986), also concentrate less upon the political ideology of the reign, and more upon the significant and lasting progress that was made in social and economic terms.

It has proved difficult to extend this revision to Napoleon III's foreign policies. Writing during the war years, the Franco-American historian, Albert Guerard (*Napoleon III*, 1943), argued that it was possible to see the Emperor as the last statesman to display a farsighted and coherent view of European politics before the advent of selfish, nationalistic preoccupations. Be that as it may, it is hard to deny that Napoleon III misread many of the most important political developments in the Europe of his day. Consistently overestimating the importance of Austrian power in the 1850s, and completely failing to counteract the rise of Prussia in the 1860s, he undoubtedly left France in a weaker diplomatic situation than it had been in the late 1840s.

1. In what ways have historians differed in their assessments of the French Second Empire?

2. What factors have caused some historians to be more critical than others when judging the overall political achievement of Napoleon III?

Source-based questions: The Plebiscite of 1851

SOURCE A

The counting of the votes was no more than a formality, it was so well known in advance what the splendid result would be. The result still surpassed all expectations, all hopes. Among the 640,000 opponents could be found intransigent legitimists, worth respecting for their inflexible convictions, militant Orleanists and honest republicans; but the dominant element was that of those involved in the rising, from which must of course be deducted those who were in safe custody, those who had thought it prudent to cross the frontier, and finally those who, having had a bone to pick with the law for robbery, bankruptcy, arson, or murder, had been deprived of their civil and political rights.

Emile de Maupas, Memoirs of the Second Empire, *published in 1885*

SOURCE B

Might we be said to claim that no one really voted for M Bonaparte? That no-one freely and knowingly accepted this man?

Far from it.

M Bonaparte had to support him the rabble of officials, the twelve hundred parasites supported by the budget, and their hangers-on; the venal, the compromised, the shifty, and following them, the half-witted, a notable crowd. He had to support him MM [*messieurs*] the cardinals, MM the bishops, MM the canons, MM the *curés*, MM the curates, MM the archdeacons, deacons and sub-deacons, and what are called 'religious' persons, who pray in these terms: O God, put up the price of Lyon shares! Sweet Saviour Jesus, let me get 25% on my Naples-Rothschild scrip! Holy apostles, sell my wine! Blessed martyrs, double my rents! Holy Mary, Mother of God, immaculate virgin, Star of the Sea, deign to look favourably on my little business on the corner of Tire-Chape street and Quincampoix street! Ivory tower, see to it that the shop opposite does badly!

The following really and undoubtedly voted for M Bonaparte: category one, officials; category two, the ignorant; category three, the Voltairean-landowner-industrialist-believer.

Victor Hugo, The Little Napoleon, *published 1852*

SOURCE C

The Bonaparte dynasty does not represent the revolutionary peasant, but the conservative peasant. It does not represent those among the peasantry who wish to escape from the narrow conditions of their farming life; it represents those who wish to perpetuate and consolidate those conditions. It does not represent the enlightenment of the peasantry, but their superstition; not their future, but their past.

The three years' rule of the parliamentary republic had freed some of the French peasants from the Napoleonic illusion, and had even revolutionised them, though superficially; but the bourgeoisie had forcibly repressed any attempt on their part to advance.

In the risings that followed the *coup d'état*, some of the peasants were making an armed protest against their own votes on 10 December 1848. Their schooling since then had taught them sense. But most of the peasants were so steeped in prejudice that in the reddest of the departments they were most frank and enthusiastic in their support for Bonaparte. In their view the National Assembly had restricted their freedom of movement, and now they were merely breaking the fetters which the towns had imposed on the will of the countryside.

Karl Marx, The 18th Brumaire of Louis Napoleon, published 1852. The title refers to the coup by which Napoleon I had originally seized power, and which his nephew now seemed to have imitated.

1. *Explain the following highlighted phrases that occur in the sources:*

(a) 'legitimists' and 'Orleanists' (Source A)

(b) 'those involved in the rising' (Source A)

(c) 'their own votes on 10 December 1848' (Source C).

2. *How far do these sources agree on the reasons for the success of Louis Napoleon in the 1851 plebiscite?*

3. *Assess the value of these sources for the historian who wishes to understand the reasons for Louis Napoleon's success in the 1851 plebiscite.*

4. *'Louis Napoleon was able to overthrow the republican constitution in 1851 simply because he enjoyed the support of a small ruling elite.' How far do these sources, and the information contained in this chapter, support this statement?*

The unification of Italy

Key Issues

● *What were the main obstacles to Italian unification in the 1850s and 1860s?*

● *Was the main aim of Piedmont to unify Italy, or merely to increase its own power?*

● *How important was foreign intervention in bringing about Italian unification?*

13.1 What were the political priorities of the Kingdom of Piedmont-Sardinia in the early 1850s?

13.2 Why did Piedmont participate in the Crimean War and what did it achieve by its participation?

13.3 How was Piedmont able to launch a war against Austria in 1859?

13.4 How successful was the war of 1859 from the point of view of the Piedmontese government?

13.5 What were the political aims and methods of Giuseppe Garibaldi?

13.6 Historical interpretation: To what extent should Cavour be regarded as a champion of Italian unification?

13.7 What problems faced the new Italian state in the 1860s?

13.8 By what means, and with what success, did the Italian state extend its influence over other Italian territories?

Framework of Events

1850	Cavour appointed Piedmontese Minister for Trade, Agriculture and the Navy
	Passage of the Siccardi Laws
1851	Cavour appointed Prime Minister of Piedmont-Sardinia
1855	Piedmont joins Britain and France in the Crimean War
1856	Congress of Paris
1857	Foundation of the National Society
1858	January: Orsini's attempted assassination of Napoleon III
	July: Pact of Plombières between Cavour and Napoleon III
1859	April: Austrian declaration of war on Piedmont-Sardinia
	June: Battle of Magenta; Battle of Solferino
	July: Armistice signed at Villafranca
	November: Treaty of Zurich
1860	March: Plebiscites in Central Duchies in favour of unity with Piedmont
	May: Garibaldi's expedition to Sicily. Battle of Calatafimi
	September: Garibaldi's forces enter Naples
	October: Meeting between Garibaldi and Victor Emmanuel at Teano
1861	March: Victor Emmanuel II proclaimed King of Italy
	June: Death of Cavour
1862	Garibaldi's attempt to capture Rome defeated by Italian forces at Aspromonte
1866	June: Italian declaration of war against Austria. Italian defeat at Custoza
	July: Defeat of Italian navy at Lissa
	October: Union of Venetia with Italy
1867	Garibaldi's attempt to capture Rome
1870	September: Occupation of Rome by the Italian army. Rome incorporated in the Kingdom of Italy.

Overview

THE events of 1848–49 had an arguably greater impact upon Italian politics than upon the politics of any other part of western Europe. Yet the changes that they brought about were subtle, and may not have been immediately obvious to many contemporaries. No significant changes were made to the boundaries of the Italian states, and the balance of power between Austrian military strength and the forces of radical nationalism remained unchanged, with Austrian control firmly re-established. Indeed, with a French garrison now lodged in Rome the influence of foreign powers over Italian politics appeared to be stronger than ever.

Yet two important changes had taken place. One of the leading Italian states, Piedmont-Sardinia (which was in two parts – the state of Piedmont and the island of Sardinia – see map on page 375), had changed direction and had established an agenda that differed significantly from the usual reactionary stances of Italian rulers. Despite the efforts of two generations of Italian nationalist historians, few authorities seriously consider now that this agenda included the unification of Italy. Instead, King Victor Emmanuel II maintained his father's vision of a more powerful Piedmontese state, capable of dominating the richer, northern regions of Italy. Such a state would be enhanced and strengthened by the modern economic and political policies implemented by his leading minister, Camillo di Cavour. Taking his lead from the recent experiences of Britain and of France, Cavour belonged to a new generation of European conservatives who sought to harness industrial and commercial progress to maintain the political authority of the traditional governing classes. The other great change had not occurred in Italy, but it had profound political significance for the peninsula. The election of Louis Napoleon Bonaparte as President (later Emperor) of France brought to power a man with a vested interest in the revision of the European balance of power. Where, before 1848, the major powers had rigidly maintained the balance and the boundaries established by the Congress of Vienna, Napoleon III based his foreign policy on their readjustment and, in particular, on the reduction of Austrian power in central and southern Europe.

Thus, in the 1850s, there were four forces at large in Italian politics, as Piedmont-Sardinia interacted with the aspirations of nationalists and of the French Emperor against the power of Austria. The alliance between Piedmont-Sardinia and France appeared to offer the best prospect for change that Italy had known since the Napoleonic Wars, but it was not successful. At least, it did not achieve the results that Cavour had anticipated. It did not drive the Austrians out of northern Italy, and did not create the strong northern Italian state that Cavour desired. Nevertheless, it did transform the political balance of Italy. Shaken, if not shattered, Austrian power was in no position to offer its traditional protection to the conservative governments of central and southern Italy. Under these circumstances, Piedmont was able to take action in the **Central Duchies** which would never have succeeded before. Piedmontese ambitions did not extend to Naples or to Rome, but those regions were firmly on the agenda of Giuseppe Garibaldi and the '**party of action**'.

In general, in the course of the *Risorgimento*, the initiatives of the radical Italian nationalists were not remarkable for their timing. The great exception

Central Duchies: The collective name given to the Duchies of Tuscany, Modena and Parma, lying just to the south of Piedmont.

'Party of Action': Term used to describe those radicals, such as Giuseppe Mazzini and Giuseppe Garibaldi, who hoped to bring about the unification of Italy by direct and popular military action.

occurred in 1860, for Garibaldi's military expedition to Sicily (and subsequently to Naples) took place at exactly the right moment. By its timing, it was able to exploit Austria's military defeat, French war-weariness, and the uncertainty and vulnerability of the conservative Italian rulers. Garibaldi's actions forced Piedmont-Sardinia, facing a deadlock in the affairs of northern Italy, to turn its attention to the south. In the final twist of a highly pragmatic career, Cavour resolved to extend Piedmont-Sardinia's control over southern Italy in order to forestall the establishment there of a dangerous, radical regime. This was enormously successful in the short term, for Garibaldi chose to hand over his conquests to the King of Italy. In the longer term, however, Cavour's actions had consequences of even greater significance. Instead of consolidating its control over the prosperous north, as had been its main aim for more than a decade, Piedmont now stretched its resources in an attempt to control territories in the south, to which it had previously never aspired.

In effect, Garibaldi's achievement in 1860 was to wrest the initiative from Piedmont-Sardinia, to impose his programme of wider unification upon Cavour, and to hasten the creation of a unitary Italian state such as the radical nationalists had always envisaged. The Italian state that emerged from the 1850s and 1860s, therefore, was a hybrid that grew from the different aspirations of its different creators. Its constitutional nature was determined by the work of Cavour and of the Piedmontese monarchy, but its geographical extent in the end was largely determined by the programme of the radical nationalists.

13.1 What were the political priorities of the Kingdom of Piedmont-Sardinia in the early 1850s?

Buffer state: A neutral state that lies between two other states, and serves to prevent their interests from clashing.

After the nationalist failures of 1848–49, Italy presented a sorry picture. Austria's military occupation was as strong as ever, political reaction was restored in the states of southern and central Italy, and most of the constitutions installed there had been suppressed. The **buffer state** of Piedmont, in the north-west corner of Italy, was the only exception to this rule. Although decisively defeated at Custoza and at Novara, it retained its constitution, the integrity of its territory and its freedom from Austrian occupation. On the face of it, these were encouraging signs for the moderate nationalists who now transferred their hopes from Pius IX to the Piedmontese monarchy. The ruler to whom Vincenzo Gioberti and others now looked, after the abdication of Charles Albert, was his son, the 29-year-old Victor Emmanuel II.

What was the political stance of Victor Emmanuel II?

The new king inherited not only his father's throne, but also the legend that Charles Albert had created by his actions in 1848–49. Victor Emmanuel's role, in the events of the next two decades, allowed later generations of Italian historians to create an even more compelling 'official' view of the king. In 1850, Victor Emmanuel was the saviour of Piedmont-Sardinia and of the Piedmontese constitution from the victorious Austrians, and his subsequent actions made him the champion of Italian constitutional monarchy, as well as the father of his country. Contemporary views of the King of Piedmont-Sardinia were often less spectacular. He was sufficiently ambiguous in his political views to be regarded as a cautious liberal by the British, and as a cautious conservative by the Austrians. He was probably just cautious. Contemporaries detected courage and good sense in him, but also found him lazy and coarse. Historian Denis Mack Smith concludes, in *Cavour* (1985), that the King was the sort of man 'always happiest in either the barracks, the stables or the hunting field'.

Victor Emmanuel's background contained little that was likely to make him a nationalist or a liberal. He was educated and trained to be heir to an autocracy, and his mother and wife were both members of the Austrian imperial family. Against claims that Victor Emmanuel bravely defended the Piedmontese constitution against the victorious Austrians, Denis Mack Smith points out that Austria had reasons of its own for favouring a compromise settlement. It was in the Austrian interest, too, that the Piedmontese monarchy should be strong enough to resist pressure from the radicals and, even more important, that Piedmont-Sardinia should have no cause to turn to France for assistance. Besides, the representative nature of the Piedmontese constitution (*il statuto*) should not be exaggerated. Of the two parliamentary chambers, the upper one was directly appointed by the king and, in the election of the lower house, the requirement that voters should be literate limited the electorate to only 2.25% of the population. Under the terms of the constitution, the king retained much personal power – the most important elements of which were command of the army and the power to appoint and dismiss his ministers at will.

The D'Azeglio ministry in Piedmont, 1849–1852

Victor Emmanuel's first domestic actions were not exactly those of a liberal. His first task was to ensure his control of the kingdom by means that included the shelling of Genoa to win it back from the radicals who remained entrenched there. His first administration included several of the 25 military men who were to hold ministerial office during his reign, although by the end of 1849 the administration was in the hands of a group of moderate conservatives under the leadership of Massimo D'Azeglio.

The first major policy of the ministry concerned one of the great liberal principles of the 19th century, the contest for power and influence between the Church and the State. Neither King nor Minister wished to tolerate the considerable influence of a body that had set its face so firmly against them both in 1848. The batch of measures, produced in 1850 and known as the Siccardi Laws, was a substantial first move in a decade of Piedmontese anti-clericalism. Church courts and other ecclesiastical privileges were abolished, the number of holy days was limited, and the senior Piedmontese churchman, Archbishop Fransoni, was imprisoned when he ordered his clergy to ignore these measures.

Such determined measures were rare from D'Azeglio. Having found a parliamentary majority hard to come by in the first place, he found it undermined, in 1852, by an opportunistic alliance between the leader of the 'middle-class party', Urbano Rattazzi, and his own Finance Minister, Camillo di Cavour. The fall of his ministry was assured when the King refused to accept the next stage of D'Azeglio's anti-clerical legislation, a bill enforcing civil marriage (May 1852). D'Azeglio was replaced by the most influential figure in the history of 19th-century Italy.

Cavour's desire for domestic political stability

Cavour's domestic administration of Piedmont, between 1852 and 1859, had as its aim the creation of a stable state prosperous enough to dominate Italy. In some respects, stability was achieved by methods that would not have been approved by the English statesmen he so much admired.

Mazzinian democrats were persecuted, the Mazzinian press was suppressed, and parliament was overridden when it did not serve the purposes of the Prime Minister. For example, in 1857, when the elections returned an unexpected right-wing majority, Cavour seized upon a series of dubious technicalities to unseat a number of the successful candidates and so reduce the right wing. In January 1855, Cavour held all three of the main posts in the administration: Prime Minister, Foreign Minister and Finance Minister.

Other policies for creating stability were more liberal. A string of administrative reforms – in the financial departments (1852), in the foreign office (1853), and those of Alphonso La Marmora in the army – increased efficiency and removed those conservative elements hostile to Cavour. Further anti-clerical measures – notably the suppression of 152 **monasteries** and 1,700 **benefices** in 1855 – further restricted the influence of the Church, but also added the equivalent of an extra £145,640 to the state's income.

Cavour and economic modernisation

The most spectacular achievement of the decade consisted of the foundations that were laid for Piedmontese commercial and industrial prosperity. Already, as Minister of Finance and Commerce, Cavour had concluded a string of free-trade treaties. These were concluded with Belgium, with France and with Britain. They had the dual purpose of forging international links with the more advanced states of western Europe, and of attracting into Piedmont the raw materials and machinery necessary for its development. In the same capacity, Cavour floated large internal and foreign loans to pay off the war indemnity owed to the Austrians and to finance the industrial projects of the government. The level of government expenditure on such projects, as well as the long-term effects of the policy, may be judged from the fact that the public debt of Piedmont rose, between 1847 and 1859, from 120 million lire (Italian currency) to 725 million.

It would, of course, be misleading to refer to Piedmont in 1859 as a 'modern industrial power', but it had produced a number of impressive projects to advertise its status as the most advanced of the Italian states. Of Italy's 1,798 kilometres of railway track in 1859, Piedmont had 819 kilometres. Italy's first steamship, the 'Sicilia', was built in Genoa in 1855, and Italy's first home-produced railway locomotives were built in the same year. Further schemes were in progress for the construction of the Mont Cenis tunnel through the Alps, and for the modernisation of the port of Genoa. In the course of the 1850s, Piedmont's trade trebled in value. By the end of the 1850s, therefore, Piedmont had effectively claimed first place in Italy, not only in terms of constitutions and of military leadership, but in material terms as well.

Alphonso La Marmora (1804–1876)
Piedmontese general, active in the wars of 1848–49. Minister of War (1849). Commanded Piedmontese forces in the Crimea (1855) and in the campaigns of 1859 and 1861. Prime Minister (1864). Defeated at Custoza (1866).

Monasteries: Buildings in which a group of monks live together and carry out their religious practices.

Benefices: Posts and offices occupied by priests, together with the income derived from them.

1. What evidence is there for regarding Piedmont as a progressive and modern state in the period 1849–1855?

2. In what respects, if any, was Piedmont better qualified to lead Italy in the early 1850s than any of the other Italian states?

13.2 Why did Piedmont participate in the Crimean War and what did it achieve by its participation?

Piedmontese motives

Cavour's most important contribution to the liberation of Italy was that he was able to place the 'Italian question' firmly into the general context of European diplomacy. This was the forum in which the 1815 settlement had been shaped, and the only forum in which that settlement could be revised. It was not until the outbreak of the Crimean War in 1854, however, that a real opportunity presented itself. It was a bold step for a minor power such as Piedmont to intervene in a European conflict such as this, and it is not surprising that some historians have seen this as a masterstroke by Cavour, supported by Victor Emmanuel. The historians Massimo Salvadori and Derek Beales, however, have laid the stress differently. In their view, much of the initiative came from the British and the French, who felt that Austria would be more likely to send troops to the Crimea if it were assured that Piedmont would be committed there too, and thus unable to attack them in the rear. Denis Mack Smith moves even further from the traditional interpretation, viewing the plan for intervention primarily as the brainchild of Victor Emmanuel who, fretting at the constitutional restraints imposed upon him, saw war as a good opportunity to reassert his royal authority.

The Piedmontese contribution

Whatever the process by which the decision was reached, by the end of 1854 Piedmont had concluded an agreement with the allies by which 18,000 Piedmontese troops would fight in the Crimea. Subsequently, Piedmont would be entitled to a place at the congress at which peace would eventually be made. Neither the military intervention nor the Congress of Paris was as successful for the Italian cause as Italian historians have sometimes claimed.

Piedmont's military contribution to the war was limited. La Marmora's troops gave a good account of themselves at the battle of the Chornaya (August 1855) and, in their own eyes, did something to restore the prestige lost at Custoza and Novara. On the other hand, they scarcely played a key role, and the official line that 'about 2,000 of them were killed or died of disease' conceals the fact that not more than 30 of that number actually died of their wounds. Similarly, Cavour travelled to Paris for the peace conference, in 1856, still greatly inexperienced in the ways of 'great power' diplomacy, and with hopes that were never likely to be realised. His first aim was for territorial compensation for Piedmont's efforts, possibly in the shape of the Duchy of Parma. Such a measure was never seriously considered by the congress. His second aim was to obtain some commitment from the powers on the subject of the Austrian presence in Italy. He could not hope to obtain this from France which had troops of its own in Rome, and who could not contemplate renewed war so soon after the campaigns against Russia.

It is true that the British representative, Lord Clarendon, attacked Austrian excesses and Papal and **Neapolitan** misgovernment in harsher terms than Cavour could have used. It was a measure of Cavour's inexperience, however, that he imagined that Clarendon might be speaking for his government. The British were soon to make it clear that they had no intention of intervening actively in so controversial a continental matter. In the context of 1856, Cavour had failed to achieve a diplomatic initiative and had not created the conditions necessary for a military solution to the problem of the Austrian presence.

Neapolitan: The adjective used to describe something or someone coming from, or relating to, Naples.

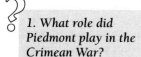

1. What role did Piedmont play in the Crimean War?

2. How successful was Piedmontese participation in the Crimean War?

13.3 How was Piedmont able to launch a war against Austria in 1859?

Relations between Piedmont and Austria, 1856–1859

One result of the events in Paris in 1856 was a significant increase in Piedmontese confidence in her dealings with Austria. As a result of the peace conference, Cavour no doubt felt that the sympathy of Britain and

France would, at the very least, be sufficient to deter Austria from any threatening ambitions. So it seemed, for Austrian policy in its provinces of Lombardy and Venetia, from 1856, was more conciliatory. The policy of confiscating the property of exiles was relaxed, and an amnesty for political prisoners was announced in 1857. Victor Emmanuel's famous speech of January 1859, in which he declared that he could not stop his ears to the 'cry of grief' (*grido di dolore*) that came from the neighbouring provinces, must have tested Austrian nerves to breaking point. It may have been instrumental in making them blunder into war later that year.

Piedmont and the nationalists

Another undoubted effect of the *grido di dolore* speech was to cement relations between the Piedmontese government and the nationalist exiles within Piedmont. Relations between Cavour and the exiled nationalists had been ambiguous since the Crimean War. The latter had formed the National Society in 1857, which boasted a membership of some 8,000 and whose main figures were Giuseppe La Farina, Giorgio Pallavicino and Daniele Manin, the hero of the former Venetian Republic. They were further convinced, by the intervention in the Crimean War, that Piedmont represented Italy's best hope, but they still entertained severe reservations about the sincerity of the state's leadership, and especially about that of Cavour. Manin had written in 1855, 'Convinced that above all Italy must be made, that this is the first and most important question, we say to the house of Savoy: "Make Italy and we are with you. If not, we are not."'

The Orsini affair and the Pact of Plombières

On the other hand, nothing was more likely to damage relations with France, certainly the most important factor in Cavour's calculations, than the assumption by Napoleon III that Piedmont was really serving the interests of a band of radicals. Although Cavour tried hard to consolidate the friendship formed in the Crimea, all was nearly ruined by Felice Orsini's terrorist attack in January 1858. The Orsini affair was a mysterious business, but there seems little doubt that Napoleon III's first reaction was one of great bitterness towards a Piedmontese government that had allowed Orsini to avoid arrest and to reach France.

At this stage, Victor Emmanuel performed one of his greatest services to Italy. In giving a brave reply to the attacks of the Emperor, he presented Piedmont as the best guarantee in Italy against the excesses of the radicals. These claims, combined with Napoleon's long-standing, if vague, desire to 'do something for Italy', calmed the Emperor. A visit by his confidant, Dr Conneau, to Turin (June 1858) raised hopes of direct co-operation between the two states against Austria. Thereafter progress was rapid, culminating in the secret meeting between Cavour and Napoleon III at Plombières in July. There plans were drawn up for French military intervention, resulting in the expulsion of Austria from Lombardy and Venetia, the enlargement of Piedmont and an Italy made up of four major power blocs. It seems highly likely that the terms of the Plombières agreement represented the views of Napoleon III, rather than those of Cavour. One is led, once more, to the view of Cavour as an **opportunist** willing to accept conditions of this sort to achieve what he had long known to be an essential precondition of the liberation of northern Italy, namely the military intervention of France.

Opportunist: A politician who does not act according to pre-established principles, but who adapts his policies to take advantage of specific opportunities as they arise.

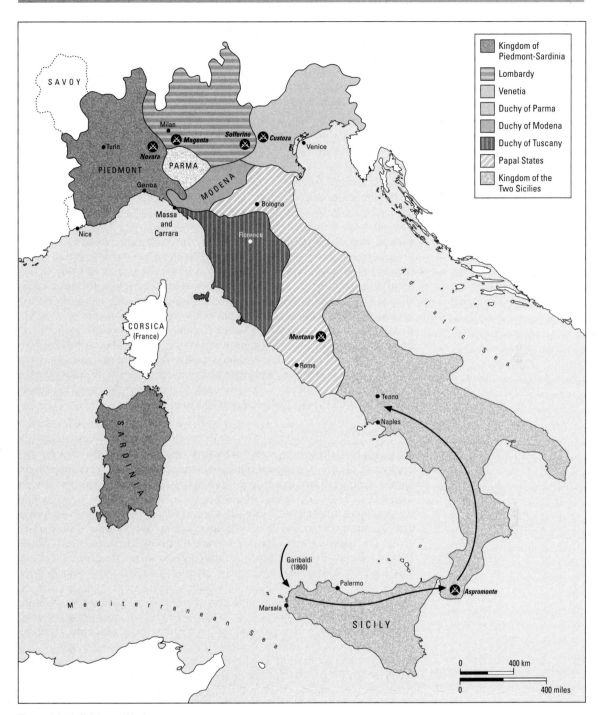

The political divisions of Italy

Legend:
- Kingdom of Piedmont-Sardinia
- Lombardy
- Venetia
- Duchy of Parma
- Duchy of Modena
- Duchy of Tuscany
- Papal States
- Kingdom of the Two Sicilies

13.4 How successful was the war of 1859 from the point of view of the Piedmontese government?

The Piedmontese war effort

For many years, the war of 1859 was traditionally viewed by Italian writers as a war of national liberation, cunningly contrived by dedicated Italians and finally betrayed at Villafranca by a cynical foreigner. Instead, study of the Piedmontese and Austrian war efforts should show how essential the part played by the French forces was to the achievement of even the limited success of 1859.

Italian reaction to the outbreak of war sheds some interesting light on the extent of Italian enthusiasm. The Piedmontese mobilisation was half-hearted. Not only was there a tendency to leave the hard work to the French, but also a distinct reluctance on the part of the conservative army officers to arm large numbers of men at a time when Piedmont was full of dangerous radical exiles. Where there was enthusiasm it was not always for the cause of nationalism. Victor Emmanuel felt himself, writes historian Mack Smith, 'a new man, powerful again, and free from interfering civilians'. Indeed, relations between King and Prime Minister were rarely worse than at this time when Victor Emmanuel directed affairs in Turin. For one reason or another, the numbers of the Piedmontese army fell 40% short of the figure agreed at Plombières, and they were not supplemented by a flood of patriotic volunteers from other parts of Italy. Victor Emmanuel had boasted of 200,000 such volunteers rallying to his cause, but only about 10% of that total materialised.

The Austrian war effort

Fortunately for Piedmont, the Austrian campaign was also faulty. The command of their forces was left by the Emperor to the 'courtier soldiers' Count von Grünne and Count Gyulai, rather than to the more able Benedek or Hess. Their mobilisation was carried out at the slow pace of the Napoleonic Wars, allowing the French ten days to move their troops into Piedmont by rail. The mobilisation could not be more than partial, given the need to leave large numbers of troops in other parts of the Empire, especially in Hungary, in anticipation of possible trouble there. The force of 90,000 that eventually assembled in Italy was considerably smaller than the Franco–Piedmontese force that faced it.

The main battles of the campaign that followed – at Magenta (4 June) and at Solferino (24 June) – were predominantly French engagements. Indeed, not a single Piedmontese soldier lost his life at Magenta, although on the day of Solferino the Piedmontese army was involved nearby in a subsidiary engagement at San Martino. It was, therefore, logical and perfectly in keeping with the previous history of the 'Italian question' that peace should be made when and how the intervening power dictated.

Villafranca and the resignation of Cavour

The armistice concluded at Villafranca on 11 July 1859 emphasises the extent to which the fate of Italy depended upon wider European considerations. Not only were the negotiations limited to the rulers of France and Austria, but Napoleon III was motivated more strongly by events in the Rhineland than by those in Italy (see Chapter 12). It seems likely, however, that he was also motivated, to some extent, by logical misgivings about Piedmont's conduct of the war. It seemed unlikely that the small kingdom would be able to fulfil its promise to pay France's campaign expenses if the war continued for much longer. Piedmont's commanders had virtually no plans nor much equipment for the prolonged siege warfare that would now be necessary if the line of Austrian fortresses on the borders of Venetia (the 'Quadrilateral') were to be attacked. Finally, it was becoming increasingly clear that Cavour had plans for the central Italian duchies that went far beyond the terms of the Plombières agreement.

The terms of the armistice transferred Lombardy, minus the important border fortresses of Peschiera and Mantua, to France on the assumption that it would transfer the territory in turn to Piedmont. The rulers of Tuscany and Modena, who had fled at the news of Magenta, were to be restored, and the principle of a **confederacy** under Papal leadership was reaffirmed. Venetia, of course, remained in Austrian hands. The attitude of Victor Emmanuel to the settlement was ambiguous; that of Cavour was not. Meeting his monarch for the first time in weeks, he railed against the terms of the armistice, called the king '"traitor" and worse', and, in desperation, advised that Piedmont should fight on alone. When the king wisely rejected such foolish advice, Cavour resigned his office.

The issue of the Central Duchies

Even as these events were taking place, it was becoming increasingly clear that the terms of Villafranca could never be implemented in full. The major difficulty would be the restoration of the rulers of central Italy. In his main piece of direct co-operation with the National Society, Cavour had connived at the establishment of provisional administrations in the central Italian territories, in the name of 'Italy and Victor Emmanuel'. By taking such action in an area designated at Plombières as strictly beyond Piedmontese control, Cavour was already violating the agreement and reinterpreting it in a fashion more favourable to his own state. The king seems to have had no prior knowledge of the operation and regarded it as madness to risk the alienation of his ally at such a vital stage in the campaign.

Cavour's resignation after Villafranca left his 'commissioners' in Tuscany, Parma and Modena in an awkward position. Faced with the alternatives of acting on their own initiatives, or abandoning their positions, they did the former. Luigi Farini had himself elected dictator in Parma, Modena and Romagna, which he declared united under their old Latin title of 'Emilia'. In Florence, the capital of Tuscany, a provisional government under Baron Ricasoli played the same role. It declared that it would never tolerate the return of the former rulers and that its intention was to become 'part of a strong Italian kingdom under the constitutional sceptre of King Victor Emmanuel'. Further reforms, in both Emilia and Tuscany, brought the currencies and customs duties of those territories into line with those of Piedmont.

The plebiscites of 1860

The actions of Farini and Ricasoli were, indeed, brave and valuable for the Italian cause, but they draw attention once again to the contribution made by Napoleon III with his military intervention. Not only were his armies indirectly responsible for the original flight of the rulers of Tuscany, Parma and Modena, but it was he, in the negotiations at Zurich to formalise the armistice of Villafranca, who insisted that no force should be used to implement the terms relating to central Italy. This ruled out the dangers of Austrian or French intervention on behalf of the former rulers, but made it hard for Piedmont to enforce its own union with the territories. The answer to this problem lay in combining this piece of unfinished business with another.

Confederacy: A political alliance or association made up of more or less equal members.

Luigi Farini (1812–1866)
Moderate nationalist and associate of Cavour. Piedmontese Minister for Public Instruction (1851). Provisional Governor of Modena (1859), in which capacity he promoted the attachment of that territory to Piedmont. Minister of Commerce in Cavour's last cabinet (1861).

Bettino, Baron Ricasoli (1809–1880)
Prominent Tuscan landowner and agriculturalist. Active in the overthrow of the Grand Duke in 1859, and as 'dictator' of Tuscany was instrumental in its attachment to the Kingdom of Italy.

Annexation: The act of incorporating new territory into a state.

1. **What factors enabled Piedmont to launch a war against Austria only ten years after the Piedmontese defeats of 1848 and 1849?**

2. **'Cavour's foreign policy in the 1850s was over-ambitious and unrealistic, and it did not achieve its aims.' Is this judgement too harsh?**

The section of the Plombières agreement whereby France would receive Nice and Savoy as repayment for its military aid, had been ignored at Villafranca as France's undertaking to clear the Austrians from Lombardy and Venetia, remained unfulfilled. Now it was resurrected in a Franco–Piedmontese agreement concluded in Turin in March 1860. It was decided that Savoy and Nice on the one hand, and Emilia and Tuscany on the other, should hold plebiscites to decide their future allegiances. In both cases, the result was emphatic. In Emilia, the voting was 426,000 to 1,506 in favour of **annexation** by Piedmont; in Tuscany, the margin was 366,571 to 14,925, although a total of 153,000 abstentions served as a reminder that Tuscans remained attached to their separate historical and cultural traditions.

The events of 1859–60 represented neither complete success nor complete disappointment for Piedmont. Its area and population were doubled as a result of war and diplomacy. Both of these methods of expansion, however, had depended, crucially, upon the aid of France, and Piedmont now faced the task of defending and consolidating her gains without the direct protection of its ally.

13.5 What were the political aims and methods of Giuseppe Garibaldi?

The rapid progress of the Italian cause from the apparent deadlock of early 1860 was largely the responsibility of one remarkable man. Giuseppe Garibaldi was born in Nice (4 July 1807) and was associated, from about 1834, with the romantic and conspiratorial nationalism of Mazzini's 'Young Italy'. His first efforts in the Italian cause – participation in an unsuccessful rising in Genoa – earned him a death sentence, passed in his absence. He fled to South America, where he established his reputation as a guerrilla fighter of genius. In 1848, his defence of Mazzini's Roman Republic earned him an international reputation. After further exile in America, and on his island home of Caprera off the coast of Sardinia, he fought for Piedmont in 1859 – or, as he saw it, for Italy against Austria.

His aims for Italy were simple. With a disregard for the constraints imposed either by international diplomacy or by economic backwardness, he worked for a free and unified state, preferably a republic, but a constitutional monarchy if necessary. His political views were confused, so confused that both the English Liberal, William Gladstone, and the Fascist dictator, Benito Mussolini, could claim him as a kindred spirit. The obituary of Garibaldi published in *The Times* (5 June 1882) passed an accurate judgement upon him.

> 'In politics, as in arms, his mind lacked the basis of a rudimentary education. He rushed to conclusions without troubling his head about arguments. His crude notions of democracy, of communism, of cosmopolitanism, or positivism, were jumbled together in his brain and jostled one another in hopeless confusion.'

Garibaldi's fame and achievement, however, rest upon his actions rather than his thought. His contribution to Italian unification falls halfway between those of the other two great Italian figures, Mazzini and Cavour. Mazzini kept the flame of Italian nationalism burning at the time of greatest adversity but, in material terms, achieved very little. Cavour achieved much, but had to dirty himself and his reputation in the murky waters of European politics to do it. By his dashing and naïve reliance on direct military action, Garibaldi seemed to many to have avoided both of these traps. His greatest admirer among historians, G.M. Trevelyan, wrote in

Giuseppe Garibaldi depicted as the 'Liberator of Sicily' – painting by Auguste Etienne

Garibaldi and the Making of Italy (1911) that his work should be 'an encouragement to all high endeavour amongst us in a later age, who, with our eyes fixed on realism and the doctrine of evolution, are in danger of losing faith in ideals'.

Why was Garibaldi able to launch a successful campaign in southern Italy in the aftermath of the 1859 war?

No event in the eleven year period (1859–70), during which the modern Italian state was effectively created, has so caught the imagination as Garibaldi's invasion of Sicily and the subsequent overthrow of the Neapolitan state. Certainly, his tactical expertise and personal charisma were major factors in the success of the Sicilian adventure but the roots of this success were more complicated.

The Sicilian revolt

Garibaldi did not initiate events in Sicily. The rising that took place on 4 April in Palermo, the chief city of the island, owed nothing to him or to Cavour. It was the work of a group of Mazzinian republicans, led by Francesco Crispi and Rosalino Pilo. As republicans, they had refused to identify with the war of the Piedmontese monarchy in the previous year, and now Cavour returned the compliment by ignoring their approaches to him. The support that the rising received in Palermo was due to a combination of national and local factors. It was partly a result of the excitement generated by the events of 1859, but more important was the disappointment felt at the continued conservatism of the young King Francis II, newly succeeded to the throne of Naples.

Francesco Crispi (1819–1901)
Sicilian radical, active in the events of 1848, and in the Sicilian revolt of 1859–60. Subsequently became a politician of national significance and served as Prime Minister of Italy (1887–90 and 1894).

The major difference between this outburst and its Mazzinian forerunners was that the Palermo revolt was quickly taken up in the countryside by the peasantry. Their motives derived entirely from local affairs, and their violent protests were directed as much against the landlords who raised their rents and charged them for the privilege of grinding their own corn, as against the Neapolitan troops who were sent to restore order.

Encouraged by these circumstances, Garibaldi began to prepare for the passage to Sicily. With just over 1,000 volunteers – mainly of middle-class and professional origin and very few of them from further south than Tuscany – he sailed from Genoa in two ancient steamers and landed at Marsala on 11 May. He was aided by the presence of a squadron of ships of the Royal Navy, actually concerned with the safety of local British property, but wrongly supposed by the patrolling Neapolitan navy to be allies of Garibaldi. The arrival of these forces proved to be too much for the harassed Neapolitan troops. On 15 May, Garibaldi had a substantial success at Calatafimi. Palermo fell to him on 30 May and, shortly afterwards, agreement was reached with the Neapolitan commanders for the withdrawal of their troops across the straits to the mainland.

The conquest of Naples

The gallant and romantic Sicilian adventure now took on a succession of more sinister international implications. If Garibaldi were to follow the fleeing troops on to the Neapolitan mainland, why should he not beat them again? If he did so, what was to prevent him from crossing the border from Naples into the Papal States? If he did that, what could prevent a major international crisis involving the French garrison in Rome and, possibly, other Catholic powers?

A cartoon which appeared in an Italian political magazine in May 1860, under the title 'A forbidden fruit'. Eve (Cavour) and the serpent (Garibaldi) discuss which of them shall pluck the apple (Sicily).

? *Why should the artist portray 'Europa' as blindfolded and unaware of the dispute over Sicily?*

Arsenal: Building where weapons
and pieces of military equipment are
stored.

None of these prospects was very attractive to the government of
Piedmont, whose attitude to the Sicilian expedition, as a whole, has been
the subject of controversy. Naturally, the 'nationalist' interpretation has
been that Cavour and his government gave Garibaldi all the help they reasonably could without raising a storm of international, diplomatic protest.
In reality, Garibaldi received so little help from the government that some
would-be volunteers had to be sent home for lack of funds to feed them,
and the ships that transported the 'thousand' to Sicily had to be stolen.
The government even refused the release of 12,000 of Garibaldi's own
guns stored in a police **arsenal** in Milan.

The role of Victor Emmanuel, in this confused period of the
Risorgimento, is difficult to define with certainty, but it seems likely that his
was the crucial contribution. He undoubtedly felt dissatisfied with the
limits imposed upon his Italian authority and influence at Villafranca, and
with France's disapproving attitude over the Central Duchies. The British
ambassador in Turin probably captured the King's state of mind when he
wrote that he 'has no head for anything but the sword and the horse, looks
forward with glee to drawing the one and riding the other, no matter where'.
There is clear evidence that Victor Emmanuel was in contact, during this
period, with Garibaldi and even with Mazzini, and he seems also to have
toyed with the idea of obtaining Venetia, either by war or by purchase. It is
hard to resist the conclusion that he did all this, not through any preconceived principles of unification, but rather through a restless desire to
continue the extension and enlargement of his political influence in Italy.

Why then, if it did not support Garibaldi, did the government allow the
expedition to gather on Piedmontese soil and to sail from a Piedmontese
port? The answer seems to be provided by Cavour in a letter to his ambassador in Paris the day after the expedition had landed in Sicily. 'I could not
stop his going, for force would have been necessary. And the ministry is in
no position to face the immense unpopularity which would have been
drawn upon it had Garibaldi been prevented.' Cavour's ministry did,
indeed, face a major cabinet revolt at that time, in protest against the
handing over of Nice and Savoy to France. Thus, torn between his dislike
for Garibaldi's radicalism and the dangers of international objections, and
the alternative danger of offending the many Italians who loved and
admired Garibaldi, Cavour kept his mouth shut and his options open and
waited upon the outcome.

How did Piedmont respond to Garibaldi's success?

Garibaldini: Term used to describe
the followers of Giuseppe Garibaldi.

The astonishing success of the 'thousand' forced Cavour's hand. A successful invasion of Naples by the *Garibaldini* would at best lead to a
prestigious, radical regime in the south, disputing the leadership of Italy
with Piedmont. At worst, it might precipitate a further international war
in Italy over the status of the Papacy. Cavour clearly outlined the dangers
of the moment. 'If Garibaldi passes over to the mainland and seizes the
Kingdom of Naples and its capital, as he has done with Sicily and
Palermo, he becomes absolute master of the situation. King Victor
Emmanuel loses more or less all his prestige; in the eyes of the great
majority of Italians he is no more than Garibaldi's friend. With the
resources of a kingdom of nine million inhabitants at his disposal,
surrounded as he is by irresistible popular prestige, it is impossible for us
to struggle against him.'

Cavour's first attempts to avert such disaster went sadly wrong.
Agents were sent into the Kingdom of the Two Sicilies to stir up a pro-
Piedmontese revolt that would pre-empt Garibaldi, but they only
encountered the general apathy that had bedevilled generations of
Italian revolutionaries. On 22 August 1860, Garibaldi finally crossed the

1. What were the results of Garibaldi's expedition to southern Italy in 1860?

2. Why did Garibaldi's tactic of direct military action achieve so much in 1860 and so little at any other time?

3. 'By the end of 1860, Garibaldi had done more than Cavour to bring about a united Italy.' Do you agree with this statement?

Straits of Messina and landed on mainland Neapolitan territory. With the general population showing no serious inclination to protect him against the invaders, Francis II abandoned Naples on 6 September, and the *Garibaldini* occupied the city the following day. Cavour rose to the occasion with probably the greatest piece of opportunism of his career. On 12 September, he informed the European powers that Piedmont had no option but to intervene in the Papal territories to restore order. Opposition from Papal forces was brushed aside six days later at Castelfidardo and, by 1 October, the Neapolitan forces between the two sets of invaders had ceased to resist.

At a dramatic meeting at Teano, north of the city of Naples (26 October), Garibaldi faced the choice of acknowledging the supremacy of the King of Piedmont, or fighting him. He chose to hand over his conquests to Victor Emmanuel and to retire, voluntarily, to his island home of Caprera. Plebiscites were held with the now customary haste. By the end of 1860 these had sanctioned the union, not only of the Kingdom of the Two Sicilies, but also of the Papal territories of Umbria and the Marches, with Piedmont-Sardinia, now dignified by the new title of the Kingdom of Italy.

13.6 To what extent should Cavour be regarded as a champion of Italian unification?
A CASE STUDY IN HISTORICAL INTERPRETATION

The events of 1850–70 created the modern state of Italy, and thus remain of great symbolic and emotional importance to it. For that reason, the history of the *Risorgimento* has often been 'borrowed' and reinterpreted by subsequent generations. Various schools of Italian historians, with very different political and intellectual agendas, have found reasons to assume that the most prominent Italian leaders of the period shared a common vision. Coming to the fore in the early days of Italian statehood, and equally acceptable under Benito Mussolini's Fascist regime, nationalist historians were concerned to establish the credentials of the new state, and to represent its creation as a coherent movement of like-minded patriots. Writers who regarded Italian unification as 'the most important fact of the 19th century' (such as D. Zanichelli) naturally regarded Cavour as a kindred spirit and as a dedicated nationalist politician.

A second sympathetic school consisted of those 'liberal' historians who saw the *Risorgimento* as an important element in the defeat of autocracy and reaction, and in the triumph of **modernism**. Such a view was promoted by the Italian historian Benedetto Croce, in *A History of Italy, 1871–1915* (1929). For Croce, the methods and tactics of Cavour and other Italian leaders were fully justified by the end-product of the *Risorgimento*: a successful, modern, and essentially liberal Italian state. This view of the *Risorgimento* was understandably popular among English-speaking historians. While the British historian, G.M. Trevelyan (*Garibaldi's Defence of the Roman Republic*, 1907; *Garibaldi and the Thousand*, 1909; *Garibaldi and the Making of Italy*, 1911) portrayed Giuseppe Garibaldi as a great European liberal, as well as the enemy of tyranny and of unrepresentative government, others performed a similar service for Cavour. A.J. Whyte (*The Political Life and Letters of Cavour*, 1930) and the American W.R. Thayer (*The Life and Times of Cavour*, 1911) emphasised the dedication of the great Piedmontese statesman to the national cause. Throughout, the dominant impression is that the statesman, the radical and the guerrilla leader may have differed in tactics and

Modernism: New ideas and methods, especially when they are contrasted with earlier thinking.

in their immediate priorities, but that each provided an essential element to the common goal of Italian unification.

The claim that Cavour should be set apart from Italian nationalist leaders has come largely from the English historian, Denis Mack Smith. Mack Smith caused controversy among Italian historians by challenging the traditional reputations of many of the Italians prominent in the movement for unification, and in particular by distancing Cavour from the nationalist cause. In *Cavour and Garibaldi, 1860* (1954) and in *Cavour* (1985), the Piedmontese statesman emerges as a cunning politician, without any ideological attachment to the principle of unification and primarily concerned with the **aggrandisement** of Piedmont-Sardinia. Similarly, Mack Smith shows little sympathy towards the view of Victor Emmanuel as an idealistic patriot and father of his country (*Victor Emmanuel, Cavour and the Risorgimento,* 1971).

Aggrandisement: The act of making oneself or one's country larger and/or more important.

In geographical terms, the origins of Garibaldi, Mazzini and Cavour were very similar. All three were born in territory which, after 1815, belonged to the kingdom of Piedmont, and each was born within five years of the others (Mazzini 1805, Garibaldi 1807, Cavour 1810). In social and economic terms, however, all the advantages lay with Cavour. Born into a family of the Piedmontese nobility, his background was as much French as it was Italian, and was open to the broader influences of western European thought. The young Cavour derived his ideas largely from the great economic theorists of the day, such as Adam Smith and David Ricardo. His extensive foreign travels – in France, Britain and Switzerland – also shaped his political and economic views. Observation of Britain's industrial growth helped to turn him into a broad-minded conservative with views similar to those of his greatest political 'hero', Sir Robert Peel. Back home, he implemented these views in economic enterprises, such as the formation of the Lake Maggiore Steamboat Company and the foundation, with others, of the Bank of Genoa and the Bank of Turin. He also spread these ideas through journalism, founding *Il Risorgimento* (1847), a liberal journal popular in Piedmont and with the Italian refugees who flocked into Piedmont from other parts of the peninsula. He came to politics relatively late, was elected to Piedmont's first constitutional assembly (June 1848), and his rapid rise owed more to his progressive economic views than to any vision of Italian nationhood.

Some historians still view Cavour as deliberately working towards the modernisation, liberation and unification of Italy. It is extremely important, therefore, to understand the nature of his 'liberalism' and his 'nationalism' correctly. Of the former, Massimo Salvadori has written, in *Cavour and the Unification of Italy* (1961), that 'Cavour believed in liberty, in responsibility, and in the ability of the educated individual to act responsibly on the basis of his own decisions.' Yet this man achieved his aims partly by bribing newspapers and rigging elections. Every major step of his diplomatic career was taken without consultation with parliament. It is perhaps easier to consider what Cavour did not believe in. As early as 1835 he had written that 'I am persuaded that the *juste milieu* is the only policy right in the circumstances, capable of saving society from the two rocks which threaten to break it – anarchy and despotism'. His 'liberal' policies, therefore, were a means of avoiding the main dangers that he felt threatened Piedmont, and perhaps Italy. These were the tyranny of the traditionalist, autocratic state and the dogmatism of a reactionary Church and, on the other hand, the dangerous extremism of Mazzini and the other left-wing radicals active in Italian politics.

The question of Cavour's nationalism has produced even greater controversy. Historians have claimed, on the one hand, that the unification of Italy was his aim from the beginning of his career and, on the other, that he was mainly interested in the expansion and consolidation of his own Piedmontese state. Denis Mack Smith has maintained that, as late as 1858, 'he [Cavour] still could not accept Mazzini's idea of a united Italy. So long as he obtained Lombardy and Venice he would dominate the peninsula, and that was enough.'

To understand Cavour's attitude to the question of Italian national unity, it may be best to view him as a man who lacked the power to dominate events, or to direct them consistently towards any preconceived goal. Rather, Cavour was a practical politician with aims, originally limited, but modified and expanded by developments over which he had little control. We find a clue, perhaps, in the letter written by Manin to Giorgio Pallavicino (September 1856). 'We must work incessantly to form public opinion, because as soon as opinion is clear and forceful, Cavour I am sure will follow it. I think Cavour to be too intelligent and too ambitious to refuse the Italian enterprise if public opinion demands it strongly enough.' It does appear to be the case that Cavour's views underwent a significant change in the last stages of his life, driven by the pressure of the events taking place around him. In 1860, with his bid for control of northern Italy checked at Villafranca, Cavour lost the initiative in Italian politics to Garibaldi. Forced to annex the southern provinces to keep them out of radical hands, he found himself having to adopt Garibaldi's nationalist programme. He seems then to have realised that the impetus towards unity – away from the greater Piedmont that had been his original goal – was unstoppable. In one of his last parliamentary speeches Cavour surprised his audience with the assertion that, in the long term, it was desirable and inevitable that Rome should become the capital of Italy.

In a sense, therefore, Cavour eventually adopted the geographical programme of Mazzini and of Garibaldi. He never accepted their political programme, however, and firmly imposed his own political vision upon the Italian peninsula as a whole. The communist writer, Antonio Gramsci, fully appreciated this fact when he wrote, in *Il Risorgimento* in 1949, that Cavour 'conceived unity as an increasing of the Piedmontese state and of the patrimony of the dynasty, not at base a national movement, but a royal conquest'.

1. What different views have historians taken of the role that Cavour played in the unification of Italy?

2. What alternatives have historians put forward to the view of Cavour as a champion of Italian unification?

13.7 What problems faced the new Italian state in the 1860s?

The death of Cavour and its aftermath

The new kingdom of Italy, officially in existence from March 1861, had to face the future without the talents of the man who had done more than anyone to establish it. Cavour died unexpectedly on 6 June 1861, exhausted by the problems and tensions of the previous few years. His aims had undoubtedly been different from those of Mazzini and Garibaldi, and his relations with his King had been cool and suspicious. By his masterly flexibility, however, in the face of great political and emotional forces that he could not control directly, he deserved the place with which he was credited by the English poet, George Meredith (1828–1909), in the creation of Italy:

'We think of those
Who blew the breath of life into her frame:
Cavour, Mazzini, Garibaldi: Three:
Her Brain, her Soul, her Sword; and set her free
From ruinous discords.'

Unfortunately, Italy was far from being 'free from ruinous discords'. It had been formed hastily, imperfectly and against the will of many, and now had to face the cost of Cavour's policies. In Cavour's place followed a succession of men: Baron Ricasoli (1861–62), Urbano Rattazzi (March–December 1862), Luigi Farini (1862–63), Marco Minghetti (1863–64) and Alphonso La Marmora (1864–66). None of these was of the calibre of their predecessor, and most of them had been kept relatively ignorant of the details of government by Cavour's virtual monopoly of the major cabinet posts.

The cost of unity

Of the three main problems that faced these men, the most glaring was the state of the Italian economy. The new kingdom had to cope with a huge deficit of 2,450 million lire, incurred by Cavour to carry through his policies of 1856 (which cost 50 million lire) and 1859 (which cost a further 250 million). It also inherited the debts of the smaller regimes that it had helped to oust from other parts of Italy. It was further assumed that a modern state would need certain trappings, such as new roads, railways and military equipment. The construction of a sizeable modern navy, in particular, was a luxury when Italy's most likely enemy, Austria, was predominantly a land power. The result was heavy and unpopular taxation, such as a flour tax proposed in 1865, and the negotiation of large foreign loans often on humiliating terms. By the middle of the 1860s, more than a third of Italian government bonds were in foreign hands and most Italian railway shares were owned by non-Italians.

Agrarian and industrial backwardness

Italy faced these problems with its main economic activity, agriculture, so deeply in debt that an estimated 30% of each year's product was eaten up by repayments. Agricultural methods were so outdated that the economist Nassau Senior considered that cereal production in the south had scarcely increased its output since the days of the Roman Empire. Furthermore, it proved impossible to extend Cavour's principles of financial and industrial modernisation to the rest of Italy. Conservative attitudes in central and southern Italy included a distrust of paper money and a condemnation of financial borrowing and lending as immoral.

Agriculture so dominated the lives of the working classes that the census of 1861 showed only three million people employed in industrial production, of whom 80% were women or children sharing their time between this and agriculture. The textile industry and the production of some chemicals, such as sulphur, had potential but, in an age dominated by coal, Italy lacked sources of energy until the development of hydro-electric power enabled it to exploit its considerable water resources.

The nature of the 'southern question'

Italy's economic difficulties were rivalled by the 'southern question': the difficulties that arose from the social, economic and political diversity of the Italian regions. The huge majorities recorded in favour of unity, in 1860–61, conveyed a misleading impression. They constituted a vote against a number of things, like the tyranny and incompetence of the previous rulers and the lawlessness of rebellious peasants. They probably also represented a considerable degree of electoral malpractice. An observer of the Nice plebiscite, for instance, noted that the slips necessary for a 'no' vote were often in short supply and were sometimes missing altogether, and this was probably true in many cases in the south. What those who voted 'yes' were actually voting for was not absolutely clear.

United Italy could have taken one of at least two forms:

● a federal state, in which the regions retained much of their local autonomy,

● or a centralised one, wholly governed from one national capital.

Cavour seems to have considered both options but, in the last months of his life, he had firmly set his face against the federal solution. The reasons are not altogether clear. It is true that, at that time, federalism seemed to have failed in the world's greatest federal state, the USA, which stood on the verge of civil war in 1861. It is difficult to avoid the conclusion, however, that federalism was seen to threaten the dominant position of Piedmont within Italy, and that Cavour's decision was taken in order to impose a rapid solution upon a problem that he had not expected to arise so suddenly.

'Piedmontisation'

Italy thus became 'piedmontised' at an almost indecent rate. The legal system of Naples, for example, was revolutionised by the passage of 53 decrees in only two days, in February 1861. 'Piedmontisation' involved the division of the new kingdom into 53 provinces on the model of the French *départements*, each governed by a prefect. Customs, coinage, weights and measures were all standardised, in theory, although the illegal use of old coinage and measures persisted at least until the end of the century. The Italian constitution was, in effect, an expanded version of the Piedmontese constitution. The new assembly comprised 443 members, elected by a mere 150,000 voters, who fulfilled the dual qualification of paying 40 lire per year in taxes, and of being literate. Thus, on average, each deputy was elected by about 300 voters.

'Piedmontisation' had two great drawbacks. One was the daunting degree of ignorance that existed in all parts of Italy about the other parts. In particular, the ignorance of the north about conditions in Naples and Sicily extended to all levels of government. Cavour himself, although he had visited France, Britain and Switzerland, never travelled further south than Tuscany. The policy resulted, therefore, in a bizarre series of misconceptions and mistakes. Compulsory education was prescribed for southern Italy, where 90% of the population was illiterate, but it could not be paid for without attacking the property of the Church. The dissolution of 2,382 monasteries and **convents**, by 1866, provided some funds, but outraged local religious feelings and deprived the localities of charitable institutions run by the monks and nuns long before the state could afford to replace them. The jury system was introduced throughout the south despite the protests of local authorities that **Mafia** activity would make the corruption and intimidation of juries a simple matter.

The second drawback was a simple lack of resources, both financial and human. The south, it was fondly imagined by men who had never been there, was rich in minerals. Instead, it had proved a drain on the resources of the north. Piedmont, unlike Prussia in the case of German unification, had neither the income nor the trained manpower to administer its new territories effectively.

'The imposition of the Piedmontese administrative system,' concludes Denis Mack Smith, 'reinforced the impression that one region had virtually conquered the rest.' Predictably, the southern regions reacted as they had done against earlier injustices. What the national government

Convents: The buildings where nuns lived and carried out their religious existence.

Mafia: A secret society originating in Sicily, and active there in opposition to Neapolitan rule.

Brigandage: The practice of bandits (brigands) who live by pillage and robbery.

1. What difficulties did the Italian government face in southern Italy as a result of the events of 1860?

2. Is it more accurate to regard the events of 1859–63 as 'Piedmontese expansion' or as 'Italian unification'?

3. To what extent, and in what respects, was the unification of Italy still incomplete at the time of Cavour's death in 1861?

referred to as 'campaigns for the suppression of **brigandage**' amounted to a full-scale civil war in the south. The issue was not effectively settled in the central government's favour until 1865, and the struggle claimed more Italian lives than all the battles of the *Risorgimento* put together. In 1863 alone the government committed 90,000 troops to peacekeeping operations in the south, far more than had ever taken the field against the Austrians.

It was not realistic to expect that such deep-rooted difficulties would be solved within a decade. The processes of road building, agricultural reform and educational improvement were still far from complete by the outbreak of the First World War. It is not surprising, therefore, that the official utterances of the Italian government sought to concentrate public attention on the third of the new kingdom's outstanding problems as far as possible.

13.8 By what means, and with what success, did the Italian state extend its influence over other Italian territories?

The Venetian question

The government of Victor Emmanuel owed much of its continued prestige, in 1861, to its opportunistic intervention in Naples, which had enabled it to be identified with the national cause. It was thus very difficult for the government, especially at a time of such extreme domestic difficulties, to ignore the fact that, in the eyes of the nationalists, there were still two very important pieces missing from the Italian 'jigsaw'. Upon taking office, Baron Ricasoli was quick to reassure Italians that 'we claim Rome as our natural capital and Venetia as an integral part of our national soil'. Rome and Venice, however, were not Naples. To gain either of them would mean dealing with one or more of the great powers at a time when nearly half of the Italian army was fighting its reluctant compatriots in the south.

The first moves towards a solution to the 'Venetian question' were therefore made by men to whom such diplomatic niceties were of little concern. Garibaldi and his 'party of action' assumed that what had worked in Naples, would work in Venetia. They were active in 1862, attempting to engineer an armed rising, and again in 1864, pinning their hopes this time on risings elsewhere in the Habsburg Empire which would draw Austrian troops out of Italy. In both cases, news leaked out. The protests of foreign diplomats caused the Italian government to intervene to thwart Garibaldi's plans.

The Prussian alliance and the war of 1866

Instead, like all the other component parts of the 'Italian question', except Naples, the Venetian question had to wait for a solution until the general mood of European politics was ready. The decline of Austria's relations with Prussia, in the course of the Schleswig-Holstein affair in 1864 (see Chapter 14), alerted both Prussians and Italians to the common ground in their foreign policies, and to the common benefits that might result from action against Austria. Italian enthusiasm was not total. Victor Emmanuel continued to believe, in Mack Smith's words, that 'the important thing was to have a war, and as soon as possible', adding to his anti-constitutional motives of 1859 the desire to distract attention from the problems in the south. La Marmora, however, recalled the pitfalls involved in playing the role of junior partner to a major power, hence his offer to purchase Venetia from an anxious Austrian government for 1,000 million lire. The military faction in Vienna overrode the initial enthusiasm of the Austrian Emperor. The Italian government was left with little option but to enter into closer negotiations with Prussia.

By April 1866, General Govone's mission to Berlin had concluded a military agreement by which both sides undertook not to conclude a separate peace, thus hoping to avoid another Villafranca, and by which Italy was to receive Venetia as the reward for its role. On 20 June, four days after Prussia, Italy formally declared itself at war with Austria once more.

After the great gains of 1859–60, Italian expectations were high and the king himself was, according to one of his ministers, 'quite drunk with overconfidence'. In theory, the confidence was justified. Italy could expect to put some 250,000 men into the field against the 130,000 that the divided Austrian army could spare from its southern front. The fleet too, after the recent 'spending spree', could count 12 ironclad battleships of the most modern design, to Austria's seven. In reality, these advantages were to be outweighed by other factors. The Italian general staff was not notable for military skill and experience. Many, like the fleet's commander, Admiral Persano, owed their positions primarily to influence and corruption at Court. It was conveniently overlooked that it was not these men, but guerrillas and Frenchmen who had won the great battles of the *Risorgimento*. Even below the highest levels of command, organisation was so bad and planning so rudimentary that only about 25% of the army ever reached the front. Once there, the unfortunate troops found strategy paralysed by bitter personal rivalries between prominent officers, and by the presence of a monarch who insisted upon taking overall personal command, despite the opinion of General Cialdini that 'the King is wholly ignorant and incompetent'.

The initial confidence did not last long. On 24 June, La Marmora's and Cialdini's forces fought an indecisive action against a strong Austrian defensive position at Custoza, close to the 1848 battlefield. They then disintegrated, due to panic and to confused orders. The engagement wrecked the reputations of La Marmora and Cialdini and burst the 'bubble' of Italian military pride. A month later, Persano's fleet engaged the Austrian fleet off the island of Lissa in the Adriatic and, in the midst of similar confusion, lost three major ships including the 'Re d'Italia', the pride of the Italian navy. It was claimed, at Persano's **court martial**, that the fleet had fired 1,450 shells without scoring a major hit on the enemy.

Despite such failures, the crushing defeat inflicted by the Prussians upon the Austrians at Sadowa (3 July) brought about an armistice (23 July) by which Italy gained Venetia after all. At the time, however, it was impossible to see the war as anything other than a miserable failure. Almost all the other aims of the government had been frustrated. It had achieved none of the heroism or glory necessary to weld the disparate parts of the country into a nationally conscious whole. The war had done great harm to the prestige of both the army and the monarchy, and Venetia had come into Italian hands, just as Lombardy had done in 1859, through

Court martial: The trial in a military court of a member of the armed forces who is charged with breaking a military law.

the triumph of a foreign army. There had been no Venetian uprising in support of the Italian forces. Even the blindest of patriots could hardly fail to notice that the huge majority, recorded in the subsequent plebiscite in favour of union with the rest of Italy, hardly squared with the apathy that Venetians had shown during the war itself.

The problem of Rome: the failure of Garibaldi

The failures of 1866 rendered even bleaker the Italian government's prospects of establishing its capital in Rome. In the five years since Garibaldi had been checked on the Pope's frontiers, two main methods had been pursued for gaining access to Rome, but with little success.

The first solution had been that of the 'party of action'. Dismissing the power of the Papacy, Garibaldi seems to have regarded Rome as an easier target than Naples. He was wrong on three counts. Firstly, he would be forced to confront the French garrison as well as the small Papal army. Secondly, he would have to face the army of his own government, who could not permit 'banditry' to prejudice their diplomatic relations with France, and could not contemplate the humiliation of acquiring their capital city from the hands of a revolutionary. Thirdly, he was once more badly mistaken in hoping that his actions might spark off a popular revolt within the Papal territories. The Church was at the heart of the region's economy, and was unlikely to be attacked by the populace that it supported. Historian A.J. Whyte concluded, in *The Political Life and Letters of Cavour* (1930), 'The Church amused them, employed them and fed them, and to her they looked alike for consolation in trouble and material help in times of stress.'

Nevertheless, the idealism of Garibaldi and the highly ambiguous attitude of the King and some of his ministers, twice tempted the 'party of action' into projects that caused the government acute embarrassment. In August 1862, an expedition that could have been intercepted easily had the Italian fleet had clearer orders, landed at Aspromonte in Calabria. It had to be checked by government troops. Five years later, in October 1867, the provisional withdrawal of the French troops gave Garibaldi another opportunity. At Mentana (3 November), however, his forces were defeated by Papal troops, reinforced at the last moment by the hastily returning Frenchmen.

The problem of Rome: the search for a diplomatic solution

The second possible solution to the Roman question was by means of diplomacy. It seemed unlikely, however, that the Italian government, after a decade of anti-clericalism, would achieve much by direct negotiation with the Church. Throughout the *Risorgimento*, the reaction of the Papacy to changing social and political circumstances was, in the words of A.J. Whyte, 'to bind her medieval robe more closely about her'. This process of restating an inflexible position culminated in the publication, in December 1864, of the **encyclical** *Quanta Cura,* which listed a 'syllabus of errors' of 80 points. Among the 'errors' were the principles of liberty of conscience, state education, liberalism, constitutional government, and opposition to the temporal power of the Pope. It was an attack upon most of the progressive ideas of western Europe in the 19th century and, as such, was an embarrassment to all progressive Catholics. It was also a manifesto of opposition to most of the professed ideas of the Italian government.

Negotiations with France were rather more fruitful. Napoleon III had long regretted the expense and political inconvenience involved in protecting a stubborn and reactionary Pope, but could not agree to abandon him to the 'bandits' who had set up the Roman republic of 1849. After

Encyclical: A letter or order issued by the Pope to the bishops of the Church.

1862, and the encounter at Aspromonte, it was possible to claim that the responsible Italian government effectively had Garibaldi under its control.

By 1864, therefore, the French were willing to enter into highly secret negotiations, which resulted in the so-called 'Convention of September'. France consented to remove its garrison from Rome, in return for an Italian undertaking to protect Papal territory from all external attack. A number of sympathetic commentators have been tempted to admire a move by which, in A.J. Whyte's words, 'the wolves were set to guard the fold'. Denis Mack Smith opposes that view, too, by pointing out that the Italian diplomats must either have been lying deliberately to the French, or else deliberately breaking their promises to the Italian electors concerning the acquisition of Rome.

The acquisition of Rome and subsequent relations with the Papacy

Whatever the motives behind it, the Convention of September did not bring the Italians any closer to making their capital in Rome. The withdrawal of French troops, in December 1866, was reversed by the Mentana fiasco less than a year later, and the situation remained one of stalemate and confrontation until 1870. Then, as usual, Italy's problems were resolved by European factors beyond Italy's control.

The drift of France towards war with Prussia offered two openings to Italy. The first was diplomatic when, in May 1870, Napoleon III sought a basis for an anti-Prussian alliance. For all its doubts about fighting against its most recent ally, Italy still suggested Rome as the price of its co-operation. For the French Catholics, that price remained too high. The outbreak of war, however, presented Italy with an opportunity that public opinion would not allow it to miss. France's Roman garrison could no longer be spared and by 19 August the evacuation was complete. The Prime Minister, Giovanni Lanza, still acted with great caution, waiting until the defeat of France at Sedan. The formal agreement of Spain, Austria and the Catholic German states, and the arrest of Mazzini, ensured that there would be no unfortunate side-effects. The modest Papal army was overcome in a brief engagement on 19 September 1870, as a result of which Rome was at last occupied by the Italian army.

The usual plebiscite (2 October) produced the usual result, a huge majority in favour of union with the rest of Italy (133,681 to 1,507). Once again, the result contradicted the previous indifference of the population, and a French officer in the Papal army, the Comte de Beaufort, published a detailed account of alleged dishonesty at the polls. This included the absence of 'no' voting slips, intimidation, plural voting and the introduction of non-qualified voters. His account is, perhaps, a fair representation of the plebiscites of the *Risorgimento*.

It was one thing to win Rome, and quite another to win the Church's acceptance of the fact. For instance, although stripped of his temporal powers, Pope Pius IX made his supreme act of defiance, in July 1870, by declaring the **doctrine of Papal Infallibility**. In May 1871, by the Law of Guarantees, the Italian government made a further gesture of conciliation as it sought to define the position of the Pope within the kingdom of Italy. The full spiritual jurisdiction of the Pope was recognised, freedom of communication with the Church throughout the world was confirmed, along with the liberty of appointment to all ecclesiastical offices, and the liberty of teaching. The Pope received an annual grant equivalent to £129,000, remained free of Italian taxation, and retained the full use of the Vatican and of Castel Gandolfo. Typically, Pius IX chose to remain 'a prisoner in the Vatican', and not until 1929 was the Italian state formally recognised by the Papacy.

Doctrine of Papal Infallibility: The teaching that, as the Pope is God's representative on Earth, his decisions and utterances on doctrine express the will of God and cannot be questioned.

1. How did Venetia and Rome become parts of the united Italian state?

2. To what extent do the events of 1861–1870 support the view that Italian unification owed more to diplomacy than to nationalist fervour and Italian military skill?

Source-based questions: Cavour and Garibaldi's expedition in 1860

SOURCE A

You will see from Fanti's note that the government is very nearly in real trouble. Fanti was not wrong, as Minister of War, to wish to safeguard the pressing needs of defence. It is evident that the treaty could be the subject of very grave censures (on 10 May). In rushing through the cession [handing over] of Nice and Savoy without the least regard for the just sensibilities of the country, the French government has succeeded in destroying the influence of the government internally as well as externally: by indefinitely prolonging the negotiations over the frontiers, it will make the existence of the government impossible, and will only give more impetus and prestige to the opposition of Rattazzi and Garibaldi. [The French government] must realise that the position in which they have put me is not sustainable. I must have at least some argument to demonstrate that we have not forgotten to safeguard the interests of the country in these unhappy negotiations. Although one might say that Italy is grateful for the power that France has given us, yet a great number of deputies are not at all inclined to forget that the Peace of Villafranca left not only Venice but also Peschiera and Mantua to Austria, and that the annexation of central Italy was made not by France but against her.

If Fanti resigns, the existing government will not last more than a single day. Fanti is the only one among the existing ministers congenial to the King – and I have reason to believe that HM, who always has a weakness for Garibaldi and Rattazzi, is secretly looking to remove me from the direction of affairs. I would be well content to retire to Leri; but I am not the man to leave the country in the middle of the immense dangers which would spring from the rejection of the treaty. I am therefore disposed to carry the burden of power for a little longer – and the unpopularity. I only ask that the Emperor gives me a little help to accomplish the thankless task I have undertaken, or at least not to make it more difficult for me.

Cavour to Nigra, Piedmontese ambassador in Paris, 24 April 1860

SOURCE B

Wednesday 2 May: Scovazzo informed me that Massimo D'Azeglio, Nigra and Hudson, the English Ambassador, were the people who are working with all their strength to keep Cavour Prime Minister. It now seems that serious opposition is being organised in the Senate over the two provinces of Nice and Savoy. The rebellion is spreading in Sicily.

Thursday 3 May: The news from Sicily is still favourable to the insurrection. Nicolari writes to me from Genoa that Garibaldi is going to leave in two days time with an elect band of young men. The Government is behaving rather passively, the clearest sign that the revolution has taken it by surprise. Public opinion in Turin is moving against Count Cavour: he may fall and never regain power.

From the political diary of the Piedmontese Senator, Asproni, May 1860

SOURCE C

Garibaldi has landed in Sicily. It is a great piece of luck that he did not pursue his idea of attacking the Pope. We cannot stop him making war against the King of Naples. Whether it turns out for the best or the worst, it was inevitable. He would have become dangerous in internal politics if he had been held back by force. What will happen now? It is impossible to predict. Will England help him? It is possible. Will France stop him? I believe not. And us? We cannot openly support him, neither can we restrain private efforts on his behalf. Therefore we have decided not to allow any new expeditions to be prepared from the ports of Genoa and Livorno, but not to stop the sending of arms and munitions, provided that it is carried out with a degree of prudence. I am not disguising all the inconvenience of this ill-defined line we are following, but I cannot think of an alternative which doesn't present more serious and dangerous prospects.

Cavour to Ricasoli, Royal Governor of Tuscany, 16 May 1860 (sent before Cavour received Source D).

Source-based questions: Cavour and Garibaldi's expedition in 1860

SOURCE D

Just as the royal government ought to stop any attack on the Papal States at the moment, so it should tolerate and even give aid to the Sicilian insurrection, if that can be done covertly, and at least without compromising ourselves too much. We cannot sufficiently proclaim towards Europe the duty that binds Italians to help their compatriots who are subject to evil governments.

Ricasoli to Cavour, 15 May 1860

SOURCE E

I entirely agree with you about Garibaldi's expedition. I have nothing to add except that we must save appearances so as not to increase our diplomatic difficulties. France has shown less displeasure than I expected.

Cavour to Ricasoli, 23 May 1860

1. Explain briefly the following highlighted references that appear in the sources.

(a) 'In rushing through the cession of Nice and Savoy without the least regard for the just sensibilities of the country' (Source A)

(b) 'the Peace of Villafranca' (Source A)

(c) 'It is a great piece of luck that he did not pursue his idea of attacking the Pope' (Source C).

2. Study Sources B and C.

Does Source B provide convincing support for Cavour's profession of weakness (Source A)?

3. Compare the trustworthiness of Cavour's remarks in Sources A and C.

4. On the strength of these sources, and any other evidence known to you, discuss the assertion that 'until long after Garibaldi had sailed for Sicily, Cavour had no policy at all towards the expedition'.

14

The unification of Germany, 1850–1871

Key Issues

● *Why was Germany unified under Prussian rather than Austrian leadership?*

● *How important was the role of Bismarck in the establishment of German unity?*

● *What were the main motives of the Prussian leadership in bringing about this form of unification?*

14.1 Why was Prussia not able to extend its political influence within Germany in the aftermath of the 1848 Revolutions?

14.2 In what ways did the balance of power between Prussia and Austria change in the years 1850–1862?

14.3 In what respects did Prussia's economy provide a basis for its dominance within Germany?

14.4 Why was there a constitutional crisis within Prussia in 1860–1862, and why did it bring Otto von Bismarck to power?

14.5 What were the bases of Bismarck's political beliefs and foreign policy?

14.6 By what means, and by what stages, was Austria excluded from German politics between 1863–1866?

14.7 What had Bismarck achieved by 1866?

14.8 What factors forced Bismarck to go beyond the settlement achieved in 1866?

14.9 Why, and with what consequences, did Prussia go to war with France in 1870?

14.10 Historical interpretation: Was German unification primarily the result of successful Bismarckian diplomacy?

Framework of Events

1850	March: Union of Erfurt
	November: Capitulation of Olmütz
1853	Commercial treaty between Prussia and Austria. Oldenburg and Hanover join *Zollverein*
1854–56	Crimean War
1858	Prince Wilhelm becomes regent of Prussia
1859	Formation of the *Nationalverein*
1860	Death of Friedrich Wilhelm IV; succession of Wilhelm I
1862	Bismarck is appointed Minister President of Prussia
1863	Polish Revolt. Prussia offers Alvensleben Convention to Russia. Schleswig incorporated into Denmark
1864	Prussia and Austria go to war with Denmark over Schleswig-Holstein
1865	Convention of Gastein. Conclusion of a new *Zollverein* treaty, from which Austria was excluded. Meetings between Bismarck and Napoleon III at Biarritz
1866	June: Outbreak of war between Prussia and Austria
	July: Prussian victory at Sadowa
	August: Peace of Prague
1867	Formation of North German Confederation. London Conference guarantees neutrality of Luxembourg
1868	Overthrow of Spanish monarchy
1870	July: Crisis over Hohenzollern candidature to the Spanish throne. Outbreak of Franco-Prussian War
	September: Defeat of French forces at Sedan
1871	Proclamation of the German Empire (Reich).

Overview

THE main forces working for and against the political unification of the German states were evident for several decades before Otto von Bismarck was called to power. Theories of German nationhood had flourished in intellectual circles throughout this period, and had occasionally been translated into action, most notably in the establishment of a German parliament in Frankfurt in 1848. As the events of 1848–49 indicated, however, such theories faced formidable opposition from several influential forces. They clashed directly with the specific political interests of the individual rulers of the German states, whose priority was invariably to resist any reduction of their own powers and prerogatives. Yet they were sometimes distracted from such preoccupations by other considerations. The experience of the Napoleonic Wars, and of the disruption of the 1840s, made it clear to them that their positions were vulnerable. They were under threat, equally, from the ambitions of a foreign power such as France, and from the radical demands of their own subjects. The desire for security jockeyed with political conservatism at the head of their agenda.

In addition to this desire for security, important economic forces worked in favour of some form of unity. German manufacturers and merchants had appreciated, for some time, the benefits to be gained from the relaxation of customs duties and the other restrictions that were involved in transporting goods and materials from one German state to another. Crucially, of course, this was a benefit that might also be enjoyed by the larger, and more economically advanced, of the German states. In particular Prussia, with territories to the west and north-east of Germany after the 1815 settlement, had a powerful vested interest in easier economic intercourse. In northern Germany, such considerations had produced a degree of economic unity as early as the 1830s, in the form of the *Zollverein*. This 'customs union' had flourished for more than two decades before Bismarck came to office.

The events of 1848 illustrated some important truths about the prospects of German unity. They made it clear, for instance, that the middle-class nationalists assembled in Frankfurt lacked the political means to impose their vision of Germany's future upon the more powerful German princes. The initiative lay with such rulers as the King of Prussia or the Emperor of Austria. For the time being, Austria remained the stronger of these two powers, with military resources and diplomatic connections that Prussia could not afford to challenge. Nor was either power greatly interested in the 'national question'. Austria was clearly preoccupied with the maintenance of its multinational Empire, while Prussia's primary concern was for its freedom of action in northern Germany, and for the maintenance of the political and economic interests of its Junker governing class. Their attitude was mirrored in neighbouring states, in France and in Russia, for instance, where the prospect of a powerful neighbour, where once there had been more than 30 lesser states, was extremely unattractive. Whatever forces worked towards German unity, they would have some thorny diplomatic or military problems to solve in this respect.

It was the following decade that transformed the prospects of German unity. In the course of the 1850s, the European context was altered in several important respects. Austria's credibility as a leader and defender of the German princes was reduced dramatically. Its decision to remain neutral in the Crimean War ruptured

Power vacuum: A term used to describe a region in which no state exercises effective control. Such areas are always liable to be occupied by expansionist forces.

the conservative alliance with Russia that had served it so well in 1848–50. Its failure to resist French forces in Italy, in 1859, not only called into question its ability to defend the German princes, but also brought home to princes and to German patriots alike the potential threat posed to them by a new Napoleon Bonaparte. At the opening of the 1860s, there was not only a **power vacuum** in the politics of German leadership, but an urgent and widespread desire that it should be filled.

Such were the circumstances that prevailed when Bismarck was appointed Minister President of Prussia in 1862. The priorities that he brought to that office have been the subject of considerable debate, but few historians today would doubt that they were primarily Prussian and conservative. Above all, he sought to defend the Prussian state, as well as the interests of his Junker class, against two major threats. These were, firstly, the domestic, political ambitions of the middle classes, with their liberal, constitutional claims, and, secondly, the continued claims of Austria to be regarded as the major political authority within the German Confederation. As a primary instrument of Austrian authority, Bismarck viewed the Confederation itself as a threat to Prussian integrity, and to its freedom of political action. In political terms, it was not hard to outmanoeuvre the liberals, and by 1867 Bismarck appeared to have done so. In part, he had achieved this by taking measures to increase the size and power of the Prussian army, the key to political power, without bothering about the approval of the parliamentary deputies. It may have been illegal, but it worked. In part, however, he achieved a working relationship with the liberals by appearing to work with them on the project closest to their hearts, the promotion of political unity within Germany.

There is a strong case for claiming that, by 1866, Bismarck had achieved all that he really wished to achieve. Austrian influence had been banished from northern Germany, where Prussia now exercised the decisive influence over the **North German Confederation**. In domestic politics, the prestige of the Prussian crown and of the Prussian army was such that it could not be challenged in the foreseeable future. In the process, Bismarck had firmly established his own political position. Yet other forces drove him further. Some of these forces were diplomatic, for he could not ignore the possibility of an Austrian recovery, and of the re-establishment of its influence over the loose confederation of states that existed in southern Germany.

North German Confederation: A revised version of the German Confederation, established as a result of Prussia's victory over Austria in 1866. It comprised those German states north of the river Main, with Prussia the dominant political influence within the confederation.

More serious, and more immediate, was the French reaction to the events of 1866. Desiring compensation and security from the new Prussian 'super state', France made demands that Bismarck hoped initially to satisfy, in order to maintain his new creation. When it proved impossible to do so, he too sought security, in military alliances with the south German states, in diplomatic intrigues with Spain, and by a pretended community of interest with the nationalists in various German states.

Otto Edouard Leopold von Bismarck-Schönhausen (1815–1898) Bismarck studied law and agriculture before becoming a member of the Prussian parliament in 1847. He was Minister	President of Prussia (1862–90) and Chancellor of the German Empire (1871–90). He became Prince von Bismarck in 1871. After successfully waging war with Denmark (1863–64), he went to war with Austria and its allies	(the Seven Weeks' War, 1866). His victory forced the unification of the north German states under his own chancellorship (1867). He was then victorious against France, under the leadership of Napoleon III, in the Franco–Prussian War	(1870–71), proclaiming the German Empire and annexing Alsace-Lorraine. He tried to preserve Prussian leadership within Germany, and to guarantee German security through alliances with Russia and Austria.

14.1 Why was Prussia not able to extend its political influence within Germany in the aftermath of the 1848 Revolutions?

The Union of Erfurt

In the short term, the revolutionary events of 1848–49 appeared to have prepared the ground for much greater Prussian influence over German politics (see Chapter 11). Following its active role in defence of German interests in Schleswig-Holstein, and against the radicalism of the Frankfurt Parliament, the prestige of the Prussian state was higher than it had been for many years in conservative circles. Austria, meanwhile, was still largely preoccupied with the affairs of its empire. The German Confederation, too, had played little part in the recent constitutional chaos, and could be regarded as obsolete. How could the vacuum in princely German politics be filled without risking the revival of radical, nationalist ideas?

This was the question that Baron Josef von Radowitz, adviser to the King of Prussia on federal reform for more than 20 years, tried to answer in a set of proposals put to a representative assembly of the German states at Erfurt in March 1850. These proposals included a union of the north German states under the presidency of the King of Prussia, and under the protection of the victorious Prussian army. For Friedrich Wilhelm, the great advantage of such a plan was that Prussian influence would be based upon sound monarchical principles and not, as the offer of the German crown had been in 1849, upon any principles of **popular sovereignty**. In general, Austria would be excluded from this 'Erfurt Union'. Radowitz proposed a compromise by which Austria might be linked to the Union by a second, wider union, based upon **free trade** and, perhaps, upon a common foreign policy.

The 'Capitulation of Olmütz'

In effect, Radowitz was moving too far, too fast. The only real basis for the Erfurt Union was the fear of the German princes at the prospect of a renewed liberal onslaught. He and Friedrich Wilhelm, as historian A.J.P. Taylor put it in *Bismarck the Man and the Statesman* (1968), 'thought the princes converted [to the idea of a *kleindeutsch* union] when they were merely frightened'. In fact, it was already evident that many of the 'middling' German states feared Prussian hegemony as much as, if not more than, liberal revolt. Hence the refusal of 11 states – including Hanover, Bavaria, Saxony and Württemberg – to send representatives to Erfurt. The weakness of the proposals was that they arose from an Austrian withdrawal from German affairs that was only temporary. By late 1850, with the Hungarian and Italian revolts under control, the Austrian premier, Felix von Schwarzenberg, was able to declare that 'we shall not let ourselves be thrown out of Germany'. He began to insist upon the reconstruction of the Confederation as it had existed before 1848.

A constitutional conflict in the small duchy of Hesse-Cassel, which formed the vital link between the two blocks of Prussian territory (see map on page 405), provided the test of nerves between the two German powers. With the alternatives of seeking aid either from the Erfurt Union or from the Confederation, Hesse-Cassel turned to the latter. For a while, Prussia seemed prepared to fight to defend its new-found prestige, but Russian support for Austria proved to be the decisive factor. 'Only the Tsar is sovereign,' wrote Karl Marx at the time. 'In the end rebellious Prussia will bow to his command.'

So, in a meeting at Olmütz (November 1850), Friedrich Wilhelm gave

Josef von Radowitz (1797–1858)
Chief of Artillery Staff in the Prussian army (1830). Adviser to Friedrich Wilhelm IV, and enthusiastic advocate of Prussian leadership of the German princes.

Popular sovereignty: The principle or belief that the people are the true rulers of the state, and that government should serve their interests.

Free trade: A system by which trading partners accept the products of the other without taxing them, confident that both would benefit from the arrangement. The benefits of free trade were felt to be considerable: wider markets for domestic products, cheaper goods from abroad, and possible stimulation of domestic industries through competition with strong foreign industries.

Kleindeutsch ('Little German'): Term used to describe the concept of a united Germany (favoured by Prussia) from which Austria is excluded.

Capitulation: Surrender (i.e. the events at Olmütz in 1850 indicated that Prussia was surrendering to the interests of Austria).

1. What factors brought about the creation of the Erfurt Union?

2. Why did it seem, in 1848–49, that Prussia might take the leading role in German politics, and why did this not turn out to be the case?

in once more to his doubts, and to the doubts of many Prussian conservatives, and agreed to abandon the Erfurt Union in favour of the revival of the German Confederation under Austrian presidency. By the so-called '**Capitulation** of Olmütz', Prussia abandoned the leadership of Germany for a decade and a half. Prussian reactions ranged from conservative satisfaction at the abandonment of a dangerous innovation, to patriotic humiliation. All were aware that German leadership lay beyond Prussia's reach until there was a change in the military balance of Germany, and in the European system of alliances.

14.2 In what ways did the balance of power between Prussia and Austria change in the years 1850–1862?

The attempted extension of Austrian hegemony

Alexander, Count von Bach (1813–1893)
Austrian politician: Minister of Justice (1848); Minister of the Interior (1849–59); Chief Minister (1852–59). Negotiated Concordat with the Papacy (1855) and served as ambassador to the Holy See (1859–67).

Karl, Count von Bruck (1798–1860)
Austrian politician: delegate to the Frankfurt Parliament (1848); Minister of Commerce (1848–51); Minister of Finance (1855–60). His projected economic and financial reforms were largely thwarted by the war in Italy (1859) and he committed suicide.

Karl Ferdinand, Count von Buol (1797–1865)
Austrian diplomat, serving as ambassador to Piedmont (1844), Russia (1848) and Britain (1851). As Foreign Minister (1852–59), he was unsuccessful in persuading the Emperor to join the Crimean War against Russia.

Between 1851 and 1853, Austrian statesmen attempted to consolidate and to exploit the position of supremacy in German affairs manifested at Olmütz. Firstly, Schwarzenberg proposed the extension of the Confederation to include Austria's non-German territories, thus forming an 'Empire of 70 millions'. When this was rejected by the German princes assembled at Dresden in mid-1851, Austrian proposals switched to an economic tack. Alexander von Bach, Minister of the Interior, and the Baron von Bruck, the former Rhineland liberal then in charge of Austrian finances, proposed the linking of the Prussian-dominated *Zollverein* with the Empire, to produce a vast central European (*Mitteleuropa* – 'Middle Europe') economic union.

The Austrians, however, were overplaying their hand. Olmütz had restored the balance between Austrian military power and Prussian economic power upon which the independence of the lesser princes depended. These princes now had no intention of seeing Austria upset that balance, and their independence, again. Austria had to be content, therefore, with a commercial treaty with Prussia, acting as spokesman for the *Zollverein*, which was signed in February 1853.

The impact of foreign affairs: the Crimea

In Germany, as in most of Europe, the Crimean War acted as a great stimulant of political change. Despite the debt that his state owed to the Russians since 1849, the Austrian Foreign Minister, Count von Buol, believed that Austria should conclude an alliance with the western powers, as a safeguard against nationalist action in Italy. He also had no desire to see Russia in control of Moldavia, Wallachia and the mouth of the river Danube. This policy required an understanding with Prussia, to ensure that it would not seek to benefit in Germany from Austria's preoccupation, as it had done in 1850. Prussian opinion, however, was bitterly divided, with conservatives following a pro-Russian policy, while the liberals favoured France and Britain.

In the end, Friedrich Wilhelm followed the least controversial line, that of neutrality. Thus, neither of the German powers played any military role in the war, although Austria maintained a kindly attitude towards the allies. The events of the Crimea, nevertheless, resulted in a number of subtle changes in the political situation within German. Firstly, Austria's concerns had been shown to be purely imperial, rather than German. Its diplomacy had been dominated by thoughts of Moldavia, the Danube and Italy, and Bismarck had ridiculed these aims as being 'to procure a few stinking Wallachians'. Secondly, Austria's failure to repay its debt to Russia had ruptured forever the 'Holy Alliance' between the two great legitimist powers, leaving Austria isolated in European diplomacy. Prussia, although also neutral, owed Russia no such debt, and its neutrality had at least guaranteed Russia security on its Polish borders. In German terms, the Crimean War was a depressing episode, proving its remoteness from the great decisions of European politics and confirming its insignificance in international affairs. German historian Helmut Böhme (1966) preferred to view the war in Prussian terms, as a period of great advance in its prestige within Germany as, proportionately, Austria's national and international prestige declined.

The impact of foreign affairs: Italy

The Italian war of 1859 (see Chapters 12 and 13) continued the process of Austrian humiliation. In Helmut Böhme's words, 'Austria now buried her plans for a customs union, her German policy and her economic policy on the battlefields of northern Italy.' As a legitimist, the Prussian regent, Prince Wilhelm, inclined towards aid for Austria, but Austria's isolation from all the other European powers made this a dangerous course to take. In the event, Prussia delayed the mobilisation of its forces until Austria's defeat was virtually assured (July 1859). It then mobilised in concert with the South German princes, with a view to protecting the Rhine frontier against any further French expansionism. Thus, Prussia appeared to be making a gesture for the protection of Germany at a time when it was becoming increasingly difficult to believe in Austrian protection.

The year 1860, with Napoleon III's annexation of Nice and Savoy, brought further cause for the princes to seek protection against French aggression. When Napoleon visited Baden-Baden in an attempt to dispel this anxiety (June 1860) he found himself faced with an array of German rulers, from Bavaria, Hanover, Saxony and Württemberg, united in their apprehension. In general, the European events of 1859–60 marked the beginning of German confidence in Prussia's military capacity, in addition to its undoubted economic capacity.

The reshaping of the Prussian army

In 1850, the prospects of far-ranging conquests by the Prussian army seemed remote. That army still rested very heavily upon the tactics and traditions of the Napoleonic wars and, as historian W. McElwee has stated, 'to the outward eye the Prussian army in 1859 was as clumsy and antiquated an instrument as any of the others'. The mobilisation, that year, seemed to confirm such reservations. In fact, at that very point, the Prussian military establishment was in the midst of a process of transformation.

The key date in this process was, perhaps, 1857, the year in which Helmut von Moltke was appointed as Chief of Staff. Moltke was an unusually cultured and humane man to lead a great national army. 'Every war,' he wrote later in his life, 'even one which is victorious, represents a great national misfortune.' Politically, his brand of romantic patriotism was closer to that of King Wilhelm than to the realism of Bismarck. He was not primarily, however, a political animal. 'For Moltke,' wrote Gerhard Ritter in *The Sword and the Sceptre* (1972), 'politics was an acquired interest rather than a congenial preoccupation and he was deeply concerned with it only when it directly touched the military sphere.'

In terms of numerical strength, the reforms proposed by Moltke in 1862 put the Prussian army squarely on terms with that of Austria. Sixty-three thousand men were called up each year, for a total period of seven years (three of them in the standing army and four in the front-line reserve), liable to instant recall in an emergency. This gave a standing army of 180,000, with a fully-trained reserve of 175,000. In 1866, therefore, Prussia could mobilise 370,000 men, including some ***Landwehr*** units. As they had fewer security commitments on other frontiers, they were able to outnumber their enemy on the Bohemian front by 278,000 to 271,000. The superior organisation of the Prussian army was equally important. The Prussian General Staff had its origins in the War Academy founded by the great military theorist Karl von Clausewitz, in the Napoleonic era. Not only did it produce officers of great expertise and professionalism, but it guaranteed a uniformity of practice and doctrine in all branches of the army. At Moltke's insistence, for example, all senior officers devoted much attention to the adaptation of modern transport and industrial methods to military needs.

By comparison, the Austrian army remained dominated by senior commanders such as Franz Gyulai and Felix von Wimpffen, who owed their rank more to influence at Court than to proven ability. At lower levels, too, the Austrian army was riddled with inefficiency. Out of a theoretical force of 600,000 men in 1866, bad reserve training and the practice of allowing the wealthy to buy themselves out of military service reduced the fighting force to about 350,000. Furthermore, basic training in the standing army was so bad that it was estimated that two troopers out of three, at the start of the Italian campaign in 1859, were unable to load and fire their muskets.

Landwehr: The part-time military force, consisting largely of middle-class recruits, which provided support for the regular army in times of crisis. The Prussian liberals regarded the *Landwehr* very favourably because it seemed to limit the overall power and authority of the aristocratic Prussian army.

Helmut von Moltke (1800–1891)	**Karl von Clausewitz (1780–1831)**	**Franz Gyulai (1798–1868)**
Joined the Prussian army in 1821 and its General Staff in 1832. Influential as *aide de camp* to the Crown Prince Friedrich (1855). As Chief of General Staff in the Prussian and German army (1857–88), he undertook significant reforms that recognised the importance of advances in technology and communications. Architect of the Prussian victories over Denmark (1863–64), Austria (1866) and France (1870).	Entered the Prussian military college in 1801, and subsequently fought in the Napoleonic Wars in the Russian army and at Waterloo (1815). Director of the Prussian Military College from 1818. In his influential book *On War*, he concentrated upon the links between war and politics, and established that the aim of war was the defeat of the enemy state as well as of the army.	Hungarian soldier in service of the Austrian Empire. As commander of the garrison at Trieste (1846) he was active against Italian rebels. Commander-in-Chief of Austrian forces during the war in Italy (1859).

Muzzle-loader/Krupp breech-loader: Terms describing two firearms. In old-fashioned firearms or cannons it was usual to insert the bullet or shell into the opening of the barrel ('muzzle') and to ram it down into place before firing. In more modern weapons, the bullet is inserted into the 'breech', an opening at the other end of the barrel, immediately above the trigger. Breech-loading enables the rifleman to load, fire and eject bullets much more rapidly.

1. *What evidence is there to suggest that Prussia occupied a stronger position in German politics in 1860 than it had held in 1850?*

2. *Why could Austria not build, in the 1850s, upon the position of strength that it had occupied in German politics at the beginning of the decade?*

3. *'It is more accurate to say that Austria got weaker in the 1850s than that Prussia became stronger.' Do you agree with this statement?*

The army and technology

Finally, the Prussian army undoubtedly led Europe in the application of industrial developments to military purposes. Not only were Prussian railways specifically planned for the swift transit of troops from one frontier to another, but the General Staff operated a special department dedicated to the study of transport by rail. In both 1866 and 1870, this swift concentration of troops was a vital factor. In 1866, Prussia's five railway lines assembled its troops on Austria's northern frontiers in five days, against 45 days taken by the Austrians. In 1870, it proved possible to transport some troops from East Prussia to Lorraine in only 36 hours.

In terms of armament, the Prussian infantry was synonymous for some years with the Dreyse 'needle gun'. First issued in 1848 and in general use by 1864, it fired at five times the rate of the old **muzzle-loader**, and its effect, at Sadowa, caused the correspondent of *The Times* to declare that 'the needle gun is king'. Nevertheless, it had its limitations in range and in accuracy, and the victory of 1870 owed more to the Prussian artillery. Equipped by the mid-1860s with a new **Krupp breech-loader**, with cooled steel barrel and a breech sealed against escaping gases, this branch of the army perfected its techniques in the new School of Gunnery founded in swift response to the superior performance of the Austrian gunners at Sadowa.

14.3 In what respects did Prussia's economy provide a basis for its dominance within Germany?

Prussian resources and government policy

Two main factors coincided to ensure that Prussia's economy would become predominant among the economies of the German states. Firstly, Prussia was blessed with remarkable natural resources, supplemented in 1814–15, by the acquisition of the richly endowed territories of the Rhineland. Through the Ruhr valley and west and south-west across the Rhine lay substantial deposits of coal and iron ore. Rich coal resources were also available in the Saar valley, in Prussian Silesia and in Upper Silesia, where zinc and iron deposits were also worked.

Secondly, although private and foreign capital was prominent in the early promotion of these industries, Prussia was remarkable for the degree of government interest and involvement in their subsequent development. The contribution of Friedrich von Motz, Finance Minister between 1825 and 1830, included tax reforms and a road building programme. P. Beuth, head of the Department of Trade and Industry (1815–45), did much to foster technical education. Meanwhile, the Prussian banking system owed much to Rother's reorganisation of the Bank of Prussia, in 1846.

The greatest monument to the economic initiative of the Prussian government was the establishment of the German Customs Union (*Zollverein*), in 1834. With an area of 415,000 square kilometres and a population of 23.5 million, the *Zollverein* was the culmination of the creation of smaller unions throughout the 1820s. Prussia benefited by securing effective links between its eastern and western territories, and by establishing its economic influence above that of Austria in German affairs. Prussia's leading position in the *Zollverein* was recognised by those clauses in the establishing treaty which accepted its tariffs as the norm for all, and which recognised the right of the Prussian government to negotiate on behalf of the union as a whole. A dramatic rise in customs revenue bore witness to the effectiveness of this leadership, from 14.4 million thalers (Prussian currency) in 1834, to 27.4 million in 1845. In addition, a string of treaties won favourable trading terms for the *Zollverein* with Piedmont-Sardinia and Holland (both 1851), Belgium (1852) and France (1862).

The development of Prussian heavy industry

Prussia also took the leading role, within Germany, in the development of those branches of heavy industry vital to a modern and militarised state. Its iron and coal industries benefited greatly from the introduction of new technology. The number of steam engines operative in Prussian industry rose from 419 (1837) to 1,444 (1848), at a time when the next best figure was Saxony's 197 (1846). Twenty-four new, deep-level mines were opened in the Ruhr coalfield between 1841 and 1849, while new sources of zinc (Dortmund and Bonn), lead (Aachen) and blackband iron (Dortmund) were discovered and exploited in the late 1840s and early 1850s. Prussia's output of iron rose sharply, from 0.5 million to 1.29 million tons between 1852 and 1857, due to rapid conversion from charcoal smelting to coke smelting.

Although private capital was of prime importance, government legislation again played a helpful role in Prussia. The Mining Laws of 1851 and 1860, for instance, freed mine owners from strict state supervision and halved taxes upon their output. The laws, subsequently, did much to free mine labour from the old guild restrictions upon mobility.

The growth of the Prussian steel industry may be measured by the rise of its greatest enterprise, the Krupp factories in Essen. Based upon a successful method of producing cast steel, Alfred Krupp's enterprise grew, between 1826 and 1861, from a single foundry employing seven men to a vast complex employing 2,000. In the next three years alone, thriving on military orders from the Prussian government, especially for modern artillery, the workforce trebled again. In all, Prussian steel production was seven times greater in 1864 than in 1848. The rate of economic growth within the *Zollverein* boundaries may be gauged from the table below.

Alfred Krupp (1812–1887)
A German industrialist whose success was founded upon a process of steel production suitable for the manufacture of improved artillery barrels (1847). He introduced the Bessemer process to Germany (1862) and founded one of the greatest industrial conglomerates in Europe.

Indicators of economic activity in the states that formed the Zollverein, 1820–1870

	1820	1840	1850	1870
Railways (km)	–	549	5,821	8,560
Coal (million tons)	1.0	–	6.9	29.4
Pig iron (million tons)	0.046	0.17	0.53	1.4

John Maynard Keynes (1883–1946)
British economist. As a delegate to the Versailles peace conference in 1919, he became convinced that the economic terms imposed upon Germany were unjust and would lead to further political difficulties in Europe. After the Wall Street Crash in 1929, he defined the principles of 'Keynesian' economics. These included the contention that a degree of government intervention would always be necessary to combat such undesirable factors as unemployment.

Railway construction

Both Bavaria (1835) and Saxony (1837) made an earlier contribution than Prussia to the construction of German railways. The Prussian government was, initially, just as suspicious about the new mode of transport as many other states had been. The 1840s and 1850s, however, saw a rapid change in this attitude. Having appreciated the advantages of east–west communications for economic and strategic purposes, Prussia constructed Germany's second state-owned line (1847), and then sought consistently to extend state influence over the system as a whole. By 1860, 55% of Prussian railways were worked by the state. Quite apart from its economic significance, the growth of the German railway system, as a whole, played a considerable role in the process of 'shrinking' the country and in stressing the insignificance of the lesser states. At every turn, therefore, in an examination of Prussian and German economic growth in the 1850s and 1860s, one is reminded of the famous judgement of John Maynard Keynes that 'the German Empire was not founded on blood and iron, but on coal and iron'.

What was the overall role of economic factors in German unification?

The claim made by Keynes raises the question of the relationship between the economic growth of Germany, and of Prussia in particular, and the political achievement of Bismarck. The traditional view has been to see Bismarck as exploiting the economic advantages of his time to gain the political ends that he sought. More recently, a school of historians led by Helmut Böhme has concluded that the dynamics of the German economy were of greater importance than the political priorities of the Prussian government. In this light, Bismarck might be seen, less realistically, as the exploiter of these economic forces, than as a politician whose course was largely determined by them and by the social forces that arose from them. Historian Geoff Eley (1992) reflects this line of thought when he summarises Böhme's views on the reduction of Austrian influence in Germany.

'The struggle for the control of the *Zollverein* was decisive between 1853 and 1868 in destroying Austrian efforts at reducing Prussia to secondary status. Therefore, 1858 and the opening of a 'New Era' in Prussian government becomes less crucial than 1857 and the economic depression, which widened the gap between the Austrian and Prussian-led economies; 1862 is important less for Bismarck's appointment as Minister-President of Prussia, than for the treaty of free trade with France; Austria's defeat in 1866 is less decisive than its exclusion from the Zollverein two years before.'

1. In what respects did the Prussian economy become stronger in the first half of the 19th century?

2. Explain the statement that 'Prussia's dominance of Germany in the late 19th century was based upon coal and iron.'

14.4 Why was there a constitutional crisis in Prussia in 1860–1862, and why did it bring Otto von Bismarck to power?

The accession of King Wilhelm I

The period 1858–62 saw a transformation of Prussian domestic politics that turned a decade of sterility into a period of crisis that threatened to bring down the monarchy. The first element in this transformation was a change of monarch. In October 1858, the mental illness of Friedrich Wilhelm required the appointment of his brother, Prince Wilhelm, as regent. He succeeded to the throne upon his brother's death in 1860. Already 63 years old, Wilhelm's first political memories dated from the

Napoleonic Wars and, by 1848, he had the reputation of a strict conservative. This, however, was an oversimplification. He was, indeed, deeply attached to the principle of legitimate monarchy and to the traditions of Prussian military glory, but he had been convinced of the need to adapt in the face of modern forces. As a man of honour, he stood by the constitution that his brother had granted, 'not,' as Golo Mann has written (*The History of Germany since 1789*, 1974), 'because he liked it, but because a king must stand by his sacred word.'

The resurgence of nationalism and liberalism

The second major development during this period was the revival of the German national movement in the last years of the 1850s. The national question, in Agatha Ramm's words (*Germany 1789–1919: a Political History*, 1968), had 'barely retained public interest' in the early 1850s. In a negative sense, the lack of any German influence over events in the Crimea played a role in its revival. More positively, the partial success of Italian nationalism in 1859 also had an impact north of the Alps. Also important were the consistent efforts of the lesser German princes to reform the Confederation with a view to increasing its influence over foreign affairs. The revival led to the formation (1859) of the National Association (*Nationalverein*), directly inspired by the Italian National Society. The Association was banned in all major German states, but continued to look to Prussia for leadership, as Italians had looked to Piedmont. The journalist J. Froebel wrote, in 1859, that 'the German nation is sick of principles and doctrines, literary greatness and theoretical existence. What it demands is power, power, power. And to the man who offers it power it will offer honour, more honour than he can imagine.'

Thirdly, whether as a cause or result of the nationalist revival, came a marked resurgence in liberal political activity. In Prussia, it had manifested itself especially in the emergence of the Progress Party (*Fortschrittpartei*). Raised upon the anti-Austrian, anti-Russian and theoretically anti-militaristic foundations of traditional Prussian liberalism, it enjoyed great success in the first elections of the new decade. In the elections to the *Landtag*, in January 1862, it won 83 seats in an assembly that contained only 16 conservatives. Three months later, its strength rose to 136 seats, while the conservatives fell to 11 and the 'old' liberals fell from 95 to 47.

Landtag: The representative assembly of an individual German state or province.

Von Roon and military reform

Such was the political temper of the *Landtag* that come to consider the proposals of the King and of his War Minister, Albrecht von Roon, for the reform of the Prussian army. These proposals were also, in part, the result of the crisis of 1859. The government's prime concern was with the size of the army for, while the Prussian population had doubled since 1814, the annual intake of recruits had remained static at 40,000. Von Roon now proposed to increase this to 63,000 and to create 53 new regiments. He also proposed to change the nature of the army by limiting the role played by the reserve militia (*Landwehr*). This was composed of part-time soldiers who had finished their three years' training and who, in his view and on the evidence of the mobilisation in 1859, 'lacked the genuine soldierly spirit and had no firm discipline'. To the liberal majority, however, the *Landwehr* had the advantage of being freer from the detested spirit of Junker militarism and of costing them far less in taxes. It also recalled fond memories of the 'people's war' against Napoleon in 1813. Thus, Roon was not only fighting a technical battle, but also facing a class struggle.

Albrecht von Roon (1803–1879)
Served in Prussian army from 1821, and wrote a number of texts on army reform. Active against radicals in 1848. As Minister of War (1859) and Minister of the Marine (1861), he collaborated with Moltke and Edwin von Manteuffel in the reform and modernisation of the Prussian Army. He became Minister President of Prussia (1871) when Bismarck vacated the post to take the office as Chancellor of the Reich.

The appointment of Otto von Bismarck

By 1862 the dispute was already two years old, and the government had twice deceived the assembly into making temporary grants of money for the army. Angry and alienated, the assembly now refused to sanction the national budget, leaving Wilhelm to contemplate the possibility of **abdication**. Only as a desperate measure, and at the prompting of von Roon, did Wilhelm take the most important political decision of his life. He summoned to office a man closely identified with the far right of Prussian politics, the ambassador to Paris, Otto von Bismarck-Schönhausen.

Bismarck was not a man to be impressed by abstract principles, whether of legitimism or of **constitutionalism**. Nevertheless, his first moves aimed at finding ground for compromise with the *Landtag*. Only when that failed did he take the determined course of adjourning their sitting (October 1862) and collecting and spending the national budget whether they liked it or not. As theoretical justification, Bismarck exploited the 'gap theory' (*Luckentheorie*). He claimed that the constitution made the budget the joint responsibility of the two houses of the assembly and the monarch, but failed to cater for the eventuality of a dispute between them. In that event, he claimed, without much justification, the executive power reverted to the king.

More important than any theory, however, was the knowledge that real power lay in the hands of the government, the more so now that it had 53 new regiments at its disposal. 'The great questions of the day', Bismarck told the *Landtag*, in the first and most famous speech of his ministerial career, 'will not be decided by speeches and the resolutions of majorities – that was the great mistake of 1848 and 1849 – but by iron and blood.' For four years, and through two wars, Bismarck was to direct Prussian affairs without a constitutionally approved budget, and in the face of continued parliamentary opposition.

Abdication: The constitutional process whereby a monarch gives up his or her throne.

Constitutionalism: Belief in a constitutional system of government.

1. **What was the Prussian constitutional crisis in the early 1860s about?**

2. **What do we learn about Bismarck's political priorities from his conduct during the constitutional crisis in 1862?**

14.5 What were the bases of Bismarck's political beliefs and foreign policy?

What were the bases of Bismarck's political beliefs?

The new Minister President of Prussia, in 1862, was a man of 47 without any ministerial experience, and with extremely limited experience of government administration. Greatly though he stressed his origins among the Prussian feudal aristocracy, Bismarck was no ordinary Junker. His middle-class mother had insisted upon an education in Berlin and at the University of Göttingen, where he acquired a veneer of student liberalism and literary radicalism, to go with his Junker swordsmanship and love of riotous living. By nature, Bismarck was intensely ambitious, rightly convinced of his superiority over the narrow-minded conservatives that made up the Junker ranks, and intolerant of criticism to an extent that often brought on physical illness. From the time of his marriage (1847), he professed a simple, personal Protestant faith, but was able to divorce personal from political morality.

This strange semi-Junker gained his first political experience almost by accident, sitting in the Prussian *Landtag* in 1847 only as a substitute for a sick member. From this experience, and from the events of 1848–49, he derived an intense hostility towards radicalism. This was matched by his disdain for parliamentary 'talking shops' and contempt for policies that were based upon abstract romanticism. Having gained a powerful reputation on the extreme right of Prussian politics, he bitterly opposed the

Germany and Central Europe, 1815–1866

Bundestag ('Federal Assembly'): The representative assembly of the German Confederation (*Bund*).

restoration of the *status quo* after Olmütz. The 1850s formed a crucial period in Bismarck's personal and political development. From 1850 to 1858, he sat as Prussian representative in the federal assembly (**Bundestag**), apparently ideally suited to aid reconciliation between the two great conservative forces in Germany. Indeed, contrary to his later autobiographical claims, his stance remained pro-Austrian until 1854. Many commentators have interpreted the transformation as the result of Austria's attempts to change the German *status quo* in its favour. For A.J.P. Taylor it was rather that the events surrounding the Crimean War convinced Bismarck that Austria was now unable effectively to protect conservative interests in Germany. Indeed, Bismarck wrote at the time, 'I should be very uneasy if we sought refuge from a possible storm by hitching our trim and sea-worthy frigate to that worm-eaten old Austrian man-of-war.'

By 1859, Bismarck was so out of sympathy with Austria that he could advise General von Alvensleben, during the Italian crisis, to 'march southwards with our whole army with boundary posts in our soldiers' knapsacks and drive them into the ground either at Lake Constance or where Protestantism ceases to prevail'. His view was so out of keeping with Prince Wilhelm's concern for legitimacy that his reward was to be packed off as ambassador, first to St Petersburg (1859) and then to Paris (1862). Despite this, and despite the outbreak of three wars in his first eight years in power, we should not regard Bismarck as a warmonger. He followed Clausewitz in believing that 'war is the continuation of politics by other means', but generally he regarded those 'other means' as dangerous and to be avoided whenever possible.

In conclusion, Bismarck's beliefs and motives may be sorted into three categories.

- Firstly, his political instincts were conservative, although his intellect taught him that conservative ends could now only be attained by harnessing more modern notions, such as industrialism and nationalism.

- Secondly, his allegiance was to Prussia. It was not an allegiance to 'the people' or to 'the nation' as that of the German nationalists was, but to the monarchical, Junker-dominated state which he valued as 'an organ of power, a principle of order and authority'. Only when that state became, nominally, a German state did Bismarck's allegiance become German.

- Thirdly, Bismarck believed unswervingly in his own superior claim to exercise political power. 'He claimed', wrote A.J.P. Taylor, 'to serve sometimes the King of Prussia, sometimes Germany, sometimes God. All three were cloaks for his own will.'

A cartoon published in 1862 in the Prussian liberal magazine *Kladderadatsch*. Bismarck holds the Prussian constitution at arm's length and declares 'I cannot govern with this'.

1. What lessons had Otto von Bismarck learned from his political experiences in the years 1848–1862?

2. Who were Bismarck's main allies and main opponents within German politics when he came to power in 1862?

What were the bases of Bismarck's foreign policy?

Principle or pragmatism?

The British statesman, Benjamin Disraeli, recounted in later years a conversation that he claimed to have had with Bismarck in 1862. According to Disraeli, Bismarck laid down a clear programme. 'As soon as the army shall be brought into such a condition as to inspire respect, I shall seize the first best pretext to declare war against Austria, dissolve the German Diet and give national unity to Germany under Prussian leadership.' Recent historians have usually reacted to this either by dismissing the conversation, or by minimising it as the barest outline of long-term aims by a man as yet unaware of the complexities of politics at the highest level. The subjection of Austria, at least in northern Germany, as well as the destruction of the Confederation, probably represent Bismarck's ultimate hopes well enough. In power, however, he found repeatedly that a master plan was impossible, and that the only means of progress was the piecemeal exploitation of external events. In the 1860s, he became the supreme realist and **pragmatist**, learning to declare in later life that 'man cannot create the current of events. He can only float with it and steer.'

It is also possible to view Bismarck's spectacular foreign policy, in the 1860s, in a completely different light. Many recent writers on German history have tended to lay stress upon the importance of domestic politics, and to interpret foreign policy mainly as a means by which politicians sought to achieve domestic ends. Accordingly, Bismarck's policies in the 1860s are now sometimes interpreted mainly as a continuation of his domestic struggle to contain liberal, constitutional trends within Prussia. No sooner had he come to power in 1862 than the conservative *Kreuzzeitung* predicted that he would 'overcome domestic difficulties by a bold foreign policy'. Bismarck himself observed, at the same time, that 'as long as we gain respect abroad, we can get away with a great deal at home'. His ambiguous attitude towards liberal principles and his bid for a *rapprochement* with the liberals from a position of great strength after the victory of Sadowa both suggest that there are grounds for viewing the events of the 1860s from this domestic angle.

Prussia and the Polish revolt

Prussia's relations with its major European neighbour, Russia, were improved by factors arising from the Polish revolt of January 1863. The reaction of the Prussian government was to send General von Alvensleben to St Petersburg (February 1863) to offer a convention whereby Russian troops would be allowed to pass through Prussian territory in pursuit of Polish rebels. It was not a startling concession, considering what Prussian Junkers stood to lose from a peasant revolt, but it contrasted favourably with France's pro-Polish stance and with Austria's Crimean 'betrayal'. Historians have found it hard to agree upon the merits of the so-called 'Alvensleben Convention'. Erich Eyck followed a traditional line in viewing it as a significant diplomatic success, guaranteeing the future goodwill of Russia. D.G. Williamson and others have disagreed, seeing the Convention in the short term as a serious error, which alienated Prussian liberals and made it harder to achieve the *rapprochement* that Bismarck was seeking with France. In the longer term, however, it remains true that Russia was to acquiesce in Prussia's destruction of the central European balance of power. There was to be no Olmütz in the 1860s.

Austria and the Zollverein, 1862–1865

Two further issues cemented Prussia's position within Germany. By signing a trade agreement with France in 1862, Prussia theoretically violated

Pragmatist: Someone who approaches problems in a practical and realistic manner, rather than with an ideal solution in mind.

Kreuzzeitung: A contemporary Prussian newspaper (*Zeitung*) that reflected the conservative views of the governing classes. It took its name from the principal military decoration of the Prussian army, the Iron Cross (*Kreuz* – cross).

Rapprochement: A French term indicating a coming together, or a resolution of different opinions. It is usually used to indicate the reestablishment of friendly relations between states or between political groups.

Fürstentag: An assembly of the
German princes, occasionally
convened by the Austrian Emperor
as a forum for the discussion of
German affairs.

*1. What did Bismarck
do between 1862 and
1865 (a) to strengthen
Prussia's position
within Germany, and
(b) to improve its
diplomatic position
within Europe?*

*2. 'Bismarck's conduct
of Prussian politics
between 1862 and
1865 was entirely
conservative.' Do you
agree with this
statement?*

existing *Zollverein* treaties. This gave Austria the chance, its last as it
happened, to make alternative economic proposals to the princes. Their
rejection of these approaches, their acceptance of the Franco–Prussian
agreement, and their conclusion of a renewed *Zollverein* treaty excluding
Austria (1865), confirmed Prussia's economic leadership of Germany.

Austria seemed to be on firmer ground in terms of political leadership.
The Emperor's decision (August 1863) to summon an Assembly of Princes
(*Fürstentag*) to discuss reform of the Confederation, seemed likely to
confirm its position and the duality of power within Germany. At
Bismarck's insistence, Wilhelm refused to acknowledge Austrian leadership by attending, and refused to accept the reform proposals drafted
there. As events were to prove, this was Austria's last attempt to unite
Germany by princely consent. Thus, Austria's traditional claim to speak
and act for the princes as a whole was already open to doubt at the
moment when the next crisis of German nationalism erupted.

14.6 By what means, and by what stages, was Austria excluded from German politics between 1863–1866?

The Schleswig-Holstein crisis of 1863–1864

The issue of the two duchies on the borders of Germany and Denmark
was an old one, and had last come to a head in 1848. The problem arose
from a mixed population and from a confusion of dynastic and semi-
feudal claims. Schleswig, to the north, was predominantly Danish, while
Holstein had a substantial German majority and was actually a member of
the German Confederation. The territories were technically subject to the
King of Denmark, but enjoyed a large degree of legal and administrative
independence. The crisis of 1848 had arisen from the support of the
middle-class nationalist Holsteiners for the Duke of Augustenburg, whose
son continued the family's bid for local power in the 1860s. The pre-1848
status of both Schleswig and Holstein was confirmed by the major powers,
in 1852, by the so-called London Protocol. This confirmed both Danish
overlordship and the liberties of the duchies and thus left both parties
dissatisfied.

A renewed crisis resulted, in 1863, from the decision of the new Danish
monarch, Christian IX, to regulate the situation in his country's favour.
The reaction of German nationalists to this initiative is well illustrated by
the declaration of the Prussian liberal, Karl Twesten, that he 'would rather
suffer the Bismarck ministry for some years longer than allow a German
land to be lost to us'. Bismarck, too, stood to benefit from intervention. In
the first place, he could not tolerate the increase in the prestige of the
German Confederation that would result from an easy victory over
Denmark. It seems clear, too, that he always had in mind the ultimate
annexation of the duchies, predominantly as a means by which to confirm
his position in the eyes of King Wilhelm.

At no stage did Bismarck pretend to be acting in the interests of nationalism, writing that 'it is no concern of ours whether the Germans of Holstein are happy'. Nor is it seriously maintained any longer that this was a trap to lure Austria into military commitment and to create the basis for future tensions. The alliance by which the two German powers agreed to joint action (January 1864) was necessary to avoid Austrian jealousy, to prevent it leading a force on behalf of the Confederation, and to minimise the fears and resentments of the other signatories of the London Protocol. The war itself was a one-sided affair, concluded by the treaty signed in Vienna, in October 1864, whereby King Christian renounced both Schleswig and Holstein. After years of wrangles in which the Confederation had put forward the German viewpoint, that body was now totally excluded from the settlement. The claims of the Duke of Augustenburg were also conveniently ignored, and the newly acquired territories were placed under the joint administration of Austria and Prussia. Squabbles, accusations and threats of war marked their ten months of joint rule. Yet, rather than start a confrontation, Bismarck accepted the conciliatory Convention of Gastein (August 1865), which formally divided the administration. Prussia took responsibility for Schleswig and Austria for Holstein.

The impact of the crisis on German politics

At the close of 1865, Bismarck had some cause for satisfaction. Quite apart from influence over Schleswig, his actions had demonstrated once more the impotence of the Confederation. Also, far from opposing him, Austria had been party to that demonstration. For the first time in German political affairs in the 19th century, Prussia had led while Austria followed.

Bismarck was also entitled to suppose that he had reduced the hostility of the Prussian liberals towards him. Otto Pflanze, in *Bismarck and the Development of Germany* (1963), has claimed that, as a result of the blow apparently struck for the German cause, 'almost overnight the Bismarck cult was born. Its devotees began to reinterpret their hero's actions during the preceding four years. They excused his infringements of the constitution in view of what they presumed to have been his hidden purpose.' Others, such as Golo Mann, do not accept that Prussia's liberals were won over so easily. There is little doubt, however, that within the next year Bismarck was to score remarkable triumphs over all his opponents within Germany.

The Austro–Prussian War: diplomatic preparations

The idea that the Gastein Convention was a trap deliberately laid by Bismarck to lure Austria into war is no longer widely accepted. It might be seen as a semi-satisfactory compromise over a delicate set of problems, which allowed Bismarck to gain time. In 1864 and in early 1865, war with Austria still posed too much of a risk. By late 1865 and early 1866, however, several of the outstanding uncertainties had been resolved in a manner satisfactory to Prussia. The first such uncertainty was the attitude of France. Bismarck's meetings with Napoleon III at Biarritz and at St Cloud (October–November 1865) left him confident of French neutrality in the event of an Austro–Prussian conflict. It is far from certain that any promises of territorial compensation were made and it may be that the most important outcome was Bismarck's realisation that Napoleon's main desire was to remain at peace.

Secondly, the attitude of Italy was clarified. A new trade treaty with the *Zollverein* (December 1865) had not fully won Italy over to the Prussian camp, but the failure of its friendly approaches to Austria had decided its course by April 1864. By the military alliance then signed, Italy agreed to fight with Prussia against Austria, with Venetia as its reward. The condition was also laid down that the war should begin within three months. Bismarck had ensured, by this diplomacy, that he would fight only on one front, while Austria fought on two. He had also ensured that the issue would be decided by war. In May, as a last bid for peace, Austria actually agreed to acknowledge Prussian supremacy in northern Germany, but demanded the retention of Venetia as a condition, forcing Bismarck to reject the offer because of his commitment to Italy.

The war and its outcome

Superficially, the war that began with the Prussian invasion of Holstein, in June, was about the administration of the duchies. Prussia accused the Austrian authorities of violating their mutual agreements by sheltering **refugees** from the harsh Prussian rule in Schleswig. Austria was also in breach of the Gastein Convention, it was claimed, when it referred this dispute to the German Confederation. These were obviously convenient excuses. The war was really a trial of Prussian strength, postponed from 1850, against Austria and against the Confederation, which was Austria's main power base within Germany. It was significant that Prussia also went to war with Saxony, Hanover, Bavaria, Würtemberg, Baden, Hesse-Darmstadt, Hesse-Cassel and Nassau. In a very real sense, this was a war for the conquest of northern Germany at least.

In the war itself, the German states proved to be ineffectual allies. Their forces failed to link effectively with those of Austria, and they were eliminated from the conflict in a series of engagements, conveniently ignored by subsequent nationalist historians, at Langensalza, Dormbach, Kissingen and Rossbrunn. On the all-important Bohemian front, the decisive action was fought at Sadowa (otherwise known as the battle of Königgrätz), on 3 July. Superior Prussian infantry tactics and **armaments** ensured heavy Austrian losses (roughly 20,000 to Prussia's 9,000), and left open the road to Vienna. The rapid conclusion of an armistice at Nikolsburg three weeks later was the result of compelling pressures on both sides. The Austrians were motivated by nationalist 'rumblings' in Bohemia and Hungary, while Bismarck had reason to fear the reactions of France and Russia to Prussia's extraordinary triumph. In combating the strong desire of King Wilhelm and his generals for territorial gains, Bismarck was thinking not only of foreign jealousy and the future balance of power, but also of the danger of the conservative Prussian state and administration overreaching itself. 'Our power finds its limits,' he wrote at the time, 'when the supply of Junkers to fill official posts gives out.'

Refugees: People who are forced to leave their country because there is a war or because of their political or religious beliefs.

Armaments: Weapons and military equipment belonging to an army or a country.

1. What steps did Bismarck take, between 1863 and 1866, to ensure that Prussia would be successful in a war against Austria?

2. How important was Bismarck's diplomacy in bringing about Prussia's victory over Austria in 1866?

14.7 What had Bismarck achieved by 1866?

The Treaty of Prague

Prussia's defeat of Austria, which was enshrined in the Treaty of Prague (23 August 1866), caused a greater disruption to the European state system, and to the balance of power, than any other event since the defeat of Napoleon. The contemporary German historian Ferdinand Gregorovius captured the importance of the event with only a little exaggeration:

'The entire Prussian campaign has no parallel in the history of the world. The consequences of the Battle of Sadowa are at least as follows:

the unification of Germany through Prussia, the consummation of Italian independence, the fall of the temporal power of the Papacy, the deposition of France from the dominion she has usurped over Europe.'

In more sober detail, the treaty allowed Prussia to annex Hanover, Hesse-Cassel, Nassau, Frankfurt and Schleswig-Holstein. By recognition of its right to form all German territories north of the river Main into a new North German Confederation, Prussia achieved the death of the old German Confederation. A seven-week military campaign had thus untied a knot that had defied decades of diplomatic wrangling. Austria suffered no territorial loss, apart from Venetia. Instead, it surrendered to Prussia the only prize that Bismarck had really desired, its prestige and status within Germany. Nevertheless, the defeat had profound long-term effects upon the Austrian Empire. At a stroke, it was banished from the political affairs of both Germany and Italy. The only direction in which it could now seek prestige and expansion was towards the south-east, towards the Balkans. This was a factor that was to have grave consequences in 1914. For the time being, it turned in on itself, reassessing its internal strength and revising its internal organisation. The most important product of these processes was the Compromise (*Ausgleich*) of 1867, by which Hungary was recognised as a constitutional monarchy, free from Austrian interference in its internal affairs and united to it only through the person of its king.

The 'surrender' of the Prussian liberals

The events of 1866 also provided Bismarck with a notable domestic triumph. The Prussian liberal movement had now to decide upon its reactions to this partial unification of Germany. It had sought unification for decades, but had consistently condemned the means by which it had now been achieved. Many were intoxicated by Bismarck's success. 'I bow before the genius of Bismarck,' wrote a previously consistent critic, von Schering. 'I have forgiven the man everything he has done up to now. More, I have convinced myself that it was necessary.' Johannes Miquel insisted that his fellow liberals should now be practical. 'Today more than ever before politicians must ask, not what is desirable, but what is attainable.'

In this atmosphere, Bismarck chose the moment perfectly to approach the **Reichstag** with an admission that he had acted illegally over the past four years. He requested their pardon in the form of an **Act of Indemnity**. He was duly pardoned by 230 votes to 75. The Progress Party split on the issue and a new political party emerged, the National Liberals. The new party remained devoted to the principles of free trade and the rule of law, but, for the time, shared common ground with Bismarck in its enthusiasm for a strong German state.

Reichstag: The parliament of the united German Empire (Reich). This name was used for the assembly of the North German Confederation even though, technically, Germany did not become an 'empire' until 1871.

Act of Indemnity: A legal act which pardons an individual, or a group, for illegal acts that he/she/they have committed in the past.

Did Prussian liberalism 'sell out' to Bismarck?
The answers of historians have tended to reflect the authors' views on liberalism, or on the German state founded by Bismarck. To Heinrich von Sybel, a patriotic contemporary, the Act of Indemnity was an enlightened and moderate compromise. More recently, Otto Pflanze has accused the liberals of surrendering to success. They were the victims, he claims, 'of their own limited ends, their lack of genuine popular support, and their lust for national power'. It is also important to understand that the relationship between Bismarck and the liberals was more complex than simple confrontation. Although the division between them over constitutional issues was deep, there was scope for genuine co-operation on other, more practical matters. Bismarck retained genuine sympathy for some of the economic priorities of the liberals, and promoted them in the aftermath of the

constitutional crisis. His succession of trade treaties, for instance, with Belgium, Britain, France and Italy served both parties, catering for the economic principles of the liberals and confirming, at the same time, Prussia's dominance within the *Zollverein*.

Equally, as the 1860s progressed, both sides could find much to attract them in a policy of *kleindeutsch* national unity. It is not satisfactory to see Bismarck's confrontation with the Prussian liberals, in 1862–63, simply as a prelude to the 'real' business of foreign policy. Until the late 1870s, it remained an important priority for Bismarck in domestic politics to maintain some form of working relationship with the liberals. This factor must be borne in mind in assessing what passed between them in 1866.

Prussian dominance of the North German Confederation

The most important characteristic of the new North German Confederation, created by the Treaty of Prague, was that it rested upon the military power of Prussia. The true nature of Prussian domination was clearly illustrated by the case of Hanover, where a long-established dynasty was deposed and the fortune of its king confiscated. Similarly, in Schleswig-Holstein, Prussia continued to ride roughshod over the Augustenburg claims. Of the 23 states that associated themselves by treaty in the North German Confederation, Prussia supplied five-sixths of the population. The constitution of the Confederation, however, was a compromise. It was a synthesis of Bismarck's original, rigidly conservative ideas, and liberal attempts to preserve some measure of parliamentary liberty. Why, given the power of his position, did Bismarck compromise? The historian Gordon Craig believes that Bismarck deliberately attempted to create a viable parliament so as to play it off against the separatist tendencies of the governments of the member states. Perhaps, as the historian Erich Eyck has suggested, Bismarck also made liberal concessions in the hope that future membership would thus be more inviting to the southern states.

As a result of these concessions, the North German Parliament (*Norddeutscher Reichstag*) was elected, by universal manhood suffrage and by secret ballot. It enjoyed both freedom of speech and the freedom to publish its debates. The liberals also succeeded in forcing the administration to submit the budget, which was nearly all for military expenditure, for the Reichstag's approval every four (later extended to every seven) years.

On the other hand, Bismarck retained substantial freedom of action. Most taxes were indirect, from *Zollverein* customs and duties, and were therefore beyond the control of the Reichstag. The Federal Chancellor (Bismarck himself) was the only 'responsible' minister, and it was far from clear to whom he was 'responsible'. Indeed, there were no other federal ministers to impede Bismarck. Finally, the initiation of legislation was in the hands of the Federal Council (*Bundesrat*), made up of appointed representatives of the states' governments. This was, effectively, the old Federal Diet, but was now firmly under the presidency and control of Prussia.

1. What did Bismarck and Prussia gain from the victory over Austria in 1866?

2. How justifiable is the claim that the North German Confederation was nothing more than an expanded version of the Prussian state?

14.8   What factors forced Bismarck to go beyond the settlement achieved in 1866?

The position of the southern states

It is probable that Bismarck had no clear plans for further action at the end of 1866. 'There is nothing more to do in our lifetime,' he had written

Friedrich Ferdinand von Beust (1809–1896)
Served in the government of his native Saxony as Foreign Minister (1849–53) and Minister of the Interior (1853–66). Upon the defeat of Saxony by Prussia in 1866, he transferred to the service of Austria. He held office as Imperial Austrian Chancellor (1867–71), in which capacity he was responsible for the early implementation of the *Ausgleich* (Compromise) with Hungary, and for important measures against the Catholic Church. Ambassador to London (1871–78) and to Paris (1878–82).

to his wife. Yet the southern German states continued to pose complex problems for Prussia. Strong separatist forces survived south of the River Main. Of four southern states, only Baden, whose Grand Duke was son-in-law to the King of Prussia, showed any real enthusiasm for union with the north. In Hesse, popular enthusiasm for union was offset by the hostility of the government while, in Bavaria and Würtemberg, opposition to the north was more general. A strong Democratic Party in Würtemberg remained hostile to Prussian absolutism, while in Bavaria dynastic jealousy and staunch anti-Protestantism combined with a widespread dislike of Prussian **militarism**. As late as 1869, the election of a large Catholic majority in the Bavarian assembly seemed to confirm the strength of **separatism**.

Why, then, could the south not be left alone? In part, there was the danger of what allies the southern states might find if they were not the friends of Prussia. The Austrian Emperor, for instance, had given clear notice that he did not necessarily regard the Treaty of Prague as a final and irreversible settlement by appointing the former Saxon premier, Friedrich Ferdinand von Beust, as his Foreign Minister. France, too, tentatively sought friends south of the Main. In addition, pressure for further progress towards unity came from the liberal nationalists of the north who, like Johannes Miquel, refused to see the river Main as more than 'a preliminary stop where the engine has to refuel and take on water in order to continue the journey'. More important still was the fact that the separate existence of the southern states was a sham. Mainly because of the mutual jealousy of Würtemberg and Bavaria, the southern states were unable to translate the vague phrases of the Treaty of Prague concerning a southern union into any form of reality. As a result, they were effectively dependent upon Prussia in both military and economic terms. As members of the *Zollverein* already, the southern states had little choice, after 1866, but to accept Prussian proposals for a 'Customs Parliament' that would add political links to existing economic ones. Even so, by electing a majority favourable to separatism, the southern states continued to keep their distance.

The most effective link between the new Confederation and the south was, therefore, the string of military treaties that Bismarck concluded with the southern states, in August 1866. These placed Prussia in the position recently vacated by Austria, as their protector. Already, by the end of 1866, war appeared the most likely cause of further German unification.

Germany and France: the Luxembourg question

The key diplomatic questions raised by the events of 1866 concerned future German relations with France. In the memoirs that he published after his fall from office, Bismarck claimed to have believed that a conflict with France was an inevitable step along the path to further national unity. In fact, his view at the time was certainly less clear than that. It was based upon the assumption that Napoleon III could not simply accept the changes of 1866, but was not based upon any clear notion of how the Emperor would respond. 'Napoleon III,' he wrote at the time, 'has lost more prestige than he can afford. To recover it he will start a dispute with us on some pretext or other. I do not believe that he personally wishes war, but his insecurity will drive him on.'

After initial probes in the direction of Belgium and the Rhineland, Napoleon's 'policy of compensation' came to focus upon the Grand Duchy of Luxembourg. The French proposals concerning Luxembourg have already been described (see Chapter 12). What concerns us here is the German reaction to those proposals. It does not seem possible, any longer, to maintain that Bismarck trapped or tricked the French Emperor over the Luxembourg question. On the contrary, most recent commentators have agreed that he was quite content to give up the territory and its fortifications to France as the price for placating it and preserving the stability of his new North German creation. What he would not do was to commit himself publicly to that policy when he badly needed the support of the liberal nationalists in the Reichstag.

The insistence of the King of Holland that he would not sell Luxembourg without the specific agreement of Prussia was thus the factor that killed the deal. Bismarck did not initiate the nationalist outcry that now condemned the loss of any 'ancient German land', but he was powerless to act against it. Prussia effectively gained nothing from the international conference (May 1867) that agreed to the neutralisation of Luxembourg and to the removal of the Prussian garrison. France was not pacified, and the strategic position of Germany was not strengthened. Bismarck's only consolation came from the increased unease that now arose in the southern states about French ambitions. When Erich Eyck wrote, in *Bismarck and the German Empire* (1968), that 'the Luxembourg affair was the turning point in Bismarck's development from a Prussian to a German statesman', he meant it, not in the sense that the Chancellor had undergone a conscious conversion, but in the sense that, for the first time, he had lost the initiative. He had been carried along further than he wished by a force that he had previously exploited with confidence.

> **1. What problems did Bismarck encounter in German politics in the years immediately after his victory over Austria?**
>
> **2. Do the political events of 1867 suggest that Bismarck was losing control of German politics?**

14.9 Why, and with what consequences, did Prussia go to war with France in 1870?

The Hohenzollern candidature

The peace of western Europe was not seriously threatened by the Luxembourg crisis, but it was shattered, three years later, by a less predictable confrontation. In September 1868, revolution in Spain overthrew the ruling house of Bourbon. By the beginning of 1869, the Spanish throne had already been rejected by a number of candidates who placed too high a value upon a quiet life. Prince Leopold von Hohenzollern-Sigmaringen, a member of the Catholic branch of the Prussian ruling house, then took up the candidature. By the following February, Spanish representatives were busy overcoming the misgivings of the prince, of his father, Prince Karl Anton, and of the Prussians. The Prussian government insisted throughout that the candidature must, at no time, appear to be official state policy. With King Wilhelm's permission grudgingly given (June 1870), the project seemed able to go ahead as long as speed and secrecy presented France with a *fait accompli*. Under such circumstances their obvious objections to a monarch with Prussian sympathies on their southern border, would be outflanked. That hope, however, was thwarted by misunderstanding and delay in Madrid. In early July, before the Spanish parliament could formally decide upon their king, the French ambassador received official confirmation of the rumours that he had already heard.

The reaction of the French foreign ministry was strong enough, and had sufficient backing elsewhere in Europe, to kill off the Hohenzollern candidature. Clumsy French attempts, however, to extract a promise from King Wilhelm that the project would never be renewed, seemed to call into question the royal and the national honour. This gave Bismarck the chance to snatch from the Spanish affair greater advantage than had ever seemed possible. By releasing to the press an edited version of the

Fait accompli: A French term signifying an 'accomplished fact', something that is over and done with, and is not subject to further negotiation.

telegram in which the king reported his conversation with the French ambassador at Bad Ems (the 'Ems Telegram'), Bismarck gave the impression that a blunt exchange of diplomatic insults had taken place. He once more took control of the nationalist forces that had served him so well in the past. Faced with the choice of retreat or further confrontation, France declared war (19 July), initiating a conflict in which a united German state was to be forged.

What was Bismarck's role in the candidature?

In his memoirs, Bismarck was eager to convey the impression of total detachment from the Hohenzollern affair, and to charge the disruption of European peace to the insolence and instability of the French government. Later research, especially by G. Bonnin and Erich Eyck, however, clearly demonstrated Bismarck's close links with the candidature. These range from the initial distribution of bribes, through the difficult process of convincing King Wilhelm of the strategic advantages of the project, to the final affair of the 'Ems Telegram'. It is difficult to doubt that Bismarck engineered the candidature, but that does not necessarily mean that he did so with a view to starting war. Indeed, it was only by accident that the French government found out about the candidature in time to react at all. It is better, therefore, to see Bismarck's aim as being to outmanoeuvre and surround France in such a way as to force it to accept further Prussian aggrandisement without a fight. The thwarting of the plan, rather than the plan itself, left him with no other means than war by which to create stronger links between the northern and southern German states. He could have had unity without war, but only through war could he guarantee that such unity would rest upon a basis of Prussian military domination. This was the only basis acceptable to Bismarck and to those he served.

Prussian troops storm a French position during the battle of Gravelotte-St Privat in 1870.

Eduard Lasker (1829–1884)
Liberal politician of Jewish origins. Active amongst student revolutionaries in Vienna in 1848. Elected to Prussian Landtag (1865) and to the assembly of the North German Confederation (1867). One of the founders of the National Liberal Party which he represented in the Reichstag from 1871. Played a major role in the drafting and codification of German law after unification.

Werner's painting draws attention to specific elements which he suggests were responsible for German unification. Identify them.

1870: the completion of German unity

The military details of the Franco–Prussian War are described in Chapter 12. Of greater importance here is the series of political developments that accompanied the war, and by which a unified German Empire was formed. At the outbreak of the war, a powerful combination of factors ensured that the southern states would honour their treaty obligations to Prussia. Not least among these was the popular enthusiasm that Karl Marx dismissed contemptuously as 'south German beer patriotism'. Much pressure also came from the leaders of the National Liberals, especially from Eduard Lasker, who organised persuasive propaganda campaigns south of the river Main. The Crown Prince of Prussia, Friedrich, was also a consistent advocate of unity and of the claim of the Hohenzollerns to the Imperial German crown. Although, once more, events were moving beyond Bismarck's control, he too played his role by the well-timed publication of France's earlier compensation proposals, a frightening revelation for the southerners.

While the generals, to the chagrin of the Chancellor, kept the conduct of the war closely under their own control, Bismarck's prime concern was to negotiate a settlement with the southern states that would turn a wartime alliance into a permanent union. In this task three main obstacles needed to be overcome: the respective desires of Würtemberg and of Bavaria to maintain their own independence, and the determination of King Wilhelm not to accept a 'popular' crown, nor to see the Prussian monarchy diminished by becoming a wider, German one. In the long run, the position of the major southern states was hopeless. They could not rely on each other, could not risk an isolated existence outside an otherwise united Germany, and could scarcely resist the growing nationalist enthusiasm inside their own boundaries. Continued separatism, as King

A painting by the German court artist, Anton von Werner, showing the acclamation of Wilhelm I as German Emperor by the German princes in the Hall of Mirrors in Versailles, 18 January 1871.

Ludwig of Bavaria conceded, 'would be completely impossible politically because of opposition from the army and the people, as a result of which the Crown would lose the support of the country'.

German unity without Austria was assured in November 1870, when a mixture of threats and bribes from Prussian state funds persuaded Ludwig to sign a treaty accepting unification. Bavaria and Würtemberg preserved a number of symbols of independence. They retained control over their postal and railway systems, and over their armies in peacetime. This was a small price for Bismarck to pay for an assurance that Wilhelm would now be offered the German crown by the princes, and not by the Reichstag. In the event, that body was merely asked to approve the offer, and did so with enthusiasm. Wilhelm, himself, had many reservations and regrets about the transformation of his beloved Prussian kingdom. He could at least console himself with the fact that the assembly that proclaimed him 'German Emperor' (not 'Emperor of Germany', for that would have offended Bavarian feelings, and would have raised awkward questions about the extent of 'Germany') at Versailles, on 18 January 1871, was an assembly of his fellow monarchs. He had thus remained true to his legitimist philosophy, and had not 'picked up a crown from the gutter'.

Conclusion

Bismarck's great achievement, by 1871, was not that he had created a united German state. Many other forces – nationalism and industrialisation, for example – had given him invaluable aid in that process. His great achievement had been to bring about German unity without damaging important conservative elements within the Prussian state. His triumph was a great one. It was a triumph over the radicals, who wanted a different kind of Germany, and over the conservatives, who had been reluctant to take Prussia into any kind of united Germany. His was a united Germany without true democracy, without parliamentarianism and without Austria.

1. What were the immediate causes of the Franco–Prussian War?

2. How convincing is the claim that Bismarck planned the Franco-Prussian War and its outcome?

3. Why did the war between Prussia and France in 1870–71 end in the declaration of a united Germany?

14.10 *Was German unification primarily the result of successful Bismarckian diplomacy?*
A CASE STUDY IN HISTORICAL INTERPRETATION

When C. Grant Robertson wrote, in *Bismarck* (1919), of German unification as a 'marvellous march of events, in which each stage seems to slip into its pre-appointed place,' he was perpetuating a tradition established some years earlier in Germany itself. A generation of German historians had interpreted German unification as the premeditated design of a master politician, and had portrayed Bismarck as the supreme statesman, leading Germany to its rightful destiny. Prominent in this school of thought was the Prussian academic Heinrich von Treitschke, whose *German History in the Nineteenth Century* (1879–94) traced the 'inevitable' rise of Prussian mastery, with Bismarck portrayed as the chosen instrument of Germany's fate. Bismarck himself was happy to convey a similar impression in his memoirs, eager as he was to maintain his status as a national hero after being forced from office. In such an interpretation, the diplomacy of the great Prussian minister is seen as the primary factor in the sequence of events that created the united German state. He successfully outmanoeuvred Austria over the Schleswig-Holstein affair, isolated it from Russia and from France in preparation for the conflict of 1866, and subsequently goaded France into the war by which the German states were finally welded together.

A very different view of Bismarck's work and of German unification was provided after the Second World War by A.J.P. Taylor, in *Bismarck: the Man and the Statesman* (1968). Taylor ascribed to Bismarck a great deal of political skill, but much more limited aims and vision. Bismarck's primary concern was merely to establish Prussian hegemony in northern Germany, as a means to guarantee that its freedom of political action would not be limited by the influence of Austria. In effect, he had achieved these goals by 1866, through the defeat of Austria, the establishment of a North German Confederation dominated by Prussia, and the acquisition of new territories in northern Germany. The subsequent confrontation with a hostile France was certainly not part of a Bismarckian master plan. On the contrary, he was surprised and frightened by it, and attempted to deflect it by concessions over Luxembourg, and by diplomatic intrigues with Spain. When these proved unsuccessful, the creation of a 'wartime coalition' involving other German states, was primarily a pragmatic measure to avert a Prussian defeat. At much the same time, the German-American historian Otto Pflanze was arguing, in *Bismarck and the Development of Germany* (1963), that the whole notion of a movement within Germany towards unification was a 'fiction of nationalistic historians'. It was not something broadly desired by public opinion, and was engineered by Bismarck mainly to serve his own political ends.

Other historians have taken a different route towards diminishing the role played by the genius of Bismarck. These have concentrated less upon the Prussian statesman himself, than upon the environment in which he operated. W.E. Mosse, in *The European Powers and the German Question* (1958), examined the wider diplomatic environment of the 1850s and 1860s, and stressed the favourable circumstances which made Bismarck's task easier. The major obstacles at the start of the 1850s to Prussian aggrandisement or to German unification were the hostility of Austria, Russia and France. In the course of the 1850s, Austria was weakened and discredited by defeats in Italy and by the breakdown of its relations with Russia, while France under Napoleon III became isolated and the object of suspicion. None of this owed anything to the work of Bismarck, or of any other German politician, but these developments created favourable circumstances, which a clever opportunist could exploit. 'If he played his hand with great skill,' Mosse concluded, 'it was a good one in the first place.'

Much as these interpretations differ over the vision and premeditation employed by Bismarck, they all view diplomacy as the primary force driving Germany towards unification. The British economist J.M. Keynes laid the foundations for a very different interpretation many years ago with his famous judgement that 'the German Empire was created more by coal and iron than by blood and iron' (*The Economic Consequences of the Peace*, 1919). Subsequently, an influential school of German historians has substituted the 'primacy of economics' for the 'primacy of diplomacy'. The most notable work, in this area, has been that of Helmut Böhme who, in *Germany's Path towards Great Power Status* (1966), concentrated upon the social and economic development of contemporary Germany. For Böhme and the writers who have followed his lead, the most important factor in German history in the 19th century was the development of its economic life, and especially the development of an industrial economy in Prussia. This emphasis leads historians to consider how far the Prussian state was in control of such forces. There is ample evidence that, in the years before 1860, Prussian ministers took important steps to exploit the growing industrial economy in the interests of the state. The creation of the *Zollverein* is a prime example of this, emphasising the growing attractions of a German national market. Indeed, Böhme believed that Prussian diplomacy, itself, was founded

1. What different views have been taken by historians of the role played by Bismarck in the unification of Germany?

2. Why have some historians in recent years attached less importance to the work of Bismarck as a cause of German unification?

upon this economic dynamic. The political struggles of the early 1860s arose largely from Prussia's awareness of the importance of such economic leadership, and the desire to protect it against economic challenges from Austria. 'The *kleindeutsch* national state,' he claimed, 'arose chiefly from the Prussian defence against the economic order conceived by Austria for the great Central European region.'

An examination of Germany's development after 1871, however, makes it equally clear that the interests of German industrialists did not fully coincide with the interests of the Prussian-dominated state. It is tempting to conclude, therefore, that although Bismarck rode such economic forces with great skill in the 1860s and the 1870s, he found himself in an unfamiliar Germany during the latter part of his political career. He governed a state with a highly traditional political structure, contrasting starkly with a modern, dynamic economy. This was not something that he had desired, and certainly not something that he had planned.

Source-based questions: *The Hohenzollern candidature*

SOURCE A

Your Majesty,
Will I trust, graciously permit me with my humble duty to summarise the motives which in my modest opinion speak in favour of the acceptance of the Spanish Crown by His Serene Highness, the Hereditary Prince of Hohenzollern, now that I have already respectfully intimated them by word of mouth.

For Germany it is desirable to have on the other side of France an ally on whose sympathies (1) we can rely and with whose feelings France is obliged to reckon. During a war between Germany and France it would be necessary to keep at least one French Corps stationed on the Spanish frontier. We have in the long run to look for the preservation of peace not to the good will of France but to the impression created by our position of strength (2).

No danger to the person of the Hereditary Prince need be anticipated. In all the revolutions which have convulsed Spain the idea of an outrage against the person of the Monarch has never arisen, no threat has ever been uttered (3).

I feel a personal need to make it plain by the present humble memorandum that if the outcome is a refusal the responsibility will not lie at my door, especially if in a near or remote future historians and public opinion were to investigate into the grounds which have led to rejection (4).

Von Bismarck (5).

Bismarck to the King of Prussia, 9 March 1870.
(The numbered notes are referred to in Source B.)

SOURCE B

(1) How long would these sympathies last?
(2) Agreed.
(3) But the expulsion of the dynasty did take place.
(4) The above marginal notes make it clear that I have strong scruples against the acceptance of the Spanish Crown by the Hereditary Prince of Hohenzollern and would only consent to his acceptance of it if his own conviction told him that it was his duty to mount the Spanish throne, in other words, that he regarded his act as a definite vocation. In these circumstances I am unable to advise the Hereditary Prince to such an act. Wilhelm.
(5) At the discussion which took place in my presence the majority gave adherence to the view put forward by the Minister-President, namely the acceptance of the Spanish throne by the Hereditary Prince. Since, however, the latter upheld his verbal and written declaration that he could only decide on acceptance on my command, the discussion was thereby brought to an end. Wilhelm.

Notes made by the King of Prussia in the margins of Bismarck's letter (Source A).

Source-based questions: The Hohenzollern candidature

SOURCE C

When the King heard that the candidature was being further discussed he said that it was 'very extraordinary that this sort of thing was going on without his authorisation'. He wanted to be informed 'of everything that Prim's agent brings either by word of mouth or in writing before any action is taken'.

Report from Thile, Bismarck's principal aide in the Foreign Office, to Bismarck, 19 June 1870

SOURCE D

That beats everything! So his Majesty wants the affair treated with official royal interference? The whole affair is only possible if it remains the limited concern of the Hohenzollern princes.
It must not turn into a Prussian concern, the King must be able to say without lying: I know nothing about it.

Bismarck's comments on Thile's report (Source C).

SOURCE E

Preparations for war on a large scale are in progress in France. The situation is, therefore, more than serious. Just as I could not bid your son accept the crown, so I cannot bid him withdraw his acceptance. Should he, however, so decide, my 'adherence' will again not be wanting.

King Wilhelm I to Prince Karl Anton, 10 July 1870

SOURCE F

During dinner at which Moltke and Roon were present, the pronouncement came from the embassy in Paris that the Prince of Hohenzollern had renounced his candidature in order to prevent the war with which France threatened us. My first idea was to retire from the service because I perceived in this extorted submission a humiliation of Germany for which I did not desire to be responsible. I was very distressed for I saw no means of repairing the corroding injury I dreaded to our national position from a timorous policy, unless by picking quarrels clumsily and seeking them artificially. I saw by that time that war was a necessity, which we could no longer avoid with honour.

Bismarck discussing the events of 12 July 1870 in his memoirs, Reflections and Reminiscences, *published in 1898.*

---

1. *Explain briefly the following references:*

(a) 'it must not turn into a Prussian concern' (Source D)

(b) 'your son' (Source E)

(c) 'the corroding injury I dreaded to our national position' (Source F)

2. *Study Sources B, C and E.*

(a) From a comparison of these sources, assess the consistency of the King's attitude to the Hohenzollern candidature.

(b) On the evidence of these sources, consider the view that Bismarck treated the opinions of the King with barely concealed contempt.

3. *Study all of the sources.*

From these documents, and any other evidence known to you, how far would you agree that by 12 July 1870 Bismarck had sustained a major diplomatic defeat entirely of his own making?

Further Reading

CHAPTER 2   ***The Enlightenment and Enlightened Despotism***

Texts designed for AS and A2 Level students

Some of the most accessible works on the Enlightenment are:

'The Enlightenment' by Hugh Dunthorne (The Historical Association, 1991)

'Europe and the Enlightened Despots' by Walter Oppenheim (Hodder, 1990) which also has good coverage of Joseph II and Catherine the Great.

For Joseph II, the best initial study is *Joseph II and Enlightened Despostism* by T.C.W. Blanning (Longman, 1970)

More advanced reading

The Enlightenment by Norman Hampson (Penguin, 1968)

'The Enlightenment' by Ray Porter (Macmillan, 1990)

Voltaire's *Candide* is well worth the effort.

'Joseph II' by Derek Beales in *The Shadow of Maria Theresa, 1741–1780* (Cambridge University Press, 1986)

From Joseph II to the Jacobin Trials by E. Wangermann (Greenwood Press, 1979)

Catherine the Great: Life and Legend by Jane Alexander (Oxford University Press, 1989)

Russia in the Age of Catherine the Great by I. de Madariaga (Weidenfeld and Nicolson, 1981)

CHAPTER 3   ***The origins of the French Revolution***

Texts designed for AS and A2 Level students

Pre-Revolutionary studies are vast in scope and number.
  To understand the nature of French government and society two books are essential:

France before the Revolution by J.H. Shennan (Methuen, Lancaster Pamphlet, 1983)

A History of Modern France, Volume 1 by Alfred Cobban (Penguin, 1957)

A general survey which is accessible is:

Revolution and Terror in France 1789–1795 by D.G. Wright (Longman, 1974)

More advanced reading

Origins of the French Revolution by William Doyle (Oxford University Press, 1989)

The Marxist interpretation is contained in *The Coming of the French Revolution* by Georges Lefebvre (Princeton University Press, 1947)

The Ancient Regime in France by Peter Robert Campbell (Blackwell for the Historical Association, 1988)

France in Revolution by Duncan Townson (Hodder and Stoughton, 1990)

France 1789–1815: Revolution and Counter-Revolution by D.M.G. Sunderland (Fontana, 1985)

A modern text which superbly sums up the interpretation of the revolution is:

The French Revolution, Class War or Culture Clash? by T.C.W. Blanning (Macmillan, 1998)

The following are 'alternative' interpretations of the origins of the Revolution:

The French Revolution by F. Furet and D. Ricet (Weidenfield and Nicolson, 1970)

Revolutionary Europe, 1783–1815 by George Rudé (Fontana, 1964)

CHAPTER 4   *The French Revolution*

Texts designed for AS and A2 Level students

The Terror and Robespierre are well covered in:

'The Terror in the French Revolution' by Norman Hampson (Historical Association pamphlet)

The Life, and Opinions of Maximilien Robespierre by Norman Hampson (Duckworth, 1974)

France in Revolution by Duncan Townson (Hodder and Stoughton, Access to History series, 1990)

Revolution and Terror in France 1789–1795 by D.G. Wright (Longman, Seminar Study in History series, 1974)

More advanced reading

Citizens. A Chronicle of the French Revolution by Simon Schama (Penguin, 1989)

The Origins of the French Revolutionary Wars by T.C.W. Blanning (Longman, 1986)

The Peasantry in the French Revolution by P.M. Jones (Cambridge University Press, 1988)

CHAPTER 5   *Napoleon, France and Europe*

Texts designed for AS and A2 Level students

Books which give access to the main ideas and events of Napoleon's career are:

Napoleon, France and Europe by Andrina Stiles (Hodder and Stoughton, Access to History series 1990)

Napoleon's First Consul and Emperor of the French by I. Collins (Historical Association, 1986)

Napoleon and Europe by D.G. Wright (Longman, Seminar Studies series 1984)

More advanced reading

Napoleon by V. Cronin (Collins, 1971) is a straightforward account but coverage is incomplete.

More detailed works which are worthy of selective use are:

Napoleon by D. Chandler (Weidenfield and Nicholson, 1973)

Napoleon by Georges Lefebvre (Paris, 1935)

A Marxist view, and more up-to-date is:

Napoleonic Empire by G. Ellis (Macmillan, 1991)

CHAPTER 6   *International relations from the Congress of Vienna to 1848*

Texts designed for AS and A2 Level students

The Concert of Europe. International Relations 1814–1870 by John Lowe (Hodder and Stoughton, Access to History series, 1990)

The Eastern Question 1774–1923 by A.L. Macfie (Longman, Seminar Studies in History series 1989; revised edition 1996)

From Vienna to Versailles by L.C.B. Seaman (Methuen, 1st published 1955, paperback 1964)

The Congress of Vienna by Tim Chapman (Routledge, 1998)

Europe 1815–1945 by Anthony Wood (Longman, 1964)

Europe 1780–1830 by Franklin Ford (Longman, 1970)

More advanced reading

The Great Powers and the European State System 1815–1914 by F.R. Bridge and R. Bullen (Longman, 1980)

Europe's Balance of Power 1815–1848 ed. A. Sked (Macmillan, 1979)

See also Volumes IX and X of the New Cambridge Modern History:

Volume IX 'War and peace in an age of upheaval 1793–1830' edited by C.W. Crawley (Cambridge University Press, 1965)

Volume X 'The Zenith of European Power 1830–1870 edited by J.P.T. Bury (Cambridge University Press, 1960)

CHAPTER 7   *France, 1814–1848*

Texts designed for AS and A2 Level students

Monarchy, Republic and Empire by Keith Randell (Hodder and Stoughton, Access to A level History Series, 1986)

For the causes of the 1848 Revolution in France:

The 1848 Revolutions by Peter Jones (Longman, Seminar Studies in History Series, 1991)

More advanced reading

A History of Modern France, Volume 2: 1799–1945 by Alfred Cobban (Penguin, 1961)

France 1814–1940 by J.P.T. Bury (Methuen, 1949)

A readable general coverage is provided in:

A Concise History of France by R. Price (Cambridge University Press, 1993)

CHAPTER 8   *The German Confederation and the Austrian Empire, 1815–1848*

Texts designed for AS and A2 Level students

The Habsburg Empire 1815–1918 by Nick Pelling (Hodder and Stoughton, Access to A level History Series, 1996)

The Unification of Germany by Andrina Stiles (Hodder and Stoughton, Access to A level History Series, 1989)

Nationmaking in Nineteenth-Century Europe by W.G. Shreeves (Nelson, Advanced Studies in History, 1984)

More advanced reading

The Decline and Fall of the Habsburg Empire 1815–1918 by A. Sked (Longman, 1989)

The Habsburg Monarchy 1809–1918 by A.J.P. Taylor (Penguin, 1948)

A History of Germany 1815–1945 by W. Carr (Arnold, 1969)

CHAPTER 9 *Italy, 1815–1848*

Texts designed for AS and A2 Level students

The Unification of Italy by Andrina Stiles (Hodder and Stoughton, Access to History Series, 1986)

Nationmaking in Nineteenth-Century Europe by W.G. Shreeves (Nelson, Advanced Studies in History, 1984)

More advanced reading

Risorgimento and the Unification of Italy by Derek Beales (Longman, 1981)

Risorgimento: The making of Italy 1815–1879 by E. Holt (Macmillan, 1970)

The making of Italy 1796–1870 by Denis Mack Smith (Macmillan, 1968)

CHAPTER 10 *Russia, 1801–1871*

Texts designed for AS and A2 Level students

Russia, 1815–1881 by Russell Sherman (Hodder and Stoughton, Access to History Series, 1991)

Nineteenth Century Russia. Opposition to Autocracy by Derek Offord (Longman, Seminar Studies in History, 1999). This is quite a difficult book, but provides some useful documents and summaries of the main opposition thinkers.

Alexander II, Emancipation and Reform in Russia 1855–1881 by Maureen Perrie (Historical Association, 1989)

More advanced reading

The Russian Empire 1801–1917 by Hugh Seton-Watson (Clarendon Press, 1988)

Russia under the Old Regime by Richard Pipes (Penguin, 1974)

Alexander II and the Modernisation of Russia by W.E. Mosse (Tauris, 1992)

Russia in the Age of Reaction and Reform by D. Saunders (London, 1992)

Also invaluable for their picture of Russian society are the works of the great Russian novelists referred to in this chapter. Particularly recommended are:

Crime and Punishment by F. Dostoevsky (Penguin, 1951)

Dead Souls by N. Gogol (Penguin, 1961)

Anna Karenina by L. Tolstoy (Penguin, 1954)

Fathers and Sons by I. Turgenev (Penguin, 1970)

CHAPTER 11   *The Revolutions of 1848 and 1849*

Texts designed for AS and A2 Level students

The 1848 Revolutions by Peter Jones (Longman, Seminar Studies series, 1981)

More advanced reading

The Revolutions of 1848–49 edited by Erich Eyck (Oliver and Boyd, 1972)

France in Revolution: 1848 by A. Denholm (Wiley, 1972)

The French Second Republic: a Social History by Roger Price (Batsford, 1972)

It would also be useful to consult general books on the history of the countries that were most affected by the events of 1848–49, such as:

France 1815–1914. The Bourgeois Century by R. Magraw (Fontana, 1983)

A History of Modern Germany, 1840–1945 by Hajo Holborn (Princeton University Press, 1982)

Italy in the Age of the Risorgimento, 1790–1870 by Harry Hearder (Longman, History of Italy series, 1984)

The Risorgimento and the Unification of Italy by Derek Beales (Longman, 1981)

The Habsburg Empire, 1790–1918 by C.A. Macartney (Weidenfeld and Nicolson, 1971)

CHAPTER 12   *France: Second Republic and Second Empire, 1848–1870*

Texts designed for AS and A2 Level students

Second Empire and Commune: 1848–1871 by W.H.C. Smith (Longman, Seminar Studies series, 1985)

France 1814–1870: Monarchy, Republic and Empire by Keith Randell (Hodder and Stoughton, Access to History series, 1991)

Napoleon III and the Second Empire by Roger Price (Routledge Lancaster Pamphlets, 1997)

More advanced reading

Napoleon III by J.F. McMillan (Longman, Profiles in Power series, 1991)

France 1815–1914; the Bourgeois Century by Roger Magraw (Fontana, History of Modern France, 1983)

The Rise and Fall of the Second Empire, 1852–1871 by A. Plessis (Cambridge University Press, 1985) – originally published in French, and provides an interesting opportunity to read a French treatment of the subject.

Louis Napoleon and the Second Empire by J.M. Thompson (Blackwell, 1965) – a more old-fashioned treatment of the subject, but still interesting for its relatively hostile attitude towards Napoleon III.

CHAPTER 13   *The unification of Italy*

Texts designed for AS and A2 Level students

Unification of Italy by John Gooch (Routledge Lancaster Pamphlets, 1990)

The Unification of Italy 1815–70 by Andrina Stiles (Hodder and Stoughton, Access to History series, 1989)

More advanced reading

A History of Italy 1700–1860: the Social Constraints of Political Change by Stuart Woolf (Routledge, 1986)

Italy in the Age of the Risorgimento by Harry Hearder (Longman, History of Italy series, 1984)

The Risorgimento and the Unification of Italy by Derek Beales (Allen and Unwin, 1972)

Cavour by Denis Mack Smith (Methuen, 1985)

Mazzini by Denis Mack Smith (Yale University Press, 1994)

Cavour by Harry Hearder (Longman, Profiles in Power series, 1994)

The Italian Risorgimento: State, Society and National Unification by Lucy Riall (Routledge, Connections in History series, 1994) offers a good brief survey of recent trends in historical writing on this subject.

CHAPTER 14   *The unification of Germany, 1850–1871*

Texts designed for AS and A2 Level students

Bismarck and Germany 1862–1890 by D.G. Williamson (Longman, Seminar Studies series, 1986)

The Unification of Germany, 1815–70 by Andrina Stiles (Hodder and Stoughton, Access to History series, 1989)

More advanced reading

Bismarck, the White Revolutionary by Lothar Gall (Allen and Unwin, 1986)

The Fontana History of Germany 1780–1918; the Long Nineteenth Century by David Blackbourn (Fontana, Harper Collins, 1997) provides an excellent introduction to recent work on German history in this period.

Bismarck and the German Empire by Erich Eyck (Allen and Unwin, 1968) provides a classic, German liberal view of the subject.

Bismarck: the Man and the Statesman by A.J.P. Taylor (New English Library, 1968) remains a classic interpretation of Bismarck's career.

Acknowledgements

Every effort has been made to contact the holders of copyright material, but if any have been inadvertently overlooked the publishers will be pleased to make the necessary arrangements at the first opportunity.

Extracts from E.N. Williams *The Ancient Regime in Europe*, Bodley Head as publisher; Hugh Dunthorne for extracts from 'The Enlightenment' pamphlet; an extract from G.R.R. Treasure *The Making of Modern Europe 1648–1780*, Routledge (1985); Pearson Education for extract from *Europe in the Eighteenth Century* by M.S. Anderson (1961); extracts from J.H. Shennan *France before the Revolution* published by Methuen (1983); *A History of Modern France Volume Three: France and the Republics* by Alfred Cobban (Penguin Books, 1965) copyright © the Estate of Alfred Cobban, 1965; extracts from *The French Revolution, Class War or Culture Clash?* by T.C.W. Blanning, Macmillan (1998); extracts from William Doyle, *Origins of the French Revolution* 1988 by permission of Oxford University Press; an extract from *Citizens* by Simon Schama (Copyright © Simon Schama 1989) reprinted by permission of PFD on behalf of Simon Schama; Pearson Education for extracts from *Europe 1780–1830* by Franklin Ford (2nd ed., 1989); Pearson Education for extract from *Napoleon and Europe* by D.G. Wright (1984); extracts from Eric Hobsbawn *The Age of Revolution*, Weidenfeld and Nicolson (1962); extracts from *The Nineteenth Century* (1970, ed. Asa Briggs) by kind permission of Thames & Hudson; extracts from C.W. Crawley *The New Cambridge Modern History volume 9: War and Peace in an Age of Upheaval, 1793–1830* (1965, Cambridge University Press); Pearson Education for extract from *The Concert of Europe* by Carsten Holbraad; extracts from Hugh Seton-Watson, *The Russian Revolution 1801–1919* (1989) by permission of Oxford University Press; Pearson Education for extracts from *Nineteenth Century Russia: Opposition to Autocracy* by Derek Offord (1999), *Europe 1815–1945* by Anthony Wood (1964), *The 1848 Revolutions* by Peter Jones (1981), *Empire and Commune: 1848–1971* by W.H.C. Smith (1985), *Napoleon III* by James McMillan (1991); extracts from Denis Mack Smith *Cavour* published by Methuen (1985); extract from *The Sword and the Sceptre Volume I: The Problem of Militarism in Germany* by Gerhard Ritter (Allen Lane, 1972) copyright © Gerhard Ritter, 1972; ITPS for extract from *Modern Germany Reconsidered, 1870–1945*, Routledge (1992).

The publishers would like to thank the following for permission to reproduce pictures on these pages.

(T=Top, B=Bottom, L=Left, R=Right)

Photo: AKG London 43, 156, 191, 195, 231, 232, 263, 277, 293, 327; Photo: AKG London/Musée de l'Armée, Paris 379; Photo: AKG London/Eric Lessing/Musée d'Orsay, Paris 415; Photo: AKG

London/Private Collection, Paris 61; Photo: AKG London/Römer, Kaisersaal, Frankfurt 33; Photo: AKG London/Tretjakov Gallery, Moscow 44; Bildarchiv Preussischer Kulturbesitz, Berlin 406, Bildarchiv Preussischer Kulturbesitz, Berlin/Bismarck-Museum, Friedrichsruh 416; Bridgeman Art Library/Bibliothèque Nationale, Paris, France 97; Bridgeman Art Library/Château de Versailles, France 114BR, Bridgeman Art Library/Louvre, Paris, France 110, 116, Bridgeman Art Library/Musée Carnavalet, Paris, France 73, 86, Bridgeman Art Library/Private Collection 114TL, 295; British Library 27; Mary Evans Picture Library 252; Mansell/Time Pix/Katz 168; Novosti (London) 273; The Punch Library 171, 209, 300, 344; © Collection Viollet 68, 164, 321. © Collection Viollet/Musée Carnavalet 102; © Collection Viollet/Musée de Versailles 208.

Cover picture: Napoleon Returning from Elba, by Vasily Ivanovich Sternberg (Wilhelm) (1818–45) Christie's Images, London, UK/Bridgeman Art Library

Index

Glossary

Abdication 404
Absolute monarchy 11, 150
Absolutism 24
Absolutist rule 167
Act of Indemnity 411
Aggrandisement 383
Agrarian depression 326
Amalgamé 124
Ambivalent 51
Amnestied 332
Amnesty 351
Anarchist 306
Anarchy 261
Ancien régime 41
Anglophiles 26
Annexation 206, 378
Anti-clericalism 190
Anti-Corn Law League 210
Anti-establishment propaganda 214
Anti-semitism 236
Arbiter 356
Arbitrary arrest 86
Aristocrats 62
Armaments 410
Armistice 177
Arsenal 381
Artisans 25
Assassins 113
Assembly of Notables 67
Assignats 90
Autocracy 33, 268, 275
Autocratic monarchy 150
Autonomy 50

Bailiffs 301
Barbarism 296
Barbary pirates 196
Barschina 268
Basques 179
Battle of Leipzig 145
Belligerent rights 172
Benefices 372
Birth rate 119
Blockade 20
Bonapartists 203, 341
Bondage 301
Bourbon 116
Bourbon monarchy 186
Bourgeois property-owners 116
Bourgeoisie 49
Brigandage 387
Brothers Grimm 233
Brunswick Manifesto 95

Budgets – deficit 221
Buffer states 150, 370
Bulletins 125
Bundestag 405
Bureaucracy 35

Cahiers 51
Cannibalism 36
Cantons 150
Capital 119
Capital offences 196
Capital punishment 274
Capitalism 56
Capitulation 397
Carbonari 193
Caricature 191
Catechism 117
Catholic 154
Censorship 122
Census 273
Central Duchies 369
Chancery 290
Charismatic 111
Charlemagne 137
Châteaux 85
Chief executive 50
Cholera 204
Civil rights 279
Civil servants 118
Civil service 343
Civil society 26
Close season 205
Coalitions 126
Codifying laws 122
Colonies 59
Commune 83
Concert of Europe 191
Concordat 120
Confederacy 377
Confession 248
Confidant 333
Congress 167
Congresses of Troppau and Laibach 253
Conservative 244
Conservatives 155
Constitution 115
Constitutional monarchy 150, 186
Constitutionalism 179, 404
Consuls 115
Continental System 119
Convents 386
Cordeliers Club 93
Cordon sanitaire 150
Cossacks 133, 292
'Cotton famine' 349
Council of Ancients 113

Counsel 61
Coup d'état 197
Court intrigue 216
Court martial 388
Curés 51
Customary law 50
Customs duties 248

Decadent 52
Decembrists 268
Dechristianisation campaign 101
Départements 88
Deputies 188
Despotism 29, 261
Despots 50
Diet 151, 216
Directory 112
Disestablished 202
Dissolution of contemplative orders 39
Divine right monarchy 26
Doctrine of Papal Infallibility 390
Domains 246
Dominions 35
Duma 268, 303
Dynasty 5

Eastern Question 18, 354
Edict 63
Egalitarian 65
Electorate 341
Emancipation of serfs 28
Emigrés 103
Enclosure 58
Encyclical 389
Enlightened despots 220
Enlightenment 277
Ennoblement 53
Epilepsy 221
Estate 33
Estates-General 49
Excommunicated 292

Fait accompli 414
Fallow 57
Federal Act 221
Federalism 99
Fédérés 95
Feudal dues 51
Feudal obligations 21
Feudal taxes 244
Feudalism 57
Feuillant Club 93
Financial bourgeoisie 201
First International 306
Franchise 186
Free market 103

Free trade 40, 396
Freemasons 251
French Legal Codes 227
French Revolutionary/'liberal' ideas 216
Fürstentag 408

Gallican 51
Garibaldini 381
Garrison 113
German Confederation 19, 216
Ghetto 247
Girondins 94
Gout 188
Grandees 56
Gross fermiers 56
Guerrillas 104
Guilds 26
Guillotined 49

Habsburgs 150
Hegemony 354
Heresy 43, 196
Historiography 49
'Holy Alliance' 249
Holy Roman Emperor 219
Holy Touch 194
Homogeneous 348
Humanitarian liberalism 149
Humanitarianism 28

Ideological 211
Illiterate 244
Imperial Guard 345
Imperialism 358
Impotent 184
Indemnity 112
Index 29
Industrial credit 346
Infantry 124
Inflation 90
Informal empire 358
'Infrastructure' 347
Inquisition 25, 247
Insurgents 317
Insurrection 86
Intelligentsia 269, 291
Intendants 36, 50
Intrigues 61
Inviolable 86
Isthmus 359

Jacobin clubs 92
Jacobins 94
Janissaries 169
Jesuit order 195